PHILIP'S

WORLD ATLAS

The World in Focus
Cartography by Philip's

Picture Acknowledgements
Page 14
Science Photo Library/NOAA

Illustrations
Stefan Chabluk

CONSULTANTS
Philip's are grateful to the following people for acting as specialist
geography consultants on '*The World in Focus*' front section:

Professor D. Brunsden, Kings College, University of London, UK
Dr C. Clarke, Oxford University, UK
Dr I. S. Evans, Durham University, UK
Professor P. Haggett, University of Bristol, UK
Professor K. McLachlan, University of London, UK
Professor M. Monmonier, Syracuse University, New York, USA
Professor M-L. Hsu, University of Minnesota, Minnesota, USA
Professor M. J. Tooley, University of St Andrews, UK
Dr T. Unwin, Royal Holloway, University of London, UK

Published in Great Britain in 1998
by George Philip Limited,
an imprint of Reed Consumer Books Limited,
Michelin House, 81 Fulham Road, London SW3 6RB,
and Auckland and Melbourne

Cartography by Philip's

ISBN 0–540–07539–6

A CIP catalogue record for this book is available
from the British Library.

Printed in China

PHILIP'S

WORLD ATLAS

EIGHTH EDITION

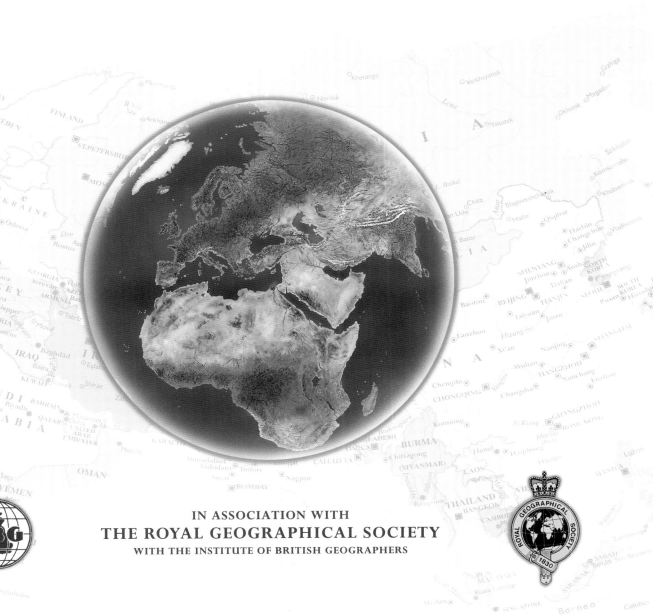

IN ASSOCIATION WITH
THE ROYAL GEOGRAPHICAL SOCIETY
WITH THE INSTITUTE OF BRITISH GEOGRAPHERS

Contents

v

World Statistics: Countries

This alphabetical list includes all the countries and territories of the world. If a territory is not completely independent, then the country it is associated with is named. The area figures give the total area of land, inland water and ice. The population figures are 1997 estimates. The annual income is the Gross National Product per capita in US dollars. The figures are the latest available, usually 1995.

Country/Territory	Area km² Thousands	Area miles² Thousands	Population Thousands	Capital	Annual Income US $
Adélie Land (France)	432	167	0.03	—	—
Afghanistan	652	252	23,000	Kabul	300
Albania	28.8	11.1	3,600	Tirana	670
Algeria	2,382	920	29,300	Algiers	1,600
American Samoa (US)	0.20	0.08	62	Pago Pago	2,600
Andorra	0.45	0.17	75	Andorra-la-Vella	14,000
Angola	1,247	481	11,200	Luanda	410
Anguilla (UK)	0.1	0.04	10	The Valley	6,800
Antigua & Barbuda	0.44	0.17	66	St John's	6,390
Argentina	2,767	1,068	35,400	Buenos Aires	8,030
Armenia	29.8	11.5	3,800	Yerevan	730
Aruba (Netherlands)	0.19	0.07	70	Oranjestad	17,500
Ascension Is. (UK)	0.09	0.03	1.5	Georgetown	—
Australia	7,687	2,968	18,400	Canberra	18,720
Austria	83.9	32.4	8,200	Vienna	26,890
Azerbaijan	86.6	33.4	7,700	Baku	480
Azores (Portugal)	2.2	0.87	238	Ponta Delgada	—
Bahamas	13.9	5.4	280	Nassau	11,940
Bahrain	0.68	0.26	605	Manama	7,840
Bangladesh	144	56	124,000	Dhaka	240
Barbados	0.43	0.17	265	Bridgetown	6,560
Belarus	207.6	80.1	10,500	Minsk	2,070
Belgium	30.5	11.8	10,200	Brussels	24,710
Belize	23	8.9	228	Belmopan	2,630
Benin	113	43	5,800	Porto-Novo	370
Bermuda (UK)	0.05	0.02	65	Hamilton	27,000
Bhutan	47	18.1	1,790	Thimphu	420
Bolivia	1,099	424	7,700	La Paz/Sucre	800
Bosnia-Herzegovina	51	20	3,600	Sarajevo	2,600
Botswana	582	225	1,500	Gaborone	3,020
Brazil	8,512	3,286	159,500	Brasília	3,640
British Indian Ocean Terr. (UK)	0.08	0.03	0	—	—
Brunei	5.8	2.2	300	Bandar Seri Begawan	14,500
Bulgaria	111	43	8,600	Sofia	1,330
Burkina Faso	274	106	10,900	Ouagadougou	230
Burma (= Myanmar)	677	261	47,500	Rangoon	1,000
Burundi	27.8	10.7	6,300	Bujumbura	160
Cambodia	181	70	10,500	Phnom Penh	270
Cameroon	475	184	13,800	Yaoundé	650
Canada	9,976	3,852	30,200	Ottawa	19,380
Canary Is. (Spain)	7.3	2.8	1,494	Las Palmas/Santa Cruz	—
Cape Verde Is.	4	1.6	410	Praia	960
Cayman Is. (UK)	0.26	0.10	35	George Town	20,000
Central African Republic	623	241	3,400	Bangui	340
Chad	1,284	496	6,800	Ndjaména	180
Chatham Is. (NZ)	0.96	0.37	0.05	Waitangi	—
Chile	757	292	14,700	Santiago	4,160
China	9,597	3,705	1,210,000	Beijing	620
Christmas Is. (Australia)	0.14	0.05	2	The Settlement	—
Cocos (Keeling) Is. (Australia)	0.01	0.005	1	West Island	—
Colombia	1,139	440	35,900	Bogotá	1,910
Comoros	2.2	0.86	630	Moroni	470
Congo	342	132	2,700	Brazzaville	680
Congo (= Zaïre)	2,345	905	47,200	Kinshasa	120
Cook Is. (NZ)	0.24	0.09	20	Avarua	900
Costa Rica	51.1	19.7	3,500	San José	2,610
Croatia	56.5	21.8	4,900	Zagreb	3,250
Cuba	111	43	11,300	Havana	1,250
Cyprus	9.3	3.6	800	Nicosia	11,500
Czech Republic	78.9	30.4	10,500	Prague	3,870
Denmark	43.1	16.6	5,400	Copenhagen	29,890
Djibouti	23.2	9	650	Djibouti	1,000
Dominica	0.75	0.29	78	Roseau	2,990
Dominican Republic	48.7	18.8	8,200	Santo Domingo	1,460
Ecuador	284	109	11,800	Quito	1,390
Egypt	1,001	387	63,000	Cairo	790
El Salvador	21	8.1	6,000	San Salvador	1,610
Equatorial Guinea	28.1	10.8	420	Malabo	380
Eritrea	94	36	3,500	Asmara	500
Estonia	44.7	17.3	1,500	Tallinn	2,860
Ethiopia	1,128	436	58,500	Addis Ababa	100
Falkland Is. (UK)	12.2	4.7	2	Stanley	—
Faroe Is. (Denmark)	1.4	0.54	45	Tórshavn	23,660
Fiji	18.3	7.1	800	Suva	2,440
Finland	338	131	5,200	Helsinki	20,580
France	552	213	58,800	Paris	24,990
French Guiana (France)	90	34.7	155	Cayenne	6,500
French Polynesia (France)	4	1.5	226	Papeete	7,500
Gabon	268	103	1,200	Libreville	3,490
Gambia, The	11.3	4.4	1,200	Banjul	320
Georgia	69.7	26.9	5,500	Tbilisi	440
Germany	357	138	82,300	Berlin/Bonn	27,510
Ghana	239	92	18,100	Accra	390
Gibraltar (UK)	0.007	0.003	28	Gibraltar Town	5,000
Greece	132	51	10,600	Athens	8,210
Greenland (Denmark)	2,176	840	57	Nuuk (Godthåb)	9,000
Grenada	0.34	0.13	99	St George's	2,980
Guadeloupe (France)	1.7	0.66	440	Basse-Terre	9,500
Guam (US)	0.55	0.21	161	Agana	6,000
Guatemala	109	42	11,300	Guatemala City	1,340
Guinea	246	95	7,500	Conakry	550
Guinea-Bissau	36.1	13.9	1,200	Bissau	250
Guyana	215	83	820	Georgetown	590
Haiti	27.8	10.7	7,400	Port-au-Prince	250
Honduras	112	43	6,300	Tegucigalpa	600
Hong Kong (China)	1.1	0.40	6,500	—	22,990
Hungary	93	35.9	10,200	Budapest	4,120
Iceland	103	40	275	Reykjavik	24,950
India	3,288	1,269	980,000	New Delhi	340
Indonesia	1,905	735	203,500	Jakarta	980
Iran	1,648	636	69,500	Tehran	4,800
Iraq	438	169	22,500	Baghdad	1,800
Ireland	70.3	27.1	3,600	Dublin	14,710
Israel	27	10.3	5,900	Jerusalem	15,920
Italy	301	116	57,800	Rome	19,020
Ivory Coast	322	125	15,100	Yamoussoukro	660
Jamaica	11	4.2	2,600	Kingston	1,510
Jan Mayen Is. (Norway)	0.38	0.15	0.06	—	—
Japan	378	146	125,900	Tokyo	39,640
Johnston Is. (US)	0.002	0.0009	1	—	—
Jordan	89.2	34.4	5,600	Amman	1,510
Kazakstan	2,717	1,049	17,000	Aqmola	1,330
Kenya	580	224	31,900	Nairobi	280
Kerguelen Is. (France)	7.2	2.8	0.7	—	—
Kermadec Is. (NZ)	0.03	0.01	0.1	—	—
Kiribati	0.72	0.28	85	Tarawa	710
Korea, North	121	47	24,500	Pyŏngyang	1,000
Korea, South	99	38.2	46,100	Seoul	9,700
Kuwait	17.8	6.9	2,050	Kuwait City	17,390
Kyrgyzstan	198.5	76.6	4,700	Bishkek	700
Laos	237	91	5,200	Vientiane	350
Latvia	65	25	2,500	Riga	2,270
Lebanon	10.4	4	3,200	Beirut	2,660
Lesotho	30.4	11.7	2,100	Maseru	770
Liberia	111	43	3,000	Monrovia	850
Libya	1,760	679	5,500	Tripoli	7,000
Liechtenstein	0.16	0.06	32	Vaduz	33,500
Lithuania	65.2	25.2	3,700	Vilnius	1,900
Luxembourg	2.6	1	400	Luxembourg	41,210
Macau (Portugal)	0.02	0.006	450	Macau	7,500
Macedonia	25.7	9.9	2,200	Skopje	860
Madagascar	587	227	15,500	Antananarivo	230
Madeira (Portugal)	0.81	0.31	253	Funchal	—
Malawi	118	46	10,300	Lilongwe	170
Malaysia	330	127	20,900	Kuala Lumpur	3,890
Maldives	0.30	0.12	275	Malé	990
Mali	1,240	479	11,000	Bamako	250
Malta	0.32	0.12	400	Valletta	11,000
Marshall Is.	0.18	0.07	60	Dalap-Uliga-Darrit	1,500
Martinique (France)	1.1	0.42	405	Fort-de-France	10,000
Mauritania	1,030	412	2,400	Nouakchott	460
Mauritius	2.0	0.72	1,200	Port Louis	3,380
Mayotte (France)	0.37	0.14	105	Mamoundzou	1,430
Mexico	1,958	756	97,400	Mexico City	3,320
Micronesia, Fed. States of	0.70	0.27	127	Palikir	1,560
Midway Is. (US)	0.005	0.002	2	—	—
Moldova	33.7	13	4,500	Chişinău	920
Monaco	0.002	0.0001	33	Monaco	16,000
Mongolia	1,567	605	2,500	Ulan Bator	310
Montserrat (UK)	0.10	0.04	12	Plymouth	4,500
Morocco	447	172	28,100	Rabat	1,110
Mozambique	802	309	19,100	Maputo	80
Namibia	825	318	1,700	Windhoek	2,000
Nauru	0.02	0.008	12	Yaren District	10,000
Nepal	141	54	22,100	Katmandu	200
Netherlands	41.5	16	15,900	Amsterdam/The Hague	24,000
Netherlands Antilles (Neths)	0.99	0.38	210	Willemstad	10,500
New Caledonia (France)	18.6	7.2	192	Nouméa	16,000
New Zealand	269	104	3,700	Wellington	14,340
Nicaragua	130	50	4,600	Managua	380
Niger	1,267	489	9,700	Niamey	220
Nigeria	924	357	118,000	Abuja	260
Niue (NZ)	0.26	0.10	2	Alofi	—
Norfolk Is. (Australia)	0.03	0.01	2	Kingston	—
Northern Mariana Is. (US)	0.48	0.18	50	Saipan	11,500
Norway	324	125	4,400	Oslo	31,250
Oman	212	82	2,400	Muscat	4,820
Pakistan	796	307	136,000	Islamabad	460
Palau	0.46	0.18	17	Koror	2,260
Panama	77.1	29.8	2,700	Panama City	2,750
Papua New Guinea	463	179	4,400	Port Moresby	1,160
Paraguay	407	157	5,200	Asunción	1,690
Peru	1,285	496	24,500	Lima	2,310
Philippines	300	116	73,500	Manila	1,050
Pitcairn Is. (UK)	0.03	0.01	0.05	Adamstown	—
Poland	313	121	38,800	Warsaw	2,790
Portugal	92.4	35.7	10,100	Lisbon	9,740
Puerto Rico (US)	9	3.5	3,800	San Juan	7,500
Qatar	11	4.2	620	Doha	11,600
Queen Maud Land (Norway)	2,800	1,081	0	—	—
Réunion (France)	2.5	0.97	680	Saint-Denis	4,500
Romania	238	92	22,600	Bucharest	1,480
Russia	17,075	6,592	147,800	Moscow	2,240
Rwanda	26.3	10.2	7,000	Kigali	180
St Helena (UK)	0.12	0.05	6	Jamestown	—
St Kitts & Nevis	0.36	0.14	42	Basseterre	4,470
St Lucia	0.62	0.24	150	Castries	3,370
St Pierre & Miquelon (France)	0.24	0.09	7	Saint Pierre	—
St Vincent & Grenadines	0.39	0.15	114	Kingstown	2,280
San Marino	0.06	0.02	26	San Marino	20,000
São Tomé & Príncipe	0.96	0.37	135	São Tomé	350
Saudi Arabia	2,150	830	19,100	Riyadh	7,040
Senegal	197	76	8,900	Dakar	600
Seychelles	0.46	0.18	78	Victoria	6,370
Sierra Leone	71.7	27.7	4,600	Freetown	180
Singapore	0.62	0.24	3,200	Singapore	26,730
Slovak Republic	49	18.9	5,400	Bratislava	2,950
Slovenia	20.3	7.8	2,000	Ljubljana	8,200
Solomon Is.	28.9	11.2	410	Honiara	910
Somalia	638	246	9,900	Mogadishu	500
South Africa	1,220	471	42,300	C. Town/Pretoria/Bloem.	3,160
South Georgia (UK)	3.8	1.4	0.05	—	—
Spain	505	195	39,300	Madrid	13,580
Sri Lanka	65.6	25.3	18,700	Colombo	700
Sudan	2,506	967	31,000	Khartoum	750
Surinam	163	63	500	Paramaribo	880
Svalbard (Norway)	62.9	24.3	4	Longyearbyen	—
Swaziland	17.4	6.7	1,000	Mbabane	1,170
Sweden	450	174	8,900	Stockholm	23,750
Switzerland	41.3	15.9	7,100	Bern	40,630
Syria	185	71	15,300	Damascus	1,120
Taiwan	36	13.9	21,700	Taipei	12,000
Tajikistan	143.1	55.2	6,000	Dushanbe	340
Tanzania	945	365	31,200	Dodoma	120
Thailand	513	198	60,800	Bangkok	2,740
Togo	56.8	21.9	4,500	Lomé	310
Tokelau (NZ)	0.01	0.005	2	Nukunonu	—
Tonga	0.75	0.29	107	Nuku'alofa	1,610
Trinidad & Tobago	5.1	2	1,300	Port of Spain	3,770
Tristan da Cunha (UK)	0.11	0.04	0.33	Edinburgh	—
Tunisia	164	63	9,200	Tunis	1,820
Turkey	779	301	63,500	Ankara	2,780
Turkmenistan	488.1	188.5	4,800	Ashkhabad	920
Turks & Caicos Is. (UK)	0.43	0.17	15	Cockburn Town	5,000
Tuvalu	0.03	0.01	10	Fongafale	600
Uganda	236	91	20,800	Kampala	240
Ukraine	603.7	233.1	51,500	Kiev	1,630
United Arab Emirates	83.6	32.3	2,400	Abu Dhabi	17,400
United Kingdom	243.3	94	58,600	London	18,700
United States of America	9,373	3,619	268,000	Washington, DC	26,980
Uruguay	177	68	3,300	Montevideo	5,170
Uzbekistan	447.4	172.7	23,800	Tashkent	970
Vanuatu	12.2	4.7	175	Port-Vila	1,200
Vatican City	0.0004	0.0002	1	—	—
Venezuela	912	352	22,500	Caracas	3,020
Vietnam	332	127	77,100	Hanoi	240
Virgin Is. (UK)	0.15	0.06	13	Road Town	—
Virgin Is. (US)	0.34	0.13	105	Charlotte Amalie	12,000
Wake Is. (US)	0.008	0.003	0.30	—	—
Wallis & Futuna Is. (France)	0.20	0.08	15	Mata-Utu	—
Western Sahara	266	103	280	El Aaiún	980
Western Samoa	2.8	1.1	175	Apia	1,120
Yemen	528	204	16,500	Sana	260
Yugoslavia	102.3	39.5	10,500	Belgrade	1,400
Zambia	753	291	9,500	Lusaka	400
Zimbabwe	391	151	12,100	Harare	540

At the time of going to press, the government of Kazakstan planned to rename the capital Aqmola to Astana.

World Statistics: Physical Dimensions

Each topic list is divided into continents and within a continent the items are listed in order of size. The bottom part of many of the lists is selective in order to give examples from as many different countries as possible. The order of the continents is the same as in the atlas, beginning with Europe and ending with South America. The figures are rounded as appropriate.

World, Continents, Oceans

	km²	miles²	%
The World	509,450,000	196,672,000	–
Land	149,450,000	57,688,000	29.3
Water	360,000,000	138,984,000	70.7
Asia	44,500,000	17,177,000	29.8
Africa	30,302,000	11,697,000	20.3
North America	24,241,000	9,357,000	16.2
South America	17,793,000	6,868,000	11.9
Antarctica	14,100,000	5,443,000	9.4
Europe	9,957,000	3,843,000	6.7
Australia & Oceania	8,557,000	3,303,000	5.7
Pacific Ocean	179,679,000	69,356,000	49.9
Atlantic Ocean	92,373,000	35,657,000	25.7
Indian Ocean	73,917,000	28,532,000	20.5
Arctic Ocean	14,090,000	5,439,000	3.9

Ocean Depths

Atlantic Ocean	m	ft
Puerto Rico (Milwaukee) Deep	9,220	30,249
Cayman Trench	7,680	25,197
Gulf of Mexico	5,203	17,070
Mediterranean Sea	5,121	16,801
Black Sea	2,211	7,254
North Sea	660	2,165

Indian Ocean	m	ft
Java Trench	7,450	24,442
Red Sea	2,635	8,454

Pacific Ocean	m	ft
Mariana Trench	11,022	36,161
Tonga Trench	10,882	35,702
Japan Trench	10,554	34,626
Kuril Trench	10,542	34,587

Arctic Ocean	m	ft
Molloy Deep	5,608	18,399

Mountains

Europe		m	ft
Mont Blanc	France/Italy	4,807	15,771
Monte Rosa	Italy/Switzerland	4,634	15,203
Dom	Switzerland	4,545	14,911
Liskamm	Switzerland	4,527	14,852
Weisshorn	Switzerland	4,505	14,780
Taschorn	Switzerland	4,490	14,730
Matterhorn/Cervino	Italy/Switzerland	4,478	14,691
Mont Maudit	France/Italy	4,465	14,649
Dent Blanche	Switzerland	4,356	14,291
Nadelhorn	Switzerland	4,327	14,196
Grandes Jorasses	France/Italy	4,208	13,806
Jungfrau	Switzerland	4,158	13,642
Grossglockner	Austria	3,797	12,457
Mulhacén	Spain	3,478	11,411
Zugspitze	Germany	2,962	9,718
Olympus	Greece	2,917	9,570
Triglav	Slovenia	2,863	9,393
Gerlachovka	Slovak Republic	2,655	8,711
Galdhöpiggen	Norway	2,468	8,100
Kebnekaise	Sweden	2,117	6,946
Ben Nevis	UK	1,343	4,406

Asia		m	ft
Everest	China/Nepal	8,848	29,029
K2 (Godwin Austen)	China/Kashmir	8,611	28,251
Kanchenjunga	India/Nepal	8,598	28,208
Lhotse	China/Nepal	8,516	27,939
Makalu	China/Nepal	8,481	27,824
Cho Oyu	China/Nepal	8,201	26,906
Dhaulagiri	Nepal	8,172	26,811
Manaslu	Nepal	8,156	26,758
Nanga Parbat	Kashmir	8,126	26,660
Annapurna	Nepal	8,078	26,502
Gasherbrum	China/Kashmir	8,068	26,469
Broad Peak	China/Kashmir	8,051	26,414
Xixabangma	China	8,012	26,286
Kangbachen	India/Nepal	7,902	25,925
Trivor	Pakistan	7,720	25,328
Pik Kommunizma	Tajikistan	7,495	24,590
Elbrus	Russia	5,642	18,510
Demavend	Iran	5,604	18,386
Ararat	Turkey	5,165	16,945
Gunong Kinabalu	Malaysia (Borneo)	4,101	13,455
Fuji-San	Japan	3,776	12,388

Africa		m	ft
Kilimanjaro	Tanzania	5,895	19,340
Mt Kenya	Kenya	5,199	17,057
Ruwenzori (Margherita)	Ug./Congo (Z.)	5,109	16,762
Ras Dashan	Ethiopia	4,620	15,157
Meru	Tanzania	4,565	14,977
Karisimbi	Rwanda/Congo (Zaïre)	4,507	14,787
Mt Elgon	Kenya/Uganda	4,321	14,176
Batu	Ethiopia	4,307	14,130
Toubkal	Morocco	4,165	13,665
Mt Cameroon	Cameroon	4,070	13,353

Oceania		m	ft
Puncak Jaya	Indonesia	5,029	16,499
Puncak Trikora	Indonesia	4,750	15,584
Puncak Mandala	Indonesia	4,702	15,427
Mt Wilhelm	Papua New Guinea	4,508	14,790
Mauna Kea	USA (Hawaii)	4,205	13,796
Mauna Loa	USA (Hawaii)	4,170	13,681
Mt Cook (Aoraki)	New Zealand	3,753	12,313
Mt Kosciuszko	Australia	2,237	7,339

North America		m	ft
Mt McKinley (Denali)	USA (Alaska)	6,194	20,321
Mt Logan	Canada	5,959	19,551
Citlaltepetl	Mexico	5,700	18,701
Mt St Elias	USA/Canada	5,489	18,008
Popocatepetl	Mexico	5,452	17,887
Mt Foraker	USA (Alaska)	5,304	17,401
Ixtaccihuatl	Mexico	5,286	17,342
Lucania	Canada	5,227	17,149
Mt Steele	Canada	5,073	16,644
Mt Bona	USA (Alaska)	5,005	16,420
Mt Whitney	USA	4,418	14,495
Tajumulco	Guatemala	4,220	13,845
Chirripó Grande	Costa Rica	3,837	12,589
Pico Duarte	Dominican Rep.	3,175	10,417

South America		m	ft
Aconcagua	Argentina	6,960	22,834
Bonete	Argentina	6,872	22,546
Ojos del Salado	Argentina/Chile	6,863	22,516
Pissis	Argentina	6,779	22,241
Mercedario	Argentina/Chile	6,770	22,211
Huascaran	Peru	6,768	22,204
Llullaillaco	Argentina/Chile	6,723	22,057
Nudo de Cachi	Argentina	6,720	22,047
Yerupaja	Peru	6,632	21,758
Sajama	Bolivia	6,542	21,463
Chimborazo	Ecuador	6,267	20,561
Pico Colon	Colombia	5,800	19,029
Pico Bolivar	Venezuela	5,007	16,427

Antarctica	m	ft
Vinson Massif	4,897	16,066
Mt Kirkpatrick	4,528	14,855

Rivers

Europe		km	miles
Volga	Caspian Sea	3,700	2,300
Danube	Black Sea	2,850	1,770
Ural	Caspian Sea	2,535	1,575
Dnepr (Dnipro)	Black Sea	2,285	1,420
Kama	Volga	2,030	1,260
Don	Black Sea	1,990	1,240
Petchora	Arctic Ocean	1,790	1,110
Oka	Volga	1,480	920
Dnister (Dniester)	Black Sea	1,400	870
Vyatka	Kama	1,370	850
Rhine	North Sea	1,320	820
N. Dvina	Arctic Ocean	1,290	800
Elbe	North Sea	1,145	710

Asia		km	miles
Yangtze	Pacific Ocean	6,380	3,960
Yenisey–Angara	Arctic Ocean	5,550	3,445
Huang He	Pacific Ocean	5,464	3,395
Ob–Irtysh	Arctic Ocean	5,410	3,360
Mekong	Pacific Ocean	4,500	2,795
Amur	Pacific Ocean	4,400	2,730
Lena	Arctic Ocean	4,400	2,730
Irtysh	Ob	4,250	2,640
Yenisey	Arctic Ocean	4,090	2,540
Ob	Arctic Ocean	3,680	2,285
Indus	Indian Ocean	3,100	1,925
Brahmaputra	Indian Ocean	2,900	1,800
Syrdarya	Aral Sea	2,860	1,775
Salween	Indian Ocean	2,800	1,740
Euphrates	Indian Ocean	2,700	1,675
Amudarya	Aral Sea	2,540	1,575

Africa		km	miles
Nile	Mediterranean	6,670	4,140
Congo	Atlantic Ocean	4,670	2,900
Niger	Atlantic Ocean	4,180	2,595
Zambezi	Indian Ocean	3,540	2,200
Oubangi/Uele	Congo (Zaïre)	2,250	1,400
Kasai	Congo (Zaïre)	1,950	1,210
Shaballe	Indian Ocean	1,930	1,200
Orange	Atlantic Ocean	1,860	1,155
Cubango	Okavango Swamps	1,800	1,120
Limpopo	Indian Ocean	1,600	995
Senegal	Atlantic Ocean	1,600	995

Australia		km	miles
Murray–Darling	Indian Ocean	3,750	2,330
Darling	Murray	3,070	1,905
Murray	Indian Ocean	2,575	1,600
Murrumbidgee	Murray	1,690	1,050

North America		km	miles
Mississippi–Missouri	Gulf of Mexico	6,020	3,740
Mackenzie	Arctic Ocean	4,240	2,630
Mississippi	Gulf of Mexico	3,780	2,350
Missouri	Mississippi	3,780	2,350
Yukon	Pacific Ocean	3,185	1,980
Rio Grande	Gulf of Mexico	3,030	1,880
Arkansas	Mississippi	2,340	1,450
Colorado	Pacific Ocean	2,330	1,445
Red	Mississippi	2,040	1,270
Columbia	Pacific Ocean	1,950	1,210
Saskatchewan	Lake Winnipeg	1,940	1,205

South America		km	miles
Amazon	Atlantic Ocean	6,450	4,010
Paraná–Plate	Atlantic Ocean	4,500	2,800
Purus	Amazon	3,350	2,080
Madeira	Amazon	3,200	1,990
São Francisco	Atlantic Ocean	2,900	1,800
Paraná	Plate	2,800	1,740
Tocantins	Atlantic Ocean	2,750	1,710
Paraguay	Paraná	2,550	1,580
Orinoco	Atlantic Ocean	2,500	1,550
Pilcomayo	Paraná	2,500	1,550
Araguaia	Tocantins	2,250	1,400

Lakes

Europe		km²	miles²
Lake Ladoga	Russia	17,700	6,800
Lake Onega	Russia	9,700	3,700
Saimaa system	Finland	8,000	3,100
Vänern	Sweden	5,500	2,100

Asia		km²	miles²
Caspian Sea	Asia	371,800	143,550
Aral Sea	Kazakstan/Uzbekistan	33,640	13,000
Lake Baykal	Russia	30,500	11,780
Tonlé Sap	Cambodia	20,000	7,700
Lake Balqash	Kazakstan	18,500	7,100

Africa		km²	miles²
Lake Victoria	East Africa	68,000	26,000
Lake Tanganyika	Central Africa	33,000	13,000
Lake Malawi/Nyasa	East Africa	29,600	11,430
Lake Chad	Central Africa	25,000	9,700
Lake Turkana	Ethiopia/Kenya	8,500	3,300
Lake Volta	Ghana	8,500	3,300

Australia		km²	miles²
Lake Eyre	Australia	8,900	3,400
Lake Torrens	Australia	5,800	2,200
Lake Gairdner	Australia	4,800	1,900

North America		km²	miles²
Lake Superior	Canada/USA	82,350	31,800
Lake Huron	Canada/USA	59,600	23,010
Lake Michigan	USA	58,000	22,400
Great Bear Lake	Canada	31,800	12,280
Great Slave Lake	Canada	28,500	11,000
Lake Erie	Canada/USA	25,700	9,900
Lake Winnipeg	Canada	24,400	9,400
Lake Ontario	Canada/USA	19,500	7,500
Lake Nicaragua	Nicaragua	8,200	3,200

South America		km²	miles²
Lake Titicaca	Bolivia/Peru	8,300	3,200
Lake Poopo	Peru	2,800	1,100

Islands

Europe		km²	miles²
Great Britain	UK	229,880	88,700
Iceland	Atlantic Ocean	103,000	39,800
Ireland	Ireland/UK	84,400	32,600
Novaya Zemlya (N.)	Russia	48,200	18,600
Sicily	Italy	25,500	9,800
Corsica	France	8,700	3,400

Asia		km²	miles²
Borneo	Southeast Asia	744,360	287,400
Sumatra	Indonesia	473,600	182,860
Honshu	Japan	230,500	88,980
Sulawesi (Celebes)	Indonesia	189,000	73,000
Java	Indonesia	126,700	48,900
Luzon	Philippines	104,700	40,400
Hokkaido	Japan	78,400	30,300

Africa		km²	miles²
Madagascar	Indian Ocean	587,040	226,660
Socotra	Indian Ocean	3,600	1,400
Réunion	Indian Ocean	2,500	965

Oceania		km²	miles²
New Guinea	Indonesia/Papua NG	821,030	317,000
New Zealand (S.)	Pacific Ocean	150,500	58,100
New Zealand (N.)	Pacific Ocean	114,700	44,300
Tasmania	Australia	67,800	26,200
Hawaii	Pacific Ocean	10,450	4,000

North America		km²	miles²
Greenland	Atlantic Ocean	2,175,600	839,800
Baffin Is.	Canada	508,000	196,100
Victoria Is.	Canada	212,200	81,900
Ellesmere Is.	Canada	212,000	81,800
Cuba	Caribbean Sea	110,860	42,800
Hispaniola	Dominican Rep./Haiti	76,200	29,400
Jamaica	Caribbean Sea	11,400	4,400
Puerto Rico	Atlantic Ocean	8,900	3,400

South America		km²	miles²
Tierra del Fuego	Argentina/Chile	47,000	18,100
Falkland Is. (E.)	Atlantic Ocean	6,800	2,600

Philip's World Maps

The reference maps which form the main body of this atlas have been prepared in accordance with the highest standards of international cartography to provide an accurate and detailed representation of the Earth. The scales and projections used have been carefully chosen to give balanced coverage of the world, while emphasizing the most densely populated and economically significant regions. A hallmark of Philip's mapping is the use of hill shading and relief colouring to create a graphic impression of landforms: this makes the maps exceptionally easy to read. However, knowledge of the key features employed in the construction and presentation of the maps will enable the reader to derive the fullest benefit from the atlas.

Map sequence

The atlas covers the Earth continent by continent: first Europe; then its land neighbour Asia (mapped north before south, in a clockwise sequence), then Africa, Australia and Oceania, North America and South America. This is the classic arrangement adopted by most cartographers since the 16th century. For each continent, there are maps at a variety of scales. First, physical relief and political maps of the whole continent; then a series of larger-scale maps of the regions within the continent, each followed, where required, by still larger-scale maps of the most important or densely populated areas. The governing principle is that by turning the pages of the atlas, the reader moves steadily from north to south through each continent, with each map overlapping its neighbours. A key map showing this sequence, and the area covered by each map, can be found on the endpapers of the atlas.

Map presentation

With very few exceptions (e.g. for the Arctic and Antarctica), the maps are drawn with north at the top, regardless of whether they are presented upright or sideways on the page. In the borders will be found the map title; a locator diagram showing the area covered and the page numbers for maps of adjacent areas; the scale; the projection used; the degrees of latitude and longitude; and the letters and figures used in the index for locating place names and geographical features. Physical relief maps also have a height reference panel identifying the colours used for each layer of contouring.

Map symbols

Each map contains a vast amount of detail which can only be conveyed clearly and accurately by the use of symbols. Points and circles of varying sizes locate and identify the relative importance of towns and cities; different styles of type are employed for administrative, geographical and regional place names. A variety of pictorial symbols denote features such as glaciers and marshes, as well as man-

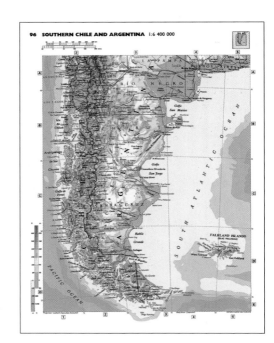

96 SOUTHERN CHILE AND ARGENTINA 1:6 400 000

made structures including roads, railways, airports and canals. International borders are shown by red lines. Where neighbouring countries are in dispute, for example in the Middle East, the maps show the *de facto* boundary between nations, regardless of the legal or historical situation. The symbols are explained on the first page of the World Maps section of the atlas.

Map scales

The scale of each map is given in the numerical form known as the 'representative fraction'. The first figure is always one, signifying one unit of distance on the map; the second figure, usually in millions, is the number by which the map unit must be multiplied to give the equivalent distance on the Earth's surface. Calculations can easily be made in centimetres and kilometres, by dividing the Earth units figure by 100 000 (i.e. deleting the last five 0s). Thus 1:1 000 000 means 1 cm = 10 km. The calculation for inches and miles is more laborious, but 1 000 000 divided by 63 360 (the number of inches in a mile) shows that the ratio 1:1 000 000 means approximately 1 inch = 16 miles. The table below provides distance equivalents for scales down to 1:50 000 000.

LARGE SCALE		
1:1 000 000	1 cm = 10 km	1 inch = 16 miles
1:2 500 000	1 cm = 25 km	1 inch = 39.5 miles
1:5 000 000	1 cm = 50 km	1 inch = 79 miles
1:6 000 000	1 cm = 60 km	1 inch = 95 miles
1:8 000 000	1 cm = 80 km	1 inch = 126 miles
1:10 000 000	1 cm = 100 km	1 inch = 158 miles
1:15 000 000	1 cm = 150 km	1 inch = 237 miles
1:20 000 000	1 cm = 200 km	1 inch = 316 miles
1:50 000 000	1 cm = 500 km	1 inch = 790 miles
SMALL SCALE		

Measuring distances

Although each map is accompanied by a scale bar, distances cannot always be measured with confidence because of the distortions involved in portraying the curved surface of the Earth on a flat page. As a general rule, the larger the map scale (i.e. the lower the number of Earth units in the representative fraction), the more accurate and reliable will be the distance measured. On small-scale maps such as those of the world and of entire continents, measurement may only be accurate along the 'standard parallels', or central axes, and should not be attempted without considering the map projection.

Latitude and longitude

Accurate positioning of individual points on the Earth's surface is made possible by reference to the geometrical system of latitude and longitude. Latitude *parallels* are drawn west-east around the Earth and numbered by degrees north and south of the Equator, which is designated 0° of latitude. Longitude *meridians* are drawn north–south and numbered by degrees east and west of the *prime meridian*, 0° of longitude, which passes through Greenwich in England. By referring to these co-ordinates and their subdivisions of minutes ($^{1}/_{60}$th of a degree) and seconds ($^{1}/_{60}$th of a minute), any place on Earth can be located to within a few hundred metres. Latitude and longitude are indicated by blue lines on the maps; they are straight or curved according to the projection employed. Reference to these lines is the easiest way of determining the relative positions of places on different maps, and for plotting compass directions.

Name forms

For ease of reference, both English and local name forms appear in the atlas. Oceans, seas and countries are shown in English throughout the atlas; country names may be abbreviated to their commonly accepted form (e.g. Germany, not The Federal Republic of Germany). Conventional English forms are also used for place names on the smaller-scale maps of the continents. However, local name forms are used on all large-scale and regional maps, with the English form given in brackets only for important cities – the large-scale map of Russia and Central Asia thus shows Moskva (Moscow). For countries which do not use a Roman script, place names have been transcribed according to the systems adopted by the British and US Geographic Names Authorities. For China, the Pin Yin system has been used, with some more widely known forms appearing in brackets, as with Beijing (Peking). Both English and local names appear in the index, the English form being cross-referenced to the local form.

The WORLD IN FOCUS

Planet Earth

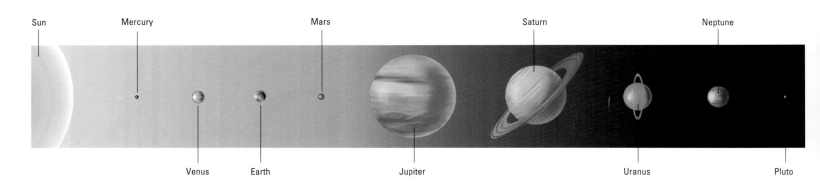

Sun · Mercury · Mars · Saturn · Neptune · Venus · Earth · Jupiter · Uranus · Pluto

The Solar System

A minute part of one of the billions of galaxies (collections of stars) that comprises the Universe, the Solar System lies some 27,000 light-years from the centre of our own galaxy, the 'Milky Way'. Thought to be over 4,700 million years old, it consists of a central sun with nine planets and their moons revolving around it, attracted by its gravitational pull. The planets orbit the Sun in the same direction – anti-clockwise when viewed from the Northern Heavens – and almost in the same plane. Their orbital paths, however, vary enormously.

The Sun's diameter is 109 times that of Earth, and the temperature at its core – caused by continuous thermonuclear fusions of hydrogen into helium – is estimated to be 15 million degrees Celsius. It is the Solar System's only source of light and heat.

Profile of the Planets

	Mean distance from Sun (million km)	Mass (Earth = 1)	Period of orbit (Earth years)	Period of rotation (Earth days)	Equatorial diameter (km)	Number of known satellites
Mercury	57.9	0.055	0.24 years	58.67	4,878	0
Venus	108.2	0.815	0.62 years	243.00	12,104	0
Earth	149.6	1.0	1.00 years	1.00	12,756	1
Mars	227.9	0.107	1.88 years	1.03	6,787	2
Jupiter	778.3	317.8	11.86 years	0.41	142,800	16
Saturn	1,427	95.2	29.46 years	0.43	120,000	20
Uranus	2,871	14.5	84.01 years	0.75	51,118	15
Neptune	4,497	17.1	164.80 years	0.80	49,528	8
Pluto	5,914	0.002	248.50 years	6.39	2,320	1

All planetary orbits are elliptical in form, but only Pluto and Mercury follow paths that deviate noticeably from a circular one. Near perihelion – its closest approach to the Sun – Pluto actually passes inside the orbit of Neptune, an event that last occurred in 1983. Pluto will not regain its station as outermost planet until February 1999.

The Seasons

Seasons occur because the Earth's axis is tilted at a constant angle of 23½°. When the northern hemisphere is tilted to a maximum extent towards the Sun, on 21 June, the Sun is overhead at the Tropic of Cancer (latitude 23½° North). This is midsummer, or the summer solstice, in the northern hemisphere.

On 22 or 23 September, the Sun is overhead at the Equator, and day and night are of equal length throughout the world. This is the autumn equinox in the northern hemisphere. On 21 or 22 December, the Sun is overhead at the Tropic of Capricorn (23½° South), the winter solstice in the northern hemisphere. The overhead Sun then tracks north until, on 21 March, it is overhead at the Equator. This is the spring (vernal) equinox in the northern hemisphere.

In the southern hemisphere, the seasons are the reverse of those in the north.

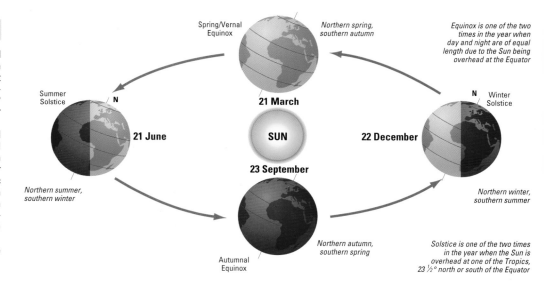

Spring/Vernal Equinox — Northern spring, southern autumn

Equinox is one of the two times in the year when day and night are of equal length due to the Sun being overhead at the Equator

Summer Solstice · 21 June · 21 March · SUN · 23 September · 22 December · Winter Solstice

Northern summer, southern winter

Autumnal Equinox — Northern autumn, southern spring

Northern winter, southern summer

Solstice is one of the two times in the year when the Sun is overhead at one of the Tropics, 23½° north or south of the Equator

Day and Night

The Sun appears to rise in the east, reach its highest point at noon, and then set in the west, to be followed by night. In reality, it is not the Sun that is moving but the Earth rotating from west to east. The moment when the Sun's upper limb first appears above the horizon is termed sunrise; the moment when the Sun's upper limb disappears below the horizon is sunset.

At the summer solstice in the northern hemisphere (21 June), the Arctic has total daylight and the Antarctic total darkness. The opposite occurs at the winter solstice (21 or 22 December). At the Equator, the length of day and night are almost equal all year.

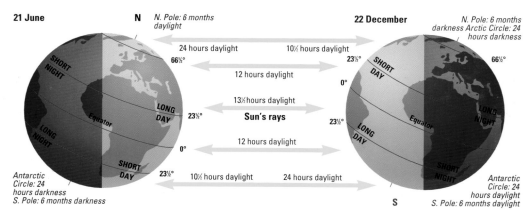

21 June — N. Pole: 6 months daylight. 24 hours daylight. 66½°. 12 hours daylight. 23½°. Sun's rays. 13½ hours daylight. 0°. 12 hours daylight. 23½°. 10½ hours daylight. Antarctic Circle: 24 hours darkness. S. Pole: 6 months darkness.

22 December — N. Pole: 6 months darkness. Arctic Circle: 24 hours darkness. 10½ hours daylight. 23½°. 66½°. 0°. 23½°. 24 hours daylight. Antarctic Circle: 24 hours daylight. S. Pole: 6 months daylight.

SHORT NIGHT · LONG DAY · LONG NIGHT · SHORT DAY

Time

Year: The time taken by the Earth to revolve around the Sun, or 365.24 days.

Leap Year: A calendar year of 366 days, 29 February being the additional day. It offsets the difference between the calendar and the solar year.

Month: The approximate time taken by the Moon to revolve around the Earth. The 12 months of the year in fact vary from 28 (29 in a Leap Year) to 31 days.

Week: An artificial period of 7 days, not based on astronomical time.

Day: The time taken by the Earth to complete one rotation on its axis.

Hour: 24 hours make one day. Usually the day is divided into hours AM (ante meridiem or before noon) and PM (post meridiem or after noon), although most timetables now use the 24-hour system, from midnight to midnight.

Sunrise

Hours AM — Spring Equinox — Autumnal Equinox — Latitude

60°N, 40°N, 20°N, 0°(Equator), 20°S, 40°S, 60°S

Months of the year: J F M A M J J A S O N D

Sunset

Hours PM — Spring Equinox — Autumnal Equinox — Latitude

60°S, 40°S, 20°S, 0°(Equator), 20°N, 40°N, 60°N

Months of the year: J F M A M J J A S O N D

The Moon

The Moon rotates more slowly than the Earth, making one complete turn on its axis in just over 27 days. Since this corresponds to its period of revolution around the Earth, the Moon always presents the same

Phases of the Moon

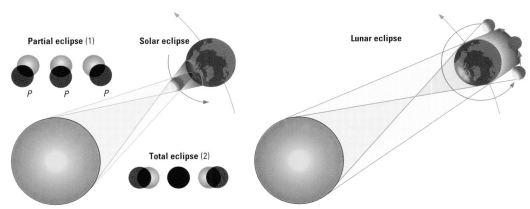

Distance from Earth: 356,410 km – 406,685 km; Mean diameter: 3,475.1 km; Mass: approx. 1/81 that of Earth; Surface gravity: one-sixth of Earth's; Daily range of temperature at lunar equator: 200°C; Average orbital speed: 3,683 km/h

New Moon — Crescent — First quarter — Gibbous — Full Moon — Gibbous — Last quarter — Crescent — New Moon

hemisphere or face to us, and we never see 'the dark side'. The interval between one full Moon and the next (and between new Moons) is about 29½ days – a lunar month. The apparent changes in the

shape of the Moon are caused by its changing position in relation to the Earth; like the planets, it produces no light of its own and shines only by reflecting the rays of the Sun.

Eclipses

When the Moon passes between the Sun and the Earth it causes a partial eclipse of the Sun (1) if the Earth passes through the Moon's outer shadow (P), or a total eclipse (2) if the inner cone shadow crosses the Earth's surface. In a lunar eclipse, the Earth's shadow crosses the Moon and, again, provides either a partial or total eclipse.

Eclipses of the Sun and the Moon do not occur every month because of the 5° difference between the plane of the Moon's orbit and the plane in which the Earth moves. In the 1990s only 14 lunar eclipses are possible, for example, seven partial and seven total; each is visible only from certain, and variable, parts of the world. The same period witnesses 13 solar eclipses – six partial (or annular) and seven total.

Partial eclipse (1) — P P P

Solar eclipse

Total eclipse (2)

Lunar eclipse

Tides

The daily rise and fall of the ocean's tides are the result of the gravitational pull of the Moon and that of the Sun, though the effect of the latter is only 46.6% as strong as that of the Moon. This effect is greatest on the hemisphere facing the Moon and causes a tidal 'bulge'. When the Sun, Earth and Moon are in line, tide-raising forces are at a maximum and Spring tides occur: high tide reaches the highest values, and low tide falls to low levels. When lunar and solar forces are least coincidental with the Sun and Moon at an angle (near the Moon's first and third quarters), Neap tides occur, which have a small tidal range.

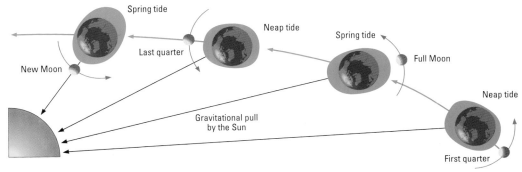

Spring tide — Neap tide — Spring tide — Full Moon — Last quarter — Neap tide — New Moon — Gravitational pull by the Sun — First quarter

Restless Earth

The Earth's Structure

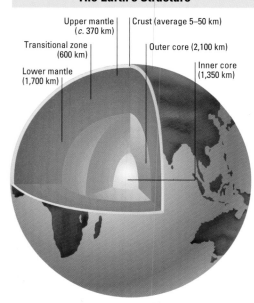

Upper mantle (c. 370 km)
Crust (average 5–50 km)
Transitional zone (600 km)
Outer core (2,100 km)
Lower mantle (1,700 km)
Inner core (1,350 km)

Continental Drift

About 200 million years ago the original Pangaea landmass began to split into two continental groups, which further separated over time to produce the present-day configuration.

180 million years ago

Laurasia
Tethys Sea
Gondwanaland

135 million years ago

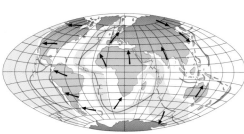

Present day

Trench
Rift
New ocean floor
Zones of slippage

Notable Earthquakes Since 1900

Year	Location	Richter Scale	Deaths
1906	San Francisco, USA	8.3	503
1906	Valparaiso, Chile	8.6	22,000
1908	Messina, Italy	7.5	83,000
1915	Avezzano, Italy	7.5	30,000
1920	Gansu (Kansu), China	8.6	180,000
1923	Yokohama, Japan	8.3	143,000
1927	Nan Shan, China	8.3	200,000
1932	Gansu (Kansu), China	7.6	70,000
1933	Sanriku, Japan	8.9	2,990
1934	Bihar, India/Nepal	8.4	10,700
1935	Quetta, India (now Pakistan)	7.5	60,000
1939	Chillan, Chile	8.3	28,000
1939	Erzincan, Turkey	7.9	30,000
1960	Agadir, Morocco	5.8	12,000
1962	Khorasan, Iran	7.1	12,230
1968	N.E. Iran	7.4	12,000
1970	N. Peru	7.7	66,794
1972	Managua, Nicaragua	6.2	5,000
1974	N. Pakistan	6.3	5,200
1976	Guatemala	7.5	22,778
1976	Tangshan, China	8.2	255,000
1978	Tabas, Iran	7.7	25,000
1980	El Asnam, Algeria	7.3	20,000
1980	S. Italy	7.2	4,800
1985	Mexico City, Mexico	8.1	4,200
1988	N.W. Armenia	6.8	55,000
1990	N. Iran	7.7	36,000
1993	Maharashtra, India	6.4	30,000
1994	Los Angeles, USA	6.6	61
1995	Kobe, Japan	7.2	5,000
1995	Sakhalin Is., Russia	7.5	2,000
1997	N.E. Iran	7.1	2,500
1998	Takhar, Afghanistan	6.1	4,200

The highest magnitude recorded on the Richter scale is 8.9 in Japan on 2 March 1933 which killed 2,990 people. The most devastating earthquake ever was at Shaanxi (Shenshi) province, central China, on 3 January 1556, when an estimated 830,000 people were killed.

Structure and Earthquakes

- Mobile land areas
- Submarine zones of mobile land areas
- Stable land platforms
- Submarine extensions of stable land platforms
- Mid-oceanic volcanic ridges
- Oceanic platforms

1976 ○ Principal earthquakes and dates

Earthquakes are a series of rapid vibrations originating from the slipping or faulting of parts of the Earth's crust when stresses within build up to breaking point. They usually happen at depths varying from 8 km to 30 km. Severe earthquakes cause extensive damage when they take place in populated areas, destroying structures and severing communications. Most initial loss of life occurs due to secondary causes such as falling masonry, fires and flooding.

Earthquakes

Earthquake magnitude is usually rated according to either the Richter or the Modified Mercalli scale, both devised by seismologists in the 1930s. The Richter scale measures absolute earthquake power with mathematical precision: each step upwards represents a tenfold increase in shockwave amplitude. Theoretically, there is no upper limit, but the largest earthquakes measured have been rated at between 8.8 and 8.9. The 12–point Mercalli scale, based on observed effects, is often more meaningful, ranging from I (earthquakes noticed only by seismographs) to XII (total destruction); intermediate points include V (people awakened at night; unstable objects overturned), VII (collapse of ordinary buildings; chimneys and monuments fall) and IX (conspicuous cracks in ground; serious damage to reservoirs).

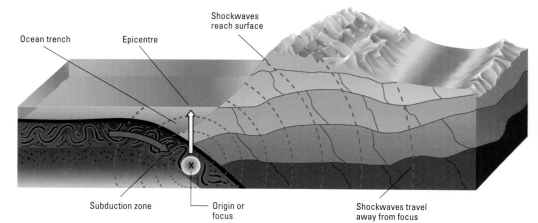

Shockwaves reach surface
Ocean trench
Epicentre
Subduction zone
Origin or focus
Shockwaves travel away from focus

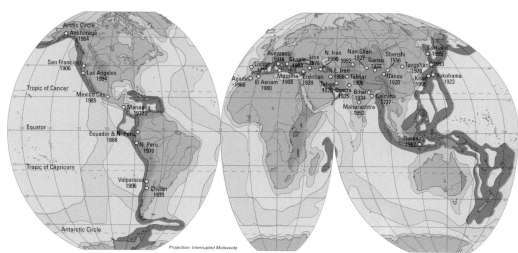

Projection: Interrupted Mollweide

Plate Tectonics

Plate boundaries   PACIFIC   Major plates

Direction of plate movements and rate of movement (cm/year)

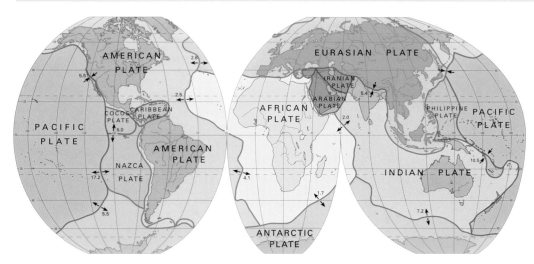

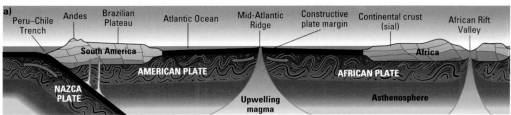

The drifting of the continents is a feature that is unique to Planet Earth. The complementary, almost jigsaw-puzzle fit of the coastlines on each side of the Atlantic Ocean inspired Alfred Wegener's theory of continental drift in 1915. The theory suggested that the ancient super-continent, which Wegener named Pangaea, incorporated all of the Earth's landmasses and gradually split up to form today's continents.

The original debate about continental drift was a prelude to a more radical idea: plate tectonics. The basic theory is that the Earth's crust is made up of a series of rigid plates which float on a soft layer of the mantle and are moved about by continental convection currents within the Earth's interior. These plates diverge and converge along margins marked by seismic activity. Plates diverge from mid-ocean ridges where molten lava pushes upwards and forces the plates apart at rates of up to 40 mm [1.6 in] a year.

The three diagrams, left, give some examples of plate boundaries from around the world. Diagram (a) shows sea-floor spreading at the Mid-Atlantic Ridge as the American and African plates slowly diverge. The same thing is happening in (b) where sea-floor spreading at the Mid-Indian Ocean Ridge is forcing the Indian plate to collide into the Eurasian plate. In (c) oceanic crust (sima) is being subducted beneath lighter continental crust (sial).

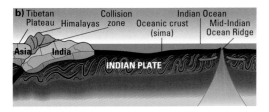

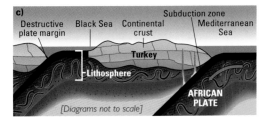

Volcanoes

Volcanoes occur when hot liquefied rock beneath the Earth's crust is pushed up by pressure to the surface as molten lava. Some volcanoes erupt in an explosive way, throwing out rocks and ash, whilst others are effusive and lava flows out of the vent. There are volcanoes which are both, such as Mount Fuji. An accumulation of lava and cinders creates cones of variable size and shape. As a result of many eruptions over centuries, Mount Etna in Sicily has a circumference of more than 120 km [75 miles].

Climatologists believe that volcanic ash, if ejected high into the atmosphere, can influence temperature and weather for several years afterwards. The 1991 eruption of Mount Pinatubo in the Philippines ejected more than 20 million tonnes of dust and ash 32 km [20 miles] into the atmosphere and is believed to have accelerated ozone depletion over a large part of the globe.

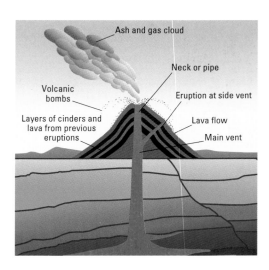

Distribution of Volcanoes

Volcanoes today may be the subject of considerable scientific study but they remain both dramatic and unpredictable: in 1991 Mount Pinatubo, 100 km [62 miles] north of the Philippines capital Manila, suddenly burst into life after lying dormant for more than six centuries. Most of the world's active volcanoes occur in a belt around the Pacific Ocean, on the edge of the Pacific plate, called the 'ring of fire'. Indonesia has the greatest concentration with 90 volcanoes, 12 of which are active. The most famous, Krakatoa, erupted in 1883 with such force that the resulting tidal wave killed 36,000 people and tremors were felt as far away as Australia.

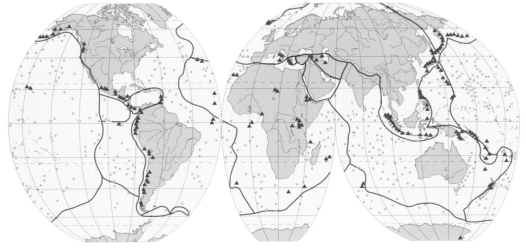

  ●   Submarine volcanoes

  ▲   Land volcanoes active since 1700

  —   Boundaries of tectonic plates

Landforms

The Rock Cycle

James Hutton first proposed the rock cycle in the late 1700s after he observed the slow but steady effects of erosion.

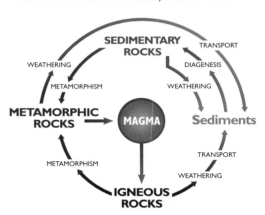

Above and below the surface of the oceans, the features of the Earth's crust are constantly changing. The phenomenal forces generated by convection currents in the molten core of our planet carry the vast segments or 'plates' of the crust across the globe in an endless cycle of creation and destruction. A continent may travel little more than 25 mm [1 in] per year, yet in the vast span of geological time this process throws up giant mountain ranges and creates new land.

Destruction of the landscape, however, begins as soon as it is formed. Wind, water, ice and sea, the main agents of erosion, mount a constant assault that even the most resistant rocks cannot withstand. Mountain peaks may dwindle by as little as a few millimetres each year, but if they are not uplifted by further movements of the crust they will eventually be reduced to rubble and transported away.

Water is the most powerful agent of erosion – it has been estimated that 100 billion tonnes of sediment are washed into the oceans every year. Three Asian rivers account for 20% of this total, the Huang He, in China, and the Brahmaputra and Ganges in Bangladesh.

Rivers and glaciers, like the sea itself, generate much of their effect through abrasion – pounding the land with the debris they carry with them. But as well as destroying they also create new landforms, many of them spectacular: vast deltas like those of the Mississippi and the Nile, or the deep fjords cut by glaciers in British Columbia, Norway and New Zealand.

Geologists once considered that landscapes evolved from 'young', newly uplifted mountainous areas, through a 'mature' hilly stage, to an 'old age' stage when the land was reduced to an almost flat plain, or peneplain. This theory, called the 'cycle of erosion', fell into disuse when it became evident that so many factors, including the effects of plate tectonics and climatic change, constantly interrupt the cycle, which takes no account of the highly complex interactions that shape the surface of our planet.

Mountain Building

Mountains are formed when pressures on the Earth's crust caused by continental drift become so intense that the surface buckles or cracks. This happens where oceanic crust is subducted by continental crust or, more dramatically, where two tectonic plates collide: the Rockies, Andes, Alps, Urals and Himalayas resulted from such impacts. These are all known as fold mountains because they were formed by the compression of the rocks, forcing the surface to bend and fold like a crumpled rug. The Himalayas are formed from the folded former sediments of the Tethys Sea which was trapped in the collision zone between the Indian and Eurasian plates.

The other main mountain-building process occurs when the crust fractures to create faults, allowing rock to be forced upwards in large blocks; or when the pressure of magma within the crust forces the surface to bulge into a dome, or erupts to form a volcano. Large mountain ranges may reveal a combination of those features; the Alps, for example, have been compressed so violently that the folds are fragmented by numerous faults and intrusions of molten igneous rock.

Over millions of years, even the greatest mountain ranges can be reduced by the agents of erosion (most notably rivers) to a low rugged landscape known as a peneplain.

Types of faults: Faults occur where the crust is being stretched or compressed so violently that the rock strata break in a horizontal or vertical movement. They are classified by the direction in which the blocks of rock have moved. A normal fault results when a vertical movement causes the surface to break apart; compression causes a reverse fault. Horizontal movement causes shearing, known as a strike-slip fault. When the rock breaks in two places, the central block may be pushed up in a horst fault, or sink (creating a rift valley) in a graben fault.

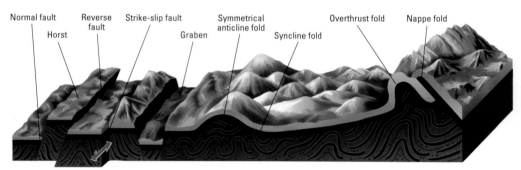

Types of fold: Folds occur when rock strata are squeezed and compressed. They are common therefore at destructive plate margins and where plates have collided, forcing the rocks to buckle into mountain ranges. Geographers give different names to the degrees of fold that result from continuing pressure on the rock. A simple fold may be symmetric, with even slopes on either side, but as the pressure builds up, one slope becomes steeper and the fold becomes asymmetric. Later, the ridge or 'anticline' at the top of the fold may slide over the lower ground or 'syncline' to form a recumbent fold. Eventually, the rock strata may break under the pressure to form an overthrust and finally a nappe fold.

Continental Glaciation

Ice sheets were at their greatest extent about 200,000 years ago. The maximum advance of the last Ice Age was about 18,000 years ago, when ice covered virtually all of Canada and reached as far south as the Bristol Channel in Britain.

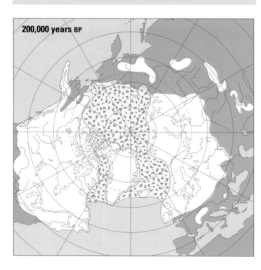

200,000 years BP

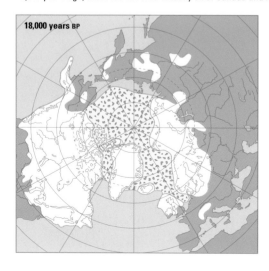

18,000 years BP

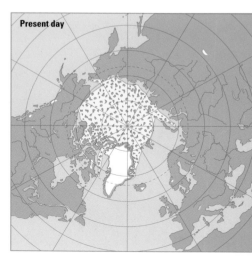

Present day

Natural Landforms

A stylized diagram to show a selection of landforms found in the mid-latitudes.

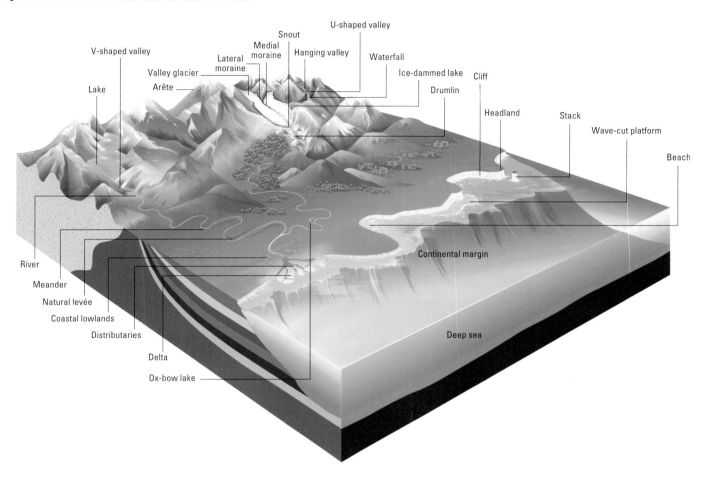

V-shaped valley · Valley glacier · Arête · Lake · Lateral moraine · Medial moraine · Snout · Hanging valley · U-shaped valley · Waterfall · Ice-dammed lake · Drumlin · Cliff · Headland · Stack · Wave-cut platform · Beach · River · Meander · Natural levée · Coastal lowlands · Distributaries · Delta · Ox-bow lake · Continental margin · Deep sea

Desert Landscapes

The popular image that deserts are all huge expanses of sand is wrong. Despite harsh conditions, deserts contain some of the most varied and interesting landscapes in the world. They are also one of the most extensive environments – the hot and cold deserts together cover almost 40% of the Earth's surface.

The three types of hot desert are known by their Arabic names: sand desert, called *erg*, covers only about one-fifth of the world's desert; the rest is divided between *hammada* (areas of bare rock) and *reg* (broad plains covered by loose gravel or pebbles).

In areas of *erg*, such as the Namib Desert, the shape of the dunes reflects the character of local winds. Where winds are constant in direction, crescent-shaped *barchan* dunes form. In areas of bare rock, wind-blown sand is a major agent of erosion. The erosion is mainly confined to within 2 m [6.5 ft] of the surface, producing characteristic, mushroom-shaped rocks.

Erg

Hammada

Reg

Surface Processes

Catastrophic changes to natural landforms are periodically caused by such phenomena as avalanches, landslides and volcanic eruptions, but most of the processes that shape the Earth's surface operate extremely slowly in human terms. One estimate, based on a study in the United States, suggested that 1 m [3 ft] of land was removed from the entire surface of the country, on average, every 29,500 years. However, the time-scale varies from 1,300 years to 154,200 years depending on the terrain and climate.

In hot, dry climates, mechanical weathering, a result of rapid temperature changes, causes the outer layers of rock to peel away, while in cold mountainous regions, boulders are prised apart when water freezes in cracks in rocks. Chemical weathering, at its greatest in warm, humid regions, is responsible for hollowing out limestone caves and decomposing granites.

The erosion of soil and rock is greatest on sloping land and the steeper the slope, the greater the tendency for mass wasting – the movement of soil and rock downhill under the influence of gravity. The mechanisms of mass wasting (ranging from very slow to very rapid) vary with the type of material, but the presence of water as a lubricant is usually an important factor.

Running water is the world's leading agent of erosion and transportation. The energy of a river depends on several factors, including its velocity and volume, and its erosive power is at its peak when it is in full flood. Sea waves also exert tremendous erosive power during storms when they hurl pebbles against the shore, undercutting cliffs and hollowing out caves.

Glacier ice forms in mountain hollows and spills out to form valley glaciers, which transport rocks shattered by frost action. As glaciers move, rocks embedded into the ice erode steep-sided, U-shaped valleys. Evidence of glaciation in mountain regions includes cirques, knife-edged ridges, or arêtes, and pyramidal peaks.

Oceans

The Great Oceans

Relative sizes of the world's oceans

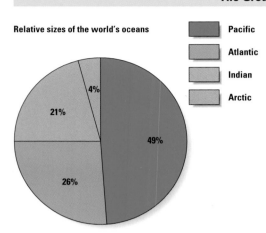

- Pacific
- Atlantic
- Indian
- Arctic

In a strict geographical sense there are only three true oceans – the Atlantic, Indian and Pacific. The legendary 'Seven Seas' would require these to be divided at the Equator and the addition of the Arctic Ocean – which accounts for less than 4% of the total sea area. The International Hydrographic Bureau does not recognize the Antarctic Ocean (even less the 'Southern Ocean') as a separate entity.

The Earth is a watery planet: more than 70% of its surface – over 360,000,000 sq km [140,000,000 sq miles] – is covered by the oceans and seas. The mighty Pacific alone accounts for nearly 36% of the total, and 49% of the sea area. Gravity holds in around 1,400 million cu. km [320 million cu. miles] of water, of which over 97% is saline.

The vast underwater world starts in the shallows of the seaside and plunges to depths of more than 11,000 m [36,000 ft]. The continental shelf, part of the landmass, drops gently to around 200 m [650 ft]; here the seabed falls away suddenly at an angle of 3° to 6° – the continental slope. The third stage, called the continental rise, is more gradual with gradients varying from 1 in 100 to 1 in 700. At an average depth of 5,000 m [16,500 ft] there begins the aptly-named abyssal plain – massive submarine depths where sunlight fails to penetrate and few creatures can survive.

From these plains rise volcanoes which, taken from base to top, rival and even surpass the tallest continental mountains in height. Mount Kea, on Hawaii, reaches a total of 10,203 m [33,400 ft], some 1,355 m [4,500 ft] more than Mount Everest, though scarcely 40% is visible above sea level.

In addition, there are underwater mountain chains up to 1,000 km [600 miles] across, whose peaks sometimes appear above sea level as islands such as Iceland and Tristan da Cunha.

The Ocean Depths

Average and maximum depths of the world's great oceans, in metres

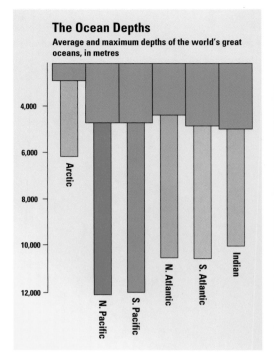

Ocean Currents

January temperatures and ocean currents

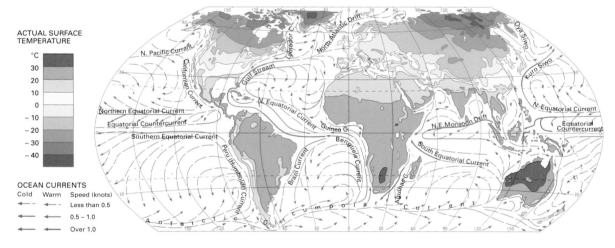

ACTUAL SURFACE TEMPERATURE

°C
- 30
- 20
- 10
- 0
- – 10
- – 20
- – 30
- – 40

OCEAN CURRENTS
Cold	Warm	Speed (knots)
		Less than 0.5
		0.5 – 1.0
		Over 1.0

July temperatures and ocean currents

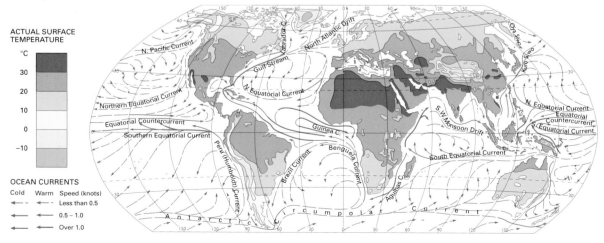

ACTUAL SURFACE TEMPERATURE

°C
- 30
- 20
- 10
- 0
- –10

OCEAN CURRENTS
Cold	Warm	Speed (knots)
		Less than 0.5
		0.5 – 1.0
		Over 1.0

Moving immense quantities of energy as well as billions of tonnes of water every hour, the ocean currents are a vital part of the great heat engine that drives the Earth's climate. They themselves are produced by a twofold mechanism. At the surface, winds push huge masses of water before them; in the deep ocean, below an abrupt temperature gradient that separates the churning surface waters from the still depths, density variations cause slow vertical movements.

The pattern of circulation of the great surface currents is determined by the displacement known as the Coriolis effect. As the Earth turns beneath a moving object – whether it is a tennis ball or a vast mass of water – it appears to be deflected to one side. The deflection is most obvious near the Equator, where the Earth's surface is spinning eastwards at 1,700 km/h [1,050 mph]; currents moving polewards are curved clockwise in the northern hemisphere and anti-clockwise in the southern.

The result is a system of spinning circles known as gyres. The Coriolis effect piles up water on the left of each gyre, creating a narrow, fast-moving stream that is matched by a slower, broader returning current on the right. North and south of the Equator, the fastest currents are located in the west and in the east respectively. In each case, warm water moves from the Equator and cold water returns to it. Cold currents often bring an upwelling of nutrients with them, supporting the world's most economically important fisheries.

Depending on the prevailing winds, some currents on or near the Equator may reverse their direction in the course of the year – a seasonal variation on which Asian monsoon rains depend, and whose occasional failure can bring disaster to millions.

World Fishing Areas

Main commercial fishing areas (numbered FAO regions)

Catch by top marine fishing areas, thousand tonnes (1992)

1.	Pacific, NW	[61]	24,199	29.3%
2.	Pacific, SE	[87]	13,899	16.8%
3.	Atlantic, NE	[27]	11,073	13.4%
4.	Pacific, WC	[71]	7,710	9.3%
5.	Indian, W	[51]	3,747	4.5%
6.	Indian, E	[57]	3,262	4.0%
7.	Atlantic, EC	[34]	3,259	3.9%
8.	Pacific, NE	[67]	3,149	3.8%

Principal fishing areas

Leading fishing nations

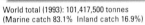

China 17.3% Peru 8.3% Japan 8.0% Chile 5.9% U.S.A. 5.9% Russia 4.4% India 4.3% Indonesia 3.6%

World total (1993): 101,417,500 tonnes
(Marine catch 83.1% Inland catch 16.9%)

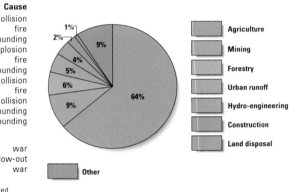

Marine Pollution

Sources of marine oil pollution (latest available year)

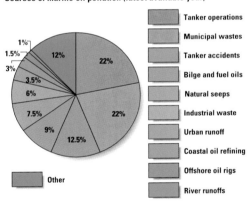

22% Tanker operations
12% Municipal wastes
1% Tanker accidents
1.5% Bilge and fuel oils
3% Natural seeps
3.5% Industrial waste
6% Urban runoff
7.5% Coastal oil refining
9% Offshore oil rigs
12.5% River runoffs
22%

Other

Oil Spills

Major oil spills from tankers and combined carriers

Year	Vessel	Location	Spill (barrels)**	Cause
1979	Atlantic Empress	West Indies	1,890,000	collision
1983	Castillo De Bellver	South Africa	1,760,000	fire
1978	Amoco Cadiz	France	1,628,000	grounding
1991	Haven	Italy	1,029,000	explosion
1988	Odyssey	Canada	1,000,000	fire
1967	Torrey Canyon	UK	909,000	grounding
1972	Sea Star	Gulf of Oman	902,250	collision
1977	Hawaiian Patriot	Hawaiian Is.	742,500	fire
1979	Independenta	Turkey	696,350	collision
1993	Braer	UK	625,000	grounding
1996	Sea Empress	UK	515,000	grounding

Other sources of major oil spills

1983	Nowruz oilfield	The Gulf	4,250,000[†]	war
1979	Ixtoc 1 oilwell	Gulf of Mexico	4,200,000	blow-out
1991	Kuwait	The Gulf	2,500,000[†]	war

** 1 barrel = 0.136 tonnes/159 lit./35 Imperial gal./42 US gal. [†] estimated

River Pollution

Sources of river pollution, USA (latest available year)

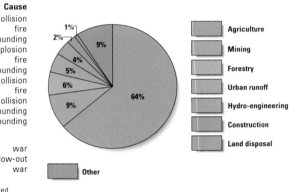

64% Agriculture
9% Mining
9% Forestry
6% Urban runoff
5% Hydro-engineering
4% Construction
2% Land disposal
1%

Other

Water Pollution

Severely polluted sea areas and lakes

Polluted sea areas and lakes

Areas of frequent oil pollution by shipping

↘ Major oil tanker spills

▲ Major oil rig blow-outs

▼ Offshore dumpsites for industrial and municipal waste

— Severely polluted rivers and estuaries

The most notorious tanker spillage of the 1980s occurred when the *Exxon Valdez* ran aground in Prince William Sound, Alaska, in 1989, spilling 267,000 barrels of crude oil close to shore in a sensitive ecological area. This rates as the world's 28th worst spill in terms of volume.

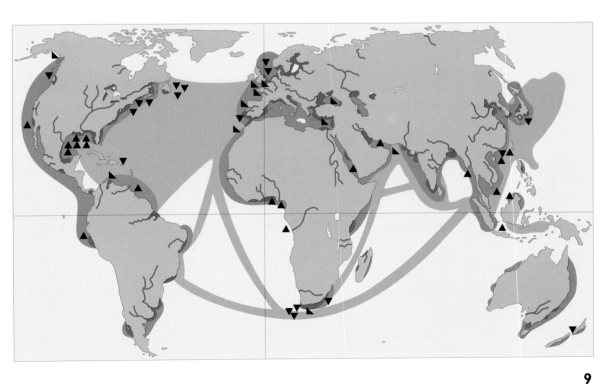

Climate

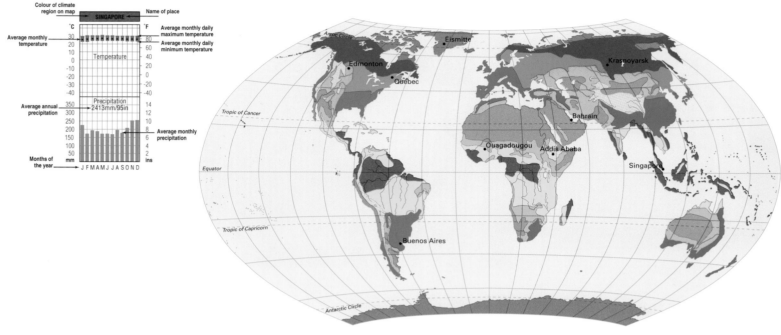

- Tropical climate (hot with rain all year)
- Desert climate (hot and very dry)
- Savanna climate (hot with dry season)
- Steppe climate (warm and dry)
- Mild climate (warm and wet)
- Continental climate (wet with cold winter)
- Subarctic climate (very cold winter)
- Polar climate (very cold and dry)
- Mountainous climate (altitude affects climate)

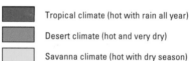
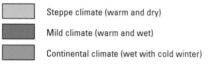
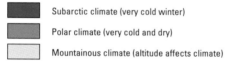

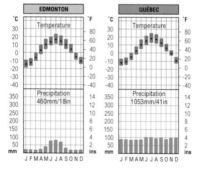
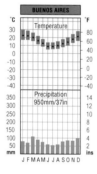
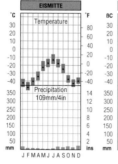
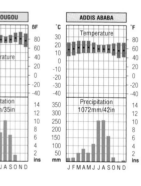
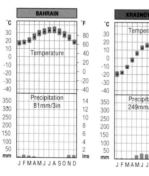
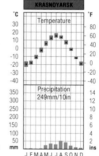

Climate Records

Temperature
Highest recorded shade temperature: Al Aziziyah, Libya, 58°C [136.4°F], 13 September 1922.

Highest mean annual temperature: Dallol, Ethiopia, 34.4°C [94°F], 1960–66.

Longest heatwave: Marble Bar, W. Australia, 162 days over 38°C [100°F], 23 October 1923 to 7 April 1924.

Lowest recorded temperature (outside poles): Verkhoyansk, Siberia, –68°C [–90°F], 6 February 1933.

Lowest mean annual temperature: Plateau Station, Antarctica, –56.6°C [–72.0°F]

Pressure
Longest drought: Calama, N. Chile, no recorded rainfall in 400 years to 1971.

Wettest place (12 months): Cherrapunji, Meghalaya, N. E. India, 26,470 mm [1,040 in], August 1860 to August 1861. Cherrapunji also holds the record for the most rainfall in one month: 2,930 mm [115 in], July 1861.

Wettest place (average): Mawsynram, India, mean annual rainfall 11,873 mm [467.4 in].

Wettest place (24 hours): Cilaos, Réunion, Indian Ocean, 1,870 mm [73.6 in], 15–16 March 1952.

Heaviest hailstones: Gopalganj, Bangladesh, up to 1.02 kg [2.25 lb], 14 April 1986 (killed 92 people).

Heaviest snowfall (continuous): Bessans, Savoie, France, 1,730 mm [68 in] in 19 hours, 5–6 April 1969.

Heaviest snowfall (season/year): Paradise Ranger Station, Mt Rainier, Washington, USA, 31,102 mm [1,224.5 in], 19 February 1971 to 18 February 1972.

Pressure and winds
Highest barometric pressure: Agata, Siberia (at 262 m [862 ft] altitude), 1,083.8 mb, 31 December 1968.

Lowest barometric pressure: Typhoon Tip, Guam, Pacific Ocean, 870 mb, 12 October 1979.

Highest recorded wind speed: Mt Washington, New Hampshire, USA, 371 km/h [231 mph], 12 April 1934. This is three times as strong as hurricane force on the Beaufort Scale.

Windiest place: Commonwealth Bay, Antarctica, where gales frequently reach over 320 km/h [200 mph].

Climate

Climate is weather in the long term: the seasonal pattern of hot and cold, wet and dry, averaged over time (usually 30 years). At the simplest level, it is caused by the uneven heating of the Earth. Surplus heat at the Equator passes towards the poles, levelling out the energy differential. Its passage is marked by a ceaseless churning of the atmosphere and the oceans, further agitated by the Earth's diurnal spin and the motion it imparts to moving air and water. The heat's means of transport – by winds and ocean currents, by the continual evaporation and recondensation of water molecules – is the weather itself. There are four basic types of climate, each of which can be further subdivided: tropical, desert (dry), temperate and polar.

Composition of Dry Air

Nitrogen	78.09%	Sulphur dioxide	trace
Oxygen	20.95%	Nitrogen oxide	trace
Argon	0.93%	Methane	trace
Water vapour	0.2–4.0%	Dust	trace
Carbon dioxide	0.03%	Helium	trace
Ozone	0.00006%	Neon	trace

El Niño

In a normal year, south-easterly trade winds drive surface waters westwards off the coast of South America, drawing cold, nutrient-rich water up from below. In an El Niño year (which occurs every 2–7 years), warm water from the west Pacific suppresses up-welling in the east, depriving the region of nutrients. The water is warmed by as much as 7°C [12°F], disturbing the tropical atmospheric circulation. During an intense El Niño, the south-east trade winds change direction and become equatorial westerlies, resulting in climatic extremes in many regions of the world, such as drought in parts of Australia and India, and heavy rainfall in south-eastern USA. An intense El Niño occurred in 1997–8, with resultant freak weather conditions across the entire Pacific region.

Normal year

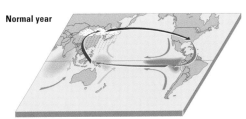

El Niño event

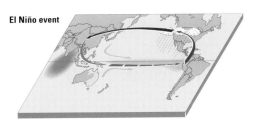

Beaufort Wind Scale

Named after the 19th-century British naval officer who devised it, the Beaufort Scale assesses wind speed according to its effects. It was originally designed as an aid for sailors, but has since been adapted for use on the land.

Scale	Wind speed km/h	mph	Effect
0	0–1	0–1	**Calm** Smoke rises vertically
1	1–5	1–3	**Light air** Wind direction shown only by smoke drift
2	6–11	4–7	**Light breeze** Wind felt on face; leaves rustle; vanes moved by wind
3	12–19	8–12	**Gentle breeze** Leaves and small twigs in constant motion; wind extends small flag
4	20–28	13–18	**Moderate** Raises dust and loose paper; small branches move
5	29–38	19–24	**Fresh** Small trees in leaf sway; wavelets on inland waters
6	39–49	25–31	**Strong** Large branches move; difficult to use umbrellas
7	50–61	32–38	**Near gale** Whole trees in motion; difficult to walk against wind
8	62–74	39–46	**Gale** Twigs break from trees; walking very difficult
9	75–88	47–54	**Strong gale** Slight structural damage
10	89–102	55–63	**Storm** Trees uprooted; serious structural damage
11	103–117	64–72	**Violent storm** Widespread damage
12	118+	73+	**Hurricane**

Conversions
°C = (°F − 32) × 5/9; °F = (°C × 9/5) + 32; 0°C = 32°F
1 in = 25.4 mm; 1 mm = 0.0394 in; 100 mm = 3.94 in

Temperature

Average temperature in January

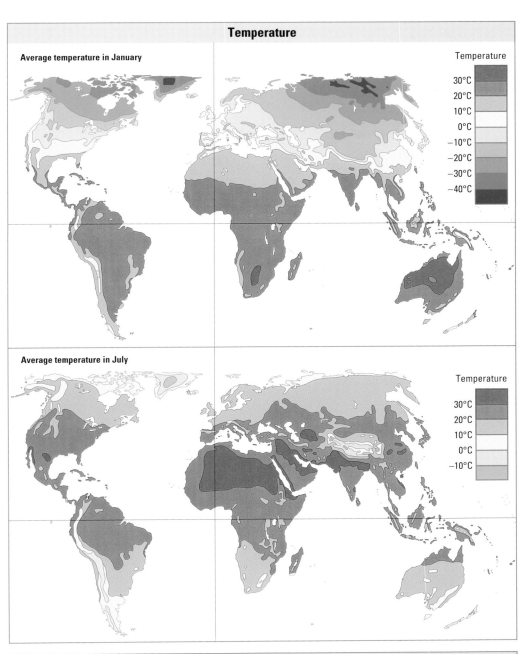

Temperature
- 30°C
- 20°C
- 10°C
- 0°C
- −10°C
- −20°C
- −30°C
- −40°C

Average temperature in July

Temperature
- 30°C
- 20°C
- 10°C
- 0°C
- −10°C

Precipitation

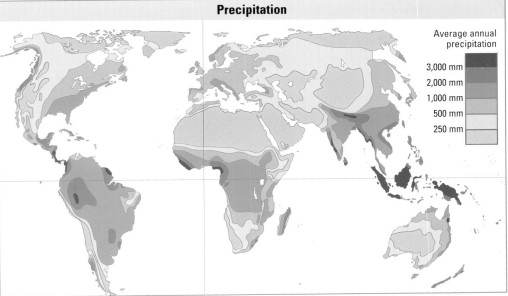

Average annual precipitation
- 3,000 mm
- 2,000 mm
- 1,000 mm
- 500 mm
- 250 mm

Water and Vegetation

The Hydrological Cycle

The world's water balance is regulated by the constant recycling of water between the oceans, atmosphere and land. The movement of water between these three reservoirs is known as the hydrological cycle. The oceans play a vital role in the hydrological cycle: 74% of the total precipitation falls over the oceans and 84% of the total evaporation comes from the oceans.

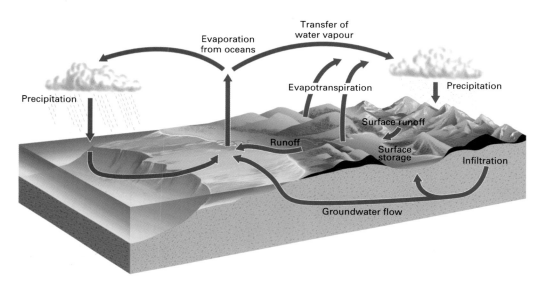

Water Distribution

The distribution of planetary water, by percentage. Oceans and ice-caps together account for more than 99% of the total; the breakdown of the remainder is estimated.

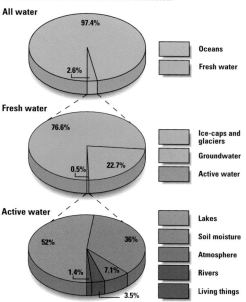

All water
- 97.4% Oceans
- 2.6% Fresh water

Fresh water
- 76.6% Ice-caps and glaciers
- 22.7% Groundwater
- 0.5% Active water

Active water
- 52% Lakes
- 36% Soil moisture
- 7.1% Atmosphere
- 3.5% Rivers
- 1.4% Living things

Water Utilization

| Domestic | Industrial | Agriculture |

The percentage breakdown of water usage by sector, selected countries (latest available year)

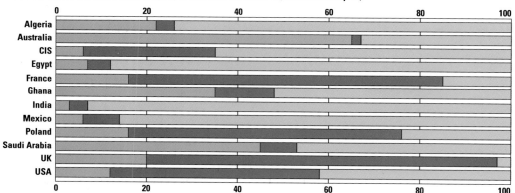

Algeria
Australia
CIS
Egypt
France
Ghana
India
Mexico
Poland
Saudi Arabia
UK
USA

Water Usage

Almost all the world's water is 3,000 million years old, and all of it cycles endlessly through the hydrosphere, though at different rates. Water vapour circulates over days, even hours, deep ocean water circulates over millennia, and ice-cap water remains solid for millions of years.

Fresh water is essential to all terrestrial life. Humans cannot survive more than a few days without it, and even the hardiest desert plants and animals could not exist without some water. Agriculture requires huge quantities of fresh water: without large-scale irrigation most of the world's people would starve. In the USA, agriculture uses 43% and industry 38% of all water withdrawals.

The United States is one of the heaviest users of water in the world. According to the latest figures the average American uses 380 litres a day and the average household uses 415,000 litres a year. This is two to four times more than in Western Europe.

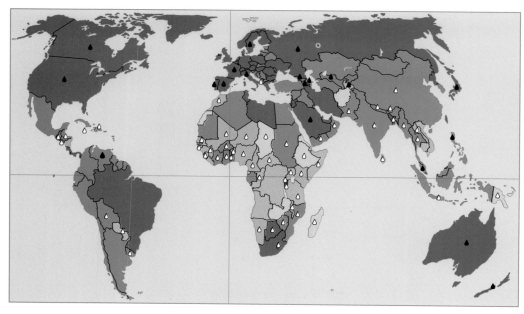

Water Supply

Percentage of total population with access to safe drinking water (average 1990–96)

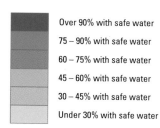

- Over 90% with safe water
- 75 – 90% with safe water
- 60 – 75% with safe water
- 45 – 60% with safe water
- 30 – 45% with safe water
- Under 30% with safe water

△ Under 80 litres per person per day domestic water consumption

▲ Over 320 litres per person per day domestic water consumption

NB: 80 litres of water a day is considered necessary for a reasonable quality of life.

Least well-provided countries

Afghanistan	23%	Papua New Guinea	28%
Chad	24%	Haiti	28%
Ethiopia	25%	Madagascar	29%

Natural Vegetation

Regional variation in vegetation

- Tundra and mountain vegetation
- Needleleaf evergreen forest
- Mixed needleleaf evergreen & broadleaf deciduous trees
- Broadleaf deciduous woodland
- Mid-latitude grassland
- Evergreen broadleaf and deciduous trees & shrubs
- Semi-desert scrub
- Desert
- Tropical grassland (savanna)
- Tropical broadleaf rainforest and monsoon forest
- Subtropical broadleaf and needleleaf forest

The map shows the natural 'climax vegetation' of regions, as dictated by climate and topography. In most cases, however, agricultural activity has drastically altered the vegetation pattern. Western Europe, for example, lost most of its broadleaf forest many centuries ago, while irrigation has turned some natural semi-desert into productive land.

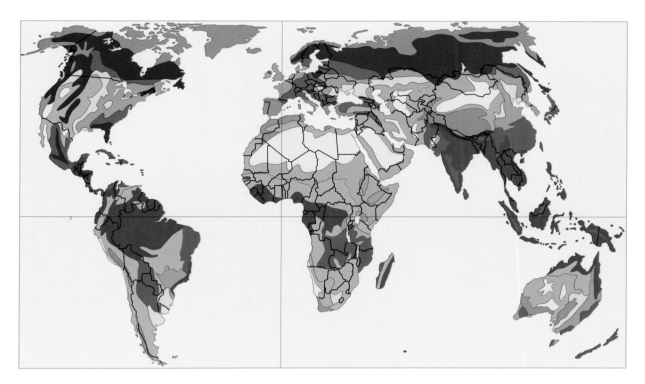

Land Use by Continent

- Forest
- Permanent pasture and rough grazing
- Permanent crops and plantations
- Arable
- Non-productive

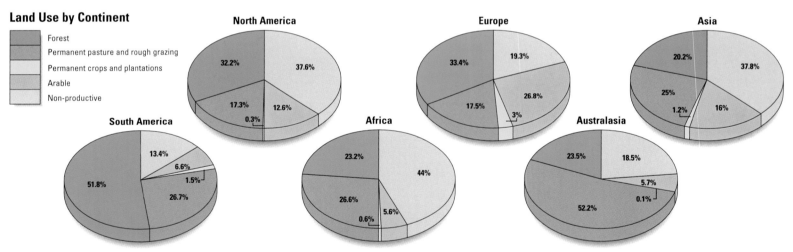

North America: 32.2%, 37.6%, 17.3%, 12.6%, 0.3%

Europe: 33.4%, 19.3%, 17.5%, 26.8%, 3%

Asia: 20.2%, 37.8%, 25%, 1.2%, 16%

South America: 13.4%, 6.6%, 1.5%, 51.8%, 26.7%

Africa: 23.2%, 44%, 26.6%, 0.6%, 5.6%

Australasia: 23.5%, 18.5%, 5.7%, 0.1%, 52.2%

Forestry: Production

Annual production (1993, million cubic metres)

	Forest and woodland (million hectares)	Fuelwood and charcoal	Industrial roundwood*
World	**3,987.9**	**1,875.8**	**1,528.5**
CIS	827.8	51.5	172.9
S. America	829.3	247.8	122.0
N. & C. America	709.8	156.7	586.7
Africa	684.6	493.6	59.5
Asia	490.2	866.4	278.1
Europe	157.3	50.9	272.2
Australasia	157.2	8.7	36.9

Paper and Board

Top producers (1993)**		Top exporters (1993)**	
USA	77,250	Canada	12,896
Japan	27,764	Finland	8,526
China	23,816	USA	7,146
Canada	17,557	Sweden	7,008
Germany	13,034	Germany	4,763

* roundwood is timber as it is felled

** in thousand tonnes

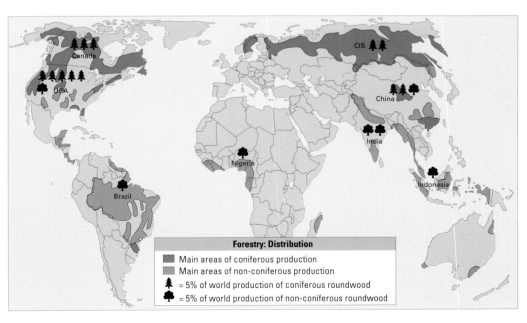

Forestry: Distribution

- Main areas of coniferous production
- Main areas of non-coniferous production
- ♠ = 5% of world production of coniferous roundwood
- ♣ = 5% of world production of non-coniferous roundwood

Environment

Humans have always had a dramatic effect on their environment, at least since the development of agriculture almost 10,000 years ago. Generally, the Earth has accepted human interference without obvious ill effects: the complex systems that regulate the global environment have been able to absorb substantial damage while maintaining a stable and comfortable home for the planet's trillions of lifeforms. But advancing human technology and the rapidly-expanding populations it supports are now threatening to overwhelm the Earth's ability to compensate.

Industrial wastes, acid rainfall, desertification and large-scale deforestation all combine to create environmental change at a rate far faster than the great slow cycles of planetary evolution can accommodate. As a result of overcultivation, overgrazing and overcutting of groundcover for firewood, desertification is affecting as much as 60% of the world's croplands. In addition, with fire and chain-saws, humans are destroying more forest in a day than their ancestors could have done in a century, upsetting the balance between plant and animal, carbon dioxide and oxygen, on which all life ultimately depends.

The fossil fuels that power industrial civilization have pumped enough carbon dioxide and other so-called greenhouse gases into the atmosphere to make climatic change a near-certainty. As a result of the combination of these factors, the Earth's average temperature has risen by approximately 0.5°C [1°F] since the beginning of the 20th century, and it is still rising.

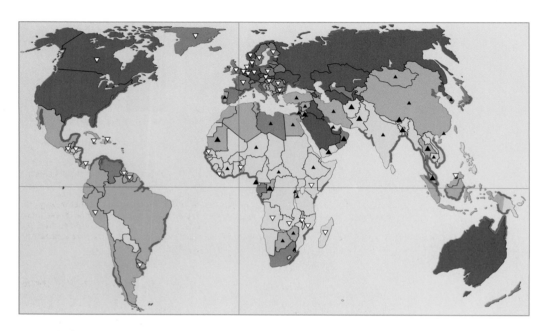

Global Warming

Carbon dioxide emissions in tonnes per person per year (1992)

- Over 10 tonnes of CO_2
- 5 – 10 tonnes of CO_2
- 1 – 5 tonnes of CO_2
- Under 1 tonne of CO_2

Changes in CO_2 emissions 1980–90

- ▲ Over 100% increase in emissions
- ▲ 50–100% increase in emissions
- ▽ Reduction in emissions
- — Coastal areas in danger of flooding from rising sea levels caused by global warming

High atmospheric concentrations of heat-absorbing gases, especially carbon dioxide, appear to be causing a steady rise in average temperatures worldwide – up to 1.5°C [3°F] by the year 2020, according to some estimates. Global warming is likely to bring with it a rise in sea levels that may flood some of the Earth's most densely populated coastal areas.

Greenhouse Power

Relative contributions to the Greenhouse Effect by the major heat-absorbing gases in the atmosphere.

The chart combines greenhouse potency and volume. Carbon dioxide has a greenhouse potential of only 1, but its concentration of 350 parts per million makes it predominate. CFC 12, with 25,000 times the absorption capacity of CO_2, is present only as 0.00044 ppm.

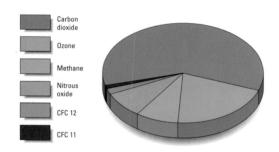

- Carbon dioxide
- Ozone
- Methane
- Nitrous oxide
- CFC 12
- CFC 11

Ozone Layer

The ozone 'hole' over the northern hemisphere on 12 March 1995.

The colours represent Dobson Units (DU). The ozone 'hole' is seen as the dark blue and purple patch in the centre, where ozone values are around 120 DU or lower. Normal levels are around 280 DU. The ozone 'hole' over Antarctica is much larger.

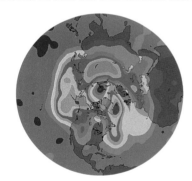

Carbon Dioxide

Carbon dioxide released in millions of tonnes (1992)

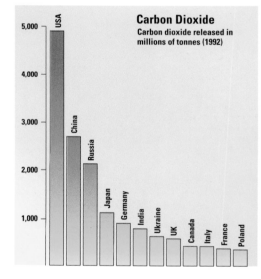

The Greenhouse Effect

Carbon dioxide is increased by burning fossil fuels and cutting forests

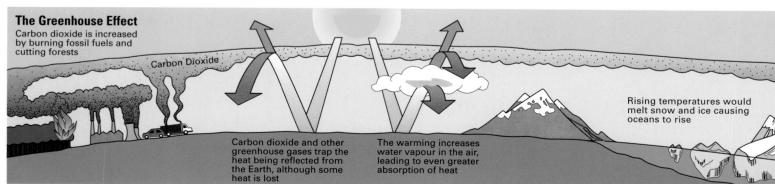

Carbon Dioxide

Carbon dioxide and other greenhouse gases trap the heat being reflected from the Earth, although some heat is lost

The warming increases water vapour in the air, leading to even greater absorption of heat

Rising temperatures would melt snow and ice causing oceans to rise

Desertification

Existing deserts

Areas with a high risk of desertification

Areas with a moderate risk of desertification

Former areas of rainforest

Existing rainforest

Forest Clearance

Thousands of hectares of forest cleared annually, tropical countries surveyed 1981–85 and 1987–90. Loss as a percentage of remaining stocks is shown in figures on each column.

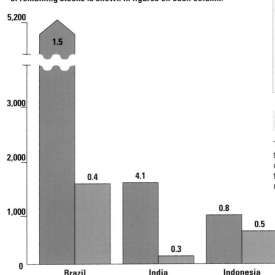

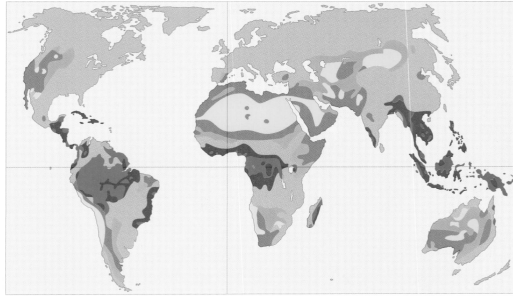

Deforestation

The Earth's remaining forests are under attack from three directions: expanding agriculture, logging, and growing consumption of fuelwood, often in combination. Sometimes deforestation is the direct result of government policy, as in the efforts made to resettle the urban poor in some parts of Brazil; just as often, it comes about despite state attempts at conservation. Loggers, licensed or unlicensed, blaze a trail into virgin forest, often destroying twice as many trees as they harvest. Landless farmers follow, burning away most of what remains to plant their crops, completing the destruction.

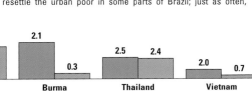

Ozone Depletion

The ozone layer, 25–30 km [15–18 miles] above sea level, acts as a barrier to most of the Sun's harmful ultra-violet radiation, protecting us from the ionizing radiation that can cause skin cancer and cataracts. In recent years, however, two holes in the ozone layer have been observed during winter: one over the Arctic and the other, the size of the USA, over Antarctica. By 1996, ozone had been reduced to around a half of its 1970 amount. The ozone (O_3) is broken down by chlorine released into the atmosphere as CFCs (chlorofluorocarbons) – chemicals used in refrigerators, packaging and aerosols.

Air Pollution

Sulphur dioxide is the main pollutant associated with industrial cities. According to the World Health Organization, at least 600 million people live in urban areas where sulphur dioxide concentrations regularly reach damaging levels. One of the world's most dangerously polluted urban areas is Mexico City, due to a combination of its enclosed valley location, three million cars and 60,000 factories. In May 1998, this lethal cocktail was added to by nearby forest fires and the resultant air pollution led to over 20% of the population (three million people) complaining of respiratory problems.

Acid Rain

Killing trees, poisoning lakes and rivers and eating away buildings, acid rain is mostly produced by sulphur dioxide emissions from industry and volcanic eruptions. By the mid 1990s, acid rain had sterilized 4,000 or more of Sweden's lakes and left 45% of Switzerland's alpine conifers dead or dying, while the monuments of Greece were dissolving in Athens' smog. Prevailing wind patterns mean that the acids often fall many hundred kilometres from where the original pollutants were discharged. In parts of Europe acid deposition has slightly decreased, following reductions in emissions, but not by enough.

World Pollution

Acid rain and sources of acidic emissions (latest available year)

Acid rain is caused by high levels of sulphur and nitrogen in the atmosphere. They combine with water vapour and oxygen to form acids (H_2SO_4 and HNO_3) which fall as precipitation.

  Regions where sulphur and nitrogen oxides are released in high concentrations, mainly from fossil fuel combustion

• Major cities with high levels of air pollution (including nitrogen and sulphur emissions)

Areas of heavy acid deposition

pH numbers indicate acidity, decreasing from a neutral 7. Normal rain, slightly acid from dissolved carbon dioxide, never exceeds a pH of 5.6.

pH less than 4.0 (most acidic)

pH 4.0 to 4.5

pH 4.5 to 5.0

Areas where acid rain is a potential problem

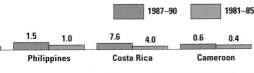

Population

Demographic Profiles

Developed nations such as the UK have populations evenly spread across the age groups and, usually, a growing proportion of elderly people. The great majority of the people in developing nations, however, are in the younger age groups, about to enter their most fertile years. In time, these population profiles should resemble the world profile (even Kenya has made recent progress with reducing its birth rate), but the transition will come about only after a few more generations of rapid population growth.

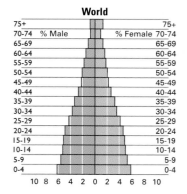

World

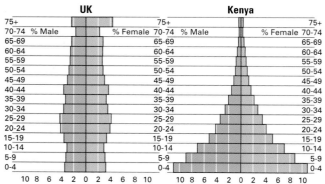

UK   **Kenya**

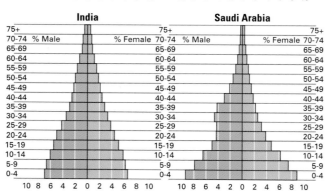

India   **Saudi Arabia**

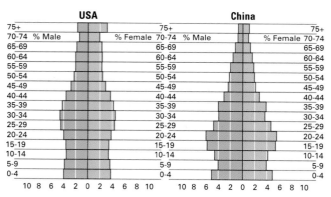

USA   **China**

Most Populous Nations [in millions (1997)]

1. China	1,210	9. Bangladesh	124	17. Egypt	63
2. India	980	10. Nigeria	118	18. Thailand	61
3. USA	268	11. Mexico	97	19. France	59
4. Indonesia	204	12. Germany	82	20. UK	59
5. Brazil	160	13. Vietnam	77	21. Ethiopia	59
6. Russia	148	14. Philippines	74	22. Italy	58
7. Pakistan	136	15. Iran	70	23. Ukraine	52
8. Japan	126	16. Turkey	64	24. Burma	48

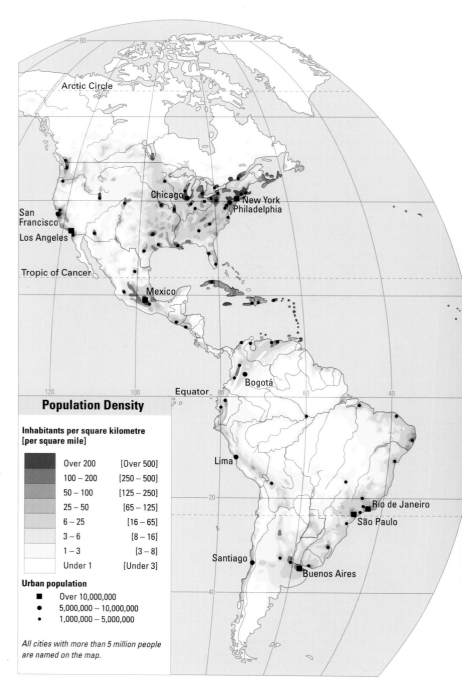

Population Density

Inhabitants per square kilometre [per square mile]

Over 200	[Over 500]
100 – 200	[250 – 500]
50 – 100	[125 – 250]
25 – 50	[65 – 125]
6 – 25	[16 – 65]
3 – 6	[8 – 16]
1 – 3	[3 – 8]
Under 1	[Under 3]

Urban population

■   Over 10,000,000

●   5,000,000 – 10,000,000

•   1,000,000 – 5,000,000

All cities with more than 5 million people are named on the map.

Continental Comparisons

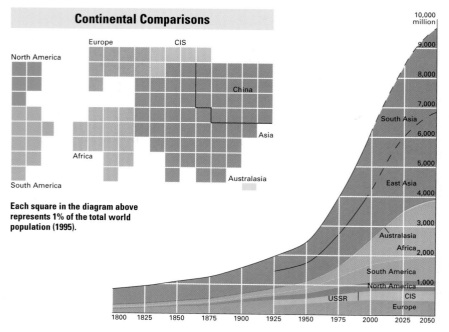

Each square in the diagram above represents 1% of the total world population (1995).

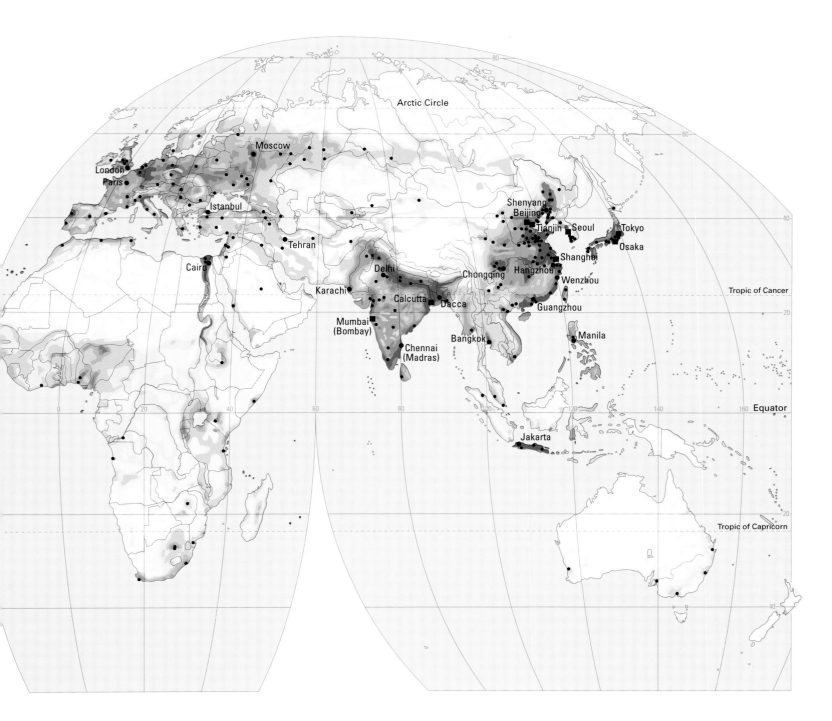

Arctic Circle

Moscow

London
Paris

Istanbul

Tehran

Cairo

Shenyang
Beijing
Tianjin   Seoul   Tokyo
Shanghai   Osaka
Hangzhou
Delhi   Wenzhou
Chongqing
Karachi
Calcutta   Dacca   Guangzhou
Mumbai
(Bombay)
Chennai   Bangkok   Manila
(Madras)

Tropic of Cancer

Equator

Jakarta

Tropic of Capricorn

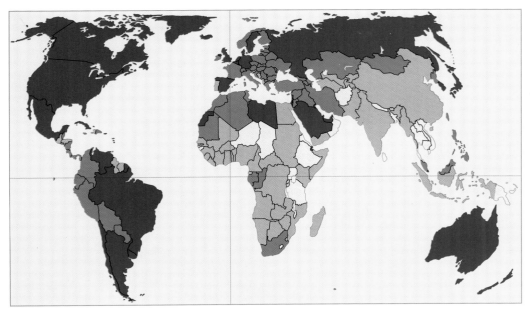

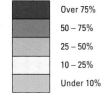

Urban Population

Percentage of total population living in towns and cities (1995)

	Over 75%
	50 – 75%
	25 – 50%
	10 – 25%
	Under 10%

Most urbanized		Least urbanized	
Singapore	100%	Rwanda	6%
Belgium	97%	Bhutan	8%
Kuwait	95%	Burundi	9%
Iceland	93%	Nepal	12%
Venezuela	91%	Uganda	12%
[UK 89%]			

The Human Family

Predominant Languages

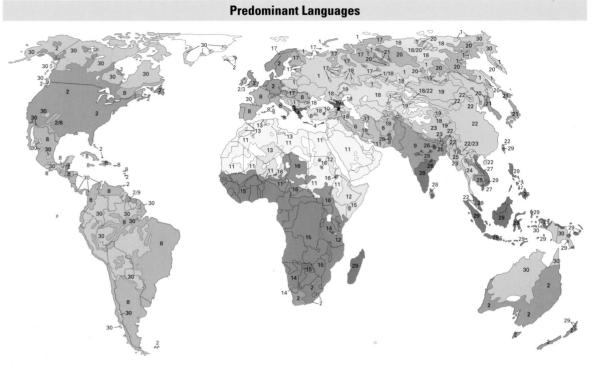

INDO-EUROPEAN FAMILY

1	Balto-Slavic group (incl. Russian, Ukrainian)
2	Germanic group (incl. English, German)
3	Celtic group
4	Greek
5	Albanian
6	Iranian group
7	Armenian
8	Romance group (incl. Spanish, Portuguese, French, Italian)
9	Indo-Aryan group (incl. Hindi, Bengali, Urdu, Punjabi, Marathi)
10	CAUCASIAN FAMILY

AFRO-ASIATIC FAMILY

11	Semitic group (incl. Arabic)
12	Kushitic group
13	Berber group
14	KHOISAN FAMILY
15	NIGER-CONGO FAMILY
16	NILO-SAHARAN FAMILY
17	URALIC FAMILY

ALTAIC FAMILY

18	Turkic group
19	Mongolian group
20	Tungus-Manchu group
21	Japanese and Korean

SINO-TIBETAN FAMILY

22	Sinitic (Chinese) languages
23	Tibetic-Burmic languages
24	TAI FAMILY

AUSTRO-ASIATIC FAMILY

25	Mon-Khmer group
26	Munda group
27	Vietnamese
28	DRAVIDIAN FAMILY (incl. Telugu, Tamil)
29	AUSTRONESIAN FAMILY (incl. Malay-Indonesian)
30	OTHER LANGUAGES

Languages of the World

Language can be classified by ancestry and structure. For example, the Romance and Germanic groups are both derived from an Indo-European language believed to have been spoken 5,000 years ago.

Mother tongues (in millions)
Chinese 1,069 (Mandarin 864), English 443, Hindi 352, Spanish 341, Russian 293, Arabic 197, Bengali 184, Portuguese 173, Malay-Indonesian 142, Japanese 125, French 121, German 118, Urdu 92, Punjabi 84, Korean 71.

Official languages (% of total population)
English 27%, Chinese 19%, Hindi 13.5%, Spanish 5.4%, Russian 5.2%, French 4.2%, Arabic 3.3%, Portuguese 3%, Malay 3%, Bengali 2.9%, Japanese 2.3%.

Predominant Religions

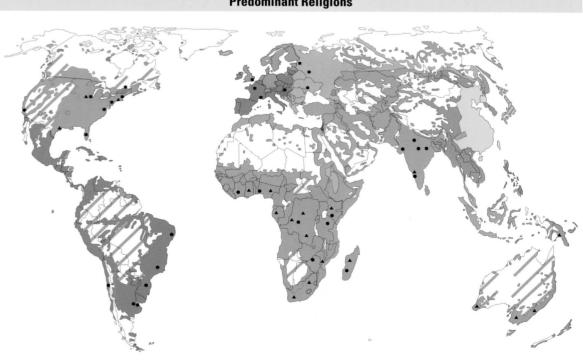

Religious Adherents

Religious adherents in millions:

Christian	1,669	Hindu	663
Roman Catholic	*952*	Buddhist	312
Protestant	*337*	Chinese Folk	172
Orthodox	*162*	Tribal	92
Anglican	*70*	Jewish	18
Other Christian	*148*	Sikhs	17
Muslim	966		
Sunni	*841*		
Shia	*125*		

▲ Roman Catholicism

Orthodox and other Eastern Churches

● Protestantism

Sunni Islam

Shia Islam

Buddhism

Hinduism

Confucianism

★ Judaism

Shintoism

Tribal Religions

United Nations

Created in 1945 to promote peace and co-operation and based in New York, the United Nations is the world's largest international organization, with 185 members and an annual budget of US $2.6 billion (1996–97). Each member of the General Assembly has one vote, while the permanent members of the 15-nation Security Council – USA, Russia, China, UK and France – hold a veto. The Secretariat is the UN's principal administrative arm. The 54 members of the Economic and Social Council are responsible for economic, social, cultural, educational, health and related matters. The UN has 16 specialized agencies – based in Canada, France, Switzerland and Italy, as well as the USA – which help members in fields such as education (UNESCO), agriculture (FAO), medicine (WHO) and finance (IFC). By the end of 1994, all the original 11 trust territories of the Trusteeship Council had become independent.

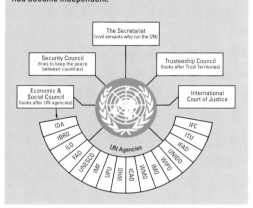

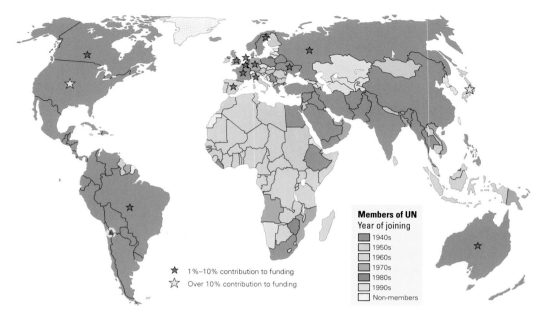

Members of UN
Year of joining
- 1940s
- 1950s
- 1960s
- 1970s
- 1980s
- 1990s
- Non-members

★ 1%–10% contribution to funding

☆ Over 10% contribution to funding

MEMBERSHIP OF THE UN In 1945 there were 51 members; by December 1994 membership had increased to 185 following the admission of Palau. There are 7 independent states which are not members of the UN – Kiribati, Nauru, Switzerland, Taiwan, Tonga, Tuvalu and the Vatican City. All the successor states of the former USSR had joined by the end of 1992. The official languages of the UN are Chinese, English, French, Russian, Spanish and Arabic.

FUNDING The UN budget for 1996–97 was US $2.6 billion. Contributions are assessed by the members' ability to pay, with the maximum 25% of the total, the minimum 0.01%. Contributions for 1996 were: USA 25.0%, Japan 15.4%, Germany 9.0%, France 6.4%, UK 5.3%, Italy 5.2%, Russia 4.5%, Canada 3.1%, Spain 2.4%, Brazil 1.6%, Netherlands 1.6%, Australia 1.5%, Sweden 1.2%, Ukraine 1.1%, Belgium 1.0%.

International Organizations

EU European Union (evolved from the European Community in 1993). The 15 members – Austria, Belgium, Denmark, Finland, France, Germany, Greece, Ireland, Italy, Luxembourg, Netherlands, Portugal, Spain, Sweden and the UK – aim to integrate economies, co-ordinate social developments and bring about political union. These members of what is now the world's biggest market share agricultural and industrial policies and tariffs on trade. The original body, the European Coal and Steel Community (ECSC), was created in 1951 following the signing of the Treaty of Paris.

EFTA European Free Trade Association (formed in 1960). Portugal left the original 'Seven' in 1989 to join what was then the EC, followed by Austria, Finland and Sweden in 1995. Only 4 members remain: Norway, Iceland, Switzerland and Liechtenstein.

ACP African-Caribbean-Pacific (formed in 1963). Members have economic ties with the EU.

NATO North Atlantic Treaty Organization (formed in 1949). It continues after 1991 despite the winding up of the Warsaw Pact. There are 16 member nations.

OAS Organization of American States (formed in 1948). It aims to promote social and economic co-operation between developed countries of North America and developing nations of Latin America.

ASEAN Association of South-east Asian Nations (formed in 1967). Burma and Laos joined in 1997.

OAU Organization of African Unity (formed in 1963). Its 53 members represent over 94% of Africa's population. Arabic, French, Portuguese and English are recognized as working languages.

LAIA Latin American Integration Association (1980). Its aim is to promote freer regional trade.

OECD Organization for Economic Co-operation and Development (formed in 1961). It comprises the 29 major Western free-market economies. Poland, Hungary and South Korea joined in 1996. 'G8' is its 'inner group' comprising Canada, France, Germany, Italy, Japan, Russia, the UK and the USA.

COMMONWEALTH The Commonwealth of Nations evolved from the British Empire; it comprises 16 Queen's realms, 32 republics and 5 indigenous monarchies, giving a total of 53.

OPEC Organization of Petroleum Exporting Countries (formed in 1960). It controls about three-quarters of the world's oil supply. Gabon left the organization in 1996.

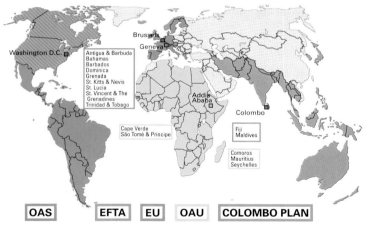

| OAS | EFTA | EU | OAU | COLOMBO PLAN |

ARAB LEAGUE (formed in 1945). The League's aim is to promote economic, social, political and military co-operation. There are 21 member nations.

COLOMBO PLAN (formed in 1951). Its 26 members aim to promote economic and social development in Asia and the Pacific.

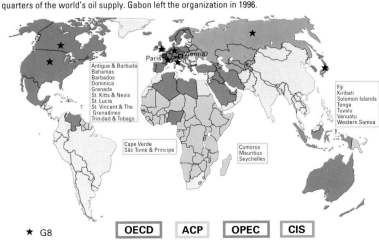

★ G8

| OECD | ACP | OPEC | CIS |

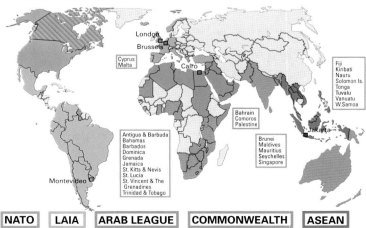

| NATO | LAIA | ARAB LEAGUE | COMMONWEALTH | ASEAN |

Wealth

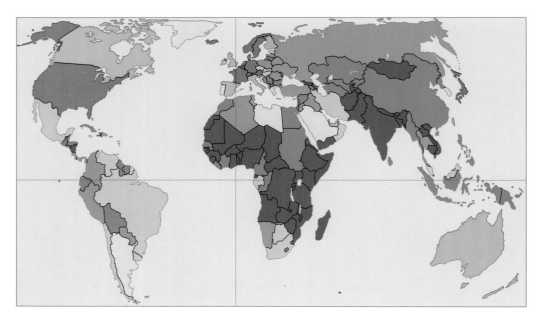

Levels of Income

Gross National Product per capita: the value of total production divided by the population (1993)

- Over 400% of world average
- 200 – 400% of world average
- 100 – 200% of world average

[World average wealth per person US $5,359]

- 50 – 100% of world average
- 25 – 50% of world average
- 10 – 25% of world average
- Under 10% of world average

GNP per capita growth rate (%), selected countries, 1985–94

Thailand	8.2	Brazil	–0.4
Chile	6.9	Zimbabwe	–0.6
Japan	3.2	USA	–1.3
Germany	1.9	UK	–1.4
Australia	1.2	Armenia	–12.9

Wealth Creation

The Gross National Product (GNP) of the world's largest economies, US $ million (1995)

1.	USA	7,100,007	23.	Indonesia	190,105
2.	Japan	4,963,587	24.	Turkey	169,452
3.	Germany	2,252,343	25.	Thailand	159,630
4.	France	1,451,051	26.	Denmark	156,027
5.	UK	1,094,734	27.	Hong Kong	142,332
6.	Italy	1,088,085	28.	Norway	136,077
7.	China	744,890	29.	Saudi Arabia	133,540
8.	Brazil	579,787	30.	South Africa	130,918
9.	Canada	573,695	31.	Poland	107,829
10.	Spain	532,347	32.	Finland	105,174
11.	South Korea	435,137	33.	Portugal	96,689
12.	Netherlands	371,039	34.	Israel	87,875
13.	Australia	337,909	35.	Greece	85,885
14.	Russia	331,948	36.	Ukraine	84,084
15.	India	319,660	37.	Singapore	79,831
16.	Mexico	304,596	38.	Malaysia	78,321
17.	Switzerland	286,014	39.	Philippines	71,865
18.	Argentina	278,431	40.	Colombia	70,263
19.	Taiwan	256,300	41.	Venezuela	65,382
20.	Belgium	250,710	42.	Pakistan	59,991
21.	Austria	216,547	43.	Chile	59,151
22.	Sweden	209,720	44.	Peru	55,019

The Wealth Gap

The world's richest and poorest countries, by Gross National Product per capita in US $ (1995)

1.	Luxembourg	41,210	1.	Mozambique	80
2.	Switzerland	40,630	2.	Ethiopia	100
3.	Japan	39,640	3.	Congo (Zaïre)	120
4.	Liechtenstein	38,520	4.	Tanzania	120
5.	Norway	31,250	5.	Burundi	160
6.	Denmark	29,890	6.	Malawi	170
7.	Germany	27,510	7.	Sierra Leone	180
8.	USA	26,980	8.	Rwanda	180
9.	Austria	26,890	9.	Chad	180
10.	Singapore	26,730	10.	Nepal	200
11.	France	24,990	11.	Niger	220
12.	Iceland	24,950	12.	Madagascar	230
13.	Belgium	24,710	13.	Burkina Faso	230
14.	Sweden	23,750	14.	Vietnam	240
15.	Hong Kong	22,990	15.	Uganda	240
16.	Finland	20,580	16.	Bangladesh	240
17.	Canada	19,380	17.	Haiti	250
18.	Italy	19,020	18.	Guinea-Bissau	250
19.	Australia	18,720	19.	Yemen	250
20.	UK	18,700	20.	Nigeria	260

GNP per capita is calculated by dividing a country's Gross National Product by its total population.

Continental Shares

Shares of population and of wealth (GNP) by continent

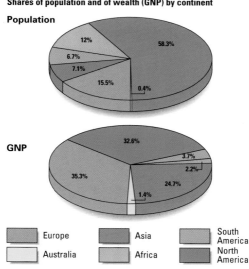

Population

GNP

- Europe
- Australia
- Asia
- Africa
- South America
- North America

Inflation

Average annual rate of inflation (1980–93)

- Over 50%
- 20 – 50%
- 7.5 – 20%
- 1 – 7.5%
- Negative inflation
- No data available

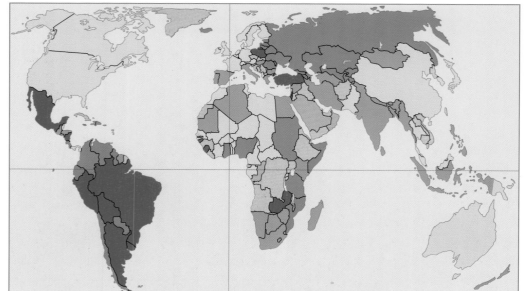

Highest average inflation		Lowest average inflation	
Nicaragua	665%	Brunei	–5.1%
Brazil	423%	Oman	–2.3%
Argentina	374%	Saudi Arabia	–2.1%
Peru	316%	Equatorial Guinea	–0.6%
Bolivia	187%	Congo	–0.6%
Israel	70%	Bahrain	–0.3%
Poland	69%	Libya	0.2%

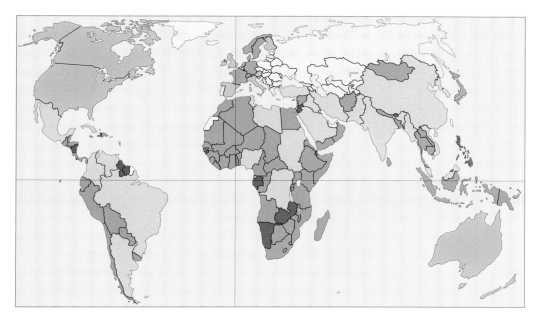

Aid provided or received, divided by the total population, in US $ (1995)

- Over $100 per person
- $10 – $100 per person
- $0 – $10 per person
- No aid given or received — Providers
- $0 – $10 per person — Receivers
- $10 – $100 per person
- Over $100 per person

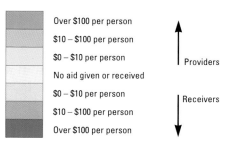

Top 5 providers per capita (1994)		Top 5 receivers per capita (1994)	
France	$279	São Tomé & P.	$378
Denmark	$260	Cape Verde	$314
Norway	$247	Djibouti	$235
Sweden	$201	Surinam	$198
Germany	$166	Mauritania	$153

Debt and Aid

International debtors and the aid they receive (1993)

Although aid grants make a vital contribution to many of the world's poorer countries, they are usually dwarfed by the burden of debt that the developing economies are expected to repay. In 1992, they had to pay US $160,000 million in debt service charges alone – more than two and a half times the amount of Official Development Assistance (ODA) the developing countries were receiving, and US $60,000 million more than total private flows of aid in the same year. In 1990, the debts of Mozambique, one of the world's poorest countries, were estimated to be 75 times its entire earnings from exports.

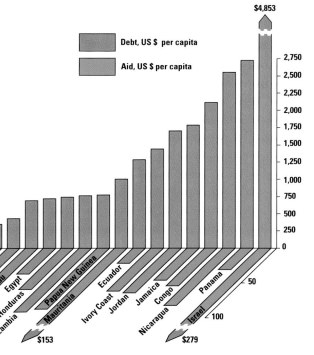

Debt, US $ per capita

Aid, US $ per capita

Distribution of Spending

Percentage share of household spending, selected countries

- Food
- Medicine & Education
- Clothing
- Transport
- Energy & Housing
- Other

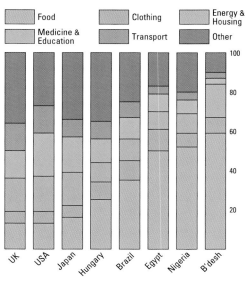

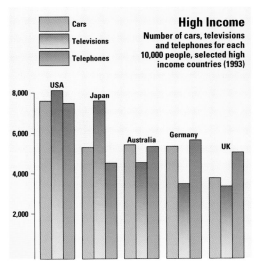

High Income

Number of cars, televisions and telephones for each 10,000 people, selected high income countries (1993)

- Cars
- Televisions
- Telephones

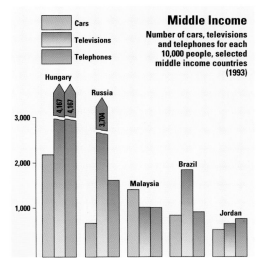

Middle Income

Number of cars, televisions and telephones for each 10,000 people, selected middle income countries (1993)

- Cars
- Televisions
- Telephones

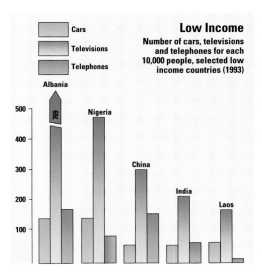

Low Income

Number of cars, televisions and telephones for each 10,000 people, selected low income countries (1993)

- Cars
- Televisions
- Telephones

Quality of Life

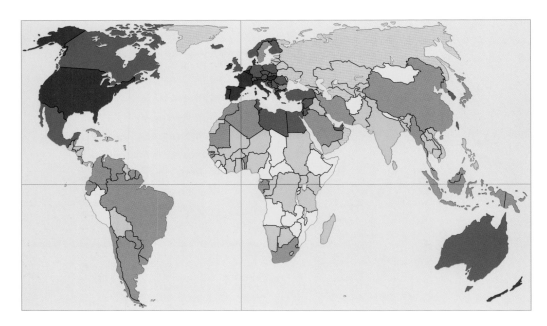

Daily Food Consumption

Average daily food intake in calories per person (latest available year)

Over 3,500 calories per person

3,000 – 3,500 calories per person

2,500 – 3,000 calories per person

2,000 – 2,500 calories per person

Under 2,000 calories per person

No available data

Top 5 countries		Bottom 5 countries	
Ireland	3,847 cal.	Mozambique	1,680 cal.
Greece	3,815 cal.	Liberia	1,640 cal.
Cyprus	3,779 cal.	Ethiopia	1,610 cal.
USA	3,732 cal.	Afghanistan	1,523 cal.
Spain	3,708 cal.	Somalia	1,499 cal.

[UK 3,317 calories]

Hospital Capacity

Hospital beds available for each 1,000 people (1993)

Highest capacity		Lowest capacity	
Japan	13.6	Bangladesh	0.2
Kazakstan	13.5	Ethiopia	0.2
Ukraine	13.5	Nepal	0.3
Russia	13.5	Burkina Faso	0.4
Latvia	13.5	Afghanistan	0.5
North Korea	13.5	Pakistan	0.6
Moldova	12.8	Niger	0.6
Belarus	12.7	Mali	0.6
Finland	12.3	Indonesia	0.6
France	12.2	Guinea	0.6

[UK 6.4] [USA 4.6]

Although the ratio of people to hospital beds gives a good approximation of a country's health provision, it is not an absolute indicator. Raw numbers may mask inefficiency and other weaknesses: the high availability of beds in Kazakstan, for example, has not prevented infant mortality rates over three times as high as in the United Kingdom and the United States.

Life Expectancy

Years of life expectancy at birth, selected countries (1990–95)

The chart shows combined data for both sexes. On average, women live longer than men worldwide, even in developing countries with high maternal mortality rates. Overall, life expectancy is steadily rising, though the difference between rich and poor nations remains dramatic.

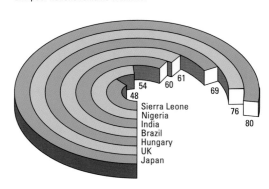

Causes of Death

Causes of death for selected countries by % (1992–94)

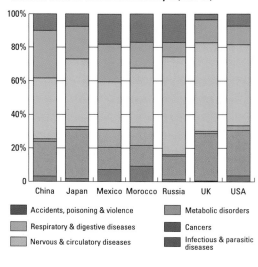

■ Accidents, poisoning & violence

■ Respiratory & digestive diseases

■ Nervous & circulatory diseases

■ Metabolic disorders

■ Cancers

■ Infectious & parasitic diseases

Child Mortality

Number of babies who will die under the age of one, per 1,000 births (average 1990–95)

Over 150 deaths per 1,000 births

100 – 150 deaths per 1,000 births

50 – 100 deaths per 1,000 births

20 – 50 deaths per 1,000 births

10 – 20 deaths per 1,000 births

Under 10 deaths per 1,000 births

Highest child mortality		Lowest child mortality	
Afghanistan	162	Hong Kong	6
Mali	159	Denmark	6
Sierra Leone	143	Japan	5
Guinea-Bissau	140	Iceland	5
Malawi	138	Finland	5

[UK 8 deaths]

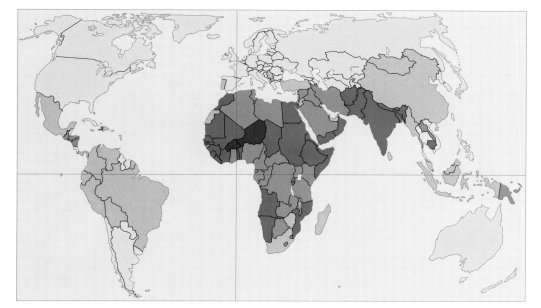

Illiteracy

Percentage of the total population unable to read or write (latest available year)

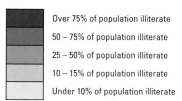

- Over 75% of population illiterate
- 50 – 75% of population illiterate
- 25 – 50% of population illiterate
- 10 – 15% of population illiterate
- Under 10% of population illiterate

Educational expenditure per person (latest available year)

Top 5 countries		Bottom 5 countries	
Sweden	$997	Chad	$2
Qatar	$989	Bangladesh	$3
Canada	$983	Ethiopia	$3
Norway	$971	Nepal	$4
Switzerland	$796	Somalia	$4

Fertility and Education

Fertility rates compared with female education, selected countries (1992–95)

Percentage of females aged 12–17 in secondary education

Fertility rate: average number of children borne per woman

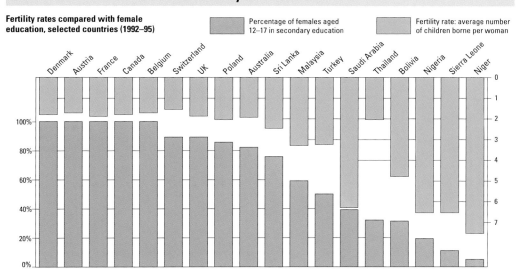

Living Standards

At first sight, most international contrasts in living standards are swamped by differences in wealth. The rich not only have more money, they have more of everything, including years of life. Those with only a little money are obliged to spend most of it on food and clothing, the basic maintenance costs of their existence; air travel and tourism are unlikely to feature on their expenditure lists. However, poverty and wealth are both relative: slum dwellers living on social security payments in an affluent industrial country have far more resources at their disposal than an average African peasant, but feel their own poverty nonetheless. A middle-class Indian lawyer cannot command a fraction of the earnings of a counterpart living in New York, London or Rome; nevertheless, he rightly sees himself as prosperous.

The rich not only live longer, on average, than the poor, they also die from different causes. Infectious and parasitic diseases, all but eliminated in the developed world, remain a scourge in the developing nations. On the other hand, more than two-thirds of the populations of OECD nations eventually succumb to cancer or circulatory disease.

Women in the Workforce

Women in paid employment as a percentage of the total workforce (latest available year)

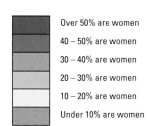

- Over 50% are women
- 40 – 50% are women
- 30 – 40% are women
- 20 – 30% are women
- 10 – 20% are women
- Under 10% are women

Most women in the workforce		Fewest women in the workforce	
Cambodia	56%	Saudi Arabia	4%
Kazakstan	54%	Oman	6%
Burundi	53%	Afghanistan	8%
Mozambique	53%	Algeria	9%
Turkmenistan	52%	Libya	9%

[USA 45] [UK 44]

23

Energy

Production

[Each square represents 1% of world energy production]

North America

Europe

CIS

Middle East

Japan

Africa

Asia

South America

Australasia

Consumption

[Each square represents 1% of world energy consumption]

North America

Europe

CIS

Middle East

Africa

Asia

South America

Japan

Australasia

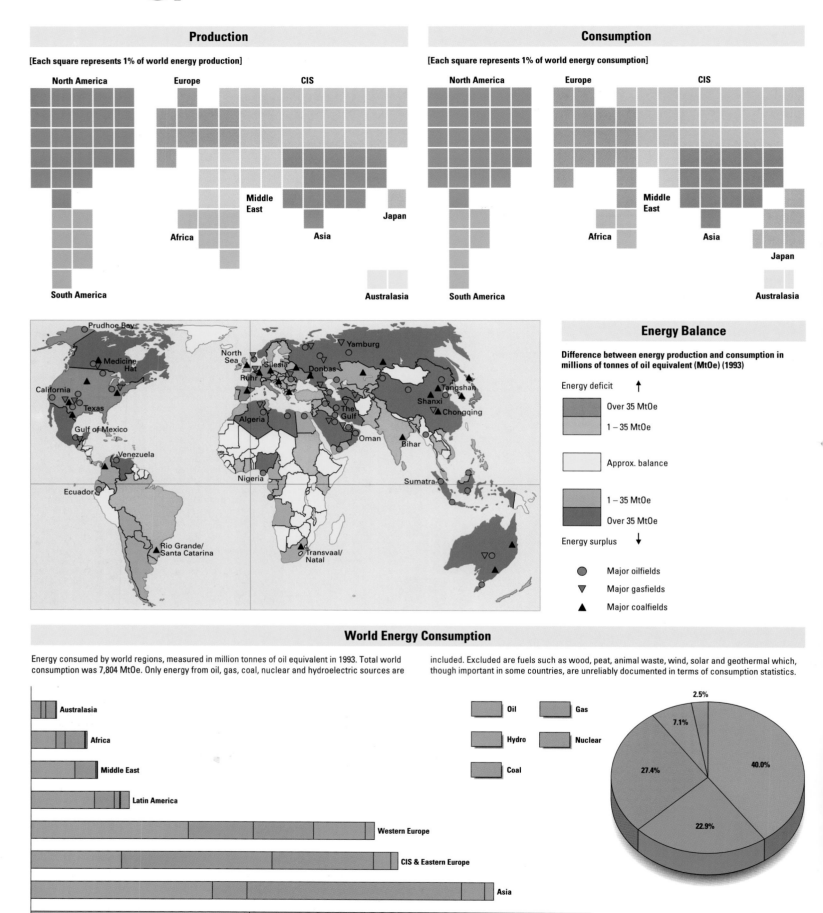

Prudhoe Bay
North Sea
Yamburg
Medicine Hat
Silesia
Ruhr
Donbas
California
Texas
Tangshan
Shanxi
Chongqing
Gulf of Mexico
The Gulf
Algeria
Venezuela
Oman
Bihar
Ecuador
Nigeria
Sumatra
Rio Grande/Santa Catarina
Transvaal/Natal

Energy Balance

Difference between energy production and consumption in millions of tonnes of oil equivalent (MtOe) (1993)

Energy deficit ↑

Over 35 MtOe

1 – 35 MtOe

Approx. balance

1 – 35 MtOe

Over 35 MtOe

Energy surplus ↓

⬤ Major oilfields

▽ Major gasfields

▲ Major coalfields

World Energy Consumption

Energy consumed by world regions, measured in million tonnes of oil equivalent in 1993. Total world consumption was 7,804 MtOe. Only energy from oil, gas, coal, nuclear and hydroelectric sources are

included. Excluded are fuels such as wood, peat, animal waste, wind, solar and geothermal which, though important in some countries, are unreliably documented in terms of consumption statistics.

Australasia

Africa

Middle East

Latin America

Western Europe

CIS & Eastern Europe

Asia

North America

Oil   Gas

Hydro   Nuclear

Coal

2.5%
7.1%
40.0%
27.4%
22.9%

5   10   15   20   25

Energy

Energy is used to keep us warm or cool, fuel our industries and our transport systems, and even feed us; high-intensity agriculture, with its use of fertilizers, pesticides and machinery, is heavily energy-dependent. Although we live in a high-energy society, there are vast discrepancies between rich and poor; for example, a North American consumes 13 times as much energy as a Chinese person. But even developing nations have more power at their disposal than was imaginable a century ago.

The distribution of energy supplies, most importantly fossil fuels (coal, oil and natural gas), is very uneven. In addition, the diagrams and map opposite show that the largest producers of energy are not necessarily the largest consumers. The movement of energy supplies around the world is therefore an important component of international trade. In 1995, total world movements in oil amounted to 1,815 million tonnes.

As the finite reserves of fossil fuels are depleted, renewable energy sources, such as solar, hydro-thermal, wind, tidal and biomass, will become increasingly important around the world.

Nuclear Power

Percentage of electricity generated by nuclear power stations, leading nations (1995)

1. Lithuania	85%	11. Spain	33%
2. France	77%	12. Finland	30%
3. Belgium	56%	13. Germany	29%
4. Slovak Rep.	49%	14. Japan	29%
5. Sweden	48%	15. UK	27%
6. Bulgaria	41%	16. Ukraine	27%
7. Hungary	41%	17. Czech Rep.	22%
8. Switzerland	39%	18. Canada	19%
9. Slovenia	38%	19. USA	18%
10. South Korea	33%	20. Russia	12%

Although the 1980s were a bad time for the nuclear power industry (major projects ran over budget, and fears of long-term environmental damage were heavily reinforced by the 1986 disaster at Chernobyl), the industry picked up in the early 1990s. However, whilst the number of reactors is still increasing, orders for new plants have shrunk. This is partly due to the increasingly difficult task of disposing of nuclear waste.

Hydroelectricity

Percentage of electricity generated by hydroelectric power stations, leading nations (1995)

1. Paraguay	99.9%	11. Rwanda	97.6%
2. Congo (Zaire)	99.7%	12. Malawi	97.6%
3. Bhutan	99.6%	13. Cameroon	96.9%
4. Zambia	99.5%	14. Nepal	96.7%
5. Norway	99.4%	15. Laos	95.3%
6. Ghana	99.3%	16. Albania	95.2%
7. Congo	99.3%	17. Iceland	94.0%
8. Uganda	99.1%	17. Brazil	92.2%
9. Burundi	98.3%	19. Honduras	87.6%
10. Uruguay	98.0%	20. Tanzania	87.1%

Countries heavily reliant on hydroelectricity are usually small and non-industrial: a high proportion of hydroelectric power more often reflects a modest energy budget than vast hydroelectric resources. The USA, for instance, produces only 9% of power requirements from hydroelectricity; yet that 9% amounts to more than three times the hydropower generated by all of Africa.

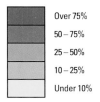

Fuel Exports

Fuels as a percentage of total value of exports (1990–94)

- Over 75%
- 50 – 75%
- 25 – 50%
- 10 – 25%
- Under 10%

Conversion Rates

1 barrel = 0.136 tonnes or 159 litres or 35 Imperial gallons or 42 US gallons

1 tonne = 7.33 barrels or 1,185 litres or 256 Imperial gallons or 261 US gallons

1 tonne oil = 1.5 tonnes hard coal or 3.0 tonnes lignite or 12,000 kWh

1 Imperial gallon = 1.201 US gallons or 4.546 litres or 277.4 cubic inches

Measurements

For historical reasons, oil is traded in 'barrels'. The weight and volume equivalents (shown right) are all based on average-density 'Arabian light' crude oil.

The energy equivalents given for a tonne of oil are also somewhat imprecise: oil and coal of different qualities will have varying energy contents, a fact usually reflected in their price on world markets.

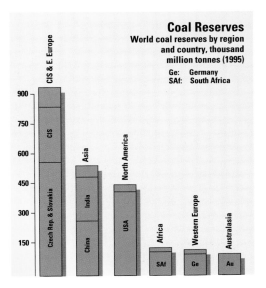

Coal Reserves
World coal reserves by region and country, thousand million tonnes (1995)

Ge: Germany
SAf: South Africa

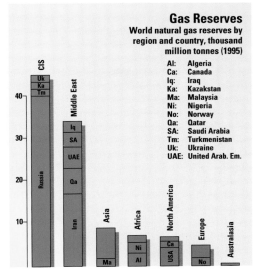

Gas Reserves
World natural gas reserves by region and country, thousand million tonnes (1995)

Al:	Algeria
Ca:	Canada
Iq:	Iraq
Ka:	Kazakstan
Ma:	Malaysia
Ni:	Nigeria
No:	Norway
Qa:	Qatar
SA:	Saudi Arabia
Tm:	Turkmenistan
Uk:	Ukraine
UAE:	United Arab. Em.

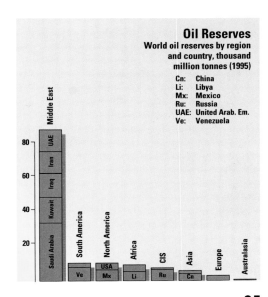

Oil Reserves
World oil reserves by region and country, thousand million tonnes (1995)

Cn:	China
Li:	Libya
Mx:	Mexico
Ru:	Russia
UAE:	United Arab. Em.
Ve:	Venezuela

Production

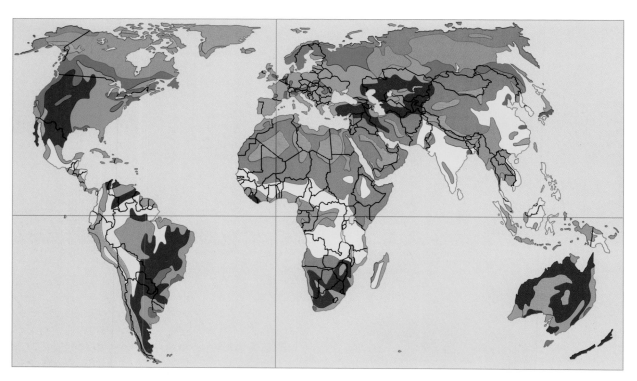

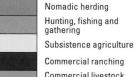

Agriculture

Predominant type of farming or land use.

- Nomadic herding
- Hunting, fishing and gathering
- Subsistence agriculture
- Commercial ranching
- Commercial livestock and grain farming
- Urban areas
- Forestry
- Unproductive land

The development of agriculture transformed human existence more than any other. The whole business of farming is constantly developing: due mainly to new varieties of rice and wheat, world grain production has increased by over 70% since 1965. New machinery and modern agricultural techniques enable relatively few farmers to produce enough food for the world's 5,800 million people.

Staple Crops

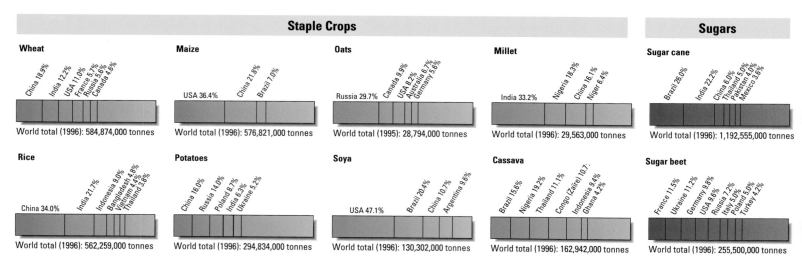

Wheat
China 18.9% India 12.2% USA 11.0% France 5.7% Russia 5.6% Canada 4.6%

World total (1996): 584,874,000 tonnes

Maize
USA 36.4% China 21.8% Brazil 7.0%

World total (1996): 576,821,000 tonnes

Oats
Russia 29.7% Canada 9.9% USA 8.2% Australia 6.7% Germany 5.6%

World total (1995): 28,794,000 tonnes

Millet
India 33.2% Nigeria 18.3% China 16.1% Niger 6.4%

World total (1996): 29,563,000 tonnes

Rice
China 34.0% India 21.7% Indonesia 9.0% Bangladesh 4.8% Vietnam 4.4% Thailand 3.8%

World total (1996): 562,259,000 tonnes

Potatoes
China 16.0% Russia 14.0% Poland 8.7% India 6.3% Ukraine 5.2%

World total (1996): 294,834,000 tonnes

Soya
USA 47.1% Brazil 20.4% China 10.7% Argentina 9.6%

World total (1996): 130,302,000 tonnes

Cassava
Brazil 15.6% Nigeria 19.2% Thailand 11.1% Congo (Zaire) 10.7% Indonesia 9.4% Ghana 4.2%

World total (1996): 162,942,000 tonnes

Sugars

Sugar cane
Brazil 26.0% India 22.2% China 6.0% Thailand 5.0% Pakistan 4.0% Mexico 3.6%

World total (1996): 1,192,555,000 tonnes

Sugar beet
France 11.5% Ukraine 11.2% Germany 9.8% USA 9.6% Russia 7.2% Italy 5.0% Poland 5.0% Turkey 4.2%

World total (1996): 255,500,000 tonnes

Balance of Employment

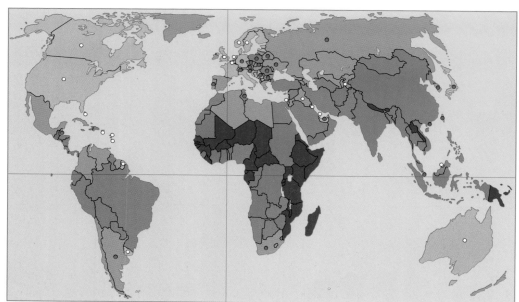

Percentage of total workforce employed in agriculture, including forestry and fishing (1990–92)

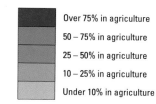

- Over 75% in agriculture
- 50 – 75% in agriculture
- 25 – 50% in agriculture
- 10 – 25% in agriculture
- Under 10% in agriculture

Employment in industry and services

- ● Over a third of total workforce employed in manufacturing

- ○ Over two-thirds of total workforce employed in service industries (work in offices, shops, tourism, transport, construction and government)

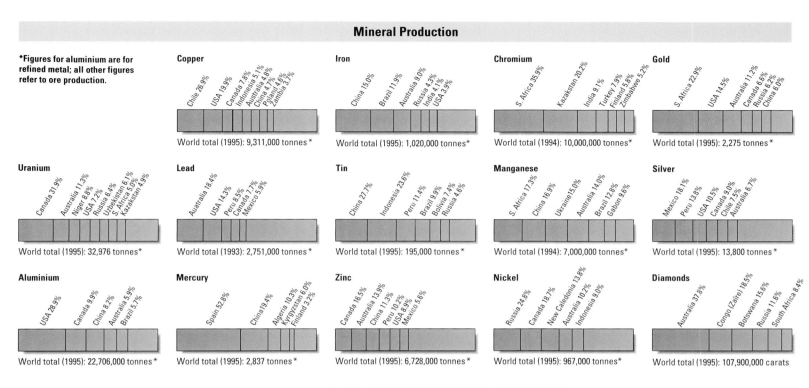

*Figures for aluminium are for refined metal; all other figures refer to ore production.

Copper
Chile 26.9% | USA 19.9% | Canada 7.8% | Indonesia 5.1% | Australia 4.8% | Russia 4.7% | Poland 4.6% | Zambia 3.7%
World total (1995): 9,311,000 tonnes *

Iron
China 15.0% | Brazil 11.9% | Australia 9.0% | Russia 4.3% | India 4.1% | USA 3.9%
World total (1995): 1,020,000 tonnes*

Chromium
S. Africa 35.9% | Kazakstan 20.2% | India 9.1% | Turkey 7.9% | Finland 5.8% | Zimbabwe 5.2%
World total (1994): 10,000,000 tonnes*

Gold
S. Africa 22.9% | USA 14.5% | Australia 11.2% | Canada 6.6% | Russia 6.2% | China 6.0%
World total (1995): 2,275 tonnes *

Uranium
Canada 31.9% | Australia 11.3% | Niger 8.8% | USA 7.2% | Russia 6.4% | Uzbekistan 6.1% | S. Africa 5.0% | Kazakstan 4.9%
World total (1995): 32,976 tonnes*

Lead
Australia 18.4% | USA 14.3% | Peru 8.5% | Canada 7.7% | Mexico 5.9%
World total (1993): 2,751,000 tonnes *

Tin
China 27.7% | Indonesia 23.6% | Peru 11.4% | Brazil 9.9% | Bolivia 7.4% | Russia 4.6%
World total (1995): 195,000 tonnes *

Manganese
S. Africa 17.3% | China 16.9% | Ukraine 15.0% | Australia 14.0% | Brazil 12.8% | Gabon 9.6%
World total (1994): 7,000,000 tonnes *

Silver
Mexico 18.1% | Peru 13.8% | USA 10.5% | Canada 9.0% | Chile 7.5% | Australia 6.7%
World total (1995): 13,800 tonnes *

Aluminium
USA 28.9% | Canada 9.9% | China 8.2% | Australia 5.9% | Brazil 5.7%
World total (1995): 22,706,000 tonnes *

Mercury
Spain 52.8% | China 19.4% | Algeria 10.3% | Kyrgyzstan 6.0% | Finland 3.2%
World total (1995): 2,837 tonnes *

Zinc
Canada 16.5% | Australia 13.9% | China 11.3% | Peru 10.2% | USA 8.9% | Mexico 5.6%
World total (1995): 6,728,000 tonnes *

Nickel
Russia 24.8% | Canada 18.7% | New Caledonia 13.8% | Australia 10.2% | Indonesia 9.0%
World total (1995): 967,000 tonnes*

Diamonds
Australia 37.8% | Congo (Zaire) 18.5% | Botswana 15.6% | Russia 11.6% | South Africa 8.4%
World total (1995): 107,900,000 carats

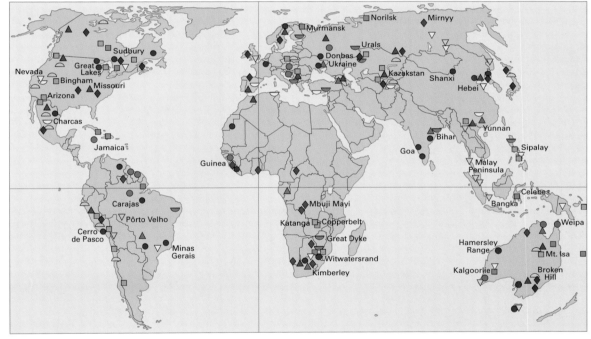

Mineral Distribution

The map shows the richest sources of the most important minerals. Major mineral locations are named.

Light metals
● Bauxite

Base metals
◻ Copper
▲ Lead
▽ Mercury
▽ Tin
◆ Zinc

Iron and ferro-alloys
● Iron
▽ Chrome
▲ Manganese
◼ Nickel

Precious metals
▽ Gold
◠ Silver

Precious stones
◆ Diamonds

The map does not show undersea deposits, most of which are considered inaccessible.

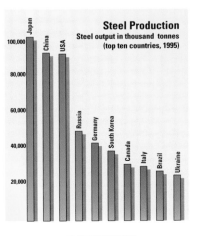

Steel Production
Steel output in thousand tonnes (top ten countries, 1995)

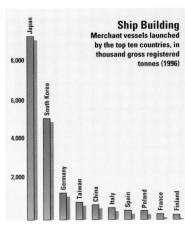

Ship Building
Merchant vessels launched by the top ten countries, in thousand gross registered tonnes (1996)

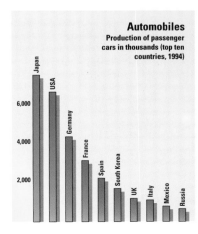

Automobiles
Production of passenger cars in thousands (top ten countries, 1994)

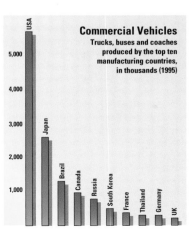

Commercial Vehicles
Trucks, buses and coaches produced by the top ten manufacturing countries, in thousands (1995)

Trade

Share of World Trade

Percentage share of total world exports by value (1995)

- Over 10% of world trade
- 5 – 10% of world trade
- 1 – 5% of world trade
- 0.5 – 1% of world trade
- 0.1 – 0.5% of world trade
- Under 0.1% of world trade

International trade is dominated by a handful of powerful maritime nations. The members of 'G8', the inner circle of OECD (see page 19), and the top seven countries listed in the diagram below, account for more than half the total. The majority of nations – including all but four in Africa – contribute less than one quarter of 1% to the worldwide total of exports; the EU countries account for 40%, the Pacific Rim nations over 35%.

The Main Trading Nations

The imports and exports of the top ten trading nations as a percentage of world trade (1994). Each country's trade in manufactured goods is shown in dark blue.

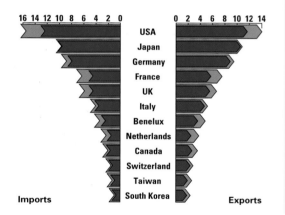

Patterns of Trade

Thriving international trade is the outward sign of a healthy world economy, the obvious indicator that some countries have goods to sell and others the means to buy them. Global exports expanded to an estimated US $3.92 trillion in 1994, an increase due partly to economic recovery in industrial nations but also to export-led growth strategies in many developing nations and lowered regional trade barriers. International trade remains dominated, however, by the rich, industrialized countries of the Organization for Economic Development: between them, OECD members account for almost 75% of world imports and exports in most years. However, continued rapid economic growth in some developing countries is altering global trade patterns. The 'tiger economies' of South-east Asia are particularly vibrant, averaging more than 8% growth between 1992 and 1994. The size of the largest trading economies means that imports and exports usually represent only a small percentage of their total wealth. In export-concious Japan, for example, trade in goods and services amounts to less than 18% of GDP. In poorer countries, trade – often in a single commodity – may amount to 50% of GDP.

Traded Products

Top ten manufactures traded, by value in billions of US $ (latest available year)

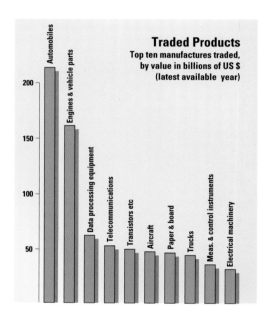

Balance of Trade

Value of exports in proportion to the value of imports (1995)

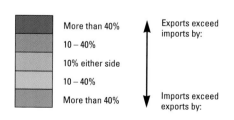

- More than 40% — Exports exceed imports by:
- 10 – 40%
- 10% either side
- 10 – 40%
- More than 40% — Imports exceed exports by:

The total world trade balance should amount to zero, since exports must equal imports on a global scale. In practice, at least $100 billion in exports go unrecorded, leaving the world with an apparent deficit and many countries in a better position than public accounting reveals. However, a favourable trade balance is not necessarily a sign of prosperity: many poorer countries must maintain a high surplus in order to service debts, and do so by restricting imports below the levels needed to sustain successful economies.

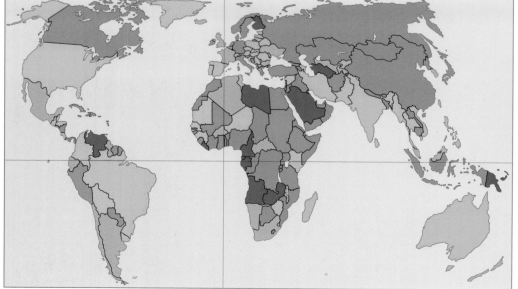

CARTOGRAPHY BY PHILIP'S. COPYRIGHT GEORGE PHILIP LTD

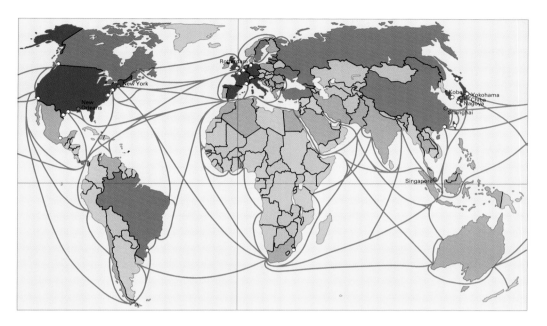

Seaborne Freight

Freight unloaded in millions of tonnes (latest available year)

- Over 100
- 50 – 100
- 10 – 50
- 5 – 10
- Under 5
- Landlocked countries

Major seaports

- Over 100 million tonnes per year
- 50–100 million tonnes per year
- Major shipping routes

Cargoes

Type of seaborne freight

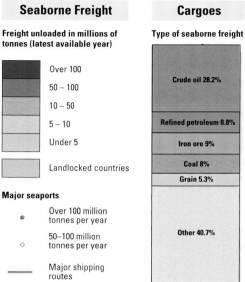

- Crude oil 28.2%
- Refined petroleum 8.8%
- Iron ore 9%
- Coal 8%
- Grain 5.3%
- Other 40.7%

Merchant Fleets

Merchant fleets in thousand gross tonnage (1994). A large number of vessels are registered in Liberia and Panama but they are not part of the national fleet.

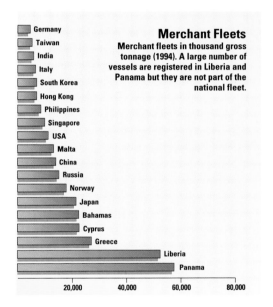

Germany, Taiwan, India, Italy, South Korea, Hong Kong, Philippines, Singapore, USA, Malta, China, Russia, Norway, Japan, Bahamas, Cyprus, Greece, Liberia, Panama

20,000   40,000   60,000   80,000

The Great Ports

Total Cargo Traffic (1995) '000 tonnes

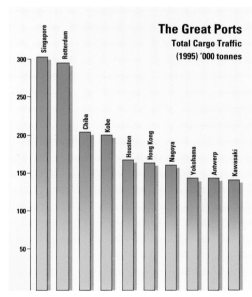

Singapore, Rotterdam, Chiba, Kobe, Houston, Hong Kong, Nagoya, Yokohama, Antwerp, Kawasaki

World Shipping

World merchant fleet by type of vessel and deadweight tonnage (latest available year)

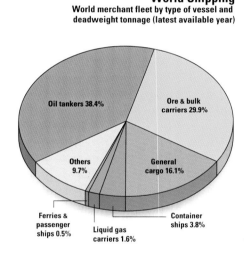

- Oil tankers 38.4%
- Ore & bulk carriers 29.9%
- Others 9.7%
- General cargo 16.1%
- Ferries & passenger ships 0.5%
- Liquid gas carriers 1.6%
- Container ships 3.8%

Dependence on Trade

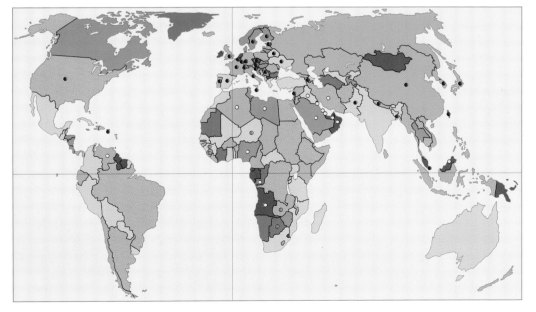

Value of exports as a percentage of Gross National Product (1995)

- Over 50% GNP from exports
- 40 – 50% GNP from exports
- 30 – 40% GNP from exports
- 20 – 30% GNP from exports
- 10 – 20% GNP from exports
- Under 10% GNP from exports

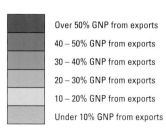

- Most dependent on industrial exports (over 75% of total exports)
- Most dependent on fuel exports (over 75% of total exports)
- Most dependent on mineral and metal exports (over 75% of total exports)

Travel and Tourism

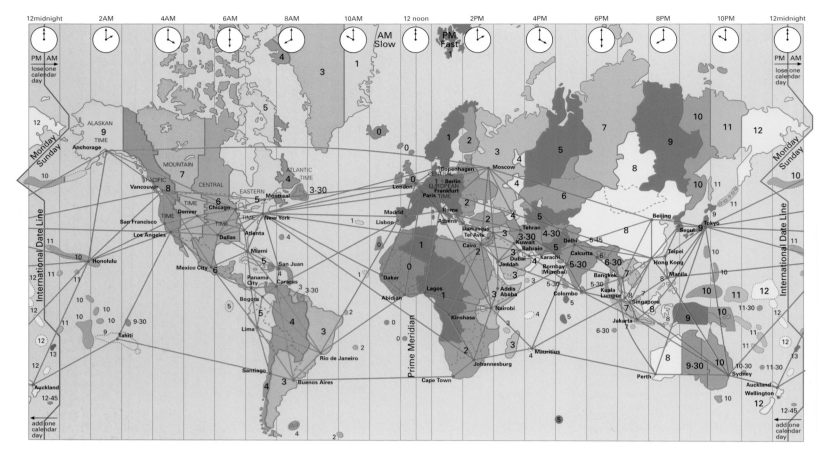

The world is divided into 24 time zones, each centred on meridians at 15° intervals, which is the longitudinal distance the sun travels every hour. The meridian running through Greenwich, London, passes through the middle of the first zone.

Time Zones

Zones using GMT	Zones fast of GMT	Certain time zones are affected by the incidence of 'summer time' in countries where it is adopted.
Zones slow of GMT	Half-hour zones	
– – – International boundaries	—— Time zone boundaries	Actual Solar Time, when it is noon at Greenwich, is shown along the top of the map.
10 Hours slow or fast of GMT	—— International Date Line	
	—— Selected air routes	

Rail and Road: The Leading Nations

Total rail network ('000 km) (1995)		Passenger km per head per year		Total road network ('000 km)		Vehicle km per head per year		Number of vehicles per km of roads	
1. USA	235.7	Japan	2,017	USA	6,277.9	USA	12,505	Hong Kong	284
2. Russia	87.4	Belarus	1,880	India	2,962.5	Luxembourg	7,989	Taiwan	211
3. India	62.7	Russia	1,826	Brazil	1,824.4	Kuwait	7,251	Singapore	152
4. China	54.6	Switzerland	1,769	Japan	1,130.9	France	7,142	Kuwait	140
5. Germany	41.7	Ukraine	1,456	China	1,041.1	Sweden	6,991	Brunei	96
6. Australia	35.8	Austria	1,168	Russia	884.0	Germany	6,806	Italy	91
7. Argentina	34.2	France	1,011	Canada	849.4	Denmark	6,764	Israel	87
8. France	31.9	Netherlands	994	France	811.6	Austria	6,518	Thailand	73
9. Mexico	26.5	Latvia	918	Australia	810.3	Netherlands	5,984	Ukraine	73
10. South Africa	26.3	Denmark	884	Germany	636.3	UK	5,738	UK	67
11. Poland	24.9	Slovak Rep.	862	Romania	461.9	Canada	5,493	Netherlands	66
12. Ukraine	22.6	Romania	851	Turkey	388.1	Italy	4,852	Germany	62

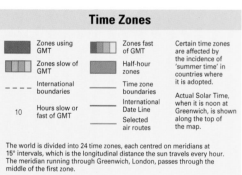

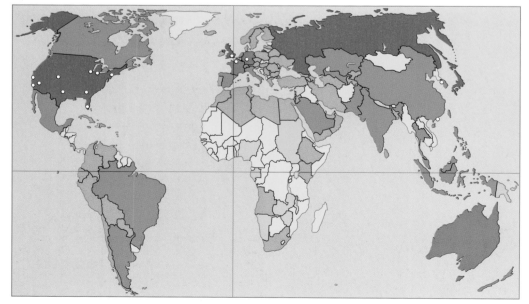

Air Travel

Passenger kilometres (the number of passengers – international and domestic – multiplied by the distance flown by each passenger from the airport of origin) (1994)

	Over 100,000 million
	50,000 – 100,000 million
	10,000 – 50,000 million
	1,000 – 10,000 million
	500 – 1,000 million
	Under 500 million
o	Major airports (handling over 25 million passengers in 1995)

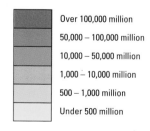

World's busiest airports (total passengers)		World's busiest airports (international passengers)	
1. Chicago	(O'Hare)	1. London	(Heathrow)
2. Atlanta	(Hatsfield)	2. London	(Gatwick)
3. Dallas	(Dallas/Ft Worth)	3. Frankfurt	(International)
4. Los Angeles	(Intern'l)	4. New York	(Kennedy)
5. London	(Heathrow)	5. Paris	(De Gaulle)

Destinations

- ■ Cultural and historical centres
- □ Coastal resorts
- □ Ski resorts
- ■ Centres of entertainment
- ■ Places of pilgrimage
- ■ Places of great natural beauty
- — Popular holiday cruise routes

Visitors to the USA

Overseas travellers to the USA, thousands (1997 projections)

1.	Canada	13,900
2.	Mexico	12,370
3.	Japan	4,640
4.	UK	3,350
5.	Germany	1,990
6.	France	1,030
7.	Taiwan	885
8.	Venezuela	860
9.	South Korea	800
10.	Brazil	785

In 1996, the USA earned the most from tourism, with receipts of more than US $64 billion.

Tourist Spending

Countries spending the most on overseas tourism, US $ million (latest available year)

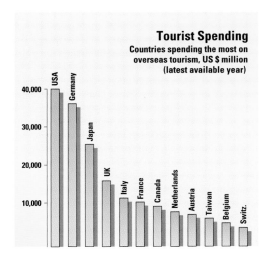

Importance of Tourism

		Arrivals from abroad (1995)	% of world total (1995)
1.	France	60,584,000	10.68%
2.	Spain	45,125,000	7.96%
3.	USA	44,730,000	7.89%
4.	Italy	29,184,000	5.15%
5.	China	23,368,000	4.12%
6.	UK	22,700,000	4.00%
7.	Hungary	22,087,000	3.90%
8.	Mexico	19,870,000	3.50%
9.	Poland	19,225,000	3.39%
10.	Austria	17,750,000	3.13%
11.	Canada	16,854,000	2.97%
12.	Czech Republic	16,600,000	2.93%

The latest figures reveal a 4.6% rise in the total number of people travelling abroad in 1996, to 593 million. Small economies in attractive areas are often completely dominated by tourism: in some West Indian islands, for example, tourist spending provides over 90% of total income.

Tourist Earning

Countries receiving the most from overseas tourism, US $ million (latest available year)

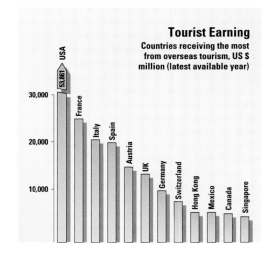

Tourism

Tourism receipts as a percentage of Gross National Product (1994)

- ■ Over 10% of GNP from tourism
- ■ 5 – 10% of GNP from tourism
- ■ 2.5 – 5% of GNP from tourism
- ■ 1 – 2.5% of GNP from tourism
- ■ 0.5 – 1% of GNP from tourism
- □ Under 0.5% of GNP from tourism

Countries spending the most on promoting tourism, millions of US $ (1996)		Fastest growing tourist destinations, % change in receipts (1994–5)	
Australia	88	South Korea	49%
Spain	79	Czech Republic	27%
UK	79	India	21%
France	73	Russia	19%
Singapore	54	Philippines	18%

The World In Focus: Index

32

WORLD MAPS

SETTLEMENTS

◻ **PARIS** ▪ **Berne** ◉ **Livorno** ◉ *Brugge* ◎ *Algeciras* ○ *Fréjus* ○ *Oberammergau* ○ *Thira*

Settlement symbols and type styles vary according to the scale of each map and indicate the importance
of towns on the map rather than specific population figures

∴ Ruins or Archæological Sites   ᵛ Wells in Desert

ADMINISTRATION

───── International Boundaries

- - - International Boundaries
(Undefined or Disputed)

········· Internal Boundaries

National Parks

Country Names

NICARAGUA

Administrative
Area Names

KENT

CALABRIA

International boundaries show the *de facto* situation where there are rival claims to territory

COMMUNICATIONS

───── Principal Roads

⌒ Other Roads

·⌒· Trails and Seasonal Roads

⋉ Passes

✿ Airfields

⌒ Principal Railroads

·-·-· Railroads
Under Construction

⌒ Other Railroads

⊐---⊏ Railroad Tunnels

········· Principal Canals

PHYSICAL FEATURES

⌒ Perennial Streams

······ Intermittent Streams

⬭ Perennial Lakes

⬭ Intermittent Lakes

Swamps and Marshes

Permanent Ice
and Glaciers

▲ 8848 Elevations (m)

▾ 8050 Sea Depths (m)

1134 Height of Lake Surface
Above Sea Level (m)

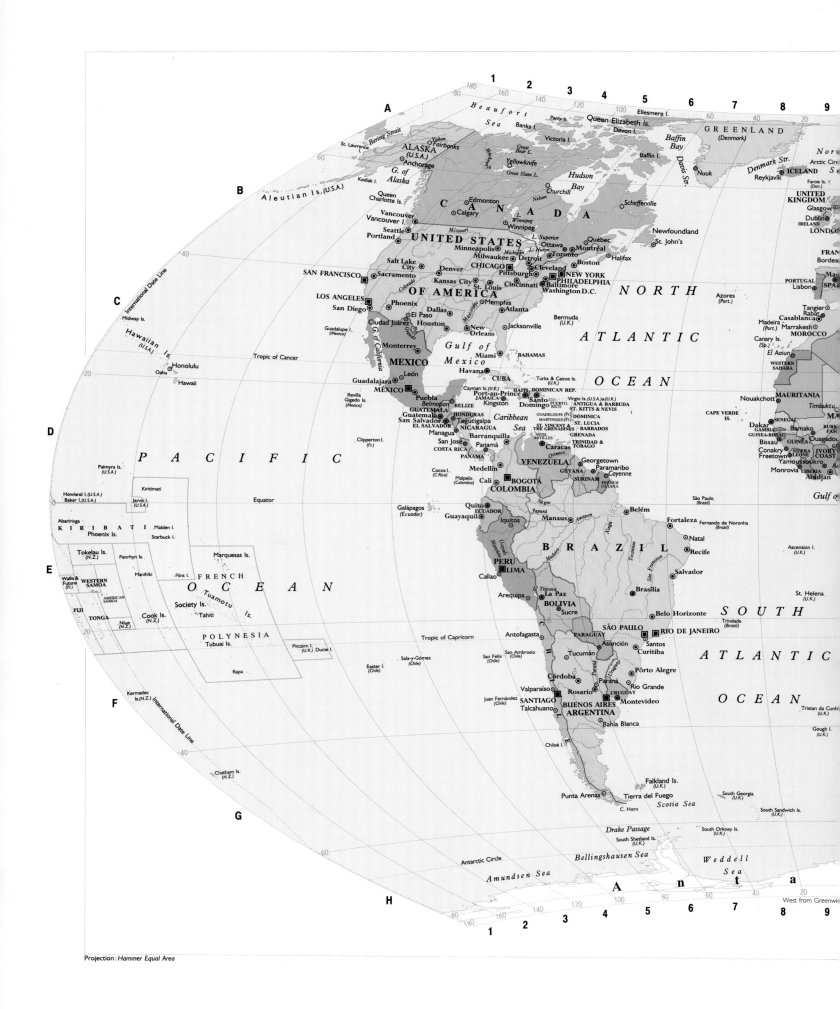

Projection: *Hammer Equal Area*

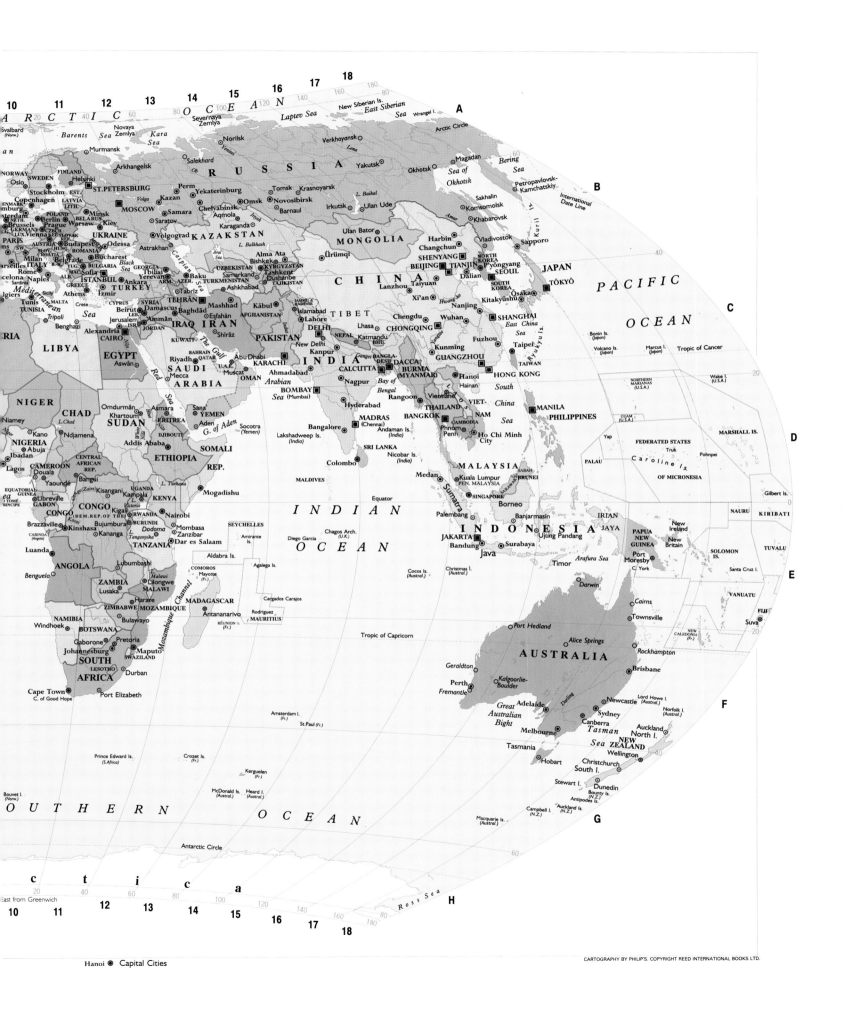

10 11 12 13 14 15 16 17 18

A R C T I C   O C E A N

40   20   60   80   100   120   140   160   180   80   60

Svalbard *(Nor.)*   Barents   Novaya Zemlya   Severnaya Zemlya   Laptev Sea   New Siberian Is.   East Siberian Sea   Wrangel I.   **A**

an   Sea   Kara Sea   Norilsk   Verkhoyansk   Lena   Arctic Circle   60

Murmansk   Salekhard   Ob   Yenisey   Yakutsk   Okhotsk   Magadan   Bering   **B**

Arkhangelsk   R U S S I A   Sea of Okhotsk   Petropavlovsk-Kamchatskly   International Date Line

NORWAY SWEDEN FINLAND Helsinki   Perm   Yekaterinburg   Tomsk Krasnoyarsk   Sakhalin   Komsomolsk   60

Oslo   ST.PETERSBURG   EST.   Volga Kazan   Omsk Novosibirsk   L. Baikal   Amur   Khabarovsk

Stockholm   Samara   Chelyabinsk   Irkutsk Ulan Ude   Vladivostok   Sapporo   40

DENMARK Copenhagen LATVIA LITH.   Saratov   Aqmola   Barnaul   Ulan Bator   Harbin   SEOUL   **C**

mburg Berlin POLAND BELARUS Minsk   Karaganda   MONGOLIA   Changchun   NORTH KOREA   Pyŏngyang   JAPAN   PACIFIC

Brussels GERMANY Prague Warsaw Kiev   Volgograd   KAZAKSTAN   L. Balkhash   Ürümqi   SHENYANG   TIANJIN Dalian   TŌKYŌ

PARIS LUX. Vienna CZECH. UKRAINE   Astrakhan   Aral Sea   Alma Ata   BEIJING   Kitakyūshū Ōsaka   OCEAN

AUSTRIA Budapest SLOVAK. ROMANIA Odessa   Bishkek KYRGYZSTAN   SOUTH KOREA

Milan CROATIA Belgrade Bucharest   Caspian Sea   GEORGIA   UZBEKISTAN Tashkent   C H I N A   Lanzhou Taiyuan

Rome ITALY YUG. BULGARIA Black Sea Tbilisi   Samarkand TAJIKISTAN   Xi'an   Hwang-ho   Nanjing   Bonin Is. *(Japan)*   20

celona ALB. Sofia Yerevan Baku TURKMENISTAN Dushanbe   Chengdu Wuhan   SHANGHAI   Volcano Is. *(Japan)*

GREECE ISTANBUL ARM. AZER. Ashkhabad   Mashhad   Kābul AFGHANISTAN   TIBET   Lhasa   CHONGQING   East China Sea   Marcus I. *(Japan)*   Tropic of Cancer

Athens TURKEY İzmir   Tabriz   JAMMU & KASHMIR   Islamabad Lahore   Kunming   GUANGZHOU   Taipei   Ryukyu Is.

Algiers Tunis MALTA Crete CYPRUS SYRIA TEHRĀN   Esfahān   DELHI   New Delhi   NEPAL BHU.   Fuzhou   TAIWAN   20

TUNISIA Tripoli Sea   Beirut Damascus Baghdād   IRAN   Kanpur   Katmandu   HONG KONG   Hainan   South   Wake I. *(U.S.A.)*

Benghazi   Jerusalem ISR. JORDAN IRAQ   KUWAIT   BAHRAIN   QATAR Abu Dhabi   PAKISTAN   I N D I A   Ganges   BANGLA-DESH   Hanoi   China   NORTHERN MARIANAS *(U.S.A.)*

LIBYA   EGYPT Alexandria CAIRO   Riyadh   U.A.E. Muscat   KARACHI   Ahmadabad   CALCUTTA   DACCA   BURMA   Sea

Aswān   Red Sea   Mecca   SAUDI   OMAN   Arabian Sea   Nagpur   Bay of Bengal   MYANMAR   Rangoon   Vientiane   VIET-   MANILA   GUAM *(U.S.A.)*   **D**

NIGER CHAD   Omdurmân Khartoum   ARABIA   BOMBAY *(Mumbai)*   Hyderabad   MADRAS *(Chennai)*   THAILAND   NAM   PHILIPPINES

Niamey   L. Chad   Asmara ERITREA   YEMEN   Sana'   BANGKOK   CAMBODIA   FEDERATED STATES

NIGERIA Kano   Ndjamena   SUDAN   DJIBOUTI   G. of Aden   Socotra *(Yemen)*   Bangalore   Andaman Is. *(India)*   Phnom   Ho Chi Minh   Yap   Truk   Pohnpei

Abuja   Aden   Lakshadweep Is. *(India)*   Penh   City   PALAU   Caroline Is.   Marcus

Ibadan   Addis Ababa   SOMALI   SRI LANKA   Nicobar Is. *(India)*   OF MICRONESIA

Lagos CAMEROON   CENTRAL AFRICAN REP.   ETHIOPIA   REP.   Colombo   Medan   MALDIVES   Kuala Lumpur SABAH   BRUNEI   NAURU

Douala   Bangui   REP.   PEN. MALAYSIA   SARAWAK   Gilbert Is.   KIRIBATI

EQUATORIAL GUINEA   Yaoundé   *(Zaïre)* Kisangani UGANDA L. Turkana   MALDIVES   MALAYSIA   SINGAPORE   Borneo

SÃO TOMÉ & PRINCIPE   Libreville GABON   CONGO   Kampala   KENYA   Mogadishu   Medan   Sumatra   Banjarmasin   IRIAN JAYA   New Ireland   SOLOMON IS.   TUVALU

CONGO (DEM.REP.OF THE)   RWANDA   Nairobi   Kigali   Palembang   I N D O N E S I A   New Britain   VANUATU

Brazzaville CABINDA *(Angola)*   Kinshasa Kananga   BURUNDI Bujumbura Dodoma L. Victoria   Mombasa   SEYCHELLES   I N D I A N   Equator   JAKARTA   Ujung Pandang   PAPUA NEW GUINEA   FIJI

Luanda   Lubumbashi   Kanji   TANZANIA   Dar es Salaam   Zanzibar   Amirante Is.   Diego Garcia Chagos Arch. *(U.K.)*   O C E A N   Bandung   Java Surabaya   Port Moresby C. York   SANTA CRUZ I.   Suva

ANGOLA   Lubumbashi   Aldabra Is.   COMOROS Mayotte *(Fr.)*   Cocos Is. *(Austral.)*   Christmas I. *(Austral.)*   Timor   Arafura Sea   Darwin   NEW CALEDONIA *(Fr.)*   **E**

Benguela   ZAMBIA   Malawi   Agalega Is.   Cairns   20

NAMIBIA   Lusaka   Lilongwe MALAWI   Cargados Carajos   Townsville

Windhoek   BOTSWANA   Harare   MOZAMBIQUE   MADAGASCAR   Rodriguez   Tropic of Capricorn   Port Hedland   Alice Springs   Rockhampton

ZIMBABWE   Antananarivo   RÉUNION *(Fr.)* MAURITIUS   A U S T R A L I A

Gaborone   Bulawayo   Pretoria   Mozambique Channel   Brisbane   **F**

Johannesburg SOUTH SWAZILAND Maputo   LESOTHO   Geraldton   Kalgoorlie-Boulder   Newcastle   Lord Howe I. *(Austral.)*

AFRICA   Durban   Perth   Adelaide   Darling   Sydney   Norfolk I. *(Austral.)*

Cape Town   Port Elizabeth   Amsterdam I. *(Fr.)*   Fremantle   Great Australian Bight   Canberra   Tasman   Auckland North I.

C. of Good Hope   St.Paul *(Fr.)*   Melbourne   NEW   20

Prince Edward Is. *(S.Africa)*   Crozet Is. *(Fr.)*   Kerguelen *(Fr.)*   Tasmania   Sea ZEALAND Wellington

Bouvet I. *(Nor.)*   McDonald Is. *(Austral.)* Heard I. *(Austral.)*   Hobart   Christchurch South I.

O U T H E R N   O C E A N   Stewart I. Antipodes Is. *(N.Z.)* Dunedin

Antarctic Circle   Macquarie Is. *(Austral.)*   Campbell I. *(N.Z.)*   Auckland I. *(N.Z.)*   **G**

60   Bounty Is. *(N.Z.)*

c   t   i   c   a   Ross Sea   **H**

20   40   60   80   100   120   140   160   180   80

East from Greenwich   10   11   12   13   14   15   16   17   18

Hanoi ⊙ Capital Cities

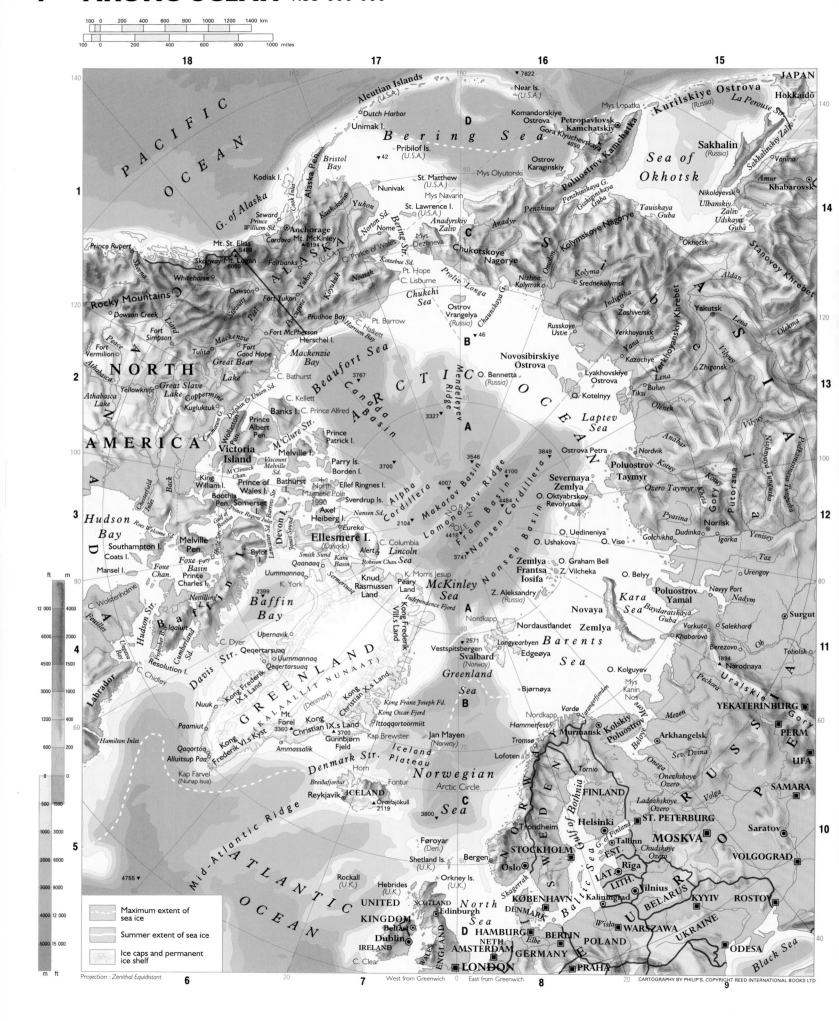

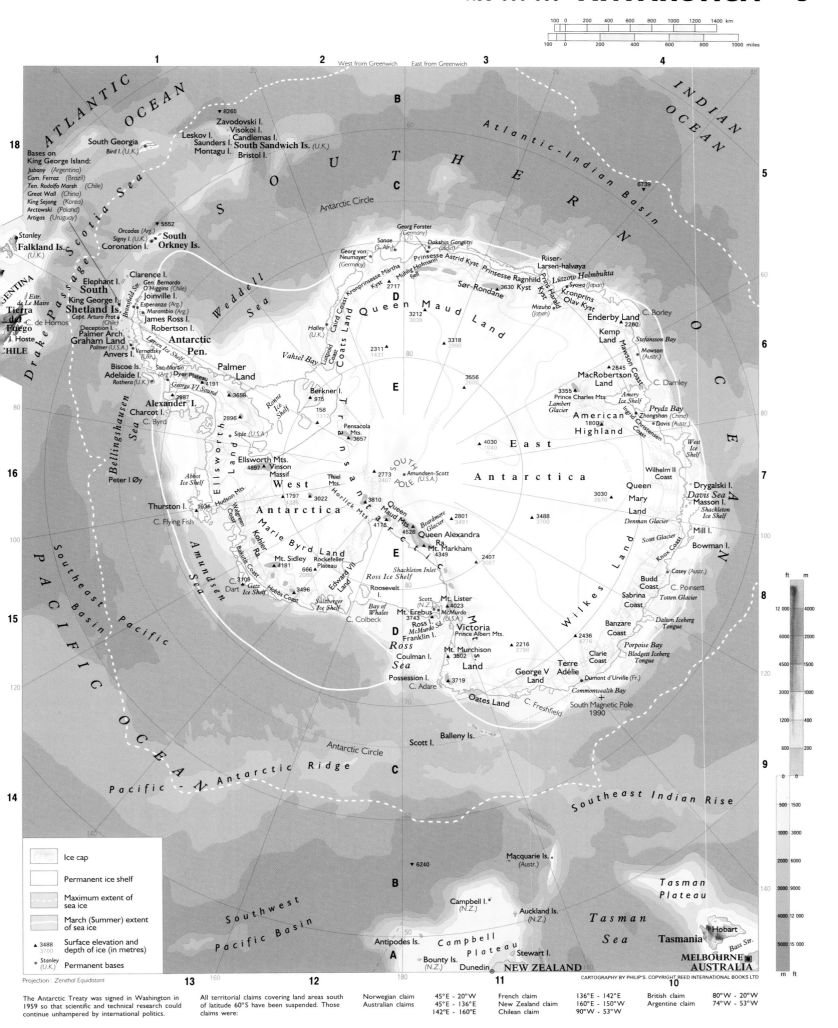

100 0 200 400 600 800 1000 1200 1400 km
100 0 200 400 600 800 1000 miles

Projection : Zenithal Equidistant

The Antarctic Treaty was signed in Washington in
1959 so that scientific and technical research could
continue unhampered by international politics.

All territorial claims covering land areas south
of latitude 60°S have been suspended. Those
claims were:

Norwegian claim	45°E - 20°W
Australian claims	45°E - 136°E
	142°E - 160°E

French claim	136°E - 142°E
New Zealand claim	160°E - 150°W
Chilean claim	90°W - 53°W

British claim	80°W - 20°W
Argentine claim	74°W - 53°W

CARTOGRAPHY BY PHILIP'S. COPYRIGHT REED INTERNATIONAL BOOKS LTD

Legend:
- Ice cap
- Permanent ice shelf
- Maximum extent of sea ice
- March (Summer) extent of sea ice
- ▲ 3488 / 3700 Surface elevation and depth of ice (in metres)
- • Stanley (U.K.) Permanent bases

ATLANTIC OCEAN
INDIAN OCEAN
SOUTHERN
Atlantic-Indian Basin
Antarctic Circle

Bases on
King George Island:
Jubany (Argentina)
Com. Ferraz (Brazil)
Ten. Rodolfo Marsh (Chile)
Great Wall (China)
King Sejong (Korea)
Arctowski (Poland)
Artigas (Uruguay)

South Georgia
Bird I. (U.K.)
Leskov I.
Visokoi I.
Zavodovski I.
Candlemas I.
Saunders I.
South Sandwich Is. (U.K.)
Montagu I.
Bristol I.
▲8265

Stanley
Falkland Is.
(U.K.)

ARGENTINA
Estr.
de Le Maire
Tierra
del
Fuego
I. Hoste
CHILE
C. de Hornos

Drake Passage
Scotia Sea
Orcadas (Arg.) ▲5552
Signy I. (U.K.)
Coronation I.
South
Orkney Is.

Clarence I.
Elephant I.
Gen. Bernardo
O'Higgins (Chile)
South
King George I.
Joinville I.
Shetland Is.
Esperanza (Arg.)
Capt. Arturo Prat (Chile)
Marambio (Arg.)
Deception I.
James Ross I.
Robertson I.
Palmer Arch.
Graham Land
Palmer (U.S.A.)
Antarctic
Vernadsky (U.K.)
Pen.
Anvers I.
San Martin
Biscoe Is.
(Arg.)
Dyer Plateau
Adelaide I.
Rothera (U.K.)
▲4191
Alexander I.
▲2987
Charcot I.
George VI Sound
C. Byrd
2896

Weddell
Sea
Larsen Ice Shelf
Palmer
Land
Vahsel Bay
Ronne
Ice
Shelf
▲3658
Berkner I.
975
158
1312
Halley
(U.K.)
Pensacola
Mts.
3657

Bellingshausen
Sea
Peter I Øy
Thurston I.
1936
C. Flying Fish
Abbot
Ice Shelf
Ellsworth
Land
Hudson Mts.
Ellsworth Mts.
▲4897 Vinson
Massif
Thiel
Mts.
2773
2407
Horlick Mts.
1797
3022
3810
4176
4528

SOUTH
POLE
Amundsen-Scott
(U.S.A.)

PACIFIC OCEAN
Southeast Pacific Basin
Pacific-Antarctic Ridge
Amundsen
Sea
Marie Byrd Land
Kohler
Ra.
Bakutis Coast
C.
Dart
3109
Getz
Ice Shelf
Hobbs Coast
3496
Mt. Sidley
▲4181
Rockefeller
Plateau
666
2080
Edward VII
Land
Sulzberger
Ice Shelf
C. Colbeck
West
Antarctica

Queen
Maud Mts.
Beardmore
Glacier
2801
3491
Queen Alexandra
Ra.
Mt. Markham
4349
Shackleton Inlet
2407
3087
Roosevelt
I.
Ross Ice Shelf
Bay of
Whales
Scott
(N.Z.)
Mt. Lister
4023
McMurdo
(U.S.A.)
Mt. Erebus
3743
Ross Sd.
McMurdo Sd.
Ross I.
Victoria
Prince Albert Mts.
Franklin I.
Ross
Sea
Coulman I.
Mt. Murchison
3502
Possession I.
C. Adare
3719

Georg Forster
(Germany)
Sanae
(S. Afr.)
Dakshin Gangotri
(India)
Georg von
Neumayer
(Germany)
Prinsesse Martha
Kyst
Kronprinsesse Martha
Prinsesse Astrid Kyst
Mühlig Hofmann
fjell
2717
Prinsesse Ragnhild
Kyst
Sør-Rondane
3630
Riiser-
Larsen-halvøya
Prins Harald
Kyst
Lützow Holmbukta
Syowa (Japan)
Kronprins
Olav Kyst
Mizuho
(Japan)

Queen Maud Land
Coats Land
Caird Coast
Luitpold Coast
3212
3039
3318
2990
2311
1431
3556
2600
T r a n s a n t a r c t i c

Enderby Land
C. Borley
Kemp
Land
Stefansson Bay
Mawson
(Austr.)
2280
Mawson Coast
MacRobertson
Land
C. Darnley
2645
Prince Charles Mts.
3355
Lambert
Glacier
Amery
Ice Shelf
American
Highland
Ingrid
Christensen
Coast
Prydz Bay
Zhongshan (China)
Davis (Austr.)
1800
1040
4030
East
Antarctica
West
Ice
Shelf
Wilhelm II
Coast
Queen
Mary
Land
3030
2570
Denman Glacier
Drygalski I.
Davis Sea
Masson I.
Shackleton
Ice Shelf
Mill I.
Bowman I.
Scott Glacier
Knox Coast
Casey (Austr.)
Budd
Coast
C. Poinsett
Sabrina
Coast
Totten Glacier
Dalton Iceberg
Tongue
Banzare
Coast
Clarie
Coast
Porpoise Bay
Blodgett Iceberg
Tongue
2436
4776
3488
3700
2216
2798
Terre
Adélie
Dumont d'Urville (Fr.)
George V
Land
Commonwealth Bay
South Magnetic Pole
1990
Oates Land
C. Freshfield

Wilkes Land

INDIAN OCEAN
6739
6240

Balleny Is.
Scott I.
Antarctic Circle

Southeast Indian Rise
Macquarie Is.
(Austr.)
Campbell I.
(N.Z.)
Auckland Is.
(N.Z.)
Tasman
Plateau
Tasman
Sea
Tasmania
Hobart
Bass Str.
MELBOURNE
AUSTRALIA

Southwest
Pacific Basin
Antipodes Is.
Campbell
Plateau
Bounty Is.
(N.Z.)
Stewart I.
Dunedin
NEW ZEALAND

ft m
12 000 4000
6000 2000
4500 1500
3000 1000
1200 400
600 200
0 0
500 1500
1000 3000
2000 6000
3000 9000
4000 12 000
5000 15 000
m ft

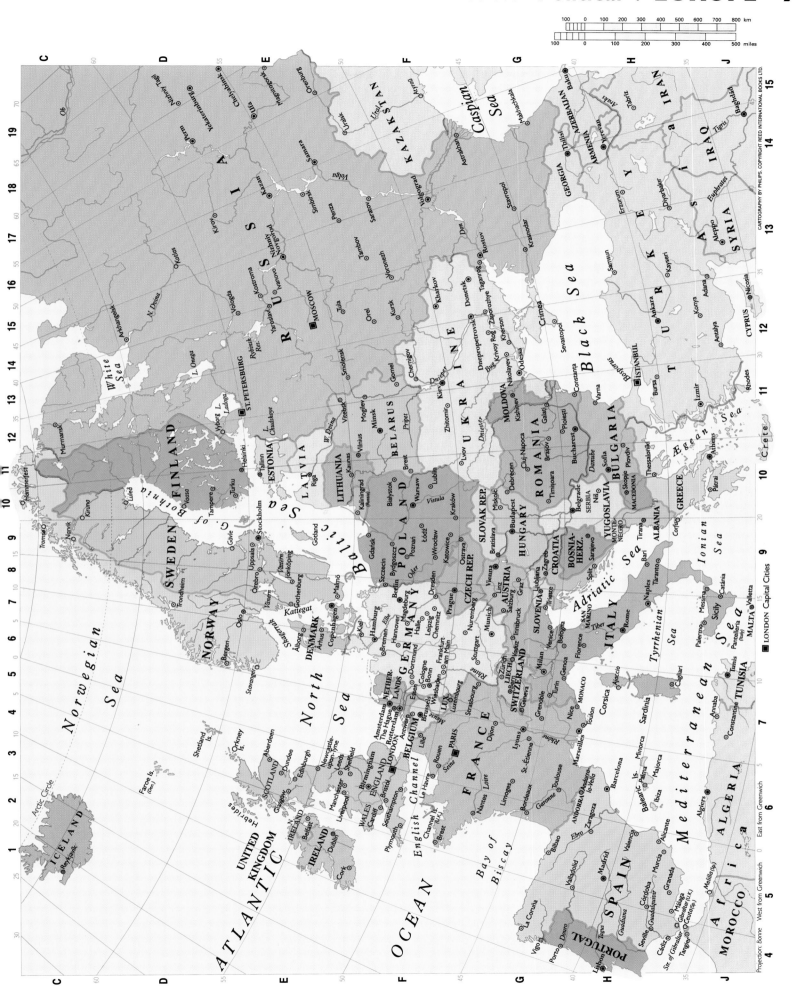

SCANDINAVIA 1:5 000 000

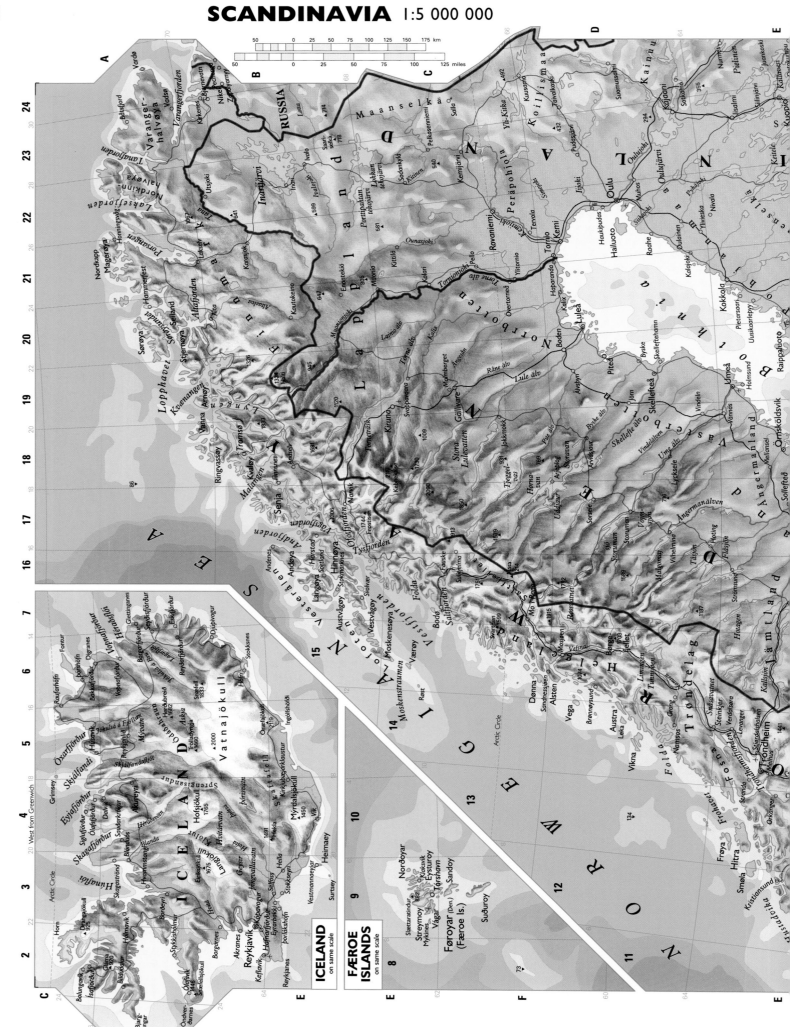

ICELAND
on same scale

FÆROE
ISLANDS
on same scale

Scandinavia and the Baltic States

FINLAND

Suomi

Pohjanmaa

Mikkeli · Savonlinna · Lappeenranta · Kouvola · Kotka
Tampere · Helsinki (Helsingfors) · Espoo · Lahti · Porvoo
Turku (Åbo) · Pori · Rauma · Uusikaupunki
Jyväskylä · Seinäjoki · Vaasa · Kokkola

ESTONIA
Tallinn · Tartu · Pärnu · Narva · Viljandi · Paide · Rapla
Hiiumaa (Dagö) · Saaremaa (Ösel) · Kuressaare · Muhu · Kärdla

LATVIA
Riga · Jelgava · Jūrmala · Ventspils · Liepāja · Daugavpils
Valmiera · Cēsis · Sigulda · Talsi · Tukums · Dobele · Saldus

LITHUANIA
Vilnius · Kaunas · Panevėžys · Šiauliai · Klaipėda
Marijampolė · Telšiai · Plungė · Tauragė · Jonava · Kėdainiai

Kaliningrad (Russia) · Gusev · Chernyakhovsk · Zelenogradsk

BELARUS

POLAND
Gdańsk · Gdynia · Elbląg · Malbork · Słupsk · Koszalin
Kołobrzeg · Słupsk · Bytów · Starogard Gdański

Gulf of Finland · Gulf of Riga

Åland (Ahvenanmaa) · Ålands hav

BALTIC SEA

Gotland · Visby · Öland · Gotska Sandön · Fårö · Bornholm

SWEDEN
STOCKHOLM · Uppsala · Västerås · Eskilstuna · Södertälje
Gävle · Sundsvall · Härnösand · Hudiksvall · Söderhamn
Örebro · Karlstad · Falun · Mora · Borlänge · Ludvika
Norrköping · Linköping · Motala · Nyköping · Mjölby
Jönköping · Växjö · Kalmar · Västervik · Oskarshamn
Halmstad · Helsingborg · Malmö · Lund · Landskrona
Kristianstad · Karlskrona · Karlshamn · Ystad · Trelleborg
Göteborg (Gothenburg) · Borås · Trollhättan · Uddevalla
Varberg · Falkenberg · Kungsbacka · Ängelholm

Svealand · Götaland · Norrland · Dalarna · Värmland
Småland · Blekinge · Halland · Skåne · Bohuslän · Dalsland
Västergötland · Östergötland · Södermanland · Uppland
Gästrikland · Hälsingland · Härjedalen · Vättern · Vänern
Mälaren · Hjälmaren

NORWAY
Oslo · Oslofjorden · Drammen · Fredrikstad · Sarpsborg
Moss · Kongsvinger · Hamar · Lillehammer · Gjøvik
Kristiansand · Arendal · Larvik · Tønsberg · Sandefjord
Skien · Porsgrunn · Stavanger · Haugesund · Bergen
Ålesund · Flekkefjord · Egersund · Sandnes

Gudbrandsdalen · Østerdalen · Valdres · Telemark
Hardangervidda · Jotunheimen · Dovrefjell · Rondane
Folgefonni · Sognefjorden · Hardangerfjorden · Nordfjord
Skagerrak

DENMARK
KØBENHAVN (Copenhagen) · Roskilde · Odense · Ålborg
Århus · Esbjerg · Randers · Kolding · Vejle · Horsens
Helsingør · Hillerød · Køge · Næstved · Slagelse · Korsør
Svendborg · Fredericia · Herning · Viborg · Silkeborg

Sjælland · Fyn · Jylland · Lolland · Falster · Møn
Langeland · Bornholm · Kattegat · Skagen · Læsø · Anholt
Store Bælt · Lille Bælt · Fehmarn Bælt

GERMANY
Kiel · Lübeck · Rostock · Stralsund · Wismar · Flensburg
Schleswig · Neumünster · Rendsburg · Husum · Cuxhaven
Rügen · Usedom · Greifswald · Nordfriesische Inseln
Ostfriesische Inseln · Helgoland · Mecklenburger Bucht
Kieler Bucht · Deutsche Bucht · Holstein · Sylt · Föhr

Projection: Conical with two standard parallels

East from Greenwich

COPYRIGHT GEORGE PHILIP LTD.

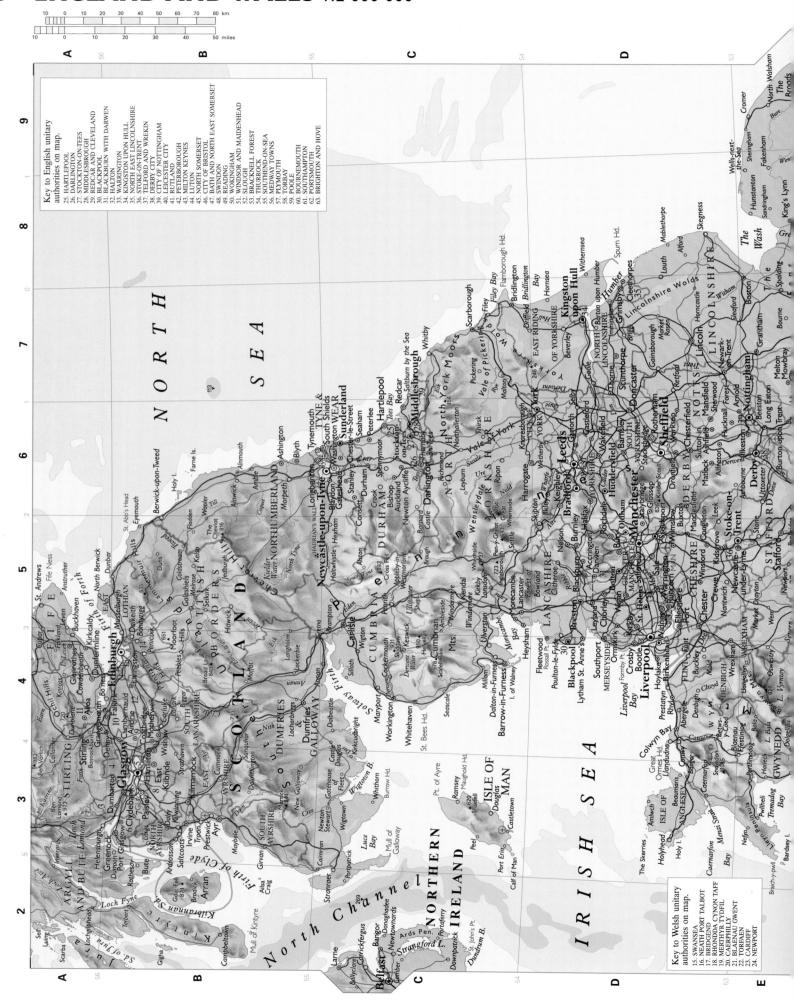

Key to English unitary authorities on map.

25. HARTLEPOOL
26. DARLINGTON
27. STOCKTON-ON-TEES
28. MIDDLESBROUGH
29. REDCAR AND CLEVELAND
30. BLACKPOOL
31. BLACKBURN WITH DARWEN
32. HALTON
33. WARRINGTON
34. KINGSTON UPON HULL
35. NORTH EAST LINCOLNSHIRE
36. STOKE-ON-TRENT
37. TELFORD AND WREKIN
38. DERBY CITY
39. CITY OF NOTTINGHAM
40. LEICESTER CITY
41. RUTLAND
42. PETERBOROUGH
43. MILTON KEYNES
44. LUTON
45. NORTH SOMERSET
46. CITY OF BRISTOL
47. BATH AND NORTH EAST SOMERSET
48. SWINDON
49. READING
50. WOKINGHAM
51. WINDSOR AND MAIDENHEAD
52. SLOUGH
53. BRACKNELL FOREST
54. THURROCK
55. SOUTHEND-ON-SEA
56. MEDWAY TOWNS
57. PLYMOUTH
58. TORBAY
59. POOLE
60. BOURNEMOUTH
61. SOUTHAMPTON
62. PORTSMOUTH
63. BRIGHTON AND HOVE

Key to Welsh unitary authorities on map.

15. SWANSEA
16. NEATH PORT TALBOT
17. BRIDGEND
18. RHONDDA CYNON TAFF
19. MERTHYR TYDFIL
20. CAERPHILLY
21. BLAENAU GWENT
22. TORFAEN
23. CARDIFF
24. NEWPORT

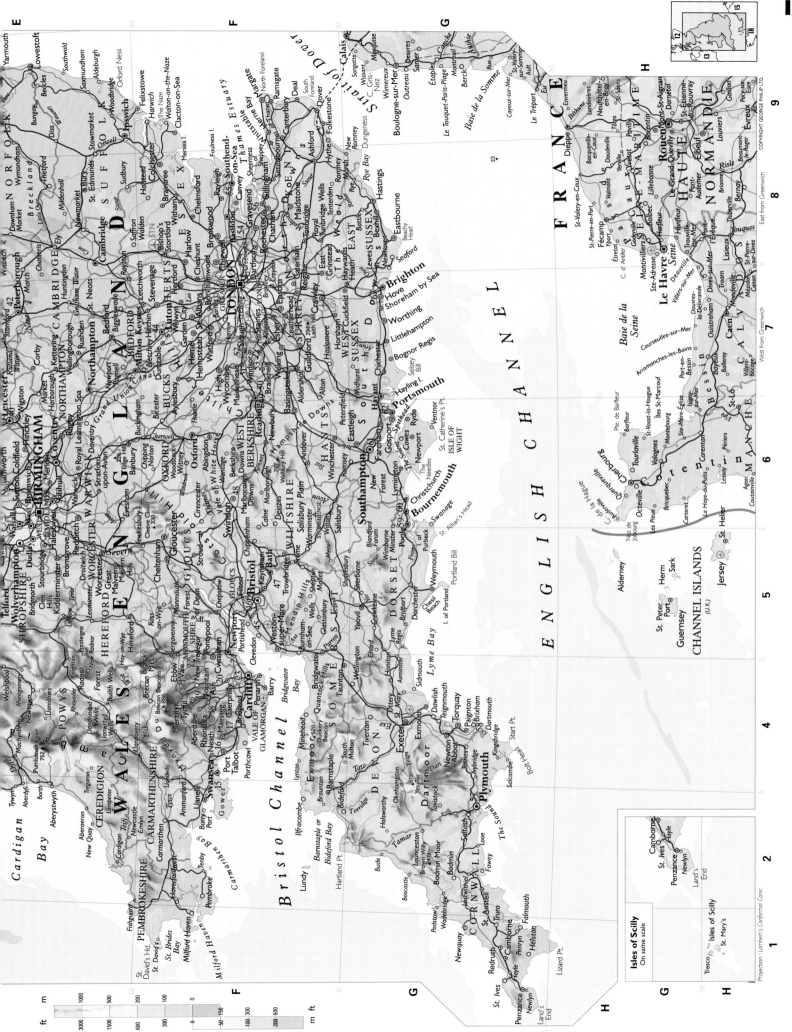

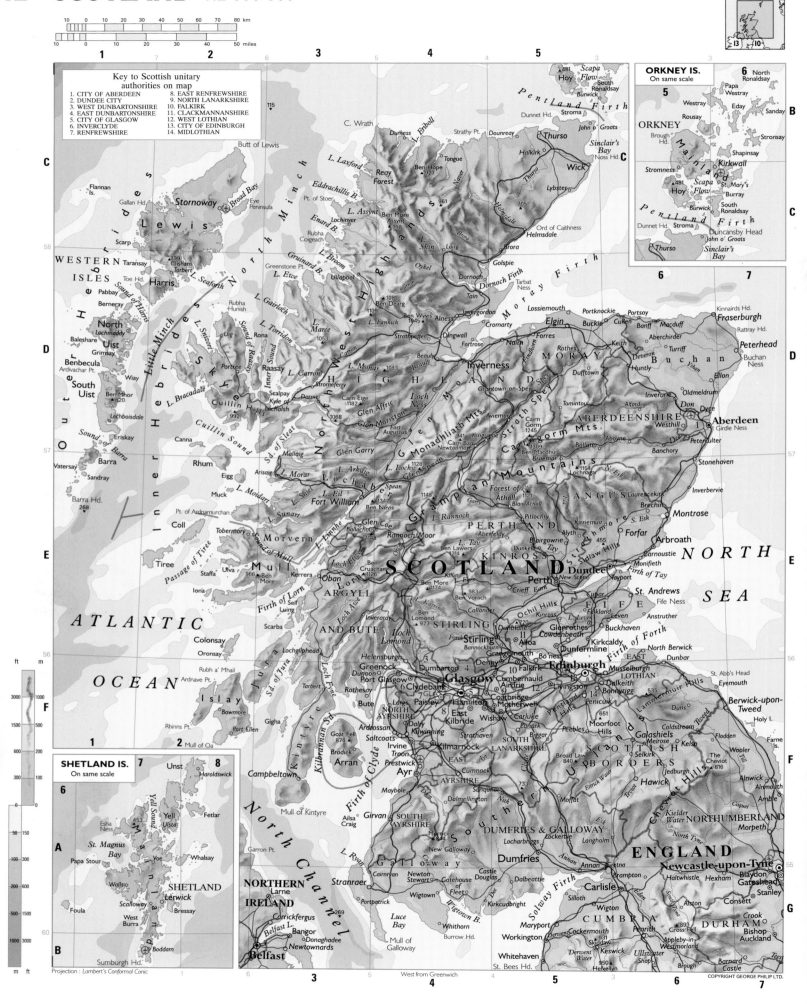

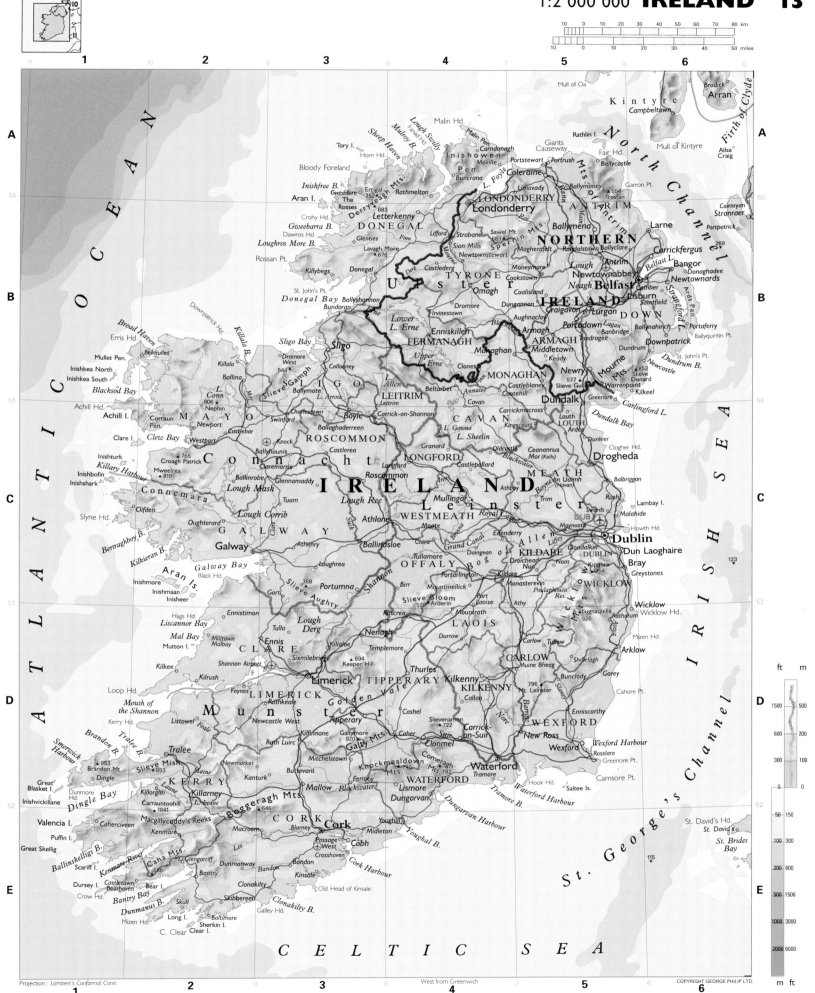

10 0 10 20 30 40 50 60 70 80 km
10 0 10 20 30 40 50 miles

A

O C E A N

A T L A N T I C

Mull of Oa
Kintyre
Campbeltown
Brodick
Arran
Firth of Clyde

Tory I.
Horn Hd.
Malin Hd.
Sheep Haven
Fanad Pt.
Lough Swilly
Malin Pen.
Carndonagh
Inishowen
Pen.
Moville
Giants
Causeway
Rathlin I.
Fair Hd.
Mull of Kintyre
Ailsa
Craig

Bloody Foreland
Muroy B.
Buncrana
L. Foyle
Coleraine
Portstewart
Portrush
Ballycastle
Cairnryan
Stranraer
Portpatrick

Inishfree B.
Gweedore
Errigal
752
The
Rosses
Derryveagh Mts
Rathmelton
Letterkenny
DONEGAL
Limavady
LONDONDERRY
Londonderry
ANTRIM
554
Trostan
Garron Pt.

55

Crohy Hd.
683
Lifford
Strabane
Sawel Mt.
683
Spermn Mts
Magherafelt
Ballymoney
Ballymena
Larne
Portpatrick

Gweebarra B.
Dawros Hd.
Glenties
Finn
Sion Mills
Newtownstewart
Moneymore
NORTHERN
Randalstown Ballyclare
Carrickfergus
269

Loughros More B.
Lavagh More
676
TYRONE
Omagh
Dromore
Cookstown
Coalisland
Dungannon
IRELAND
Antrim
Neagh
Belfast
Bangor
Donaghadee
Newtownards

Rossan Pt.
Killybegs
Donegal
St. John's Pt.
Ballyshannon
Bundoran
Castlederg
Derg
Irvinestown
Enniskillen
Aughnacloy
Armagh
Craigavon
Portadown
Lurgan
Lagan
Lisburn
DOWN
Comber
Strangford L.
Ards Pen.
Ballyquintin Pt.

B

Erris Hd.
Belmullet
Downpatrick Hd.
Killala B.
Sligo Bay
Lower
L. Erne
FERMANAGH
Monaghan
ARMAGH
Middletown
Keady
Banbridge
Portaferry

Mullet Pen.
Inishkea North
Killala
Ballina
Collooney
Upper
L. Erne
Clones
MONAGHAN
Newry
577
Slieve Gullion
Mourne Mts.
852
Slieve
Donard
Dundrum B.
St. John's Pt.

B

Inishkea South
Blacksod Bay
544
Sligo
SLIGO
Ballymote
L. Arrow
Belturbet
Annalee
Castleblaney
Cootehill
Dundalk
Warrenpoint
Kilkeel
Newcastle

Achill Hd.
L.
Conn
806
Nephin
Swinford
Boyle
Carrick-on-Shannon
Carrickmacross
LOUTH
Ardee
Carlingford L.
Greenore

54

Achill I.
Corraun
Pen.
Newport
Castlebar
Knock
Ballaghaderreen
LEITRIM
Leitrim
CAVAN
L. Gowna
L. Sheelin
Kingscourt
Oldcastle
Ceanannus
Mor (Kells)
Clogher Hd.
Dunleer
Dundalk Bay

Clare I.
Clew Bay
Westport
MAYO
Ballyhaunis
ROSCOMMON
Castlerea
Cavan
Granard
Blackwater
Drogheda

Inishturk
Killary Harbour
765
Croagh Patrick
Claremorris
Roscommon
LONGFORD
Castlepollard
MEATH
An Uaimh
(Navan)
Balbriggan

Inishbofin
Inishshark
819
Mweelrea
Ballinrobe
Glennamaddy
Longford
Inny
Boyne
Athboy
Royal Canal
Rush

C

Slyne Hd.
Connemara
Lough Mask
Tuam
IRELAND
Mullingar
WESTMEATH
Trim
Lambay I.
Malahide

Clifden
Oughterard
Lough Corrib
Leinster
Moate
DUB
Swords
Howth Hd.

Bertraghboy B.
Kilkieran B.
GALWAY
Corrib
Athlone
Edenderry
Grand Canal
Bog of Allen
Clondalkin
Dublin
Dun Laoghaire

C

Slyne Hd.
Galway
Athenry
Ballinasloe
Clara
Daingean
Naas
KILDARE
DUBLIN
Bray

Aran Is.
Galway Bay
Black Hd.
Loughrea
Tullamore
OFFALY
Droichead
Nua
Monasterevin
Kippure
754
Greystones

Inishmore
Inishmaan
Inisheer
Gort
368
Slieve Aughty
Portumna
Birr
Mountmellick
Portarlington
Port
Laoise
Poulaphouca
Res.
WICKLOW
123

Hags Hd.
Liscannor Bay
Ennistimon
Shannon
Lough
Derg
Slieve Bloom
Arderin
528
Athy
Mountrath
Wicklow
Mts
Lugnaquilla
926
Wicklow
Wicklow Hd.

53

Mal Bay
Mutton I.
Tulla
CLARE
Nenagh
Roscrea
LAOIS
Durrow
Carlow
Tullow
Mizen Hd.
Rathdrum
Avoca
Arklow

Kilkee
Ennis
Killaloe
Templemore
Thurles
Carlow
Shillelagh
Gorey

Loop Hd.
Kilrush
Shannon Airport
Sixmilebridge
694
Keeper Hill
TIPPERARY
Kilkenny
CARLOW
Muine Bheag
Bunclody
796
Mt. Leinster
Cahore Pt.

D

Mouth of
the Shannon
Kerry Hd.
Foynes
Limerick
LIMERICK
Golden
Vale
KILKENNY
Callan
Enniscorthy

Listowel
Rathkeale
Tipperary
Cashel
Slievenamon
722
Nore
WEXFORD

D

Smerwick
Harbour
Brandon B.
Tralee B.
953
Brandon Mt.
853
Tralee
Slieve Mish
Maine
Newmarket
Newcastle West
Kilfinnane
Galtymore
920
Galty Mts.
Caher
Clonmel
Comeragh
Mts.
792
New Ross
Wexford

Great
Blasket I.
Dunmore
Hd.
Dingle
Slieve Mish
Feale
Rath Luirc
Mitchelstown
Knockmealdown
Mts.
795
Carrick-
on-Suir
Waterford
Tramore
Rosslare
Greenore Pt.

52

Inishvickillane
Dingle Bay
Killorglin
Laune
KERRY
Kanturk
Buttevant
Fermoy
WATERFORD
Dungarvan
Carnsore Pt.

Valencia I.
Caherciveen
Carrauntoohill
1041
L. Leane
Killarney
Mallow
Blackwater
Lismore
Dungarvan
Tramore B.
Waterford Harbour
Saltee Is.

Puffin I.
Macgillycuddy's Reeks
646
Boggeragh Mts
CORK
Youghal
Midleton
Youghal B.
Dungarvan Harbour
Hook Hd.

Great Skellig
Kenmare
Caha Mts.
686
Macroom
Cork
Blarney
Lee
Passage
West
Cobh
Crosshaven
Cork Harbour
115

E

Ballinskellig B.
Scariff I.
Glengarriff
Dunmanway
Bandon
Kinsale
Old Head of Kinsale

Great Skellig
Dursey I.
Castletown
Bearhaven
Bear I.
Bantry
Clonakilty
Clonakilty B.
St. George's Channel

E

Crow Hd.
Bantry Bay
Dunmanus B.
Skull
Long I.
Baltimore
Sherkin I.
Galley Hd.

Mizen Hd.
C. Clear
Clear I.

C E L T I C   S E A

ft m
1500 500
600 200
300 100
0 0
50 150
100 300
200 600
500 1500
1000 3000
2000 6000
m ft

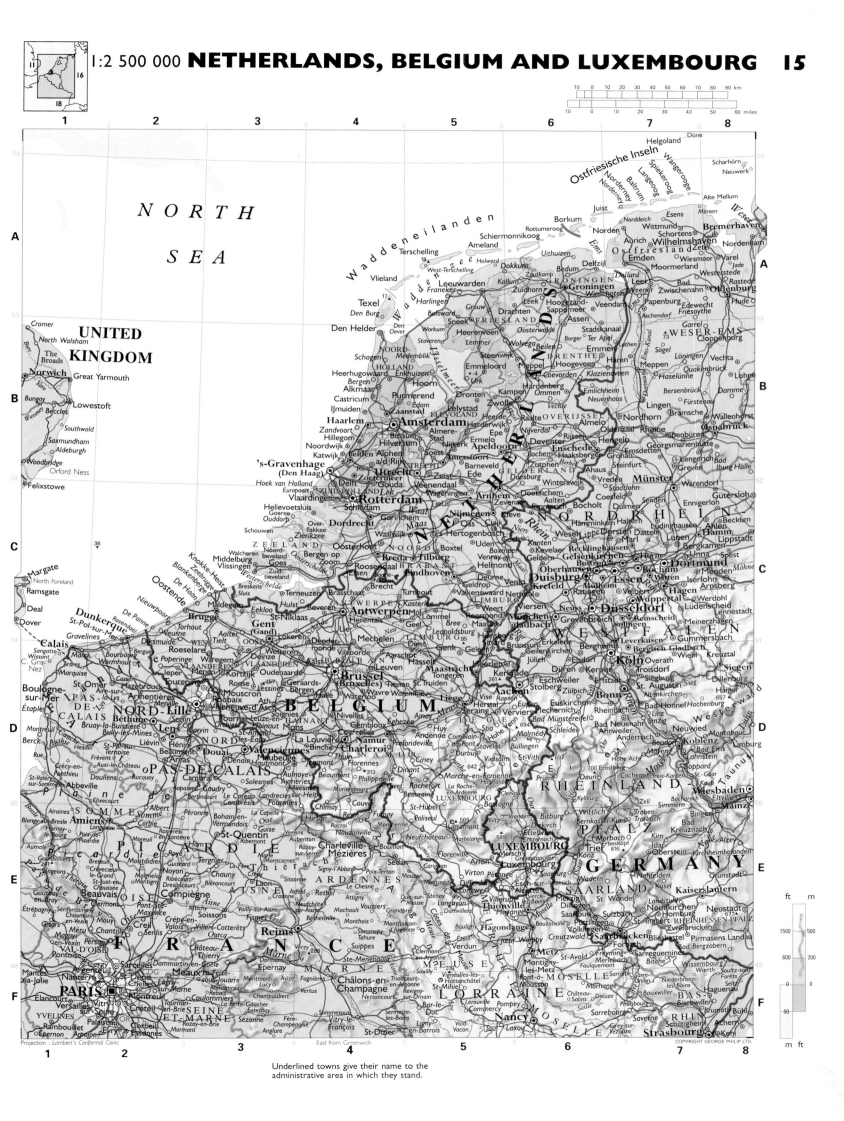

Underlined towns give their name to the
administrative area in which they stand.

Projection : Lambert's Conformal Conic

East from Greenwich

COPYRIGHT GEORGE PHILIP LTD.

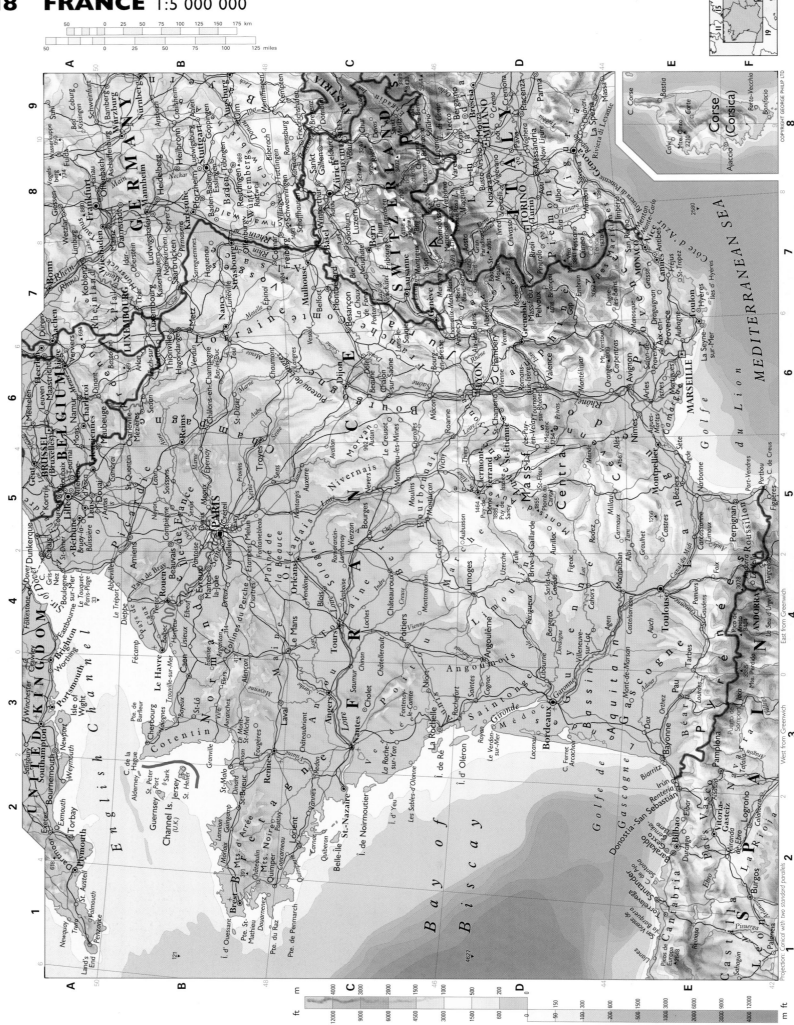

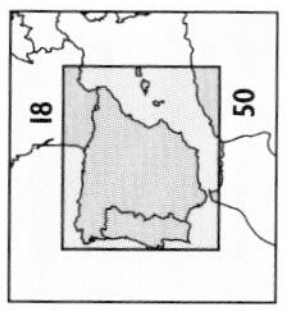

Projection: Conical with two standard parallels

COPYRIGHT GEORGE PHILIP LTD

West from Greenwich   East from Greenwich

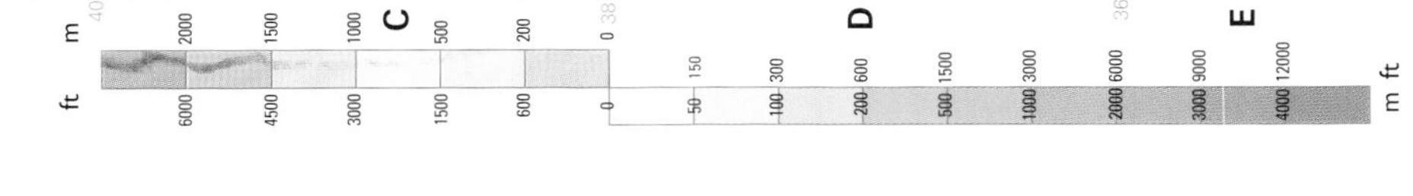

FRANCE

SPAIN

PORTUGAL

ALGERIA

MOROCCO

MEDITERRANEAN SEA

Balearic Islands

ATLANTIC OCEAN

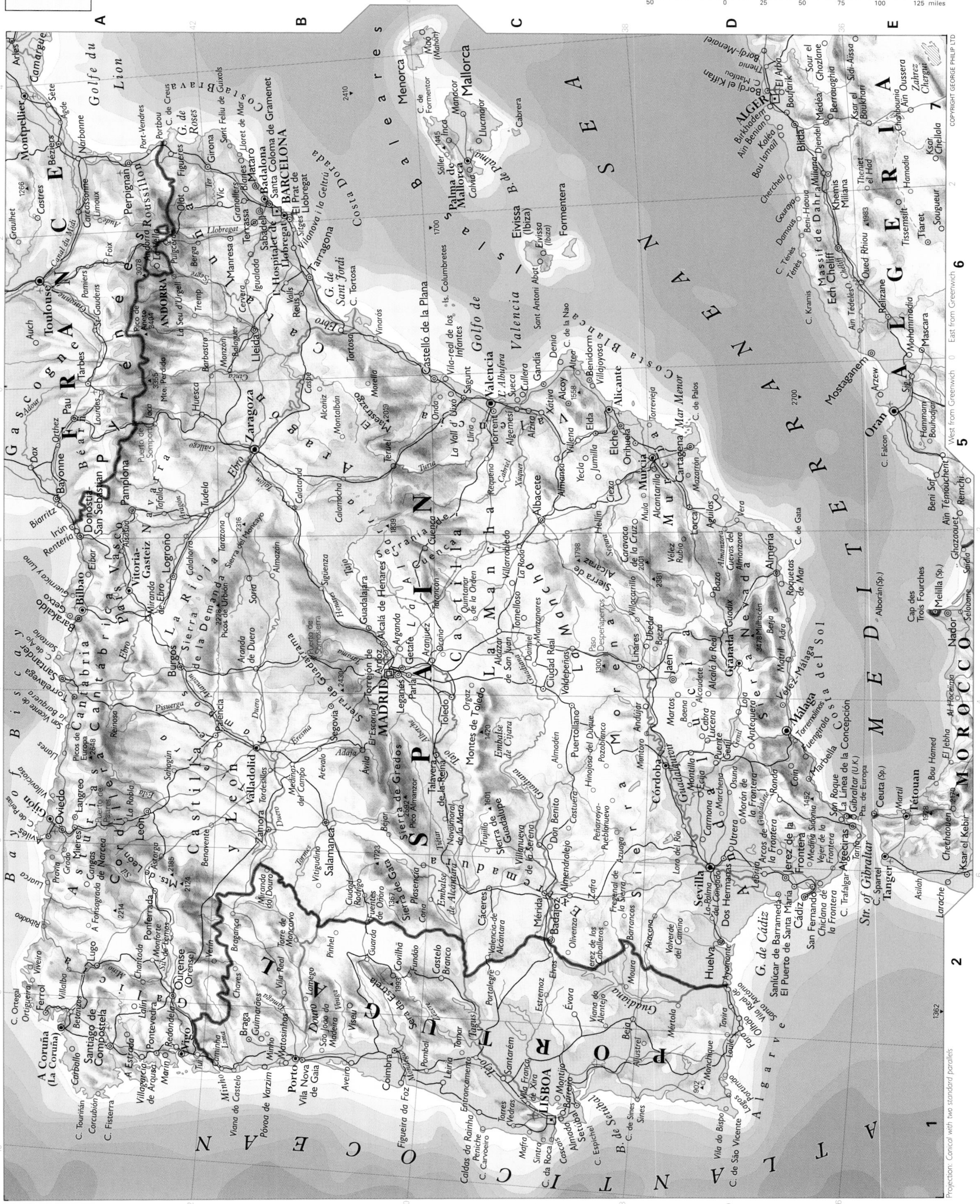

Bay of Biscay

Golfe du Lion

G. de Cádiz

Str. of Gibraltar

MADRID
BARCELONA
LISBOA
Valencia
Sevilla
Zaragoza
Málaga
Bilbao
Porto
Valladolid
Granada
Córdoba
Murcia
Alicante
Oviedo
Pamplona
Vitoria-Gasteiz
Logroño
Burgos
León
Salamanca
Cáceres
Badajoz
Huelva
Cádiz
Almería
Cartagena
Albacete
Toledo
Guadalajara
Cuenca
Teruel
Lleida
Girona
Tarragona
Castelló de la Plana
Alacant
Palma de Mallorca
Eivissa (Ibiza)
Menorca
Mallorca
Formentera

ANDORRA

Santiago de Compostela
A Coruña (La Coruña)
Vigo
Ourense (Orense)
Lugo
Ferrol
Pontevedra
Santander
Gijón
Donostia-San Sebastián
Coimbra
Évora
Faro
Setúbal

Toulouse
Perpignan
Bayonne
Pau
Tarbes
Montpellier
Narbonne
Béziers

ORAN
ALGER (ALGIERS)
Mostaganem
Tlemcen
Mascara
Oujda
Tetouan
Ceuta (Sp.)
Melilla (Sp.)
Tanger
Nador

Pyrénées
Cordillera Cantábrica
Picos de Europa
Sierra de Gredos
Sierra Nevada
Sierra Morena
Montes de Toledo
La Mancha
Castilla y León
Castilla-La Mancha
Costa Brava
Costa Dorada
Costa Blanca
Costa del Sol

Ebro
Duero
Tajo
Guadiana
Guadalquivir

m ft
6000 / 2000
4500 / 1500
3000 / 1000
1500 / 500
600 / 200
150 / 50
0
0
50 / 150
300 / 600
1500 / 3000
3000 / 6000
9000 / 12000
ft m

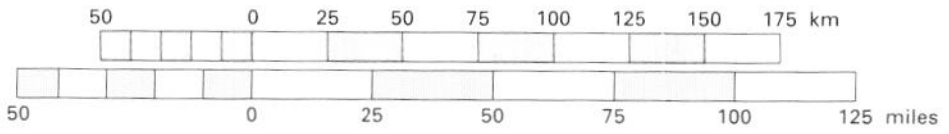

50 0 25 50 75 100 125 150 175 km
50 0 25 50 75 100 125 miles

SWITZERLAND • AUSTRIA • SLOVENIA • CROATIA

FRANCE • PROVENCE • LYON • Grenoble • Valence • MARSEILLE • Toulon • MONACO • Nice • Cannes

TORINO (Turin) • MILANO • Genova • La Spezia • Bologna • Ravenna • Rimini • Venézia (Venice) • Padova • Verona • Trieste • Ljubljana • Zagreb • Maribor

Firenze (Florence) • Livorno • Pisa • Siena • Perugia • Ancona • Pescara • ROMA • VATICAN CITY • SAN MARINO

LIGURIAN SEA • Golfo di Génova • Corse • Ajaccio • Bonifacio • Bouches de Bonifacio

Sardegna • Sassari • Olbia • Núoro • Oristano • Cágliari • Iglésias

TYRRHENIAN SEA

NÁPOLI • Salerno • Potenza • Bari • Táranto • Golfo di Táranto • Cosenza • Catanzaro • Réggio di Calábria • Messina

Palermo • Trápani • Marsala • Catánia • Siracusa • Ragusa • Agrigento • Caltanissetta • Etna • Sicília

ADRIATIC SEA • Split • Hvar • Korčula

ALGERIA • Constantine • Annaba • Skikda

TUNISIA • Tunis • Bizerte • Sousse • Kairouan

MALTA • Valletta • Gozo

MEDITERRANEAN

Ísole Eólie • Strómboli • Pantelleria (Italy) • Lampedusa • Ísole Pelagie (Italy)

Projection: Conical with two standard parallels

A

HUNGARY
posvár
Szekszárd
Kalocsa
Kiskőrös
Kiskunhalas
Oroszháza
Hódmezővásárhely
Crişul Alb
Muntii Bihor 1848
Aiud
Tîrnăveni
Odorheiu Secuiesc
Mercurea Ciuc
Oneşti
Buhai
Bârlad
Cedar-Lunga
Tatarbunary
UKRAINE
Ozero Sasyk
Baja
Szeged
Makó
Arad
Brad
Alba-Iulia
Medias
Sighişoara
Sfântu Gheorghe
1783
Focşani
Tecuci
Vulcaneşti
Cahul
Bolhrad
Kiliya
Vylkove
Pécs
Mohács
Subotica
Sânnicolau Maré
Mureş
Lugoj
Deva
Simeria
Sibiu
Făgăraş
Braşov
Râmnicu Sărat
Galaţi
Reni
Izmayil
Sulina

ROMANIA
Senta
Kikinda
Timişoara
Caransebes
Hunedoara
1380
Carpatii Meridionali
Câmpulung
Cămpina
Buzău
Brăila
Tulcea
Babadag
B
Sombor
Bečej
Zrenjanin
Vršac
Reşiţa
VI. Peleaga 2509
P. Turnu 2505
Moldoveanu 2543
M. Omu
Dâmbova
Dunărea (Danube)
44

Osijek
Vukovar
Vojvodina
Novi Sad
Petrovaradin
Vulcan
Parângul Mare
Târgu-Jiu
Curtea de Argeş
Târgovişte
Ploieşti
Slobozia
Lacul Razelm
Slavonski Brod
Sava
Vinkovci
Sremska Mitrovica
Pančevo
Bela Crkva
Porta Orientalis
Portile de Fier
Drobeta-Turnu-Severin
Orşoval
Dunav
Pitesti
BUCUREŞTI
(Bucharest)
Feteşti
Medgidia
Năvodari
Doboj
Brčko
Bijeljina
Zemun
BEOGRAD
(Belgrade)
Smederevo
Požarevac
1226
Drăgăşani
Slatina
Oltenita
Silistra
Călăraşi
Constanţa

SNIA-
Tuzla
Drina
Valjevo
YUGOSLAVIA
Craiova
Roşiori-de-Vede
Alexandria
Tutrakan
Dobrich
Mangalia
Travnik
Zenica
Šabac
1366
Băileşti
Caracal
Turnu Măgurele
Giurgiu
Zimnicea
Ruse
Balchik
EGOVINA
2112
Han Pijesak
Kragujevac
Jagodina
Bor
Vidin
Corabia
Lom
Oryakhovo
Svishtov
Razgrad
Nos Kaliakra
Sarajevo
Užice
Čačak
Zaječar
Montana
Vratsa
Pleven
Veliko Tŭrnovo
Shumen
Varna
C
Konjic
Goražde
SERBIA
Niš
2168 Midžor
Timok
Lovech
Gorna Oryakhovitsa
Sevlievo
Gabrovo
Tŭrgovişte
Sliven
Nos Emine
**BLACK
SEA**
Mostar
1969
Plevlja
1833
Prokuplje
2017
Pirot
P. Dragoman
Teteven
Stara Planina
Aytos
Stolac
2522 Durmitor
Novi Pazar
Leskovac
1409
Suva Planina
SOFIYA
Vezhen
Shipchenski P.
1636
Kazanlŭk
Burgas
Trebinje
Nikšić
Kosovska Mitrovica
Priština
Vranje
Kyustendil
Karlovo
Nova Zagora
Yambol
42
1210
Peć
Uroševac
2198
Samokov
BULGARIA
Stara Zagora
Elkhovo
Michurin
Herceg-Novi
MONTENEGRO
Podgorica
Cetinje
Skadarsko Jezero
Dakovica
Đeneral Drin
Prizren
Kumanovo
2252
Blagoevgrad
Dupnitsa
Samokov
Maritsa
Pazardzhik
Plovdiv
Dimitrovgrad
Igneada Burnu
Demirköy
brovnik
Bar
Ulcinj
Bojana
Shkodër
Kukës
Sar Planina
Skopje
Kočani
2925 Musala
2186
Rhodopi Planina
Asenovgrad
Khaskovo
Kŭrdzhali
Kŭrklareli
Yildiz Daglari
**İstanbul
Boğazı
(Bosporus)**
Peshkopi
Kolmb
2764
Tetovo
Veles
Štip
Pirin Planina
Smilyan
Arda
Momchilgrad
Zlatograd
Edirne
Pinarhisar
Vize
Çerkezköy
İSTANBUL
D
ALBANIA
Lezhe
Debar
Solunska Glava 2540
Sandanski
Metju
2031
Komotini
Orestiás
Babaeski
Lüleburgaz
Saray
Hayrabolu
Çorlu
Silivri
Kartal
Durrës
Tiranë
Elbasan
2225
MACEDONIA
Prilep
Strumica
Petrich
Xánthi
Drama
Uzunköprü
Malkara
Tekirdağ
Büyükçekmece
1220 Gebze
Ohridsko Jezero
Ohrid
Bitola
Valandovo
Makedhonia
Sérrai
Strimón
Kavála
Ipsala
Enez
Keşan
Marmara
Şarköy
**Marmara
Denizi
(Sea of Marmara)**
Yalova
İznik Gölü

Shkumbini
Lushnjë
Prespansko Jezero
Kilkís
Yiannitsá
Thásos
Alexandroúpolis
Évros
Saros Körfezi
Gelibolu
(Dardanelles)
Erdek
Bandirma
Gemlik
İznik
E
Seman
Berat
Florina
Véroia
Édhessa
Thessaloniki
Smetrikós Kólpos
Samothráki
1600
Gökçeada
Eceabat
Çanakkale Boğazı
Lápseki
Karabiğa
Kuş Gölü
Karacabey
Bursa
2543
Fier
Vlorë
Korçë
Ptolemais
Kozáni
Poliyiros
Athos 2033
Ákra Pinnes
Moúdhros
Bozcaada
Çanakkale
Can
Yenice
Mustafakemalpaşa
Susurluk
Uludağ
Orhaneli
Sazanit
Kastoria
Smólikas 2637
Mt. Olympus 2917
Thermaïkós Kólpos
Toronaios Kólpos
Ákra Palioúrion
Límnos
TROY
M
Ezine
Bayramiç
Edremit
Balıkesir
Brindisi
Francavilla
Fontana
Gjirokastër
Delvinë
2520
Pindos
Olimbos
Ossa 1978
Toronios Kólpos
Ayios Evstrátios
Baba Burnu
Ayvacik
Burhaniye
Ayvalik
Bigadiç
Alacam Daglar
2089
Emet
Ostuni
Lecce
C. Santa Maria di Leuca
Mathráki
Ioánnina
Tírnavos
1280
Voriai Sporádhes
Lésvos
Soma
Bergama
Kinik
Dursunbey
Nardò
allipoli
C. d'Otranto
Kérkira
(Corfu)
Kérkira
Igoumenítsa
Trikkala
Lárisa
Vólos
Pagastikós Kólpos
Skiathos
Skópelos
1766 Mitilini
Demirci
Simav
E
Otranto
Párga
Páxoi
2469
Kardhitsa
Fársala
Istiaia
AE
968
TURKEY
Akhisar
Lydia
ONIAN
Préveza
Árta
Tríkeri
Óros Óssa
Lamia
Évvoia
Skíros
Psará
Manisa
SARDIS
Menemen
Salihli
Alaşehir
Eşme
Sandiğ
Levkás
1158
Óros Gióna 2510
2457 Parnassós
Dhirfis 1743
Khalkís
Khíos
1297 Khíos
**İZMİR
(Smyrna)**
Urla
Çeşme
Seferihisar
Boz Daglar 2137
Ödemis
Buldan
38
SEA
Kefallinía
Mesolóngion
Návpaktos
Leivádhia
Thívai
1413
Akharnai
Ákra Kafirévs
1396
Ákra Kafirévs
Foça
Karaburun
Torbali
Selçuk
Bayindir
Tire
Nazilli
Sarayköy
Argostólion
1628
Ithaki
Pátraikós Kólpos
Pátrai
Aiyion
Korinthiakós Kólpos
Thívai
Piraiévs
ATHINAI
(Athens)
Lávrion
Ándros
Ándros
EPHESUS
MILETUS
Sámos
Kuşadasi
Söke
1153
Aydın
Incirliova
Karacasu
Çine
Bozdoğan
Zákinthos
Zákinthos
Amaliás
2224
Erimanthos
Killini
Mégara
Salamis
Saronikós Kólpos
Kéa
Tínos
Tínos
Mikonos
Ikaría
Foúrnoi
Pátmos
Milas
Yatağan
Köyceğiz
Pelopónnisos
Korinthos
Korinthos
MYCENAE
Argos
Návplion
Idhra
Kíthnos
Síros
Páros
Náxos
Kálimnos
Kos
Güllük
Bodrum
Ören
Muğla
Gö15eli Daglari
Pirgos
Trípolis
OLYMPIA
Sérifos
Páros
1001 Náxos
Astipálaia
Dhodhekánisos
Gökova Körfezi
Marmaris
Datça
Bozburun
F
Kiparissiakós Kólpos
Kiparissía
Filiatrá
Spárti
Taíyetos Óros
Argolikós Kólpos
Ídhra
Sífnos
Sikinos
Íos
Amorgós
Tilos
Simi
Ródhos
Messini
Kalámai
2407 Taíyetos Óros
Yíthion
Ákra Maléa
Páros
Sífnos
Milos
Thíra
Astipálaia
1215
Líndhos
**Ródhos
(Rhodes)**
Pilos
Messiniakós Kólpos
Lakonikós Kólpos
Ákra Tainaron
Kíthira
Kíthira
1480
Kárpathos
G
RANEAN SEA
4070
Andikíthira
Ákra Spátha
Kólpos Khaníon
Kólpos Soúdhas
Kríti
Iráklion
Kólpos Merabéllou
Ákra Plaka
Kásos
Khaniá
KNOSSOS
Dhikti Óros
Réthimnon
Léka Óri
Khóra Sfakíon
Idhi Óros 2456
Sitía
Ierápetra
2453 Léka Óri
2148
Gávdhos
Lithínon

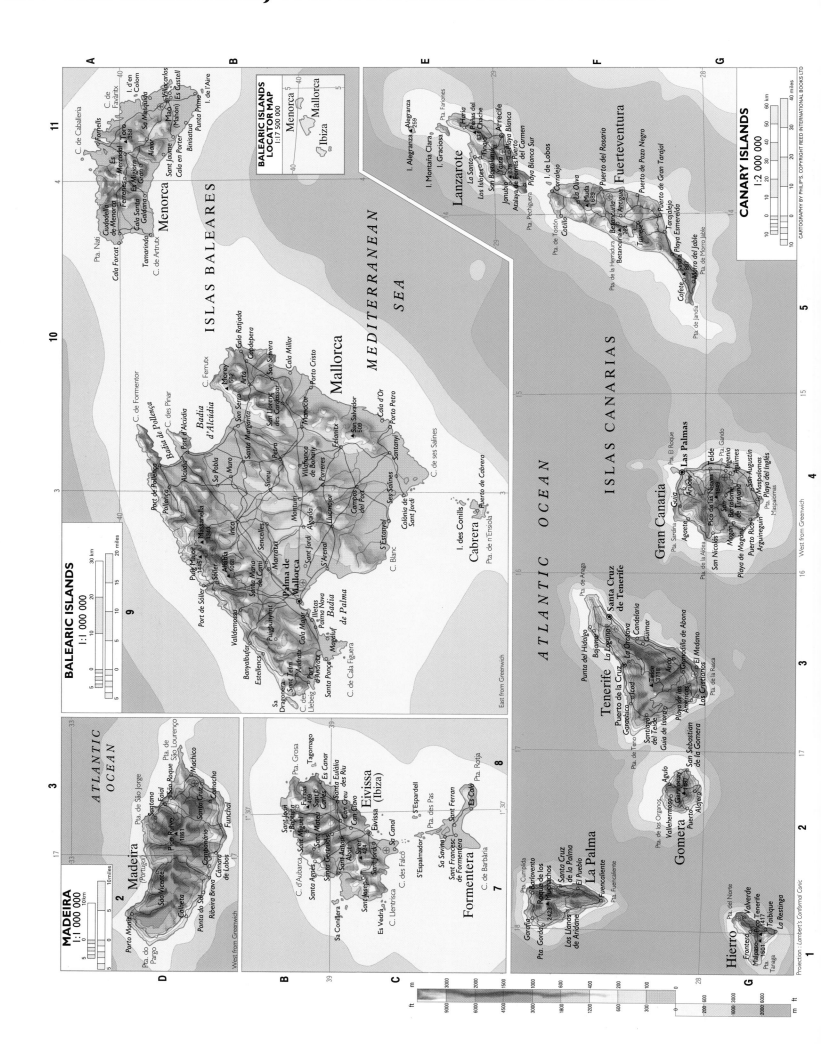

BALEARIC ISLANDS
1:1 000 000

MADEIRA
1:1 000 000

BALEARIC ISLANDS LOCATOR MAP
1:17 500 000

CANARY ISLANDS
1:2 000 000

CARTOGRAPHY BY PHILIP'S. COPYRIGHT REED INTERNATIONAL BOOKS LTD

Projection: Lambert's Conformal Conic

ISLAS BALEARES

MEDITERRANEAN SEA

Menorca

Mallorca

Cabrera

Eivissa (Ibiza)

Formentera

Madeira (Portugal)

ATLANTIC OCEAN

ISLAS CANARIAS

Lanzarote

Fuerteventura

Gran Canaria

Tenerife

Gomera

La Palma

Hierro

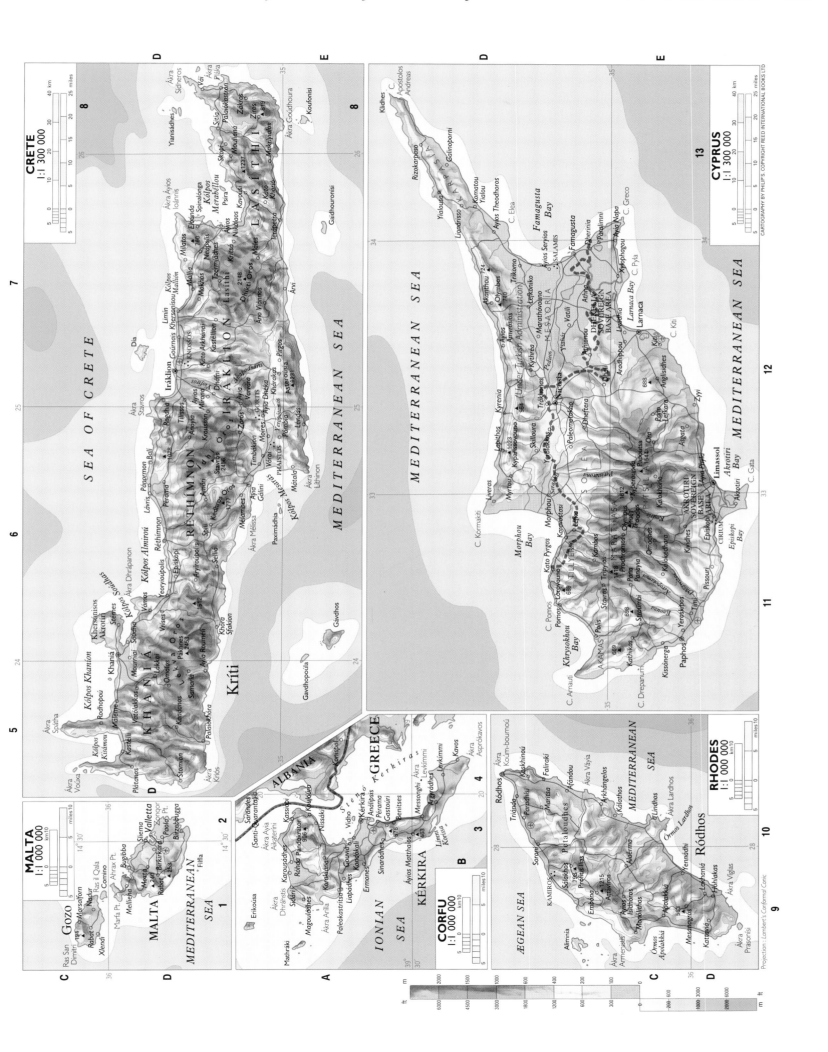

CRETE
1:1 300 000

CYPRUS
1:1 300 000

MALTA
1:1 000 000

CORFU
1:1 000 000

RHODES
1:1 000 000

Projection : Lambert's Conformal Conic

Projection : Conical with two standard parallels

Division between Greeks and Turkis
in Cyprus; Turkis to the North.

East from Greenwich

RUSSIA
1 Adygea
2 Karachey-Cherkessia
3 Kabardino-Balkaria
4 North Ossetia
5 Ingushetia
6 Chechenia
7 Dagestan
8 Mordvinia
9 Chuvashia
10 Mari El
11 Tatarstan
12 Udmurtia
13 Khakassia
AZERBAIJAN
14 Naxçivan
GEORGIA   UKRAINE
15 Ajaria   17 Crimea
16 Abkhazia

Projection: Conical Orthomorphic with two standard parallels

East from Greenwich

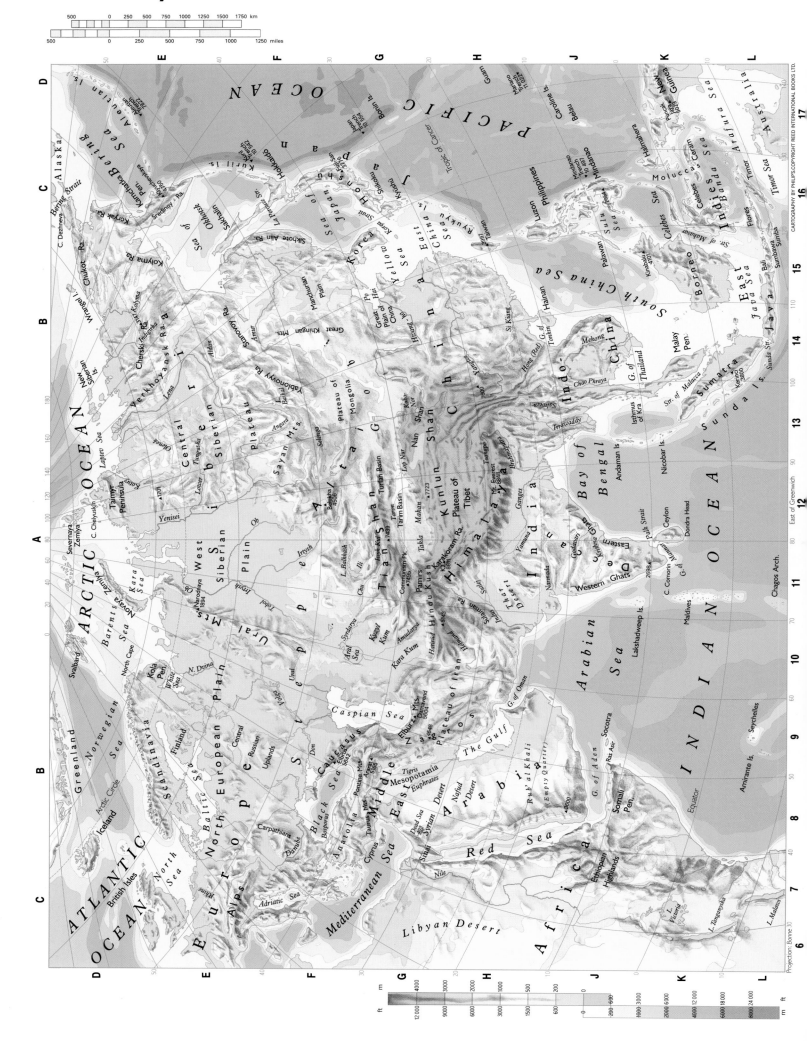

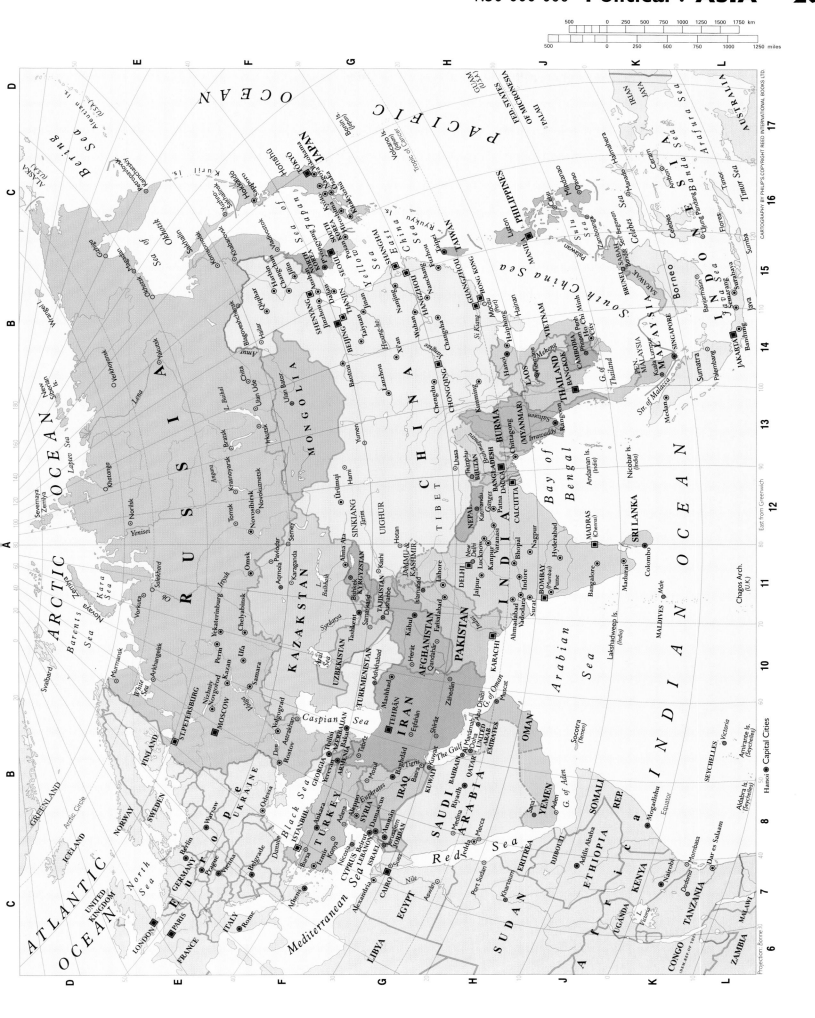

JAPAN 1:5 000 000

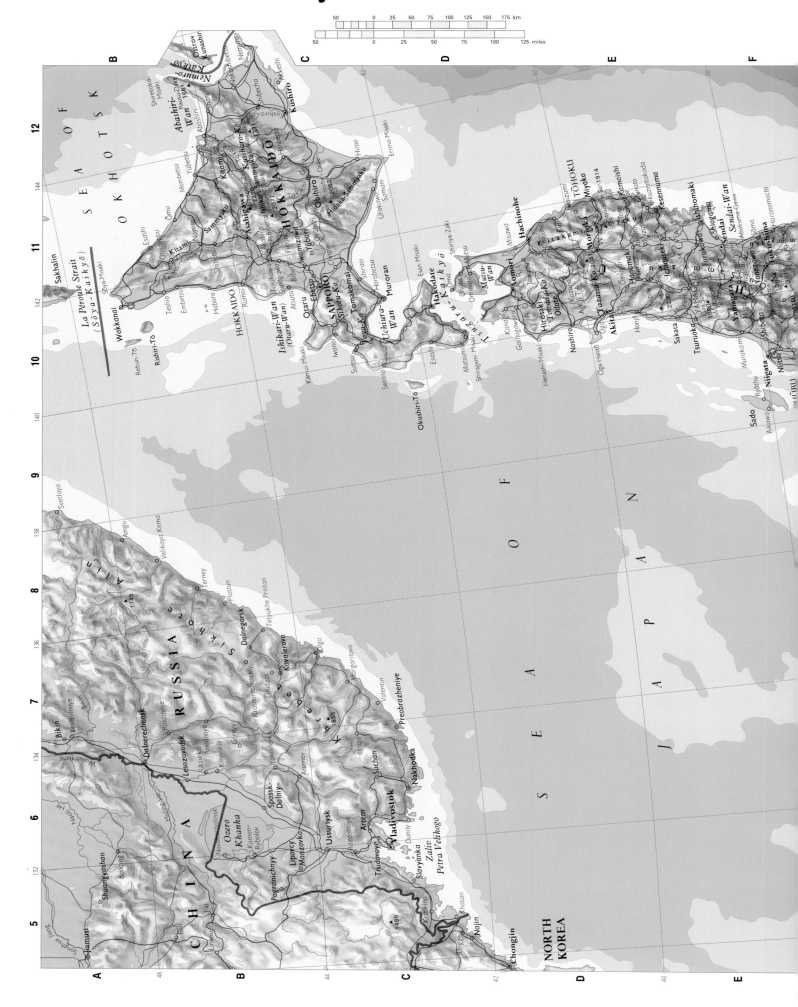

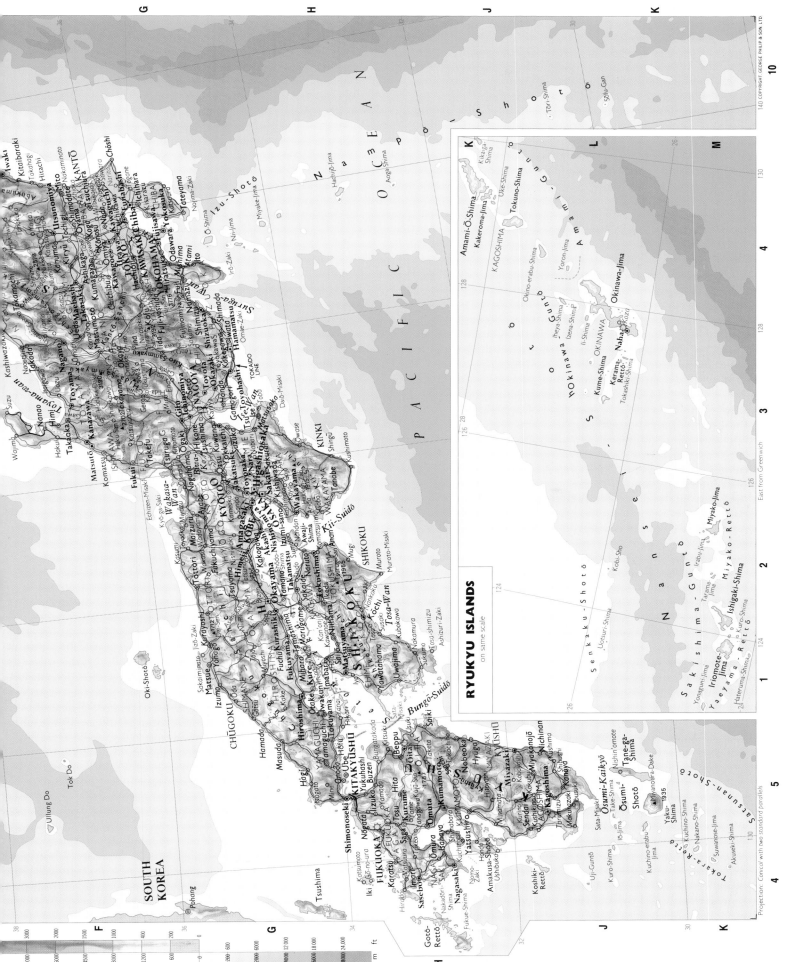

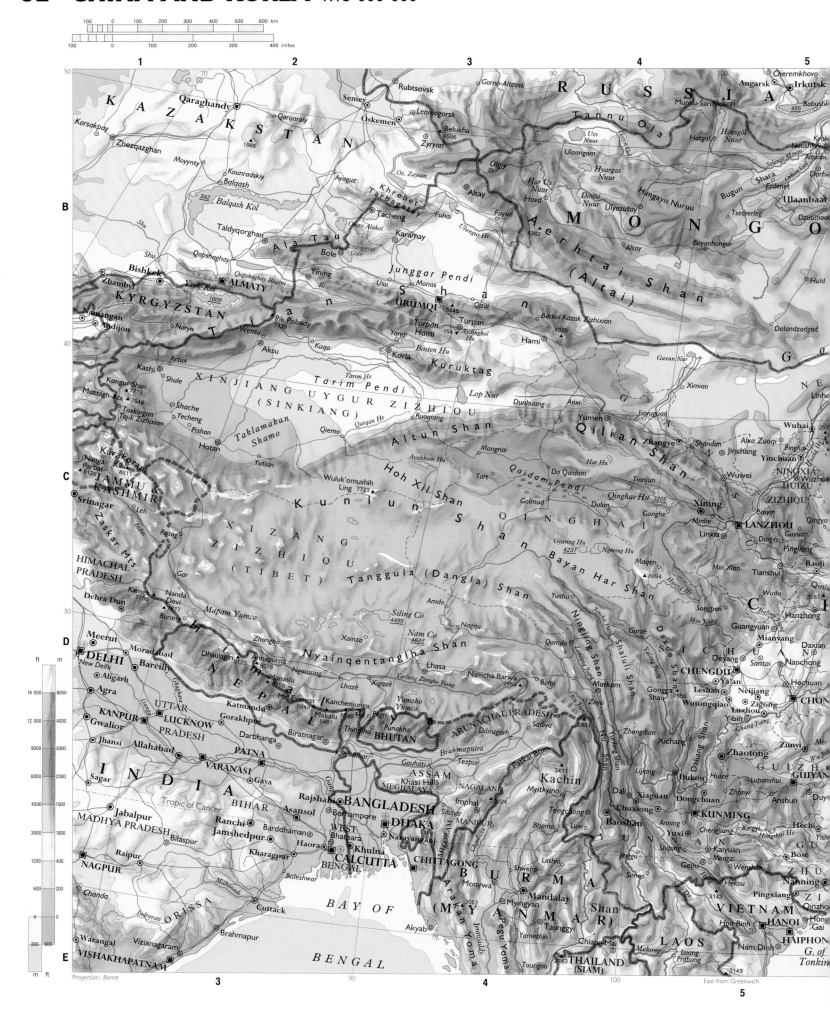

East from Greenwich

27
40
38 37

6

7

8

9

Oz. Baykal
Ulan Ude
Chita
Bukachacha
Nerchinsk
Sretensk
Gulian
Shimanovsk
Svobodnyy
Chegdomyn
Komsomolsk
Aleksandrovsk-
Sakhalinskiy
Poronaysk
Mys Terpeniya

Olovyannaya
Borzya
Yilehuli Shan
Blagoveshchensk
Aihui
Bureya
Birobidzhan
Khabarovsk
Vanino
Sakhalin

-baykalskiy
Manzhouli
Priargunsk
Orogen Zizhiqi
Nenjiang
Obluchye
Amur
Qianjin
Kholmsk
Yuzhno-Sakhalinsk

LIA
Hailar
Arxan
Solon
Butha Qi
Bei'an
Yichun
Hegang
Jiamusi
Bikin
Hulin
Mishan
Wakkanai
Kitami
B

Buir Nur
Choybalsan
Tamsagbulag
QIQIHAR
Daqing
Anda
Suihua
Shuangyashan
L. Khanka
Asahigawa
2290
Kushiro

Saynshand
Horqin Youyi Qianqi
Baicheng
HARBIN
Fuyu
Jixi
Ussuriysk
Otaru
SAPPORO
HOKKAIDO
Muroran

Dzamin Üüd
Xilinhot
Tao'an
CHANGCHUN
JILIN
Mudanjiang
Dunhua
Vladivostok
Artem
Partizansk
Hakodate
Erimo-misaki

Sonid Youqi
Erenhot
Linxi
Duolun
Tongliao
Siping
Liaoyuan
Yanji
Hunchun
Nakhodka
Tsugaru-Kaikyō
Aomori
Hachinohe

Chifeng
Fuxin
Tieling
FUSHUN
Changbai Shan
2744
Chŏngjin
Akita
Morioka

Chaoyang
Liaoyang
SHENYANG
Benxi
Tonghua
SEA OF
Sakata
Ishinomaki

Hohhot
Zhangjiakou
Chengde
Jinzhou
ANSHAN
NORTH
Kimchaek
Yamagata
Sendai

Baotou
Datong
Xuanhua
Yingkou
Qinhuangdao
Dandong
KOREA
Hamhung
Hŭngnam
JAPAN
Niigata
Fukushima

BEIJING
(PEKING)
BEIJING SHI
Liaodong Wan
P'YŎNGYANG
Wŏnsan
Wajima
Jōetsu
Kōriyama

TAIYUAN
Baoding
Anci
TANGSHAN
TIANJIN SHI
DALIAN
Nampo
Haeju
Kaesong
Chunchon
Kangnŭng
Takaoka
TOKYO

3058
TIANJIN
Cangzhou
Bo Hai
Yantai
Weihai
SŎUL (SEOUL)
Takaoka
Kanazawa
NAGOYA
KAWASAKI

SHIJIAZHUANG
INCH'ŎN
SOUTH
Komatsu
ŌSAKA
YOKOHAMA
C

Yangquan
Dezhou
Huang He
Ye Xian
Shandong Bandao
TAEJŎN
KOREA
TAEGU
Matsue
KYŌTO
Fuji-San
Shizuoka

Fenyang
Yuci
Weifang
QINGDAO
Kunsan
Chŏnju
PUSAN
KŌBE
Sakai
Hamamatsu

XI'AN
JINAN
ZIBO
YELLOW
KWANGJU
Masan
Okayama
HIROSHIMA
Kure
Shikoku
Wakayama

Handan
Anyang
Tai'an
SEA
Mokpo
Tsushima
Shimonoseki
Matsuyama
Kōchi

Linfen
Jincheng
Xinxiang
Jining
Rizhao
KITAKYUSHU
FUKUOKA
Kagoshima

Tongchuan
Luoyang
Kaifeng
Zaozhuang
Lianyungang
Cheju Do
1950
Sasebo
Kumamoto

ZHENGZHOU
Shangqiu
Huaibei
Xuzhou
Yancheng
Nagasaki
Kyūshū
Miyazaki

Pingdingshan
HENAN
Shangshui
Bengbu
Yangzhou
Taizhou
Kagoshima
Tane-ga-Shima

Nanyang
Zhumadian
Fuyang
Huainan
NANJING
Changzhou
Nantong
SHANGHAI SHI
Yaku-Shima

Shiyan
Xiangfan
Xinyang
HEFEI
Ma'anshan
Wuxi
Suzhou
SHANGHAI
EAST CHINA

Dabie Shan
Zhongxiang
Tongling
Wuhu
Wuxing
Jiaxing
Amami-Ō-Shima

WUHAN
Anqing
HANGZHOU
Hangzhou Wan
SEA
Tokuno-Shima

Huangshi
Jiujiang
Jingdezhen
Shaoxing
NINGBO

Yueyang
Dongting Hu
Jinhua
LINHAI
PACIFIC

Changde
Yiyang
Poyang Hu
Shangrao
Quzhou
Wenzhou

NANCHANG
ZHEJIANG

HUNAN
CHANGSHA
JIANGXI
Nanping
Naha
Okinawa-Jima
D

Xiangtan
Pingxiang
Fuzhou
Ji'an
Nanping
Ryūkyū-rettō
7507

Shaoyang
Hengyang
Sanming
Min Jiang

Hongjiang
FUZHOU
FUJIAN
Chilung
Sakishima-Guntō
Miyako-Jima

Guilin
Ganzhou
Ruijin
Longyan
Putian
TAIPEI
Ishigaki-Shima
Iriomote-Jima

Nan Ling
Shaoguan
Zhangzhou
Quanzhou
Hsinchu
T'aichung
Tropic of Cancer

GXI
Wuzhou
GUANGDONG
Mei Xian
Xiamen
Changhua
Chiai
Yu Shan
3997
TAIWAN
(FORMOSA)

GZU
Zhaoqing
Foshan
Huizhou
Chao'an
T'ainan
T'aitung
Pingtung

Yangjiang
GUANGZHOU
(CANTON)
Shantou
KAOHSIUNG
Pingtung

Macau
(Port.)
HONG KONG
Batan Is.

Maoming
Zhanjiang
SOUTH CHINA
PACIFIC

Hainan Dao
1879
Haikou
SEA
PHILIPPINES
Babuyan Is.
OCEAN
E

Yacheng
HAINAN

110

120

130

140

6

7

8

120

130

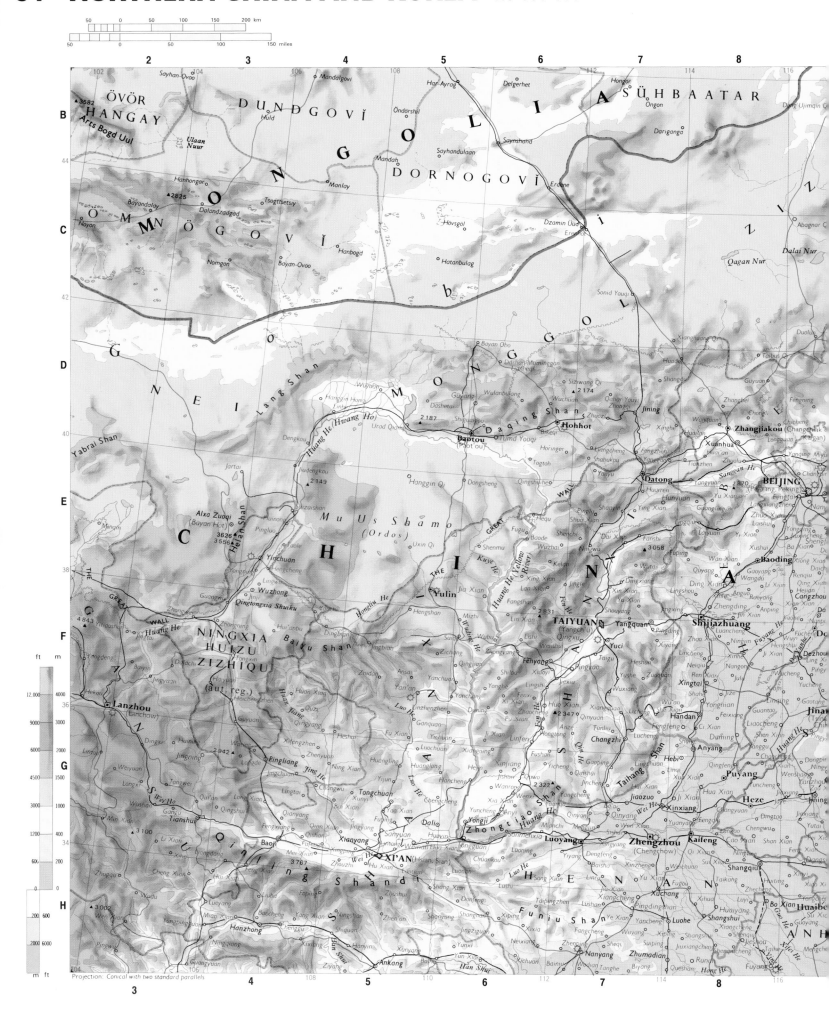

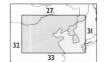

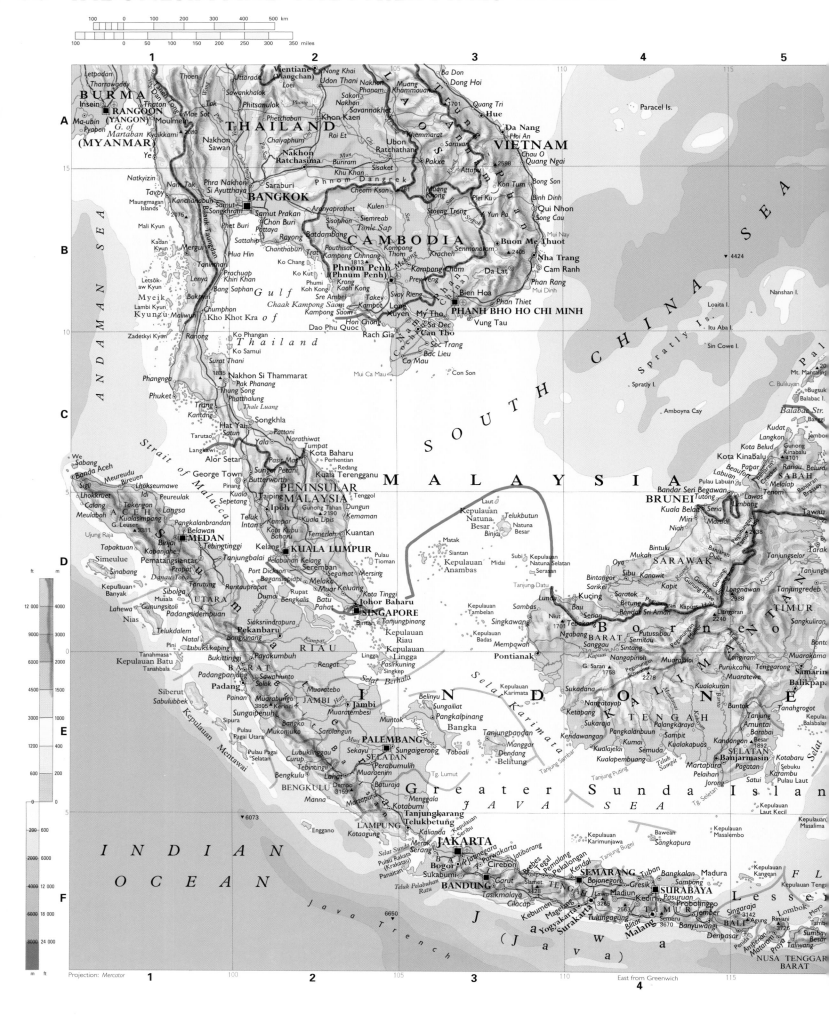

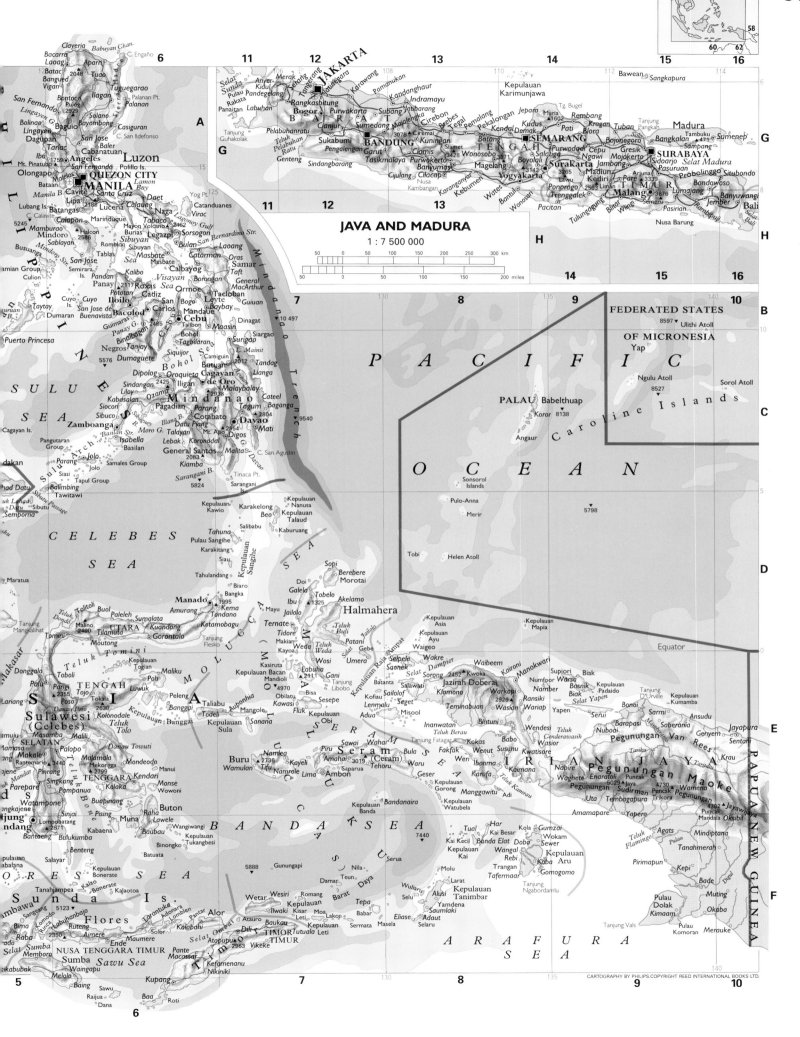

JAVA AND MADURA

1 : 7 500 000

CARTOGRAPHY BY PHILIPS.COPYRIGHT REED INTERNATIONAL BOOKS LTD.

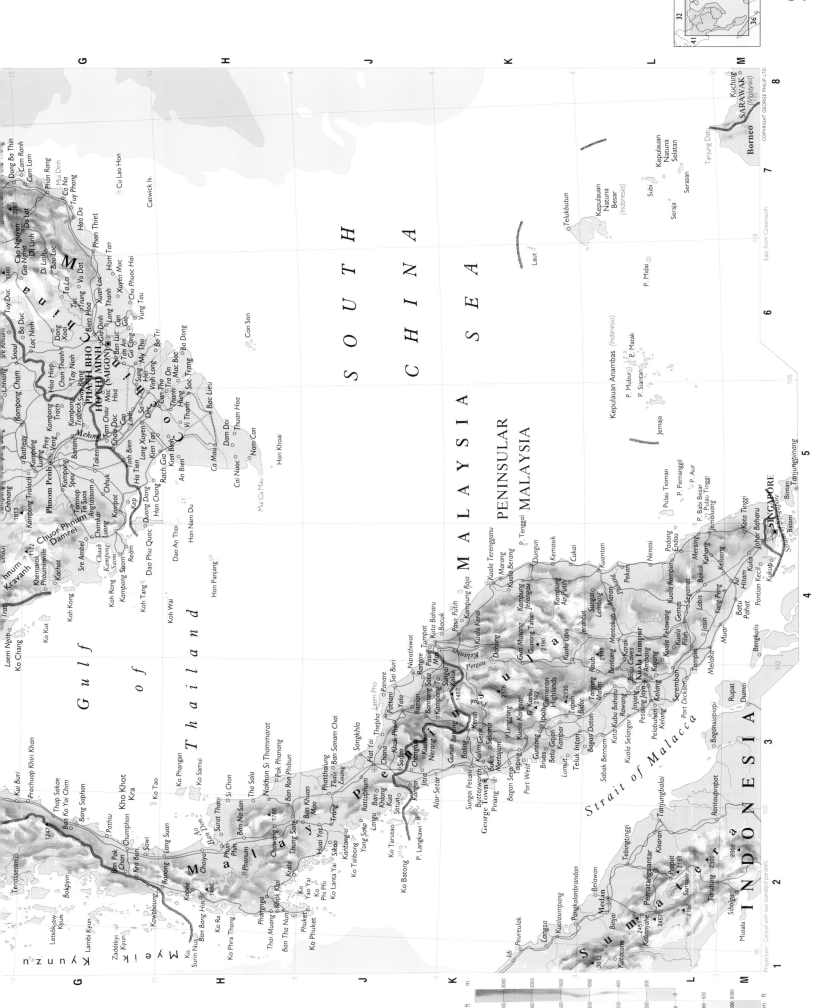

SARAWAK (Malaysia)

Borneo

Tanjung Datu

Kuching

Kepulauan Natuna Besar (Indonesia)

Subi

Serasan

Seraja

Telukbutun

Laut

P. Midai

SOUTH

CHINA

SEA

Kepulauan Anambas (Indonesia)

P. Mubur
P. Matak
P. Siantan

Jemaja

MALAYSIA

PENINSULAR MALAYSIA

Kuala Terengganu
Marang
Kuala Berang
Dungun
Kemasik
Cukai
Kuantan
Nenasi
Pekan

P. Tenggol

Kampung Raja
Kampung Jerangau
Kampung Air Putih
Dabong
Kuala Kerai

Gua Musang
Gunong Tahan 2190
Kuala Lipis

Kuala Rompin
Endau
Padang
Pulau Tioman
P. Pemanggil
P. Aur
P. Babi Besar
Pulau Tinggi
Mersing
Kota Tinggi

SINGAPORE
Singapore
Batam
Bintan
Johor Baharu

Kukup
Pontian Kecil
Batu Pahat
Muar
Bengkalis
Bagansiapiapi
Dumai
Rupat

Strait of Malacca

INDONESIA

Tanjungpinang

Tanjungbalai
Rantauprapat
Kisaran
Tebingtinggi
Pematangsiantar
Prapat 2151
Samosir
Tarutung 2300
Kabanjahe 2451
Kutacane 3012
Kualasimpang
Pangkalanbrandan
Binjai
Medan
Belawan
Musala
Sibolga
Barus

Sumatera

Langsa
Peureulak
Idi

East from Greenwich

Port Dickson
Port Weld
Kuala Selangor
Sabak Bernam
Teluk Intan
Lumut
Bagan Serai
Sungai Petani
Butterworth
George Town
Pinang
P. Langkawi

Kuala Kubu Baharu
Kota Bharu
Bagan Datoh
Kampar
Tapah
Bidor
Cameron Highlands 2130
Ipoh
Kuala Kangsar 2182
Taiping
Bruas
Selama

Kelang
Petaling Jaya
Kuala Lumpur
Ampang
Kajang
Seremban
Melaka
Tampin
Gemas
Labis
Segamat
Yong Peng
Kluang
Kota Baharu
Kulai

Bentong
Raub
Karak
Mentakab
Temerloh
Jerantut
Kuala Krau
Kerau

Guntong
Gerik
Kuala Kangsar

George Town

Butterworth

Kangar
Alor Setar
Kodiang
Jitra

Kroh
Baling
Sik
Kulim

Hat Yai
Songkhla
Sadao
Chana
Nerang
Sungai Kolok
Rangae
Tak Bai
Tumpat
Pasir Mas
Pasir Putih
Bachok

Narathiwat
Sai Buri
Pattani
Thepha
Laem Pho
Panare
Yala
Raman
Kabang
Betong
Yaha

Phatthalung
Thale Luang
Ranot
Ban Khuan Mao
Trang
Huai Yot
Sikao
Kantang
Ban Sanam Chai
Nakhon Si Thammarat
Pak Phanang
Chian Yai
Thung Song
Ban Na San
Surat Thani
Ban Don
Chaiya

Ko Samui
Ko Phangan
Phunphin

Si Chon
Tha Sala

Ko Tao

Chumphon
Lang Suan
Sawi

Prachuap Khiri Khan
Thap Sakae
Bang Saphan
Pathiu

Kui Buri

Kho Khot Kra

Ban Ko Yai Chim

Thailand

Gulf

of

Thailand

Krabi
Ko Lanta Yai
Phi Phi
Ko Yao Yai
Phangnga
Ban Tha Num
Phuket
Ko Phuket

Malay

Ko Kradan
P. Langkawi
Langu
Yong Sata
Satun
Ko Tarutao
Ko Talibong
Ko Batong

Ko Phra Thong
Khao Lak
Thai Muang

Ban Bang Hin
Takua Pa
Ko Ra
Kapoe
Ranong
Kra Buri
Bang Saphan

Kawthaung
Surin Nua
Lambi Kyun
Letsok-aw Kyun
Zadetkyi Kyun

Tenasserim

Ko Chang
Ko Kut
Laem Ngop
Ko Kong

Gulf

of

Kompong Som
Sre Ambel
Kampong Saom
Kachot
Kampot
Ream
Kep
Duong Dong
Dao Phu Quoc
Hon Chong
Ha Tien
Rach Gia
Kien Tan
Long Xuyen

Koh Kong
Koh Rong
Koh Tang
Koh Wai

Chuor Phnum Damrei 1172

Khemarak Phouminville

Kompong Speu
Tonnop
Ta Suos
Angtassom
Takeo
Chhuk
Chamkar Luong
Banam
Prey Veng

Chuor Phnum Kravanh

Phnom Penh
1813

Kampong Tralach
Kompong Chhnang
Batheay
Kompong Thom

Kompong Cham
Hoa Hiep
Chon Thanh
Tay Ninh
Go Dau
Ben Luc
Tan An
My Tho
Cho Phuoc Hai
Vung Tau

Trach
Trabeck
Svay Rieng
Chau Doc
Tan Chau

Long
Loc Ninh
Bien Hoa
GIA DINH
HO CHI MINH (SAIGON)
THANH PHO

Dong Xoai

M o i

Bu

Cao Nguyen 2287
Di Linh 1580
Da Lat
Gia Nghia
Bao Loc
Xuan Loc
Vo Dat
Ta Lai
Tuy Duc
Dinh Quan

Cam Ranh
Cam Lam
Phan Rang
Phan Thiet
Mui Dinh
Tuy Phong
Hoa Da

Dong Ba Thin

Cu Lao Hon

Catwick Is.

Con Son

Vi Thanh
Soc Trang
Bac Lieu
Ca Mau
Nam Can
Dam Doi
Thuan Hoa
Hon Khoai

Mui Ca Mau

An Bien
Kien Binh

Can Tho
Vinh Long
Tra On
Tra Vinh
Mac Bac
Hung
Ben Tre
Ba Dong
Go Cong
Cao Lanh
Sa Dec
Tinh Bien
Long Xuyen
Vinh Chau
Ba Tri

Hon Nam Du
Dao An Thoi
Hon Panjang

Mekong

ft   m

9000
6000
4500
3000
1500
1200
600
200
0

m   ft

200
2000
4000
6000

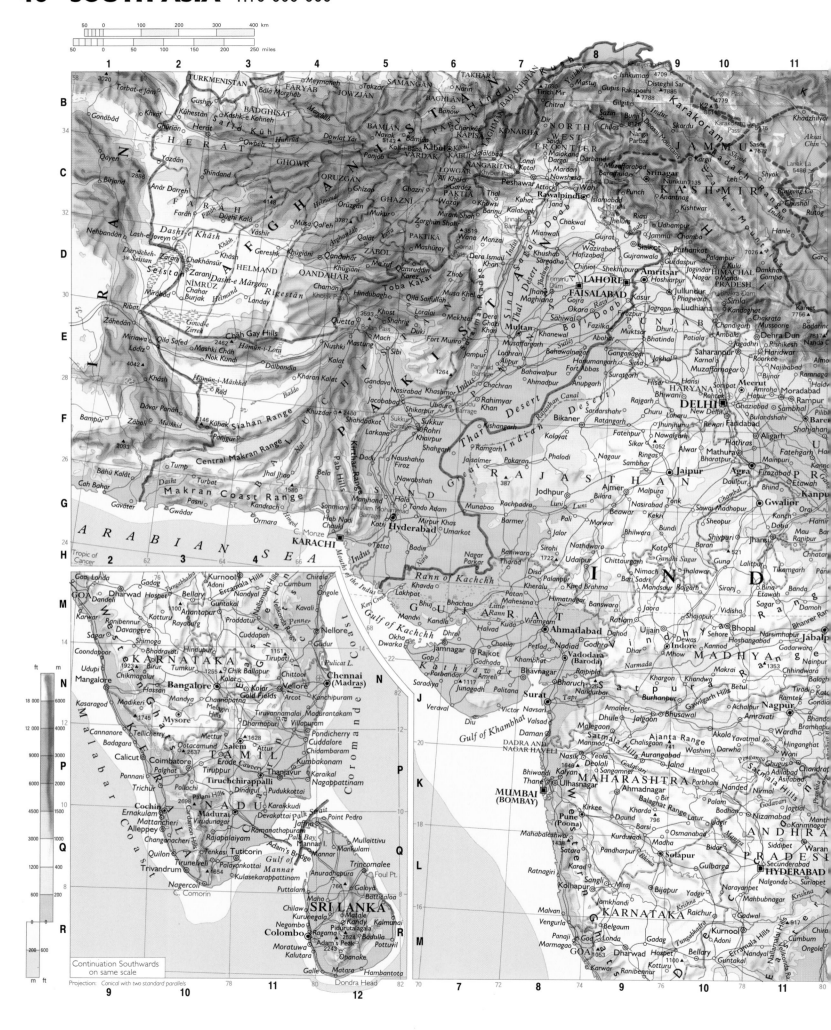

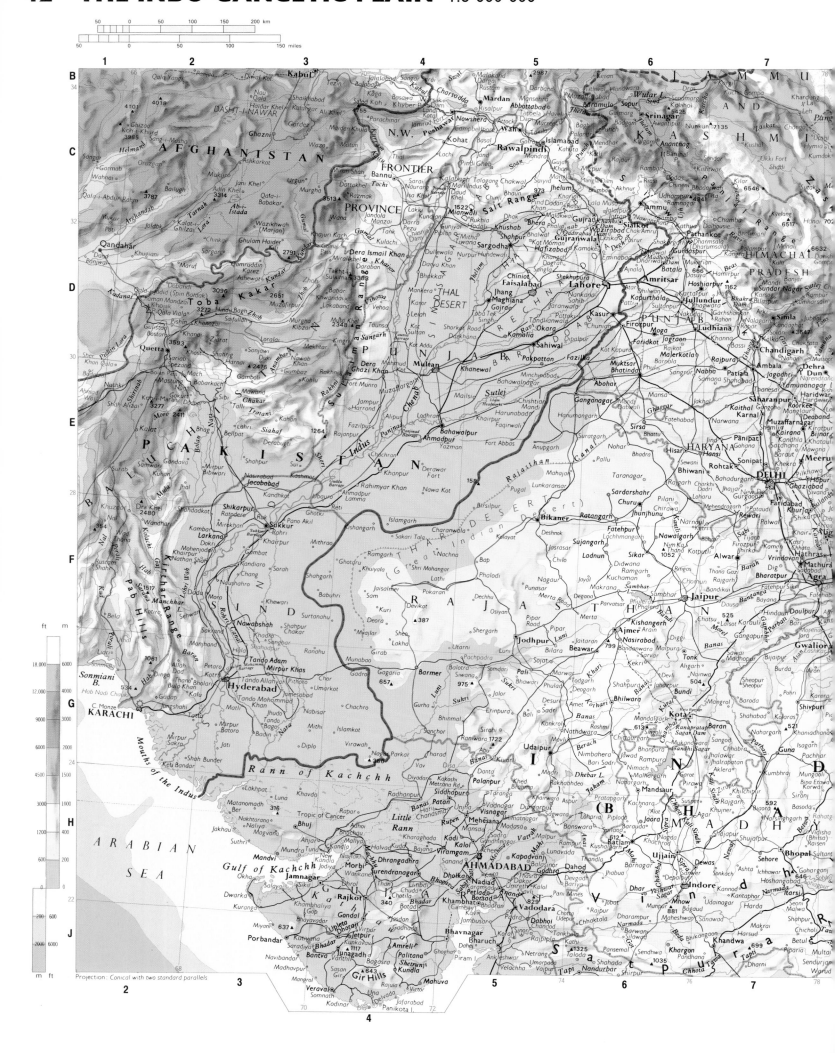

Projection : Conical with two standard parallels

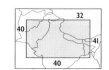

JAMMU AND KASHMIR
On same scale as Main Map

COPYRIGHT GEORGE PHILIP & SON LTD

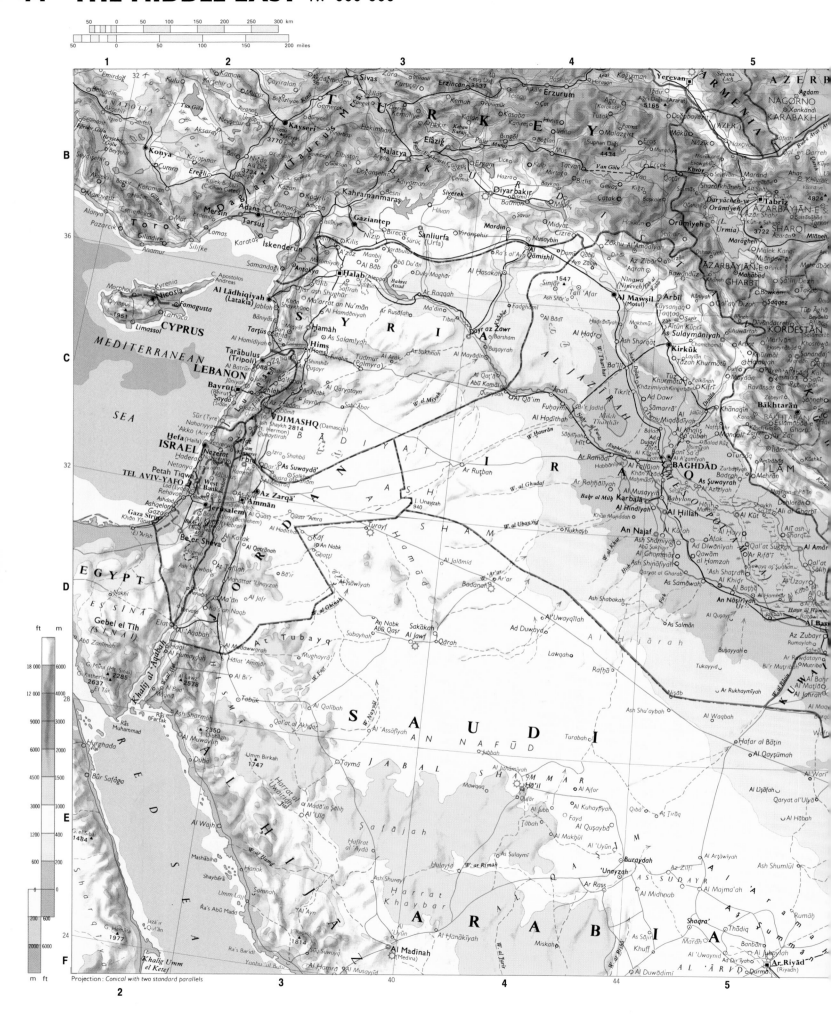

Projection : Conical with two standard parallels

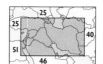

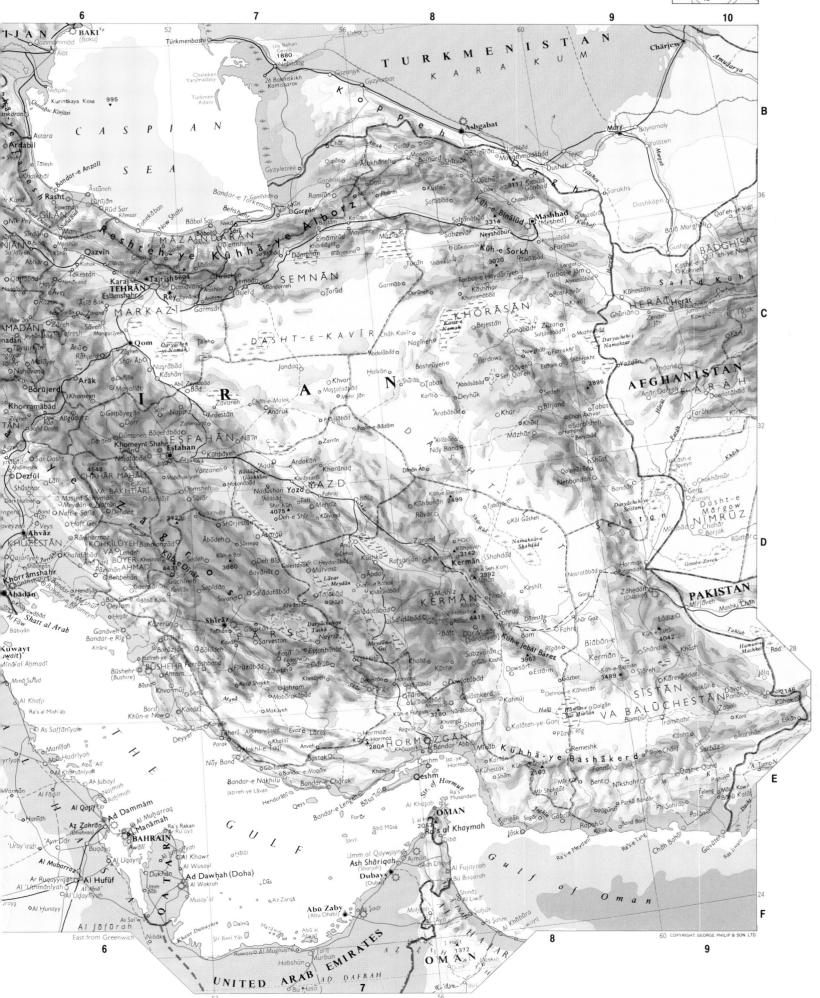

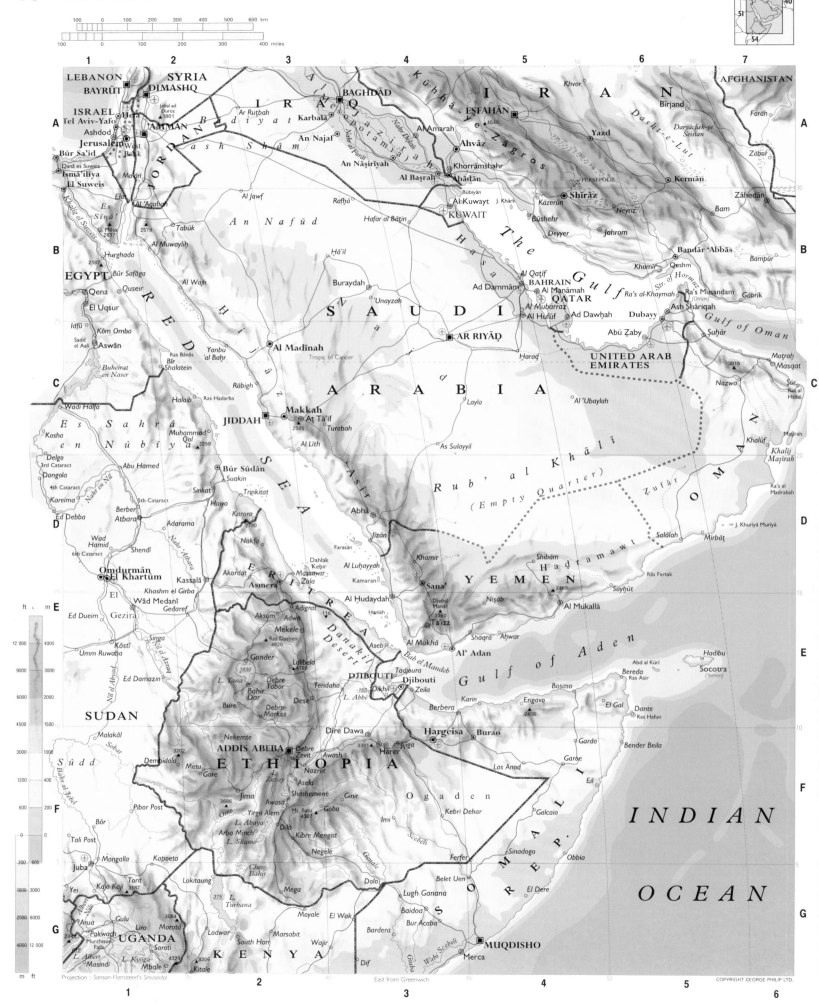

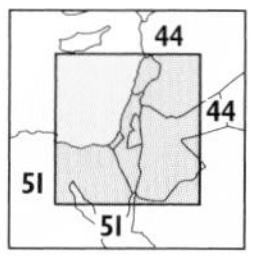

44
44
51
51

10 0 10 20 30 40 50 60 70 80 100 km
10 0 10 20 30 40 50 60 miles

1 2 3 4 5 6

Paphos Episkopi Limassol **CYPRUS**
Episkopi Bay Akrotiri C. Gata

M E D I T E R R A N E A N

S E A

LEBANON

Al Ḥamidiyah Tall Kalakh Shinshār **Ḥimṣ** (Homs) Furqlus
Halba Al Hirmil Al Quṣayr ḤIMṢ
ASH SHAMĀL
Ṭarābulus (Tripoli) Zgharta Qurnat as Sawdā' 3088 Al Burayj Al Qaryatayn
Al Batrūn Bsharri 2464
Jubayl Qarṭabā Al Labwah 2616 An Nabk Bi'r Ghadīr
Ibrāhīm 2628 Ba'labakk Yabrūd
Jūniyah Sannin Sirghāya **SYRIA**
BAYRŪT (Beirut) Bikfayyā Zaḥlah Al Qutayfah Khān Abū Shāmat
Ash Shuwayfāt Alayh Hawsh Mussá Dumayr DIMASHQ
Ad Dāmūr Az Zabadānī **DIMASHQ** (Damascus)
Saydā (Sidon) Jazzīn 1942 Al Bārūk 2814 ash Shayk (Mt. Hermon) Dūmā A'waj
An Nabaṭīyah at Taḥtā Marj 'Uyūn Dārayyā Qaṭanā Al Ḥājānah
AL Al Khiyām Burāq Aṣ Ṣafā
Sūr (Tyre) JANŪB Qiryat Shemona Golan Heights 1197 Al Qunayṭirah As Sanamayn
Nahariyya Me'ona Ar Rafid DAR'Ā Shahbā JABAL AD DURŪZ AS SUWAYDĀ
'Akko (Acre) Zefat Fiq Shaykh Miskin Izra 1800
Mifraz Hefa **Hagalil** Yam -210 Saham al Jawlān As Suwaydā Sālah
Hefa (Haifa) Qiryat Yam Karmi'el Teverya (Tiberias) Dar'ā
Qiryat Ata Kinneret Yarmūk Busrā ash Shām Salkhad
Dāliyat el Karmel Nazerat (Nazareth) HAZAFON Afula Ṭabaqa Irbid Ar Ramthā Umm al Qittayn
TEL MEGIDDO Bet She'an IRBID
Umm el Fahm Jenin Ailūn 1247 Al-Mafraq Umm ad Dan
CAESAREA Hadera Ṭulkarm SAMARIA Nahr az Zarqā' Jarash
ISRAEL Hanna-Karkur Shomrōn Tūbās Nāblus AL BALQĀ' As Salt Az Zarqā
Netanya HAMERKAZ Kefar Sava SHILO Wadi as Sīr **'AMMĀN**
Herzliyya Benē Beraq Petah Tiqwa As Salṭ Karama Azraq ash Shishan
Tel Aviv-Yafo Ramat Gan 289 Nā'ūr
Bat Yam **West Bank** 'AMMĀN
Rishon le Ziyyon Lōd Rām Allāh El Arīḥa (Jericho) At Tunayb
Ashdod Ramla Rehovot Ma'daba
Yavne **Jerusalem** (Yerushalayim) (Al Quds) Ma'daba
Qiryat Mal'akhi Bet Shemesh Bayt Laḥm (Bethlehem) W. al Ḥaydān Dhībān
Ashqelon Qiryat Gat TEL LAKHISH Al Khalīl (Hebron) -403 W. al Mawjib Al Hadithah
Gaza Strip Gaza N. Shiqma Az Ẓāhiriyah W. al Ghadaf Al Qaṭrānah
Khān Yūnis Sederot Arad Sedom Al Karak W. al Madhui
Rafaḥ Be'er Sheva (Beersheba) 1305 Al Mazār
Bûr Sa'îd (Port Said) El Daheir Bor Mashash Sedom JORDAN W. Ba'ir
Bûr Fu'ad Rās Burūn El 'Arīsh Dimona 333 W. al Ḥasā
Khalīg El Tîna Sabkhet el Bardawîl HADAROM
Romāni Bîr el 'Abd Bîr Lahfān At Ṭafilah Bā'ir
El Qantara Bîr Qaṭia Bîr el Gararât Qezi'ot Sedé Boqér 1072 J. ash Shawmari
El Duweidar Bîr Kaseiba Birein -121 Ma'ān
Wâḥid Bîr el Jafir 892 Mizpe Ramon Nijil Mahaṭṭat 'Unayzah
Ismâ'iliya Bîr Madkûr Muweilih Birein Bîr ad Dabbāghāt W. Abu Ṣafāt
Talâta Bîr el Mālḥi El Quṣeima **Hanegev** Rujm Tal'at al Jamā'ah 1736 Qa'el Jafr
Khamsa Bîr Ḥasana El 'Agrūd Sedé Boqér PETRA As Sūwaydā
El Buheirat el Murrat el Kubra (Great Bitter L.) G. Y. 'Allaq 1094 N. Paran Ma'ān
Gineifo El Thamāda W. el Brūk N. Ḥiyyon Bi'r al Mārī
EGYPT W. Maḥasham N. Hiyyon MA'ĀN
El Suweis (Suez) Bûr Taufiq Bîr Gebeil Hisn El Kuntilla Ra's an Naqb
Adabiya W. El Sadeira Nakhl W. El 'Aqaba Yotvata 1435 Mahaṭṭat ash Shidīyah
Uyûn Mûsa **Es Sina** (Sinai) W. El Tamarāni Ra's an Naqb
Bîr Bad' Ain Sudr W. Girāfi 'En Avrona Bi'r al Buṭayyiḥāt Bi'r al Qaṭṭār
Mamarr Mitlā 948 G. el Kabrît Bîr Abu Muḥammad Baṭn al Ghūl **SAUDI**
Ghubbet el Bûs Gebel el Tîh El Thamad 1592 At Ṭubayq **ARABIA**
Râs Matarma El Wabeira Elat Al 'Aqabah
Bîr Abu Sandûq 1272 Al Ṭāba Al Mudawwarah
EL SUWEIS **Shibh Jazîrat Sînâ'** Bîr el Biarāt Ḥaql
Bîr Abu Ga'da 1165 Gulf of Aqaba W. an Nīchin
Bîr Wuseit Bîr el Ḥeisi

ft m
9000 3000
6000 2000
4500 1500
3000 1000
1200 400
600 200
0 0
200 600
2000 6000
m ft

Projection: Polyconic East from Greenwich CARTOGRAPHY BY PHILIP'S COPYRIGHT REED INTERNATIONAL BOOKS LTD.

═ ═ ═ 1974 Cease Fire Lines

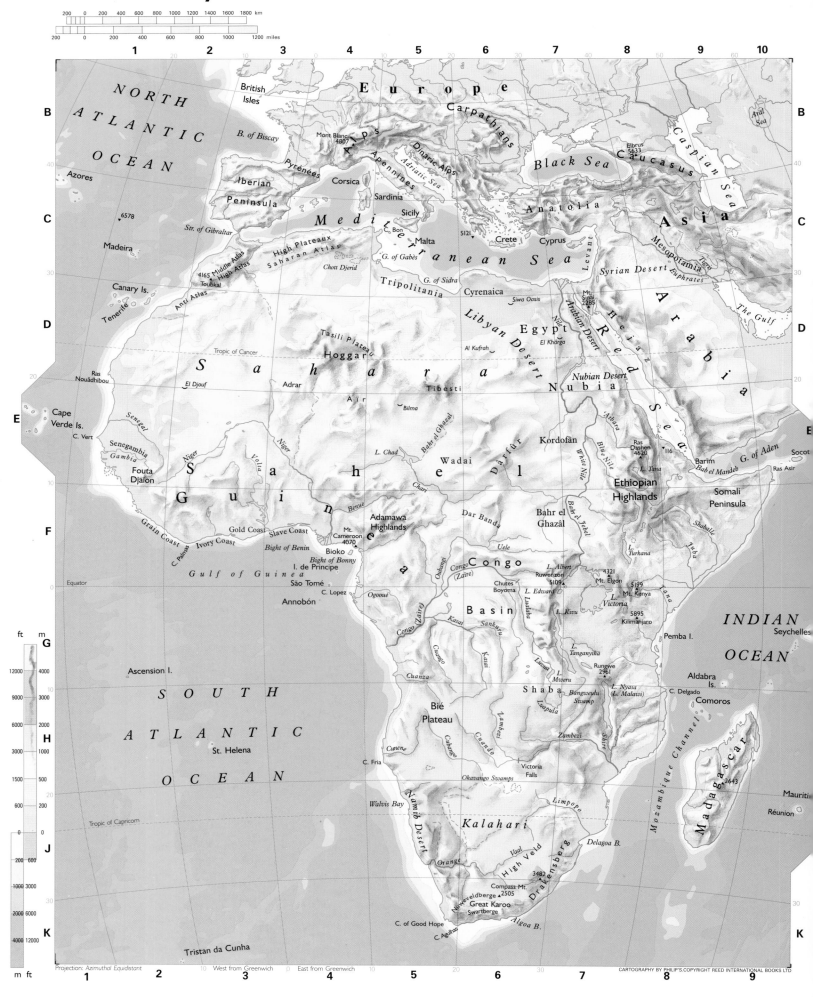

NORTH

ATLANTIC

OCEAN

British Isles

Europe

Carpathians

Alps

Mont Blanc 4807

Pyrénées

B. of Biscay

Iberian Peninsula

Corsica

Apennines

Dinaric Alps

Adriatic Sea

Black Sea

Caucasus

Elbrus 5633

Caspian Sea

Aral Sea

Asia

Azores

Madeira

6578

Str. of Gibraltar

Sardinia

Sicily

C. Bon

Malta

5121

Crete

Cyprus

Anatolia

Levant

Mesopotamia

Tigris

Mediterranean Sea

Canary Is.

Tenerife

High Plateaux

Saharan Atlas

Middle Atlas

4165

High Atlas

Toubkal

Anti Atlas

Chott Djerid

G. of Gabès

G. of Sidra

Tripolitania

Cyrenaica

Mt. Sinai 2285

Siwa Oasis

Egypt

El Khârga

Arabian Desert

Red Sea

Syrian Desert

Euphrates

Arabia

The Gulf

Hejaz

Ras Nouâdhibou

Tropic of Cancer

Tasili Plateau

Hoggar

Adrar

Aïr

Tibesti

Libyan Desert

Nubian Desert

Nubia

El Djouf

Bilma

S a h a r a

Cape Verde Is.

C. Vert

Senegal

Senegambia

Gambia

Fouta Djalon

Niger

Niger

Volta

L. Chad

Bahr el Ghazal

Wadai

Darfûr

Kordofân

Atbara

Ras Dashen 4620

116

Barim

Bab el Mandeb

G. of Aden

Ras Asir

Socot

S a h e l

White Nile

Blue Nile

L. Tana

Ethiopian Highlands

Somali Peninsula

G u i n e a

Grain Coast

C. Palmas

Ivory Coast

Gold Coast

Slave Coast

Bight of Benin

Mt. Cameroon 4070

Bioko

Bight of Bonny

I. de Principe

Adamawa Highlands

Benue

Dar Banda

Bahr el Ghazâl

Bahr el Jebel

Uele

São Tomé

C. Lopez

Equator

Annobón

Ogooué

Onbangi

Congo (Zaire)

Congo

Chutes Boyoma

L. Albert

Ruwenzori 5109

L. Edward

L. Kivu

Mt. Elgon

4321

5199

Mt. Kenya

L. Victoria

5895

Kilimanjaro

Turkana

Shabelle

Juba

Tana

Pemba I.

INDIAN

OCEAN

Seychelles

Gulf of Guinea

Congo

Basin

Kasai

Sankuru

Lualaba

L. Tanganyika

Aldabra Is.

C. Delgado

Comoros

Ascension I.

SOUTH

Cuango

Cuanza

Shaba

L. Mweru

Lucua

Bangweulu Swamp

Rungwe 2961

L. Nyasa (L. Malawi)

St. Helena

ATLANTIC

Bié

Plateau

Zambezi

Lualaba

Zambezi

Shire

Mozambique Channel

MADAGASCAR

2643

Mauritie

Réunion

OCEAN

C. Fria

Cunene

Cabango

Cuando

Victoria Falls

Tropic of Capricorn

Walvis Bay

Namib Desert

Okavango Swamps

Kalahari

Limpopo

Delagoa B.

Orange

Vaal

High Veld

Drakensberg

3482

Nuweveldberge

Compass Mt. 2505

Great Karoo

Swartberge

Algoa B.

C. of Good Hope

C. Agulhas

Tristan da Cunha

Projection: Azimuthal Equidistant

West from Greenwich

East from Greenwich

ft m

12000 4000

9000 3000

6000 2000

3000 1000

1500 500

600 200

0 0

200 600

1000 3000

2000 6000

4000 12000

m ft

200   0   200 400 600 800 1000 1200 1400 1600 1800 km
200   0   200   400   600   800   1000 1200 miles

1   2   3   4   5   6   7   8   9   10

NORTH
ATLANTIC
OCEAN

B. of Biscay

UNITED
KINGDOM
LONDON
NETH.
BELG.
GERMANY POLAND
Warsaw
Kiev
RUSSIA
PARIS
FRANCE
SWITZ.
CZECH REP.
Prague
Vienna
AUSTRIA
HUNGARY
SLOVAK REP.
ROMANIA
UKRAINE
Odessa
Volgograd
KAZAKSTAN
Aral
Sea

Azores
(Port.)

Madrid
PORTUGAL
SPAIN
Lisbon
Corsica
Rome
Sardinia
ITALY
CROATIA
BOS.
HERZ.
YUG.
N.
MAC.
Adriatic Sea
BULGARIA
GREECE
Athens
Crete
Black Sea
Sicily
Ankara
TURKEY
GEORGIA
ARM.
AZER.
Baku
TURKMEN.
Caspian Sea

Madeira
(Port.)
Algiers
Annaba
Constantine
Tunis
TUNISIA
Sfax
MALTA
Tripoli
Misrátah
Mediterranean Sea
CYPRUS
LEB.
SYRIA
Aleppo
Mosul
Damascus
Tel Aviv-
Jaffa
Jerusalem
ISRAEL
JORDAN
Tigris
Euphrates
I R A Q
Baghdad
Esfahán
Tehrán
IRAN

Casablanca
Rabat
Tétouan
Fès
MOROCCO
Marrakesh
Chott Djerid

Canary Is.
(Sp.)

Benghazi
Alexandria
Port Said
CAIRO
Suez
El Faiyûm

Dakhla

WESTERN SAHARA
El Aaiún
Fdérik
Tropic of Cancer

ALGERIA
In Salah
LIBYA
Marzúq
Al Jawf
EGYPT
Asyût
Aswán
Wadi Halfa

S a h a r a

Ras
Nouâdhibou

Medina
SAUDI
ARABIA
Riyadh
BAHRAIN
QATAR
The Gulf
KUWAIT
Basra

VERDE IS.

MAURITANIA
Nouakchott

St-Louis
C. Vert
Dakar
SENEGAL
GAMBIA
Banjul
GUINEA-
BISSAU
Bissau

Praia

Senegal
Tombouctou
NIGER
Agadès
Niger
Niamey
MALI
Bamako
BURKINA
FASO
Ouagadougou
Bobo-
Dioulasso
BENIN
Kano
L. Chad
CHAD
Abéché
Ndjamena
Maiduguri
Chari
NIGERIA
Abuja
SUDAN
El Fasher
El Obeid
Omdurmán
Khartoum
Wád Medani
Atbara
Atbara
ERITREA
Mesewa
Asmera
L. Tana
YEMEN
G. of Aden
Socotra
(Yemen)
Ras Asir
DJIBOUTI
Djibouti
Berbera

GUINEA
Conakry
Freetown
SIERRA
LEONE
Monrovia
LIBERIA
Abidjan
IVORY
COAST
Yamoussoukro
Bouaké
GHANA
Kumasi
TOGO
Lomé
Accra
Sekondi-
Takoradi
Porto
Novo
Ibadan
Lagos
Enugu
Benue
CAMEROON
Douala
Yaoundé
CENTRAL
AFRICAN REP.
Bangui
Wau
Bahr el Jebel
White Nile
Blue Nile
Malakál
ETHIOPIA
Addis Ababa
Harer
Shabelle
SOMALI REP.
Mogadishu
Kismayu

Bight of Benin
Port
Harcourt
Malabo
EQUATORIAL
GUINEA
SÃO TOMÉ & PRINCIPE
Libreville
Annobón
C. Lopez
GABON
Congo
(Zaïre)
Oubangi
CONGO
Mbandaka
Congo
(Zaïre)
Kisangani
L. Albert
L. Edward
L. Kivu
RWANDA
Kigali
BURUNDI
Bujumbura
UGANDA
Kampala
Kisumu
L.
Victoria
KENYA
Nairobi
Mombasa
L.
Turkana

Gulf of Guinea

Equator

CONGO
(DEM. REP. OF THE)
Brazzaville
Kinshasa
Matadi
Pointe-Noire
CABINDA
(Angola)
Kasai
Lualaba
Kananga
TANZANIA
Dodoma
Zanzibar
Dar es Salaam
L. Tanganyika

SEYCHELLES

INDIAN
OCEAN

Ascension I.
(U.K.)

Luanda
Lobito
Namibe
Huambo
ANGOLA
Cubango
Cunene
Cuanza
L. Mweru
Likasi
Lubumbashi
Ndola
ZAMBIA
Lusaka
Livingstone
L. Malawi
C. Delgado
COMOROS
Mayotte
(Fr.)
Antsiranana
Mahajanga

SOUTH
ATLANTIC
OCEAN

St. Helena
(U.K.)
C. Fria

NAMIBIA
Windhoek
BOTSWANA
Gaborone
Zambezi
Limpopo
Lilongwe
MALAWI
Blantyre
MOZAMBIQUE
Moçambique
Beira
ZIMBABWE
Harare
Bulawayo
Mozambique Channel
Toamasina
Antananarivo
MADAGASCAR
Fianarantsoa
MAURITIUS
Réunion
(Fr.)
Aldabra
Is.

Tropic of Capricorn

Johannesburg
Pretoria
Maputo
Mbabane
SWAZ.
Vaal
Orange
Kimberley
Maseru
LESOTHO
Durban
SOUTH AFRICA
Cape Town
C. of Good Hope
C. Agulhas
East
London
Port
Elizabeth

Tristan da Cunha
(U.K.)

Projection: Azimuthal Equidistant
West from Greenwich   East from Greenwich

1   2   3   4   5   6   7   8   9

Dakar Capital Cities

CARTOGRAPHY BY PHILIP'S COPYRIGHT REED INTERNATIONAL BOOKS LTD

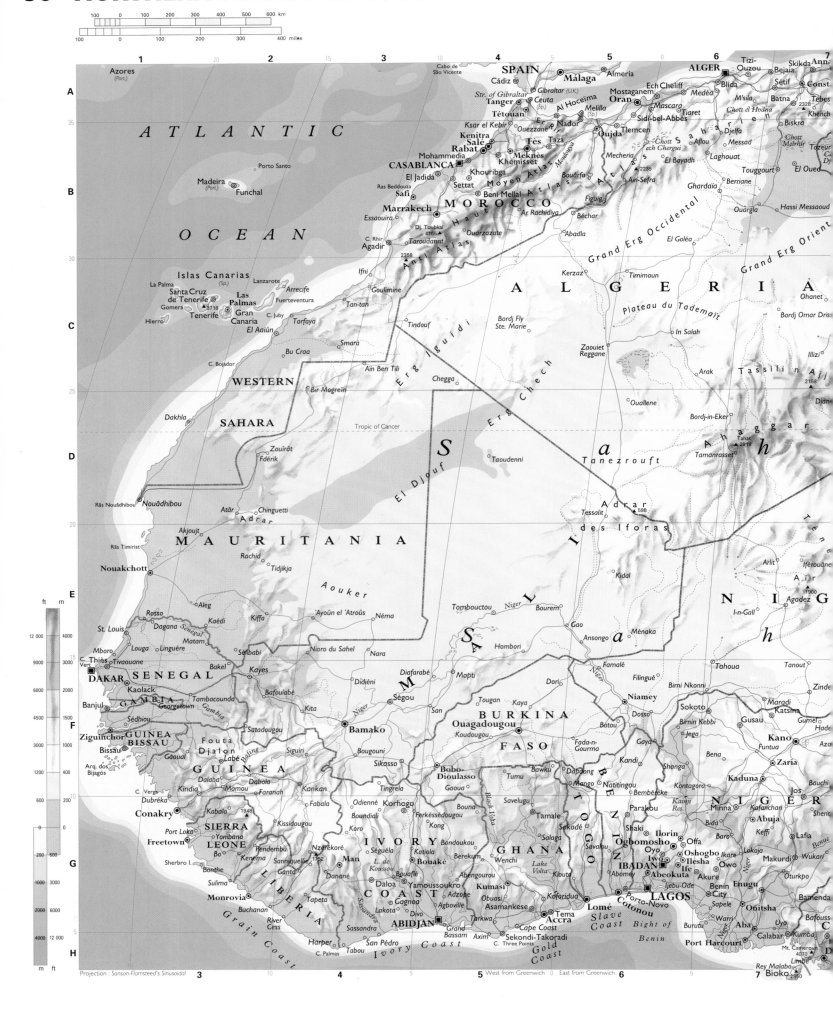

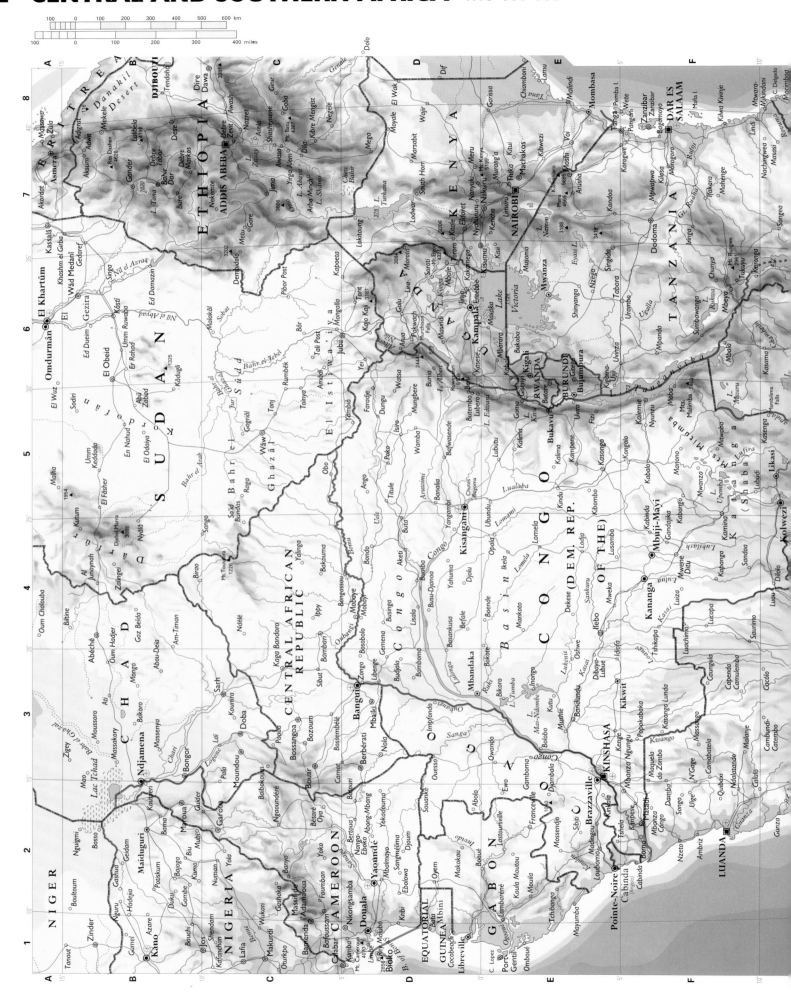

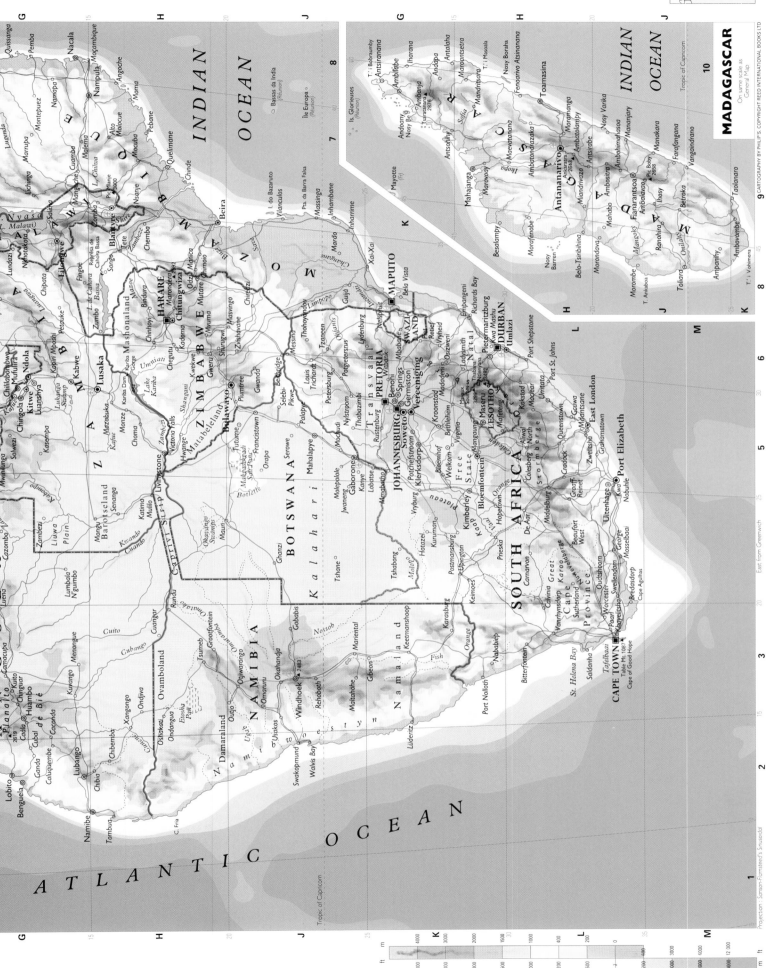

MADAGASCAR

On same scale as
General Map

INDIAN

OCEAN

Tropic of Capricorn

CARTOGRAPHY BY PHILIP'S. COPYRIGHT REED INTERNATIONAL BOOKS LTD

INDIAN

OCEAN

ATLANTIC OCEAN

SOUTH AFRICA

BOTSWANA

NAMIBIA

ZIMBABWE

Projection: Sanson-Flamsteed's Sinusoidal

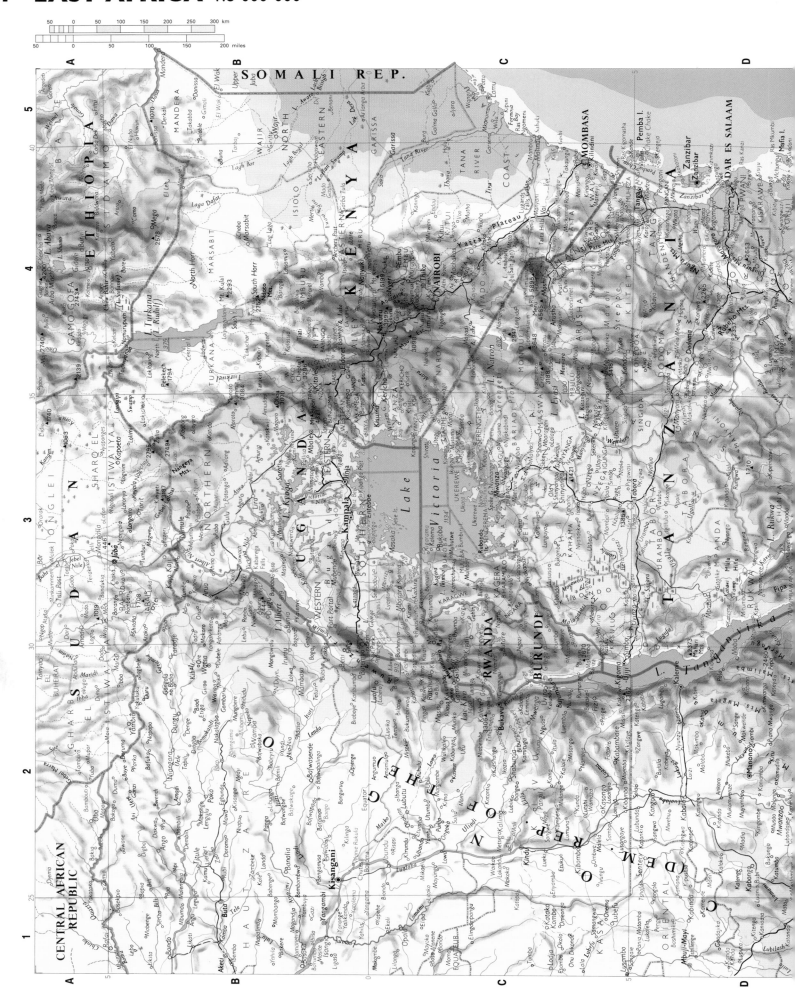

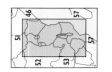

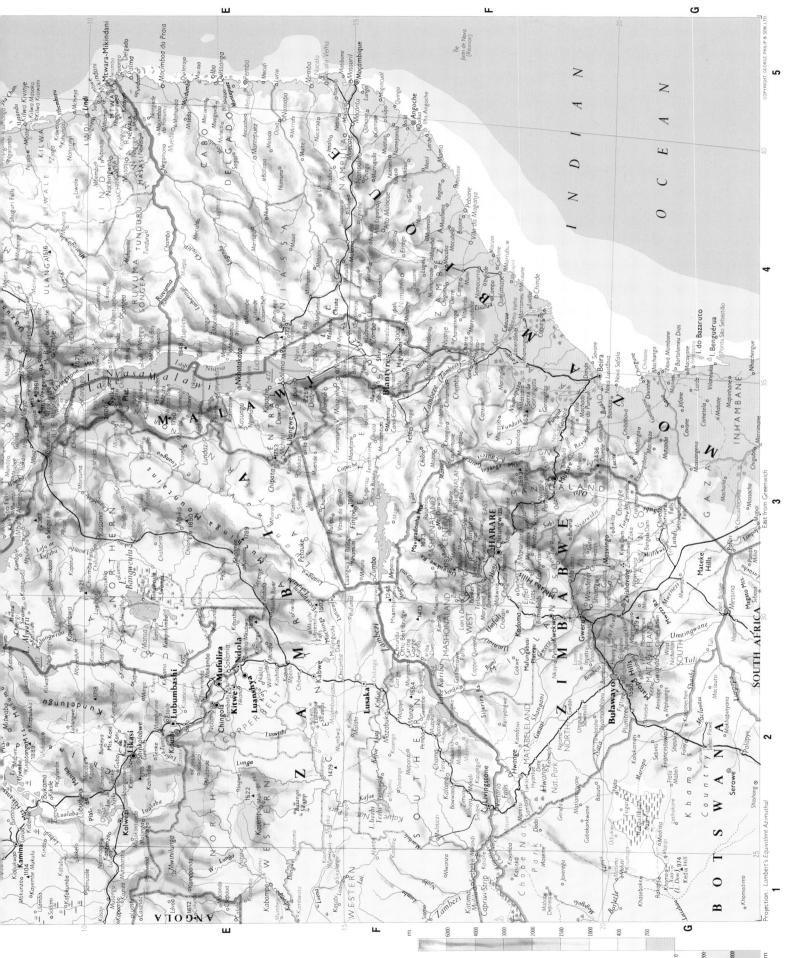

Projection: Lambert's Equivalent Azimuthal

East from Greenwich

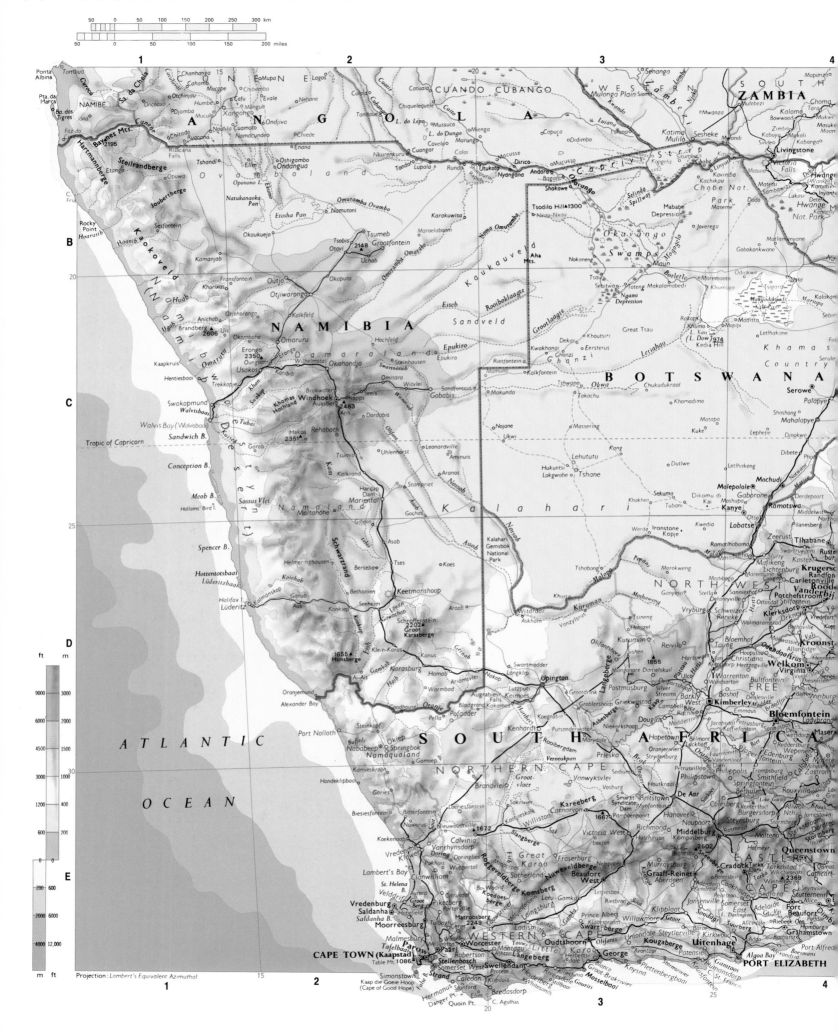

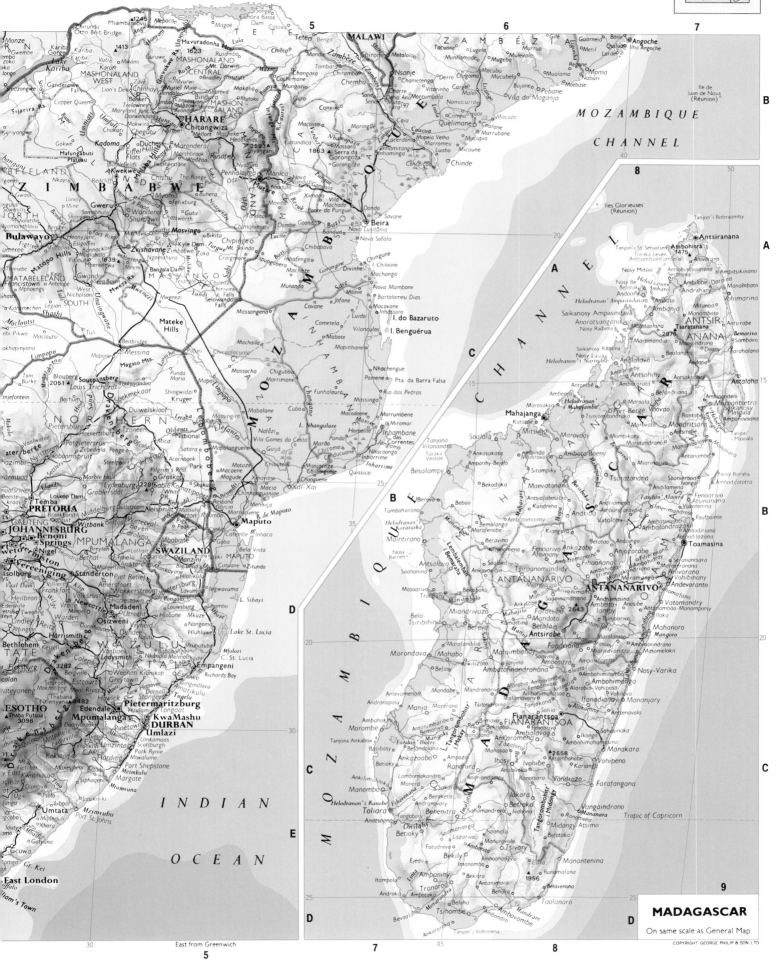

MOZAMBIQUE

CHANNEL

INDIAN

OCEAN

MADAGASCAR

On same scale as General Map

East from Greenwich

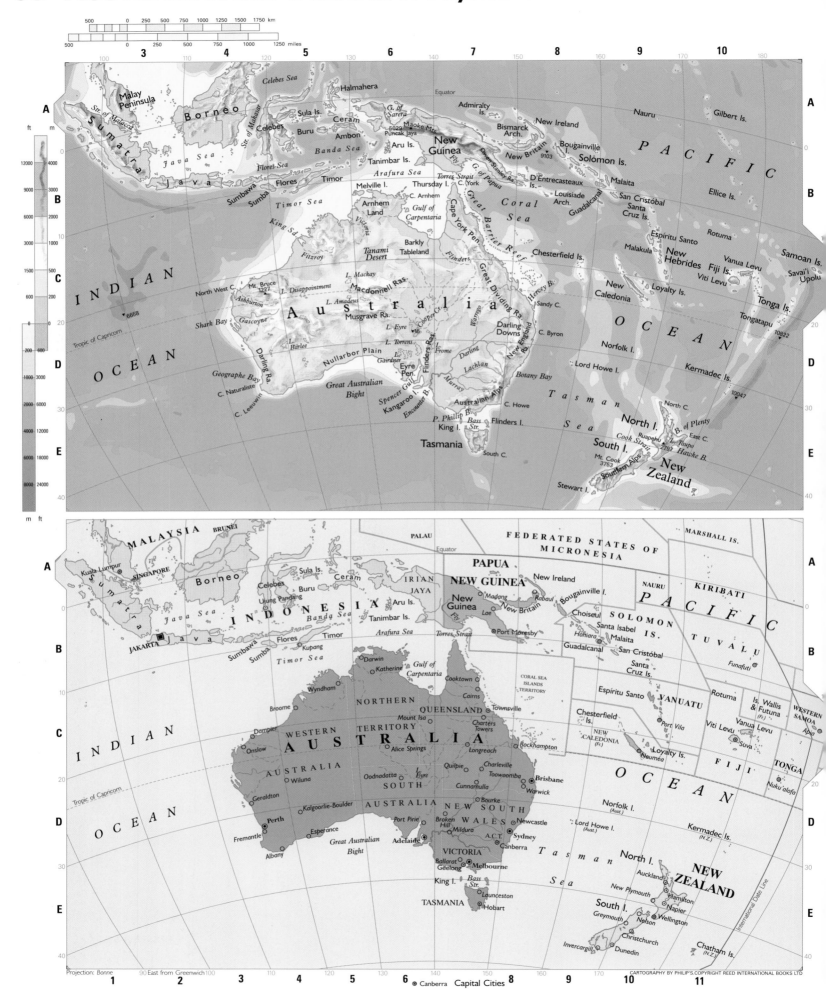

● Canberra   Capital Cities

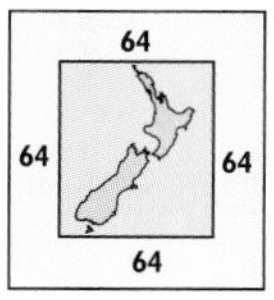

64

64   64

64

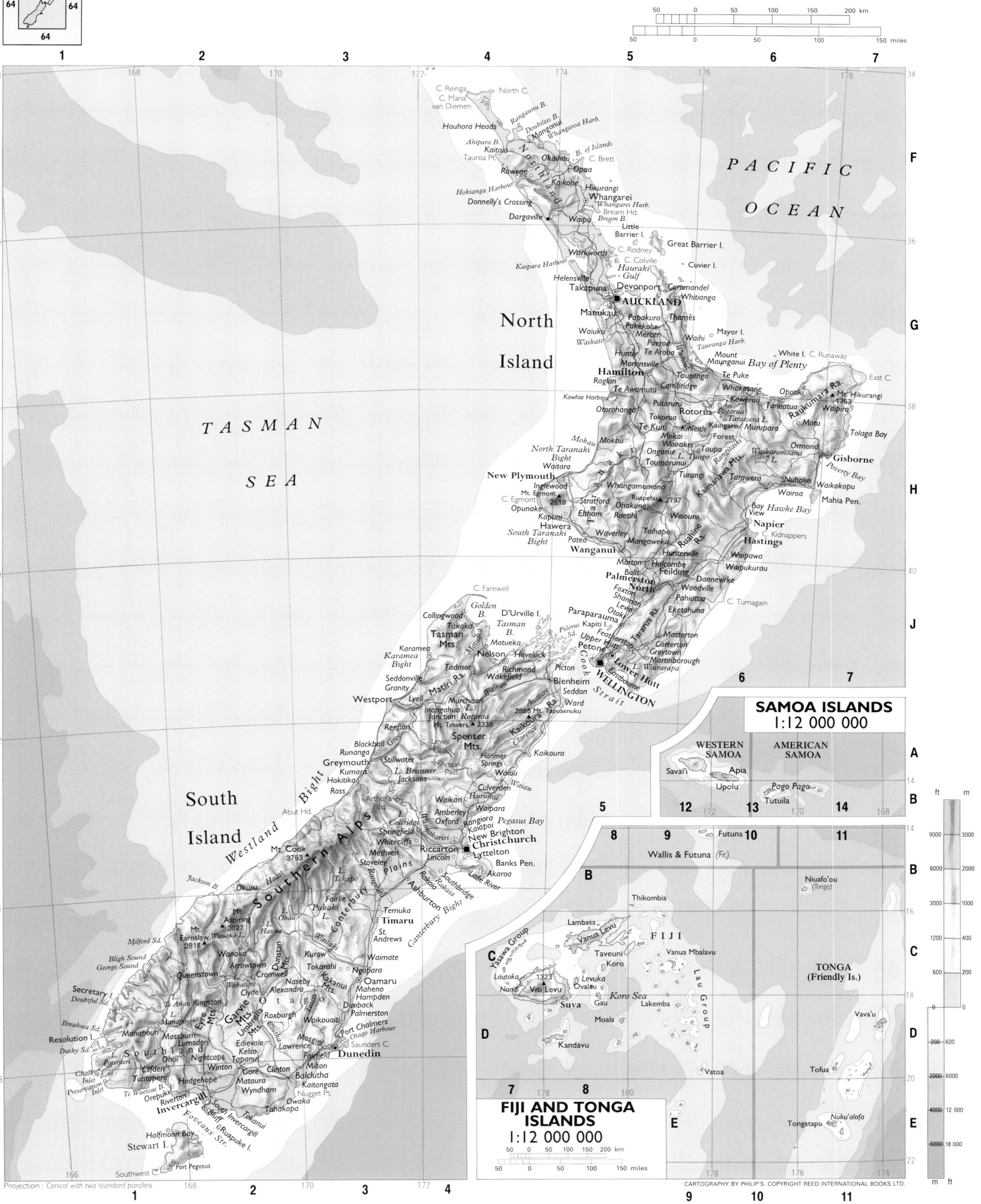

50   0   50   100   150   200 km
50   0   50   100   150 miles

1   2   3   4   5   6   7

34   34
168   170   172   174   176   178

F   C. Reinga   North C.   **F**
C. Maria van Diemen
Rangaunu B.
Houhora Heads   Doubtless B.
Mangonui
Ahipara B.   Whangaroa Harb.
Kaitaia   Okaihau   B. of Islands
Tauroa Pt.   Opua
Rawene   Kaikohe   C. Brett
Hokianga Harbour   Hikurangi
Donnelly's Crossing   Whangarei
Whangarei Harb.
Dargaville   Waipu   Bream Hd.
Bream B.

P A C I F I C

O C E A N

Little Barrier I.

G   Great Barrier I.   **G**
Kaipara Harbour   C. Rodney
Helensville   C. Colville   Cuvier I.
Hauraki   Coromandel
North   Gulf   Whitianga
Takapuna   Devonport
Island   Manukau   **AUCKLAND**
Papakura   Thames
Waiuku   Pukekohe   Waihi   Mayor I.
Waikato   Mercer   Tauranga Harb.
Huntly   Paeroa   White I.   C. Runaway
Morrinsville   Mount
Raglan   Te Aroha   Maunganui   *Bay of Plenty*   East C.
Hamilton   Tauranga
Cambridge   Te Puke
Kawhia Harbour   Te Awamutu   Whakatane
Kawerau   Opotiki   Raukumara Ra.   Mt. Hikurangi
1763
Otorohanga   Putaruru   Taneatua   Waipiro
Rotorua   Rotorua L.   Murupara
38   Mokau   Te Kuiti   Kinleith   Kaingaroa   Tarawera L.   Tolaga Bay   38
Mokai   Waikaremoana   Motu
North Taranaki   Mokau   Waraker   Forest
Bight   Ongarue   L. Taupo   Waikaremoana L.   Ormond
Waitara   Taumarunui   Taupo   Ruatahuna Mts.   Gisborne
New Plymouth   Turangi   Poverty Bay
Inglewood   Whangamomona   Kaimanawa Mts.   Nuhaka   Waikokopu
Mt. Egmont   Ruapehu   Tarawera   Mahia Pen.
H   C. Egmont   2518   Stratford   2797   Bay   Hawke Bay   **H**
Opunake   Ohakune   Waiouru   View
Kapuni   Eltham   Raetihi   **Napier**
Hawera   Waioru   C. Kidnappers
Waverley   Taihape   Ruahine Ra.   **Hastings**
South Taranaki   Mangaweka   Waipawa
Bight   Patea   Hunterville   Waipukurau
Wanganui   Marton   Halcombe   Dannevirke
40   Bulls   Feilding   Woodville   40
Palmerston   Foxton   **North**   Pahiatua
Shannon   Eketahuna
Levin   Tararua Ra.
Otaki   C. Turnagain
J   C. Farewell   Paraparaumu   Kapiti I.   **J**
Golden   D'Urville I.   Masterton
B.   Tasman   Pelorus Sd.   Featherston   Carterton
Collingwood   Tasman   B.   Upper Hutt   Greytown
Takaka   Motueka   Cook   Petone   Martinborough
Tasman   Mts.   Havelock   Lower Hutt   Wairarapa
Karamea   Nelson   Picton   Eastbourne
Karamea   Richmond   **WELLINGTON**
Bight   Matiri Ra.   Wakefield   Blenheim   Strait
Seddonville   Seddon
Granity   Lyell   Murchison   Ward   6   7
Westport   Inangahua   Rotoroa   2885 Mt. Tapuaenuku
42   Junction   L. Rotoroa   42
Reefton   Mt. Travers   2338   Kaikoura
Blackball   Spenser   Clarence   **SAMOA ISLANDS**
Runanga   Mts.   1:12 000 000
Greymouth   Stillwater   Hanmer   Waiau   **A**   WESTERN   AMERICAN
Kumara   L. Brunner   Springs   SAMOA   SAMOA
Hokitika   Jacksons   Arthur's   Waiau   Savai'i   Apia
Ross   Pass   Culverden   Upolu   Pago Pago
South   Waikari   Hurunui   5   Tutuila   14
Abut Hd.   Amberley   Waipara   12   13
K   Island   Oxford   Pegasus Bay   **B**
Rangiora   8   9   Futuna   10   11
Westland   Coldridge   Kaiapoi   14
Springfield   New Brighton   Wallis & Futuna (Fr.)
Methven   **Christchurch**   **B**
Whitecliffs   Riccarton   Lyttelton   Niuafo'ou
Mt. Cook   Staveley   Lincoln   Banks Pen.   (Tonga)
3763   Rakaia   Akaroa   Thikombia
Southern Alps   Southbridge   Little River
L. Tekapo   Ashburton   Yasawa Group   Vanua Levu   FIJI
Jackson B.   Fairlie   Bight   Lambasa
44   Mt.   Pukaki   **C**   44
Aspiring   L.   Taveuni   Koro   Vanua Mbalavu
3027   Ohau   Temuka   Lautoka   1323   Levuka
Mt.   Geraldine   Nanai   Viti Levu   Ovalau   TONGA
Earnslaw   2818   **Timaru**   Koro Sea   (Friendly Is.)
Milford Sd.   Wanaka   Waitaki   St. Andrews   Suva   Gau   Lakemba   Vava'u
Bligh Sound   Arrowtown   Kurow   Waimate   Moala   Lau
George Sound   Cromwell   Tokarahi   Kandavu   Group   Vatoa
Queenstown   Ngapara   Tofua
L   Dunstan Mts.   Oamaru   **D**
Secretary I.   Clyde   Naseby   Maheno
Doubtful Sd.   Te Anau   Kingston   Alexandra   Dunback   Palmerston
L.   Wakatipu   Roxburgh   7   8
Garvie   Waikouaiti   176   174
Manapouri   Mts.   Port Chalmers   **FIJI AND TONGA**
Breaksea Sd.   Mossburn   Edievale   Mosgiel   Saunders C.   **ISLANDS**
Resolution I.   Manapouri   Lumsden   Kelso   Fairfield   **Dunedin**   1:12 000 000
Dusky Sd.   Eyre   Ohai   Milton   50   0   50   100   150   200 km
Chalky   Nightcaps   Lawrence   Balclutha   50   0   50   100   150 miles
Inlet   Clifden   Winton   Gore   Kaitangata
Preservation   Tuatapere   Mataura   Owaka   Nuku'alofa
Inlet   Te Waewae B.   Hedgehope   Wyndham   Tongatapu
Orepuki   Riverton   Tokanui
M   Clinton   **M**
Invercargill
Bluff   Invercargill
Ruapuke I.   Foveaux Str.
Halfmoon Bay
Stewart I.   Port Pegasus
Southwest C.

166   168   170   172   174
1   2   3   4

ft   m
9000   3000
6000   2000
3000   1000
1200   400
600   200
0   0
200   600
2000   6000
4000   12 000
6000   18 000
m   ft

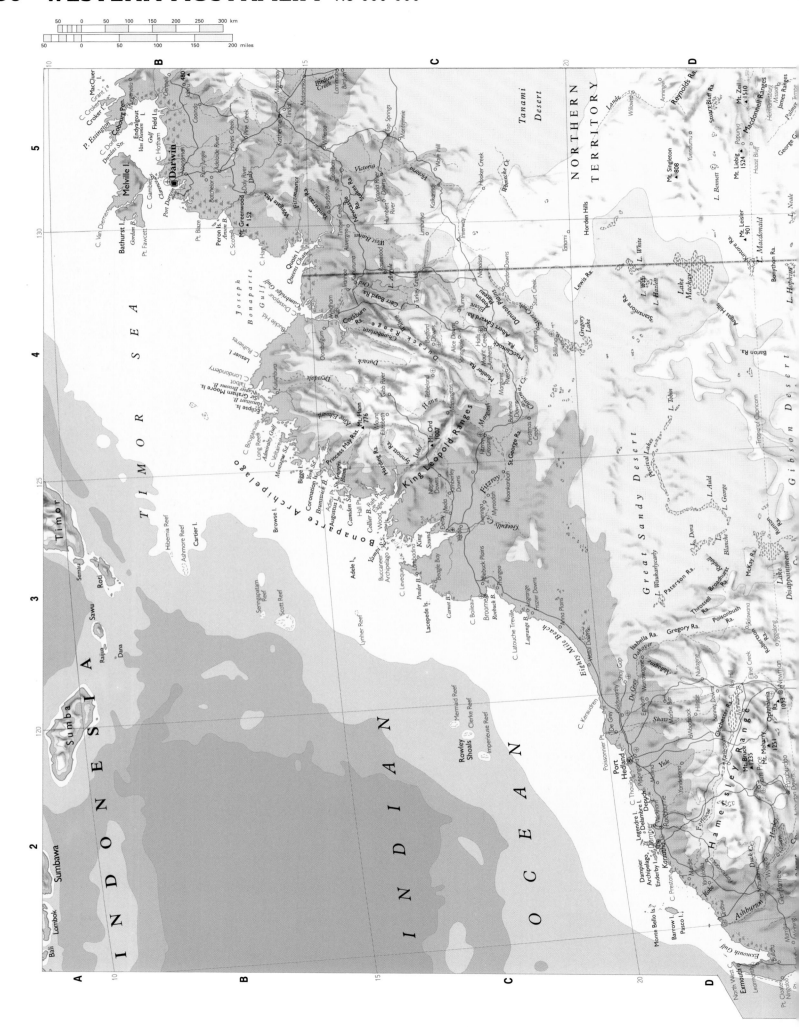

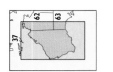

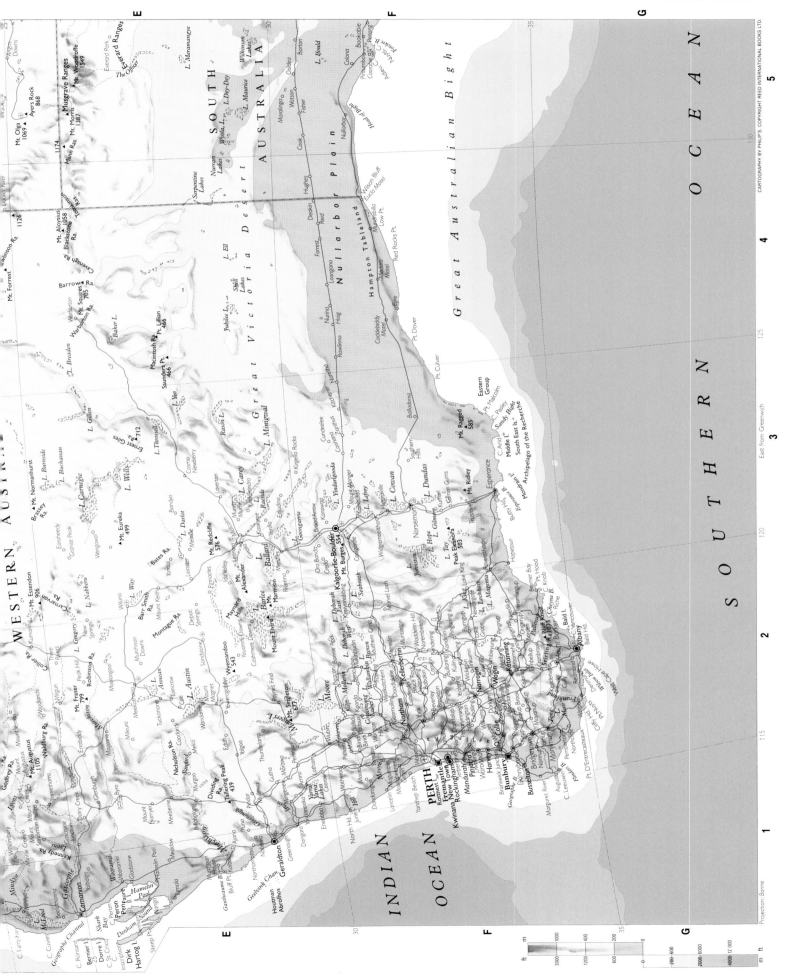

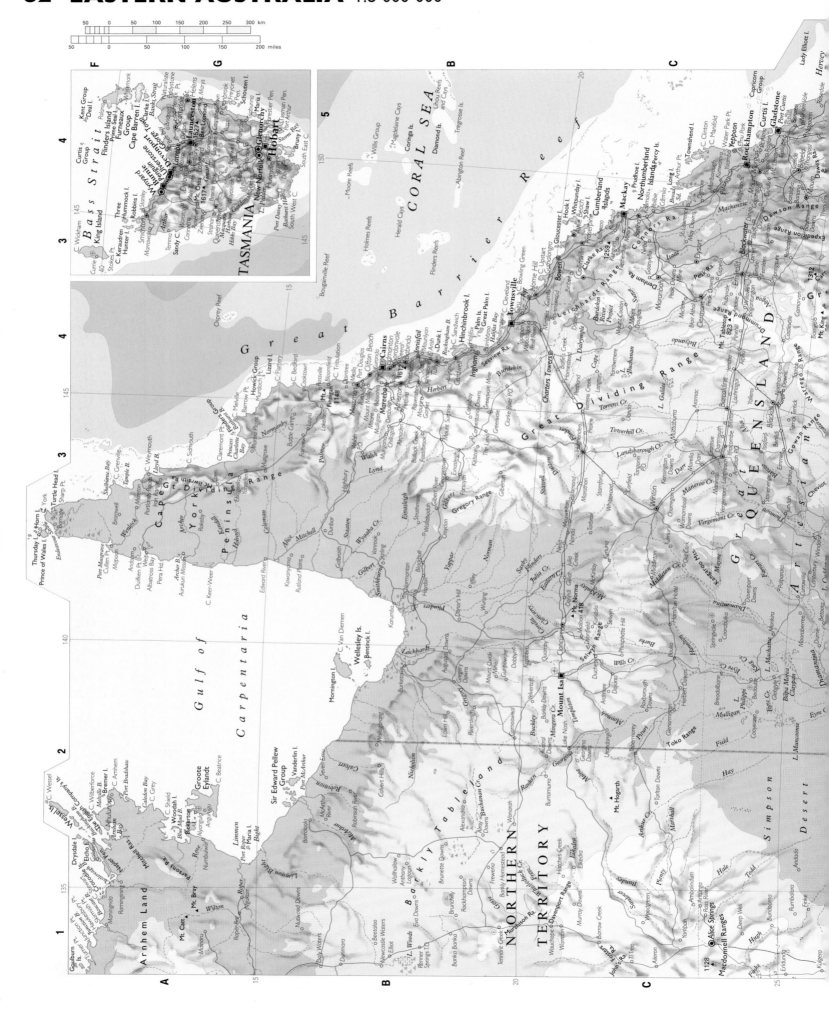

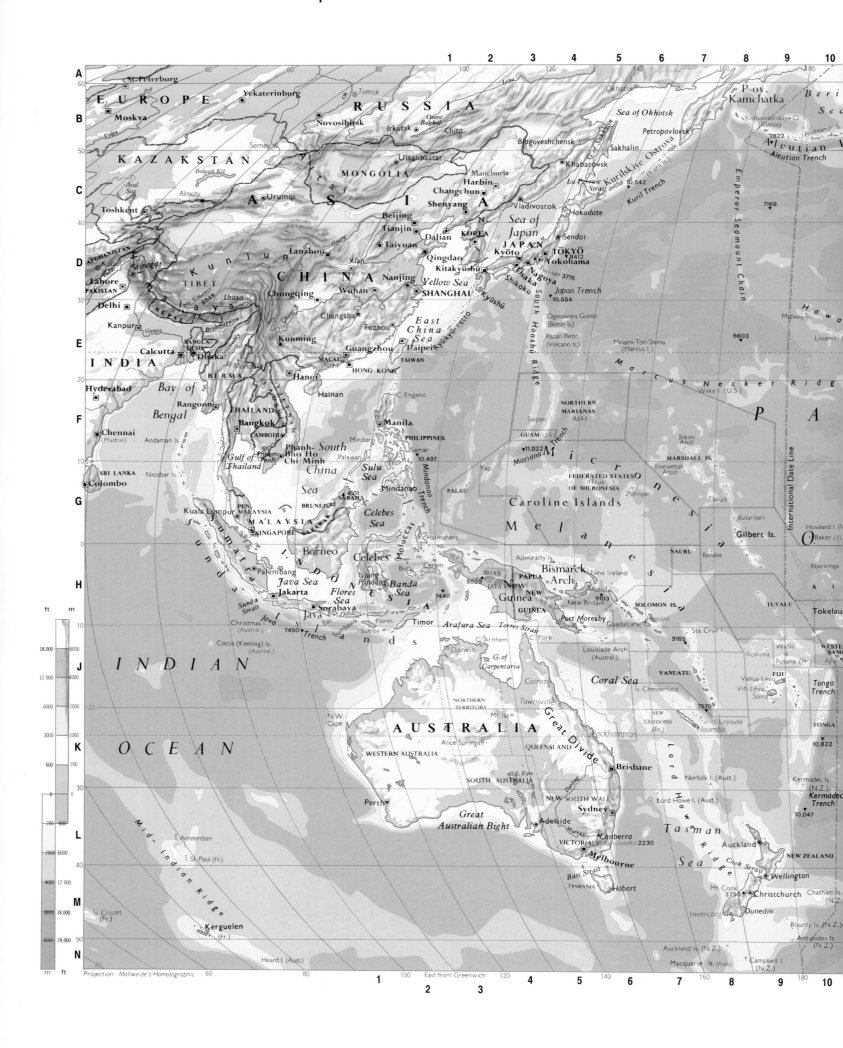

ALASKA (U.S.)

Bristol Bay

Gulf of Alaska

Prince of Wales I.
Prince Rupert
Queen Charlotte Is.
Kitimat
Juneau

GREENLAND

C. Farewell

NORTH AMERICA

CANADA

Hudson
Bay

Edmonton

L. Winnipeg

Labrador

Newfoundland

NORTH

Vancouver
Vancouver I.
Victoria
Seattle
Calgary
Regina
Winnipeg

Portland

Montréal
Ottawa
Toronto
Quebec
St. Lawrence
Pr. Edward I.
Saint John
C. Sable

Rocky Mountains

Boise
Snake

Salt Lake
City

L. Superior
L. Huron
L. Michigan
L. Ontario
L. Erie
Buffalo
Detroit
Pittsburgh
Boston
NEW YORK
Philadelphia
Baltimore
Washington

San Francisco
4418

Denver
Kansas
City
St. Louis

Cincinnati

UNITED STATES

Oklahoma

Memphis

Appalachian Mts.

Atlanta

C. Hatteras

Bermuda (U.K.)

ATLANTIC

Los Angeles
San Diego

Dallas

Mississippi

Jacksonville

Ciudad
Juárez

6225
I. Guadalupe
(Mexico)

Sierra Madre

M E X I C O

San Antonio
Houston
New
Orleans

Gulf of Mexico Miami

OCEAN

Tropic of Cancer

Hawaiian Is.
(U.S.)

Honolulu
Oahu

4205
Hawaii

Is. Revilla Gigedo
(Mexico)

Guadalajara

Gulf of California

Monterrey

La Habana

Florida Strait

BAHAMAS

CUBA

Yucatan Channel
Mérida

México
5700
Puebla
Acapulco

Yucatan

BELIZE

7680
JAMAICA
Kingston

West Indies
Hispaniola
DOM.
REP.
HAITI
9200

PUERTO
RICO
(U.S.)

Leeward
Is.

PACIFIC

I F I C

Christmas Island Ridge

Palmyra Is. (U.S.)

Teraina
P. Tabuaeran
Kiritimati

Jarvis I.
(U.S.)

O C E A N

Equator

GUATEMALA
Guatemala
San Salvador
EL SALVADOR

HONDURAS

NICARAGUA
Managua

**CENTRAL
AMERICA**

COSTA RICA
Colón
PANAMA
Panama Canal

San José
Barranquilla

Caribbean Sea

BARBADOS

Windward
Is.
TRINIDAD &
TOBAGO

Maracaibo
Caracas
Orinoco
VENEZUELA

I. Clipperton (Fr.)

I. del Coco
(Costa Rica)

I. de Malpelo
(Colombia)

Medellín
Bogotá
Cali
COLOMBIA

KIRIBATI

Malden I.

Starbuck I.

Galápagos
(Ecuador)

Guayaquil

Quito
ECUADOR

Iquitos

Manaus

Amazonas

BRAZIL

Îs. Marquises

C. Pariñas

6369

Trujillo

SOUTH

Tongareva
Penrhyn Is.
Manihiki
Suwarrow Is.

Vostok
I.
Caroline I.
Flint I.

Îs. de la
Société
Îs. Tuamotu

PERU
Lima

AMERICA

Cuzco

Cook
Islands
(N.Z.)

Tahiti
FRENCH POLYNESIA

Manuae

Tuamotu Ridge

Arequipa

Titicaca
Illampu & Ancohuma
6550
La Paz
BOLIVIA

Austral

Rarotonga

6866
Peru-
Iquique
Chile

Seamount Chain

Îs. Tubuai
(Îs. Australes)

Rapa

Pitcairn I. (U.K.)

Ducie I.
(U.K.)

East Pacific Ridge

Tropic of Capricorn

8050
Antofagasta
Trench

PARAGUAY

Asunción

I. de Pascua
(Easter I.)
(Chile)

Sala-y-Gomez
(Chile)

San Félix (Chile)

San Ambrosio (Chile)

Tucumán

Pto. Alegre

Pacific-Antarctic Ridge

Arch. de Juan Fernández
(Chile)

Valparaíso
Santiago

6960
Córdoba
Rosario

URUGUAY
Montevideo

Andes

Río de la Plata

Chile Rise

Concepción
ARGENTINA

SOUTH

Patagonia

ATLANTIC

OCEAN

6212

Falkland Is. (U.K.)

Punta Arenas
Str. of Magellan
Tierra del Fuego
C. Horn

South Georgia (U.K.)

West from Greenwich

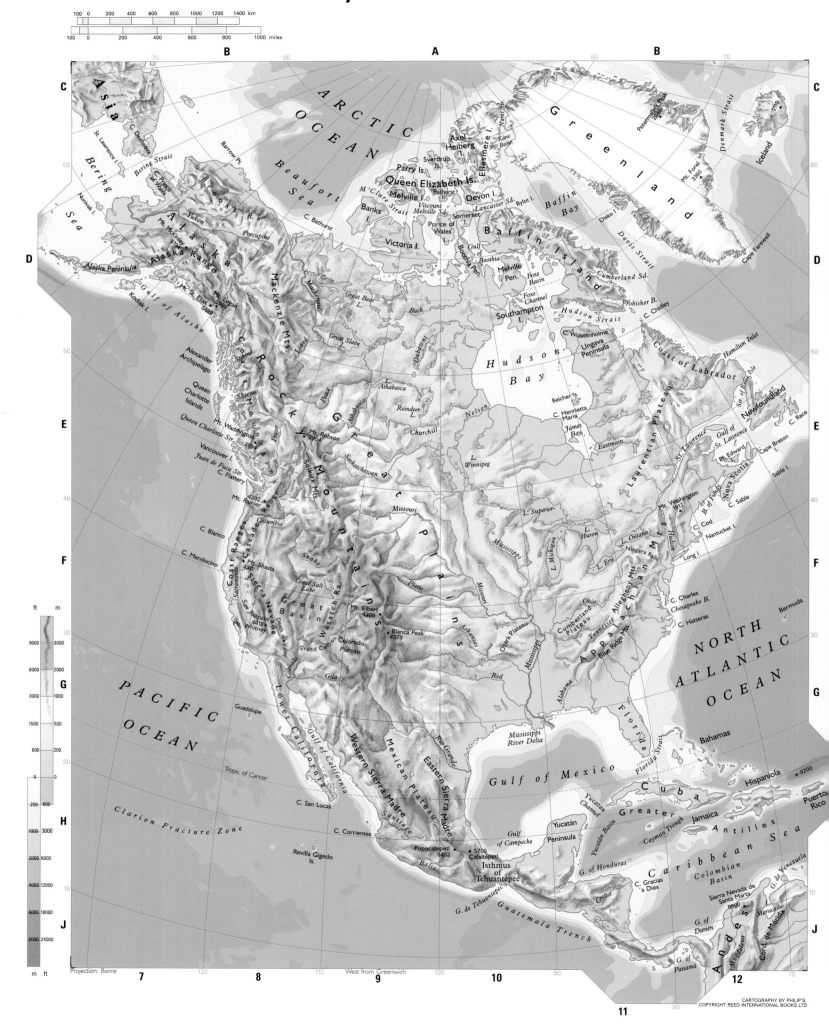

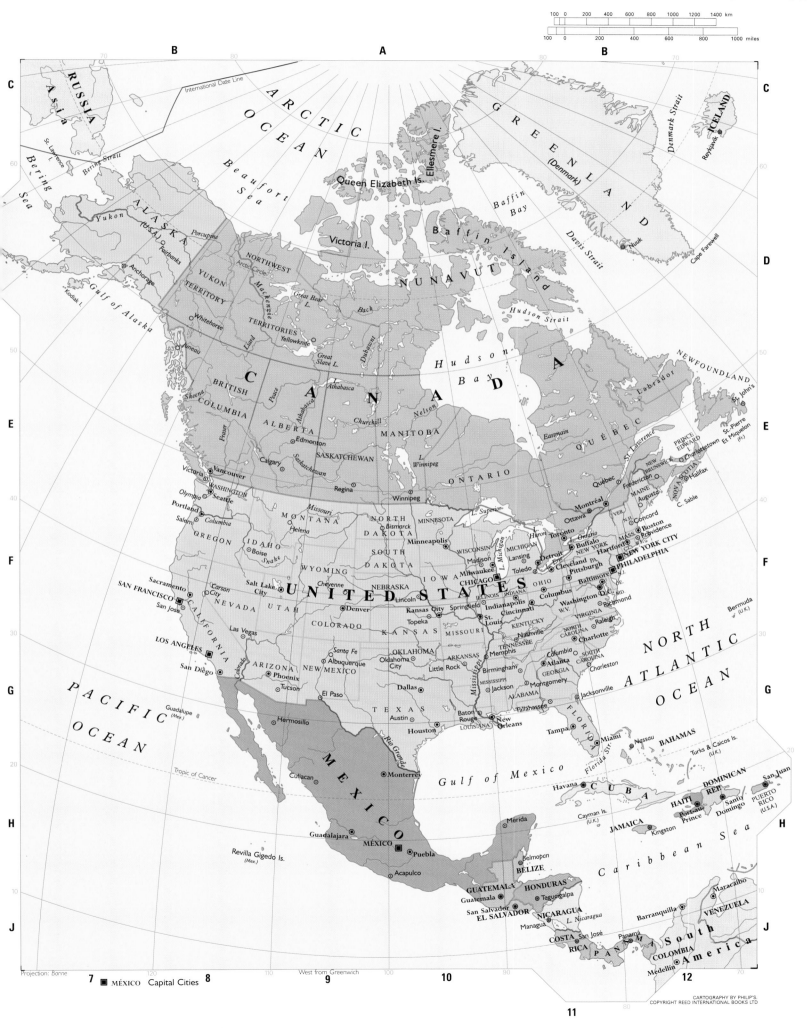

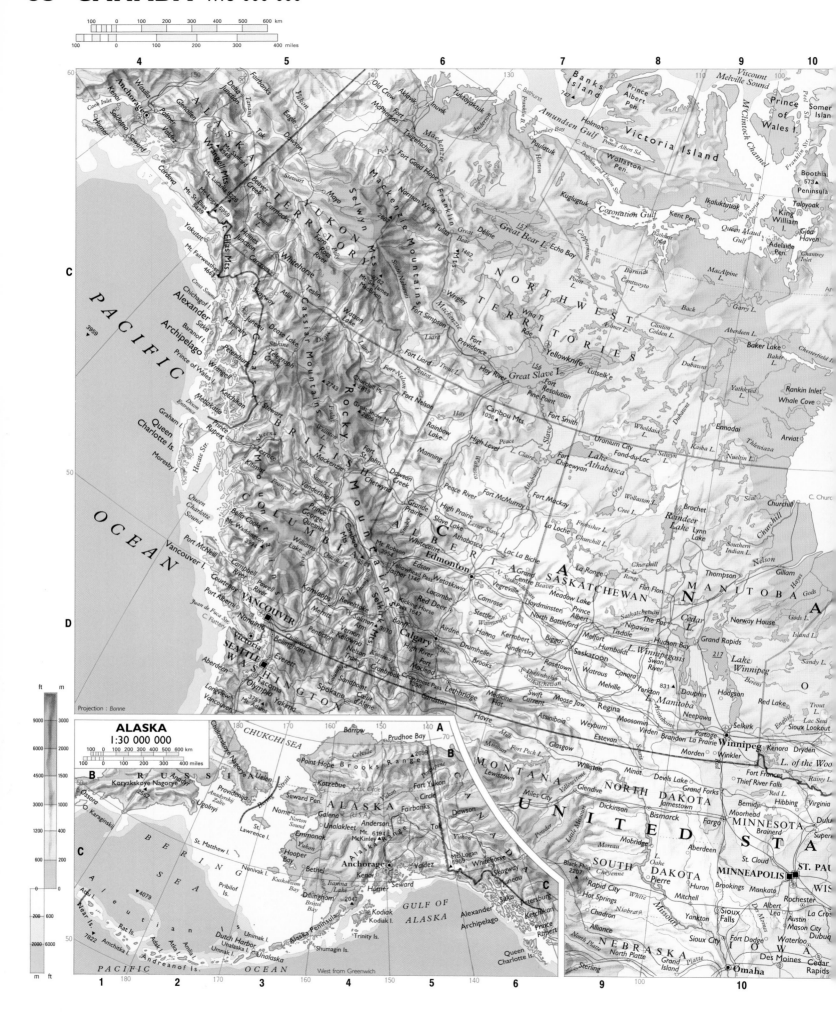

ALASKA 1:30 000 000

Projection : Bonne

West from Greenwich

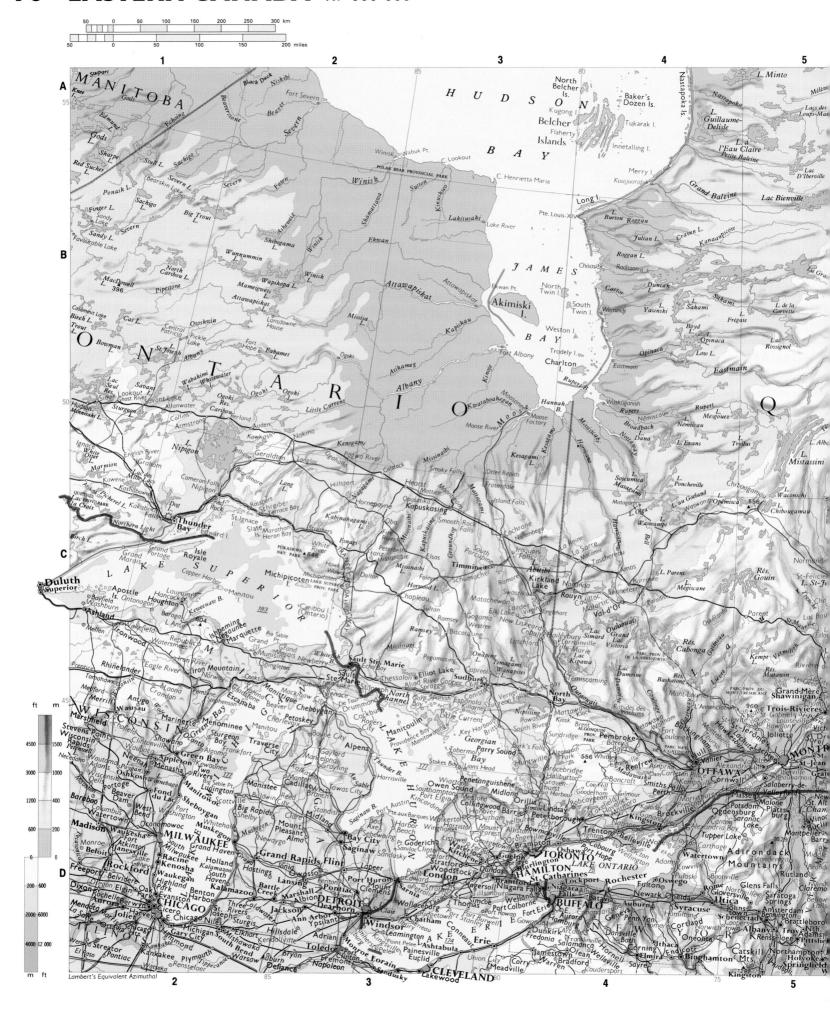

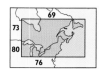

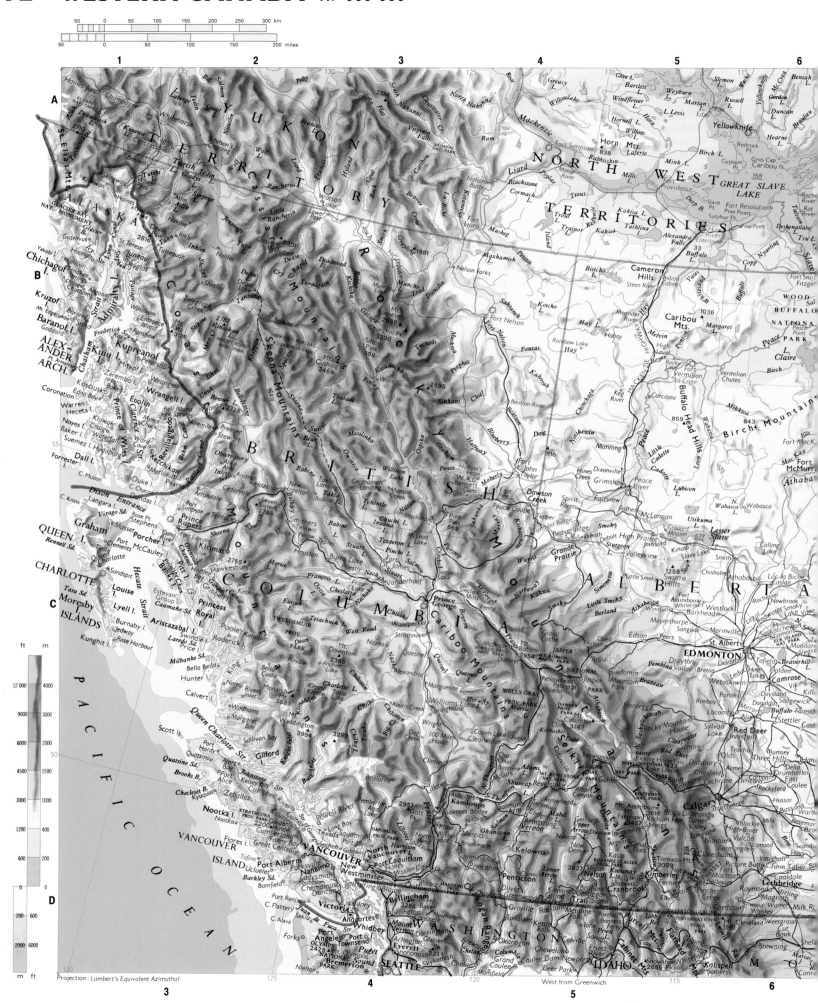

Projection: Lambert's Equivalent Azimuthal

West from Greenwich

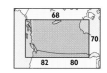

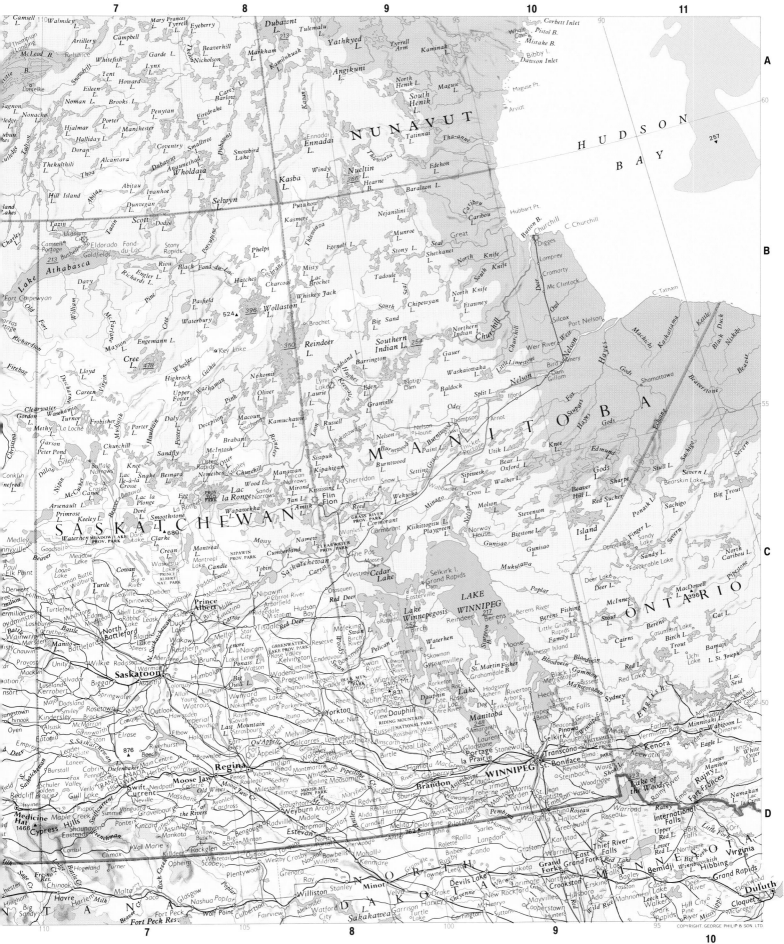

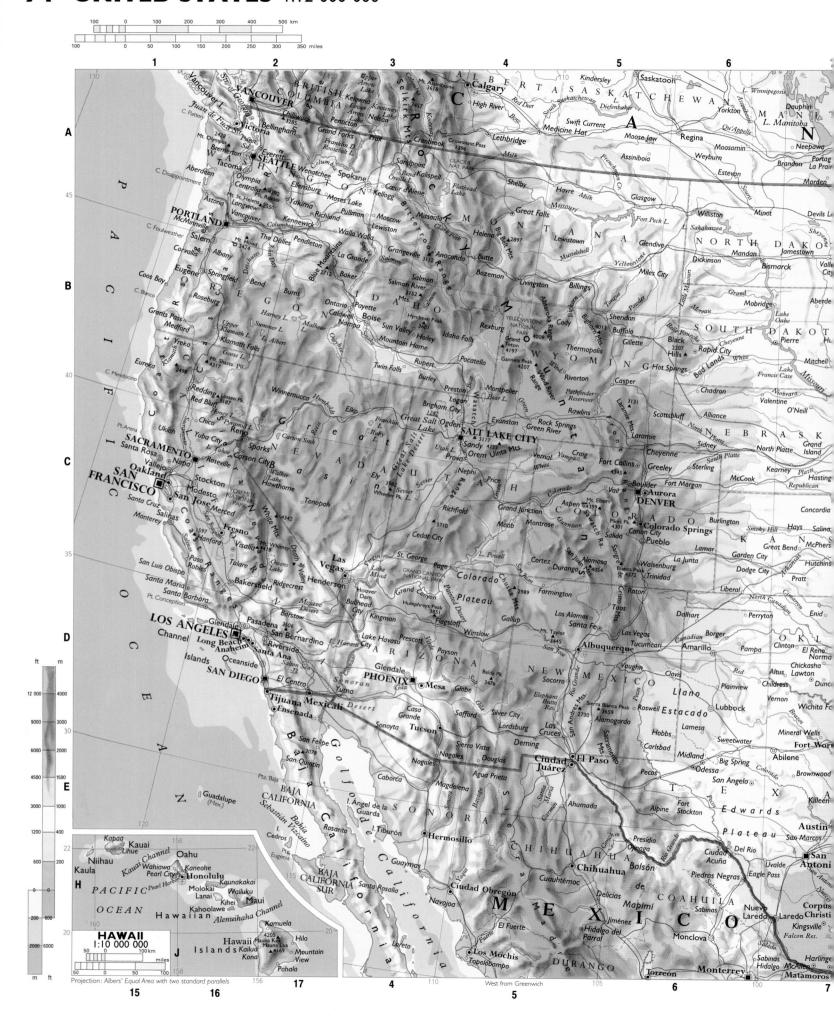

Continuation Eastwards
On same scale.

NEW HAMPSHIRE

MAINE

ATLANTIC OCEAN

BAHAMAS

GULF OF MEXICO

TENNESSEE

NORTH CAROLINA

SOUTH CAROLINA

GEORGIA

ALABAMA

MISSISSIPPI

FLORIDA

KENTUCKY

Projection: Alber's Equal Area with two standard parallels

West from Greenwich

COPYRIGHT GEORGE PHILIP & SON LTD

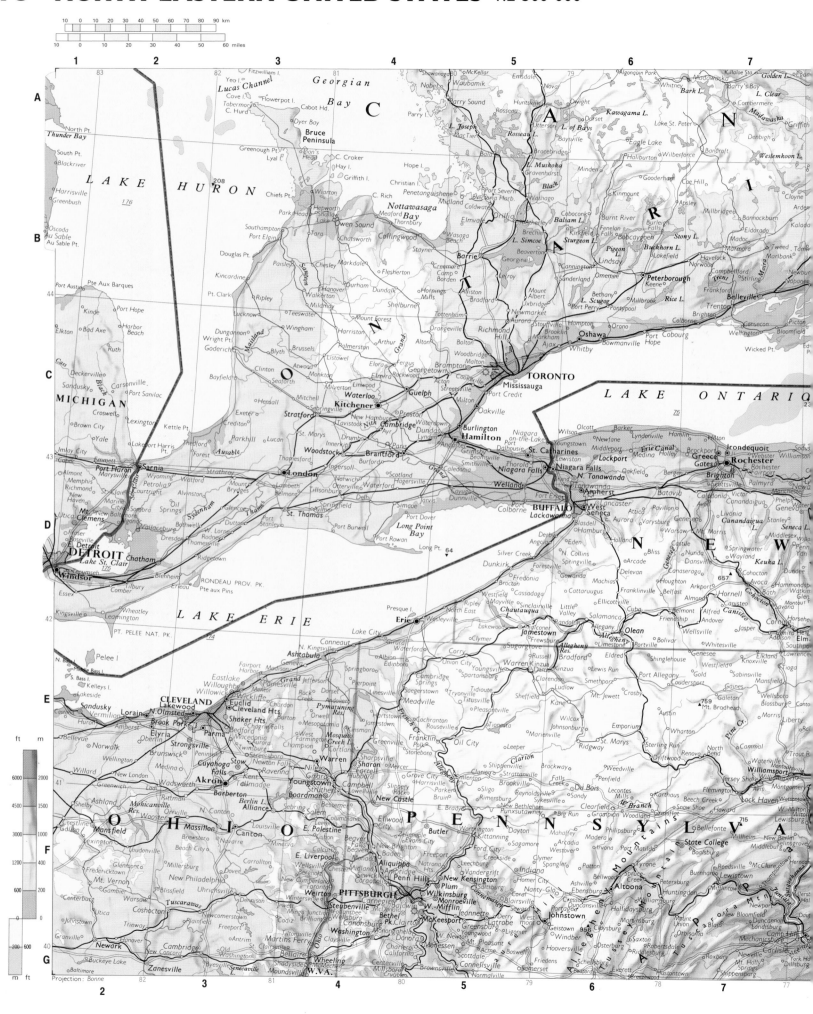

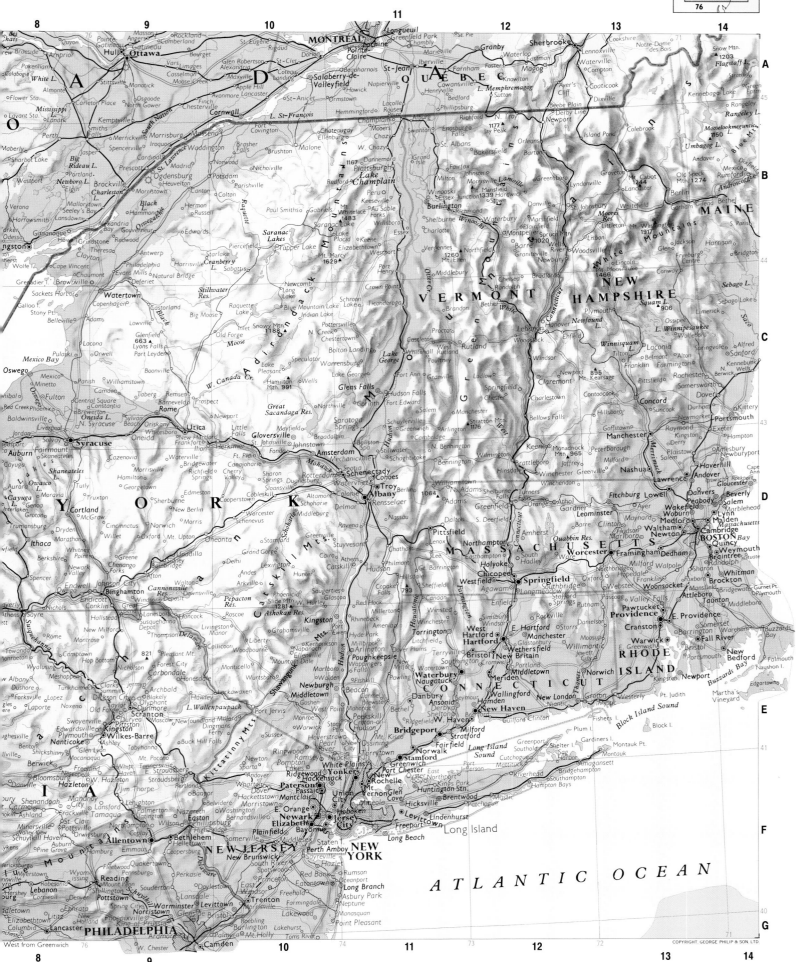

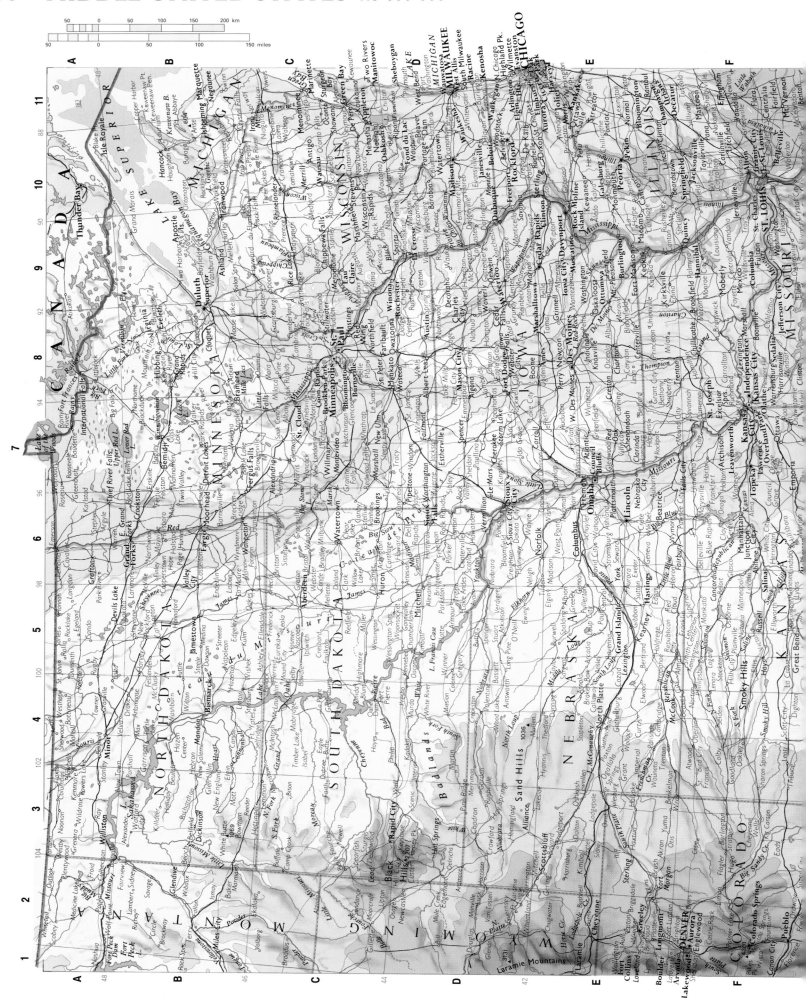

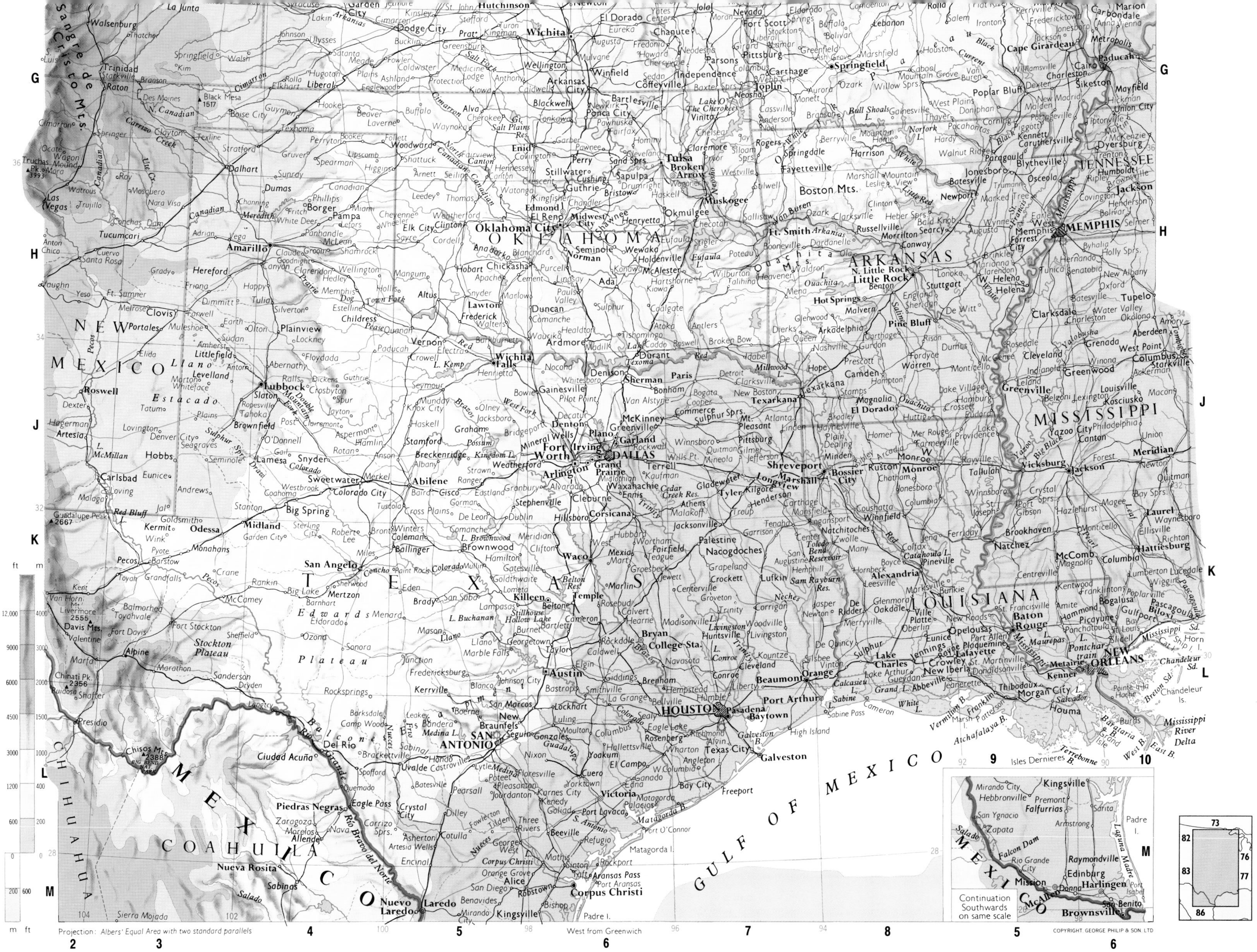
NEW MEXICO
TEXAS
OKLAHOMA
ARKANSAS
LOUISIANA
MISSISSIPPI
TENNESSEE
MEXICO
COAHUILA
CHIHUAHUA
GULF OF MEXICO
Sangre de Cristo Mts.
Llano Estacado
Edwards Plateau
Stockton Plateau
Boston Mts.
Ouachita Mts.
Oklahoma City
Tulsa
Wichita
Amarillo
Lubbock
Dallas
Fort Worth
Austin
San Antonio
Houston
Corpus Christi
El Paso
Shreveport
Little Rock
Memphis
Jackson
Baton Rouge
New Orleans
Mobile
Continuation Southwards on same scale
Projection: Albers' Equal Area with two standard parallels
West from Greenwich
COPYRIGHT GEORGE PHILIP & SON, LTD

West from Greenwich

Projection: Albers' Equal Area with two standard parallels

WESTERN WASHINGTON
REGION
On same scale

COPYRIGHT GEORGE PHILIP & SON LTD

Projection: Bonne

West from Greenwich

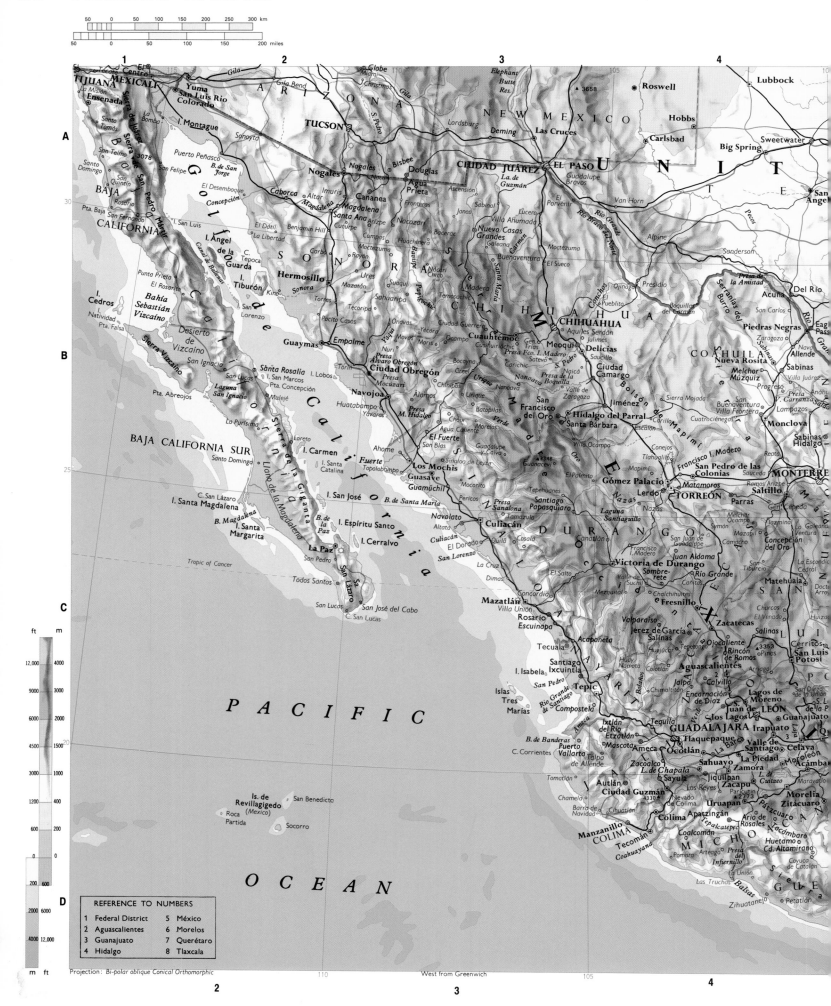

REFERENCE TO NUMBERS

1	Federal District	5	México
2	Aguascalientes	6	Morelos
3	Guanajuato	7	Querétaro
4	Hidalgo	8	Tlaxcala

Projection: Bi-polar oblique Conical Orthomorphic

West from Greenwich

5 6 7 8

GULF OF MEXICO

Golfo de Campeche

Wichita Falls
Denison
Sherman
Paris
Texarkana
Texarkana
Camden
Hope
Greenville
Greenville
Tuscaloosa
Opelika
Columbus
McRae
Ocmulgee

Denton
Greenville
El Dorado
ARKANSAS
MISSISSIPPI
Selma
Phenix City
Americus
Cordele
Tifton

FORT WORTH
DALLAS
Marshall
Monroe
Vicksburg
Meridian
Montgomery
Troy
ALABAMA
Albany
GEORGIA
Waycross

Cleburne
Longview
Tyler
Shreveport
Tallulah
Jackson
Natchez
Laurel
Dothan
Jim Woodruff Res.
Valdosta

Brownwood
Hillsboro
Corsicana
Palestine
Nacogdoches
Alexandria
McComb
Hattiesburg
Flomaton
Chattahoochee
Tallahassee
Lake City

Waco
Lufkin
Sam Rayburn Res.
Bogalusa
Biloxi
Pensacola
Panama City
Apalachee Bay
Suwannee
FLORIDA

Temple
Huntsville
Bryan
Beaumont
Lake Charles
Lafayette
Baton Rouge
Hammond
Gulfport
MOBILE
C. San Blas

Austin
HOUSTON
Port Arthur
NEW ORLEANS
Breton Sound
Mississippi Delta
Clearwater

SAN ANTONIO
Victoria
Galveston
Rosenberg
Atchafalaya Bay
Terrebonne B.

Alice
Corpus Christi

Laredo
Kingsville
Nuevo Laredo
Zapata

Camargo
McAllen
Harlingen
Brownsville
Laguna Madre

M.R. Reynosa
Matamoros
Valle Hermoso
China
Santa Teresa
Laguna Madre

Montemorelos
Méndez
San Fernando

Linares
Villagrán

Ciudad Victoria
La Pesca
Soto la Marina
CUBA
Guane
La Fé

Ciudad Mante
Áldama
Pta. Jerez
C. San Antonio
C. Corrientes

Ciudad Madero
Altamira
Isla Desterrada
Isla Pérez
Pta. Yalkubul
Río Lagartos
C. Catoche
Cancún
Canal de Yucatán

Tampico
Pánuco
Dzilam de Bravo
El Cuyo
Pto. Juárez

Ciudad de Valles
Laguna de Tamiahua
Progreso
Motul
Temax
Tizimín
Espita
Puerto Morelos

Tamazunchale
Tantoyuca
C. Rojo
Mérida
Izamal
YUCATÁN
Valladolid
Isla Cozumel
Cozumel

Tuxpan
Maxcanú
Sotuta

Poza Rica
Papantla
Ticul
Tekax
Peto
Vigía Chico
B. de la Ascensión

Huauchinango
Uxmal
Tenabo
Bolonchenticul
B. del Espíritu Santo

Pachuca
Tulancingo
Teziutlán
Campeche
Hopelchén
QUINTANA ROO

Jalapa Enríquez
Champotón
Chenkán
Bacalar
Chetumal
Banco Chinchorro

MÉXICO
PUEBLA
Coatepec
Veracruz Llave
Ciudad del Carmen
Laguna de Términos
Matamoros
B. de Chetumal

Amecameca
Orizaba
Córdoba
Alvarado
San Andrés Tuxtla
Frontera
Pital
Corozal
Orange Walk
Ambergris Cay

Cuernavaca
Tehuacán
Cosamaloapan
Coatzacoalcos
Paraíso
Palizada
CAMPECHE
Concepción
Río Hondo
Turneffe Is.

Iguala
Acatlán
Acayucan
Minatitlán
La Venta
Cárdenas
TABASCO
Villahermosa
Tenosique
Uaxactún
Tikal
Belize City
Belmopan
BELIZE
Islas de la Bahía

Chilapa
Chilpancingo
Oaxaca
OAXACA
Tuxtla Gutiérrez
San Cristóbal de las Casas
CHIAPAS
Comitán
L. Petén Itzá
Flores
Benque Viejo
Dangriga
Maya Mts.
Golfo de Honduras
Roatán
Puerto Castilla

Acapulco
Ocotlán
Ixtepec
Juchitán
Arriaga
Tonalá
San Luis
Punta Gorda
Livingston
Puerto Barrios
Tela
La Ceiba

Tehuantepec
Salina Cruz
Golfo de Tehuantepec
Mar Muerto
GUATEMALA
Cobán
Zacapa
HONDURAS

Tapachula
Coatepeque
Quez.
GUATEMALA
Huehuetenango
Chiquimula
Tegucigalpa

COPYRIGHT, GEORGE PHILIP & SON, LTD.

5 6 7

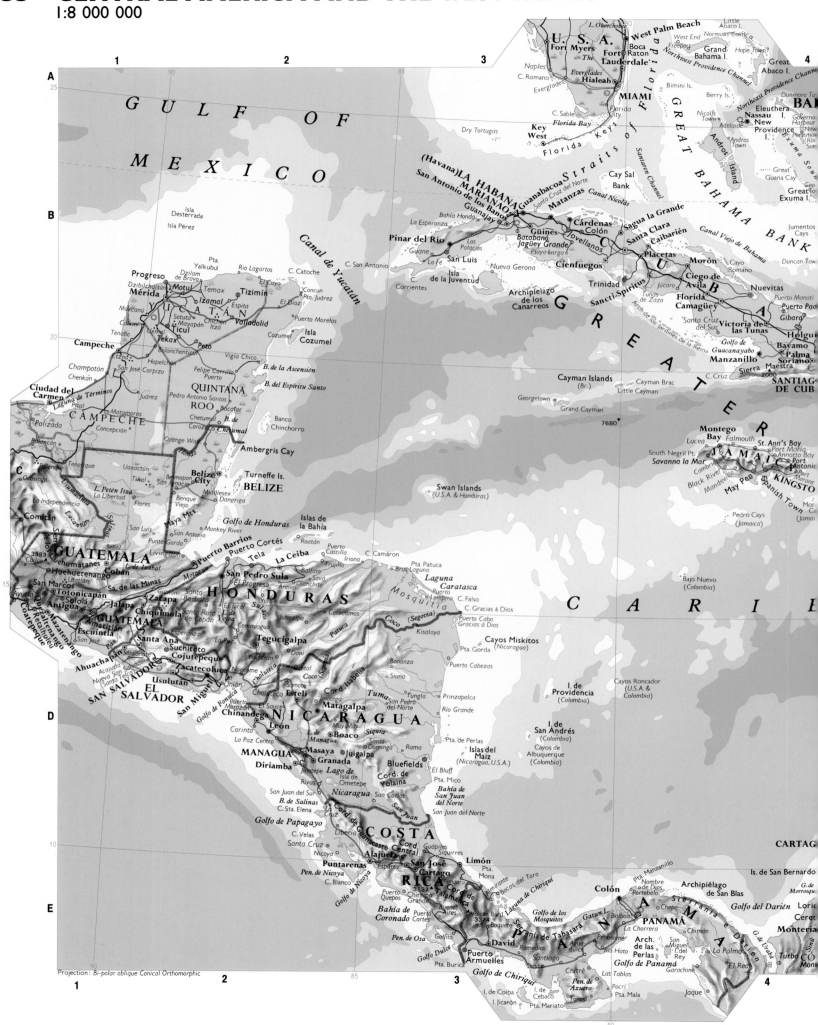

GULF OF MEXICO

U.S.A.
Fort Myers
Fort Lauderdale
West Palm Beach
Boca Raton
MIAMI
Hialeah
Everglades
Naples
C. Romano
C. Sable
Florida Bay
Dry Tortugas
Key West
Florida Keys

Little Abaco I.
Northwest Providence Channel
Freeport
Grand Bahama I.
Hope Town
Great Abaco I.
Eleuthera
Nassau
New Providence
Andros Island
Andros Town

BAHAMA BANK
GREAT

(Havana) LA HABANA
San Antonio de los Baños
Guanabacoa
Matanzas
Cárdenas
Colón
Sagua la Grande
Santa Clara
Caibarién
MARIANAO
Guanajay
Bahía Honda
La Esperanza
Pinar del Río
Los Palacios
Güines
Jovellanos
Batabanó
Jagüey Grande
Playa Larga
Cienfuegos
Placetas
Morón
Cayo Romano
Ciego de Ávila
Sancti-Spíritus
Trinidad
CUBA
GREATER
Camagüey
Florida
Nuevitas
Puerto Padre
Gibara
Holguín
Bayamo
Manzanillo
Palma Soriano
SANTIAGO DE CUB
Sierra Maestra

Guane
La Fé
San Luis
Nueva Gerona
Isla de la Juventud
Archipiélago de los Canarreos
Júcaro
Tunas de Zaza
Arch. de los Jardines de la Reina
Golfo de Guacanayabo
Santa Cruz del Sur

Cay Sal Bank

Cayman Islands (Br.)
Georgetown
Grand Cayman
Cayman Brac
Little Cayman
C. Cruz

7680

JAMAICA
Montego Bay
Lucea
Falmouth
St. Ann's Bay
Savanna la Mar
Black River
Mandeville
May Pen
Spanish Town
KINGSTON

Pedro Cays (Jamaica)

CARIBE

Swan Islands (U.S.A. & Honduras)

Isla Desterrada
Isla Pérez
Canal de Yucatán

Progreso
Dzilam de Bravo
Mérida
Motul
Temax
Tizimín
Izamal
Espita
Chichén Itzá
Valladolid
Cancún
Pto. Juárez
Puerto Morelos
Isla Cozumel
YUCATÁN
Campeche
QUINTANA ROO
CAMPECHE
Champotón
Ciudad del Carmen
Chetumal
Ambergris Cay
Turneffe Is.
BELIZE
Belize City
BELIZE
Dangriga

GUATEMALA
HONDURAS
San Pedro Sula
La Ceiba
Tela
Puerto Cortés
Puerto Barrios
Islas de la Bahía
Roatán
Mosquitia
Laguna Caratasca
C. Falso
C. Gracias á Dios
Puerto Cabo Gracias á Dios
Tegucigalpa
Comayagua
Juticalpa
Catacamas
Cayos Miskitos (Nicaragua)
Pta. Gorda
Puerto Cabezas

EL SALVADOR
SAN SALVADOR
NICARAGUA
Estelí
Matagalpa
Prinzapolca
Río Grande
Cord. Isabelia
MANAGUA
Masaya
Granada
Juigalpa
Boaco
Bluefields
El Bluff
Lago de Nicaragua
Pta. de Perlas
Islas del Maíz (Nicaragua, U.S.A.)
Cord. de Yolaina
San Carlos
San Juan del Norte
Bahía de San Juan del Norte

I. de Providencia (Colombia)
I. de San Andrés (Colombia)
Cayos de Albuquerque (Colombia)
Cayos Roncador (U.S.A. & Colombia)

COSTA RICA
San José
Cartago
Limón
Puntarenas
Pen. de Nicoya
Golfo de Nicoya
Alajuela
Golfo de Papagayo
Liberia

PANAMÁ
Colón
David
Golfo de Chiriquí
Golfo de Panamá
Archipiélago de San Blas
Golfo del Darién
Arch. de las Perlas

CARTAG

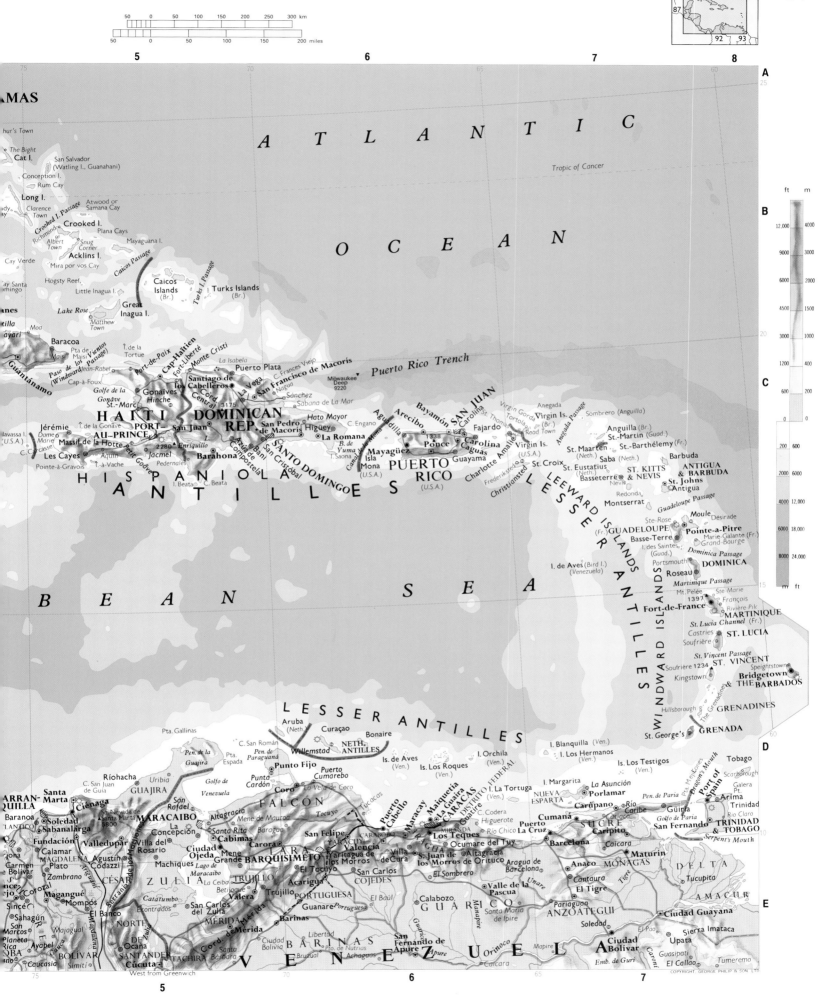

ft m

12,000 4000

9000 3000

6000 2000

4500 1500

3000 1000

1200 400

600 200

0 0

200 600

2000 6000

4000 12,000

6000 18,000

8000 24,000

m ft

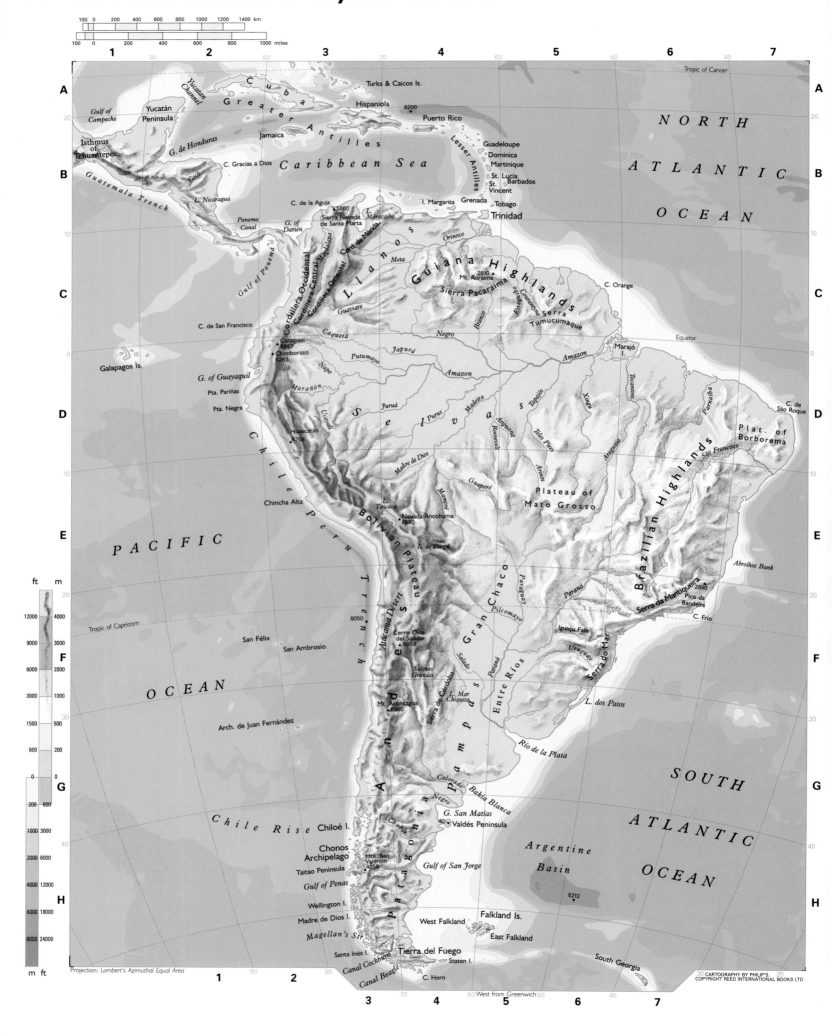

100 0 200 400 600 800 1000 1200 1400 km
100 0 200 400 600 800 1000 miles

1 2 3 4 5 6 7

ft m

12000 4000
9000 3000
6000 2000
3000 1000
1500 500
600 200
0 0
200 600
1000 3000
2000 6000
4000 12000
6000 18000
8000 24000

m ft

Projection: Lambert's Azimuthal Equal Area

Tropic of Cancer

A Yucatán Channel, Cuba, Greater Antilles, Turks & Caicos Is., Hispaniola, 9200

Gulf of Campeche, Yucatán Peninsula, Puerto Rico

B Isthmus of Tehuantepec, Guatemala Trench, G. de Honduras, C. Gracias a Dios, Coco, Jamaica, Caribbean Sea, Lesser Antilles, Guadeloupe, Dominica, Martinique, St. Lucia, St. Vincent, Barbados, Grenada, Tobago, Trinidad

L. Nicaragua, Panama Canal, G. of Darién, C. de la Aguja, 5800, Sierra Nevada de Santa Marta, Maracaibo, I. Margarita

NORTH ATLANTIC OCEAN

C Gulf of Panamá, Cordillera Occidental, Cordillera Central, Cordillera Oriental, Cord. de Mérida, Llanos, Orinoco, Meta, Guiana Highlands, Mt. Roraima 2810, Sierra Pacaraima, Caroni, Cuyuni, Serra Tumucumaque, C. Orange

C. de San Francisco, Guaviare, Caquetá, Negro, Branco, Equator

D Cotopaxi 5897, Chimborazo 6267, G. of Guayaquil, Pta. Pariñas, Pta. Negra, Napo, Marañón, Putumayo, Japurá, Amazon, Amazon, Tocantins, Marajó I., Xingu, Parnaíba, C. de São Roque, Plat. of Borborema

Selvas, Juruá, Purus, Madeira, Roosevelt, Araguaia, Tapajós, Tocantins, Teles Pires

Huascarán 6768, Ucayali, Madre de Dios, Mamoré, Guaporé, Plateau of Mato Grosso, São Francisco

E PACIFIC, Chile Peru Trench, Chincha Alta, L. Titicaca, Nevada Ancohuma 6550, Bolivian Plateau, L. de Poopó, Paraguay, Brazilian Highlands, Abrolhos Bank

F Tropic of Capricorn, San Félix, San Ambrosio, Atacama Desert, Cerro Ojos del Salado 6863, Salinas Grandes, Salado, Gran Chaco, Pilcomayo, Paraná, Iguaçu Falls, Serra da Mantiqueira 2890, Pico da Bandeira, C. Frio, Serra do Mar

OCEAN, 8050

G Arch. de Juan Fernández, Mt. Aconcagua 6960, Sierra de Córdoba, L. Mar Chiquita, Entre Ríos, Paraná, Uruguay, L. dos Patos, Río de la Plata

Colorado, Bahía Blanca, SOUTH ATLANTIC OCEAN

H Chile Rise, Chiloé I., Chonos Archipelago, Taitao Peninsula, Mte. San Valentin 4058, Gulf of Penas, Wellington I., Madre de Dios I., Magellan's Str., Santa Inés I., Canal Cockburn, Tierra del Fuego, Canal Beagle, C. Horn, Staten I.

Negro, G. San Matias, Valdés Peninsula, Pampas, Patagonia, G. San Jorge, Argentine Basin, 6212

West Falkland, Falkland Is., East Falkland, South Georgia

PACIFIC OCEAN, Andes, Pampas

West from Greenwich

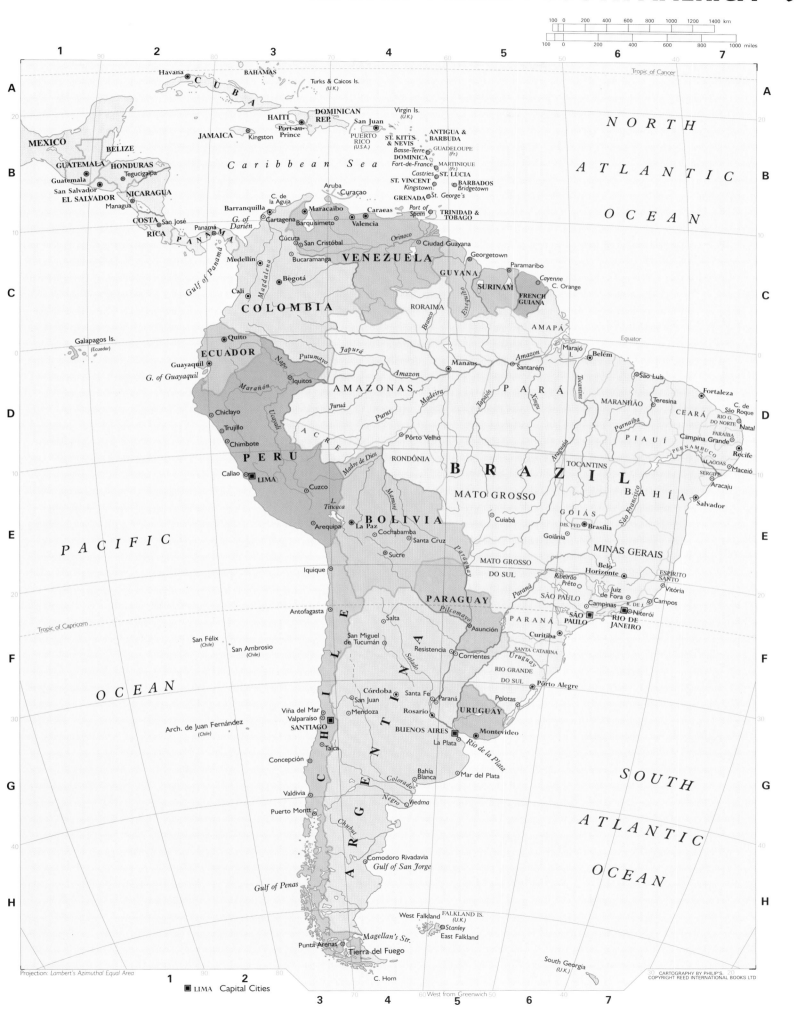

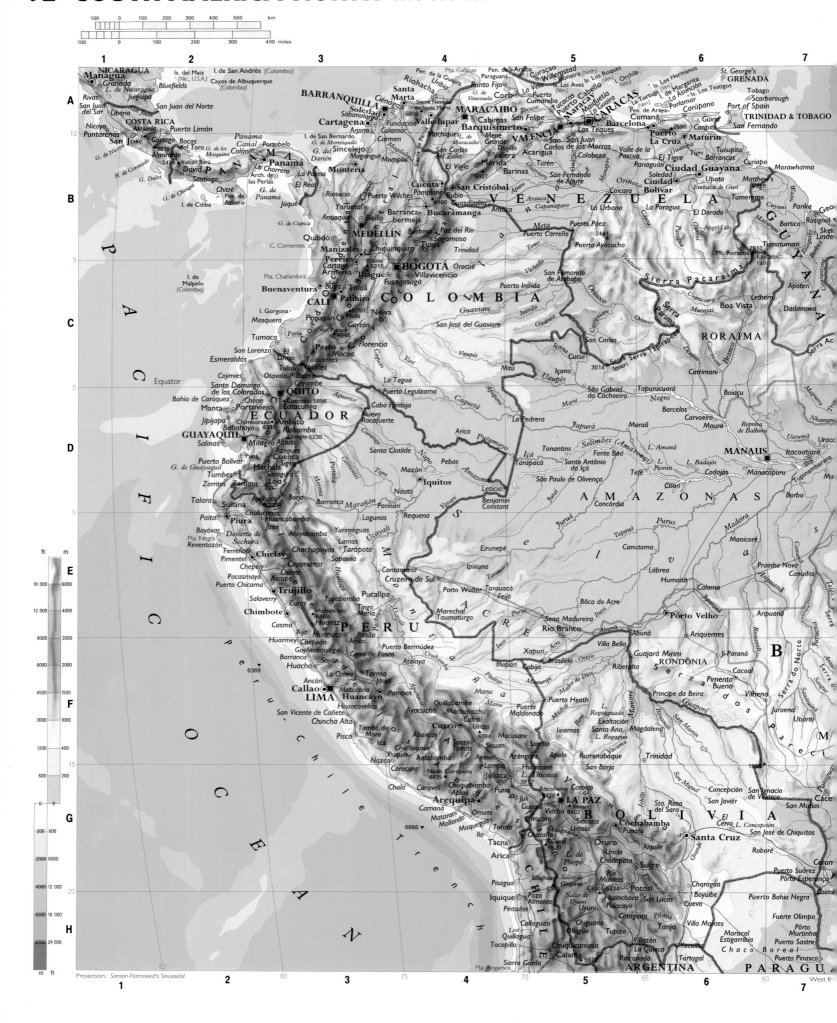

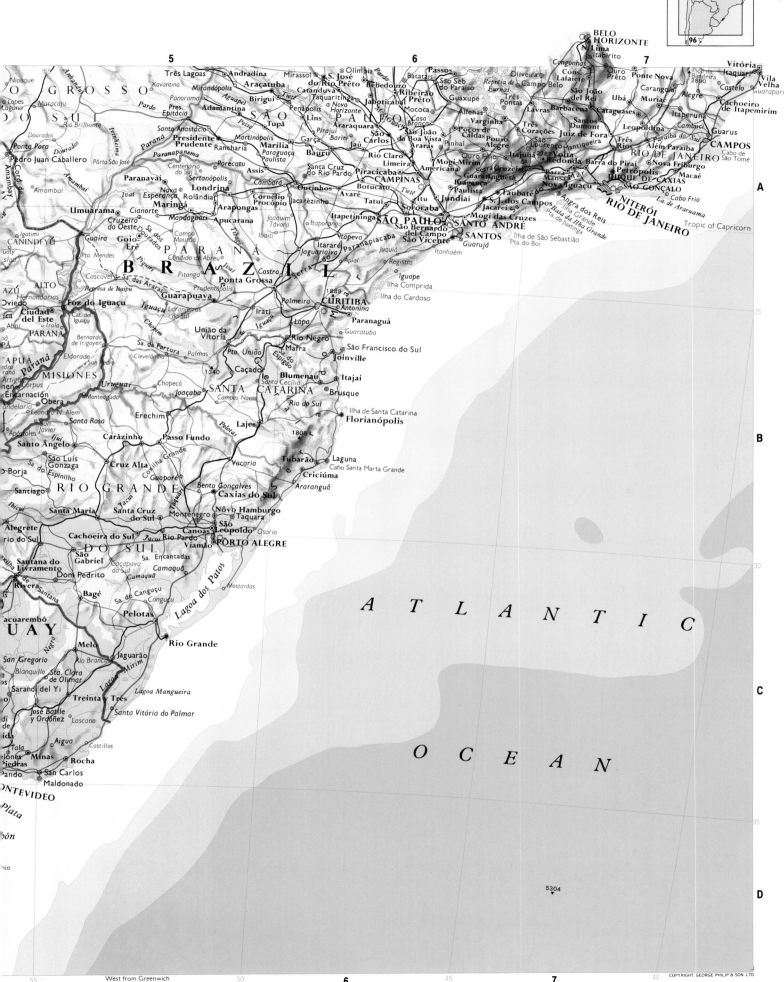

West from Greenwich

COPYRIGHT. GEORGE PHILIP & SON. LTD

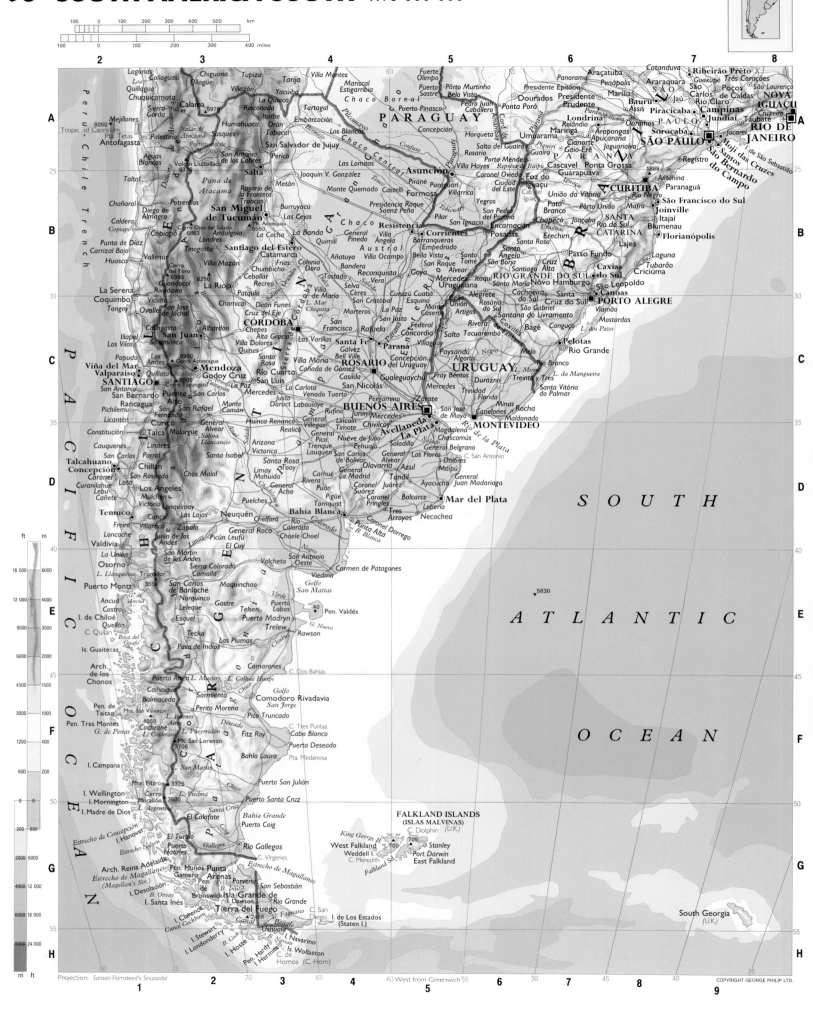

INDEX

The index contains the names of all the principal places and features shown on the World Maps. Each name is followed by an additional entry in italics giving the country or region within which it is located. The alphabetical order of names composed of two or more words is governed primarily by the first word and then by the second. This is an example of the rule:

Mīr Kūh, *Iran*	**45 E8**	26 22N	58 55 E
Mīr Shahdād, *Iran*	**45 E8**	26 15N	58 29 E
Mira, *Italy*	**20 B5**	45 26N	12 8 E
Mira por vos Cay, *Bahamas*	**89 B5**	22 9N	74 30W
Miraj, *India*	**40 L9**	16 50N	74 45 E

Physical features composed of a proper name (Erie) and a description (Lake) are positioned alphabetically by the proper name. The description is positioned after the proper name and is usually abbreviated:

Erie, L., *N. Amer.*	**78 D4**	42 15N	81 0W

Where a description forms part of a settlement or administrative name however, it is always written in full and put in its true alphabetic position:

Mount Morris, *U.S.A.*	**78 D7**	42 44N	77 52W

Names beginning with M' and Mc are indexed as if they were spelled Mac. Names beginning St. are alphabetised under Saint, but Sankt, Sint, Sant', Santa and San are all spelt in full and are alphabetised accordingly. If the same place name occurs two or more times in the index and all are in the same country, each is followed by the name of the administrative subdivision in which it is located. The names are placed in the alphabetical order of the subdivisions. For example:

Jackson, *Ky., U.S.A.*	**76 G4**	37 33N	83 23W
Jackson, *Mich., U.S.A.*	**76 D3**	42 15N	84 24W
Jackson, *Minn., U.S.A.*	**80 D7**	43 37N	95 1W

The number in bold type which follows each name in the index refers to the number of the map page where that feature or place will be found. This is usually the largest scale at which the place or feature appears.

The letter and figure which are in bold type immediately after the page number give the grid square on the map page, within which the feature is situated. The letter represents the latitude and the figure the longitude.

In some cases the feature itself may fall within the specified square, while the name is outside. This is usually the case only with features which are larger than a grid square.

For a more precise location the geographical coordinates which follow the letter/figure references give the latitude and the longitude of each place. The first set of figures represent the latitude which is the distance north or south of the Equator measured as an angle at the centre of the earth. The Equator is latitude 0°, the North Pole is 90°N, and the South Pole 90°S.

The second set of figures represent the longitude, which is the distance East or West of the prime meridian, which runs through Greenwich, England. Longitude is also measured as an angle at the centre of the earth and is given East or West of the prime meridian, from 0° to 180° in either direction.

The unit of measurement for latitude and longitude is the degree, which is subdivided into 60 minutes. Each index entry states the position of a place in degrees and minutes, a space being left between the degrees and the minutes.

The latitude is followed by N(orth) or S(outh) and the longitude by E(ast) or W(est).

Rivers are indexed to their mouths or confluences, and carry the symbol ➔ after their names. A solid square ■ follows the name of a country, while an open square ☐ refers to a first order administrative area.

Abbreviations used in the index

A.C.T. – Australian Capital Territory
Afghan. – Afghanistan
Ala. – Alabama
Alta. – Alberta
Amer. – America(n)
Arch. – Archipelago
Ariz. – Arizona
Ark. – Arkansas
Atl. Oc. – Atlantic Ocean
B. – Baie, Bahía, Bay, Bucht, Bugt
B.C. – British Columbia
Bangla. – Bangladesh
Barr. – Barrage
Bos.-H. – Bosnia-Herzegovina
C. – Cabo, Cap, Cape, Coast
C.A.R. – Central African Republic
C. Prov. – Cape Province
Calif. – California
Cent. – Central
Chan. – Channel
Colo. – Colorado
Conn. – Connecticut
Cord. – Cordillera
Cr. – Creek
Czech. – Czech Republic
D.C. – District of Columbia
Del. – Delaware
Dep. – Dependency
Des. – Desert
Dist. – District
Dj. – Djebel
Domin. – Dominica
Dom. Rep. – Dominican Republic
E. – East

E. Salv. – El Salvador
Eq. Guin. – Equatorial Guinea
Fla. – Florida
Falk. Is. – Falkland Is.
G. – Golfe, Golfo, Gulf, Guba, Gebel
Ga. – Georgia
Gt. – Great, Greater
Guinea-Biss. – Guinea-Bissau
H.K. – Hong Kong
H.P. – Himachal Pradesh
Hants. – Hampshire
Harb. – Harbor, Harbour
Hd. – Head
Hts. – Heights
I.(s). – Île, Ilha, Insel, Isla, Island, Isle
Ill. – Illinois
Ind. – Indiana
Ind. Oc. – Indian Ocean
Ivory C. – Ivory Coast
J. – Jabal, Jebel, Jazira
Junc. – Junction
K. – Kap, Kapp
Kans. – Kansas
Kep. – Kepulauan
Ky. – Kentucky
L. – Lac, Lacul, Lago, Lagoa, Lake, Limni, Loch, Lough
La. – Louisiana
Liech. – Liechtenstein
Lux. – Luxembourg
Mad. P. – Madhya Pradesh
Madag. – Madagascar
Man. – Manitoba
Mass. – Massachusetts

Md. – Maryland
Me. – Maine
Medit. S. – Mediterranean Sea
Mich. – Michigan
Minn. – Minnesota
Miss. – Mississippi
Mo. – Missouri
Mont. – Montana
Mozam. – Mozambique
Mt.(e) – Mont, Monte, Monti, Montaña, Mountain
N. – Nord, Norte, North, Northern, Nouveau
N.B. – New Brunswick
N.C. – North Carolina
N. Cal. – New Caledonia
N. Dak. – North Dakota
N.H. – New Hampshire
N.I. – North Island
N.J. – New Jersey
N. Mex. – New Mexico
N.S. – Nova Scotia
N.S.W. – New South Wales
N.W.T. – North West Territory
N.Y. – New York
N.Z. – New Zealand
Nebr. – Nebraska
Neths. – Netherlands
Nev. – Nevada
Nfld. – Newfoundland
Nic. – Nicaragua
O. – Oued, Ouadi
Occ. – Occidentale
Okla. – Oklahoma
Ont. – Ontario
Or. – Orientale

Oreg. – Oregon
Os. – Ostrov
Oz. – Ozero
P. – Pass, Passo, Pasul, Pulau
P.E.I. – Prince Edward Island
Pa. – Pennsylvania
Pac. Oc. – Pacific Ocean
Papua N.G. – Papua New Guinea
Pass. – Passage
Pen. – Peninsula, Péninsule
Phil. – Philippines
Pk. – Park, Peak
Plat. – Plateau
Prov. – Province, Provincial
Pt. – Point
Pta. – Ponta, Punta
Pte. – Pointe
Qué. – Québec
Queens. – Queensland
R. – Rio, River
R.I. – Rhode Island
Ra.(s). – Range(s)
Raj. – Rajasthan
Reg. – Region
Rep. – Republic
Res. – Reserve, Reservoir
S. – San, South, Sea
Si. Arabia – Saudi Arabia
S.C. – South Carolina
S. Dak. – South Dakota
S.I. – South Island
S. Leone – Sierra Leone
Sa. – Serra, Sierra
Sask. – Saskatchewan
Scot. – Scotland
Sd. – Sound

Sev. – Severnaya
Sib. – Siberia
Sprs. – Springs
St. – Saint
Sta. – Santa, Station
Ste. – Sainte
Sto. – Santo
Str. – Strait, Stretto
Switz. – Switzerland
Tas. – Tasmania
Tenn. – Tennessee
Tex. – Texas
Tg. – Tanjung
Trin. & Tob. – Trinidad & Tobago
U.A.E. – United Arab Emirates
U.K. – United Kingdom
U.S.A. – United States of America
Ut. P. – Uttar Pradesh
Va. – Virginia
Vdkhr. – Vodokhranilishche
Vf. – Vírful
Vic. – Victoria
Vol. – Volcano
Vt. – Vermont
W. – Wadi, West
W. Va. – West Virginia
Wash. – Washington
Wis. – Wisconsin
Wlkp. – Wielkopolski
Wyo. – Wyoming
Yorks. – Yorkshire
Yug. – Yugoslavia

A Coruña

A

A Coruña, *Spain* **19 A1** 43 20N 8 25W
A Estrada, *Spain* **19 A1** 42 43N 8 27W
A Fonsagrada, *Spain* **19 A2** 43 8N 7 4W
Aachen, *Germany* **16 C4** 50 45N 6 6 E
Aalborg = Ålborg, *Denmark* **9 H13** 57 2N 9 54 E
Aalen, *Germany* **16 D6** 48 51N 10 6 E
Aalst, *Belgium* **15 D4** 50 56N 4 2 E
Aalten, *Neths.* **15 C6** 51 56N 6 35 E
Aalter, *Belgium* **15 C3** 51 5N 3 28 E
Äänekoski, *Finland* **9 E21** 62 36N 25 44 E
Aarau, *Switz.* **18 C8** 47 23N 8 4 E
Aare →, *Switz.* **18 C8** 47 33N 8 14 E
Aarhus = Århus, *Denmark* **9 H14** 56 8N 10 11 E
Aarschot, *Belgium* **15 D4** 50 59N 4 49 E
Aba, *Dem. Rep. of the Congo* **54 B3** 3 58N 30 17 E
Aba, *Nigeria* **50 G7** 5 10N 7 19 E
Ābādān, *Iran* **45 D6** 30 22N 48 20 E
Ābādeh, *Iran* **45 D7** 31 8N 52 40 E
Abadla, *Algeria* **50 B5** 31 2N 2 45W
Abaetetuba, *Brazil* **93 D9** 1 40S 48 50W
Abagnar Qi, *China* **34 C9** 43 52N 116 2 E
Abai, *Paraguay* **95 B4** 25 58S 55 54W
Abakan, *Russia* **27 D10** 53 40N 91 10 E
Abancay, *Peru* **92 F4** 13 35S 72 55W
Abariringa, *Kiribati* **64 H10** 2 50S 171 40W
Abarqū, *Iran* **45 D7** 31 10N 53 20 E
Abashiri, *Japan* **30 C12** 44 0N 144 15 E
Abashiri-Wan, *Japan* **30 C12** 44 0N 144 30 E
Abay, *Kazakstan* **26 E8** 49 38N 72 53 E
Abaya, L., *Ethiopia* **46 F2** 6 30N 37 50 E
Abaza, *Russia* **26 D10** 52 39N 90 6 E
'Abbāsābād, *Iran* **45 C8** 33 34N 58 23 E
Abbay = Nîl el Azraq →, *Sudan* **51 E12** 15 38N 32 31 E
Abbaye, Pt., *U.S.A.* **76 B1** 46 58N 88 8W
Abbeville, *France* **18 A4** 50 6N 1 49 E
Abbeville, *La., U.S.A.* **81 L8** 29 58N 92 8W
Abbeville, *S.C., U.S.A.* **77 H4** 34 11N 82 23W
Abbieglassie, *Australia* **63 D4** 27 15S 147 28 E
Abbot Ice Shelf, *Antarctica* **5 D16** 73 0S 92 0W
Abbotsford, *Canada* **72 D4** 49 5N 122 20W
Abbotsford, *U.S.A.* **80 C9** 44 57N 90 19W
Abbottabad, *Pakistan* **42 B5** 34 10N 73 15 E
Abd al Kūrī, *Ind. Oc.* **46 E5** 12 5N 52 20 E
Ābdar, *Iran* **45 D7** 30 16N 55 19 E
'Abdolābād, *Iran* **45 C8** 34 12N 56 30 E
Abéché, *Chad* **51 F10** 13 50N 20 35 E
Åbenrå, *Denmark* **9 J13** 55 3N 9 25 E
Abeokuta, *Nigeria* **50 G6** 7 3N 3 19 E
Aber, *Uganda* **54 B3** 2 12N 32 25 E
Aberaeron, *U.K.* **11 E3** 52 15N 4 15W
Aberayron = Aberaeron, *U.K.* **11 E3** 52 15N 4 15W
Aberchirder, *U.K.* **12 D6** 57 34N 2 37W
Abercorn = Mbala, *Zambia* **55 D3** 8 46S 31 24 E
Abercorn, *Australia* **63 D5** 25 12S 151 5 E
Aberdare, *U.K.* **11 F4** 51 43N 3 27W
Aberdare Ra., *Kenya* **54 C4** 0 15S 36 50 E
Aberdeen, *Australia* **63 E5** 32 9S 150 56 E
Aberdeen, *Canada* **73 C7** 52 20N 106 8W
Aberdeen, *S. Africa* **56 E3** 32 28S 24 2 E
Aberdeen, *U.K.* **12 D6** 57 9N 2 5W
Aberdeen, *Ala., U.S.A.* **77 J1** 33 49N 88 33W
Aberdeen, *Idaho, U.S.A.* **82 E7** 42 57N 112 50W
Aberdeen, *S. Dak., U.S.A.* **80 C5** 45 28N 98 29W
Aberdeen, *Wash., U.S.A.* **84 D3** 46 59N 123 50W
Aberdeen, City of □, *U.K.* **12 D6** 57 10N 2 10W
Aberdeenshire □, *U.K.* **12 D6** 57 17N 2 36W
Aberdovey = Aberdyfi, *U.K.* **11 E3** 52 33N 4 3W
Aberdyfi, *U.K.* **11 E3** 52 33N 4 3W
Aberfeldy, *U.K.* **12 E5** 56 37N 3 51W
Abergavenny, *U.K.* **11 F4** 51 49N 3 1W
Abergele, *U.K.* **10 D4** 53 17N 3 35W
Abernathy, *U.S.A.* **81 J4** 33 50N 101 51W
Abert, L., *U.S.A.* **82 E3** 42 38N 120 14W
Aberystwyth, *U.K.* **11 E3** 52 25N 4 5W
Abhar, *Iran* **45 B6** 36 9N 49 13 E
Abhayapuri, *India* **43 F14** 26 24N 90 38 E
Abidjan, *Ivory C.* **50 G5** 5 26N 3 58W
Abilene, *Kans., U.S.A.* **80 F6** 38 55N 97 13W
Abilene, *Tex., U.S.A.* **81 J5** 32 28N 99 43W
Abingdon, *U.K.* **11 F6** 51 40N 1 17W
Abingdon, *Ill., U.S.A.* **80 E9** 40 48N 90 24W
Abingdon, *Va., U.S.A.* **77 G5** 36 43N 81 59W
Abington Reef, *Australia* **62 B4** 18 0S 149 35 E
Abitau →, *Canada* **73 B7** 59 53N 109 3W
Abitau L., *Canada* **73 A7** 60 27N 107 15W
Abitibi L., *Canada* **70 C4** 48 40N 79 40W
Abkhaz Republic □ = Abkhazia □, *Georgia* **25 F7** 43 12N 41 5 E
Abkhazia □, *Georgia* **25 F7** 43 12N 41 5 E
Abminga, *Australia* **63 D1** 26 8S 134 51 E
Åbo = Turku, *Finland* **9 F20** 60 30N 22 19 E
Abohar, *India* **42 D6** 30 10N 74 10 E
Abomey, *Benin* **50 G6** 7 10N 2 5 E
Abong-Mbang, *Cameroon* **52 D2** 4 0N 13 8 E
Abou-Deïa, *Chad* **51 F9** 11 20N 19 20 E
Aboyne, *U.K.* **12 D6** 57 4N 2 47W
Abra Pampa, *Argentina* **94 A2** 22 43S 65 42W
Abreojos, Pta., *Mexico* **86 B2** 26 50N 113 40W
Abrud, *Romania* **17 E12** 46 19N 23 5 E
Absaroka Range, *U.S.A.* **82 D9** 44 45N 109 50W
Abū al Khaṣīb, *Iraq* **45 D6** 30 25N 48 0 E
Abū 'Alī, *Si. Arabia* **45 E6** 27 20N 49 27 E
Abū 'Alī →, *Lebanon* **47 A4** 34 25N 35 50 E
Abu Dhabi = Abū Ẓāby, *U.A.E.* **45 E7** 24 28N 54 22 E
Abū Du'ān, *Syria* **44 B3** 36 25N 38 15 E
Abu el Gairi, W. →, *Egypt* **47 F2** 29 35N 33 30 E
Abu Ga'da, W. →, *Egypt* **47 F1** 29 15N 32 53 E
Abū Ḥadrīyah, *Si. Arabia* **45 E6** 27 20N 48 58 E
Abu Hamed, *Sudan* **51 E12** 19 32N 33 13 E
Abū Kamāl, *Syria* **44 C4** 34 30N 41 0 E
Abū Madd, Ra's, *Si. Arabia* **44 E3** 24 50N 37 7 E
Abu Ṣafāt, W. →, *Jordan* **47 E5** 30 24N 36 7 E
Abū Ṣukhayr, *Iraq* **44 D5** 31 54N 44 30 E
Abū Zabad, *Sudan* **51 F11** 12 25N 29 10 E
Abū Ẓāby, *U.A.E.* **45 E7** 24 28N 54 22 E
Abū Zeydābād, *Iran* **45 C6** 33 54N 51 45 E
Abuja, *Nigeria* **50 G7** 9 16N 7 2 E
Abukuma-Gawa →, *Japan* **30 E10** 38 6N 140 52 E
Abukuma-Sammyaku, *Japan* **30 F10** 37 30N 140 45 E
Abunã, *Brazil* **92 E5** 9 40S 65 20W
Abunã →, *Brazil* **92 E5** 9 41S 65 20W
Aburo, *Dem. Rep. of the Congo* **54 B3** 2 4N 30 53 E
Abut Hd., *N.Z.* **59 K3** 43 7S 170 15 E
Açailândia, *Brazil* **93 D9** 4 57S 47 0W
Acajutla, *El Salv.* **88 D2** 13 36N 89 50W
Acámbaro, *Mexico* **86 D4** 20 0N 100 40W
Acaponeta, *Mexico* **86 C3** 22 30N 105 20W
Acapulco, *Mexico* **87 D5** 16 51N 99 56W
Acarai, Serra, *Brazil* **92 C7** 1 50N 57 50W
Acarigua, *Venezuela* **92 B5** 9 33N 69 12W
Acatlán, *Mexico* **87 D5** 18 10N 98 3W
Acayucan, *Mexico* **87 D6** 17 59N 94 58W
Accomac, *U.S.A.* **76 G8** 37 43N 75 40W
Accra, *Ghana* **50 G5** 5 35N 0 6W
Accrington, *U.K.* **10 D5** 53 45N 2 22W
Acebal, *Argentina* **94 C3** 33 20S 60 50W
Aceh □, *Indonesia* **36 D1** 4 15N 97 30 E
Achalpur, *India* **40 J10** 21 22N 77 32 E
Acheng, *China* **35 B14** 45 30N 126 58 E
Acher, *India* **42 H5** 23 10N 72 32 E
Achill Hd., *Ireland* **13 C1** 53 58N 10 15W
Achill I., *Ireland* **13 C1** 53 58N 10 1W
Achinsk, *Russia* **27 D10** 56 20N 90 20 E
Acireale, *Italy* **20 F6** 37 37N 15 10 E
Ackerman, *U.S.A.* **81 J10** 33 19N 89 11W
Acklins I., *Bahamas* **89 B5** 22 30N 74 0W
Acme, *Canada* **72 C6** 51 33N 113 30W
Aconcagua, Cerro, *Argentina* **94 C2** 32 39S 70 0W
Aconquija, Mt., *Argentina* **94 B2** 27 0S 66 0W
Açores, Is. dos = Azores, *Atl. Oc.* **48 C1** 38 44N 29 0W
Acraman, L., *Australia* **63 E2** 32 2S 135 23 E
Acre = 'Akko, *Israel* **47 C4** 32 55N 35 4 E
Acre □, *Brazil* **92 E4** 9 1S 71 0W
Acre →, *Brazil* **92 E5** 8 45S 67 22W
Acton, *Canada* **78 C4** 43 38N 80 3W
Ad Dammām, *Si. Arabia* **45 E6** 26 20N 50 5 E
Ad Dawhah, *Qatar* **46 B5** 25 15N 51 35 E
Ad Dawr, *Iraq* **44 C4** 34 27N 43 47 E
Ad Dir'īyah, *Si. Arabia* **44 E5** 24 44N 46 35 E
Ad Dīwānīyah, *Iraq* **44 D5** 32 0N 45 0 E
Ad Dujayl, *Iraq* **44 C5** 33 51N 44 14 E
Ada, *Minn., U.S.A.* **80 B6** 47 18N 96 31W
Ada, *Okla., U.S.A.* **81 H6** 34 46N 96 41W
Adaja →, *Spain* **19 B3** 41 32N 4 52W
Adamaoua, Massif de l', *Cameroon* **52 C2** 7 20N 12 20 E
Adamawa Highlands = Adamaoua, Massif de l', *Cameroon* **52 C2** 7 20N 12 20 E
Adamello, Mte., *Italy* **18 C9** 46 9N 10 30 E
Adaminaby, *Australia* **63 F4** 36 0S 148 45 E
Adams, *Mass., U.S.A.* **79 D11** 42 38N 73 7W
Adams, *N.Y., U.S.A.* **79 C8** 43 49N 76 1W
Adams, *Wis., U.S.A.* **80 D10** 43 57N 89 49W
Adam's Bridge, *Sri Lanka* **40 Q11** 9 15N 79 40 E
Adams L., *Canada* **72 C5** 51 10N 119 40W
Adams Mt., *U.S.A.* **84 D5** 46 12N 121 30W
Adam's Peak, *Sri Lanka* **40 R12** 6 48N 80 30 E
Adana, *Turkey* **25 G6** 37 0N 35 16 E
Adapazarı, *Turkey* **25 F5** 40 48N 30 25 E
Adarama, *Sudan* **51 E12** 17 10N 34 52 E
Adare, C., *Antarctica* **5 D11** 71 0S 171 0 E
Adaut, *Indonesia* **37 F8** 8 8S 131 7 E
Adavale, *Australia* **63 D3** 25 52S 144 32 E
Adda →, *Italy* **18 D8** 45 8N 9 53 E
Addis Ababa = Addis Abeba, *Ethiopia* **46 F2** 9 2N 38 42 E
Addis Abeba, *Ethiopia* **46 F2** 9 2N 38 42 E
Addison, *U.S.A.* **78 D7** 42 1N 77 14W
Addo, *S. Africa* **56 E4** 33 32S 25 45 E
Ādeh, *Iran* **44 B5** 37 42N 45 11 E
Adel, *U.S.A.* **77 K4** 31 8N 83 25W
Adelaide, *Australia* **63 E2** 34 52S 138 30 E
Adelaide, *Bahamas* **88 A4** 25 4N 77 31W
Adelaide, *S. Africa* **56 E4** 32 42S 26 20 E
Adelaide I., *Antarctica* **5 C17** 67 15S 68 30W
Adelaide Pen., *Canada* **68 B10** 68 15N 97 30W
Adelaide River, *Australia* **60 B5** 13 15S 131 7 E
Adelanto, *U.S.A.* **85 L9** 34 35N 117 22W
Adele I., *Australia* **60 C3** 15 32S 123 9 E
Adélie, Terre, *Antarctica* **5 C10** 68 0S 140 0 E
Adélie Land = Adélie, Terre, *Antarctica* **5 C10** 68 0S 140 0 E
Aden = Al 'Adan, *Yemen* **46 E4** 12 45N 45 0 E
Aden, G. of, *Asia* **46 E4** 12 30N 47 30 E
Adendorp, *S. Africa* **56 E3** 32 15S 24 30 E
Adh Dhayd, *U.A.E.* **45 E7** 25 17N 55 53 E
Adhoi, *India* **42 H4** 23 26N 70 32 E
Adi, *Indonesia* **37 E8** 4 15S 133 30 E
Adieu, C., *Australia* **61 F5** 32 0S 132 10 E
Adieu Pt., *Australia* **60 C3** 15 14S 124 35 E
Adige →, *Italy* **20 B5** 45 9N 12 20 E
Adilabad, *India* **40 K11** 19 33N 78 20 E
Adin, *U.S.A.* **82 F3** 41 12N 120 57W
Adin Khel, *Afghan.* **40 C6** 32 45N 68 5 E
Adirondack Mts., *U.S.A.* **79 C10** 44 0N 74 0W
Adjumani, *Uganda* **54 B3** 3 20N 31 50 E
Adlavik Is., *Canada* **71 A8** 55 2N 57 45W
Admiralty G., *Australia* **60 B4** 14 20S 125 55 E
Admiralty I., *U.S.A.* **68 C6** 57 30N 134 30W
Admiralty Inlet, *U.S.A.* **82 C2** 48 8N 122 58W
Admiralty Is., *Papua N. G.* **64 H6** 2 0S 147 0 E
Adonara, *Indonesia* **37 F6** 8 15S 123 5 E
Adoni, *India* **40 M10** 15 33N 77 18 E
Adour →, *France* **18 E3** 43 32N 1 32W
Adra, *India* **43 H12** 23 30N 86 42 E
Adra, *Spain* **19 D4** 36 43N 3 3W
Adrano, *Italy* **20 F6** 37 40N 14 50 E
Adrar, *Algeria* **48 D4** 27 51N 0 11 E
Adrian, *Mich., U.S.A.* **76 E3** 41 54N 84 2W
Adrian, *Tex., U.S.A.* **81 H3** 35 16N 102 40W
Adriatic Sea, *Medit. S.* **20 C6** 43 0N 16 0 E
Adua, *Indonesia* **37 E7** 1 45S 129 50 E
Adwa, *Ethiopia* **46 E2** 14 15N 38 52 E
Adzhar Republic □ = Ajaria □, *Georgia* **25 F7** 41 30N 42 0 E
Ægean Sea, *Medit. S.* **21 E11** 38 30N 25 0 E
Aerhtai Shan, *Mongolia* **32 B4** 46 40N 92 45 E
'Afak, *Iraq* **44 C5** 32 4N 45 15 E
Afándou, *Greece* **23 C10** 36 18N 28 12 E
Afghanistan ■, *Asia* **40 C4** 33 0N 65 0 E
'Afrīn, *Syria* **44 B3** 36 32N 36 50 E
Afton, *U.S.A.* **79 D9** 42 14N 75 32W
Afuá, *Brazil* **93 D8** 0 15S 50 20W
'Afula, *Israel* **47 C4** 32 37N 35 17 E
Afyon, *Turkey* **25 G5** 38 45N 30 33 E
Afyonkarahisar = Afyon, *Turkey* **25 G5** 38 45N 30 33 E
Agadès = Agadez, *Niger* **50 E7** 16 58N 7 59 E
Agadez, *Niger* **50 E7** 16 58N 7 59 E
Agadir, *Morocco* **50 B4** 30 28N 9 55W
Agaete, *Canary Is.* **22 F4** 28 6N 15 43W
Agar, *India* **42 H7** 23 40N 76 2 E
Agartala, *India* **41 H17** 23 50N 91 23 E
Agassiz, *Canada* **72 D4** 49 14N 121 46W
Agats, *Indonesia* **37 F9** 5 33S 138 0 E
Agboville, *Ivory C.* **50 G5** 5 55N 4 15W
Agde, *France* **18 E5** 43 19N 3 28 E
Agen, *France* **18 D4** 44 12N 0 38 E
Āgh Kand, *Iran* **45 B6** 37 15N 48 4 E
Aginskoye, *Russia* **27 D12** 51 6N 114 32 E
Agra, *India* **42 F7** 27 17N 77 58 E
Agri →, *Italy* **20 D7** 40 13N 16 44 E
Ağrı Dağı, *Turkey* **25 G7** 39 50N 44 15 E
Ağrı Karakose, *Turkey* **25 G7** 39 44N 43 3 E
Agrigento, *Italy* **20 F5** 37 19N 13 34 E
Agrínion, *Greece* **21 E9** 38 37N 21 27 E
Agua Caliente, *Baja Calif., Mexico* **85 N10** 32 29N 116 59W
Agua Caliente, *Sinaloa, Mexico* **86 B3** 26 30N 108 20W
Agua Caliente Springs, *U.S.A.* **85 N10** 32 56N 116 19W
Água Clara, *Brazil* **93 H8** 20 25S 52 45W
Agua Hechicero, *Mexico* **85 N10** 32 26N 116 14W
Agua Prieta, *Mexico* **86 A3** 31 20N 109 32W
Aguadilla, *Puerto Rico* **89 C6** 18 26N 67 10W
Aguadulce, *Panama* **88 E3** 8 15N 80 32W
Aguanga, *U.S.A.* **85 M10** 33 27N 116 51W
Aguanish, *Canada* **71 B7** 50 14N 62 2W
Aguanus →, *Canada* **71 B7** 50 13N 62 5W
Aguapey →, *Argentina* **94 B4** 29 7S 56 36W
Aguaray Guazú →, *Paraguay* **94 A4** 24 47S 57 19W
Aguarico →, *Ecuador* **92 D3** 0 59S 75 11W
Aguas Blancas, *Chile* **94 A2** 24 15S 69 55W
Aguas Calientes, Sierra de, *Argentina* **94 B2** 25 26S 66 40W
Aguascalientes, *Mexico* **86 C4** 21 53N 102 12W
Aguascalientes □, *Mexico* **86 C4** 22 0N 102 20W
Aguilares, *Argentina* **94 B2** 27 26S 65 35W
Aguilas, *Spain* **19 D5** 37 23N 1 35W
Agüimes, *Canary Is.* **22 G4** 27 58N 15 27W
Aguja, C. de la, *Colombia* **90 B3** 11 18N 74 12W
Agulhas, C., *S. Africa* **56 E3** 34 52S 20 0 E
Agulo, *Canary Is.* **22 F2** 28 11N 17 12W
Agung, *Indonesia* **36 F5** 8 20S 115 28 E
Agur, *Uganda* **54 B3** 2 28N 32 55 E
Agusan →, *Phil.* **37 C7** 9 0N 125 30 E
Aha Mts., *Botswana* **56 B3** 19 45S 21 0 E
Ahaggar, *Algeria* **50 D7** 23 0N 6 30 E
Ahar, *Iran* **44 B5** 38 35N 47 0 E
Ahipara B., *N.Z.* **59 F4** 35 5S 173 5 E
Ahiri, *India* **40 K12** 19 30N 80 0 E
Ahmad Wal, *Pakistan* **42 E1** 29 18N 65 58 E
Ahmadabad, *India* **42 H5** 23 0N 72 40 E
Aḥmadābād, *Khorāsān, Iran* **45 C9** 35 3N 60 50 E
Aḥmadābād, *Khorāsān, Iran* **45 C8** 35 49N 59 42 E
Aḥmadī, *Iran* **45 E8** 27 56N 56 42 E
Ahmadnagar, *India* **40 K9** 19 7N 74 46 E
Ahmadpur, *Pakistan* **42 E4** 29 12N 71 10 E
Ahmedabad = Ahmadabad, *India* **42 H5** 23 0N 72 40 E
Ahmednagar = Ahmadnagar, *India* **40 K9** 19 7N 74 46 E
Ahome, *Mexico* **86 B3** 25 55N 109 11W
Ahram, *Iran* **45 D6** 28 52N 51 16 E
Ahrax Pt., *Malta* **23 D1** 35 59N 14 22 E
Āhū, *Iran* **45 C6** 34 33N 50 2 E
Ahuachapán, *El Salv.* **88 D2** 13 54N 89 52W
Ahvāz, *Iran* **45 D6** 31 20N 48 40 E
Ahvenanmaa = Åland, *Finland* **9 F19** 60 15N 20 0 E
Aḥwar, *Yemen* **46 E4** 13 30N 46 40 E
Aichi □, *Japan* **31 G8** 35 0N 137 15 E
Aigua, *Uruguay* **95 C5** 34 13S 54 46W
Aigues-Mortes, *France* **18 E6** 43 35N 4 12 E
Aihui, *China* **33 A7** 50 10N 127 30 E
Aija, *Peru* **92 E3** 9 50S 77 45W
Aikawa, *Japan* **30 E9** 38 2N 138 15 E
Aiken, *U.S.A.* **77 J5** 33 34N 81 43W
Aillik, *Canada* **71 A8** 55 11N 59 18W
Ailsa Craig, *U.K.* **12 F3** 55 15N 5 6W
'Ailūn, *Jordan* **47 C4** 32 18N 35 47 E
Aim, *Russia* **27 D14** 59 0N 133 55 E
Aimere, *Indonesia* **37 F6** 8 45S 121 3 E
Aimogasta, *Argentina* **94 B2** 28 33S 66 50W
Aïn Ben Tili, *Mauritania* **50 C4** 25 59N 9 27W
Aïn-Sefra, *Algeria* **50 B5** 32 47N 0 37W
'Ain Sudr, *Egypt* **47 F2** 29 50N 33 6 E
Ainaži, *Latvia* **9 H21** 57 50N 24 24 E
Ainsworth, *U.S.A.* **80 D5** 42 33N 99 52W
Aiquile, *Bolivia* **92 G5** 18 10S 65 10W
Aïr, *Niger* **50 E7** 18 30N 8 0 E
Air Hitam, *Malaysia* **39 M4** 1 55N 103 11 E
Airdrie, *U.K.* **12 F5** 55 52N 3 57W
Aire →, *U.K.* **10 D7** 53 43N 0 55W
Aire, I. de l', *Spain* **22 B11** 39 48N 4 16 E
Airlie Beach, *Australia* **62 C4** 20 16S 148 43 E
Aisne →, *France* **18 B5** 49 26N 2 50 E
Aitkin, *U.S.A.* **80 B8** 46 32N 93 42W
Aiud, *Romania* **17 E12** 46 19N 23 44 E
Aix-en-Provence, *France* **18 E6** 43 32N 5 27 E
Aix-la-Chapelle = Aachen, *Germany* **16 C4** 50 45N 6 6 E
Aix-les-Bains, *France* **18 D6** 45 41N 5 53 E
Aiyansh, *Canada* **72 B3** 55 17N 129 2W
Aiyion, *Greece* **21 E10** 38 15N 22 5 E
Aizawl, *India* **41 H18** 23 40N 92 44 E
Aizkraukle, *Latvia* **9 H21** 56 36N 25 11 E
Aizpute, *Latvia* **9 H19** 56 43N 21 40 E
Aizuwakamatsu, *Japan* **30 F9** 37 30N 139 56 E
Ajaccio, *France* **18 F8** 41 55N 8 40 E
Ajalpan, *Mexico* **87 D5** 18 22N 97 15W
Ajanta Ra., *India* **40 J9** 20 28N 75 50 E
Ajari Rep. = Ajaria □, *Georgia* **25 F7** 41 30N 42 0 E
Ajaria □, *Georgia* **25 F7** 41 30N 42 0 E
Ajax, *Canada* **78 C5** 43 50N 79 1W
Ajdâbiyah, *Libya* **51 B10** 30 54N 20 4 E
Ajka, *Hungary* **17 E9** 47 4N 17 31 E
'Ajmān, *U.A.E.* **45 E7** 25 25N 55 30 E
Ajmer, *India* **42 F6** 26 28N 74 37 E
Ajo, *U.S.A.* **83 K7** 32 22N 112 52W
Ajo, C. de, *Spain* **19 A4** 43 31N 3 35W
Akabira, *Japan* **30 C11** 43 33N 142 5 E
Akamas □, *Cyprus* **23 D11** 35 3N 32 18 E
Akanthou, *Cyprus* **23 D12** 35 22N 33 45 E
Akaroa, *N.Z.* **59 K4** 43 49S 172 59 E
Akashi, *Japan* **31 G7** 34 45N 134 58 E
Akelamo, *Indonesia* **37 D7** 1 35N 129 40 E
Aketi, *Dem. Rep. of the Congo* **52 D4** 2 38N 23 47 E
Akharnaí, *Greece* **21 E10** 38 5N 23 44 E
Akhelóös →, *Greece* **21 E9** 38 19N 21 7 E
Akhisar, *Turkey* **21 E12** 38 56N 27 48 E
Akhnur, *India* **43 C6** 32 52N 74 45 E
Aki, *Japan* **31 H6** 33 30N 133 54 E
Akimiski I., *Canada* **70 B3** 52 50N 81 30W
Akita, *Japan* **30 E10** 39 45N 140 7 E
Akita □, *Japan* **30 E10** 39 40N 140 30 E
Akjoujt, *Mauritania* **50 E3** 19 45N 14 15W
Akkeshi, *Japan* **30 C12** 43 2N 144 51 E
'Akko, *Israel* **47 C4** 32 55N 35 4 E
Aklavik, *Canada* **68 B6** 68 12N 135 0W
Akmolinsk = Aqmola, *Kazakstan* **26 D8** 51 10N 71 30 E
Akō, *Japan* **31 G7** 34 45N 134 24 E
Akola, *India* **40 J10** 20 42N 77 2 E
Akordat, *Eritrea* **46 D2** 15 30N 37 40 E
Akpatok I., *Canada* **69 B13** 60 25N 68 8W
Åkrahamn, *Norway* **9 G11** 59 15N 5 10 E
Akranes, *Iceland* **8 D2** 64 19N 22 5W
Akron, *Colo., U.S.A.* **80 E3** 40 10N 103 13W
Akron, *Ohio, U.S.A.* **78 E3** 41 5N 81 31W
Akrotiri, *Cyprus* **23 E11** 34 36N 32 57 E
Akrotiri Bay, *Cyprus* **23 E12** 34 35N 33 10 E
Aksai Chin, *India* **43 B8** 35 15N 79 55 E
Aksay, *Kazakstan* **24 D9** 51 11N 53 0 E
Aksu, *China* **32 B3** 41 5N 80 10 E
Aksum, *Ethiopia* **46 E2** 14 5N 38 40 E
Aktogay, *Kazakstan* **26 E8** 46 57N 79 40 E
Aktsyabrski, *Belarus* **17 B15** 52 38N 28 53 E
Aktyubinsk = Aqtöbe, *Kazakstan* **25 D10** 50 17N 57 10 E
Akure, *Nigeria* **50 G7** 7 15N 5 5 E
Akureyri, *Iceland* **8 D4** 65 40N 18 6W
Akuseki-Shima, *Japan* **31 K4** 29 27N 129 37 E
Akyab = Sittwe, *Burma* **41 J18** 20 18N 92 45 E
Al 'Adan, *Yemen* **46 E4** 12 45N 45 0 E
Al Aḥsā, *Si. Arabia* **45 E6** 25 50N 49 0 E
Al Ajfar, *Si. Arabia* **44 E4** 27 26N 43 0 E
Al Amādīyah, *Iraq* **44 B4** 37 5N 43 30 E
Al Amārah, *Iraq* **44 D5** 31 55N 47 15 E
Al 'Aqabah, *Jordan* **47 F4** 29 31N 35 0 E
Al Arak, *Syria* **44 C3** 34 38N 38 35 E
Al 'Aramah, *Si. Arabia* **44 E5** 25 30N 46 0 E
Al Arṭāwīyah, *Si. Arabia* **44 E5** 26 31N 45 20 E
Al 'Āṣimah = 'Ammān □, *Jordan* **47 D5** 31 40N 36 30 E
Al 'Assāfīyah, *Si. Arabia* **44 D3** 28 17N 38 59 E
Al 'Ayn, *Oman* **45 E7** 24 15N 55 45 E
Al 'Ayn, *Si. Arabia* **44 E3** 25 4N 38 6 E
Al A'ẓamīyah, *Iraq* **44 C5** 33 22N 44 22 E
Al 'Azīzīyah, *Iraq* **44 C5** 32 54N 45 4 E
Al Bāb, *Syria* **44 B3** 36 23N 37 29 E
Al Bad', *Si. Arabia* **44 D2** 28 28N 35 1 E
Al Bādī, *Iraq* **44 C4** 35 56N 41 32 E
Al Baḥrah, *Kuwait* **44 D5** 29 40N 47 52 E
Al Baḥral Mayyit = Dead Sea, *Asia* **47 D4** 31 30N 35 30 E
Al Balqā' □, *Jordan* **47 C4** 32 5N 35 45 E
Al Bārūk, J., *Lebanon* **47 B4** 33 39N 35 40 E
Al Başrah, *Iraq* **44 D5** 30 30N 47 50 E
Al Baṭḥā, *Iraq* **44 D5** 31 6N 45 53 E
Al Batrūn, *Lebanon* **47 A4** 34 15N 35 40 E
Al Bayḍā, *Libya* **51 B10** 32 50N 21 44 E
Al Biqā □, *Lebanon* **47 A5** 34 10N 36 10 E
Al Bi'r, *Si. Arabia* **44 D3** 28 51N 36 16 E
Al Burayj, *Syria* **47 A5** 34 15N 36 46 E
Al Fallūjah, *Iraq* **44 C4** 33 20N 43 55 E
Al Fāw, *Iraq* **45 D6** 30 0N 48 30 E
Al Fujayrah, *U.A.E.* **45 E8** 25 7N 56 18 E
Al Ghadaf, W. →, *Jordan* **47 D5** 31 26N 36 43 E
Al Ghammās, *Iraq* **44 D5** 31 45N 44 37 E
Al Hābah, *Si. Arabia* **44 E5** 27 10N 47 0 E
Al Ḥadīthah, *Iraq* **44 C4** 34 0N 41 13 E
Al Ḥadīthah, *Si. Arabia* **44 D3** 31 28N 37 8 E
Al Ḥājānah, *Syria* **47 B5** 33 20N 36 33 E
Al Hāmad, *Si. Arabia* **44 D3** 31 30N 39 30 E
Al Hamdānīyah, *Syria* **44 C3** 35 25N 36 50 E
Al Ḥamīdīyah, *Syria* **47 A4** 34 42N 35 57 E
Al Ḥammār, *Iraq* **44 D5** 30 57N 46 51 E
Al Ḥarīr, W. →, *Syria* **47 C4** 32 44N 35 59 E
Al Ḥasā, W. →, *Jordan* **47 D4** 31 4N 35 29 E
Al Ḥasakah, *Syria* **44 B4** 36 35N 40 45 E
Al Haydān, W. →, *Jordan* **47 D4** 31 29N 35 34 E
Al Ḥayy, *Iraq* **44 C5** 32 5N 46 5 E
Al Ḥillah, *Iraq* **44 C5** 32 30N 44 25 E
Al Hirmil, *Lebanon* **47 A5** 34 26N 36 24 E
Al Hoceïma, *Morocco* **50 A5** 35 8N 3 58W

Amargosa Range

Al Ḥudaydah, *Yemen* **46 E3** 14 50N 43 0 E
Al Hufūf, *Si. Arabia* **45 E6** 25 25N 49 45 E
Al Ḥumayḍah, *Si. Arabia* **44 D2** 29 14N 34 56 E
Al Ḥunayy, *Si. Arabia* **45 E6** 25 58N 48 45 E
Al ʻĪsāwīyah, *Si. Arabia* **44 D3** 30 43N 37 59 E
Al Jafr, *Jordan* **47 E5** 30 18N 36 14 E
Al Jaghbūb, *Libya* **51 C10** 29 42N 24 38 E
Al Jahrah, *Kuwait* **44 D5** 29 25N 47 40 E
Al Jalāmīd, *Si. Arabia* **44 D3** 31 20N 39 45 E
Al Jamalīyah, *Qatar* **45 E6** 25 37N 51 5 E
Al Janūb □, *Lebanon* **47 B4** 33 20N 35 20 E
Al Jawf, *Libya* **51 D10** 24 10N 23 24 E
Al Jawf, *Si. Arabia* **44 D3** 29 55N 39 40 E
Al Jazirah, *Iraq* **44 C5** 33 30N 44 0 E
Al Jithāmīyah, *Si. Arabia* **44 E4** 27 41N 41 43 E
Al Jubayl, *Si. Arabia* **45 E6** 27 0N 49 50 E
Al Jubaylah, *Si. Arabia* **44 E5** 24 55N 46 25 E
Al Jubb, *Si. Arabia* **44 E4** 27 11N 42 17 E
Al Junaynah, *Sudan* **51 F10** 13 27N 22 45 E
Al Kabā'ish, *Iraq* **44 D5** 30 58N 47 0 E
Al Karak, *Jordan* **47 D4** 31 11N 35 42 E
Al Karak □, *Jordan* **47 E5** 31 0N 36 0 E
Al Kāzim Tyah, *Iraq* **44 C5** 33 22N 44 12 E
Al Khalīl, *West Bank* **47 D4** 31 32N 35 6 E
Al Khawr, *Qatar* **45 E6** 25 41N 51 30 E
Al Khiḍr, *Iraq* **44 D5** 31 12N 45 33 E
Al Khiyām, *Lebanon* **47 B4** 33 20N 35 36 E
Al Kiswah, *Syria* **47 B5** 33 23N 36 14 E
Al Kufrah, *Libya* **51 D10** 24 17N 23 15 E
Al Kuhayfiyah, *Si. Arabia* **44 E4** 27 12N 43 3 E
Al Kūt, *Iraq* **44 C5** 32 30N 46 0 E
Al Kuwayt, *Kuwait* **44 D5** 29 30N 48 0 E
Al Labwah, *Lebanon* **47 A5** 34 11N 36 20 E
Al Lādhiqīyah, *Syria* **44 C2** 35 30N 35 45 E
Al Liwā', *Oman* **45 E8** 24 31N 56 36 E
Al Luḥayyah, *Yemen* **46 D3** 15 45N 42 40 E
Al Madīnah, *Iraq* **44 D5** 30 57N 47 16 E
Al Madīnah, *Si. Arabia* **46 C2** 24 35N 39 52 E
Al Mafraq, *Jordan* **47 C5** 32 17N 36 14 E
Al Maḥmūdīyah, *Iraq* **44 C5** 33 3N 44 21 E
Al Majma'ah, *Si. Arabia* **44 E5** 25 57N 45 22 E
Al Makhruq, W. ⟶,
Jordan **47 D6** 31 28N 37 0 E
Al Makḥūl, *Si. Arabia* **44 E4** 26 37N 42 39 E
Al Manāmah, *Bahrain* **45 E6** 26 10N 50 30 E
Al Maqwa', *Kuwait* **44 D5** 29 10N 47 59 E
Al Marj, *Libya* **51 B10** 32 25N 20 30 E
Al Maṭlā, *Kuwait* **44 D5** 29 24N 47 40 E
Al Mawjib, W. ⟶, *Jordan* **47 D4** 31 28N 35 36 E
Al Mawṣil, *Iraq* **44 B4** 36 15N 43 5 E
Al Mayādin, *Syria* **44 C4** 35 1N 40 27 E
Al Mazār, *Jordan* **47 D4** 31 4N 35 41 E
Al Midhnab, *Si. Arabia* **44 E5** 25 50N 44 18 E
Al Minā', *Lebanon* **47 A4** 34 24N 35 49 E
Al Miqdādīyah, *Iraq* **44 C5** 34 0N 45 0 E
Al Mubarraz, *Si. Arabia* **45 E6** 25 30N 49 40 E
Al Mughayrā', *U.A.E.* **45 E7** 24 5N 53 32 E
Al Muḥarraq, *Bahrain* **45 E6** 26 15N 50 40 E
Al Mukallā, *Yemen* **46 E4** 14 33N 49 2 E
Al Mukhā, *Yemen* **46 E3** 13 18N 43 15 E
Al Musayjīd, *Si. Arabia* **44 E3** 24 5N 39 5 E
Al Musayyib, *Iraq* **44 C5** 32 49N 44 20 E
Al Muwayliḥ, *Si. Arabia* **44 E2** 27 40N 35 30 E
Al Qā'im, *Iraq* **44 C4** 34 21N 41 7 E
Al Qalībah, *Si. Arabia* **44 D3** 28 24N 37 42 E
Al Qaryatayn, *Syria* **47 A6** 34 12N 37 13 E
Al Qaṭ'ā, *Syria* **44 C4** 34 40N 40 48 E
Al Qaṭīf, *Si. Arabia* **45 E6** 26 35N 50 0 E
Al Qatrānah, *Jordan* **47 D5** 31 12N 36 6 E
Al Qaṭrūn, *Libya* **51 D9** 24 56N 15 3 E
Al Qayṣūmah, *Si. Arabia* **44 D5** 28 20N 46 7 E
Al Quds = Jerusalem,
Israel **47 D4** 31 47N 35 10 E
Al Qunayṭirah, *Syria* **47 C4** 32 55N 35 45 E
Al Qurnah, *Iraq* **44 D5** 31 1N 47 25 E
Al Quṣayr, *Iraq* **44 D5** 30 39N 45 50 E
Al Quṣayr, *Syria* **47 A5** 34 31N 36 34 E
Al Qutayfah, *Syria* **47 B5** 33 44N 36 36 E
Al 'Uḍaylīyah, *Si. Arabia* **45 E6** 25 8N 49 18 E
Al 'Ulā, *Si. Arabia* **44 E3** 26 35N 38 0 E
Al Uqayr, *Si. Arabia* **45 E6** 25 40N 50 15 E
Al 'Uwaynid, *Si. Arabia* **44 E5** 24 50N 46 0 E
Al 'Uwayqīlah, *Si. Arabia* **44 D4** 30 30N 42 10 E
Al 'Uyūn, *Ḥijāz, Si. Arabia* **44 E3** 24 33N 39 35 E
Al 'Uyūn, *Najd, Si. Arabia* **44 E4** 26 30N 43 50 E
Al 'Uzayr, *Iraq* **44 D5** 31 19N 47 25 E
Al Wajh, *Si. Arabia* **44 E3** 26 10N 36 30 E
Al Wakrah, *Qatar* **45 E6** 25 10N 51 40 E
Al Wannān, *Si. Arabia* **45 E6** 26 55N 48 24 E
Al Waqbah, *Si. Arabia* **44 D5** 28 48N 45 33 E
Al Wari'āh, *Si. Arabia* **44 E5** 27 51N 47 25 E
Al Wusayl, *Qatar* **45 E6** 25 29N 51 29 E
Ala Tau Shankou =
Dzungarian Gates,
Kazakstan **32 B3** 45 0N 82 0 E
Alabama □, *U.S.A.* **77 J2** 33 0N 87 0W
Alabama ⟶, *U.S.A.* **77 K2** 31 8N 87 57W
Alaçam Dağları, *Turkey* **21 E13** 39 18N 28 49 E
Alaérma, *Greece* **23 C9** 36 9N 27 57 E
Alagoa Grande, *Brazil* **93 E11** 7 3S 35 35W
Alagoas □, *Brazil* **93 E11** 9 0S 36 0W
Alagoinhas, *Brazil* **93 F11** 12 7S 38 20W
Alaior, *Spain* **22 B11** 39 57N 4 8 E
Alajero, *Canary Is.* **22 F2** 28 3N 17 13W
Alajuela, *Costa Rica* **88 D3** 10 2N 84 8W
Alakamisy, *Madag.* **57 C8** 21 19S 47 14 E
Alakurtti, *Russia* **24 A5** 67 0N 30 30 E
Alameda, *Calif., U.S.A.* **84 H4** 37 46N 122 15W
Alameda, *N. Mex., U.S.A.* **83 J10** 35 11N 106 37W
Alamo, *U.S.A.* **85 J11** 36 21N 115 10W
Alamo Crossing, *U.S.A.* **85 L13** 34 16N 113 33W
Alamogordo, *U.S.A.* **83 K11** 32 54N 105 57W
Alamos, *Mexico* **86 B3** 27 0N 109 0W
Alamosa, *U.S.A.* **83 H11** 37 28N 105 52W
Åland, *Finland* **9 F19** 60 15N 20 0 E
Ålands hav, *Sweden* **9 F18** 60 0N 19 30 E
Alandur, *India* **40 N12** 13 0N 80 15 E
Alania = North Ossetia □,
Russia **25 F7** 43 30N 44 30 E
Alanya, *Turkey* **25 G5** 36 38N 32 0 E
Alaotra, Farihin', *Madag.* **57 B8** 17 30S 48 30 E
Alapayevsk, *Russia* **26 D7** 57 52N 61 42 E
Alaşehir, *Turkey* **25 G4** 38 23N 28 30 E
Alaska □, *U.S.A.* **68 B5** 64 0N 154 0W
Alaska, G. of, *Pac. Oc.* **68 C5** 58 0N 145 0W
Alaska Peninsula, *U.S.A.* **68 C4** 56 0N 159 0W
Alaska Range, *U.S.A.* **68 B4** 62 50N 151 0W
Älät, *Azerbaijan* **25 G8** 39 58N 49 25 E
Alatyr, *Russia* **24 D8** 54 55N 46 35 E
Alausi, *Ecuador* **92 D3** 2 0S 78 50W
Alava, C., *U.S.A.* **82 B1** 48 10N 124 44W
Alavus, *Finland* **9 E20** 62 35N 23 36 E
Alawoona, *Australia* **63 E3** 34 45S 140 30 E
'Alayh, *Lebanon* **47 B4** 33 46N 35 33 E
Alba, *Italy* **18 D8** 44 42N 8 2 E
Alba-Iulia, *Romania* **17 E12** 46 8N 23 39 E
Albacete, *Spain* **19 C5** 39 0N 1 50W
Albacutya, L., *Australia* **63 F3** 35 45S 141 58 E
Albania ■, *Europe* **21 D9** 41 0N 20 0 E
Albany, *Australia* **61 G2** 35 1S 117 58 E
Albany, *Ga., U.S.A.* **77 K3** 31 35N 84 10W
Albany, *Minn., U.S.A.* **80 C7** 45 38N 94 34W
Albany, *N.Y., U.S.A.* **79 D11** 42 39N 73 45W
Albany, *Oreg., U.S.A.* **82 D2** 44 38N 123 6W
Albany, *Tex., U.S.A.* **81 J5** 32 44N 99 18W
Albany ⟶, *Canada* **70 B3** 52 17N 81 31W
Albardón, *Argentina* **94 C2** 31 20S 68 30W
Albatross B., *Australia* **62 A3** 12 45S 141 30 E
Albemarle, *U.S.A.* **77 H5** 35 21N 80 11W
Albemarle Sd., *U.S.A.* **77 H7** 36 5N 76 0W
Alberche ⟶, *Spain* **19 C3** 39 58N 4 46W
Alberdi, *Paraguay* **94 B4** 26 14S 58 20W
Albert, L., *Australia* **63 F2** 35 30S 139 10 E
Albert Canyon, *Canada* **72 C5** 51 8N 117 41W
Albert Edward Ra.,
Australia **60 C4** 18 17S 127 57 E
Albert L., *Africa* **54 B3** 1 30N 31 0 E
Albert Lea, *U.S.A.* **80 D8** 43 39N 93 22W
Albert Nile ⟶, *Uganda* **54 B3** 3 36N 32 2 E
Albert Town, *Bahamas* **89 B5** 22 37N 74 33W
Alberta □, *Canada* **72 C6** 54 40N 115 0W
Alberti, *Argentina* **94 D3** 35 1S 60 16W
Albertinia, *S. Africa* **56 E3** 34 11S 21 34 E
Alberton, *Canada* **71 C7** 46 50N 64 0W
Albertville = Kalemie,
Dem. Rep. of the Congo **54 D2** 5 55S 29 9 E
Albertville, *France* **18 D7** 45 40N 6 22 E
Albi, *France* **18 E5** 43 56N 2 9 E
Albia, *U.S.A.* **80 E8** 41 2N 92 48W
Albina, *Surinam* **93 B8** 5 37N 54 15W
Albina, Ponta, *Angola* **56 B1** 15 52S 11 44 E
Albion, *Idaho, U.S.A.* **82 E7** 42 25N 113 35W
Albion, *Mich., U.S.A.* **76 D3** 42 15N 84 45W
Albion, *Nebr., U.S.A.* **80 E6** 41 42N 98 0W
Albion, *Pa., U.S.A.* **78 E4** 41 53N 80 22W
Alborán, *Medit. S.* **19 E4** 35 57N 3 0W
Ålborg, *Denmark* **9 H13** 57 2N 9 54 E
Alborz, Reshteh-ye Kūhhā-
ye, *Iran* **45 C7** 36 0N 52 0 E
Albreda, *Canada* **72 C5** 52 35N 119 10W
Albuquerque, *U.S.A.* **83 J10** 35 5N 106 39W
Albuquerque, Cayos de,
Caribbean **88 D3** 12 10N 81 50W
Alburg, *U.S.A.* **79 B11** 44 59N 73 18W
Albury, *Australia* **63 F4** 36 3S 146 56 E
Alcalá de Henares, *Spain* **19 B4** 40 28N 3 22W
Alcalá la Real, *Spain* **19 D4** 37 27N 3 57W
Álcamo, *Italy* **20 F5** 37 59N 12 55 E
Alcañiz, *Spain* **19 B5** 41 2N 0 8W
Alcântara, *Brazil* **93 D10** 2 20S 44 30W
Alcántara, Embalse de,
Spain **19 C2** 39 44N 6 50W
Alcantara L., *Canada* **73 A7** 60 57N 108 9W
Alcantarilla, *Spain* **19 D5** 37 59N 1 12W
Alcaraz, Sierra de, *Spain* **19 C4** 38 40N 2 20W
Alcaudete, *Spain* **19 D3** 37 35N 4 5W
Alcázar de San Juan,
Spain **19 C4** 39 24N 3 12W
Alchevsk, *Ukraine* **25 E6** 48 30N 38 45 E
Alcira = Alzira, *Spain* **19 C5** 39 9N 0 30W
Alcoa, *U.S.A.* **77 H4** 35 48N 83 59W
Alcova, *U.S.A.* **82 E10** 42 34N 106 43W
Alcoy, *Spain* **19 C5** 38 43N 0 30W
Alcúdia, *Spain* **22 B10** 39 51N 3 7 E
Alcúdia, B. d', *Spain* **22 B10** 39 47N 3 15 E
Aldabra Is., *Seychelles* **49 G8** 9 22S 46 28 E
Aldama, *Mexico* **87 C5** 23 0N 98 4W
Aldan, *Russia* **27 D13** 58 40N 125 30 E
Aldan ⟶, *Russia* **27 C13** 63 28N 129 35 E
Aldea, Pta. de la,
Canary Is. **22 G4** 28 0N 15 50W
Aldeburgh, *U.K.* **11 E9** 52 10N 1 37 E
Alder, *U.S.A.* **82 D7** 45 19N 112 6W
Alder Pk., *U.S.A.* **84 K5** 35 53N 121 22W
Alderney, *U.K.* **11 H5** 49 42N 2 11W
Aldershot, *U.K.* **11 F7** 51 15N 0 44W
Aledo, *U.S.A.* **80 E9** 41 12N 90 45W
Aleg, *Mauritania* **50 E3** 17 3N 13 55W
Alegranza, *Canary Is.* **22 E6** 29 23N 13 32W
Alegranza, I., *Canary Is.* **22 E6** 29 23N 13 32W
Alegre, *Brazil* **95 A7** 20 50S 41 30W
Alegrete, *Brazil* **95 B4** 29 40S 56 0W
Aleisk, *Russia* **26 D9** 52 40N 83 0 E
Aleksandriya =
Oleksandriya, *Ukraine* **17 C14** 50 37N 26 19 E
Aleksandrovsk-
Sakhalinskiy, *Russia* **27 D15** 50 50N 142 20 E
Além Paraíba, *Brazil* **95 A7** 21 52S 42 41W
Alemania, *Argentina* **94 B2** 25 40S 65 30W
Alemania, *Chile* **94 B2** 25 10S 69 55W
Alençon, *France* **18 B4** 48 27N 0 4 E
Alenquer, *Brazil* **93 D8** 1 56S 54 46W
Alenuihaha Channel,
U.S.A. **74 H17** 20 30N 156 0W
Aleppo = Ḥalab, *Syria* **44 B3** 36 10N 37 15 E
Alert Bay, *Canada* **72 C3** 50 30N 126 55W
Alès, *France* **18 D6** 44 9N 4 5 E
Alessándria, *Italy* **18 D8** 44 54N 8 37 E
Ålesund, *Norway* **9 E12** 62 28N 6 12 E
Aleutian Is., *Pac. Oc.* **68 C2** 52 0N 175 0W
Aleutian Trench, *Pac. Oc.* **64 C10** 48 0N 180 0 E
Alexander, *U.S.A.* **80 B3** 47 51N 103 39W
Alexander, Mt., *Australia* **61 E3** 28 58S 120 16 E
Alexander Arch., *U.S.A.* **72 B2** 56 0N 136 0W
Alexander Bay, *S. Africa* **56 D2** 28 40S 16 30 E
Alexander City, *U.S.A.* **77 J3** 32 56N 85 58W
Alexander I., *Antarctica* **5 C17** 69 0S 70 0W
Alexandra, *Australia* **63 F4** 37 8S 145 40 E
Alexandra, *N.Z.* **59 L2** 45 14S 169 25 E
Alexandra Falls, *Canada* **72 A5** 60 29N 116 18W
Alexandria = El
Iskandarîya, *Egypt* **51 B11** 31 13N 29 58 E
Alexandria, *Australia* **62 B2** 19 5S 136 40 E
Alexandria, *B.C., Canada* **72 C4** 52 35N 122 27W
Alexandria, *Ont., Canada* **70 C5** 45 19N 74 38W
Alexandria, *Romania* **17 G13** 43 57N 25 24 E
Alexandria, *S. Africa* **56 E4** 33 38S 26 28 E
Alexandria, *U.K.* **12 F4** 55 59N 4 35W
Alexandria, *Ind., U.S.A.* **76 E3** 40 16N 85 41W
Alexandria, *La., U.S.A.* **81 K8** 31 18N 92 27W
Alexandria, *Minn., U.S.A.* **80 C7** 45 53N 95 22W
Alexandria, *S. Dak., U.S.A.* **80 D6** 43 39N 97 47W
Alexandria, *Va., U.S.A.* **76 F7** 38 48N 77 3W
Alexandria Bay, *U.S.A.* **79 B9** 44 20N 75 55W
Alexandrina, L., *Australia* **63 F2** 35 25S 139 10 E
Alexandroúpolis, *Greece* **21 D11** 40 50N 25 54 E
Alexis ⟶, *Canada* **71 B8** 52 33N 56 8W
Alexis Creek, *Canada* **72 C4** 52 10N 123 20W
Alfabia, *Spain* **22 B9** 39 44N 2 44 E
Alfenas, *Brazil* **95 A6** 21 20S 46 10W
Alford, *Aberds., U.K.* **12 D6** 57 14N 2 41W
Alford, *Lincs., U.K.* **10 D8** 53 15N 0 10 E
Alfred, *Maine, U.S.A.* **79 C14** 43 29N 70 43W
Alfred, *N.Y., U.S.A.* **78 D7** 42 16N 77 48W
Alfreton, *U.K.* **10 D6** 53 6N 1 24W
Alga, *Kazakstan* **25 E10** 49 53N 57 20 E
Algaida, *Spain* **22 B9** 39 33N 2 53 E
Ålgård, *Norway* **9 G11** 58 46N 5 53 E
Algarve, *Portugal* **19 D1** 36 58N 8 20W
Algeciras, *Spain* **19 D3** 36 9N 5 28W
Algemesí, *Spain* **19 C5** 39 11N 0 27W
Alger, *Algeria* **50 A6** 36 42N 3 8 E
Algeria ■, *Africa* **50 C6** 28 30N 2 0 E
Alghero, *Italy* **20 D3** 40 33N 8 19 E
Algiers = Alger, *Algeria* **50 A6** 36 42N 3 8 E
Algoa B., *S. Africa* **56 E4** 33 50S 25 45 E
Algoma, *U.S.A.* **76 C2** 44 36N 87 26W
Algona, *U.S.A.* **80 D7** 43 4N 94 14W
Algonac, *U.S.A.* **78 D2** 42 37N 82 32W
Algorta, *Uruguay* **96 C5** 32 25S 57 23W
Alhambra, *U.S.A.* **85 L8** 34 8N 118 6W
Alhucemas = Al Hoceïma,
Morocco **50 A5** 35 8N 3 58W
'Alī al Gharbī, *Iraq* **44 C5** 32 30N 46 45 E
'Alī ash Sharqī, *Iraq* **44 C5** 32 7N 46 44 E
'Alī Khēl, *Afghan.* **42 C3** 33 57N 69 43 E
Alī Shāh, *Iran* **44 B5** 38 9N 45 50 E
'Alīābād, *Khorāsān, Iran* **45 C8** 32 30N 57 30 E
'Alīābād, *Kordestān, Iran* **44 C5** 35 4N 46 58 E
'Alīābād, *Yazd, Iran* **45 D7** 31 41N 53 49 E
Aliağa, *Turkey* **21 E12** 38 47N 26 59 E
Aliákmon ⟶, *Greece* **21 D10** 40 30N 22 36 E
Alicante, *Spain* **19 C5** 38 23N 0 30W
Alice, *S. Africa* **56 E4** 32 48S 26 55 E
Alice, *U.S.A.* **81 M5** 27 45N 98 5W
Alice ⟶, *Queens.,*
Australia **62 C3** 24 2S 144 50 E
Alice ⟶, *Queens.,*
Australia **62 B3** 15 35S 142 20 E
Alice Arm, *Canada* **72 B3** 55 29N 129 31W
Alice Downs, *Australia* **60 C4** 17 45S 127 56 E
Alice Springs, *Australia* **62 C1** 23 40S 133 50 E
Alicedale, *S. Africa* **56 E4** 33 15S 26 4 E
Aliceville, *U.S.A.* **77 J1** 33 8N 88 9W
Alick Cr. ⟶, *Australia* **62 C3** 20 55S 142 20 E
Alida, *Canada* **73 D8** 49 25N 101 55W
Aligarh, *Raj., India* **42 G7** 25 55N 76 15 E
Aligarh, *Ut. P., India* **42 F8** 27 55N 78 10 E
Alīgūdarz, *Iran* **45 C6** 33 25N 49 45 E
Alimnía, *Greece* **23 C9** 36 16N 27 43 E
Alingsås, *Sweden* **9 H15** 57 56N 12 31 E
Alipur, *Pakistan* **42 E4** 29 25N 70 55 E
Alipur Duar, *India* **41 F16** 26 30N 89 35 E
Aliquippa, *U.S.A.* **78 F4** 40 37N 80 15W
Alitus = Alytus, *Lithuania* **9 J21** 54 24N 24 3 E
Aliwal North, *S. Africa* **56 E4** 30 45S 26 45 E
Alix, *Canada* **72 C6** 52 24N 113 11W
Aljustrel, *Portugal* **19 D1** 37 55N 8 10W
Alkmaar, *Neths.* **15 B4** 52 37N 4 45 E
All American Canal, *U.S.A.* **83 K6** 32 45N 115 15W
Allah Dad, *Pakistan* **42 G2** 25 38N 67 34 E
Allahabad, *India* **43 G9** 25 25N 81 58 E
Allan, *Canada* **73 C7** 51 53N 106 4W
Allanmyo, *Burma* **41 K19** 19 30N 95 17 E
Allanridge, *S. Africa* **56 D4** 27 45S 26 40 E
Allanwater, *Canada* **70 B1** 50 14N 90 10W
Allegan, *U.S.A.* **76 D3** 42 32N 85 51W
Allegany, *U.S.A.* **78 D6** 42 6N 78 30W
Allegheny ⟶, *U.S.A.* **78 F5** 40 27N 80 1W
Allegheny Mts., *U.S.A.* **66 F11** 38 15N 80 10W
Allegheny Plateau, *U.S.A.* **76 G6** 38 0N 80 0W
Allegheny Reservoir,
U.S.A. **78 E6** 41 50N 79 0W
Allen, Bog of, *Ireland* **13 C5** 53 15N 7 0W
Allen, L., *Ireland* **13 B3** 54 8N 8 4W
Allende, *Mexico* **86 B4** 28 20N 100 50W
Allentown, *U.S.A.* **79 F9** 40 37N 75 29W
Alleppey, *India* **40 Q10** 9 30N 76 28 E
Aller ⟶, *Germany* **16 B5** 52 56N 9 12 E
Alliance, *Nebr., U.S.A.* **80 D3** 42 6N 102 52W
Alliance, *Ohio, U.S.A.* **78 F3** 40 55N 81 6W
Allier ⟶, *France* **18 C5** 46 57N 3 4 E
Alliston, *Canada* **70 D4** 44 9N 79 52W
Alloa, *U.K.* **12 E5** 56 7N 3 47W
Allora, *Australia* **63 D5** 28 2S 152 0 E
Alma, *Canada* **71 C5** 48 35N 71 40W
Alma, *Ga., U.S.A.* **77 K4** 31 33N 82 28W
Alma, *Kans., U.S.A.* **80 F6** 39 1N 96 17W
Alma, *Mich., U.S.A.* **76 D3** 43 23N 84 39W
Alma, *Nebr., U.S.A.* **80 E5** 40 6N 99 22W
Alma, *Wis., U.S.A.* **80 C9** 44 20N 91 55W
Alma Ata = Almaty,
Kazakstan **26 E8** 43 15N 76 57 E
Almada, *Portugal* **19 C1** 38 40N 9 9W
Almaden, *Australia* **62 B3** 17 22S 144 40 E
Almadén, *Spain* **19 C3** 38 49N 4 52W
Almanor, L., *U.S.A.* **82 F3** 40 14N 121 9W
Almansa, *Spain* **19 C5** 38 51N 1 5W
Almanzor, Pico, *Spain* **19 B3** 40 15N 5 18W
Almanzora ⟶, *Spain* **19 D5** 37 14N 1 46W
Almaty, *Kazakstan* **26 E8** 43 15N 76 57 E
Almazán, *Spain* **19 B4** 41 30N 2 30W
Almeirim, *Brazil* **93 D8** 1 30S 52 34W
Almelo, *Neths.* **15 B6** 52 22N 6 42 E
Almendralejo, *Spain* **19 C2** 38 41N 6 26W
Almere-Stad, *Neths.* **15 B5** 52 20N 5 15 E
Almería, *Spain* **19 D4** 36 52N 2 27W
Almirante, *Panama* **88 E3** 9 10N 82 30W
Almiroú, Kólpos, *Greece* **23 D6** 35 23N 24 20 E
Almont, *U.S.A.* **78 D1** 42 55N 83 3W
Almonte, *Canada* **79 A8** 45 14N 76 12W
Almora, *India* **43 E8** 29 38N 79 40 E
Alness, *U.K.* **12 D4** 57 41N 4 16W
Alnmouth, *U.K.* **10 B6** 55 24N 1 37W
Alnwick, *U.K.* **10 B6** 55 24N 1 42W
Aloi, *Uganda* **54 B3** 2 16N 33 10 E
Alon, *Burma* **41 H19** 22 12N 95 5 E
Alor, *Indonesia* **37 F6** 8 15S 124 30 E
Alor Setar, *Malaysia* **39 J3** 6 7N 100 22 E
Aloysius, Mt., *Australia* **61 E4** 26 0S 128 38 E
Alpaugh, *U.S.A.* **84 K7** 35 53N 119 29W
Alpena, *U.S.A.* **76 C4** 45 4N 83 27W
Alpha, *Australia* **62 C4** 23 39S 146 37 E
Alphen aan den Rijn,
Neths. **15 B4** 52 7N 4 40 E
Alpine, *Ariz., U.S.A.* **83 K9** 33 51N 109 9W
Alpine, *Calif., U.S.A.* **85 N10** 32 50N 116 46W
Alpine, *Tex., U.S.A.* **81 K3** 30 22N 103 40W
Alps, *Europe* **18 C8** 46 30N 9 30 E
Alroy Downs, *Australia* **62 B2** 19 20S 136 5 E
Alsace, *France* **18 B7** 48 15N 7 25 E
Alsask, *Canada* **73 C7** 51 21N 109 59W
Alsasua, *Spain* **19 A4** 42 54N 2 10W
Alsten, *Norway* **8 D15** 65 58N 12 40 E
Alston, *U.K.* **10 C5** 54 49N 2 25W
Alta, *Norway* **8 B20** 69 57N 23 10 E
Alta Gracia, *Argentina* **94 C3** 31 40S 64 30W
Alta Lake, *Canada* **72 C4** 50 10N 123 0W
Alta Sierra, *U.S.A.* **85 K8** 35 42N 118 33W
Altaelva ⟶, *Norway* **8 B20** 69 54N 23 17 E
Altafjorden, *Norway* **8 A20** 70 5N 23 5 E
Altai = Aerhtai Shan,
Mongolia **32 B4** 46 40N 92 45 E
Altamaha ⟶, *U.S.A.* **77 K5** 31 20N 81 20W
Altamira, *Chile* **94 B2** 25 47S 69 51W
Altamira, *Mexico* **87 C5** 22 24N 97 55W
Altamont, *U.S.A.* **79 D10** 42 43N 74 3W
Altamura, *Italy* **20 D7** 40 49N 16 33 E
Altanbulag, *Mongolia* **32 A5** 50 16N 106 30 E
Altar, *Mexico* **86 A2** 30 40N 111 50W
Altata, *Mexico* **86 C3** 24 30N 108 0W
Altavista, *U.S.A.* **76 G6** 37 6N 79 17W
Altay, *China* **32 B3** 47 48N 88 10 E
Altea, *Spain* **19 C5** 38 38N 0 2W
Alto Araguaia, *Brazil* **93 G8** 17 15S 53 20W
Alto Cuchumatanes =
Cuchumatanes, Sierra
de los, *Guatemala* **88 C1** 15 35N 91 25W
Alto del Inca, *Chile* **94 A2** 24 10S 68 10W
Alto Ligonha, *Mozam.* **55 F4** 15 30S 38 11 E
Alto Molocue, *Mozam.* **55 F4** 15 50S 37 35 E
Alto Paraguay □,
Paraguay **94 A4** 21 0S 58 30W
Alto Paraná □, *Paraguay* **95 B5** 25 30S 54 50W
Alton, *Canada* **78 C4** 43 54N 80 5W
Alton, *U.K.* **11 F7** 51 9N 0 59W
Alton, *U.S.A.* **80 F9** 38 53N 90 11W
Alton Downs, *Australia* **63 D2** 26 7S 138 57 E
Altoona, *U.S.A.* **78 F6** 40 31N 78 24W
Altūn Kūprī, *Iraq* **44 C5** 35 45N 44 9 E
Altun Shan, *China* **32 C3** 38 30N 88 0 E
Alturas, *U.S.A.* **82 F3** 41 29N 120 32W
Altus, *U.S.A.* **81 H5** 34 38N 99 20W
Alūksne, *Latvia* **9 H22** 57 24N 27 3 E
Alunite, *U.S.A.* **85 K12** 35 59N 114 55W
Alusi, *Indonesia* **37 F8** 7 35S 131 40 E
Alva, *U.S.A.* **81 G5** 36 48N 98 40W
Alvarado, *Mexico* **87 D5** 18 40N 95 50W
Alvarado, *U.S.A.* **81 J6** 32 24N 97 13W
Alvaro Obregón, Presa,
Mexico **86 B3** 27 55N 109 52W
Alvear, *Argentina* **94 B4** 29 5S 56 30W
Alvesta, *Sweden* **9 H16** 56 54N 14 35 E
Alvie, *Australia* **63 F3** 38 14S 143 30 E
Alvin, *U.S.A.* **81 L7** 29 26N 95 15W
Alvinston, *Canada* **78 D3** 42 49N 81 52W
Älvkarleby, *Sweden* **9 F17** 60 34N 17 26 E
Älvsbyn, *Sweden* **8 D19** 65 40N 21 0 E
Alwar, *India* **42 F7** 27 38N 76 34 E
Alxa Zuoqi, *China* **34 E3** 38 50N 105 40 E
Alyata = Älät, *Azerbaijan* **25 G8** 39 58N 49 25 E
Alyth, *U.K.* **12 E5** 56 38N 3 13W
Alytus, *Lithuania* **9 J21** 54 24N 24 3 E
Alzada, *U.S.A.* **80 C2** 45 2N 104 25W
Alzira, *Spain* **19 C5** 39 9N 0 30W
Am-Timan, *Chad* **51 F10** 11 0N 20 10 E
Amadeus, L., *Australia* **61 D5** 24 54S 131 0 E
Amadi,
Dem. Rep. of the Congo **54 B2** 3 40N 26 40 E
Amâdi, *Sudan* **51 G12** 5 29N 30 25 E
Amadjuak L., *Canada* **69 B12** 65 0N 71 8W
Amagasaki, *Japan* **31 G7** 34 42N 135 20 E
Amakusa-Shotō, *Japan* **31 H5** 32 15N 130 10 E
Åmål, *Sweden* **9 G15** 59 3N 12 42 E
Amaliás, *Greece* **21 F9** 37 47N 21 22 E
Amalner, *India* **40 J9** 21 5N 75 5 E
Amambaí, *Brazil* **95 A4** 23 5S 55 13W
Amambaí ⟶, *Brazil* **95 A5** 23 22S 53 56W
Amambay □, *Paraguay* **95 A4** 23 0S 56 0W
Amambay, Cordillera de,
S. Amer. **95 A4** 23 0S 55 45W
Amami-Guntō, *Japan* **31 L4** 27 16N 129 21 E
Amami-Ō-Shima, *Japan* **31 L4** 28 0N 129 0 E
Amaná, L., *Brazil* **92 D6** 2 35S 64 40W
Amanda Park, *U.S.A.* **84 C3** 47 28N 123 55W
Amangeldy, *Kazakstan* **26 D7** 50 10N 65 10 E
Amapá, *Brazil* **93 C8** 2 5N 50 50W
Amapá □, *Brazil* **93 C8** 1 40N 52 0W
Amarante, *Brazil* **93 E10** 6 14S 42 50W
Amaranth, *Canada* **73 C9** 50 36N 98 43W
Amargosa ⟶, *U.S.A.* **85 J10** 36 14N 116 51W
Amargosa Range, *U.S.A.* **85 J10** 36 20N 116 45W

Amári

Amári, *Greece* .... **23 D6** 35 13N 24 40 E
Amarillo, *U.S.A.* **81 H4** 35 13N 101 50W
Amaro, Mte., *Italy* ...... **20 C6** 42 5N 14 5 E
Amarpur, *India* .... **43 G12** 25 5N 87 0 E
Amatikulu, *S. Africa* ..... **57 D5** 29 3S 31 33 E
Amatitlán, *Guatemala* ... **88 D1** 14 29N 90 38W
Amay, *Belgium* .... **15 D5** 50 33N 5 19 E
Amazon = Amazonas →,
S. Amer. **93 D9** 0 5S 50 0W
Amazonas →, *S. Amer.* **93 D9** 0 5S 50 0W
Ambahakily, *Madag.* .... **57 C7** 21 36S 43 41 E
Ambala, *India* .... **42 D7** 30 23N 76 56 E
Ambalavao, *Madag.* .... **57 C8** 21 50S 46 56 E
Ambalindum, *Australia* .. **62 C2** 23 23S 135 0 E
Ambanja, *Madag.* ...... **57 A8** 13 40S 48 27 E
Ambarchik, *Russia* ...... **27 C17** 69 40N 162 20 E
Ambarijeby, *Madag.* .... **57 A8** 14 56S 47 41 E
Ambaro, Helodranon',
Madag. .... **57 A8** 13 23S 48 38 E
Ambato, *Ecuador* **92 D3** 1 5S 78 42W
Ambato, Sierra de,
Argentina **94 B2** 28 25S 66 10W
Ambato Boeny, *Madag.* . **57 B8** 16 28S 46 43 E
Ambatofinandrahana,
Madag. .... **57 C8** 20 33S 46 48 E
Ambatolampy, *Madag.* .. **57 B8** 19 20S 47 35 E
Ambatondrazaka, *Madag.* **57 B8** 17 55S 48 28 E
Ambatosoratra, *Madag.* . **57 B8** 17 37S 48 31 E
Ambenja, *Madag.* ...... **57 B8** 15 17S 46 58 E
Amberg, *Germany* ...... **16 D6** 49 26N 11 52 E
Ambergris Cay, *Belize* ... **87 D7** 18 0N 88 0W
Amberley, *N.Z.* .... **59 K4** 43 9S 172 44 E
Ambikapur, *India* .... **43 H10** 23 15N 83 15 E
Ambilobé, *Madag.* ...... **57 A8** 13 10S 49 3 E
Ambinanindrano, *Madag.* **57 C8** 20 5S 48 23 E
Amble, *U.K.* **10 B6** 55 20N 1 36W
Ambleside, *U.K.* **10 C5** 54 26N 2 58W
Ambo, *Peru* **92 F3** 10 5S 76 10W
Ambodifototra, *Madag.* .. **57 B8** 16 59S 49 52 E
Ambodilazana, *Madag.* .. **57 B8** 18 6S 49 10 E
Ambohimahasoa, *Madag.* **57 C8** 21 7S 47 13 E
Ambohimanga, *Madag.* . **57 C8** 20 52S 47 36 E
Ambohitra, *Madag.* ..... **57 A8** 12 30S 49 10 E
Amboise, *France* .... **18 C4** 47 24N 1 2 E
Amboseli, L., *Kenya* ..... **54 C4** 2 40S 37 10 E
Ambositra, *Madag.* ..... **57 C8** 20 31S 47 25 E
Ambovombé, *Madag.* ... **57 D8** 25 11S 46 5 E
Amboy, *U.S.A.* **85 L11** 34 33N 115 45W
Amboyna Cay,
S. China Sea .... **36 C4** 7 50N 112 50 E
Ambridge, *U.S.A.* **78 F4** 40 36N 80 14W
Ambriz, *Angola* .... **52 F2** 7 48S 13 8 E
Amby, *Australia* .... **63 D4** 26 30S 148 11 E
Amchitka I., *U.S.A.* ...... **68 C1** 51 32N 179 0 E
Amderma, *Russia* ...... **26 C7** 69 45N 61 30 E
Ameca, *Mexico* **86 C4** 20 30N 104 0W
Ameca →, *Mexico* **86 C3** 20 40N 105 15W
Amecameca, *Mexico* **87 D5** 19 7N 98 46W
Ameland, *Neths.* .... **15 A5** 53 27N 5 45 E
American Falls, *U.S.A.* .. **82 E7** 42 47N 112 51W
American Falls Reservoir,
U.S.A. **82 E7** 42 47N 112 52W
American Highland,
Antarctica .... **5 D6** 73 0S 75 0 E
American Samoa ■,
Pac. Oc. **59 B13** 14 20S 170 40W
Americana, *Brazil* **95 A6** 22 45S 47 20W
Americus, *U.S.A.* **77 K3** 32 4N 84 14W
Amersfoort, *Neths.* ..... **15 B5** 52 9N 5 23 E
Amersfoort, *S. Africa* ... **57 D4** 26 59S 29 53 E
Amery, *Australia* .... **61 F2** 31 9S 117 5 E
Amery, *Canada* **73 B10** 56 34N 94 3W
Amery Ice Shelf,
Antarctica .... **5 C6** 69 30S 72 0 E
Ames, *U.S.A.* **80 E8** 42 2N 93 37W
Amesbury, *U.S.A.* **79 D14** 42 51N 70 56W
Amga, *Russia* .... **27 C14** 60 50N 132 0 E
Amga →, *Russia* ...... **27 C14** 62 38N 134 32 E
Amgu, *Russia* .... **30 B8** 45 45N 137 15 E
Amgun →, *Russia* .... **27 D14** 52 56N 139 38 E
Amherst, *Burma* .... **41 L20** 16 2N 97 20 E
Amherst, *Canada* **71 C7** 45 48N 64 8W
Amherst, *Mass., U.S.A.* .. **79 D12** 42 23N 72 31W
Amherst, *N.Y., U.S.A.* ... **78 D6** 42 59N 78 48W
Amherst, *Ohio, U.S.A.* ... **78 E2** 41 24N 82 14W
Amherst, *Tex., U.S.A.* ... **81 J3** 34 1N 102 25W
Amherst I., *Canada* **79 B8** 44 8N 76 43W
Amherstburg, *Canada* ... **70 D3** 42 6N 83 6W
Amiata, Mte., *Italy* ...... **20 C4** 42 53N 11 37 E
Amiens, *France* .... **18 B5** 49 54N 2 16 E
Amīrābād, *Iran* .... **44 C5** 33 20N 46 16 E
Amirante Is., *Seychelles* . **28 K9** 6 0S 53 0 E
Amisk L., *Canada* **73 C8** 54 35N 102 15W
Amistad, Presa de la,
Mexico **86 B4** 29 24N 101 0W
Amite, *U.S.A.* **81 K9** 30 44N 90 30W
Amlwch, *U.K.* **10 D3** 53 24N 4 20W
'Ammān, *Jordan* .... **47 D4** 31 57N 35 52 E
'Ammān □, *Jordan* .... **47 D5** 31 40N 36 30 E
Ammanford, *U.K.* **11 F4** 51 48N 3 59W
Amnat Charoen, *Thailand* **38 E5** 15 51N 104 38 E
Āmol, *Iran* .... **45 B7** 36 23N 52 20 E
Amory, *U.S.A.* **77 J1** 33 59N 88 29W
Amos, *Canada* **70 C4** 48 35N 78 5W
Åmot, *Norway* .... **9 G13** 59 57N 9 54 E
Amoy = Xiamen, *China* . **33 D6** 24 25N 118 4 E
Ampang, *Malaysia* ..... **39 L3** 3 8N 101 45 E
Ampanihy, *Madag.* ..... **57 C7** 24 40S 44 45 E
Ampasindava,
Helodranon', *Madag.* .. **57 A8** 13 40S 48 15 E
Ampasindava, Saikanosy,
Madag. .... **57 A8** 13 42S 47 55 E
Ampenan, *Indonesia* ... **36 F5** 8 35S 116 13 E
Amper →, *Germany* ... **16 D6** 48 29N 11 55 E
Ampotaka, *Madag.* ..... **57 D7** 25 3S 44 41 E
Ampoza, *Madag.* .... **57 C7** 22 20S 44 44 E
Amqui, *Canada* **71 C6** 48 28N 67 27W
Amravati, *India* .... **40 J10** 20 55N 77 45 E
Amreli, *India* .... **42 J4** 21 35N 71 17 E
Amritsar, *India* .... **42 D6** 31 35N 74 57 E
Amroha, *India* .... **43 E8** 28 53N 78 30 E
Amsterdam, *Neths.* ..... **15 B4** 52 23N 4 54 E
Amsterdam, *U.S.A.* **79 D10** 42 56N 74 11W
Amsterdam, I., *Ind. Oc.* .. **3 F13** 38 30S 77 30 E
Amstetten, *Austria* ...... **16 D8** 48 7N 14 51 E
Amudarya →, *Uzbekistan* **26 E6** 43 58N 59 34 E
Amundsen Gulf, *Canada* . **68 A7** 71 0N 124 0W
Amundsen Sea, *Antarctica* **5 D15** 72 0S 115 0W
Amuntai, *Indonesia* ..... **36 E5** 2 28S 115 25 E
Amur →, *Russia* ...... **27 D15** 52 56N 141 10 E
Amurang, *Indonesia* .... **37 D6** 1 5N 124 40 E
Amuri Pass, *N.Z.* .... **59 K4** 42 31S 172 11 E
Amursk, *Russia* .... **27 D14** 50 14N 136 54 E
Amyderya =
Amudarya →,
Uzbekistan .... **26 E6** 43 58N 59 34 E
An Bien, *Vietnam* .... **39 H5** 9 45N 105 0 E
An Hoa, *Vietnam* .... **38 E7** 15 40N 108 5 E
An Nabatīyah at Tahta,
Lebanon .... **47 B4** 33 23N 35 27 E
An Nabk, *Si. Arabia* ..... **44 D3** 31 20N 37 20 E
An Nabk, *Syria* .... **47 A5** 34 2N 36 44 E
An Nabk Abū Qaşr,
Si. Arabia .... **44 D3** 30 21N 38 34 E
An Nafūd, *Si. Arabia* .... **44 D4** 28 15N 41 0 E
An Najaf, *Iraq* .... **44 C5** 32 3N 44 15 E
An Nāşirīyah, *Iraq* ...... **44 D5** 31 0N 46 15 E
An Nhon, *Vietnam* ...... **38 F7** 13 55N 109 7 E
An Nu'ayrīyah, *Si. Arabia* **45 E6** 27 30N 48 30 E
An Nuwaybʻī, W. →,
Si. Arabia .... **47 F3** 29 18N 34 57 E
An Thoi, Dao, *Vietnam* .. **39 H5** 9 58N 104 0 E
An Uaimh, *Ireland* **13 C5** 53 39N 6 41W
Anabar →, *Russia* ..... **27 B12** 73 8N 113 36 E
'Anabtā, *West Bank* ..... **47 C4** 32 19N 35 7 E
Anaconda, *U.S.A.* **82 C7** 46 8N 112 57W
Anacortes, *U.S.A.* **84 B4** 48 30N 122 37W
Anadarko, *U.S.A.* **81 H5** 35 4N 98 15W
Anadolu, *Turkey* .... **25 G5** 39 0N 30 0 E
Anadyr, *Russia* .... **27 C18** 64 35N 177 20 E
Anadyr →, *Russia* ..... **27 C18** 64 55N 176 5 E
Anadyrskiy Zaliv, *Russia* . **27 C19** 64 0N 180 0 E
Anaga, Pta. de, *Canary Is.* **22 F3** 28 34N 16 9W
'Ānah, *Iraq* .... **44 C4** 34 25N 42 0 E
Anaheim, *U.S.A.* **85 M9** 33 50N 117 55W
Anahim Lake, *Canada* ... **72 C3** 52 28N 125 18W
Anáhuac, *Mexico* **86 B4** 27 14N 100 9W
Anakapalle, *India* ...... **41 L13** 17 42N 83 6 E
Anakie, *Australia* .... **62 C4** 23 32S 147 45 E
Analalava, *Madag.* ..... **57 A8** 14 35S 48 0 E
Análipsis, *Greece* ...... **23 A3** 39 36N 19 55 E
Anambar →, *Pakistan* .. **42 D3** 30 15N 68 50 E
Anambas, Kepulauan,
Indonesia .... **39 L6** 3 20N 106 30 E
Anambas Is. = Anambas,
Kepulauan, *Indonesia* . **39 L6** 3 20N 106 30 E
Anamoose, *U.S.A.* **80 B4** 47 53N 100 15W
Anamosa, *U.S.A.* **80 D9** 42 7N 91 17W
Anamur, *Turkey* .... **25 G5** 36 8N 32 58 E
Anan, *Japan* .... **31 H7** 33 54N 134 40 E
Anand, *India* .... **42 H5** 22 32N 72 59 E
Anantnag, *India* .... **43 C6** 33 45N 75 10 E
Ananyiv, *Ukraine* .... **17 E15** 47 44N 29 58 E
Anapodháris →, *Greece* **23 E7** 34 59N 25 20 E
Anápolis, *Brazil* **93 G9** 16 15S 48 50W
Anapu →, *Brazil* **93 D8** 1 53S 50 53W
Anār, *Iran* .... **45 D7** 30 55N 55 13 E
Anārak, *Iran* .... **45 C7** 33 25N 53 40 E
Anatolia = Anadolu,
Turkey .... **25 G5** 39 0N 30 0 E
Anatone, *U.S.A.* **82 C5** 46 8N 117 8W
Anatsogno, *Madag.* ..... **57 C7** 23 33S 43 46 E
Añatuya, *Argentina* **94 B3** 28 20S 62 50W
Anaunethad L., *Canada* .. **73 A8** 60 55N 104 25W
Anbyŏn, *N. Korea* ...... **35 E14** 39 1N 127 35 E
Anchor Bay, *U.S.A.* **84 G3** 38 48N 123 34W
Anchorage, *U.S.A.* **68 B5** 61 13N 149 54W
Anci, *China* .... **34 E9** 39 20N 116 40 E
Ancohuma, Nevada,
Bolivia **92 G5** 16 0S 68 50W
Ancón, *Peru* **92 F3** 11 50S 77 10W
Ancona, *Italy* .... **20 C5** 43 38N 13 30 E
Ancud, *Chile* **96 E2** 42 0S 73 50W
Ancud, G. de, *Chile* **96 E2** 42 0S 73 0W
Anda, *China* .... **33 B7** 46 24N 125 19 E
Andacollo, *Argentina* ... **94 D1** 37 10S 70 42W
Andacollo, *Chile* **94 C1** 30 5S 71 10W
Andado, *Australia* ...... **62 D2** 25 25S 135 15 E
Andalgalá, *Argentina* ... **94 B2** 27 40S 66 30W
Åndalsnes, *Norway* ..... **9 E12** 62 35N 7 43 E
Andalucía □, *Spain* **19 D3** 37 35N 5 0W
Andalusia, *U.S.A.* **77 K2** 31 18N 86 29W
Andalusia □ =
Andalucía □, *Spain* ... **19 D3** 37 35N 5 0W
Andaman Is., *Ind. Oc.* ... **28 H13** 12 30N 92 30 E
Andaman Sea, *Ind. Oc.* .. **36 B1** 13 0N 96 0 E
Andara, *Namibia* .... **56 B3** 18 2S 21 9 E
Andenes, *Norway* ...... **8 B17** 69 19N 16 18 E
Andenne, *Belgium* ...... **15 D5** 50 28N 5 5 E
Anderson, *Calif., U.S.A.* .. **82 F2** 40 27N 122 18W
Anderson, *Ind., U.S.A.* ... **76 E3** 40 10N 85 41W
Anderson, *Mo., U.S.A.* ... **81 G7** 36 39N 94 27W
Anderson, *S.C., U.S.A.* ... **77 H4** 34 31N 82 39W
Anderson →, *Canada* ... **68 B7** 69 42N 129 0W
Andes, Cord. de los,
S. Amer. **92 H5** 20 0S 68 0W
Andfjorden, *Norway* .... **8 B17** 69 10N 16 20 E
Andhra Pradesh □, *India* **40 L11** 18 0N 79 0 E
Andijon, *Uzbekistan* .... **26 E8** 41 10N 72 15 E
Andikíthira, *Greece* ..... **21 G10** 35 52N 23 15 E
Andīmeshk, *Iran* .... **45 C6** 32 27N 48 21 E
Andizhan = Andijon,
Uzbekistan .... **26 E8** 41 10N 72 15 E
Andoany, *Madag.* ...... **57 A8** 13 25S 48 16 E
Andong, *S. Korea* ...... **35 F15** 36 40N 128 43 E
Andongwei, *China* ...... **35 G10** 35 6N 119 20 E
Andorra ■, *Europe* ..... **18 E4** 42 30N 1 30 E
Andorra La Vella, *Andorra* **18 E4** 42 31N 1 32 E
Andover, *U.K.* **11 F6** 51 12N 1 29W
Andover, *Mass., U.S.A.* .. **79 D13** 42 40N 71 8W
Andover, *N.Y., U.S.A.* ... **78 D7** 42 10N 77 48W
Andover, *Ohio, U.S.A.* ... **78 E4** 41 36N 80 34W
Andøya, *Norway* .... **8 B16** 69 10N 15 50 E
Andradina, *Brazil* **93 H8** 20 54S 51 23W
Andrahary, Mt., *Madag.* . **57 A8** 13 37S 49 17 E
Andramasina, *Madag.* ... **57 B8** 19 11S 47 35 E
Andranopasy, *Madag.* ... **57 C7** 21 17S 43 44 E
Andratx, *Spain* .... **22 B9** 39 39N 2 25 E
Andreanof Is., *U.S.A.* **68 C2** 51 30N 176 0W
Andrewilla, *Australia* .... **63 D2** 26 31S 139 17 E
Andrews, *S.C., U.S.A.* ... **77 J6** 33 27N 79 34W
Andrews, *Tex., U.S.A.* ... **81 J3** 32 19N 102 33W
Ándria, *Italy* .... **20 D7** 41 13N 16 17 E
Andriba, *Madag.* .... **57 B8** 17 30S 46 58 E
Androka, *Madag.* .... **57 C7** 24 58S 44 2 E
Andropov = Rybinsk,
Russia .... **24 C6** 58 5N 38 50 E
Andros I., *Bahamas* **88 B4** 24 30N 78 0W
Andros Town, *Bahamas* . **88 B4** 24 43N 77 47W
Andselv, *Norway* .... **8 B18** 69 4N 18 34 E
Andújar, *Spain* **19 C3** 38 3N 4 5W
Andulo, *Angola* .... **52 G3** 11 25S 16 45 E
Anegada I., *Virgin Is.* ... **89 C7** 18 45N 64 20W
Anegada Passage,
W. Indies **89 C7** 18 15N 63 45W
Aneto, Pico de, *Spain* ... **19 A6** 42 37N 0 40 E
Ang Thong, *Thailand* ... **38 E3** 14 35N 100 31 E
Angamos, Punta, *Chile* . **94 A1** 23 1S 70 32W
Angara →, *Russia* ..... **27 D10** 58 5N 94 20 E
Angarsk, *Russia* .... **27 D11** 52 30N 104 0 E
Angas Downs, *Australia* . **61 E5** 25 2S 132 14 E
Angas Hills, *Australia* ... **60 D4** 23 0S 127 50 E
Angaston, *Australia* .... **63 E2** 34 30S 139 8 E
Ånge, *Sweden* .... **9 E16** 62 31N 15 35 E
Ángel, Salto = Angel
Falls, *Venezuela* **92 B6** 5 57N 62 30W
Ángel de la Guarda, I.,
Mexico **86 B2** 29 30N 113 30W
Angel Falls, *Venezuela* .. **92 B6** 5 57N 62 30W
Angeles, *Phil.* .... **37 A6** 15 9N 120 33 E
Ängelholm, *Sweden* .... **9 H15** 56 15N 12 58 E
Angellala, *Australia* .... **63 D4** 26 24S 146 54 E
Angels Camp, *U.S.A.* ... **84 G6** 38 4N 120 32W
Ångermanälven →,
Sweden .... **8 E17** 62 40N 18 0 E
Ångermanland, *Sweden* . **8 E18** 63 36N 17 45 E
Angers, *Canada* **79 A9** 45 31N 75 29W
Angers, *France* **18 C3** 47 30N 0 35W
Ängesån →, *Sweden* ... **8 C20** 66 16N 22 47 E
Angikuni L., *Canada* **73 A9** 62 0N 100 0W
Angkor, *Cambodia* ..... **38 F4** 13 22N 103 50 E
Anglesey, *U.K.* **10 D3** 53 17N 4 20W
Anglesey, Isle of □, *U.K.* . **10 D3** 53 16N 4 18W
Angleton, *U.S.A.* **81 L7** 29 10N 95 26W
Anglisidhes, *Cyprus* .... **23 E12** 34 51N 33 27 E
Ango,
Dem. Rep. of the Congo **54 B2** 4 10N 26 5 E
Angoche, *Mozam.* ...... **55 F4** 16 8S 39 55 E
Angoche, I., *Mozam.* .... **55 F4** 16 20S 39 50 E
Angol, *Chile* **94 D1** 37 56S 72 45W
Angola, *Ind., U.S.A.* **76 E3** 41 38N 85 0W
Angola, *N.Y., U.S.A.* **78 D5** 42 38N 79 2W
Angola ■, *Africa* ...... **53 G3** 12 0S 18 0 E
Angoon, *U.S.A.* **72 B2** 57 30N 134 35W
Angoulême, *France* .... **18 D4** 45 39N 0 10 E
Angoumois, *France* .... **18 D3** 45 50N 0 25 E
Angra dos Reis, *Brazil* .. **95 A7** 23 0S 44 10W
Angren, *Uzbekistan* ..... **26 E8** 41 1N 70 12 E
Angtassom, *Cambodia* .. **39 G5** 11 1N 104 41 E
Angu,
Dem. Rep. of the Congo **54 B1** 3 25N 24 28 E
Anguang, *China* .... **35 B12** 45 15N 123 45 E
Anguilla ■, *W. Indies* ... **89 C7** 18 14N 63 5W
Anguo, *China* .... **34 E8** 38 28N 115 15 E
Angurugu, *Australia* .... **62 A2** 14 0S 136 25 E
Angus □, *U.K.* **12 E6** 56 46N 2 56W
Anhanduí →, *Brazil* **95 A5** 21 46S 52 9W
Anholt, *Denmark* .... **9 H14** 56 42N 11 33 E
Anhui □, *China* .... **33 C6** 32 0N 117 0 E
Anhwei □ = Anhui □,
China .... **33 C6** 32 0N 117 0 E
Anichab, *Namibia* ...... **56 C1** 21 0S 14 46 E
Animas, *U.S.A.* **83 L9** 31 57N 108 48W
Anivorano, *Madag.* ..... **57 B8** 18 44S 48 58 E
Anjalankoski, *Finland* ... **9 F22** 60 45N 26 51 E
Anjar, *India* .... **42 H4** 23 6N 70 10 E
Anjidiv I., *India* .... **40 M9** 14 40N 74 10 E
Anjou, *France* **18 C3** 47 20N 0 15W
Anjozorobe, *Madag.* .... **57 B8** 18 22S 47 52 E
Anju, *N. Korea* .... **35 E13** 39 36N 125 40 E
Ankaboa, Tanjona, *Madag.* **57 C7** 21 58S 43 20 E
Ankang, *China* .... **34 H5** 32 40N 109 1 E
Ankara, *Turkey* .... **25 G5** 39 57N 32 54 E
Ankaramena, *Madag.* ... **57 C8** 21 57S 46 39 E
Ankazoabo, *Madag.* .... **57 C7** 22 18S 44 31 E
Ankazobe, *Madag.* ..... **57 B8** 18 20S 47 10 E
Ankisabe, *Madag.* ...... **57 B8** 19 17S 46 29 E
Ankoro,
Dem. Rep. of the Congo **54 D2** 6 45S 26 55 E
Anmyŏn-do, *S. Korea* ... **35 F14** 36 25N 126 25 E
Ann, C., *U.S.A.* **79 D14** 42 38N 70 35W
Ann Arbor, *U.S.A.* **76 D4** 42 17N 83 45W
Anna, *U.S.A.* **81 G10** 37 28N 89 15W
Anna Plains, *Australia* .. **60 C3** 19 17S 121 37 E
Annaba, *Algeria* .... **50 A7** 36 50N 7 46 E
Annalee →, *Ireland* **13 B4** 54 2N 7 24W
Annam, *Vietnam* .... **38 E7** 16 0N 108 0 E
Annamitique, Chaîne, *Asia* **38 D6** 17 0N 106 0 E
Annan, *U.K.* **12 G5** 54 59N 3 16W
Annan →, *U.K.* **12 G5** 54 58N 3 16W
Annapolis, *U.S.A.* **76 F7** 38 59N 76 30W
Annapolis Royal, *Canada* **71 D6** 44 44N 65 32W
Annapurna, *Nepal* ...... **43 E10** 28 34N 83 50 E
Annean, L., *Australia* ... **61 E2** 26 54S 118 14 E
Annecy, *France* .... **18 D7** 45 55N 6 8 E
Anning, *China* .... **32 D5** 24 55N 102 26 E
Anningie, *Australia* ..... **60 D5** 21 50S 133 7 E
Anniston, *U.S.A.* **77 J3** 33 39N 85 50W
Annobón, *Atl. Oc.* ...... **49 G4** 1 25S 5 36 E
Annotto Bay, *Jamaica* ... **88 C4** 18 17N 76 45W
Annuello, *Australia* ..... **63 E3** 34 53S 142 55 E
Annville, *U.S.A.* **79 F8** 40 20N 76 31W
Áno Viánnos, *Greece* ... **23 D7** 35 2N 25 21 E
Anoka, *U.S.A.* **75 A8** 45 12N 93 23W
Anorotsangana, *Madag.* . **57 A8** 13 56S 47 55 E
Anóyia, *Greece* .... **23 D6** 35 16N 24 52 E
Anping, *Hebei, China* ... **34 E8** 38 15N 115 30 E
Anping, *Liaoning, China* . **35 D12** 41 5N 123 30 E
Anqing, *China* .... **33 C6** 30 30N 117 3 E
Anqiu, *China* .... **35 F10** 36 25N 119 10 E
Ansai, *China* .... **34 F5** 36 50N 109 20 E
Ansbach, *Germany* ..... **16 D6** 49 28N 10 34 E
Anshan, *China* .... **35 D12** 41 5N 122 58 E
Anshun, *China* .... **32 D5** 26 18N 105 57 E
Ansley, *U.S.A.* **80 E5** 41 18N 99 23W
Anson, *U.S.A.* **81 J5** 32 45N 99 54W
Anson B., *Australia* ..... **60 B5** 13 20S 130 6 E
Ansongo, *Mali* .... **50 E6** 15 25N 0 35 E
Ansonia, *U.S.A.* **79 E11** 41 21N 73 5W
Anstruther, *U.K.* **12 E6** 56 14N 2 41W
Ansudu, *Indonesia* ..... **37 E9** 2 11S 139 22 E
Antabamba, *Peru* **92 F4** 14 40S 73 0W
Antakya, *Turkey* .... **25 G6** 36 14N 36 10 E
Antalaha, *Madag.* ...... **57 A9** 14 57S 50 20 E
Antalya, *Turkey* .... **25 G5** 36 52N 30 45 E
Antalya Körfezi, *Turkey* .. **25 G5** 36 15N 31 30 E
Antananarivo, *Madag.* ... **57 B8** 18 55S 47 31 E
Antananarivo □, *Madag.* . **57 B8** 19 0S 47 0 E
Antanimbaribe, *Madag.* . **57 C7** 21 30S 44 48 E
Antarctic Pen., *Antarctica* **5 C18** 67 0S 60 0W
Antarctica .... **5 E3** 90 0S 0 0 E
Antelope, *Zimbabwe* .... **55 G2** 21 2S 28 31 E
Antequera, *Paraguay* ... **94 A4** 24 8S 57 7W
Antequera, *Spain* **19 D3** 37 5N 4 33W
Antero, Mt., *U.S.A.* **83 G10** 38 41N 106 15W
Anthony, *Kans., U.S.A.* .. **81 G5** 37 9N 98 2W
Anthony, *N. Mex., U.S.A.* **83 K10** 32 0N 106 36W
Anthony Lagoon, *Australia* **62 B2** 18 0S 135 30 E
Anti Atlas, *Morocco* **50 C4** 30 0N 8 30W
Anti-Lebanon = Ash
Sharqi, Al Jabal,
Lebanon .... **47 B5** 33 40N 36 10 E
Antibes, *France* .... **18 E7** 43 34N 7 6 E
Anticosti, Î. d', *Canada* .. **71 C7** 49 30N 63 0W
Antigo, *U.S.A.* **80 C10** 45 9N 89 9W
Antigonish, *Canada* **71 C7** 45 38N 61 58W
Antigua, *Canary Is.* **22 F5** 28 24N 14 1W
Antigua, *W. Indies* **89 C7** 17 0N 61 50W
Antigua & Barbuda ■,
W. Indies **89 C7** 17 20N 61 48W
Antigua Guatemala,
Guatemala **88 D1** 14 34N 90 41W
Antilla, *Cuba* **88 B4** 20 40N 75 50W
Antimony, *U.S.A.* **83 G8** 38 7N 112 0W
Antioch, *U.S.A.* **84 G5** 38 1N 121 48W
Antioquia, *Colombia* **92 B3** 6 40N 75 55W
Antipodes Is., *Pac. Oc.* .. **64 M9** 49 45S 178 40 E
Antler, *U.S.A.* **80 A4** 48 59N 101 17W
Antler →, *Canada* **73 D8** 49 8N 101 0W
Antlers, *U.S.A.* **81 H7** 34 14N 95 37W
Antofagasta, *Chile* **94 A1** 23 50S 70 30W
Antofagasta □, *Chile* ... **94 A2** 24 0S 69 0W
Antofagasta de la Sierra,
Argentina **94 B2** 26 5S 67 20W
Antofalla, *Argentina* **94 B2** 25 30S 68 5W
Antofalla, Salar de,
Argentina **94 B2** 25 40S 67 45W
Anton, *U.S.A.* **81 J3** 33 49N 102 10W
Anton Chico, *U.S.A.* **83 J11** 35 12N 105 9W
Antongila, Helodrano,
Madag. .... **57 B8** 15 30S 49 50 E
Antonibé, *Madag.* ...... **57 B8** 15 7S 47 24 E
Antonibé, Presqu'île d',
Madag. .... **57 A8** 14 55S 47 20 E
Antonina, *Brazil* **95 B6** 25 26S 48 42W
Antonito, *U.S.A.* **83 H10** 37 5N 106 0W
Antrim, *U.K.* **13 B5** 54 43N 6 14W
Antrim □, *U.K.* **13 B5** 54 56N 6 25W
Antrim, Mts. of, *U.K.* **13 A5** 55 3N 6 14W
Antrim Plateau, *Australia* **60 C4** 18 8S 128 20 E
Antsalova, *Madag.* ..... **57 B7** 18 40S 44 37 E
Antsirabe, *Madag.* ..... **57 B8** 19 55S 47 2 E
Antsiranana, *Madag.* ... **57 A8** 12 25S 49 20 E
Antsohihy, *Madag.* ..... **57 A8** 14 50S 47 59 E
Antsohimbondrona
Seranana, *Madag.* .... **57 A8** 13 7S 48 48 E
Antu, *China* .... **35 C15** 42 30N 128 20 E
Antwerp = Antwerpen,
Belgium .... **15 C4** 51 13N 4 25 E
Antwerp, *U.S.A.* **79 B9** 44 12N 75 37W
Antwerpen, *Belgium* .... **15 C4** 51 13N 4 25 E
Antwerpen □, *Belgium* . **15 C4** 51 15N 4 40 E
Anupgarh, *India* .... **42 E5** 29 10N 73 10 E
Anuradhapura, *Sri Lanka* **40 Q12** 8 22N 80 28 E
Anveh, *Iran* .... **45 E7** 27 23N 54 11 E
Anvers = Antwerpen,
Belgium .... **15 C4** 51 13N 4 25 E
Anvers I., *Antarctica* **5 C17** 64 30S 63 40W
Anxi, *China* .... **32 B4** 40 30N 95 43 E
Anxious B., *Australia* ... **63 E1** 33 24S 134 45 E
Anyang, *China* .... **34 F8** 36 5N 114 21 E
Anyi, *China* .... **34 G6** 35 2N 111 2 E
Anza, *U.S.A.* **85 M10** 33 35N 116 39W
Anze, *China* .... **34 F7** 36 10N 112 12 E
Anzhero-Sudzhensk,
Russia .... **26 D9** 56 10N 86 0 E
Ánzio, *Italy* .... **20 D5** 41 27N 12 37 E
Aoga-Shima, *Japan* .... **31 H9** 32 28N 139 46 E
Aomori, *Japan* .... **30 D10** 40 45N 140 45 E
Aomori □, *Japan* ...... **30 D10** 40 45N 140 40 E
Aonla, *India* .... **43 E8** 28 16N 79 11 E
Aosta, *Italy* .... **18 D7** 45 45N 7 20 E
Apa →, *S. Amer.* **94 A4** 22 6S 58 2W
Apache, *U.S.A.* **81 H5** 34 54N 98 22W
Apalachee B., *U.S.A.* ... **77 L4** 30 0N 84 0W
Apalachicola, *U.S.A.* **77 L3** 29 43N 84 59W
Apalachicola →, *U.S.A.* . **77 L3** 29 43N 84 58W
Apaporis →, *Colombia* . **92 D5** 1 23S 69 25W
Aparri, *Phil.* .... **37 A6** 18 22N 121 38 E
Apàtity, *Russia* .... **24 A5** 67 34N 33 22 E
Apatzingán, *Mexico* **86 D4** 19 0N 102 20W
Apeldoorn, *Neths.* ...... **15 B5** 52 13N 5 57 E
Apennines = Appennini,
Italy .... **20 B4** 44 0N 10 0 E
Apia, *W. Samoa* **59 A13** 13 50S 171 50W
Apiacás, Serra dos, *Brazil* **92 E7** 9 50S 57 0W
Apizaco, *Mexico* **87 D5** 19 26N 98 9W
Aplao, *Peru* **92 G4** 16 0S 72 40W
Apo, Mt., *Phil.* .... **37 C7** 6 53N 125 14 E
Apolakkiá, *Greece* ..... **23 C9** 36 5N 27 48 E
Apolakkiá, Órmos, *Greece* **23 C9** 36 5N 27 45 E

Astara

Apolo, *Bolivia* **92 F5** 14 30S 68 30W
Aporé →, *Brazil* **93 G8** 19 27S 50 57W
Apostle Is., *U.S.A.* **80 B9** 47 0N 90 40W
Apóstoles, *Argentina* **95 B4** 28 0S 56 0W
Apostolos Andreas, C., *Cyprus* **23 D13** 35 42N 34 35 E
Apoteri, *Guyana* **92 C7** 4 2N 58 32W
Appalachian Mts., *U.S.A.* **76 G6** 38 0N 80 0W
Appennini, *Italy* **20 B4** 44 0N 10 0 E
Apple Hill, *Canada* **79 A10** 45 13N 74 46W
Apple Valley, *U.S.A.* **85 L9** 34 32N 117 14W
Appleby-in-Westmorland, *U.K.* **10 C5** 54 35N 2 29W
Appleton, *U.S.A.* **76 C1** 44 16N 88 25W
Approuague →, *Fr. Guiana* **93 C8** 4 30N 51 57W
Aprília, *Italy* **20 D5** 41 36N 12 39 E
Apucarana, *Brazil* **95 A5** 23 55S 51 33W
Apure →, *Venezuela* **92 B5** 7 37N 66 25W
Apurimac →, *Peru* **92 F4** 12 17S 73 56W
Aqaba = Al 'Aqabah, *Jordan* **47 F4** 29 31N 35 0 E
Aqaba, G. of, *Red Sea* **44 D2** 28 15N 33 20 E
'Aqabah, Khalīj al = Aqaba, G. of, *Red Sea* **44 D2** 28 15N 33 20 E
'Aqdā, *Iran* **45 C7** 32 26N 53 37 E
Aqmola, *Kazakstan* **26 D8** 51 10N 71 30 E
Aqrah, *Iraq* **44 B4** 36 46N 43 45 E
Aqtöbe, *Kazakstan* **25 D10** 50 17N 57 10 E
Aquidauana, *Brazil* **93 H7** 20 30S 55 50W
Aquiles Serdán, *Mexico* **86 B3** 28 37N 105 54W
Aquin, *Haiti* **89 C5** 18 16N 73 24W
Aquitain, Bassin, *France* **18 D3** 44 0N 0 30W
Ar Rachidiya, *Morocco* **50 B5** 31 58N 4 20W
Ar Rafid, *Syria* **47 C4** 32 57N 35 52 E
Ar Raḥḥālīyah, *Iraq* **44 C4** 32 44N 43 23 E
Ar Ramādī, *Iraq* **44 C4** 33 25N 43 20 E
Ar Ramthā, *Jordan* **47 C5** 32 34N 36 0 E
Ar Raqqah, *Syria* **44 C3** 35 59N 39 8 E
Ar Rass, *Si. Arabia* **44 E4** 25 50N 43 40 E
Ar Rifā'ī, *Iraq* **44 D5** 31 50N 46 10 E
Ar Riyāḍ, *Si. Arabia* **46 C4** 24 41N 46 42 E
Ar Ru'ays, *Qatar* **45 E6** 26 8N 51 12 E
Ar Rukhaymīyah, *Iraq* **44 D5** 29 22N 45 38 E
Ar Ruqayyidah, *Si. Arabia* **45 E6** 25 21N 49 34 E
Ar Ruşāfah, *Syria* **44 C3** 35 45N 38 49 E
Ar Ruṭbah, *Iraq* **44 C4** 33 0N 40 15 E
Ara, *India* **43 G11** 25 35N 84 32 E
'Arab, Bahr el →, *Sudan* **51 G11** 9 0N 29 30 E
'Arabābād, *Iran* **45 C8** 33 2N 57 41 E
Arabia, *Asia* **28 G8** 25 0N 45 0 E
Arabian Desert = Es Sahrâ' Esh Sharqîya, *Egypt* **51 C12** 27 30N 32 30 E
Arabian Gulf = Gulf, The, *Asia* **45 E6** 27 0N 50 0 E
Arabian Sea, *Ind. Oc.* **29 H10** 16 0N 65 0 E
Aracaju, *Brazil* **93 F11** 10 55S 37 4W
Aracati, *Brazil* **93 D11** 4 30S 37 44W
Araçatuba, *Brazil* **95 A5** 21 10S 50 30W
Aracena, *Spain* **19 D2** 37 53N 6 38W
Araçuai, *Brazil* **93 G10** 16 52S 42 4W
'Arad, *Israel* **47 D4** 31 15N 35 12 E
Arad, *Romania* **17 E11** 46 10N 21 20 E
Aradhippou, *Cyprus* **23 E12** 34 57N 33 36 E
Arafura Sea, *E. Indies* **37 F9** 9 0S 135 0 E
Aragón □, *Spain* **19 B5** 41 25N 0 40W
Aragón →, *Spain* **19 A5** 42 13N 1 44W
Araguacema, *Brazil* **93 E9** 8 50S 49 20W
Araguaia →, *Brazil* **93 E9** 5 21S 48 41W
Araguaína, *Brazil* **93 E9** 7 12S 48 12W
Araguari, *Brazil* **93 G9** 18 38S 48 11W
Araguari →, *Brazil* **93 C9** 1 15N 49 55W
Arak, *Algeria* **50 C6** 25 20N 3 45 E
Arāk, *Iran* **45 C6** 34 0N 49 40 E
Arakan Coast, *Burma* **41 K19** 19 0N 94 0 E
Arakan Yoma, *Burma* **41 K19** 20 0N 94 40 E
Araks = Aras, Rūd-e →, *Azerbaijan* **44 B5** 40 5N 48 29 E
Aral, *Kazakstan* **26 E7** 46 41N 61 45 E
Aral Sea, *Asia* **26 E7** 44 30N 60 0 E
Aral Tengizi = Aral Sea, *Asia* **26 E7** 44 30N 60 0 E
Aralsk = Aral, *Kazakstan* **26 E7** 46 41N 61 45 E
Aralskoye More = Aral Sea, *Asia* **26 E7** 44 30N 60 0 E
Aramac, *Australia* **62 C4** 22 58S 145 14 E
Arambag, *India* **43 H12** 22 53N 87 48 E
Aran I., *Ireland* **13 A3** 55 0N 8 30W
Aran Is., *Ireland* **13 C2** 53 6N 9 38W
Aranda de Duero, *Spain* **19 B4** 41 39N 3 42W
Arandān, *Iran* **44 C5** 35 23N 46 55 E
Aranjuez, *Spain* **19 B4** 40 1N 3 40W
Aranos, *Namibia* **56 C2** 24 9S 19 7 E
Aransas Pass, *U.S.A.* **81 M6** 27 55N 97 9W
Aranyaprathet, *Thailand* **38 F4** 13 41N 102 30 E
Arapahoe, *U.S.A.* **80 E5** 40 18N 99 54W
Arapey Grande →, *Uruguay* **94 C4** 30 55S 57 49W
Arapiraca, *Brazil* **93 E11** 9 45S 36 39W
Arapongas, *Brazil* **95 A5** 23 29S 51 28W
Ar'ar, *Si. Arabia* **44 D4** 30 59N 41 2 E
Araranguá, *Brazil* **95 B6** 29 0S 49 30W
Araraquara, *Brazil* **93 H9** 21 50S 48 0W
Ararás, Serra das, *Brazil* **95 B5** 25 0S 53 10W
Ararat, *Australia* **63 F3** 37 16S 143 0 E
Ararat, Mt. = Ağrı Dağı, *Turkey* **25 G7** 39 50N 44 15 E
Araria, *India* **43 F12** 26 9N 87 33 E
Araripe, Chapada do, *Brazil* **93 E11** 7 20S 40 0W
Araruama, L. de, *Brazil* **95 A7** 22 53S 42 12W
Aras, Rūd-e →, *Azerbaijan* **44 B5** 40 5N 48 29 E
Arauca, *Colombia* **92 B4** 7 0N 70 40W
Arauca →, *Venezuela* **92 B5** 7 24N 66 35W
Arauco, *Chile* **94 D1** 37 16S 73 25W
Arauco □, *Chile* **94 D1** 37 40S 73 25W
Araxá, *Brazil* **93 G9** 19 35S 46 55W
Araya, Pen. de, *Venezuela* **92 A6** 10 40N 64 0W
Arbat, *Iraq* **44 C5** 35 25N 45 35 E
Árbatax, *Italy* **20 E3** 39 56N 9 42 E
Arbīl, *Iraq* **44 B5** 36 15N 44 5 E
Arborfield, *Canada* **73 C8** 53 6N 103 39W
Arborg, *Canada* **73 C9** 50 54N 97 13W
Arbroath, *U.K.* **12 E6** 56 34N 2 35W
Arbuckle, *U.S.A.* **84 F4** 39 1N 122 3W
Arcachon, *France* **18 D3** 44 40N 1 10W
Arcade, *U.S.A.* **78 D6** 42 32N 78 25W
Arcadia, *Fla., U.S.A.* **77 M5** 27 13N 81 52W
Arcadia, *La., U.S.A.* **81 J8** 32 33N 92 55W
Arcadia, *Nebr., U.S.A.* **80 E5** 41 25N 99 8W
Arcadia, *Pa., U.S.A.* **78 F6** 40 47N 78 51W
Arcadia, *Wis., U.S.A.* **80 C9** 44 15N 91 30W
Arcata, *U.S.A.* **82 F1** 40 52N 124 5W
Archangel = Arkhangelsk, *Russia* **24 B7** 64 38N 40 36 E
Archbald, *U.S.A.* **79 E9** 41 30N 75 32W
Archer →, *Australia* **62 A3** 13 28S 141 41 E
Archer B., *Australia* **62 A3** 13 20S 141 30 E
Archers Post, *Kenya* **54 B4** 0 35N 37 35 E
Arckaringa, *Australia* **63 D1** 27 56S 134 45 E
Arckaringa Cr. →, *Australia* **63 D2** 28 10S 135 22 E
Arco, *U.S.A.* **82 E7** 43 38N 113 18W
Arcola, *Canada* **73 D8** 49 40N 102 30W
Arcos de la Frontera, *Spain* **19 D3** 36 45N 5 49W
Arcot, *India* **40 N11** 12 53N 79 20 E
Arctic Bay, *Canada* **69 A11** 73 1N 85 7W
Arda →, *Bulgaria* **21 D12** 41 40N 26 30 E
Ardabīl, *Iran* **45 B6** 38 15N 48 18 E
Ardakān = Sepīdān, *Iran* **45 D7** 30 20N 52 5 E
Ardee, *Ireland* **13 C5** 53 52N 6 33W
Arden, *Canada* **78 B8** 44 43N 76 56W
Arden, *Calif., U.S.A.* **84 G5** 38 36N 121 33W
Arden, *Nev., U.S.A.* **85 J11** 36 1N 115 14W
Ardenne, *Belgium* **16 D3** 49 50N 5 5 E
Ardennes = Ardenne, *Belgium* **16 D3** 49 50N 5 5 E
Arderin, *Ireland* **13 C4** 53 2N 7 39W
Ardestān, *Iran* **45 C7** 33 20N 52 25 E
Ardivachar Pt., *U.K.* **12 D1** 57 23N 7 26W
Ardlethan, *Australia* **63 E4** 34 22S 146 53 E
Ardmore, *Australia* **62 C2** 21 39S 139 11 E
Ardmore, *Okla., U.S.A.* **81 H6** 34 10N 97 8W
Ardmore, *Pa., U.S.A.* **79 G9** 39 58N 75 18W
Ardmore, *S. Dak., U.S.A.* **80 D3** 43 1N 103 40W
Ardnamurchan, Pt. of, *U.K.* **12 E2** 56 43N 6 14W
Ardnave Pt., *U.K.* **12 F2** 55 53N 6 20W
Ardrossan, *Australia* **63 E2** 34 26S 137 53 E
Ardrossan, *U.K.* **12 F4** 55 39N 4 49W
Ards Pen., *U.K.* **13 B6** 54 33N 5 34W
Arecibo, *Puerto Rico* **89 C6** 18 29N 66 43W
Areia Branca, *Brazil* **93 E11** 5 0S 37 0W
Arena, Pt., *U.S.A.* **84 G3** 38 57N 123 44W
Arendal, *Norway* **9 G13** 58 28N 8 46 E
Arequipa, *Peru* **92 G4** 16 20S 71 30W
Arévalo, *Spain* **19 B3** 41 3N 4 43W
Arezzo, *Italy* **20 C4** 43 25N 11 53 E
Arganda, *Spain* **19 B4** 40 19N 3 26W
Argentan, *France* **18 B3** 48 45N 0 1W
Argentário, Mte., *Italy* **20 C4** 42 24N 11 9 E
Argentia, *Canada* **71 C9** 47 18N 53 58W
Argentina ■, *S. Amer.* **96 D3** 35 0S 66 0W
Argentina Is., *Antarctica* **5 C17** 66 0S 64 0W
Argentino, L., *Argentina* **96 G2** 50 10S 73 0W
Argeş →, *Romania* **17 F14** 44 5N 26 38 E
Arghandab →, *Afghan.* **42 D1** 31 30N 64 15 E
Argolikós Kólpos, *Greece* **21 F10** 37 20N 22 52 E
Árgos, *Greece* **21 F10** 37 40N 22 43 E
Argostólion, *Greece* **21 E9** 38 12N 20 33 E
Arguello, Pt., *U.S.A.* **85 L6** 34 35N 120 39W
Arguineguín, *Canary Is.* **22 G4** 27 46N 15 41W
Argun →, *Russia* **27 D13** 53 20N 121 28 E
Argus Pk., *U.S.A.* **85 K9** 35 52N 117 26W
Argyle, *U.S.A.* **80 A6** 48 20N 96 49W
Argyle, L., *Australia* **60 C4** 16 20S 128 40 E
Argyll & Bute □, *U.K.* **12 E3** 56 13N 5 28W
Århus, *Denmark* **9 H14** 56 8N 10 11 E
Ariadnoye, *Russia* **30 B7** 45 8N 134 25 E
Ariamsvlei, *Namibia* **56 D2** 28 9S 19 51 E
Arica, *Chile* **92 G4** 18 32S 70 20W
Arica, *Colombia* **92 D4** 2 0S 71 50W
Arico, *Canary Is.* **22 F3** 28 9N 16 29W
Arid, C., *Australia* **61 F3** 34 1S 123 10 E
Arida, *Japan* **31 G7** 34 5N 135 8 E
Arílla, Ákra, *Greece* **23 A3** 39 43N 19 39 E
Arima, *Trin. & Tob.* **89 D7** 10 38N 61 17W
Arinos →, *Brazil* **92 F7** 10 25S 58 20W
Ario de Rosales, *Mexico* **86 D4** 19 12N 102 0W
Aripuanã, *Brazil* **92 E6** 9 25S 60 30W
Aripuanã →, *Brazil* **92 E6** 5 7S 60 25W
Ariquemes, *Brazil* **92 E6** 9 55S 63 6W
Arisaig, *U.K.* **12 E3** 56 55N 5 51W
Aristazabal I., *Canada* **72 C3** 52 40N 129 10W
Arivaca, *U.S.A.* **83 L8** 31 37N 111 25W
Arivonimamo, *Madag.* **57 B8** 19 1S 47 11 E
Arizaro, Salar de, *Argentina* **94 A2** 24 40S 67 50W
Arizona, *Argentina* **94 D2** 35 45S 65 25W
Arizona □, *U.S.A.* **83 J8** 34 0N 112 0W
Arizpe, *Mexico* **86 A2** 30 20N 110 11W
Arjeplog, *Sweden* **8 D18** 66 3N 18 2 E
Arjona, *Colombia* **92 A3** 10 14N 75 22W
Arjuna, *Indonesia* **37 G15** 7 49S 112 34 E
Arka, *Russia* **27 C15** 60 15N 142 0 E
Arkadelphia, *U.S.A.* **81 H8** 34 7N 93 4W
Arkaig, L., *U.K.* **12 E3** 56 59N 5 10W
Arkalyk = Arqalyk, *Kazakstan* **26 D7** 50 13N 66 50 E
Arkansas □, *U.S.A.* **81 H8** 35 0N 92 30W
Arkansas →, *U.S.A.* **81 J9** 33 47N 91 4W
Arkansas City, *U.S.A.* **81 G6** 37 4N 97 2W
Arkhángelos, *Greece* **23 C10** 36 13N 28 7 E
Arkhangelsk, *Russia* **24 B7** 64 38N 40 36 E
Arklow, *Ireland* **13 D5** 52 48N 6 10W
Arkticheskiy, Mys, *Russia* **27 A10** 81 10N 95 0 E
Arlanzón →, *Spain* **19 A3** 42 3N 4 17W
Arlbergpass, *Austria* **16 E6** 47 9N 10 12 E
Arlee, *U.S.A.* **82 C6** 47 10N 114 5W
Arles, *France* **18 E6** 43 41N 4 40 E
Arlington, *S. Africa* **57 D4** 28 1S 27 53 E
Arlington, *Oreg., U.S.A.* **82 D3** 45 43N 120 12W
Arlington, *S. Dak., U.S.A.* **80 C6** 44 22N 97 8W
Arlington, *Va., U.S.A.* **76 F7** 38 53N 77 7W
Arlington, *Wash., U.S.A.* **84 B4** 48 12N 122 8W
Arlington Heights, *U.S.A.* **76 D2** 42 5N 87 59W
Arlon, *Belgium* **15 E5** 49 42N 5 49 E
Armagh, *U.K.* **13 B5** 54 21N 6 39W
Armagh □, *U.K.* **13 B5** 54 18N 6 37W
Armavir, *Russia* **25 E7** 45 2N 41 7 E
Armenia, *Colombia* **92 C3** 4 35N 75 45W
Armenia ■, *Asia* **25 F7** 40 20N 45 0 E
Armenistís, Ákra, *Greece* **23 C9** 36 8N 27 42 E
Armidale, *Australia* **63 E5** 30 30S 151 40 E
Armour, *U.S.A.* **80 D5** 43 19N 98 21W
Armstrong, *B.C., Canada* **72 C5** 50 25N 119 10W
Armstrong, *Ont., Canada* **70 B2** 50 18N 89 4W
Armstrong, *U.S.A.* **81 M6** 26 56N 97 47W
Armstrong →, *Australia* **60 C5** 16 35S 131 40 E
Arnarfjörður, *Iceland* **8 D2** 65 48N 23 40W
Arnaud →, *Canada* **69 C13** 60 0N 70 0W
Arnauti, C., *Cyprus* **23 D11** 35 6N 32 17 E
Arnett, *U.S.A.* **81 G5** 36 8N 99 46W
Arnhem, *Neths.* **15 C5** 51 58N 5 55 E
Arnhem, C., *Australia* **62 A2** 12 20S 137 30 E
Arnhem B., *Australia* **62 A2** 12 20S 136 10 E
Arnhem Land, *Australia* **62 A1** 13 10S 134 30 E
Arno →, *Italy* **20 C4** 43 41N 10 17 E
Arno Bay, *Australia* **63 E2** 33 54S 136 34 E
Arnold, *U.K.* **10 D6** 53 1N 1 7W
Arnold, *Calif., U.S.A.* **84 G6** 38 15N 120 20W
Arnold, *Nebr., U.S.A.* **80 E4** 41 26N 100 12W
Arnot, *Canada* **73 B9** 55 56N 96 41W
Arnøy, *Norway* **8 A19** 70 9N 20 40 E
Arnprior, *Canada* **70 C4** 45 26N 76 21W
Arnsberg, *Germany* **16 C5** 51 24N 8 5 E
Aroab, *Namibia* **56 D2** 26 41S 19 39 E
Arqalyk, *Kazakstan* **26 D7** 50 13N 66 50 E
Arrabury, *Australia* **63 D3** 26 45S 141 0 E
Arrah = Ara, *India* **43 G11** 25 35N 84 32 E
Arran, *U.K.* **12 F3** 55 34N 5 12W
Arrandale, *Canada* **72 C3** 54 57N 130 0W
Arras, *France* **18 A5** 50 17N 2 46 E
Arrecife, *Canary Is.* **22 F6** 28 57N 13 37W
Arrecifes, *Argentina* **94 C3** 34 6S 60 9W
Arrée, Mts. d', *France* **18 B2** 48 26N 3 55W
Arriaga, *Chiapas, Mexico* **87 D6** 16 15N 93 52W
Arriaga, *San Luis Potosí, Mexico* **86 C4** 21 55N 101 23W
Arrilalah P.O., *Australia* **62 C3** 23 43S 143 54 E
Arrino, *Australia* **61 E2** 29 30S 115 40 E
Arrow, L., *Ireland* **13 B3** 54 3N 8 19W
Arrow Rock Res., *U.S.A.* **82 E6** 43 45N 115 50W
Arrowhead, *Canada* **72 C5** 50 40N 117 55W
Arrowhead, L., *U.S.A.* **85 L9** 34 16N 117 10W
Arrowtown, *N.Z.* **59 L2** 44 57S 168 50 E
Arroyo Grande, *U.S.A.* **85 K6** 35 7N 120 35W
Ars, *Iran* **44 B5** 37 9N 47 46 E
Arsenault L., *Canada* **73 B7** 55 6N 108 32W
Arsenev, *Russia* **30 B6** 44 10N 133 15 E
Árta, *Greece* **21 E9** 39 8N 21 2 E
Artà, *Spain* **22 B10** 39 41N 3 21 E
Arteaga, *Mexico* **86 D4** 18 50N 102 20W
Artem, *Russia* **30 C6** 43 22N 132 13 E
Artemovsk, *Russia* **27 D10** 54 45N 93 35 E
Artesia = Mosomane, *Botswana* **56 C4** 24 2S 26 19 E
Artesia, *U.S.A.* **81 J2** 32 51N 104 24W
Artesia Wells, *U.S.A.* **81 L5** 28 17N 99 17W
Artesian, *U.S.A.* **80 C6** 44 1N 97 55W
Arthur →, *Australia* **62 G3** 41 2S 144 40 E
Arthur Cr. →, *Australia* **62 C2** 22 30S 136 25 E
Arthur Pt., *Australia* **62 C5** 22 7S 150 3 E
Arthur's Pass, *N.Z.* **59 K3** 42 54S 171 35 E
Arthur's Town, *Bahamas* **89 B4** 24 38N 75 42W
Artigas, *Uruguay* **94 C4** 30 20S 56 30W
Artillery L., *Canada* **73 A7** 63 9N 107 52W
Artois, *France* **18 A5** 50 20N 2 30 E
Artsyz, *Ukraine* **17 E15** 46 4N 29 26 E
Artvin, *Turkey* **25 F7** 41 14N 41 44 E
Aru, Kepulauan, *Indonesia* **37 F8** 6 0S 134 30 E
Aru Is. = Aru, Kepulauan, *Indonesia* **37 F8** 6 0S 134 30 E
Aru Meru □, *Tanzania* **54 C4** 3 20S 36 50 E
Arua, *Uganda* **54 B3** 3 1N 30 58 E
Aruanã, *Brazil* **93 F8** 14 54S 51 10W
Aruba ■, *W. Indies* **89 D6** 12 30N 70 0W
Arucas, *Canary Is.* **22 F4** 28 7N 15 32W
Arumpo, *Australia* **63 E3** 33 48S 142 55 E
Arun →, *Nepal* **43 F12** 26 55N 87 10 E
Arun →, *U.K.* **11 G7** 50 49N 0 33W
Arunachal Pradesh □, *India* **41 F19** 28 0N 95 0 E
Arusha, *Tanzania* **54 C4** 3 20S 36 40 E
Arusha □, *Tanzania* **54 C4** 4 0S 36 30 E
Arusha Chini, *Tanzania* **54 C4** 3 32S 37 20 E
Aruwimi →, *Dem. Rep. of the Congo* **54 B1** 1 13N 23 36 E
Arvada, *U.S.A.* **82 D10** 44 39N 106 8W
Árvi, *Greece* **23 E7** 34 59N 25 28 E
Arvida, *Canada* **71 C5** 48 25N 71 14W
Arvidsjaur, *Sweden* **8 D18** 65 35N 19 10 E
Arvika, *Sweden* **9 G15** 59 40N 12 36 E
Arvin, *U.S.A.* **85 K8** 35 12N 118 50W
Arxan, *China* **33 B6** 47 11N 119 57 E
Aryirádhes, *Greece* **23 B3** 39 27N 19 58 E
Aryiroúpolis, *Greece* **23 D6** 35 17N 24 20 E
Arys, *Kazakstan* **26 E7** 42 26N 68 48 E
Arzamas, *Russia* **24 C7** 55 27N 43 55 E
Aş Şadr, *U.A.E.* **45 E7** 24 40N 54 41 E
Aş Şafā, *Syria* **47 B6** 33 10N 37 0 E
'As Saffānīyah, *Si. Arabia* **45 D6** 28 5N 48 50 E
As Safīrah, *Syria* **44 B3** 36 5N 37 21 E
Aş Şahm, *Oman* **45 E8** 24 10N 56 53 E
As Sājir, *Si. Arabia* **44 E5** 25 11N 44 36 E
As Salamīyah, *Syria* **44 C3** 35 1N 37 2 E
As Salṭ, *Jordan* **47 C4** 32 2N 35 43 E
As Sal'w'a, *Qatar* **45 E6** 24 23N 50 50 E
As Samāwah, *Iraq* **44 D5** 31 15N 45 15 E
As Sanamayn, *Syria* **47 B5** 33 3N 36 10 E
As Sohar = Şuḩār, *Oman* **45 E8** 24 20N 56 40 E
As Sukhnah, *Syria* **44 C3** 34 52N 38 52 E
As Sulaymānīyah, *Iraq* **44 C5** 35 35N 45 29 E
As Sulaymī, *Si. Arabia* **44 E4** 26 17N 41 21 E
As Summān, *Si. Arabia* **44 E5** 25 0N 47 0 E
As Suwaydā', *Syria* **47 C5** 32 40N 36 30 E
As Suwaydā' □, *Syria* **47 C5** 32 45N 36 45 E
As Şuwayrah, *Iraq* **44 C5** 32 55N 45 0 E
Asab, *Namibia* **56 D2** 25 30S 18 0 E
Asahi-Gawa →, *Japan* **31 G6** 34 36N 133 58 E
Asahigawa, *Japan* **30 C11** 43 46N 142 22 E
Asansol, *India* **43 H12** 23 40N 87 1 E
Asbesberge, *S. Africa* **56 D3** 29 0S 23 0 E
Asbestos, *Canada* **71 C5** 45 47N 71 58W
Asbury Park, *U.S.A.* **79 F10** 40 13N 74 1W
Ascensión, *Mexico* **86 A3** 31 6N 107 59W
Ascensión, B. de la, *Mexico* **87 D7** 19 50N 87 20W
Ascension I., *Atl. Oc.* **49 G2** 8 0S 14 15W
Aschaffenburg, *Germany* **16 D5** 49 58N 9 6 E
Aschersleben, *Germany* **16 C6** 51 45N 11 29 E
Áscoli Piceno, *Italy* **20 C5** 42 51N 13 34 E
Ascope, *Peru* **92 E3** 7 46S 79 8W
Ascotán, *Chile* **94 A2** 21 45S 68 17W
Aseb, *Eritrea* **46 E3** 13 0N 42 40 E
Asela, *Ethiopia* **46 F2** 8 0N 39 0 E
Asenovgrad, *Bulgaria* **21 C11** 42 1N 24 51 E
Asgata, *Cyprus* **23 E12** 34 46N 33 15 E
Ash Fork, *U.S.A.* **83 J7** 35 13N 112 29W
Ash Grove, *U.S.A.* **81 G8** 37 19N 93 35W
Ash Shām, Bādiyat, *Asia* **28 F7** 32 0N 40 0 E
Ash Shamāl □, *Lebanon* **47 A5** 34 25N 36 0 E
Ash Shāmīyah, *Iraq* **44 D5** 31 55N 44 35 E
Ash Shāriqah, *U.A.E.* **45 E7** 25 23N 55 26 E
Ash Sharmah, *Si. Arabia* **44 D2** 28 1N 35 16 E
Ash Sharqāt, *Iraq* **44 C4** 35 27N 43 16 E
Ash Sharqi, Al Jabal, *Lebanon* **47 B5** 33 40N 36 10 E
Ash Shaṭrah, *Iraq* **44 D5** 31 30N 46 10 E
Ash Shawbak, *Jordan* **44 D2** 30 32N 35 34 E
Ash Shawmari, J., *Jordan* **47 E5** 30 35N 36 35 E
Ash Shaykh, J., *Lebanon* **47 B4** 33 25N 35 50 E
Ash Shināfīyah, *Iraq* **44 D5** 31 35N 44 39 E
Ash Shu'aybah, *Si. Arabia* **44 E5** 27 53N 44 43 E
Ash Shumlūl, *Si. Arabia* **44 E5** 26 31N 47 20 E
Ash Shūr'a, *Iraq* **44 C4** 35 58N 43 13 E
Ash Shurayf, *Si. Arabia* **44 E3** 25 43N 39 14 E
Ash Shuwayfāt, *Lebanon* **47 B4** 33 45N 35 30 E
Asha, *Russia* **24 D10** 55 0N 57 16 E
Ashau, *Vietnam* **38 D6** 16 6N 107 22 E
Ashbourne, *U.K.* **10 D6** 53 2N 1 43W
Ashburn, *U.S.A.* **77 K4** 31 43N 83 39W
Ashburton, *N.Z.* **59 K3** 43 53S 171 48 E
Ashburton →, *Australia* **60 D1** 21 40S 114 56 E
Ashburton Downs, *Australia* **60 D2** 23 25S 117 4 E
Ashcroft, *Canada* **72 C4** 50 40N 121 20W
Ashdod, *Israel* **47 D3** 31 49N 34 35 E
Asheboro, *U.S.A.* **77 H6** 35 43N 79 49W
Asherton, *U.S.A.* **81 L5** 28 27N 99 46W
Asheville, *U.S.A.* **77 H4** 35 36N 82 33W
Asheweig →, *Canada* **70 B2** 54 17N 87 12W
Ashford, *Australia* **63 D5** 29 15S 151 3 E
Ashford, *U.K.* **11 F8** 51 8N 0 53 E
Ashford, *U.S.A.* **82 C2** 46 46N 122 2W
Ashgabat, *Turkmenistan* **26 F6** 38 0N 57 50 E
Ashibetsu, *Japan* **30 C11** 43 31N 142 11 E
Ashikaga, *Japan* **31 F9** 36 28N 139 29 E
Ashington, *U.K.* **10 B6** 55 11N 1 33W
Ashizuri-Zaki, *Japan* **31 H6** 32 44N 133 0 E
Ashkarkot, *Afghan.* **42 C2** 33 3N 67 58 E
Ashkhabad = Ashgabat, *Turkmenistan* **26 F6** 38 0N 57 50 E
Ashland, *Kans., U.S.A.* **81 G5** 37 11N 99 46W
Ashland, *Ky., U.S.A.* **76 F4** 38 28N 82 38W
Ashland, *Maine, U.S.A.* **71 C6** 46 38N 68 24W
Ashland, *Mont., U.S.A.* **82 D10** 45 36N 106 16W
Ashland, *Nebr., U.S.A.* **80 E6** 41 3N 96 23W
Ashland, *Ohio, U.S.A.* **78 F2** 40 52N 82 19W
Ashland, *Oreg., U.S.A.* **82 E2** 42 12N 122 43W
Ashland, *Pa., U.S.A.* **79 F8** 40 45N 76 22W
Ashland, *Va., U.S.A.* **76 G7** 37 46N 77 29W
Ashland, *Wis., U.S.A.* **80 B9** 46 35N 90 53W
Ashley, *N. Dak., U.S.A.* **80 B5** 46 2N 99 22W
Ashley, *Pa., U.S.A.* **79 E9** 41 12N 75 55W
Ashmont, *Canada* **72 C6** 54 7N 111 35W
Ashmore Reef, *Australia* **60 B3** 12 14S 123 5 E
Ashmyany, *Belarus* **9 J21** 54 26N 25 52 E
Ashqelon, *Israel* **47 D3** 31 42N 34 35 E
Ashtabula, *U.S.A.* **78 E4** 41 52N 80 47W
Ashton, *S. Africa* **56 E3** 33 50S 20 5 E
Ashton, *U.S.A.* **82 D8** 44 4N 111 27W
Ashuanipi, L., *Canada* **71 B6** 52 45N 66 15W
Asia, Kepulauan, *Indonesia* **37 D8** 1 0N 131 13 E
Āsīā Bak, *Iran* **45 C6** 35 19N 50 30 E
Asifabad, *India* **40 K11** 19 20N 79 24 E
Asinara, *Italy* **20 D3** 41 4N 8 16 E
Asinara, G. dell', *Italy* **20 D3** 41 0N 8 30 E
Asino, *Russia* **26 D9** 57 0N 86 0 E
Asipovichy, *Belarus* **17 B15** 53 19N 28 33 E
'Asīr □, *Si. Arabia* **46 D3** 18 40N 42 30 E
Asir, Ras, *Somali Rep.* **46 E5** 11 55N 51 10 E
Askersund, *Sweden* **9 G16** 58 53N 14 55 E
Askham, *S. Africa* **56 D3** 26 59S 20 47 E
Askim, *Norway* **9 G14** 59 35N 11 10 E
Askja, *Iceland* **8 D5** 65 3N 16 48W
Askøy, *Norway* **9 F11** 60 29N 5 10 E
Asmara = Asmera, *Eritrea* **46 D2** 15 19N 38 55 E
Asmera, *Eritrea* **46 D2** 15 19N 38 55 E
Åsnen, *Sweden* **9 H16** 56 37N 14 45 E
Asotin, *U.S.A.* **82 C5** 46 20N 117 3W
Aspen, *U.S.A.* **83 G10** 39 11N 106 49W
Aspermont, *U.S.A.* **81 J4** 33 8N 100 14W
Aspiring, Mt., *N.Z.* **59 L2** 44 23S 168 46 E
Asprókavos, Ákra, *Greece* **23 B4** 39 21N 20 6 E
Aspur, *India* **42 H6** 23 58N 74 7 E
Asquith, *Canada* **73 C7** 52 8N 107 13W
Assad, Bahret, *Syria* **44 C3** 36 0N 38 15 E
Assam □, *India* **41 G18** 26 0N 93 0 E
Asse, *Belgium* **15 D4** 50 24N 4 10 E
Assen, *Neths.* **15 A6** 53 0N 6 35 E
Assiniboia, *Canada* **73 D7** 49 40N 105 59W
Assiniboine →, *Canada* **73 D9** 49 53N 97 8W
Assis, *Brazil* **95 A5** 22 40S 50 20W
Assisi, *Italy* **20 C5** 43 4N 12 37 E
Assynt, L., *U.K.* **12 C3** 58 10N 5 3W
Astana = Aqmola, *Kazakstan* **26 D8** 51 10N 71 30 E
Astara, *Azerbaijan* **25 G8** 38 30N 48 50 E

Barnard Castle

Barnard Castle, U.K. 10 C6 54 33N 1 55W
Barnato, Australia 63 E4 31 38S 145 0 E
Barnaul, Russia 26 D9 53 20N 83 40 E
Barnesville, U.S.A. 77 J3 33 3N 84 9W
Barnet, U.K. 11 F7 51 38N 0 9W
Barneveld, Neths. 15 B5 52 7N 5 36 E
Barneveld, U.S.A. 79 C9 43 16N 75 14W
Barngo, Australia 62 D4 25 3S 147 20 E
Barnhart, U.S.A. 81 K4 31 8N 101 10W
Barnsley, U.K. 10 D6 53 34N 1 27W
Barnstaple, U.K. 11 F3 51 5N 4 4W
Barnstaple Bay = Bideford Bay, U.K. 11 F3 51 5N 4 20W
Barnsville, U.S.A. 80 B6 46 43N 96 28W
Baro, Nigeria 50 G7 8 35N 6 18 E
Baroda = Vadodara, India 42 H5 22 20N 73 10 E
Baroda, India 42 G7 25 29N 76 35 E
Baroe, S. Africa 56 E3 33 13S 24 33 E
Baron Ra., Australia 60 D4 23 30S 127 45 E
Barpeta, India 41 F17 26 20N 91 10 E
Barques, Pt. Aux, U.S.A. 76 C4 44 4N 82 58W
Barquísimeto, Venezuela 92 A5 10 4N 69 19W
Barra, Brazil 93 F10 11 5S 43 10W
Barra, U.K. 12 E1 57 0N 7 29W
Barra, Sd. of, U.K. 12 E1 57 4N 7 25W
Barra de Navidad, Mexico 86 D4 19 12N 104 41W
Barra do Corda, Brazil 93 E9 5 30S 45 10W
Barra do Piraí, Brazil 95 A7 22 30S 43 50W
Barra Falsa, Pta. da, Mozam. 57 C6 22 58S 35 37 E
Barra Hd., U.K. 12 E1 56 47N 7 40W
Barra Mansa, Brazil 95 A7 22 35S 44 12W
Barraba, Australia 63 E5 30 21S 150 35 E
Barrackpur = Barakpur, India 43 H13 22 44N 88 30 E
Barraigh = Barra, U.K. 12 E1 57 0N 7 29W
Barranca, Lima, Peru 92 F3 10 45S 77 50W
Barranca, Loreto, Peru 92 D3 4 50S 76 50W
Barrancabermeja, Colombia 92 B4 7 0N 73 50W
Barrancos, Portugal 19 C2 38 10N 6 58W
Barranqueras, Argentina 94 B4 27 30S 59 0W
Barranquilla, Colombia 92 A4 11 0N 74 50W
Barraute, Canada 70 C4 48 26N 77 38W
Barre, Mass., U.S.A. 79 D12 42 25N 72 6W
Barre, Vt., U.S.A. 79 B12 44 12N 72 30W
Barreal, Argentina 94 C2 31 33S 69 28W
Barreiras, Brazil 93 F10 12 8S 45 0W
Barreirinhas, Brazil 93 D10 2 30S 42 50W
Barreiro, Portugal 19 C1 38 40N 9 6W
Barren, Nosy, Madag. 57 B7 18 25S 43 40 E
Barretos, Brazil 93 H9 20 30S 48 35W
Barrhead, Canada 72 C6 54 10N 114 24W
Barrie, Canada 70 D4 44 24N 79 40W
Barrier Ra., Australia 63 E3 31 0S 141 30 E
Barrière, Canada 72 C4 51 12N 120 7W
Barrington, U.S.A. 79 E13 41 44N 71 18W
Barrington L., Canada 73 B8 56 55N 100 15W
Barrington Tops, Australia 63 E5 32 6S 151 28 E
Barringun, Australia 63 D4 29 1S 145 41 E
Barro do Garças, Brazil 93 G8 15 54S 52 16W
Barrow, U.S.A. 68 A4 71 18N 156 47W
Barrow →, Ireland 13 D5 52 25N 6 58W
Barrow Creek, Australia 62 C1 21 30S 133 55 E
Barrow I., Australia 60 D2 20 45S 115 20 E
Barrow-in-Furness, U.K. 10 C4 54 7N 3 14W
Barrow Pt., Australia 62 A3 14 20S 144 40 E
Barrow Pt., U.S.A. 66 B4 71 24N 156 29W
Barrow Ra., Australia 61 E4 26 0S 127 40 E
Barry, U.K. 11 F4 51 24N 3 16W
Barry's Bay, Canada 70 C4 45 29N 77 41W
Barsat, Pakistan 43 A5 36 10N 72 45 E
Barsham, Syria 44 C4 35 21N 40 33 E
Barsi, India 40 K9 18 10N 75 50 E
Barsoi, India 41 G15 25 48N 87 57 E
Barstow, Calif., U.S.A. 85 L9 34 54N 117 1W
Barstow, Tex., U.S.A. 81 K3 31 28N 103 24W
Barthélemy, Col, Vietnam 38 C5 19 26N 104 6 E
Bartica, Guyana 92 B7 6 25N 58 40W
Bartlesville, U.S.A. 81 G7 36 45N 95 59W
Bartlett, Calif., U.S.A. 84 J8 36 29N 118 2W
Bartlett, Tex., U.S.A. 81 K6 30 48N 97 26W
Bartlett, L., Canada 72 A5 63 5N 118 20W
Bartolomeu Dias, Mozam. 55 G4 21 10S 35 8 E
Barton, Australia 61 F5 30 31S 132 39 E
Barton upon Humber, U.K. 10 D7 53 41N 0 25W
Bartow, U.S.A. 77 M5 27 54N 81 50W
Barú, Volcan, Panama 88 E3 8 55N 82 35W
Barumba, Dem. Rep. of the Congo 54 B1 1 3N 23 37 E
Barwani, India 42 H6 22 2N 74 57 E
Barysaw, Belarus 24 D4 54 17N 28 28 E
Barzān, Iraq 44 B5 36 55N 44 3 E
Bāsa'idū, Iran 45 E7 26 35N 55 20 E
Basal, Pakistan 42 C5 33 33N 72 13 E
Basankusa, Dem. Rep. of the Congo 52 D3 1 5N 19 50 E
Basarabeasca, Moldova 17 E15 46 21N 28 58 E
Basawa, Afghan. 42 B4 34 15N 70 50 E
Bascuñán, C., Chile 94 B1 28 52S 71 35W
Basel, Switz. 18 C7 47 35N 7 35 E
Bāshī, Iran 45 D6 28 41N 51 4 E
Bashkir Republic = Bashkortostan □, Russia 24 D10 54 0N 57 0 E
Bashkortostan □, Russia 24 D10 54 0N 57 0 E
Basilan, Phil. 37 C6 6 35N 122 0 E
Basilan Str., Phil. 37 C6 6 50N 122 0 E
Basildon, U.K. 11 F8 51 34N 0 28 E
Basim = Washim, India 40 J10 20 3N 77 0 E
Basin, U.S.A. 82 D9 44 23N 108 2W
Basingstoke, U.K. 11 F6 51 15N 1 5W
Baskatong, Rés., Canada 70 C4 46 46N 75 50W
Basle = Basel, Switz. 18 C7 47 35N 7 35 E
Basoda, India 42 H7 23 52N 77 54 E
Basoka, Dem. Rep. of the Congo 54 B1 1 16N 23 40 E
Basque Provinces = País Vasco □, Spain 19 A4 42 50N 2 45W
Basra = Al Başrah, Iraq 44 D5 30 30N 47 50 E
Bass Str., Australia 62 F4 39 15S 146 30 E
Bassano, Canada 72 C6 50 48N 112 20W
Bassano del Grappa, Italy 20 B4 45 46N 11 44 E
Bassas da India, Ind. Oc. 53 J7 22 0S 39 0 E
Basse-Terre, Guadeloupe 89 C7 16 0N 61 44W
Bassein, Burma 41 L19 16 45N 94 30 E
Basseterre, St. Kitts & Nevis 89 C7 17 17N 62 43W
Bassett, Nebr., U.S.A. 80 D5 42 35N 99 32W
Bassett, Va., U.S.A. 77 G6 36 46N 79 59W
Bassi, India 42 D7 30 44N 76 21 E
Bastak, Iran 45 E7 27 15N 54 25 E
Baştām, Iran 45 B7 36 29N 55 4 E
Bastar, India 41 K12 19 15N 81 40 E
Basti, India 43 F10 26 52N 82 55 E
Bastia, France 18 E8 42 40N 9 30 E
Bastogne, Belgium 15 D5 50 1N 5 43 E
Bastrop, U.S.A. 81 K6 30 7N 97 19W
Bat Yam, Israel 47 C3 32 2N 34 44 E
Bata, Eq. Guin. 52 D1 1 57N 9 50 E
Bataan, Phil. 37 B6 14 40N 120 25 E
Batabanó, Cuba 88 B3 22 40N 82 20W
Batabanó, G. de, Cuba 88 B3 22 30N 82 30W
Batac, Phil. 37 A6 18 3N 120 34 E
Batagai, Russia 27 C14 67 38N 134 38 E
Batama, Dem. Rep. of the Congo 54 B2 0 58N 26 33 E
Batamay, Russia 27 C13 63 30N 129 15 E
Batang, Indonesia 37 G13 6 55S 109 45 E
Batangas, Phil. 37 B6 13 35N 121 10 E
Batanta, Indonesia 37 E8 0 55S 130 40 E
Batatais, Brazil 95 A6 20 54S 47 37W
Batavia, U.S.A. 78 D6 43 0N 78 11W
Batchelor, Australia 60 B5 13 4S 131 1 E
Batdambang, Cambodia 38 F4 13 7N 103 12 E
Bateman's B., Australia 63 F5 35 40S 150 12 E
Batemans Bay, Australia 63 F5 35 44S 150 11 E
Bates Ra., Australia 61 E3 27 27S 121 5 E
Batesburg, U.S.A. 77 J5 33 54N 81 33W
Batesville, Ark., U.S.A. 81 H9 35 46N 91 39W
Batesville, Miss., U.S.A. 81 H10 34 19N 89 57W
Batesville, Tex., U.S.A. 81 L5 28 58N 99 37W
Bath, U.K. 11 F5 51 23N 2 22W
Bath, Maine, U.S.A. 71 D6 43 55N 69 49W
Bath, N.Y., U.S.A. 78 D7 42 20N 77 19W
Bath & North East Somerset □, U.K. 11 F5 51 21N 2 27W
Batheay, Cambodia 39 G5 11 59N 104 57 E
Bathurst = Banjul, Gambia 50 F2 13 28N 16 40W
Bathurst, Australia 63 E4 33 25S 149 31 E
Bathurst, Canada 71 C6 47 37N 65 43W
Bathurst, S. Africa 56 E4 33 30S 26 50 E
Bathurst, C., Canada 68 A7 70 34N 128 0W
Bathurst B., Australia 62 A3 14 16S 144 25 E
Bathurst Harb., Australia 62 G4 43 15S 146 10 E
Bathurst I., Australia 60 B5 11 30S 130 10 E
Bathurst I., Canada 66 B9 76 0N 100 30W
Bathurst Inlet, Canada 68 B9 66 50N 108 1W
Batlow, Australia 63 F4 35 31S 148 9 E
Batna, Algeria 50 A7 35 34N 6 15 E
Batoka, Zambia 55 F2 16 45S 27 15 E
Baton Rouge, U.S.A. 81 K9 30 27N 91 11W
Batong, Ko, Thailand 39 J2 6 32N 99 12 E
Batopilas, Mexico 86 B3 27 0N 107 45W
Batouri, Cameroon 52 D2 4 30N 14 25 E
Båtsfjord, Norway 8 A23 70 38N 29 39 E
Battambang = Batdambang, Cambodia 38 F4 13 7N 103 12 E
Batticaloa, Sri Lanka 40 R12 7 43N 81 45 E
Battipáglia, Italy 20 D6 40 37N 14 58 E
Battle, U.K. 11 G8 50 55N 0 30 E
Battle →, Canada 73 C7 52 43N 108 15W
Battle Camp, Australia 62 B3 15 20S 144 40 E
Battle Creek, U.S.A. 76 D3 42 19N 85 11W
Battle Ground, U.S.A. 84 E4 45 47N 122 32W
Battle Harbour, Canada 71 B8 52 16N 55 35W
Battle Lake, U.S.A. 80 B7 46 17N 95 43W
Battle Mountain, U.S.A. 82 F5 40 38N 116 56W
Battlefields, Zimbabwe 55 F2 18 37S 29 47 E
Battleford, Canada 73 C7 52 45N 108 15W
Batu, Kepulauan, Indonesia 36 E1 0 30S 98 25 E
Batu, Mt., Ethiopia 46 F2 6 55N 39 45 E
Batu Caves, Malaysia 39 L3 3 15N 101 40 E
Batu Gajah, Malaysia 39 K3 4 28N 101 3 E
Batu Is. = Batu, Kepulauan, Indonesia 36 E1 0 30S 98 25 E
Batu Pahat, Malaysia 39 M4 1 50N 102 56 E
Batuata, Indonesia 37 F6 6 12S 122 42 E
Batumi, Georgia 25 F7 41 39N 41 44 E
Baturaja, Indonesia 36 E2 4 11S 104 15 E
Baturité, Brazil 93 D11 4 28S 38 45W
Bau, Malaysia 36 D4 1 25N 110 9 E
Baubau, Indonesia 37 F6 5 25S 122 38 E
Bauchi, Nigeria 50 F7 10 22N 9 48 E
Baudette, U.S.A. 80 A7 48 43N 94 36W
Bauer, C., Australia 63 E1 32 44S 134 4 E
Bauhinia Downs, Australia 62 C4 24 35S 149 18 E
Baukau, Indonesia 37 F7 8 27S 126 27 E
Bauru, Brazil 95 A6 22 10S 49 0W
Bauska, Latvia 9 H21 56 24N 24 15 E
Bautzen, Germany 16 C8 51 10N 14 26 E
Bavānāt, Iran 45 D7 30 28N 53 27 E
Bavaria = Bayern □, Germany 16 D6 48 50N 12 0 E
Bavi Sadri, India 42 G6 24 28N 74 30 E
Bavispe →, Mexico 86 B3 29 30N 109 11W
Bawdwin, Burma 41 H20 23 5N 97 20 E
Bawean, Indonesia 36 F4 5 46S 112 35 E
Bawku, Ghana 50 F5 11 3N 0 19W
Bawlake, Burma 41 K20 19 11N 97 21 E
Baxley, U.S.A. 77 K4 31 47N 82 21W
Baxter Springs, U.S.A. 81 G7 37 2N 94 44W
Bay Bulls, Canada 71 C9 47 19N 52 50W
Bay City, Mich., U.S.A. 76 D4 43 36N 83 54W
Bay City, Oreg., U.S.A. 82 D2 45 31N 123 53W
Bay City, Tex., U.S.A. 81 L7 28 59N 95 58W
Bay de Verde, Canada 71 C9 48 5N 52 54W
Bay Minette, U.S.A. 77 K2 30 53N 87 46W
Bay St. Louis, U.S.A. 81 K10 30 19N 89 20W
Bay Springs, U.S.A. 81 K10 31 59N 89 17W
Bay View, N.Z. 59 H6 39 25S 176 50 E
Baya, Dem. Rep. of the Congo 55 E2 11 53S 27 25 E
Bayamo, Cuba 88 B4 20 20N 76 40W
Bayamón, Puerto Rico 89 C6 18 24N 66 10W
Bayan Har Shan, China 32 C4 34 0N 98 0 E
Bayan Hot = Alxa Zuoqi, China 34 E3 38 50N 105 40 E
Bayan Obo, China 34 D5 41 52N 109 59 E
Bayan-Ovoo, Mongolia 34 C4 42 55N 106 5 E
Bayana, India 42 F7 26 55N 77 18 E
Bayanaūyl, Kazakstan 26 D8 50 45N 75 45 E
Bayandalay, Mongolia 34 C2 43 30N 103 29 E
Bayanhongor, Mongolia 32 B5 46 8N 102 43 E
Bayard, U.S.A. 80 E3 41 45N 103 20W
Baybay, Phil. 37 B6 10 40N 124 55 E
Bayern □, Germany 16 D6 48 50N 12 0 E
Bayeux, France 18 B3 49 17N 0 42W
Bayfield, Canada 78 C3 43 34N 81 42W
Bayfield, U.S.A. 80 B9 46 49N 90 49W
Bayındır, Turkey 21 E12 38 13N 27 39 E
Baykal, Oz., Russia 27 D11 53 0N 108 0 E
Baykonur = Bayqongyr, Kazakstan 26 E7 47 48N 65 50 E
Baymak, Russia 24 D10 52 36N 58 19 E
Baynes Mts., Namibia 56 B1 17 15S 13 0 E
Bayombong, Phil. 37 A6 16 30N 121 10 E
Bayonne, France 18 E3 43 30N 1 28W
Bayonne, U.S.A. 79 F10 40 40N 74 7W
Bayovar, Peru 92 E2 5 50S 81 0W
Bayqongyr, Kazakstan 26 E7 47 48N 65 50 E
Bayram-Ali = Bayramaly, Turkmenistan 26 F7 37 37N 62 10 E
Bayramaly, Turkmenistan 26 F7 37 37N 62 10 E
Bayramiç, Turkey 21 E12 39 48N 26 36 E
Bayreuth, Germany 16 D6 49 56N 11 35 E
Bayrūt, Lebanon 47 B4 33 53N 35 31 E
Bayt Lahm, West Bank 47 D4 31 43N 35 12 E
Baytown, U.S.A. 81 L7 29 43N 94 59W
Baza, Spain 19 D4 37 30N 2 47W
Bazaruto, I. do, Mozam. 57 C6 21 40S 35 28 E
Bazmān, Kūh-e, Iran 45 D9 28 4N 60 1 E
Beach, U.S.A. 80 B3 46 58N 104 0W
Beach City, U.S.A. 78 F3 40 39N 81 35W
Beachport, Australia 63 F3 37 29S 140 0 E
Beachy Hd., U.K. 11 G8 50 44N 0 15 E
Beacon, Australia 61 F2 30 26S 117 52 E
Beacon, U.S.A. 79 E11 41 30N 73 58W
Beaconia, Canada 73 C9 50 25N 96 31W
Beagle, Canal, S. Amer. 96 H3 55 0S 68 30W
Beagle Bay, Australia 60 C3 16 58S 122 40 E
Bealanana, Madag. 57 A8 14 33S 48 44 E
Beamsville, Canada 78 C5 43 12N 79 28W
Bear →, U.S.A. 84 G5 38 56N 121 36W
Bear I., Ireland 13 E2 51 38N 9 50W
Bear L., B.C., Canada 72 B3 56 10N 126 52W
Bear L., Man., Canada 73 B9 55 8N 96 0W
Bear L., U.S.A. 82 F8 41 59N 111 21W
Bearcreek, U.S.A. 82 D9 45 11N 109 6W
Beardmore, Canada 70 C2 49 36N 87 57W
Beardmore Glacier, Antarctica 5 E11 84 30S 170 0 E
Beardstown, U.S.A. 80 F9 40 1N 90 26W
Béarn, France 18 E3 43 20N 0 30W
Bearpaw Mts., U.S.A. 82 B9 48 12N 109 30W
Bearskin Lake, Canada 70 B1 53 58N 91 2W
Beata, C., Dom. Rep. 89 C5 17 40N 71 30W
Beata, I., Dom. Rep. 89 C5 17 34N 71 31W
Beatrice, U.S.A. 80 E6 40 16N 96 45W
Beatrice, Zimbabwe 55 F3 18 15S 30 55 E
Beatrice, C., Australia 62 A2 14 20S 136 55 E
Beatton →, Canada 72 B4 56 15N 120 45W
Beatton River, Canada 72 B4 57 26N 121 20W
Beatty, U.S.A. 84 J10 36 54N 116 46W
Beauce, Plaine de la, France 18 B4 48 10N 1 45 E
Beauceville, Canada 71 C5 46 13N 70 46W
Beaudesert, Australia 63 D5 27 59S 153 0 E
Beaufort, Malaysia 36 C5 5 30N 115 40 E
Beaufort, N.C., U.S.A. 77 H7 34 43N 76 40W
Beaufort, S.C., U.S.A. 77 J5 32 26N 80 40W
Beaufort Sea, Arctic 66 B5 72 0N 140 0W
Beaufort West, S. Africa 56 E3 32 18S 22 36 E
Beauharnois, Canada 70 C5 45 20N 73 52W
Beaulieu →, Canada 72 A6 62 3N 113 11W
Beauly, U.K. 12 D4 57 30N 4 28W
Beauly →, U.K. 12 D4 57 29N 4 27W
Beaumaris, U.K. 10 D3 53 16N 4 6W
Beaumont, Belgium 15 D4 50 15N 4 14 E
Beaumont, U.S.A. 81 K7 30 5N 94 6W
Beaune, France 18 C6 47 2N 4 50 E
Beauraing, Belgium 15 D4 50 7N 4 57 E
Beauséjour, Canada 73 C9 50 5N 96 35W
Beauvais, France 18 B5 49 25N 2 8 E
Beauval, Canada 73 B7 55 9N 107 37W
Beaver, Okla., U.S.A. 81 G4 36 49N 100 31W
Beaver, Pa., U.S.A. 78 F4 40 42N 80 19W
Beaver, Utah, U.S.A. 83 G7 38 17N 112 38W
Beaver →, B.C., Canada 72 B4 59 52N 124 20W
Beaver →, Ont., Canada 70 A2 55 55N 87 48W
Beaver →, Sask., Canada 73 B7 55 26N 107 45W
Beaver City, U.S.A. 80 E5 40 8N 99 50W
Beaver Dam, U.S.A. 80 D10 43 28N 88 50W
Beaver Falls, U.S.A. 78 F4 40 46N 80 20W
Beaver Hill L., Canada 73 C10 54 5N 94 50W
Beaver I., U.S.A. 76 C3 45 40N 85 33W
Beaverhill L., Alta., Canada 72 C6 53 27N 112 32W
Beaverhill L., N.W.T., Canada 73 A8 63 2N 104 22W
Beaverlodge, Canada 72 B5 55 11N 119 29W
Beavermouth, Canada 72 C5 51 32N 117 23W
Beaverstone →, Canada 70 B2 54 59N 89 25W
Beaverton, Canada 78 B5 44 26N 79 9W
Beaverton, U.S.A. 84 E4 45 29N 122 48W
Beawar, India 42 F6 26 3N 74 18 E
Bebedouro, Brazil 95 A6 21 0S 48 25W
Beboa, Madag. 57 B7 17 22S 44 33 E
Beccles, U.K. 11 E9 52 27N 1 35 E
Bečej, Serbia, Yug. 21 B9 45 36N 20 3 E
Béchar, Algeria 50 B5 31 38N 2 18W
Beckley, U.S.A. 76 G5 37 47N 81 11W
Bedford, Canada 70 C5 45 7N 72 59W
Bedford, S. Africa 56 E4 32 40S 26 10 E
Bedford, U.K. 11 E7 52 8N 0 28W
Bedford, Ind., U.S.A. 76 F2 38 52N 86 29W
Bedford, Iowa, U.S.A. 80 E7 40 40N 94 44W
Bedford, Ohio, U.S.A. 78 E3 41 23N 81 32W
Bedford, Pa., U.S.A. 78 F6 40 1N 78 30W
Bedford, Va., U.S.A. 76 G6 37 20N 79 31W
Bedford, C., Australia 62 B4 15 14S 145 21 E
Bedford Downs, Australia 60 C4 17 19S 127 20 E
Bedfordshire □, U.K. 11 E7 52 4N 0 28W
Bedourie, Australia 62 C2 24 30S 139 30 E
Bedum, Neths. 15 A6 53 18N 6 36 E
Beech Grove, U.S.A. 76 F2 39 44N 86 3W
Beechy, Canada 73 C7 50 53N 107 24W
Beenleigh, Australia 63 D5 27 43S 153 10 E
Be'er Menuḥa, Israel 44 D2 30 19N 35 8 E
Be'er Sheva, Israel 47 D3 31 15N 34 48 E
Beersheba = Be'er Sheva, Israel 47 D3 31 15N 34 48 E
Beeston, U.K. 10 E6 52 56N 1 14W
Beetaloo, Australia 62 B1 17 15S 133 50 E
Beeville, U.S.A. 81 L6 28 24N 97 45W
Befale, Dem. Rep. of the Congo 52 D4 0 25N 20 45 E
Befandriana, Madag. 57 C7 21 55S 44 0 E
Befotaka, Madag. 57 C8 23 49S 47 0 E
Bega, Australia 63 F4 36 41S 149 51 E
Begusarai, India 43 G12 25 24N 86 9 E
Behābād, Iran 45 C8 32 24N 59 47 E
Behara, Madag. 57 C8 24 55S 46 20 E
Behbehān, Iran 45 D6 30 30N 50 15 E
Behshahr, Iran 45 B7 36 45N 53 35 E
Bei Jiang →, China 33 D6 23 2N 112 58 E
Bei'an, China 33 B7 48 10N 126 20 E
Beihai, China 33 D5 21 28N 109 6 E
Beijing, China 34 E9 39 55N 116 20 E
Beijing □, China 34 E9 39 55N 116 20 E
Beilen, Neths. 15 B6 52 52N 6 27 E
Beilpajah, Australia 63 E3 32 54S 143 52 E
Beinn na Faoghla = Benbecula, U.K. 12 D1 57 26N 7 21W
Beipiao, China 35 D11 41 52N 120 32 E
Beira, Mozam. 55 F3 19 50S 34 52 E
Beirut = Bayrūt, Lebanon 47 B4 33 53N 35 31 E
Beitaolaizhao, China 35 B13 44 58N 125 58 E
Beitbridge, Zimbabwe 55 G3 22 12S 30 0 E
Beizhen, Liaoning, China 35 D11 41 38N 121 54 E
Beizhen, Shandong, China 35 F10 37 20N 118 2 E
Beizhengzhen, China 35 B12 44 31N 123 30 E
Beja, Portugal 19 C2 38 2N 7 53W
Béja, Tunisia 51 A7 36 43N 9 12 E
Bejaia, Algeria 50 A7 36 42N 5 2 E
Béjar, Spain 19 B3 40 23N 5 46W
Bejestān, Iran 45 C8 34 30N 58 5 E
Békéscsaba, Hungary 17 E11 46 40N 21 5 E
Bekily, Madag. 57 C8 24 13S 45 19 E
Bekok, Malaysia 39 L4 2 20N 103 7 E
Bela, India 43 G10 25 50N 82 0 E
Bela, Pakistan 42 F2 26 12N 66 20 E
Bela Crkva, Serbia, Yug. 21 B9 44 55N 21 27 E
Bela Vista, Brazil 94 A4 22 12S 56 20W
Bela Vista, Mozam. 57 D5 26 10S 32 44 E
Belarus ■, Europe 24 D4 53 30N 27 0 E
Belau = Palau ■, Pac. Oc. 64 G5 7 30N 134 30 E
Belavenona, Madag. 57 C8 24 50S 47 4 E
Belawan, Indonesia 36 D1 3 33N 98 32 E
Belaya →, Russia 24 C9 54 40N 56 0 E
Belaya Tserkov = Bila Tserkva, Ukraine 25 E5 49 45N 30 10 E
Belcher Is., Canada 69 C12 56 15N 78 45W
Belden, U.S.A. 84 E5 40 2N 121 17W
Belebey, Russia 24 D9 54 7N 54 7 E
Belém, Brazil 93 D9 1 20S 48 30W
Belén, Argentina 94 B2 27 40S 67 5W
Belén, Paraguay 94 A4 23 30S 57 6W
Belen, U.S.A. 83 J10 34 40N 106 46W
Belet Uen, Somali Rep. 46 G4 4 30N 45 5 E
Belev, Russia 24 D6 53 50N 36 5 E
Belfair, U.S.A. 84 C4 47 27N 122 50W
Belfast, S. Africa 57 D5 25 42S 30 2 E
Belfast, U.K. 13 B6 54 37N 5 56W
Belfast, Maine, U.S.A. 71 D6 44 26N 69 1W
Belfast, N.Y., U.S.A. 78 D6 42 21N 78 7W
Belfast L., U.K. 13 B6 54 40N 5 50W
Belfield, U.S.A. 80 B3 46 53N 103 12W
Belfort, France 18 C7 47 38N 6 50 E
Belfry, U.S.A. 82 D9 45 9N 109 1W
Belgaum, India 40 M9 15 55N 74 35 E
Belgium ■, Europe 15 D4 50 30N 5 0 E
Belgorod, Russia 25 D6 50 35N 36 35 E
Belgorod-Dnestrovskiy = Bilhorod-Dnistrovskyy, Ukraine 25 E5 46 11N 30 23 E
Belgrade = Beograd, Serbia, Yug. 21 B9 44 50N 20 37 E
Belgrade, U.S.A. 82 D8 45 47N 111 11W
Belhaven, U.S.A. 77 H7 35 33N 76 37W
Beli Drim →, Europe 21 C9 42 6N 20 25 E
Belinyu, Indonesia 36 E3 1 35S 105 50 E
Beliton Is. = Belitung, Indonesia 36 E3 3 10S 107 50 E
Belitung, Indonesia 36 E3 3 10S 107 50 E
Belize ■, Cent. Amer. 87 D7 17 0N 88 30W
Belize City, Belize 87 D7 17 25N 88 0W
Belkovskiy, Ostrov, Russia 27 B14 75 32N 135 44 E
Bell →, Canada 70 C4 49 48N 77 38W
Bell Bay, Australia 62 G4 41 6S 146 53 E
Bell I., Canada 71 B8 50 46N 55 35W
Bell-Irving →, Canada 72 B3 56 12N 129 5W
Bell Peninsula, Canada 69 B11 63 50N 82 0W
Bell Ville, Argentina 94 C3 32 40S 62 40W
Bella Bella, Canada 72 C3 52 10N 128 10W
Bella Coola, Canada 72 C3 52 25N 126 40W
Bella Unión, Uruguay 94 C4 30 15S 57 40W
Bella Vista, Corrientes, Argentina 94 B4 28 33S 59 0W
Bella Vista, Tucuman, Argentina 94 B2 27 10S 65 25W
Bellaire, U.S.A. 78 F4 40 1N 80 45W
Bellary, India 40 M10 15 10N 76 56 E
Bellata, Australia 63 D4 29 53S 149 46 E
Belle Fourche, U.S.A. 80 C3 44 40N 103 51W
Belle Fourche →, U.S.A. 80 C3 44 26N 102 18W
Belle Glade, U.S.A. 77 M5 26 41N 80 40W
Belle-Île, France 18 C2 47 20N 3 10W
Belle Isle, Canada 71 B8 51 57N 55 25W
Belle Isle, Str. of, Canada 71 B8 51 30N 56 30W
Belle Plaine, Iowa, U.S.A. 80 E8 41 54N 92 17W
Belle Plaine, Minn., U.S.A. 80 C8 44 37N 93 46W
Belledune, Canada 71 C6 47 55N 65 50W

Bilyana

Bellefontaine, *U.S.A.* **76 E4** 40 22N 83 46W
Bellefonte, *U.S.A.* **78 F7** 40 55N 77 47W
Belleoram, *Canada* **71 C8** 47 31N 55 25W
Belleville, *Canada* **70 D4** 44 10N 77 23W
Belleville, *Ill., U.S.A.* **80 F10** 38 31N 89 59W
Belleville, *Kans., U.S.A.* **80 F6** 39 50N 97 38W
Belleville, *N.Y., U.S.A.* **79 C8** 43 46N 76 10W
Bellevue, *Canada* **72 D6** 49 35N 114 22W
Bellevue, *Idaho, U.S.A.* **82 E6** 43 28N 114 16W
Bellevue, *Ohio, U.S.A.* **78 E2** 41 17N 82 51W
Bellevue, *Wash., U.S.A.* **84 C4** 47 37N 122 12W
Bellin = Kangirsuk, *Canada* **69 C13** 60 0N 70 0W
Bellingen, *Australia* **63 E5** 30 25S 152 50 E
Bellingham, *U.S.A.* **84 B4** 48 46N 122 29W
Bellingshausen Sea, *Antarctica* **5 C17** 66 0S 80 0W
Bellinzona, *Switz.* **18 C8** 46 11N 9 1 E
Bello, *Colombia* **92 B3** 6 20N 75 33W
Bellows Falls, *U.S.A.* **79 C12** 43 8N 72 27W
Bellpat, *Pakistan* **42 E3** 29 0N 68 5 E
Belluno, *Italy* **20 A5** 46 9N 12 13 E
Bellville, *U.S.A.* **81 L6** 29 57N 96 15W
Bellwood, *U.S.A.* **78 F6** 40 36N 78 20W
Belmont, *Australia* **63 E5** 33 4S 151 42 E
Belmont, *Canada* **78 D3** 42 53N 81 5W
Belmont, *S. Africa* **56 D3** 29 28S 24 22 E
Belmont, *U.S.A.* **78 D6** 42 14N 78 2W
Belmonte, *Brazil* **93 G11** 16 0S 39 0W
Belmopan, *Belize* **87 D7** 17 18N 88 30W
Belmullet, *Ireland* **13 B2** 54 14N 9 58W
Belo Horizonte, *Brazil* **93 G10** 19 55S 43 56W
Belo-sur-Mer, *Madag.* **57 C7** 20 42S 44 0 E
Belo-Tsiribihina, *Madag.* **57 B7** 19 40S 44 30 E
Belogorsk, *Russia* **27 D13** 51 0N 128 20 E
Beloha, *Madag.* **57 D8** 25 10S 45 3 E
Beloit, *Kans., U.S.A.* **80 F5** 39 28N 98 6W
Beloit, *Wis., U.S.A.* **80 D10** 42 31N 89 2W
Belokorovichi, *Ukraine* **17 C15** 51 7N 28 2 E
Belomorsk, *Russia* **24 B5** 64 35N 34 54 E
Belonia, *India* **41 H17** 23 15N 91 30 E
Beloretsk, *Russia* **24 D10** 53 58N 58 24 E
Belorussia = Belarus ■, *Europe* **24 D4** 53 30N 27 0 E
Belovo, *Russia* **26 D9** 54 30N 86 0 E
Beloye, Ozero, *Russia* **24 B6** 60 10N 37 35 E
Beloye More, *Russia* **24 A6** 66 30N 38 0 E
Belozersk, *Russia* **24 B6** 60 1N 37 45 E
Beltana, *Australia* **63 E2** 30 48S 138 25 E
Belterra, *Brazil* **93 D8** 2 45S 55 0W
Belton, *S.C., U.S.A.* **77 H4** 34 31N 82 30W
Belton, *Tex., U.S.A.* **81 K6** 31 3N 97 28W
Belton Res., *U.S.A.* **81 K6** 31 8N 97 32W
Beltsy = Bălţi, *Moldova* **25 E4** 47 48N 27 58 E
Belturbet, *Ireland* **13 B4** 54 6N 7 26W
Belukha, *Russia* **26 E9** 49 50N 86 50 E
Beluran, *Malaysia* **36 C5** 5 48N 117 35 E
Belvidere, *Ill., U.S.A.* **80 D10** 42 15N 88 50W
Belvidere, *N.J., U.S.A.* **79 F9** 40 50N 75 5W
Belyando →, *Australia* **62 C4** 21 38S 146 50 E
Belyy, Ostrov, *Russia* **26 B8** 73 30N 71 0 E
Belyy Yar, *Russia* **26 D9** 58 26N 84 39 E
Belzoni, *U.S.A.* **81 J9** 33 11N 90 29W
Bemaraha, Lembalemban' i, *Madag.* **57 B7** 18 40S 44 45 E
Bemarivo, *Madag.* **57 C7** 21 45S 44 45 E
Bemarivo →, *Madag.* **57 B8** 15 27S 47 40 E
Bemavo, *Madag.* **57 C8** 21 33S 45 25 E
Bembéréke, *Benin* **50 F6** 10 11N 2 43 E
Bembesi, *Zimbabwe* **55 G2** 20 0S 28 58 E
Bembesi →, *Zimbabwe* **55 F2** 18 57S 27 47 E
Bemidji, *U.S.A.* **80 B7** 47 28N 94 53W
Ben, *Iran* **45 C6** 32 32N 50 45 E
Ben Cruachan, *U.K.* **12 E3** 56 26N 5 8W
Ben Dearg, *U.K.* **12 D4** 57 47N 4 56W
Ben Hope, *U.K.* **12 C4** 58 25N 4 36W
Ben Lawers, *U.K.* **12 E4** 56 32N 4 14W
Ben Lomond, *N.S.W., Australia* **63 E5** 30 1S 151 43 E
Ben Lomond, *Tas., Australia* **62 G4** 41 38S 147 42 E
Ben Lomond, *U.K.* **12 E4** 56 11N 4 38W
Ben Luc, *Vietnam* **39 G6** 10 39N 106 29 E
Ben Macdhui, *U.K.* **12 D5** 57 4N 3 40W
Ben Mhor, *U.K.* **12 D1** 57 15N 7 18W
Ben More, *Arg. & Bute, U.K.* **12 E2** 56 26N 6 1W
Ben More, *Stirl., U.K.* **12 E4** 56 23N 4 32W
Ben More Assynt, *U.K.* **12 C4** 58 8N 4 52W
Ben Nevis, *U.K.* **12 E3** 56 48N 5 1W
Ben Quang, *Vietnam* **38 D6** 17 3N 106 55 E
Ben Vorlich, *U.K.* **12 E4** 56 21N 4 14W
Ben Wyvis, *U.K.* **12 D4** 57 40N 4 35W
Bena, *Nigeria* **50 F7** 11 20N 5 50 E
Benagerie, *Australia* **63 E3** 31 25S 140 22 E
Benalla, *Australia* **63 F4** 36 30S 146 0 E
Benambra, Mt., *Australia* **63 F4** 36 31S 147 34 E
Benares = Varanasi, *India* **43 G10** 25 22N 83 0 E
Benavente, *Spain* **19 A3** 42 2N 5 43W
Benavides, *U.S.A.* **81 M5** 27 36N 98 25W
Benbecula, *U.K.* **12 D1** 57 26N 7 21W
Benbonyathe, *Australia* **63 E2** 30 25S 139 11 E
Bencubbin, *Australia* **61 F2** 30 48S 117 52 E
Bend, *U.S.A.* **82 D3** 44 4N 121 19W
Bender Beila, *Somali Rep.* **46 F5** 9 30N 50 48 E
Bendering, *Australia* **61 F2** 32 23S 118 18 E
Bendery = Tighina, *Moldova* **25 E4** 46 50N 29 30 E
Bendigo, *Australia* **63 F3** 36 40S 144 15 E
Benë Beraq, *Israel* **47 C3** 32 6N 34 51 E
Benenitra, *Madag.* **57 C8** 23 27S 45 5 E
Benevento, *Italy* **20 D6** 41 8N 14 45 E
Benga, *Mozam.* **55 F3** 16 11S 33 40 E
Bengal, Bay of, *Ind. Oc.* **41 M17** 15 0N 90 0 E
Bengbu, *China* **35 H9** 32 58N 117 20 E
Benghazi = Banghāzī, *Libya* **51 B10** 32 11N 20 3 E
Bengkalis, *Indonesia* **36 D2** 1 30N 102 10 E
Bengkulu, *Indonesia* **36 E2** 3 50S 102 12 E
Bengkulu □, *Indonesia* **36 E2** 3 48S 102 16 E
Bengough, *Canada* **73 D7** 49 25N 105 10W
Benguela, *Angola* **53 G2** 12 37S 13 25 E
Benguérua, I., *Mozam.* **57 C6** 21 58S 35 28 E
Beni, *Dem. Rep. of the Congo* **54 B2** 0 30N 29 27 E
Beni →, *Bolivia* **92 F5** 10 23S 65 24W
Beni Mellal, *Morocco* **50 B4** 32 21N 6 21W
Beni Suef, *Egypt* **51 C12** 29 5N 31 6 E
Beniah L., *Canada* **72 A6** 63 23N 112 17W
Benicia, *U.S.A.* **84 G4** 38 3N 122 9W
Benidorm, *Spain* **19 C5** 38 33N 0 9W
Benin ■, *Africa* **50 G6** 10 0N 2 0 E
Benin, Bight of, *W. Afr.* **50 H6** 5 0N 3 0 E
Benin City, *Nigeria* **50 G7** 6 20N 5 31 E
Benitses, *Greece* **23 A3** 39 32N 19 55 E
Benjamin Aceval, *Paraguay* **94 A4** 24 58S 57 34W
Benjamin Constant, *Brazil* **92 D4** 4 40S 70 15W
Benjamin Hill, *Mexico* **86 A2** 30 10N 111 10W
Benkelman, *U.S.A.* **80 E4** 40 3N 101 32W
Benlidi, *Australia* **62 C3** 24 35S 144 50 E
Bennett, *Canada* **72 B2** 59 56N 134 53W
Bennett, L., *Australia* **60 D5** 22 50S 131 2 E
Bennetta, Ostrov, *Russia* **27 B15** 76 21N 148 56 E
Bennettsville, *U.S.A.* **77 H6** 34 37N 79 41W
Bennington, *U.S.A.* **79 D11** 43 0N 71 55W
Benoni, *S. Africa* **57 D4** 26 11S 28 18 E
Benque Viejo, *Belize* **87 D7** 17 5N 89 8W
Benson, *U.S.A.* **83 L8** 31 58N 110 18W
Bent, *Iran* **45 E8** 26 20N 59 31 E
Benteng, *Indonesia* **37 F6** 6 10S 120 30 E
Bentinck I., *Australia* **62 B2** 17 3S 139 35 E
Bento Gonçalves, *Brazil* **95 B5** 29 10S 51 31W
Benton, *Ark., U.S.A.* **81 H8** 34 34N 92 35W
Benton, *Calif., U.S.A.* **84 H8** 37 48N 118 32W
Benton, *Ill., U.S.A.* **80 G10** 38 0N 88 55W
Benton Harbor, *U.S.A.* **76 D2** 42 6N 86 27W
Bentung, *Malaysia* **39 L3** 3 31N 101 55 E
Benue →, *Nigeria* **50 G7** 7 48N 6 46 E
Benxi, *China* **35 D12** 41 20N 123 48 E
Beo, *Indonesia* **37 D7** 4 25N 126 50 E
Beograd, *Serbia, Yug.* **21 B9** 44 50N 20 37 E
Beowawe, *U.S.A.* **82 F5** 40 35N 116 29W
Beppu, *Japan* **31 H5** 33 15N 131 30 E
Beqaa Valley = Al Biqā □, *Lebanon* **47 A5** 34 10N 36 10 E
Berati, *Albania* **21 D8** 40 43N 19 59 E
Berau, Teluk, *Indonesia* **37 E8** 2 30S 132 30 E
Berber, *Sudan* **51 E12** 18 0N 34 0 E
Berbera, *Somali Rep.* **46 E4** 10 30N 45 2 E
Berbérati, *C.A.R.* **52 D3** 4 15N 15 40 E
Berbice →, *Guyana* **92 B7** 6 20N 57 32W
Berdichev = Berdychiv, *Ukraine* **25 E4** 49 57N 28 30 E
Berdsk, *Russia* **26 D9** 54 47N 83 2 E
Berdyansk, *Ukraine* **25 E6** 46 45N 36 50 E
Berdychiv, *Ukraine* **25 E4** 49 57N 28 30 E
Berea, *U.S.A.* **76 G3** 37 34N 84 17W
Berebere, *Indonesia* **37 D7** 2 25N 128 45 E
Bereda, *Somali Rep.* **46 E5** 11 45N 51 0 E
Berehove, *Ukraine* **17 D12** 48 15N 22 35 E
Berekum, *Ghana* **50 G5** 7 29N 2 34W
Berens →, *Canada* **73 C9** 52 25N 97 2W
Berens I., *Canada* **73 C9** 52 18N 97 18W
Berens River, *Canada* **73 C9** 52 25N 97 0W
Berestechko, *Ukraine* **17 C13** 50 22N 25 5 E
Berevo, *Mahajanga, Madag.* **57 B7** 17 14S 44 17 E
Berevo, *Toliara, Madag.* **57 B7** 19 44S 44 58 E
Bereza, *Belarus* **17 B13** 52 31N 24 51 E
Berezhany, *Ukraine* **17 D13** 49 26N 24 58 E
Berezina = Byarezina →, *Belarus* **24 D5** 52 33N 30 14 E
Berezniki, *Russia* **26 D6** 59 24N 56 46 E
Berezovo, *Russia* **24 B12** 64 0N 65 0 E
Berga, *Spain* **19 A6** 42 6N 1 48 E
Bergama, *Turkey* **21 E12** 39 8N 27 11 E
Bérgamo, *Italy* **18 D8** 45 41N 9 43 E
Bergen, *Neths.* **15 B4** 52 40N 4 43 E
Bergen, *Norway* **9 F11** 60 20N 5 20 E
Bergen, *U.S.A.* **78 C7** 43 5N 77 57W
Bergen op Zoom, *Neths.* **15 C4** 51 28N 4 18 E
Bergerac, *France* **18 D4** 44 51N 0 30 E
Bergisch Gladbach, *Germany* **15 D7** 50 59N 7 8 E
Bergville, *S. Africa* **57 D4** 28 52S 29 18 E
Berhala, Selat, *Indonesia* **36 E2** 1 0S 104 15 E
Berhampore = Baharampur, *India* **43 G13** 24 2N 88 27 E
Berhampur = Brahmapur, *India* **41 K14** 19 15N 84 54 E
Bering Sea, *Pac. Oc.* **68 C1** 58 0N 171 0 E
Bering Strait, *Pac. Oc.* **68 B3** 65 30N 169 0W
Beringovskiy, *Russia* **27 C18** 63 3N 179 19 E
Berisso, *Argentina* **94 C4** 34 56S 57 50W
Berja, *Spain* **19 D4** 36 50N 2 56W
Berkeley, *U.S.A.* **84 H4** 37 52N 122 16W
Berkeley Springs, *U.S.A.* **76 F6** 39 38N 78 14W
Berkner I., *Antarctica* **5 D18** 79 30S 50 0W
Berkshire Downs, *U.K.* **11 F6** 51 33N 1 29W
Berland →, *Canada* **72 C5** 54 0N 116 50W
Berlin, *Germany* **16 B7** 52 30N 13 25 E
Berlin, *Md., U.S.A.* **76 F8** 38 20N 75 13W
Berlin, *N.H., U.S.A.* **79 B13** 44 28N 71 11W
Berlin, *Wis., U.S.A.* **76 D1** 43 58N 88 57W
Bermejo →, *Formosa, Argentina* **94 B4** 26 51S 58 23W
Bermejo →, *San Juan, Argentina* **94 C2** 32 30S 67 30W
Bermuda ■, *Atl. Oc.* **66 F13** 32 45N 65 0W
Bern, *Switz.* **18 C7** 46 57N 7 28 E
Bernado, *U.S.A.* **83 J10** 34 30N 106 53W
Bernalillo, *U.S.A.* **83 J10** 35 18N 106 33W
Bernardo de Irigoyen, *Argentina* **95 B5** 26 15S 53 40W
Bernardo O'Higgins □, *Chile* **94 C1** 34 15S 70 45W
Bernasconi, *Argentina* **94 D3** 37 55S 63 44W
Bernburg, *Germany* **16 C6** 51 47N 11 44 E
Berne = Bern, *Switz.* **18 C7** 46 57N 7 28 E
Berneray, *U.K.* **12 D1** 57 43N 7 11W
Bernier I., *Australia* **61 D1** 24 50S 113 12 E
Bernina, Piz, *Switz.* **18 C8** 46 20N 9 54 E
Beroroha, *Madag.* **57 C8** 21 40S 45 10 E
Beroun, *Czech Rep.* **16 D8** 49 57N 14 5 E
Berri, *Australia* **63 E3** 34 14S 140 35 E
Berry, *Australia* **63 E5** 34 46S 150 43 E
Berry, *France* **18 C5** 46 50N 2 0 E
Berry Is., *Bahamas* **88 A4** 25 40N 77 50W
Berryessa L., *U.S.A.* **84 G4** 38 31N 122 6W
Berryville, *U.S.A.* **81 G8** 36 22N 93 34W
Bershad, *Ukraine* **17 D15** 48 22N 29 31 E
Berthold, *U.S.A.* **80 A4** 48 19N 101 44W
Berthoud, *U.S.A.* **80 E2** 40 19N 105 5W
Bertoua, *Cameroon* **52 D2** 4 30N 13 45 E
Bertraghboy B., *Ireland* **13 C2** 53 22N 9 54W
Bertrand, *U.S.A.* **80 E5** 40 32N 99 38W
Berwick, *U.S.A.* **79 E8** 41 3N 76 14W
Berwick-upon-Tweed, *U.K.* **10 B6** 55 46N 2 0W
Berwyn Mts., *U.K.* **10 E4** 52 54N 3 26W
Besal, *Pakistan* **43 B5** 35 4N 73 56 E
Besalampy, *Madag.* **57 B7** 16 43S 44 29 E
Besançon, *France* **18 C7** 47 15N 6 2 E
Besar, *Indonesia* **36 E5** 2 40S 116 0 E
Besnard L., *Canada* **73 B7** 55 25N 106 0W
Besor, N. →, *Egypt* **47 D3** 31 28N 34 22 E
Bessarabiya, *Moldova* **17 E15** 47 0N 28 10 E
Bessarabka = Basarabeasca, *Moldova* **17 E15** 46 21N 28 58 E
Bessemer, *Ala., U.S.A.* **77 J2** 33 24N 86 58W
Bessemer, *Mich., U.S.A.* **80 B9** 46 29N 90 3W
Bet She'an, *Israel* **47 C4** 32 30N 35 30 E
Bet Shemesh, *Israel* **47 D4** 31 44N 35 0 E
Betafo, *Madag.* **57 B8** 19 50S 46 51 E
Betancuria, *Canary Is.* **22 F5** 28 25N 14 3W
Betanzos, *Spain* **19 A1** 43 15N 8 12W
Bétaré Oya, *Cameroon* **52 C2** 5 40N 14 5 E
Bethal, *S. Africa* **57 D4** 26 27S 29 28 E
Bethanien, *Namibia* **56 D2** 26 31S 17 8 E
Bethany, *U.S.A.* **80 E7** 40 16N 94 2W
Bethel, *Alaska, U.S.A.* **68 B3** 60 48N 161 45W
Bethel, *Vt., U.S.A.* **79 C12** 43 50N 72 38W
Bethel Park, *U.S.A.* **78 F4** 40 20N 80 1W
Bethlehem = Bayt Lahm, *West Bank* **47 D4** 31 43N 35 12 E
Bethlehem, *S. Africa* **57 D4** 28 14S 28 18 E
Bethlehem, *U.S.A.* **79 F9** 40 37N 75 23W
Bethulie, *S. Africa* **56 E4** 30 30S 25 59 E
Béthune, *France* **18 A5** 50 30N 2 38 E
Bethungra, *Australia* **63 E4** 34 45S 147 51 E
Betioky, *Madag.* **57 C7** 23 48S 44 20 E
Betong, *Thailand* **39 K3** 5 45N 101 5 E
Betoota, *Australia* **62 D3** 25 45S 140 42 E
Betroka, *Madag.* **57 C8** 23 16S 46 0 E
Betsiamites, *Canada* **71 C6** 48 56N 68 40W
Betsiamites →, *Canada* **71 C6** 48 56N 68 38W
Betsiboka →, *Madag.* **57 B8** 16 3S 46 36 E
Bettiah, *India* **43 F11** 26 48N 84 33 E
Betul, *India* **40 J10** 21 58N 77 59 E
Betung, *Malaysia* **36 D4** 1 24N 111 31 E
Betws-y-Coed, *U.K.* **10 D4** 53 5N 3 48W
Beulah, *U.S.A.* **80 B4** 47 16N 101 47W
Beveren, *Belgium* **15 C4** 51 12N 4 16 E
Beverley, *Australia* **61 F2** 32 9S 116 56 E
Beverley, *U.K.* **10 D7** 53 51N 0 26W
Beverly, *Mass., U.S.A.* **79 D14** 42 33N 70 53W
Beverly, *Wash., U.S.A.* **82 C4** 46 50N 119 56W
Beverly Hills, *U.S.A.* **85 L8** 34 4N 118 25W
Bexhill, *U.K.* **11 G8** 50 51N 0 29 E
Beyānlū, *Iran* **44 C5** 36 0N 47 51 E
Beyneu, *Kazakstan* **25 E10** 45 18N 55 9 E
Beypazan, *Turkey* **25 F5** 40 10N 31 56 E
Beyşehir Gölü, *Turkey* **25 G5** 37 41N 31 33 E
Bezhitsa, *Russia* **24 D5** 53 19N 34 17 E
Béziers, *France* **18 E5** 43 20N 3 12 E
Bezwada = Vijayawada, *India* **41 L12** 16 31N 80 39 E
Bhachau, *India* **40 H7** 23 20N 70 16 E
Bhadarwah, *India* **43 C6** 32 58N 75 46 E
Bhadrakh, *India* **41 J15** 21 10N 86 30 E
Bhadravati, *India* **40 N9** 13 49N 75 40 E
Bhagalpur, *India* **43 G12** 25 10N 87 0 E
Bhakkar, *Pakistan* **42 D4** 31 40N 71 5 E
Bhakra Dam, *India* **42 D7** 31 30N 76 45 E
Bhamo, *Burma* **41 G20** 24 15N 97 15 E
Bhandara, *India* **40 J11** 21 5N 79 42 E
Bhanrer Ra., *India* **42 H8** 23 40N 79 45 E
Bharat = India ■, *Asia* **40 K11** 20 0N 78 0 E
Bharatpur, *India* **42 F7** 27 15N 77 30 E
Bhatinda, *India* **42 D6** 30 15N 74 57 E
Bhatpara, *India* **43 H13** 22 50N 88 25 E
Bhaun, *Pakistan* **42 C5** 32 55N 72 40 E
Bhaunagar = Bhavnagar, *India* **42 J5** 21 45N 72 10 E
Bhavnagar, *India* **42 J5** 21 45N 72 10 E
Bhawanipatna, *India* **41 K12** 19 55N 80 10 E
Bhera, *Pakistan* **42 C5** 32 29N 72 57 E
Bhilsa = Vidisha, *India* **42 H7** 23 28N 77 53 E
Bhilwara, *India* **42 G6** 25 25N 74 38 E
Bhima →, *India* **40 L10** 16 25N 77 17 E
Bhimavaram, *India* **41 L12** 16 30N 81 30 E
Bhimbar, *Pakistan* **43 C6** 32 59N 74 3 E
Bhind, *India* **43 F8** 26 30N 78 46 E
Bhiwandi, *India* **40 K8** 19 20N 73 0 E
Bhiwani, *India* **42 E7** 28 50N 76 9 E
Bhola, *Bangla.* **41 H17** 22 45N 90 35 E
Bhopal, *India* **42 H7** 23 20N 77 30 E
Bhubaneshwar, *India* **41 J14** 20 15N 85 50 E
Bhuj, *India* **42 H3** 23 15N 69 49 E
Bhusaval, *India* **40 J9** 21 3N 75 46 E
Bhutan ■, *Asia* **41 F17** 27 25N 90 30 E
Biafra, B. of = Bonny, Bight of, *Africa* **52 D1** 3 30N 9 20 E
Biak, *Indonesia* **37 E9** 1 10S 136 6 E
Biała Podlaska, *Poland* **17 B12** 52 4N 23 6 E
Białogard, *Poland* **16 A8** 54 2N 15 58 E
Białystok, *Poland* **17 B12** 53 10N 23 10 E
Biārjmand, *Iran* **45 B7** 36 6N 55 53 E
Biaro, *Indonesia* **37 D7** 2 5N 125 26 E
Biarritz, *France* **18 E3** 43 29N 1 33W
Bibai, *Japan* **30 C10** 43 19N 141 52 E
Bibby I., *Canada* **73 A10** 61 55N 93 0W
Biberach, *Germany* **16 D5** 48 5N 9 47 E
Biboohra, *Australia* **62 B4** 16 56S 145 25 E
Bibungwa, *Dem. Rep. of the Congo* **54 C2** 2 40S 28 15 E
Bic, *Canada* **71 C6** 48 20N 68 41W
Bicester, *U.K.* **11 F6** 51 54N 1 9W
Bickerton I., *Australia* **62 A2** 13 45S 136 10 E
Bicknell, *Ind., U.S.A.* **76 F2** 38 47N 87 19W
Bicknell, *Utah, U.S.A.* **83 G8** 38 20N 111 33W
Bida, *Nigeria* **50 G7** 9 3N 5 58 E
Bidar, *India* **40 L10** 17 55N 77 35 E
Biddeford, *U.S.A.* **71 D5** 43 30N 70 28W
Bideford, *U.K.* **11 F3** 51 1N 4 13W
Bideford Bay, *U.K.* **11 F3** 51 5N 4 20W
Bidor, *Malaysia* **39 K3** 4 6N 101 15 E
Bié, Planalto de, *Angola* **53 G3** 12 0S 16 0 E
Bieber, *U.S.A.* **82 F3** 41 7N 121 8W
Biel, *Switz.* **18 C7** 47 8N 7 14 E
Bielefeld, *Germany* **16 B5** 52 1N 8 33 E
Biella, *Italy* **18 D8** 45 34N 8 3 E
Bielsk Podlaski, *Poland* **17 B12** 52 47N 23 12 E
Bielsko-Biała, *Poland* **17 D10** 49 50N 19 2 E
Bien Hoa, *Vietnam* **39 G6** 10 57N 106 49 E
Bienfait, *Canada* **73 D8** 49 10N 102 50W
Bienne = Biel, *Switz.* **18 C7** 47 8N 7 14 E
Bienville, L., *Canada* **70 A5** 55 5N 72 40W
Biesiesfontein, *S. Africa* **56 E2** 30 57S 17 58 E
Big →, *Canada* **71 B8** 54 50N 58 55W
Big B., *Canada* **71 A7** 55 43N 60 35W
Big Bear City, *U.S.A.* **85 L10** 34 16N 116 51W
Big Bear Lake, *U.S.A.* **85 L10** 34 15N 116 56W
Big Beaver, *Canada* **73 D7** 49 10N 105 10W
Big Belt Mts., *U.S.A.* **82 C8** 46 30N 111 25W
Big Bend, *Swaziland* **57 D5** 26 50S 31 58 E
Big Bend National Park, *U.S.A.* **81 L3** 29 20N 103 5W
Big Black →, *U.S.A.* **81 K9** 32 3N 91 4W
Big Blue →, *U.S.A.* **80 F6** 39 35N 96 34W
Big Cr. →, *Canada* **72 C4** 51 42N 122 41W
Big Creek, *U.S.A.* **84 H7** 37 11N 119 14W
Big Cypress Swamp, *U.S.A.* **77 M5** 26 12N 81 10W
Big Falls, *U.S.A.* **80 A8** 48 12N 93 48W
Big Fork →, *U.S.A.* **80 A8** 48 31N 93 43W
Big Horn Mts. = Bighorn Mts., *U.S.A.* **82 D10** 44 30N 107 30W
Big Lake, *U.S.A.* **81 K4** 31 12N 101 28W
Big Moose, *U.S.A.* **79 C10** 43 49N 74 58W
Big Muddy Cr. →, *U.S.A.* **80 A2** 48 8N 104 36W
Big Pine, *U.S.A.* **84 H8** 37 10N 118 17W
Big Piney, *U.S.A.* **82 E8** 42 32N 110 7W
Big Quill L., *Canada* **73 C8** 51 55N 104 50W
Big Rapids, *U.S.A.* **76 D3** 43 42N 85 29W
Big River, *Canada* **73 C7** 53 50N 107 0W
Big Run, *U.S.A.* **78 F6** 40 57N 78 55W
Big Sable Pt., *U.S.A.* **76 C2** 44 3N 86 1W
Big Sand L., *Canada* **73 B9** 57 45N 99 45W
Big Sandy, *U.S.A.* **82 B8** 48 11N 110 7W
Big Sandy Cr. →, *U.S.A.* **80 F3** 38 7N 102 29W
Big Sioux →, *U.S.A.* **80 D6** 42 29N 96 27W
Big Spring, *U.S.A.* **81 J4** 32 15N 101 28W
Big Springs, *U.S.A.* **80 E3** 41 4N 102 5W
Big Stone City, *U.S.A.* **80 C6** 45 18N 96 28W
Big Stone Gap, *U.S.A.* **77 G4** 36 52N 82 47W
Big Stone L., *U.S.A.* **80 C6** 45 30N 96 35W
Big Sur, *U.S.A.* **84 J5** 36 15N 121 48W
Big Timber, *U.S.A.* **82 D9** 45 50N 109 57W
Big Trout L., *Canada* **70 B2** 53 40N 90 0W
Biğa, *Turkey* **21 D12** 40 13N 27 14 E
Bigadiç, *Turkey* **21 E13** 39 22N 28 7 E
Bigfork, *U.S.A.* **82 B6** 48 4N 114 4W
Biggar, *Canada* **73 C7** 52 4N 108 0W
Biggar, *U.K.* **12 F5** 55 38N 3 32W
Bigge I., *Australia* **60 B4** 14 35S 125 10 E
Biggenden, *Australia* **63 D5** 25 31S 152 4 E
Biggleswade, *U.K.* **11 E7** 52 5N 0 14W
Biggs, *U.S.A.* **84 F5** 39 25N 121 43W
Bighorn, *U.S.A.* **82 C10** 46 10N 107 27W
Bighorn →, *U.S.A.* **82 C10** 46 10N 107 28W
Bighorn Mts., *U.S.A.* **82 D10** 44 30N 107 30W
Bigstone L., *Canada* **73 C9** 53 42N 95 44W
Bigwa, *Tanzania* **54 D4** 7 10S 39 10 E
Bihać, *Bos.-H.* **16 F8** 44 49N 15 57 E
Bihar, *India* **43 G11** 25 5N 85 40 E
Bihar □, *India* **43 G12** 25 0N 86 0 E
Biharamulo, *Tanzania* **54 C3** 2 25S 31 25 E
Biharamulo □, *Tanzania* **54 C3** 2 30S 31 20 E
Bihor, Munţii, *Romania* **17 E12** 46 29N 22 47 E
Bijagós, Arquipélago dos, *Guinea-Biss.* **50 F2** 11 15N 16 10W
Bijaipur, *India* **42 F7** 26 2N 77 20 E
Bijapur, *Karnataka, India* **40 L9** 16 50N 75 55 E
Bijapur, *Mad. P., India* **41 K12** 18 50N 80 50 E
Bījār, *Iran* **44 C5** 35 52N 47 35 E
Bijeljina, *Bos.-H.* **21 B8** 44 46N 19 14 E
Bijnor, *India* **42 E8** 29 27N 78 11 E
Bikaner, *India* **42 E5** 28 2N 73 18 E
Bikapur, *India* **43 F10** 26 30N 82 7 E
Bikeqi, *China* **34 D6** 40 43N 111 20 E
Bikfayyā, *Lebanon* **47 B4** 33 55N 35 41 E
Bikin, *Russia* **27 E14** 46 50N 134 20 E
Bikin →, *Russia* **30 A7** 46 51N 134 2 E
Bikini Atoll, *Pac. Oc.* **64 F8** 12 0N 167 30 E
Bila Tserkva, *Ukraine* **25 E5** 49 45N 30 10 E
Bilara, *India* **42 F5** 26 14N 73 53 E
Bilaspur, *Mad. P., India* **43 H10** 22 2N 82 15 E
Bilaspur, *Punjab, India* **42 D7** 31 19N 76 50 E
Bilauk Taungdan, *Thailand* **38 F2** 13 0N 99 0 E
Bilbao, *Spain* **19 A4** 43 16N 2 56W
Bilbo = Bilbao, *Spain* **19 A4** 43 16N 2 56W
Bildudalur, *Iceland* **8 D2** 65 41N 23 36W
Bílé Karpaty, *Europe* **17 D9** 49 5N 18 0 E
Bilecik, *Turkey* **25 F5** 40 5N 30 5 E
Bilhorod-Dnistrovskyy, *Ukraine* **25 E5** 46 11N 30 23 E
Bilibino, *Russia* **27 C17** 68 3N 166 20 E
Bilibiza, *Mozam.* **55 E5** 12 30S 40 20 E
Bill, *U.S.A.* **80 D2** 43 14N 105 16W
Billabalong, *Australia* **61 E2** 27 25S 115 49 E
Billiluna, *Australia* **60 C4** 19 37S 127 41 E
Billings, *U.S.A.* **82 D9** 45 47N 108 30W
Billiton Is. = Belitung, *Indonesia* **36 E3** 3 10S 107 50 E
Bilma, *Niger* **51 E8** 18 50N 13 30 E
Biloela, *Australia* **62 C5** 24 24S 150 31 E
Biloxi, *U.S.A.* **81 K10** 30 24N 88 53W
Bilpa Morea Claypan, *Australia* **62 D3** 25 0S 140 0 E
Biltine, *Chad* **51 F10** 14 40N 20 50 E
Bilyana, *Australia* **62 B4** 18 5S 145 50 E

Brookmere

Bontang, *Indonesia* ..... **36 D5** 0 10N 117 30 E
Bonthe, *S. Leone* **50 G3** 7 30N 12 33W
Bontoc, *Phil.* .... **37 A6** 17 7N 120 58 E
Bonython Ra., *Australia* . **60 D4** 23 40S 128 45 E
Bookabie, *Australia* ..... **61 F5** 31 50S 132 41 E
Booker, *U.S.A.* **81 G4** 36 27N 100 32W
Boolaboolka L., *Australia* **63 E3** 32 38S 143 10 E
Booligal, *Australia* ...... **63 E3** 33 58S 144 53 E
Boonah, *Australia* ...... **63 D5** 27 58S 152 41 E
Boone, *Iowa, U.S.A.* **80 D8** 42 4N 93 53W
Boone, *N.C., U.S.A.* **77 G5** 36 13N 81 41W
Booneville, *Ark., U.S.A.* .. **81 H8** 35 8N 93 55W
Booneville, *Miss., U.S.A.* . **77 H1** 34 39N 88 34W
Boonville, *Calif., U.S.A.* .. **84 F3** 39 1N 123 22W
Boonville, *Ind., U.S.A.* ... **76 F2** 38 3N 87 16W
Boonville, *Mo., U.S.A.* ... **80 F8** 38 58N 92 44W
Boonville, *N.Y., U.S.A.* .. **79 C9** 43 29N 75 20W
Boorindal, *Australia* ..... **63 E4** 30 22S 146 11 E
Boorowa, *Australia* ...... **63 E4** 34 28S 148 44 E
Boothia, Gulf of, *Canada* . **69 A11** 71 0N 90 0W
Boothia Pen., *Canada* ... **68 A10** 71 0N 94 0W
Bootle, *U.K.* **10 D4** 53 28N 3 1W
Booué, *Gabon* .... **52 E2** 0 5S 11 55 E
Boquete, *Panama* **88 E3** 8 46N 82 27W
Boquilla, Presa de la, *Mexico* **86 B3** 27 40N 105 30W
Boquillas del Carmen, *Mexico* **86 B4** 29 17N 102 53W
Bor, *Serbia, Yug.* .... **21 B10** 44 5N 22 7 E
Bôr, *Sudan* .... **51 G12** 6 10N 31 40 E
Bor Mashash, *Israel* ..... **47 D3** 31 7N 34 50 E
Borah Peak, *U.S.A.* **82 D7** 44 8N 113 47W
Borås, *Sweden* .... **9 H15** 57 43N 12 56 E
Borāzjān, *Iran* .... **45 D6** 29 22N 51 10 E
Borba, *Brazil* **92 D7** 4 12S 59 34W
Borborema, Planalto da, *Brazil* **90 D7** 7 0S 37 0W
Bord Khūn-e Now, *Iran* .. **45 D6** 28 3N 51 28 E
Borda, C., *Australia* ..... **63 F2** 35 45S 136 34 E
Bordeaux, *France* **18 D3** 44 50N 0 36W
Borden, *Australia* ...... **61 F2** 34 3S 118 12 E
Borden, *Canada* **71 C7** 46 18N 63 47W
Bordertown, *Australia* ... **63 F3** 36 19S 140 45 E
Borðeyri, *Iceland* **8 D3** 65 12N 21 6W
Bordj Fly Ste. Marie, *Algeria* **50 C5** 27 19N 2 32W
Bordj-in-Eker, *Algeria* ... **50 D7** 24 9N 5 3 E
Bordj Omar Driss, *Algeria* **50 C7** 28 10N 6 40 E
Borehamwood, *U.K.* **11 F7** 51 40N 0 15W
Borgå = Porvoo, *Finland* **9 F21** 60 24N 25 40 E
Borgarfjörður, *Iceland* ... **8 D7** 65 31N 13 49W
Borgarnes, *Iceland* **8 D3** 64 32N 21 55W
Børgefjellet, *Norway* .... **8 D15** 65 20N 13 45 E
Borger, *Neths.* .... **15 B6** 52 54N 6 44 E
Borger, *U.S.A.* **81 H4** 35 39N 101 24W
Borgholm, *Sweden* ...... **9 H17** 56 52N 16 39 E
Borikhane, *Laos* .... **38 C4** 18 33N 103 43 E
Borisoglebsk, *Russia* .... **25 D7** 51 27N 42 5 E
Borisov = Barysaw, *Belarus* .... **24 D4** 54 17N 28 28 E
Borja, *Peru* **92 D3** 4 20S 77 40W
Borkou, *Chad* .... **51 E9** 18 15N 18 50 E
Borkum, *Germany* .... **16 B4** 53 34N 6 40 E
Borlänge, *Sweden* ...... **9 F16** 60 29N 15 26 E
Borley, C., *Antarctica* ... **5 C5** 66 15S 52 30 E
Borneo, *E. Indies* .... **36 D5** 1 0N 115 0 E
Bornholm, *Denmark* ..... **9 J16** 55 10N 15 0 E
Borogontsy, *Russia* ..... **27 C14** 62 42N 131 8 E
Boron, *U.S.A.* **85 L9** 35 0N 117 39W
Borongan, *Phil.* .... **37 B7** 11 37N 125 26 E
Bororen, *Australia* ...... **62 C5** 24 13S 151 33 E
Borovichi, *Russia* ...... **24 C5** 58 25N 33 55 E
Borrego Springs, *U.S.A.* . **85 M10** 33 15N 116 23W
Borroloola, *Australia* .... **62 B2** 16 4S 136 17 E
Borşa, *Romania* .... **17 E13** 47 41N 24 50 E
Borth, *U.K.* **11 E3** 52 29N 4 2W
Borūjerd, *Iran* .... **45 C6** 33 55N 48 50 E
Boryslav, *Ukraine* ...... **17 D12** 49 18N 23 28 E
Borzya, *Russia* .... **27 D12** 50 24N 116 31 E
Bosa, *Italy* .... **20 D3** 40 18N 8 30 E
Bosanska Gradiška, *Bos.-H.* .... **20 B7** 45 10N 17 15 E
Bosaso, *Somali Rep.* .... **46 E4** 11 12N 49 18 E
Boscastle, *U.K.* **11 G3** 50 41N 4 42W
Boshan, *China* .... **35 F9** 36 28N 117 49 E
Boshof, *S. Africa* .... **56 D4** 28 31S 25 13 E
Boshrūyeh, *Iran* .... **45 C8** 33 50N 57 30 E
Bosna →, *Bos.-H.* ...... **21 B8** 45 4N 18 29 E
Bosna i Hercegovina = Bosnia-Herzegovina ■, *Europe* .... **20 B7** 44 0N 18 0 E
Bosnia-Herzegovina ■, *Europe* .... **20 B7** 44 0N 18 0 E
Bosnik, *Indonesia* ...... **37 E9** 1 5S 136 10 E
Bosobolo, *Dem. Rep. of the Congo* **52 D3** 4 15N 19 50 E
Bosporus = İstanbul Boğazı, *Turkey* .... **25 F4** 41 10N 29 10 E
Bossangoa, *C.A.R.* ...... **52 C3** 6 35N 17 30 E
Bossier City, *U.S.A.* **81 J8** 32 31N 93 44W
Bosso, *Niger* .... **51 F8** 13 43N 13 19 E
Bostānābād, *Iran* .... **44 B5** 37 50N 46 50 E
Bosten Hu, *China* .... **32 B3** 41 55N 87 40 E
Boston, *U.K.* **10 E7** 52 59N 0 2W
Boston, *U.S.A.* **79 D13** 42 22N 71 4W
Boston Bar, *Canada* **72 D4** 49 52N 121 30W
Boswell, *Canada* **72 D5** 49 28N 116 45W
Boswell, *Okla., U.S.A.* ... **81 H7** 34 2N 95 52W
Boswell, *Pa., U.S.A.* **78 F5** 40 10N 79 2W
Botad, *India* .... **42 H4** 22 15N 71 40 E
Botany B., *Australia* ..... **63 E5** 34 0S 151 14 E
Botene, *Laos* .... **38 D3** 17 35N 101 12 E
Bothaville, *S. Africa* .... **56 D4** 27 23S 26 34 E
Bothnia, G. of, *Europe* ... **8 E19** 63 0N 20 15 E
Bothwell, *Australia* ..... **62 G4** 42 20S 147 1 E
Bothwell, *Canada* **78 D3** 42 38N 81 52W
Botletle →, *Botswana* .. **56 C3** 20 10S 23 15 E
Botoşani, *Romania* ..... **17 E14** 47 42N 26 41 E
Botswana ■, *Africa* ..... **56 C3** 22 0S 24 0 E
Bottineau, *U.S.A.* **80 A4** 48 50N 100 27W
Bottrop, *Germany* ...... **15 C6** 51 31N 6 58 E
Botucatu, *Brazil* **95 A6** 22 55S 48 30W
Botwood, *Canada* **71 C8** 49 6N 55 23W
Bouaké, *Ivory C.* **50 G4** 7 40N 5 2W
Bouar, *C.A.R.* .... **52 C3** 6 0N 15 40 E
Bouârfa, *Morocco* **50 B5** 32 32N 1 58W
Boucaut B., *Australia* ... **62 A1** 12 0S 134 25 E
Bougainville, C., *Australia* **60 B4** 13 57S 126 4 E
Bougainville Reef, *Australia* .... **62 B4** 15 30S 147 5 E
Bougie = Bejaia, *Algeria* . **50 A7** 36 42N 5 2 E
Bougouni, *Mali* **50 F4** 11 30N 7 20W
Bouillon, *Belgium* ...... **15 E5** 49 44N 5 3 E
Boulder, *Colo., U.S.A.* ... **80 E2** 40 1N 105 17W
Boulder, *Mont., U.S.A.* ... **82 C7** 46 14N 112 7W
Boulder City, *U.S.A.* **85 K12** 35 59N 114 50W
Boulder Creek, *U.S.A.* ... **84 H4** 37 7N 122 7W
Boulder Dam = Hoover Dam, *U.S.A.* **85 K12** 36 1N 114 44W
Boulia, *Australia* .... **62 C2** 22 52S 139 51 E
Boulogne-sur-Mer, *France* **18 A4** 50 42N 1 36 E
Boultoum, *Niger* .... **51 F8** 14 45N 10 25 E
Boun Neua, *Laos* .... **38 B3** 21 38N 101 54 E
Boun Tai, *Laos* .... **38 B3** 21 23N 101 58 E
Bouna, *Ivory C.* **50 G5** 9 10N 3 0W
Boundary Peak, *U.S.A.* ... **84 H8** 37 51N 118 21W
Boundiali, *Ivory C.* **50 G4** 9 30N 6 20W
Bountiful, *U.S.A.* **82 F8** 40 53N 111 53W
Bounty Is., *Pac. Oc.* ..... **64 M9** 48 0S 178 30 E
Bourbonnais, *France* .... **18 C5** 46 28N 3 0 E
Bourem, *Mali* **50 E5** 17 0N 0 24W
Bourg-en-Bresse, *France* . **18 C6** 46 13N 5 12 E
Bourg-St-Maurice, *France* **18 D7** 45 35N 6 46 E
Bourges, *France* .... **18 C5** 47 9N 2 25 E
Bourget, *Canada* **79 A9** 45 26N 75 9W
Bourgogne, *France* ...... **18 C6** 47 0N 4 50 E
Bourke, *Australia* .... **63 E4** 30 8S 145 55 E
Bourne, *U.K.* **10 E7** 52 47N 0 22W
Bournemouth, *U.K.* **11 G6** 50 43N 1 52W
Bournemouth □, *U.K.* **11 G6** 50 43N 1 52W
Bouse, *U.S.A.* **85 M13** 33 56N 114 0W
Bouvet I. = Bouvetøya, *Antarctica* .... **3 G10** 54 26S 3 24 E
Bouvetøya, *Antarctica* ... **3 G10** 54 26S 3 24 E
Bovill, *U.S.A.* **82 C5** 46 51N 116 24W
Bow Island, *Canada* **72 D6** 49 50N 111 23W
Bowbells, *U.S.A.* **80 A3** 48 48N 102 15W
Bowdle, *U.S.A.* **80 C5** 45 27N 99 39W
Bowelling, *Australia* .... **61 F2** 33 25S 116 30 E
Bowen, *Australia* .... **62 C4** 20 0S 148 16 E
Bowen Mts., *Australia* ... **63 F4** 37 0S 147 50 E
Bowie, *Ariz., U.S.A.* **83 K9** 32 19N 109 29W
Bowie, *Tex., U.S.A.* **81 J6** 33 34N 97 51W
Bowkān, *Iran* .... **44 B5** 36 31N 46 12 E
Bowland, Forest of, *U.K.* . **10 D5** 54 0N 2 30W
Bowling Green, *Ky., U.S.A.* **76 G2** 36 59N 86 27W
Bowling Green, *Ohio, U.S.A.* **76 E4** 41 23N 83 39W
Bowling Green, C., *Australia* .... **62 B4** 19 19S 147 25 E
Bowman, *U.S.A.* **80 B3** 46 11N 103 24W
Bowman I., *Antarctica* ... **5 C8** 65 0S 104 0 E
Bowmans, *Australia* ..... **63 E2** 34 10S 138 17 E
Bowmanville, *Canada* **70 D4** 43 55N 78 41W
Bowmore, *U.K.* **12 F2** 55 45N 6 17W
Bowral, *Australia* .... **63 E5** 34 26S 150 27 E
Bowraville, *Australia* .... **63 E5** 30 37S 152 52 E
Bowron →, *Canada* **72 C4** 54 3N 121 50W
Bowser L., *Canada* **72 B3** 56 30N 129 30W
Bowsman, *Canada* **73 C8** 52 14N 101 12W
Bowwood, *Zambia* ...... **55 F2** 17 5S 26 20 E
Boxmeer, *Neths.* .... **15 C5** 51 38N 5 56 E
Boxtel, *Neths.* .... **15 C5** 51 36N 5 20 E
Boyce, *U.S.A.* **81 K8** 31 23N 92 40W
Boyer →, *Canada* **72 B5** 58 27N 115 57W
Boyle, *Ireland* **13 C3** 53 59N 8 18W
Boyne →, *Ireland* **13 C5** 53 43N 6 15W
Boyne City, *U.S.A.* **76 C3** 45 13N 85 1W
Boynton Beach, *U.S.A.* .. **77 M5** 26 32N 80 4W
Boyoma, Chutes, *Dem. Rep. of the Congo* **54 B2** 0 35N 25 23 E
Boyuibe, *Bolivia* **92 G6** 20 25S 63 17W
Boyup Brook, *Australia* .. **61 F2** 33 50S 116 23 E
Boz Dağlan, *Turkey* ..... **21 E13** 38 20N 28 0 E
Bozburun, *Turkey* ...... **21 F13** 36 43N 28 4 E
Bozdoğan, *Turkey* ...... **21 F13** 37 40N 28 17 E
Bozeman, *U.S.A.* **82 D8** 45 41N 111 2W
Bozen = Bolzano, *Italy* .. **20 A4** 46 31N 11 22 E
Bozoum, *C.A.R.* .... **52 C3** 6 25N 16 35 E
Bra, *Italy* .... **18 D7** 44 42N 7 51 E
Brabant □, *Belgium* ..... **15 D4** 50 46N 4 30 E
Brabant L., *Canada* **73 B8** 55 58N 103 43W
Brač, *Croatia* .... **20 C7** 43 20N 16 40 E
Bracadale, L., *U.K.* **12 D2** 57 20N 6 30W
Bracciano, L. di, *Italy* ... **20 C5** 42 7N 12 14 E
Bracebridge, *Canada* **70 C4** 45 2N 79 19W
Brach, *Libya* .... **51 C8** 27 31N 14 20 E
Bräcke, *Sweden* .... **9 E16** 62 45N 15 26 E
Brackettville, *U.S.A.* **81 L4** 29 19N 100 25W
Bracknell, *U.K.* **11 F7** 51 25N 0 43W
Bracknell Forest □, *U.K.* . **11 F7** 51 25N 0 44W
Brad, *Romania* .... **17 E12** 46 10N 22 50 E
Bradenton, *U.S.A.* **77 M4** 27 30N 82 34W
Bradford, *Canada* **78 B5** 44 7N 79 34W
Bradford, *U.K.* **10 D6** 53 47N 1 45W
Bradford, *Pa., U.S.A.* **78 E6** 41 58N 78 38W
Bradford, *Vt., U.S.A.* **79 C12** 43 59N 72 9W
Bradley, *Ark., U.S.A.* **81 J8** 33 6N 93 39W
Bradley, *Calif., U.S.A.* ... **84 K6** 35 52N 120 48W
Bradley, *S. Dak., U.S.A.* .. **80 C6** 45 5N 97 39W
Bradley Institute, *Zimbabwe* .... **55 F3** 17 7S 31 25 E
Bradore Bay, *Canada* **71 B8** 51 27N 57 18W
Bradshaw, *Australia* .... **60 C5** 15 21S 130 16 E
Brady, *U.S.A.* **81 K5** 31 9N 99 20W
Braemar, *Australia* ...... **63 E2** 33 12S 139 35 E
Braemar, *U.K.* **12 D5** 57 0N 3 23W
Braeside, *Canada* **79 A8** 45 28N 76 24W
Braga, *Portugal* **19 B1** 41 35N 8 25W
Bragado, *Argentina* **94 D3** 35 2S 60 27W
Bragança, *Brazil* **93 D9** 1 0S 47 2W
Bragança, *Portugal* **19 B2** 41 48N 6 50W
Bragança Paulista, *Brazil* . **95 A6** 22 55S 46 32W
Brahmanbaria, *Bangla.* ... **41 H17** 23 58N 91 15 E
Brahmani →, *India* ..... **41 J15** 20 39N 86 46 E
Brahmapur, *India* .... **41 K14** 19 15N 84 54 E
Brahmaputra →, *India* .. **43 H13** 23 58N 89 50 E
Braich-y-pwll, *U.K.* **10 E3** 52 47N 4 46W
Braidwood, *Australia* .... **63 F4** 35 27S 149 49 E
Brăila, *Romania* .... **17 F14** 45 19N 27 59 E
Brainerd, *U.S.A.* **80 B7** 46 22N 94 12W
Braintree, *U.K.* .... **11 F8** 51 53N 0 34 E
Braintree, *U.S.A.* **79 D14** 42 13N 71 0W
Brak →, *S. Africa* ...... **56 D3** 29 35S 22 55 E
Brakwater, *Namibia* ..... **56 C2** 22 28S 17 3 E
Bralorne, *Canada* **72 C4** 50 50N 122 50W
Brampton, *Canada* **70 D4** 43 45N 79 45W
Brampton, *U.K.* **10 C5** 54 57N 2 44W
Bramwell, *Australia* ..... **62 A3** 12 8S 142 37 E
Branco →, *Brazil* **92 D6** 1 20S 61 50W
Brandenburg = Neubrandenburg, *Germany* .... **16 B7** 53 33N 13 15 E
Brandenburg, *Germany* .. **16 B7** 52 25N 12 33 E
Brandenburg □, *Germany* **16 B6** 52 50N 13 0 E
Brandfort, *S. Africa* ..... **56 D4** 28 40S 26 30 E
Brandon, *Canada* **73 D9** 49 50N 99 57W
Brandon, *U.S.A.* **79 C11** 43 48N 73 4W
Brandon B., *Ireland* **13 D1** 52 17N 10 8W
Brandon Mt., *Ireland* **13 D1** 52 15N 10 15W
Brandsen, *Argentina* **94 D4** 35 10S 58 15W
Brandvlei, *S. Africa* ..... **56 E3** 30 25S 20 30 E
Branford, *U.S.A.* **79 E12** 41 17N 72 49W
Braniewo, *Poland* .... **17 A10** 54 25N 19 50 E
Bransfield Str., *Antarctica* **5 C18** 63 0S 59 0W
Branson, *Colo., U.S.A.* ... **81 G3** 37 1N 103 53W
Branson, *Mo., U.S.A.* **81 G8** 36 39N 93 13W
Brantford, *Canada* **70 D3** 43 10N 80 15W
Branxholme, *Australia* ... **63 F3** 37 52S 141 49 E
Bras d'Or, L., *Canada* ... **71 C7** 45 50N 60 50W
Brasil, Planalto, *Brazil* ... **90 E6** 18 0S 46 30W
Brasiléia, *Brazil* **92 F5** 11 0S 68 45W
Brasília, *Brazil* **93 G9** 15 47S 47 55W
Brasília Legal, *Brazil* **93 D7** 3 49S 55 36W
Braslaw, *Belarus* .... **9 J22** 55 38N 27 0 E
Braşov, *Romania* .... **17 F13** 45 38N 25 35 E
Brasschaat, *Belgium* .... **15 C4** 51 19N 4 27 E
Brassey, Banjaran, *Malaysia* .... **36 D5** 5 0N 117 15 E
Brassey Ra., *Australia* ... **61 E3** 25 8S 122 15 E
Brasstown Bald, *U.S.A.* .. **77 H4** 34 53N 83 49W
Brastad, *Sweden* .... **9 G14** 58 23N 11 30 E
Bratislava, *Slovak Rep.* .. **17 D9** 48 10N 17 7 E
Bratsk, *Russia* .... **27 D11** 56 10N 101 30 E
Brattleboro, *U.S.A.* **79 D12** 42 51N 72 34W
Braunau, *Austria* .... **16 D7** 48 15N 13 3 E
Braunschweig, *Germany* . **16 B6** 52 15N 10 31 E
Braunton, *U.K.* **11 F3** 51 7N 4 10W
Bravo del Norte →, *Mexico* **86 B5** 25 57N 97 9W
Bravo del Norte, Rio → = Grande, Rio →, *U.S.A.* **81 N6** 25 58N 97 9W
Brawley, *U.S.A.* **85 N11** 32 59N 115 31W
Bray, *Ireland* **13 C5** 53 13N 6 7W
Bray, Mt., *Australia* ..... **62 A1** 14 0S 134 30 E
Bray, Pays de, *France* ... **18 B4** 49 46N 1 26 E
Brazeau →, *Canada* **72 C5** 52 55N 115 14W
Brazil, *U.S.A.* **76 F2** 39 32N 87 8W
Brazil ■, *S. Amer.* **93 F9** 12 0S 50 0W
Brazilian Highlands = Brasil, Planalto, *Brazil* . **90 E6** 18 0S 46 30W
Brazo Sur →, *S. Amer.* .. **94 B4** 25 21S 57 42W
Brazos →, *U.S.A.* **81 L7** 28 53N 95 23W
Brazzaville, *Congo* ...... **52 E3** 4 9S 15 12 E
Brčko, *Bos.-H.* .... **21 B8** 44 54N 18 46 E
Breadalbane, *Australia* .. **62 C2** 23 50S 139 35 E
Breaden, L., *Australia* ... **61 E4** 25 51S 125 28 E
Breaksea Sd., *N.Z.* ...... **59 L1** 45 35S 166 35 E
Bream B., *N.Z.* .... **59 F5** 35 56S 174 28 E
Bream Hd., *N.Z.* .... **59 F5** 35 51S 174 36 E
Breas, *Chile* **94 B1** 25 29S 70 24W
Brebes, *Indonesia* ...... **37 G13** 6 52S 109 3 E
Brechin, *Canada* **78 B5** 44 32N 79 10W
Brechin, *U.K.* **12 E6** 56 44N 2 39W
Brecht, *Belgium* .... **15 C4** 51 21N 4 38 E
Breckenridge, *Colo., U.S.A.* **82 G10** 39 29N 106 3W
Breckenridge, *Minn., U.S.A.* **80 B6** 46 16N 96 35W
Breckenridge, *Tex., U.S.A.* **81 J5** 32 45N 98 54W
Breckland, *U.K.* .... **11 E8** 52 30N 0 40 E
Brecon, *U.K.* **11 F4** 51 57N 3 23W
Brecon Beacons, *U.K.* ... **11 F4** 51 53N 3 26W
Breda, *Neths.* .... **15 C4** 51 35N 4 45 E
Bredasdorp, *S. Africa* ... **56 E3** 34 33S 20 2 E
Bredbo, *Australia* ...... **63 F4** 35 58S 149 10 E
Bree, *Belgium* .... **15 C5** 51 8N 5 35 E
Bregenz, *Austria* .... **16 E5** 47 30N 9 45 E
Breiðafjörður, *Iceland* .. **8 D2** 65 15N 23 15W
Brejo, *Brazil* **93 D10** 3 41S 42 47W
Bremen, *Germany* ...... **16 B5** 53 4N 8 47 E
Bremer I., *Australia* ..... **62 A2** 12 5S 136 45 E
Bremerhaven, *Germany* .. **16 B5** 53 33N 8 36 E
Bremerton, *U.S.A.* **84 C4** 47 34N 122 38W
Brenham, *U.S.A.* **81 K6** 30 10N 96 24W
Brennerpass, *Austria* .... **16 E6** 47 2N 11 30 E
Brent, *Canada* **70 C4** 46 2N 78 29W
Brentwood, *U.K.* .... **11 F8** 51 37N 0 19 E
Brentwood, *U.S.A.* **79 F11** 40 47N 73 15W
Bréscia, *Italy* .... **18 D9** 45 33N 10 15 E
Breskens, *Neths.* .... **15 C3** 51 23N 3 33 E
Breslau = Wrocław, *Poland* .... **17 C9** 51 5N 17 5 E
Bressanone, *Italy* ...... **20 A4** 46 43N 11 39 E
Bressay, *U.K.* **12 A7** 60 9N 1 6W
Brest, *Belarus* .... **24 D3** 52 10N 23 40 E
Brest, *France* **18 B1** 48 24N 4 31W
Brest-Litovsk = Brest, *Belarus* .... **24 D3** 52 10N 23 40 E
Bretagne, *France* **18 B2** 48 10N 3 0W
Breton, *Canada* **72 C6** 53 7N 114 28W
Breton Sd., *U.S.A.* **81 L10** 29 35N 89 15W
Brett, C., *N.Z.* .... **59 F5** 35 10S 174 20 E
Brevard, *U.S.A.* **77 H4** 35 14N 82 44W
Breves, *Brazil* **93 D8** 1 40S 50 29W
Brewarrina, *Australia* ... **63 E4** 30 0S 146 51 E
Brewer, *U.S.A.* **71 D6** 44 48N 68 46W
Brewer, Mt., *U.S.A.* **84 J8** 36 44N 118 28W
Brewster, *N.Y., U.S.A.* ... **79 E11** 41 23N 73 37W
Brewster, *Wash., U.S.A.* . **82 B4** 48 6N 119 47W
Brewton, *U.S.A.* **77 K2** 31 7N 87 4W
Breyten, *S. Africa* .... **57 D5** 26 16S 30 0 E
Brezhnev = Naberezhnyye Chelny, *Russia* .... **24 C9** 55 42N 52 19 E
Briançon, *France* .... **18 D7** 44 54N 6 39 E
Bribie I., *Australia* ..... **63 D5** 27 0S 153 10 E
Bridgehampton, *U.S.A.* .. **79 F12** 40 56N 72 19W
Bridgend, *U.K.* **11 F4** 51 30N 3 34W
Bridgend □, *U.K.* **11 F4** 51 36N 3 36W
Bridgeport, *Calif., U.S.A.* . **84 G7** 38 15N 119 14W
Bridgeport, *Conn., U.S.A.* **79 E11** 41 11N 73 12W
Bridgeport, *Nebr., U.S.A.* . **80 E3** 41 40N 103 6W
Bridgeport, *Tex., U.S.A.* .. **81 J6** 33 13N 97 45W
Bridger, *U.S.A.* **82 D9** 45 18N 108 55W
Bridgeton, *U.S.A.* **76 F8** 39 26N 75 14W
Bridgetown, *Australia* ... **61 F2** 33 58S 116 7 E
Bridgetown, *Barbados* ... **89 D8** 13 5N 59 30W
Bridgetown, *Canada* **71 D6** 44 55N 65 18W
Bridgewater, *Canada* **71 D7** 44 25N 64 31W
Bridgewater, *Mass., U.S.A.* **79 E14** 41 59N 70 58W
Bridgewater, *S. Dak., U.S.A.* **80 D6** 43 33N 97 30W
Bridgewater, C., *Australia* **63 F3** 38 23S 141 23 E
Bridgnorth, *U.K.* **11 E5** 52 32N 2 25W
Bridgton, *U.S.A.* **79 B14** 44 3N 70 42W
Bridgwater, *U.K.* **11 F5** 51 8N 2 59W
Bridgwater B., *U.K.* **11 F4** 51 15N 3 15W
Bridlington, *U.K.* **10 C7** 54 5N 0 12W
Bridlington B., *U.K.* **10 C7** 54 4N 0 10W
Bridport, *Australia* ...... **62 G4** 40 59S 147 23 E
Bridport, *U.K.* **11 G5** 50 44N 2 45W
Brig, *Switz.* .... **18 C7** 46 18N 7 59 E
Brigg, *U.K.* **10 D7** 53 34N 0 28W
Briggsdale, *U.S.A.* **80 E2** 40 38N 104 20W
Brigham City, *U.S.A.* **82 F7** 41 31N 112 1W
Bright, *Australia* .... **63 F4** 36 42S 146 56 E
Brighton, *Australia* ..... **63 F2** 35 5S 138 30 E
Brighton, *Canada* **70 D4** 44 2N 77 44W
Brighton, *U.K.* **11 G7** 50 49N 0 7W
Brighton, *U.S.A.* **80 F2** 39 59N 104 49W
Brilliant, *Canada* **72 D5** 49 19N 117 38W
Brilliant, *U.S.A.* **78 F4** 40 15N 80 39W
Bríndisi, *Italy* .... **21 D7** 40 39N 17 55 E
Brinkley, *U.S.A.* **81 H9** 34 53N 91 12W
Brinkworth, *Australia* ... **63 E2** 33 42S 138 26 E
Brinnon, *U.S.A.* **84 C4** 47 41N 122 54W
Brion, I., *Canada* **71 C7** 47 46N 61 26W
Brisbane, *Australia* ..... **63 D5** 27 25S 153 2 E
Brisbane →, *Australia* . **63 D5** 27 24S 153 9 E
Bristol, *U.K.* **11 F5** 51 26N 2 35W
Bristol, *Conn., U.S.A.* ... **79 E12** 41 40N 72 57W
Bristol, *Pa., U.S.A.* **79 F10** 40 6N 74 51W
Bristol, *R.I., U.S.A.* **79 E13** 41 40N 71 16W
Bristol, *S. Dak., U.S.A.* .. **80 C6** 45 21N 97 45W
Bristol, *Tenn., U.S.A.* ... **77 G4** 36 36N 82 11W
Bristol, City of □, *U.K.* ... **11 F5** 51 27N 2 36W
Bristol B., *U.S.A.* **68 C4** 58 0N 160 0W
Bristol Channel, *U.K.* **11 F3** 51 18N 4 30W
Bristol I., *Antarctica* **5 B1** 58 45S 28 0W
Bristol L., *U.S.A.* **83 J5** 34 23N 116 50W
Bristow, *U.S.A.* **81 H6** 35 50N 96 23W
British Columbia □, *Canada* **72 C3** 55 0N 125 15W
British Isles, *Europe* **6 E5** 54 0N 4 0W
Brits, *S. Africa* .... **57 D4** 25 37S 27 48 E
Britstown, *S. Africa* ..... **56 E3** 30 37S 23 30 E
Britt, *Canada* **70 C3** 45 46N 80 34W
Brittany = Bretagne, *France* **18 B2** 48 10N 3 0W
Britton, *U.S.A.* **80 C6** 45 48N 97 45W
Brive-la-Gaillarde, *France* **18 D4** 45 10N 1 32 E
Brixen = Bressanone, *Italy* **20 A4** 46 43N 11 39 E
Brixham, *U.K.* **11 G4** 50 23N 3 31W
Brixton, *Australia* ...... **62 C3** 23 32S 144 57 E
Brno, *Czech Rep.* .... **17 D9** 49 10N 16 35 E
Broad →, *U.S.A.* **77 J5** 34 1N 81 4W
Broad Arrow, *Australia* . **61 F3** 30 23S 121 15 E
Broad B., *U.K.* **12 C2** 58 14N 6 18W
Broad Haven, *Ireland* **13 B2** 54 20N 9 55W
Broad Law, *U.K.* **12 F5** 55 30N 3 21W
Broad Sd., *Australia* ..... **62 C4** 22 0S 149 45 E
Broadhurst Ra., *Australia* **60 D3** 22 30S 122 30 E
Broads, The, *U.K.* ...... **10 E9** 52 45N 1 30 E
Broadus, *U.S.A.* **80 C2** 45 27N 105 25W
Broadview, *Canada* **73 C8** 50 22N 102 35W
Brochet, *Canada* **73 B8** 57 53N 101 40W
Brochet, L., *Canada* **73 B8** 58 36N 101 35W
Brock, *Canada* **73 C7** 51 26N 108 43W
Brocken, *Germany* ...... **16 C6** 51 47N 10 37 E
Brockport, *U.S.A.* **78 C7** 43 13N 77 56W
Brockton, *U.S.A.* **79 D13** 42 5N 71 1W
Brockville, *Canada* **70 D4** 44 35N 75 41W
Brockway, *Mont., U.S.A.* . **80 B2** 47 18N 105 45W
Brockway, *Pa., U.S.A.* ... **78 E6** 41 15N 78 47W
Brocton, *U.S.A.* **78 D5** 42 23N 79 26W
Brodeur Pen., *Canada* ... **69 A11** 72 30N 88 10W
Brodick, *U.K.* **12 F3** 55 35N 5 9W
Brodnica, *Poland* .... **17 B10** 53 15N 19 25 E
Brody, *Ukraine* .... **17 C13** 50 5N 25 10 E
Brogan, *U.S.A.* **82 D5** 44 15N 117 31W
Broken Arrow, *U.S.A.* ... **81 G7** 36 3N 95 48W
Broken Bow, *Nebr., U.S.A.* **80 E5** 41 24N 99 38W
Broken Bow, *Okla., U.S.A.* **81 H7** 34 2N 94 44W
Broken Hill = Kabwe, *Zambia* .... **55 E2** 14 30S 28 29 E
Broken Hill, *Australia* ... **63 E3** 31 58S 141 29 E
Bromley, *U.K.* .... **11 F8** 51 24N 0 2 E
Bromsgrove, *U.K.* **11 E5** 52 21N 2 2W
Brønderslev, *Denmark* ... **9 H13** 57 16N 9 57 E
Bronkhorstspruit, *S. Africa* **57 D4** 25 46S 28 45 E
Brønnøysund, *Norway* .... **8 D15** 65 28N 12 14 E
Bronte, *U.S.A.* **81 K4** 31 53N 100 18W
Bronte Park, *Australia* ... **62 G4** 42 8S 146 30 E
Brook Park, *U.S.A.* **78 E4** 41 24N 80 51W
Brookfield, *U.S.A.* **80 F8** 39 47N 93 4W
Brookhaven, *U.S.A.* **81 K9** 31 35N 90 26W
Brookings, *Oreg., U.S.A.* . **82 E1** 42 3N 124 17W
Brookings, *S. Dak., U.S.A.* **80 C6** 44 19N 96 48W
Brooklin, *Canada* **78 C6** 43 55N 78 55W
Brooklyn Park, *U.S.A.* ... **80 C8** 45 6N 93 23W
Brookmere, *Canada* **72 D4** 49 52N 120 53W

Carei

Cache Cr. →, U.S.A. 84 G5 38 42N 121 42W
Cachi, Argentina 94 B2 25 5S 66 10W
Cachimbo, Serra do, Brazil 93 E7 9 30S 55 30W
Cachoeira, Brazil 93 F11 12 30S 39 0W
Cachoeira de Itapemirim, Brazil 95 A7 20 51S 41 7W
Cachoeira do Sul, Brazil 95 C5 30 3S 52 53W
Cacoal, Brazil 92 F6 11 32S 61 18W
Cacólo, Angola 52 G3 10 9S 19 21 E
Caconda, Angola 53 G3 13 48S 15 8 E
Caddo, U.S.A. 81 H6 34 7N 96 16W
Cadell Cr. →, Australia 62 C3 22 35S 141 51 E
Cader Idris, U.K. 11 E4 52 42N 3 53W
Cadibarrawirracanna, L., Australia 63 D2 28 52S 135 27 E
Cadillac, Canada 70 C4 48 14N 78 23W
Cadillac, U.S.A. 76 C3 44 15N 85 24W
Cadiz, Phil. 37 B6 10 57N 123 15 E
Cádiz, Spain 19 D2 36 30N 6 20W
Cadiz, U.S.A. 78 F4 40 22N 81 0W
Cádiz, G. de, Spain 19 D2 36 40N 7 0W
Cadney Park, Australia 63 D1 27 55S 134 3 E
Cadomin, Canada 72 C5 53 2N 117 20W
Cadotte →, Canada 72 B5 56 43N 117 10W
Cadoux, Australia 61 F2 30 46S 117 7 E
Caen, France 18 B3 49 10N 0 22W
Caernarfon, U.K. 10 D3 53 8N 4 16W
Caernarfon B., U.K. 10 D3 53 4N 4 40W
Caernarvon = Caernarfon, U.K. 10 D3 53 8N 4 16W
Caerphilly, U.K. 11 F4 51 35N 3 13W
Caerphilly □, U.K. 11 F4 51 37N 3 12W
Caesarea, Israel 47 C3 32 30N 34 53 E
Caetité, Brazil 93 F10 13 50S 42 32W
Cafayate, Argentina 94 B2 26 2S 66 0W
Cafu, Angola 56 B2 16 30S 15 8 E
Cagayan de Oro, Phil. 37 C6 8 30N 124 40 E
Cágliari, Italy 20 E3 39 13N 9 7 E
Cágliari, G. di, Italy 20 E3 39 8N 9 11 E
Caguán →, Colombia 92 D4 0 8S 74 18W
Caguas, Puerto Rico 89 C6 18 14N 66 2W
Caha Mts., Ireland 13 E2 51 45N 9 40W
Cahama, Angola 56 B1 16 17S 14 19 E
Caher, Ireland 13 D4 52 22N 7 56W
Caherciveen, Ireland 13 E1 51 56N 10 14W
Cahora Bassa, Représa de, Mozam. 55 F3 15 20S 32 50 E
Cahore Pt., Ireland 13 D5 52 33N 6 12W
Cahors, France 18 D4 44 27N 1 27 E
Cahul, Moldova 17 F15 45 50N 28 15 E
Cai Bau, Dao, Vietnam 38 B6 21 10N 107 27 E
Cai Nuoc, Vietnam 39 H5 8 56N 105 1 E
Caia, Mozam. 55 F4 17 51S 35 24 E
Caianda, Angola 55 E1 11 2S 23 31 E
Caibarién, Cuba 88 B4 22 30N 79 30W
Caicó, Brazil 93 E11 6 20S 37 0W
Caicos Is., W. Indies 89 B5 21 40N 71 40W
Caicos Passage, W. Indies 89 B5 22 45N 72 45W
Caird Coast, Antarctica 5 D1 75 0S 25 0W
Cairn Gorm, U.K. 12 D5 57 7N 3 39W
Cairngorm Mts., U.K. 12 D5 57 6N 3 42W
Cairnryan, U.K. 12 G3 54 59N 5 1W
Cairns, Australia 62 B4 16 57S 145 45 E
Cairo = El Qâhira, Egypt 51 B12 30 1N 31 14 E
Cairo, Ga., U.S.A. 77 K3 30 52N 84 13W
Cairo, Ill., U.S.A. 81 G10 37 0N 89 11W
Caithness, Ord of, U.K. 12 C5 58 8N 3 36W
Cajamarca, Peru 92 E3 7 5S 78 28W
Cajàzeiras, Brazil 93 E11 6 52S 38 30W
Cala d'Or, Spain 22 B10 39 23N 3 14 E
Cala Figuera, C. de, Spain 22 B9 39 27N 2 31 E
Cala Forcat, Spain 22 B10 40 0N 3 47 E
Cala Mayor, Spain 22 B9 39 33N 2 37 E
Cala Mezquida, Spain 22 B11 39 55N 4 16 E
Cala Millor, Spain 22 B10 39 35N 3 22 E
Cala Ratjada, Spain 22 B10 39 43N 3 27 E
Calabar, Nigeria 50 H7 4 57N 8 20 E
Calabozo, Venezuela 92 B5 9 0N 67 28W
Calábria □, Italy 20 E7 39 0N 16 30 E
Calafate, Argentina 96 G2 50 19S 72 15W
Calahorra, Spain 19 A5 42 18N 1 59W
Calais, France 18 A4 50 57N 1 56 E
Calais, U.S.A. 71 C6 45 11N 67 17W
Calalaste, Cord. de, Argentina 94 B2 25 0S 67 0W
Calama, Brazil 92 E6 8 0S 62 50W
Calama, Chile 94 A2 22 30S 68 55W
Calamian Group, Phil. 37 B5 11 50N 119 55 E
Calamocha, Spain 19 B5 40 50N 1 17W
Calán Porter, Spain 22 B11 39 52N 4 8 E
Calang, Indonesia 36 D1 4 37N 95 37 E
Calapan, Phil. 37 B6 13 25N 121 7 E
Călăraşi, Romania 17 F14 44 12N 27 20 E
Calatayud, Spain 19 B5 41 20N 1 40W
Calauag, Phil. 37 B6 13 55N 122 15 E
Calavite, C., Phil. 37 B6 13 26N 120 20 E
Calbayog, Phil. 37 B6 12 4N 124 38 E
Calca, Peru 92 F4 13 22S 72 0W
Calcasieu L., U.S.A. 81 L8 29 55N 93 18W
Calcutta, India 43 H13 22 36N 88 24 E
Caldas da Rainha, Portugal 19 C1 39 24N 9 8W
Calder →, U.K. 10 D6 53 44N 1 22W
Caldera, Chile 94 B1 27 5S 70 55W
Caldwell, Idaho, U.S.A. 82 E5 43 40N 116 41W
Caldwell, Kans., U.S.A. 81 G6 37 2N 97 37W
Caldwell, Tex., U.S.A. 81 K6 30 32N 96 42W
Caledon, S. Africa 56 E2 34 14S 19 26 E
Caledon →, S. Africa 56 E4 30 31S 26 5 E
Caledon B., Australia 62 A2 12 45S 137 0 E
Caledonia, Canada 78 C5 43 7N 79 58W
Caledonia, U.S.A. 78 D7 42 58N 77 51W
Calemba, Angola 56 B2 16 0S 15 44 E
Calexico, U.S.A. 85 N11 32 40N 115 30W
Calf of Man, U.K. 10 C3 54 3N 4 48W
Calgary, Canada 72 C6 51 0N 114 10W
Calheta, Madeira 22 D2 32 44N 17 11W
Calhoun, U.S.A. 77 H3 34 30N 84 57W
Cali, Colombia 92 C3 3 25N 76 35W
Calicut, India 40 P9 11 15N 75 43 E
Caliente, U.S.A. 83 H6 37 37N 114 31W
California, Mo., U.S.A. 80 F8 38 38N 92 34W
California, Pa., U.S.A. 78 F5 40 4N 79 54W
California □, U.S.A. 83 H4 37 30N 119 30W
California, Baja, Mexico 86 A1 32 10N 115 12W
California, Baja, T.N. □ = Baja California □, Mexico 86 B2 30 0N 115 0W
California, Baja, T.S. □ = Baja California Sur □, Mexico 86 B2 25 50N 111 50W
California, G. de, Mexico 86 B2 27 0N 111 0W
California City, U.S.A. 85 K9 35 10N 117 55W
California Hot Springs, U.S.A. 85 K8 35 51N 118 41W
Calingasta, Argentina 94 C2 31 15S 69 30W
Calipatria, U.S.A. 85 M11 33 8N 115 31W
Calistoga, U.S.A. 84 G4 38 35N 122 35W
Calitzdorp, S. Africa 56 E3 33 33S 21 42 E
Callabonna, L., Australia 63 D3 29 40S 140 5 E
Callan, Ireland 13 D4 52 32N 7 24W
Callander, U.K. 12 E4 56 15N 4 13W
Callao, Peru 92 F3 12 0S 77 0W
Callaway, U.S.A. 80 E5 41 18N 99 56W
Calles, Mexico 87 C5 23 2N 98 42W
Callide, Australia 62 C5 24 18S 150 28 E
Calling Lake, Canada 72 B6 55 15N 113 12W
Calliope, Australia 62 C5 24 0S 151 16 E
Calne, U.K. 11 F6 51 26N 2 0W
Calola, Angola 56 B2 16 25S 17 48 E
Caloundra, Australia 63 D5 26 45S 153 10 E
Calpella, U.S.A. 84 F3 39 14N 123 12W
Calpine, U.S.A. 84 F6 39 40N 120 27W
Calstock, Canada 70 C3 49 47N 84 9W
Caltagirone, Italy 20 F6 37 14N 14 31 E
Caltanissetta, Italy 20 F6 37 29N 14 4 E
Calulo, Angola 52 G2 10 1S 14 56 E
Calumet, U.S.A. 76 B1 47 14N 88 27W
Calvert, U.S.A. 81 K6 30 59N 96 40W
Calvert →, Australia 62 B2 16 17S 137 44 E
Calvert Hills, Australia 62 B2 17 15S 137 20 E
Calvert I., Canada 72 C3 51 30N 128 0W
Calvert Ra., Australia 60 D3 24 0S 122 30 E
Calvi, France 18 E8 42 34N 8 45 E
Calviá, Spain 19 C7 39 34N 2 31 E
Calvillo, Mexico 86 C4 21 51N 102 43W
Calvinia, S. Africa 56 E2 31 28S 19 45 E
Calwa, U.S.A. 84 J7 36 42N 119 46W
Cam →, U.K. 11 E8 52 21N 0 16 E
Cam Lam, Vietnam 39 G7 11 54N 109 10 E
Cam Pha, Vietnam 38 B6 21 7N 107 18 E
Cam Ranh, Vietnam 39 G7 11 54N 109 12 E
Cam Xuyen, Vietnam 38 C6 18 15N 106 0 E
Camabatela, Angola 52 F3 8 20S 15 26 E
Camacha, Madeira 22 D3 32 41N 16 49W
Camacho, Mexico 86 C4 24 25N 102 18W
Camacupa, Angola 53 G3 11 58S 17 22 E
Camagüey, Cuba 88 B4 21 20N 78 0W
Camaná, Peru 92 G4 16 30S 72 50W
Camanche Reservoir, U.S.A. 84 G6 38 14N 121 1W
Camaquã →, Brazil 95 C5 31 17S 51 47W
Câmara de Lobos, Madeira 22 D3 32 39N 16 59W
Camargue, France 18 E6 43 34N 4 34 E
Camarillo, U.S.A. 85 L7 34 13N 119 2W
Camarón, C., Honduras 88 C2 16 0N 85 5W
Camarones, Argentina 96 E3 44 50S 65 40W
Camas, U.S.A. 84 E4 45 35N 122 24W
Camas Valley, U.S.A. 82 E2 43 2N 123 40W
Cambará, Brazil 95 A5 23 2S 50 5W
Cambay = Khambhat, India 42 H5 22 23N 72 33 E
Cambay, G. of = Khambhat, G. of, India 42 J5 20 45N 72 30 E
Cambodia ■, Asia 38 F5 12 15N 105 0 E
Camborne, U.K. 11 G2 50 12N 5 19W
Cambrai, France 18 A5 50 11N 3 14 E
Cambria, U.S.A. 84 K5 35 34N 121 5W
Cambrian Mts., U.K. 11 E4 52 3N 3 57W
Cambridge, Canada 70 D3 43 23N 80 15W
Cambridge, Jamaica 88 C4 18 18N 77 54W
Cambridge, N.Z. 59 G5 37 54S 175 29 E
Cambridge, U.K. 11 E8 52 12N 0 8 E
Cambridge, Idaho, U.S.A. 82 D5 44 34N 116 41W
Cambridge, Mass., U.S.A. 79 D13 42 22N 71 6W
Cambridge, Md., U.S.A. 76 F7 38 34N 76 5W
Cambridge, Minn., U.S.A. 80 C8 45 34N 93 13W
Cambridge, N.Y., U.S.A. 79 C11 43 2N 73 22W
Cambridge, Nebr., U.S.A. 80 E4 40 17N 100 10W
Cambridge, Ohio, U.S.A. 78 F3 40 2N 81 35W
Cambridge G., Australia 60 B4 14 55S 128 15 E
Cambridge Springs, U.S.A. 78 E4 41 48N 80 4W
Cambridgeshire □, U.K. 11 E7 52 25N 0 7W
Cambuci, Brazil 95 A7 21 35S 41 55W
Cambundi-Catembo, Angola 52 G3 10 10S 17 35 E
Camden, Ala., U.S.A. 77 K2 31 59N 87 17W
Camden, Ark., U.S.A. 81 J8 33 35N 92 50W
Camden, Maine, U.S.A. 71 D6 44 13N 69 4W
Camden, N.J., U.S.A. 79 G9 39 56N 75 7W
Camden, S.C., U.S.A. 77 H5 34 16N 80 36W
Camden Sd., Australia 60 C3 15 27S 124 25 E
Camdenton, U.S.A. 81 F8 38 1N 92 45W
Cameron, Ariz., U.S.A. 83 J8 35 53N 111 25W
Cameron, La., U.S.A. 81 L8 29 48N 93 20W
Cameron, Mo., U.S.A. 80 F7 39 44N 94 14W
Cameron, Tex., U.S.A. 81 K6 30 51N 96 59W
Cameron Falls, Canada 70 C2 49 8N 88 19W
Cameron Highlands, Malaysia 39 K3 4 27N 101 22 E
Cameron Hills, Canada 72 B5 59 48N 118 0W
Cameroon ■, Africa 52 C2 6 0N 12 30 E
Cameroun, Mt., Cameroon 52 D1 4 13N 9 10 E
Cametá, Brazil 93 D9 2 12S 49 30W
Caminha, Portugal 19 B1 41 50N 8 50W
Camino, U.S.A. 84 G6 38 44N 120 41W
Camira Creek, Australia 63 D5 29 15S 152 58 E
Cammal, U.S.A. 78 E7 41 24N 77 28W
Camocim, Brazil 93 D10 2 55S 40 50W
Camooweal, Australia 62 B2 19 56S 138 7 E
Camopi, Fr. Guiana 93 C8 3 12N 52 17W
Camp Crook, U.S.A. 80 C3 45 33N 103 59W
Camp Nelson, U.S.A. 85 J8 36 8N 118 39W
Camp Wood, U.S.A. 81 L5 29 40N 100 1W
Campana, Argentina 94 C4 34 10S 58 55W
Campana, I., Chile 96 F1 48 20S 75 20W
Campanário, Madeira 22 D2 32 39N 17 2W
Campánia □, Italy 20 D6 41 0N 14 30 E
Campbell, S. Africa 56 D3 28 48S 23 44 E
Campbell, Calif., U.S.A. 84 H5 37 17N 121 57W
Campbell, Ohio, U.S.A. 78 E4 41 5N 80 37W
Campbell I., Pac. Oc. 64 N8 52 30S 169 0 E
Campbell L., Canada 73 A7 63 14N 106 55W
Campbell River, Canada 72 C3 50 5N 125 20W
Campbell Town, Australia 62 G4 41 52S 147 30 E
Campbellford, Canada 78 B7 44 18N 77 48W
Campbellpur, Pakistan 42 C5 33 46N 72 26 E
Campbellsville, U.S.A. 76 G3 37 21N 85 20W
Campbellton, Canada 71 C6 47 57N 66 43W
Campbelltown, Australia 63 E5 34 4S 150 49 E
Campbeltown, U.K. 12 F3 55 26N 5 36W
Campeche, Mexico 87 D6 19 50N 90 32W
Campeche □, Mexico 87 D6 19 50N 90 32W
Campeche, B. de, Mexico 87 D6 19 30N 93 0W
Camperdown, Australia 63 F3 38 14S 143 9 E
Camperville, Canada 73 C8 51 59N 100 9W
Câmpina, Romania 17 F13 45 10N 25 45 E
Campina Grande, Brazil 93 E11 7 20S 35 47W
Campinas, Brazil 95 A6 22 50S 47 0W
Campo Grande, Brazil 93 H8 20 25S 54 40W
Campo Maíor, Brazil 93 D10 4 50S 42 12W
Campo Mourão, Brazil 95 A5 24 3S 52 22W
Campobasso, Italy 20 D6 41 34N 14 39 E
Campos, Brazil 95 A7 21 50S 41 20W
Campos Belos, Brazil 93 F9 13 10S 47 3W
Campos del Puerto, Spain 22 B10 39 26N 3 1 E
Campos Novos, Brazil 95 B5 27 21S 51 50W
Camptonville, U.S.A. 84 F5 39 27N 121 3W
Câmpulung, Romania 17 F13 45 17N 25 3 E
Camrose, Canada 72 C6 53 0N 112 50W
Camsell Portage, Canada 73 B7 59 37N 109 15W
Çan, Turkey 21 D12 40 2N 27 3 E
Can Clavo, Spain 22 C7 38 57N 1 27 E
Can Creu, Spain 22 C7 38 58N 1 28 E
Can Gio, Vietnam 39 G6 10 25N 106 58 E
Can Tho, Vietnam 39 G5 10 2N 105 46 E
Canaan, U.S.A. 79 D11 42 2N 73 20W
Canada ■, N. Amer. 68 C10 60 0N 100 0W
Cañada de Gómez, Argentina 94 C3 32 40S 61 30W
Canadian, U.S.A. 81 H4 35 55N 100 23W
Canadian →, U.S.A. 81 H7 35 28N 95 3W
Çanakkale, Turkey 25 F4 40 8N 26 24 E
Çanakkale Boğazı, Turkey 25 F4 40 17N 26 32 E
Canal Flats, Canada 72 C5 50 10N 115 48W
Canalejas, Argentina 94 D2 35 15S 66 34W
Canals, Argentina 94 C3 33 35S 62 53W
Canandaigua, U.S.A. 78 D7 42 54N 77 17W
Cananea, Mexico 86 A2 31 0N 110 20W
Canarias, Is., Atl. Oc. 22 F4 28 30N 16 0W
Canarreos, Arch. de los, Cuba 88 B3 21 35N 81 40W
Canary Is. = Canarias, Is., Atl. Oc. 22 F4 28 30N 16 0W
Canatlán, Mexico 86 C4 24 31N 104 47W
Canaveral, C., U.S.A. 77 L5 28 27N 80 32W
Canavieiras, Brazil 93 G11 15 39S 39 0W
Canbelego, Australia 63 E4 31 32S 146 18 E
Canberra, Australia 63 F4 35 15S 149 8 E
Canby, Calif., U.S.A. 82 F3 41 27N 120 52W
Canby, Minn., U.S.A. 80 C6 44 43N 96 16W
Canby, Oreg., U.S.A. 84 E4 45 16N 122 42W
Cancún, Mexico 87 C7 21 8N 86 44W
Candelaria, Argentina 95 B4 27 29S 55 44W
Candelaria, Canary Is. 22 F3 28 22N 16 22W
Candelo, Australia 63 F4 36 47S 149 43 E
Candia = Iráklion, Greece 23 D7 35 20N 25 12 E
Candle L., Canada 73 C7 53 50N 105 18W
Candlemas I., Antarctica 5 B1 57 3S 26 40W
Cando, U.S.A. 80 A5 48 32N 99 12W
Canea = Khaniá, Greece 23 D6 35 30N 24 4 E
Canelones, Uruguay 95 C4 34 32S 56 17W
Cañete, Chile 94 D1 37 50S 73 30W
Cañete, Peru 92 F3 13 8S 76 30W
Cangas de Narcea, Spain 19 A2 43 10N 6 32W
Canguaretama, Brazil 93 E11 6 20S 35 5W
Canguçu, Brazil 95 C5 31 22S 52 43W
Cangzhou, China 34 E9 38 19N 116 52 E
Caniapiscau = Kaniapiskau →, Canada 71 A6 56 40N 69 30W
Caniapiscau, L. = Kaniapiskau L., Canada 71 B6 54 10N 69 55W
Canicattì, Italy 20 F5 37 21N 13 51 E
Canim Lake, Canada 72 C4 51 47N 120 54W
Canindeyu □, Paraguay 95 A5 24 10S 55 0W
Canisteo, U.S.A. 78 D7 42 16N 77 36W
Canisteo →, U.S.A. 78 D7 42 7N 77 8W
Cañitas, Mexico 86 C4 23 36N 102 43W
Çankırı, Turkey 25 F5 40 40N 33 37 E
Cankuzo, Burundi 54 C3 3 10S 30 31 E
Canmore, Canada 72 C5 51 7N 115 18W
Cann River, Australia 63 F4 37 35S 149 7 E
Canna, U.K. 12 D2 57 3N 6 33W
Cannanore, India 40 P9 11 53N 75 27 E
Cannes, France 18 E7 43 32N 7 1 E
Canning Town = Port Canning, India 43 H13 22 23N 88 40 E
Cannington, Canada 78 B5 44 20N 79 2W
Cannock, U.K. 11 E5 52 41N 2 1W
Cannon Ball →, U.S.A. 80 B4 46 20N 100 38W
Cannondale Mt., Australia 62 D4 25 13S 148 57 E
Canoas, Brazil 95 B5 29 56S 51 11W
Canoe L., Canada 73 B7 55 10N 108 15W
Canon City, U.S.A. 80 F2 38 27N 105 14W
Canora, Canada 73 C8 51 40N 102 30W
Canowindra, Australia 63 E4 33 35S 148 38 E
Canso, Canada 71 C7 45 20N 61 0W
Cantabria □, Spain 19 A4 43 10N 4 0W
Cantabrian Mts. = Cantábrica, Cordillera, Spain 19 A3 43 0N 5 10W
Cantábrica, Cordillera, Spain 19 A3 43 0N 5 10W
Cantal, Plomb du, France 18 D5 45 3N 2 45 E
Canterbury, Australia 62 D3 25 23S 141 53 E
Canterbury, U.K. 11 F9 51 16N 1 6 E
Canterbury □, N.Z. 59 K3 43 45S 171 19 E
Canterbury Bight, N.Z. 59 L3 44 16S 171 55 E
Canterbury Plains, N.Z. 59 K3 43 55S 171 22 E
Cantil, U.S.A. 85 K9 35 18N 117 58W
Canton = Guangzhou, China 33 D6 23 5N 113 10 E
Canton, Ga., U.S.A. 77 H3 34 14N 84 29W
Canton, Ill., U.S.A. 80 E9 40 33N 90 2W
Canton, Miss., U.S.A. 81 J9 32 37N 90 2W
Canton, Mo., U.S.A. 80 E9 40 8N 91 32W
Canton, N.Y., U.S.A. 79 B9 44 36N 75 10W
Canton, Ohio, U.S.A. 78 F3 40 48N 81 23W
Canton, Okla., U.S.A. 81 G5 36 3N 98 35W
Canton, S. Dak., U.S.A. 80 D6 43 18N 96 35W
Canton L., U.S.A. 81 G5 36 6N 98 35W
Canudos, Brazil 92 E7 7 13S 58 5W
Canumã →, Brazil 92 D7 3 55S 59 10W
Canutama, Brazil 92 E6 6 30S 64 20W
Canutillo, U.S.A. 83 L10 31 55N 106 36W
Canvey, U.K. 11 F8 51 31N 0 37 E
Canyon, Tex., U.S.A. 81 H4 34 59N 101 55W
Canyon, Wyo., U.S.A. 82 D8 44 43N 110 36W
Canyonlands National Park, U.S.A. 83 G9 38 15N 110 0W
Canyonville, U.S.A. 82 E2 42 56N 123 17W
Cao Bang, Vietnam 38 A6 22 40N 106 15 E
Cao He →, China 35 D13 40 10N 124 32 E
Cao Lanh, Vietnam 39 G5 10 27N 105 38 E
Cao Xian, China 34 G8 34 50N 115 35 E
Cap-aux-Meules, Canada 71 C7 47 23N 61 52W
Cap-Chat, Canada 71 C6 49 6N 66 40W
Cap-de-la-Madeleine, Canada 70 C5 46 22N 72 31W
Cap-Haïtien, Haiti 89 C5 19 40N 72 20W
Capanaparo →, Venezuela 92 B5 7 1N 67 7W
Cape →, Australia 62 C4 20 59S 146 51 E
Cape Barren I., Australia 62 G4 40 25S 148 15 E
Cape Breton Highlands Nat. Park, Canada 71 C7 46 50N 60 40W
Cape Breton I., Canada 71 C7 46 0N 60 30W
Cape Charles, U.S.A. 76 G8 37 16N 76 1W
Cape Coast, Ghana 50 G5 5 5N 1 15W
Cape Coral, U.S.A. 77 M5 26 33N 81 57W
Cape Dorset, Canada 69 B12 64 14N 76 32W
Cape Fear →, U.S.A. 77 H6 33 53N 78 1W
Cape Girardeau, U.S.A. 81 G10 37 19N 89 32W
Cape Jervis, Australia 63 F2 35 40S 138 5 E
Cape May, U.S.A. 76 F8 38 56N 74 56W
Cape May Point, U.S.A. 75 C12 38 56N 74 58W
Cape Tormentine, Canada 71 C7 46 8N 63 47W
Cape Town, S. Africa 56 E2 33 55S 18 22 E
Cape Verde Is. ■, Atl. Oc. 49 E1 17 10N 25 20W
Cape Vincent, U.S.A. 79 B8 44 8N 76 20W
Cape York Peninsula, Australia 62 A3 12 0S 142 30 E
Capela, Brazil 93 F11 10 30S 37 0W
Capella, Australia 62 C4 23 2S 148 1 E
Capim →, Brazil 93 D9 1 40S 47 47W
Capitan, U.S.A. 83 K11 33 35N 105 35W
Capitola, U.S.A. 84 J5 36 59N 121 57W
Capoche →, Mozam. 55 F3 15 35S 33 0 E
Capraia, Italy 18 E8 43 2N 9 50 E
Capreol, Canada 70 C3 46 43N 80 56W
Capri, Italy 20 D6 40 33N 14 14 E
Capricorn Group, Australia 62 C5 23 30S 151 55 E
Capricorn Ra., Australia 60 D2 23 20S 116 50 E
Caprivi Strip, Namibia 56 B3 18 0S 23 0 E
Captainganj, India 43 F10 26 55N 83 45 E
Captain's Flat, Australia 63 F4 35 35S 149 27 E
Caquetá →, Colombia 92 D5 1 15S 69 15W
Caracal, Romania 17 F13 44 8N 24 22 E
Caracas, Venezuela 92 A5 10 30N 66 55W
Caracol, Brazil 93 E10 9 15S 43 22W
Caradoc, Australia 63 E3 30 35S 143 5 E
Carajas, Brazil 93 E8 6 5S 50 23W
Carajás, Serra dos, Brazil 93 E8 6 0S 51 30W
Carangola, Brazil 95 A7 20 44S 42 5W
Carani, Australia 61 F2 30 57S 116 28 E
Caransebeş, Romania 17 F12 45 28N 22 18 E
Caras, Peru 92 E3 9 3S 77 47W
Caratasca, L., Honduras 88 C3 15 20N 83 40W
Caratinga, Brazil 93 G10 19 50S 42 10W
Caraúbas, Brazil 93 E11 5 43S 37 33W
Caravaca = Caravaca de la Cruz, Spain 19 C5 38 8N 1 52W
Caravaca de la Cruz, Spain 19 C5 38 8N 1 52W
Caravelas, Brazil 93 G11 17 45S 39 15W
Caraveli, Peru 92 G4 15 45S 73 25W
Caràzinho, Brazil 95 B5 28 16S 52 46W
Carballo, Spain 19 A1 43 13N 8 41W
Carberry, Canada 73 D9 49 50N 99 25W
Carbó, Mexico 86 B2 29 42N 110 58W
Carbon, Canada 72 C6 51 30N 113 9W
Carbonara, C., Italy 20 E3 39 6N 9 31 E
Carbondale, Colo., U.S.A. 82 G10 39 24N 107 13W
Carbondale, Ill., U.S.A. 81 G10 37 44N 89 13W
Carbondale, Pa., U.S.A. 79 E9 41 35N 75 30W
Carbonear, Canada 71 C9 47 42N 53 13W
Carbónia, Italy 20 E3 39 10N 8 30 E
Carcajou, Canada 72 B5 57 47N 117 6W
Carcasse, C., Haiti 89 C5 18 30N 74 28W
Carcassonne, France 18 E5 43 13N 2 20 E
Carcross, Canada 68 B6 60 13N 134 45W
Cardabia, Australia 60 D1 23 2S 113 48 E
Cardamon Hills, India 40 Q10 9 30N 77 15 E
Cárdenas, Cuba 88 B3 23 0N 81 30W
Cárdenas, San Luis Potosí, Mexico 87 C5 22 0N 99 41W
Cárdenas, Tabasco, Mexico 87 D6 17 59N 93 21W
Cardiff, U.K. 11 F4 51 29N 3 10W
Cardiff □, U.K. 11 F4 51 31N 3 12W
Cardiff-by-the-Sea, U.S.A. 85 M9 33 1N 117 17W
Cardigan, U.K. 11 E3 52 5N 4 40W
Cardigan B., U.K. 11 E3 52 30N 4 30W
Cardinal, Canada 79 B9 44 47N 75 23W
Cardona, Uruguay 94 C4 33 53S 57 18W
Cardross, Canada 73 D7 49 50N 105 40W
Cardston, Canada 72 D6 49 15N 113 20W
Cardwell, Australia 62 B4 18 14S 146 2 E
Careen L., Canada 73 B7 57 0N 108 11W
Carei, Romania 17 E12 47 40N 22 29 E

Chinle

Chamical, Argentina 94 C2 30 22S 66 27W
Chamkar Luong, Cambodia 39 G4 11 0N 103 45 E
Chamonix-Mont Blanc, France 18 D7 45 55N 6 51 E
Champa, India 43 H10 22 2N 82 43 E
Champagne, Canada 72 A1 60 49N 136 30W
Champagne, France 18 B6 48 40N 4 20 E
Champaign, U.S.A. 76 E1 40 7N 88 15W
Champassak, Laos 38 E5 14 53N 105 52 E
Champlain, Canada 76 B9 46 27N 72 24W
Champlain, U.S.A. 79 B11 44 59N 73 27W
Champlain, L., U.S.A. 79 B11 44 40N 73 20W
Champotón, Mexico 87 D6 19 20N 90 50W
Chana, Thailand 39 J3 6 55N 100 44 E
Chañaral, Chile 94 B1 26 23S 70 40W
Chanārān, Iran 45 B8 36 39N 59 6 E
Chanasma, India 42 H5 23 44N 72 5 E
Chandannagar, India 43 H13 22 52N 88 24 E
Chandausi, India 43 E8 28 27N 78 49 E
Chandeleur Is., U.S.A. 81 L10 29 55N 88 57W
Chandeleur Sd., U.S.A. 81 L10 29 55N 89 0W
Chandigarh, India 42 D7 30 43N 76 47 E
Chandler, Australia 63 D1 27 0S 133 19 E
Chandler, Canada 71 C7 48 18N 64 46W
Chandler, Ariz., U.S.A. 83 K8 33 18N 111 50W
Chandler, Okla., U.S.A. 81 H6 35 42N 96 53W
Chandpur, Bangla. 41 H17 23 8N 90 45 E
Chandpur, India 42 E8 29 8N 78 19 E
Chandrapur, India 40 K11 19 57N 79 25 E
Chānf, Iran 45 E9 26 38N 60 29 E
Chang, Pakistan 42 F3 26 59N 68 30 E
Chang, Ko, Thailand 39 G4 12 0N 102 23 E
Ch'ang Chiang = Chang Jiang →, China 33 C7 31 48N 121 10 E
Chang Jiang →, China 33 C7 31 48N 121 10 E
Changa, India 43 C7 33 53N 77 35 E
Changanacheri, India 40 Q10 9 25N 76 31 E
Changane →, Mozam. 57 C5 24 30S 33 30 E
Changbai, China 35 D15 41 25N 128 5 E
Changbai Shan, China 35 C15 42 20N 129 0 E
Changchiak'ou = Zhangjiakou, China 34 D8 40 48N 114 55 E
Ch'angchou = Changzhou, China 33 C6 31 47N 119 58 E
Changchun, China 35 C13 43 57N 125 17 E
Changchunling, China 35 B13 45 18N 125 27 E
Changde, China 33 D6 29 4N 111 35 E
Changdo-ri, N. Korea 35 E14 38 30N 127 40 E
Changhai = Shanghai, China 33 C7 31 15N 121 26 E
Changhua, Taiwan 33 D7 24 2N 120 30 E
Changhŭng, S. Korea 35 G14 34 41N 126 52 E
Changhŭngni, N. Korea 35 D15 40 24N 128 19 E
Changjiang, China 38 C7 19 20N 108 55 E
Changjin, N. Korea 35 D14 40 23N 127 15 E
Changjin-chŏsuji, N. Korea 35 D14 40 30N 127 15 E
Changli, China 35 E10 39 40N 119 13 E
Changling, China 35 B12 44 20N 123 58 E
Changlun, Malaysia 39 J3 6 25N 100 26 E
Changping, China 34 D9 40 14N 116 12 E
Changsha, China 33 D6 28 12N 113 0 E
Changwu, China 34 G4 35 10N 107 45 E
Changyi, China 35 F10 36 40N 119 30 E
Changyŏn, N. Korea 35 E13 38 15N 125 6 E
Changyuan, China 34 G8 35 15N 114 42 E
Changzhi, China 34 F7 36 10N 113 6 E
Changzhou, China 33 C6 31 47N 119 58 E
Chanhanga, Angola 56 B1 16 0S 14 8 E
Channapatna, India 40 N10 12 40N 77 15 E
Channel Is., U.K. 11 H5 49 19N 2 24W
Channel Is., U.S.A. 85 M7 33 40N 119 15W
Channel-Port aux Basques, Canada 71 C8 47 30N 59 9W
Channing, Mich., U.S.A. 76 B1 46 9N 88 5W
Channing, Tex., U.S.A. 81 H3 35 41N 102 20W
Chantada, Spain 19 A2 42 36N 7 46W
Chanthaburi, Thailand 38 F4 12 38N 102 12 E
Chantrey Inlet, Canada 68 B10 67 48N 96 20W
Chanute, U.S.A. 81 G7 37 41N 95 27W
Chao Phraya →, Thailand 38 F3 13 32N 100 36 E
Chao Phraya Lowlands, Thailand 38 E3 15 30N 100 0 E
Chao'an, China 33 D6 23 42N 116 32 E
Chaocheng, China 34 F8 36 4N 115 37 E
Chaoyang, China 35 D11 41 35N 120 22 E
Chapala, Mozam. 55 F4 15 50S 37 35 E
Chapala, L. de, Mexico 86 C4 20 10N 103 20W
Chapayev, Kazakstan 25 D9 50 25N 51 10 E
Chapayevsk, Russia 24 D8 53 0N 49 40 E
Chapecó, Brazil 95 B5 27 14S 52 41W
Chapel Hill, U.S.A. 77 H6 35 55N 79 4W
Chapleau, Canada 70 C3 47 50N 83 24W
Chaplin, Canada 73 C7 50 28N 106 40W
Chapra = Chhapra, India 43 G11 25 48N 84 44 E
Chara, Russia 27 D12 56 54N 118 20 E
Charadai, Argentina 94 B4 27 35S 59 55W
Charagua, Bolivia 92 G6 19 45S 63 10W
Charambirá, Punta, Colombia 92 C3 4 16N 77 32W
Charaña, Bolivia 92 G5 17 30S 69 25W
Charata, Argentina 94 B3 27 13S 61 14W
Charcas, Mexico 86 C4 23 10N 101 20W
Charcoal L., Canada 73 B8 58 49N 102 22W
Chard, U.K. 11 G5 50 52N 2 58W
Chardon, U.S.A. 78 E3 41 35N 81 12W
Chardzhou = Chärjew, Turkmenistan 26 F7 39 6N 63 34 E
Charente →, France 18 D3 45 57N 1 5W
Chari →, Chad 51 F8 12 58N 14 31 E
Chārīkār, Afghan. 40 B6 35 0N 69 10 E
Chariton →, U.S.A. 80 F8 39 19N 92 58W
Chärjew, Turkmenistan 26 F7 39 6N 63 34 E
Charkhari, India 43 G8 25 24N 79 45 E
Charkhi Dadri, India 42 E7 28 37N 76 17 E
Charleroi, Belgium 15 D4 50 24N 4 27 E
Charleroi, U.S.A. 78 F5 40 9N 79 57W
Charles, C., U.S.A. 76 G8 37 7N 75 58W
Charles City, U.S.A. 80 D8 43 4N 92 41W
Charles L., Canada 73 B6 59 50N 110 33W
Charles Town, U.S.A. 76 F7 39 17N 77 52W
Charleston, Ill., U.S.A. 76 F1 39 30N 88 10W
Charleston, Miss., U.S.A. 81 H9 34 1N 90 4W
Charleston, Mo., U.S.A. 81 G10 36 55N 89 21W
Charleston, S.C., U.S.A. 77 J6 32 46N 79 56W
Charleston, W. Va., U.S.A. 76 F5 38 21N 81 38W
Charleston Peak, U.S.A. 85 J11 36 16N 115 42W
Charlestown, Ireland 13 C3 53 58N 8 48W
Charlestown, S. Africa 57 D4 27 26S 29 53 E
Charlestown, U.S.A. 76 F3 38 27N 85 40W
Charleville = Rath Luirc, Ireland 13 D3 52 21N 8 40W
Charleville, Australia 63 D4 26 24S 146 15 E
Charleville-Mézières, France 18 B6 49 44N 4 40 E
Charlevoix, U.S.A. 76 C3 45 19N 85 16W
Charlotte, Mich., U.S.A. 76 D3 42 34N 84 50W
Charlotte, N.C., U.S.A. 77 H5 35 13N 80 51W
Charlotte Amalie, Virgin Is. 89 C7 18 21N 64 56W
Charlotte Harbor, U.S.A. 77 M4 26 50N 82 10W
Charlottesville, U.S.A. 76 F6 38 2N 78 30W
Charlottetown, Canada 71 C7 46 14N 63 8W
Charlton, Australia 63 F3 36 16S 143 24 E
Charlton, U.S.A. 80 E8 40 59N 93 20W
Charlton I., Canada 70 B4 52 0N 79 20W
Charny, Canada 71 C5 46 43N 71 15W
Charolles, France 18 C6 46 27N 4 16 E
Charre, Mozam. 55 F4 17 13S 35 10 E
Charsadda, Pakistan 42 B4 34 7N 71 45 E
Charters Towers, Australia 62 C4 20 5S 146 13 E
Chartres, France 18 B4 48 29N 1 30 E
Chascomús, Argentina 94 D4 35 30S 58 0W
Chasefu, Zambia 55 E3 11 55S 33 8 E
Chāt, Iran 45 B7 37 59N 55 16 E
Châteaubriant, France 18 C3 47 43N 1 23W
Châteaulin, France 18 B1 48 11N 4 8W
Châteauroux, France 18 C4 46 50N 1 40 E
Châtellerault, France 18 C4 46 50N 0 30 E
Chatfield, U.S.A. 80 D9 43 51N 92 11W
Chatham, N.B., Canada 71 C6 47 2N 65 28W
Chatham, Ont., Canada 70 D3 42 24N 82 11W
Chatham, U.K. 11 F8 51 22N 0 32 E
Chatham, La., U.S.A. 81 J8 32 18N 92 27W
Chatham, N.Y., U.S.A. 79 D11 42 21N 73 36W
Chatham Is., Pac. Oc. 64 M10 44 0S 176 40W
Chatham Str., U.S.A. 72 B2 57 0N 134 40W
Chatmohar, Bangla. 43 G13 24 15N 89 15 E
Chatra, India 43 G11 24 12N 84 56 E
Chatrapur, India 41 K14 19 22N 85 2 E
Chats, L. des, Canada 79 A8 45 30N 76 20W
Chatsworth, Canada 78 B4 44 27N 80 54W
Chatsworth, Zimbabwe 55 F3 19 38S 31 13 E
Chattahoochee →, U.S.A. 77 K3 30 54N 84 57W
Chattanooga, U.S.A. 77 H3 35 3N 85 19W
Chatteris, U.K. 11 E8 52 28N 0 2 E
Chaturat, Thailand 38 E3 15 40N 101 51 E
Chau Doc, Vietnam 39 G5 10 42N 105 7 E
Chauk, Burma 41 J19 20 53N 94 49 E
Chaukan La, Burma 41 F20 27 0N 97 15 E
Chaumont, France 18 B6 48 7N 5 8 E
Chaumont, U.S.A. 79 B8 44 4N 76 8W
Chautauqua L., U.S.A. 78 D5 42 10N 79 24W
Chauvin, Canada 73 C6 52 45N 110 10W
Chaves, Brazil 93 D9 0 15S 49 55W
Chaves, Portugal 19 B2 41 45N 7 32W
Chawang, Thailand 39 H2 8 25N 99 30 E
Chaykovskiy, Russia 24 C9 56 47N 54 9 E
Chazy, U.S.A. 79 B11 44 53N 73 26W
Cheb, Czech Rep. 16 C7 50 9N 12 28 E
Cheboksary, Russia 24 C8 56 8N 47 12 E
Cheboygan, U.S.A. 76 C3 45 39N 84 29W
Chech, Erg, Africa 50 D5 25 0N 2 15W
Chechenia □, Russia 25 F8 43 30N 45 29 E
Checheno-Ingush Republic = Chechenia □, Russia 25 F8 43 30N 45 29 E
Chechnya = Chechenia □, Russia 25 F8 43 30N 45 29 E
Chechon, S. Korea 35 F15 37 8N 128 12 E
Checleset B., Canada 72 C3 50 5N 127 35W
Checotah, U.S.A. 81 H7 35 28N 95 31W
Chedabucto B., Canada 71 C7 45 25N 61 8W
Cheduba I., Burma 41 K18 18 45N 93 40 E
Cheepie, Australia 63 D4 26 33S 145 1 E
Chegdomyn, Russia 27 D14 51 7N 133 1 E
Chegga, Mauritania 50 C4 25 27N 5 40W
Chegutu, Zimbabwe 55 F3 18 10S 30 14 E
Chehalis, U.S.A. 84 D4 46 40N 122 58W
Cheju Do, S. Korea 35 H14 33 29N 126 34 E
Chekiang = Zhejiang □, China 33 D7 29 0N 120 0 E
Chela, Sa. da, Angola 56 B1 16 20S 13 20 E
Chelan, U.S.A. 82 C4 47 51N 120 1W
Chelan, L., U.S.A. 82 B3 48 11N 120 30W
Cheleken, Turkmenistan 25 G9 39 34N 53 16 E
Chelforó, Argentina 96 D3 39 0S 66 33W
Chelkar = Shalqar, Kazakstan 26 E6 47 48N 59 39 E
Chelkar Tengiz, Solonchak, Kazakstan 26 E7 48 5N 63 7 E
Chełm, Poland 17 C12 51 8N 23 30 E
Chełmno, Poland 17 B10 53 20N 18 30 E
Chelmsford, U.K. 11 F8 51 44N 0 29 E
Chelsea, Okla., U.S.A. 81 G7 36 32N 95 26W
Chelsea, Vt., U.S.A. 79 C12 43 59N 72 27W
Cheltenham, U.K. 11 F5 51 54N 2 4W
Chelyabinsk, Russia 26 D7 55 10N 61 24 E
Chelyuskin, C., Russia 28 B14 77 30N 103 0 E
Chemainus, Canada 72 D4 48 55N 123 42W
Chemnitz, Germany 16 C7 50 51N 12 54 E
Chemult, U.S.A. 82 E3 43 14N 121 47W
Chen, Gora, Russia 27 C15 65 16N 141 50 E
Chenab →, Pakistan 42 D4 30 23N 71 2 E
Chenango Forks, U.S.A. 79 D9 42 15N 75 51W
Cheney, U.S.A. 82 C5 47 30N 117 35W
Cheng Xian, China 34 H3 33 43N 105 42 E
Chengcheng, China 34 G5 35 8N 109 56 E
Chengchou = Zhengzhou, China 34 G7 34 45N 113 34 E
Chengde, China 35 D9 40 59N 117 58 E
Chengdu, China 32 C5 30 38N 104 2 E
Chenggu, China 34 H4 33 10N 107 21 E
Chengjiang, China 32 D5 24 39N 103 0 E
Ch'engtu = Chengdu, China 32 C5 30 38N 104 2 E
Chengwu, China 34 G8 34 58N 115 50 E
Chengyang, China 35 F11 36 18N 120 21 E
Chenjiagang, China 35 G10 34 23N 119 47 E
Chenkán, Mexico 87 D6 19 8N 90 58W
Chennai, India 40 N12 13 8N 80 19 E
Cheom Ksan, Cambodia 38 E5 14 13N 104 56 E
Chepén, Peru 92 E3 7 15S 79 23W
Chepes, Argentina 94 C2 31 20S 66 35W
Chepo, Panama 88 E4 9 10N 79 6W
Chepstow, U.K. 11 F5 51 38N 2 41W
Cheptulil, Mt., Kenya 54 B4 1 25N 35 35 E
Chequamegon B., U.S.A. 80 B9 46 40N 90 30W
Cher →, France 18 C4 47 21N 0 29 E
Cheraw, U.S.A. 77 H6 34 42N 79 53W
Cherbourg, France 18 B3 49 39N 1 40W
Cherdyn, Russia 24 B10 60 24N 56 29 E
Cheremkhovo, Russia 27 D11 53 8N 103 1 E
Cherepanovo, Russia 26 D9 54 15N 83 30 E
Cherepovets, Russia 24 C6 59 5N 37 55 E
Chergui, Chott ech, Algeria 50 B6 34 21N 0 25 E
Cherikov = Cherykaw, Belarus 17 B16 53 32N 31 20 E
Cherkasy, Ukraine 25 E5 49 27N 32 4 E
Cherlak, Russia 26 D8 54 15N 74 55 E
Chernaya, Russia 27 B9 70 30N 89 10 E
Chernigov = Chernihiv, Ukraine 24 D5 51 28N 31 20 E
Chernihiv, Ukraine 24 D5 51 28N 31 20 E
Chernikovsk, Russia 24 D10 54 48N 56 8 E
Chernivtsi, Ukraine 25 E4 48 15N 25 52 E
Chernobyl = Chornobyl, Ukraine 17 C16 51 20N 30 15 E
Chernogorsk, Russia 27 D10 53 49N 91 18 E
Chernovtsy = Chernivtsi, Ukraine 25 E4 48 15N 25 52 E
Chernyakhovsk, Russia 9 J19 54 36N 21 48 E
Chernysheyskiy, Russia 27 C12 63 0N 112 30 E
Cherokee, Iowa, U.S.A. 80 D7 42 45N 95 33W
Cherokee, Okla., U.S.A. 81 G5 36 45N 98 21W
Cherokees, Lake O' The, U.S.A. 81 G7 36 28N 95 2W
Cherrapunji, India 41 G17 25 17N 91 47 E
Cherry Creek, U.S.A. 82 G6 39 54N 114 53W
Cherry Valley, U.S.A. 85 M10 33 59N 116 57W
Cherryvale, U.S.A. 81 G7 37 16N 95 33W
Cherskiy, Russia 27 C17 68 45N 161 18 E
Cherskogo Khrebet, Russia 27 C15 65 0N 143 0 E
Cherven, Belarus 17 B15 53 45N 28 28 E
Chervonohrad, Ukraine 17 C13 50 25N 24 10 E
Cherwell →, U.K. 11 F6 51 44N 1 14W
Cherykaw, Belarus 17 B16 53 32N 31 20 E
Chesapeake, U.S.A. 76 G7 36 50N 76 17W
Chesapeake B., U.S.A. 76 G7 38 0N 76 10W
Cheshire □, U.K. 10 D5 53 14N 2 30W
Cheshskaya Guba, Russia 24 A8 67 20N 47 0 E
Cheshunt, U.K. 11 F7 51 43N 0 1W
Chesil Beach, U.K. 11 G5 50 37N 2 33W
Cheslatta L., Canada 72 C3 53 49N 125 20W
Chesley, Canada 78 B3 44 17N 81 5W
Chester, U.K. 10 D5 53 12N 2 53W
Chester, Calif., U.S.A. 82 F3 40 19N 121 14W
Chester, Ill., U.S.A. 81 G10 37 55N 89 49W
Chester, Mont., U.S.A. 82 B8 48 31N 110 58W
Chester, Pa., U.S.A. 76 F8 39 51N 75 22W
Chester, S.C., U.S.A. 77 H5 34 43N 81 12W
Chester-le-Street, U.K. 10 C6 54 51N 1 34W
Chesterfield, U.K. 10 D6 53 15N 1 25W
Chesterfield, Is., N. Cal. 64 J7 19 52S 158 15 E
Chesterfield Inlet, Canada 68 B10 63 30N 90 45W
Chesterton Ra., Australia 63 D4 25 30S 147 27 E
Chesterville, Canada 79 A9 45 6N 75 14W
Chesuncook L., U.S.A. 71 C6 46 0N 69 21W
Chéticamp, Canada 71 C7 46 37N 60 59W
Chetumal, B. de, Mexico 87 D7 18 40N 88 10W
Chetwynd, Canada 72 B4 55 45N 121 36W
Cheviot, The, U.K. 10 B5 55 29N 2 9W
Cheviot Hills, U.K. 10 B5 55 20N 2 30W
Cheviot Ra., Australia 62 D3 25 20S 143 45 E
Chew Bahir, Ethiopia 46 G2 4 40N 36 50 E
Chewelah, U.S.A. 82 B5 48 17N 117 43W
Cheyenne, Okla., U.S.A. 81 H5 35 37N 99 40W
Cheyenne, Wyo., U.S.A. 80 E2 41 8N 104 49W
Cheyenne →, U.S.A. 80 C4 44 41N 101 18W
Cheyenne Wells, U.S.A. 80 F3 38 49N 102 21W
Cheyne B., Australia 61 F2 34 35S 118 50 E
Chhabra, India 42 G7 24 40N 76 54 E
Chhapra, India 43 G11 25 48N 84 44 E
Chhata, India 42 F7 27 42N 77 30 E
Chhatarpur, India 43 G8 24 55N 79 35 E
Chhep, Cambodia 38 F5 13 45N 105 24 E
Chhindwara, India 43 H8 22 2N 78 59 E
Chhlong, Cambodia 39 F5 12 15N 105 58 E
Chhuk, Cambodia 39 G5 10 46N 104 28 E
Chi →, Thailand 38 E5 15 11N 104 43 E
Chiai, Taiwan 33 D7 23 29N 120 25 E
Chiamussu = Jiamusi, China 33 B8 46 40N 130 26 E
Chiang Dao, Thailand 38 C2 19 22N 98 58 E
Chiang Kham, Thailand 38 C3 19 32N 100 18 E
Chiang Khan, Thailand 38 D3 17 52N 101 36 E
Chiang Khong, Thailand 38 B3 20 17N 100 24 E
Chiang Mai, Thailand 38 C2 18 47N 98 59 E
Chiang Saen, Thailand 38 B3 20 16N 100 5 E
Chiapa →, Mexico 87 D6 16 42N 93 0W
Chiapa de Corzo, Mexico 87 D6 16 42N 93 0W
Chiapas □, Mexico 87 D6 17 0N 92 45W
Chiautla, Mexico 87 D5 18 18N 98 34W
Chiávari, Italy 18 D8 44 19N 9 19 E
Chiavenna, Italy 18 C8 46 19N 9 24 E
Chiba, Japan 31 G10 35 30N 140 7 E
Chibabava, Mozam. 57 C5 20 17S 33 35 E
Chibemba, Cunene, Angola 53 H2 15 48S 14 8 E
Chibemba, Huila, Angola 56 B2 16 20S 15 20 E
Chibia, Angola 53 H2 15 10S 13 42 E
Chibougamau, Canada 70 C5 49 56N 74 24W
Chibougamau L., Canada 70 C5 49 50N 74 20W
Chic-Chocs, Mts., Canada 71 C6 48 55N 66 0W
Chicacole = Srikakulam, India 41 K13 18 14N 83 58 E
Chicago, U.S.A. 76 E2 41 53N 87 38W
Chicago Heights, U.S.A. 76 E2 41 30N 87 38W
Chichagof I., U.S.A. 72 B1 57 30N 135 30W
Chicheng, China 34 D8 40 55N 115 55 E
Chichester, U.K. 11 G7 50 50N 0 47W
Chichibu, Japan 31 F9 36 5N 139 10 E
Ch'ich'ihaerh = Qiqihar, China 27 E13 47 26N 124 0 E
Chickasha, U.S.A. 81 H6 35 3N 97 58W
Chiclana de la Frontera, Spain 19 D2 36 26N 6 9W
Chiclayo, Peru 92 E3 6 42S 79 50W
Chico, U.S.A. 84 F5 39 44N 121 50W
Chico →, Chubut, Argentina 96 E3 44 0S 67 0W
Chico →, Santa Cruz, Argentina 96 G3 50 0S 68 30W
Chicomo, Mozam. 57 C5 24 31S 34 6 E
Chicontepec, Mexico 87 C5 20 58N 98 10W
Chicopee, U.S.A. 79 D12 42 9N 72 37W
Chicoutimi, Canada 71 C5 48 28N 71 5W
Chicualacuala, Mozam. 57 C5 22 6S 31 42 E
Chidambaram, India 40 P11 11 20N 79 45 E
Chidenguele, Mozam. 57 C5 24 55S 34 11 E
Chidley, C., Canada 69 B13 60 23N 64 26W
Chiede, Angola 56 B2 17 15S 16 22 E
Chiefs Pt., Canada 78 B3 44 41N 81 18W
Chiem Hoa, Vietnam 38 A5 22 12N 105 17 E
Chiemsee, Germany 16 E7 47 53N 12 28 E
Chiengi, Zambia 55 D2 8 45S 29 10 E
Chiengmai = Chiang Mai, Thailand 38 C2 18 47N 98 59 E
Chiese →, Italy 18 D9 45 8N 10 25 E
Chieti, Italy 20 C6 42 21N 14 10 E
Chifeng, China 35 C10 42 18N 118 58 E
Chignecto B., Canada 71 C7 45 30N 64 40W
Chiguana, Bolivia 94 A2 21 0S 67 58W
Chigwell, U.K. 11 F8 51 37N 0 5 E
Chiha-ri, N. Korea 35 E14 38 40N 126 30 E
Chihli, G. of = Bo Hai, China 35 E10 39 0N 119 0 E
Chihuahua, Mexico 86 B3 28 40N 106 3W
Chihuahua □, Mexico 86 B3 28 40N 106 3W
Chiili, Kazakstan 26 E7 44 20N 66 15 E
Chik Bollapur, India 40 N10 13 25N 77 45 E
Chikmagalur, India 40 N9 13 15N 75 45 E
Chikwawa, Malawi 55 F3 16 2S 34 50 E
Chilac, Mexico 87 D5 18 20N 97 24W
Chilako →, Canada 72 C4 53 53N 122 57W
Chilam Chavki, Pakistan 43 B6 35 5N 75 5 E
Chilanga, Zambia 55 F2 15 33S 28 16 E
Chilapa, Mexico 87 D5 17 40N 99 11W
Chilas, Pakistan 43 B6 35 25N 74 5 E
Chilaw, Sri Lanka 40 R11 7 30N 79 50 E
Chilcotin →, Canada 72 C4 51 44N 122 23W
Childers, Australia 63 D5 25 15S 152 17 E
Childress, U.S.A. 81 H4 34 25N 100 13W
Chile ■, S. Amer. 96 D2 35 0S 72 0W
Chile Rise, Pac. Oc. 65 L18 38 0S 92 0W
Chilecito, Argentina 94 B2 29 10S 67 30W
Chilete, Peru 92 E3 7 10S 78 50W
Chililabombwe, Zambia 55 E2 12 18S 27 43 E
Chilin = Jilin, China 35 C14 43 44N 126 30 E
Chilka L., India 41 K14 19 40N 85 25 E
Chilko →, Canada 72 C4 52 0N 123 40W
Chilko, L., Canada 72 C4 51 20N 124 10W
Chillagoe, Australia 62 B3 17 7S 144 33 E
Chillán, Chile 94 D1 36 40S 72 10W
Chillicothe, Ill., U.S.A. 80 E10 40 55N 89 29W
Chillicothe, Mo., U.S.A. 80 F8 39 48N 93 33W
Chillicothe, Ohio, U.S.A. 76 F4 39 20N 82 59W
Chilliwack, Canada 72 D4 49 10N 121 54W
Chilo, India 42 F5 27 25N 73 32 E
Chiloane, I., Mozam. 57 C5 20 40S 34 55 E
Chiloé, I. de, Chile 96 E2 42 30S 73 50W
Chilpancingo, Mexico 87 D5 17 30N 99 30W
Chiltern Hills, U.K. 11 F7 51 40N 0 53W
Chilton, U.S.A. 76 C1 44 2N 88 10W
Chilubi, Zambia 55 E2 11 5S 29 58 E
Chilubula, Zambia 55 E3 10 14S 30 51 E
Chilumba, Malawi 55 E3 10 28S 34 12 E
Chilung, Taiwan 33 D7 25 3N 121 45 E
Chilwa, L., Malawi 55 F4 15 15S 35 40 E
Chimaltitán, Mexico 86 C4 21 46N 103 50W
Chimán, Panama 88 E4 8 45N 78 40W
Chimay, Belgium 15 D4 50 3N 4 20 E
Chimbay, Uzbekistan 26 E6 42 57N 59 47 E
Chimborazo, Ecuador 92 D3 1 29S 78 55W
Chimbote, Peru 92 E3 9 0S 78 35W
Chimkent = Shymkent, Kazakstan 26 E7 42 18N 69 36 E
Chimoio, Mozam. 55 F3 19 4S 33 30 E
Chimpembe, Zambia 55 D2 9 31S 29 33 E
Chin □, Burma 41 J18 22 0N 93 0 E
Chin Ling Shan = Qinling Shandi, China 34 H5 33 50N 108 10 E
China, Mexico 87 B5 25 40N 99 20W
China ■, Asia 34 E3 30 0N 110 0 E
China Lake, U.S.A. 85 K9 35 44N 117 37W
Chinan = Jinan, China 34 F9 36 38N 117 1 E
Chinandega, Nic. 88 D2 12 35N 87 12W
Chinati Peak, U.S.A. 81 L2 29 57N 104 29W
Chincha Alta, Peru 92 F3 13 25S 76 7W
Chinchilla, Australia 63 D5 26 45S 150 38 E
Chinchorro, Banco, Mexico 87 D7 18 35N 87 20W
Chinchou = Jinzhou, China 35 D11 41 5N 121 3 E
Chincoteague, U.S.A. 76 G8 37 56N 75 23W
Chinde, Mozam. 55 F4 18 35S 36 30 E
Chindo, S. Korea 35 G14 34 28N 126 15 E
Chindwin →, Burma 41 J19 21 26N 95 15 E
Chineni, India 43 C6 33 2N 75 15 E
Chinga, Mozam. 55 F4 15 13S 38 35 E
Chingola, Zambia 55 E2 12 31S 27 53 E
Chingole, Malawi 55 E3 13 4S 34 17 E
Ch'ingtao = Qingdao, China 35 F11 36 5N 120 20 E
Chinguetti, Mauritania 50 D3 20 25N 12 24W
Chingune, Mozam. 57 C5 20 33S 34 58 E
Chinhae, S. Korea 35 G15 35 9N 128 47 E
Chinhanguanine, Mozam. 57 D5 25 21S 32 30 E
Chinhoyi, Zimbabwe 55 F3 17 20S 30 8 E
Chiniot, Pakistan 42 D5 31 45N 73 0 E
Chínipas, Mexico 86 B3 27 22N 108 32W
Chinju, S. Korea 35 G15 35 12N 128 2 E
Chinle, U.S.A. 83 H9 36 9N 109 33W

Coronel Dorrego

Cocanada = Kakinada, *India* **41 L13** 16 57N 82 11 E
Cochabamba, *Bolivia* **92 G5** 17 26S 66 10W
Cochemane, *Mozam.* **55 F3** 17 0S 32 54 E
Cochin, *India* **40 Q10** 9 59N 76 22 E
Cochin China, *Vietnam* **39 G6** 10 30N 106 0 E
Cochise, *U.S.A.* **83 K9** 32 7N 109 55W
Cochran, *U.S.A.* **77 J4** 32 23N 83 21W
Cochrane, *Alta., Canada* **72 C6** 51 11N 114 30W
Cochrane, *Ont., Canada* **70 C3** 49 0N 81 0W
Cochrane, *Chile* **96 F2** 47 15S 72 33W
Cochrane →, *Canada* **73 B8** 59 0N 103 40W
Cochrane, L., *Chile* **96 F2** 47 10S 72 0W
Cockburn, *Australia* **63 E3** 32 5S 141 0 E
Cockburn, Canal, *Chile* **96 G2** 54 30S 72 0W
Cockburn I., *Canada* **70 C3** 45 55N 83 22W
Cockburn Ra., *Australia* **60 C4** 15 46S 128 0 E
Cockermouth, *U.K.* **10 C4** 54 40N 3 22W
Cocklebiddy Motel, *Australia* **61 F4** 32 0S 126 3 E
Coco →, *Cent. Amer.* **88 D3** 15 0N 83 8W
Cocoa, *U.S.A.* **77 L5** 28 21N 80 44W
Cocobeach, *Gabon* **52 D1** 0 59N 9 34 E
Cocos, I. del, *Pac. Oc.* **65 G19** 5 25N 87 55W
Cocos Is., *Ind. Oc.* **64 J1** 12 10S 96 55 E
Cod, C., *U.S.A.* **75 B12** 42 5N 70 10W
Codajás, *Brazil* **92 D6** 3 55S 62 0W
Coderre, *Canada* **73 C7** 50 11N 106 31W
Codó, *Brazil* **93 D10** 4 30S 43 55W
Cody, *U.S.A.* **82 D9** 44 32N 109 3W
Coe Hill, *Canada* **70 D4** 44 52N 77 50W
Coelemu, *Chile* **94 D1** 36 30S 72 48W
Coen, *Australia* **62 A3** 13 52S 143 12 E
Cœur d'Alene, *U.S.A.* **82 C5** 47 45N 116 51W
Cœur d'Alene L., *U.S.A.* **82 C5** 47 32N 116 48W
Coevorden, *Neths.* **15 B6** 52 40N 6 44 E
Cofete, *Canary Is.* **22 F5** 28 6N 14 23W
Coffeyville, *U.S.A.* **81 G7** 37 2N 95 37W
Coffin B., *Australia* **63 E2** 34 38S 135 28 E
Coffin Bay Peninsula, *Australia* **63 E2** 34 32S 135 15 E
Coffs Harbour, *Australia* **63 E5** 30 16S 153 5 E
Cognac, *France* **18 D3** 45 41N 0 20W
Cohagen, *U.S.A.* **82 C10** 47 3N 106 37W
Cohoes, *U.S.A.* **79 D11** 42 46N 73 42W
Cohuna, *Australia* **63 F3** 35 45S 144 15 E
Coiba, I., *Panama* **88 E3** 7 30N 81 40W
Coig →, *Argentina* **96 G3** 51 0S 69 10W
Coigeach, Rubha, *U.K.* **12 C3** 58 6N 5 26W
Coihaique, *Chile* **96 F2** 45 30S 71 45W
Coimbatore, *India* **40 P10** 11 2N 76 59 E
Coimbra, *Brazil* **92 G7** 19 55S 57 48W
Coimbra, *Portugal* **19 B1** 40 15N 8 27W
Coín, *Spain* **19 D3** 36 40N 4 48W
Coipasa, Salar de, *Bolivia* **92 G5** 19 26S 68 9W
Cojimies, *Ecuador* **92 C3** 0 20N 80 0W
Cojutepequé, *El Salv.* **88 D2** 13 41N 88 54W
Cokeville, *U.S.A.* **82 E8** 42 5N 110 57W
Colac, *Australia* **63 F3** 38 21S 143 35 E
Colatina, *Brazil* **93 G10** 19 32S 40 37W
Colbeck, C., *Antarctica* **5 D13** 77 6S 157 48W
Colbinabbin, *Australia* **63 F3** 36 38S 144 48 E
Colborne, *Canada* **78 C7** 44 0N 77 53W
Colby, *U.S.A.* **80 F4** 39 24N 101 3W
Colchagua □, *Chile* **94 C1** 34 30S 71 0W
Colchester, *U.K.* **11 F8** 51 54N 0 55 E
Coldstream, *U.K.* **12 F6** 55 39N 2 15W
Coldwater, *Canada* **78 B5** 44 42N 79 40W
Coldwater, *U.S.A.* **81 G5** 37 16N 99 20W
Colebrook, *Australia* **62 G4** 42 31S 147 21 E
Colebrook, *U.S.A.* **79 B13** 44 54N 71 30W
Coleman, *Canada* **72 D6** 49 40N 114 30W
Coleman, *U.S.A.* **81 K5** 31 50N 99 26W
Coleman →, *Australia* **62 B3** 15 6S 141 38 E
Colenso, *S. Africa* **57 D4** 28 44S 29 50 E
Coleraine, *Australia* **63 F3** 37 36S 141 40 E
Coleraine, *U.K.* **13 A5** 55 8N 6 41W
Coleridge, L., *N.Z.* **59 K3** 43 17S 171 30 E
Colesberg, *S. Africa* **56 E4** 30 45S 25 5 E
Coleville, *U.S.A.* **84 G7** 38 34N 119 30W
Colfax, *Calif., U.S.A.* **84 F6** 39 6N 120 57W
Colfax, *La., U.S.A.* **81 K8** 31 31N 92 42W
Colfax, *Wash., U.S.A.* **82 C5** 46 53N 117 22W
Colhué Huapi, L., *Argentina* **96 F3** 45 30S 69 0W
Coligny, *S. Africa* **57 D4** 26 17S 26 15 E
Colima, *Mexico* **86 D4** 19 14N 103 43W
Colima □, *Mexico* **86 D4** 19 10N 103 40W
Colima, Nevado de, *Mexico* **86 D4** 19 35N 103 45W
Colina, *Chile* **94 C1** 33 13S 70 45W
Coll, *U.K.* **12 E2** 56 39N 6 34W
Collaguasi, *Chile* **94 A2** 21 5S 68 45W
Collarenebri, *Australia* **63 D4** 29 33S 148 34 E
Collbran, *U.S.A.* **83 G10** 39 14N 107 58W
Colleen Bawn, *Zimbabwe* **55 G2** 21 0S 29 12 E
College Park, *U.S.A.* **77 J3** 33 40N 84 27W
College Station, *U.S.A.* **81 K6** 30 37N 96 21W
Collette, *Canada* **71 C6** 46 40N 65 30W
Collie, *Australia* **61 F2** 33 22S 116 8 E
Collier B., *Australia* **60 C3** 16 10S 124 15 E
Collier Ra., *Australia* **60 D2** 24 45S 119 10 E
Collina, Passo di, *Italy* **20 B4** 44 2N 10 56 E
Collingwood, *Canada* **78 B4** 44 29N 80 13W
Collingwood, *N.Z.* **59 J4** 40 41S 172 40 E
Collins, *Canada* **70 B2** 50 17N 89 27W
Collinsville, *Australia* **62 C4** 20 30S 147 56 E
Collipulli, *Chile* **94 D1** 37 55S 72 30W
Collooney, *Ireland* **13 B3** 54 11N 8 29W
Colmar, *France* **18 B7** 48 5N 7 20 E
Colo →, *Australia* **63 E5** 33 25S 150 52 E
Cologne = Köln, *Germany* **16 C4** 50 56N 6 57 E
Colom, I., *Spain* **22 B11** 39 58N 4 16 E
Coloma, *U.S.A.* **84 G6** 38 48N 120 53W
Colomb-Béchar = Béchar, *Algeria* **50 B5** 31 38N 2 18W
Colombia ■, *S. Amer.* **92 C4** 3 45N 73 0W
Colombian Basin, *S. Amer.* **66 H12** 14 0N 76 0W
Colombo, *Sri Lanka* **40 R11** 6 56N 79 58 E
Colome, *U.S.A.* **80 D5** 43 16N 99 43W
Colón, *Argentina* **94 C4** 32 12S 58 10W
Colón, *Cuba* **88 B3** 22 42N 80 54W
Colón, *Panama* **88 E4** 9 20N 79 54W
Colona, *Australia* **61 F5** 31 38S 132 4 E
Colonia de San Jordi, *Spain* **22 B9** 39 19N 2 59 E
Colonia del Sacramento, *Uruguay* **94 C4** 34 25S 57 50W
Colonia Dora, *Argentina* **94 B3** 28 34S 62 59W
Colonial Heights, *U.S.A.* **76 G7** 37 15N 77 25W
Colonsay, *Canada* **73 C7** 51 59N 105 52W
Colonsay, *U.K.* **12 E2** 56 5N 6 12W
Colorado □, *U.S.A.* **83 G10** 39 30N 105 30W
Colorado →, *Argentina* **96 D4** 39 50S 62 8W
Colorado →, *N. Amer.* **83 L6** 31 45N 114 40W
Colorado →, *U.S.A.* **81 L7** 28 36N 95 59W
Colorado City, *U.S.A.* **81 J4** 32 24N 100 52W
Colorado Desert, *U.S.A.* **74 D3** 34 20N 116 0W
Colorado Plateau, *U.S.A.* **83 H8** 37 0N 111 0W
Colorado River Aqueduct, *U.S.A.* **85 L12** 34 17N 114 10W
Colorado Springs, *U.S.A.* **80 F2** 38 50N 104 49W
Colotlán, *Mexico* **86 C4** 22 6N 103 16W
Colton, *N.Y., U.S.A.* **79 B10** 44 33N 74 56W
Colton, *Wash., U.S.A.* **82 C5** 46 34N 117 8W
Columbia, *La., U.S.A.* **81 J8** 32 6N 92 5W
Columbia, *Miss., U.S.A.* **81 K10** 31 15N 89 50W
Columbia, *Mo., U.S.A.* **80 F8** 38 57N 92 20W
Columbia, *Pa., U.S.A.* **79 F8** 40 2N 76 30W
Columbia, *S.C., U.S.A.* **77 J5** 34 0N 81 2W
Columbia, *Tenn., U.S.A.* **77 H2** 35 37N 87 2W
Columbia →, *U.S.A.* **82 C1** 46 15N 124 5W
Columbia, District of □, *U.S.A.* **76 F7** 38 55N 77 0W
Columbia, Mt., *Canada* **72 C5** 52 8N 117 20W
Columbia Basin, *U.S.A.* **82 C4** 46 45N 119 5W
Columbia Falls, *U.S.A.* **82 B6** 48 23N 114 11W
Columbia Heights, *U.S.A.* **80 C8** 45 3N 93 15W
Columbiana, *U.S.A.* **78 F4** 40 53N 80 42W
Columbretes, Is., *Spain* **19 C6** 39 50N 0 50 E
Columbus, *Ga., U.S.A.* **77 J3** 32 28N 84 59W
Columbus, *Ind., U.S.A.* **76 F3** 39 13N 85 55W
Columbus, *Kans., U.S.A.* **81 G7** 37 10N 94 50W
Columbus, *Miss., U.S.A.* **77 J1** 33 30N 88 25W
Columbus, *Mont., U.S.A.* **82 D9** 45 38N 109 15W
Columbus, *N. Dak., U.S.A.* **80 A3** 48 54N 102 47W
Columbus, *N. Mex., U.S.A.* **83 L10** 31 50N 107 38W
Columbus, *Nebr., U.S.A.* **80 E6** 41 26N 97 22W
Columbus, *Ohio, U.S.A.* **76 F4** 39 58N 83 0W
Columbus, *Tex., U.S.A.* **81 L6** 29 42N 96 33W
Columbus, *Wis., U.S.A.* **80 D10** 43 21N 89 1W
Colusa, *U.S.A.* **84 F4** 39 13N 122 1W
Colville, *U.S.A.* **82 B5** 48 33N 117 54W
Colville →, *U.S.A.* **68 A4** 70 25N 150 30W
Colville, C., *N.Z.* **59 G5** 36 29S 175 21 E
Colwyn Bay, *U.K.* **10 D4** 53 18N 3 44W
Comácchio, *Italy* **20 B5** 44 42N 12 11 E
Comalcalco, *Mexico* **87 D6** 18 16N 93 13W
Comallo, *Argentina* **96 E2** 41 0S 70 5W
Comanche, *Okla., U.S.A.* **81 H6** 34 22N 97 58W
Comanche, *Tex., U.S.A.* **81 K5** 31 54N 98 36W
Comayagua, *Honduras* **88 D2** 14 25N 87 37W
Combahee →, *U.S.A.* **77 J5** 32 30N 80 31W
Comber, *Canada* **78 D2** 42 14N 82 33W
Comber, *U.K.* **13 B6** 54 33N 5 45W
Comblain-au-Pont, *Belgium* **15 D5** 50 29N 5 35 E
Comeragh Mts., *Ireland* **13 D4** 52 18N 7 34W
Comet, *Australia* **62 C4** 23 36S 148 38 E
Comilla, *Bangla.* **41 H17** 23 28N 91 10 E
Comino, *Malta* **23 C1** 36 2N 14 20 E
Comino, C., *Italy* **20 D3** 40 32N 9 49 E
Comitán, *Mexico* **87 D6** 16 18N 92 9W
Commerce, *Ga., U.S.A.* **77 H4** 34 12N 83 28W
Commerce, *Tex., U.S.A.* **81 J7** 33 15N 95 54W
Committee B., *Canada* **69 B11** 68 30N 86 30W
Commonwealth B., *Antarctica* **5 C10** 67 0S 144 0 E
Commoron Cr. →, *Australia* **63 D5** 28 22S 150 8 E
Communism Pk. = Kommunizma, Pik, *Tajikistan* **26 F8** 39 0N 72 2 E
Como, *Italy* **18 D8** 45 47N 9 5 E
Como, L. di, *Italy* **18 D8** 46 0N 9 11 E
Comodoro Rivadavia, *Argentina* **96 F3** 45 50S 67 40W
Comorin, C., *India* **40 Q10** 8 3N 77 40 E
Comoro Is. = Comoros ■, *Ind. Oc.* **49 H8** 12 10S 44 15 E
Comoros ■, *Ind. Oc.* **49 H8** 12 10S 44 15 E
Comox, *Canada* **72 D4** 49 42N 124 55W
Compiègne, *France* **18 B5** 49 24N 2 50 E
Compostela, *Mexico* **86 C4** 21 15N 104 53W
Comprida, I., *Brazil* **95 A6** 24 50S 47 42W
Compton, *U.S.A.* **85 M8** 33 54N 118 13W
Compton Downs, *Australia* **63 E4** 30 28S 146 30 E
Comrat, *Moldova* **17 E15** 46 18N 28 40 E
Con Cuong, *Vietnam* **38 C5** 19 2N 104 54 E
Con Son, *Vietnam* **39 H6** 8 41N 106 37 E
Conakry, *Guinea* **50 G3** 9 29N 13 49W
Conara Junction, *Australia* **62 G4** 41 50S 147 26 E
Concarneau, *France* **18 C2** 47 52N 3 56W
Conceição, *Mozam.* **55 F4** 18 47S 36 7 E
Conceição da Barra, *Brazil* **93 G11** 18 35S 39 45W
Conceição do Araguaia, *Brazil* **93 E9** 8 0S 49 2W
Concepción, *Argentina* **94 B2** 27 20S 65 35W
Concepción, *Chile* **94 D1** 36 50S 73 0W
Concepción, *Mexico* **87 D6** 18 15N 90 5W
Concepción, *Paraguay* **94 A4** 23 22S 57 26W
Concepción □, *Chile* **94 D1** 37 0S 72 30W
Concepción →, *Mexico* **86 A2** 30 32N 113 2W
Concepción, Est. de, *Chile* **96 G2** 50 30S 74 55W
Concepción, L., *Bolivia* **92 G6** 17 20S 61 20W
Concepción, Punta, *Mexico* **86 B2** 26 55N 111 59W
Concepción del Oro, *Mexico* **86 C4** 24 40N 101 30W
Concepción del Uruguay, *Argentina* **94 C4** 32 35S 58 20W
Conception, Pt., *U.S.A.* **85 L6** 34 27N 120 28W
Conception B., *Namibia* **56 C1** 23 55S 14 22 E
Conception I., *Bahamas* **89 B4** 23 52N 75 9W
Concession, *Zimbabwe* **55 F3** 17 27S 30 56 E
Conchas Dam, *U.S.A.* **81 H2** 35 22N 104 11W
Conche, *Canada* **71 B8** 50 55N 55 58W
Concho, *U.S.A.* **83 J9** 34 28N 109 36W
Concho →, *U.S.A.* **81 K5** 31 34N 99 43W
Conchos →, *Chihuahua, Mexico* **86 B4** 29 32N 105 0W
Conchos →, *Tamaulipas, Mexico* **87 B5** 25 9N 98 35W
Concord, *Calif., U.S.A.* **84 H4** 37 59N 122 2W
Concord, *N.C., U.S.A.* **77 H5** 35 25N 80 35W
Concord, *N.H., U.S.A.* **79 C13** 43 12N 71 32W
Concordia, *Argentina* **94 C4** 31 20S 58 2W
Concórdia, *Brazil* **92 D5** 4 36S 66 36W
Concordia, *Mexico* **86 C3** 23 18N 106 2W
Concordia, *U.S.A.* **80 F6** 39 34N 97 40W
Concrete, *U.S.A.* **82 B3** 48 32N 121 45W
Condamine, *Australia* **63 D5** 26 56S 150 9 E
Conde, *U.S.A.* **80 C5** 45 9N 98 6W
Condeúba, *Brazil* **93 F10** 14 52S 42 0W
Condobolin, *Australia* **63 E4** 33 4S 147 6 E
Condon, *U.S.A.* **82 D3** 45 14N 120 11W
Conegliano, *Italy* **20 B5** 45 53N 12 18 E
Conejera, I. = Conills, I. des, *Spain* **22 B9** 39 11N 2 58 E
Conejos, *Mexico* **86 B4** 26 14N 103 53W
Confuso →, *Paraguay* **94 B4** 25 9S 57 34W
Congleton, *U.K.* **10 D5** 53 10N 2 13W
Congo (Kinshasa) = Congo, Dem. Rep. of the ■, *Africa* **52 E4** 3 0S 23 0 E
Congo ■, *Africa* **52 E3** 1 0S 16 0 E
Congo →, *Africa* **52 F2** 6 4S 12 24 E
Congo, Dem. Rep. of the ■, *Africa* **52 E4** 3 0S 23 0 E
Congo Basin, *Africa* **48 G6** 0 10S 24 30 E
Congonhas, *Brazil* **95 A7** 20 30S 43 52W
Congress, *U.S.A.* **83 J7** 34 9N 112 51W
Conills, I. des, *Spain* **22 B9** 39 11N 2 58 E
Coniston, *Canada* **70 C3** 46 29N 80 51W
Conjeeveram = Kanchipuram, *India* **40 N11** 12 52N 79 45 E
Conjuboy, *Australia* **62 B3** 18 35S 144 35 E
Conklin, *Canada* **73 B6** 55 38N 111 5W
Conlea, *Australia* **63 E3** 30 7S 144 35 E
Conn, L., *Ireland* **13 B2** 54 3N 9 15W
Connacht □, *Ireland* **13 C2** 53 43N 9 12W
Conneaut, *U.S.A.* **78 E4** 41 57N 80 34W
Connecticut □, *U.S.A.* **79 E12** 41 30N 72 45W
Connecticut →, *U.S.A.* **79 E12** 41 16N 72 20W
Connell, *U.S.A.* **82 C4** 46 40N 118 52W
Connellsville, *U.S.A.* **78 F5** 40 1N 79 35W
Connemara, *Ireland* **13 C2** 53 29N 9 45W
Connemaugh →, *U.S.A.* **78 F5** 40 28N 79 19W
Connersville, *U.S.A.* **76 F3** 39 39N 85 8W
Connors Ra., *Australia* **62 C4** 21 40S 149 10 E
Conoble, *Australia* **63 E3** 32 55S 144 33 E
Conquest, *Canada* **73 C7** 51 32N 107 14W
Conrad, *U.S.A.* **82 B8** 48 10N 111 57W
Conran, C., *Australia* **63 F4** 37 49S 148 44 E
Conroe, *U.S.A.* **81 K7** 30 19N 95 27W
Conselheiro Lafaiete, *Brazil* **95 A7** 20 40S 43 48W
Consett, *U.K.* **10 C6** 54 51N 1 50W
Consort, *Canada* **73 C6** 52 1N 110 46W
Constance = Konstanz, *Germany* **16 E5** 47 40N 9 10 E
Constance, L. = Bodensee, *Europe* **18 C8** 47 35N 9 25 E
Constanța, *Romania* **17 F15** 44 14N 28 38 E
Constantine, *Algeria* **50 A7** 36 25N 6 42 E
Constitución, *Chile* **94 D1** 35 20S 72 30W
Constitución, *Uruguay* **94 C4** 31 0S 57 50W
Consul, *Canada* **73 D7** 49 20N 109 30W
Contact, *U.S.A.* **82 F6** 41 46N 114 45W
Contai, *India* **43 J12** 21 54N 87 46 E
Contamana, *Peru* **92 E4** 7 19S 74 55W
Contas →, *Brazil* **93 F11** 14 17S 39 1W
Contoocook, *U.S.A.* **79 C13** 43 13N 71 45W
Contra Costa, *Mozam.* **57 D5** 25 9S 33 30 E
Conway = Conwy, *U.K.* **10 D4** 53 17N 3 50W
Conway = Conwy →, *U.K.* **10 D4** 53 17N 3 50W
Conway, *Ark., U.S.A.* **81 H8** 35 5N 92 26W
Conway, *N.H., U.S.A.* **79 C13** 43 59N 71 7W
Conway, *S.C., U.S.A.* **77 J6** 33 51N 79 3W
Conway, L., *Australia* **63 D2** 28 17S 135 35 E
Conwy, *U.K.* **10 D4** 53 17N 3 50W
Conwy □, *U.K.* **10 D4** 53 10N 3 44W
Conwy →, *U.K.* **10 D4** 53 17N 3 50W
Coober Pedy, *Australia* **63 D1** 29 1S 134 43 E
Cooch Behar = Koch Bihar, *India* **41 F16** 26 22N 89 29 E
Coodardy, *Australia* **61 E2** 27 15S 117 39 E
Cook, *Australia* **61 F5** 30 37S 130 25 E
Cook, *U.S.A.* **80 B8** 47 49N 92 39W
Cook, B., *Chile* **96 H3** 55 10S 70 0W
Cook, Mt., *N.Z.* **59 K3** 43 36S 170 9 E
Cook Inlet, *U.S.A.* **68 C4** 60 0N 152 0W
Cook Is., *Pac. Oc.* **65 J12** 17 0S 160 0W
Cook Strait, *N.Z.* **59 J5** 41 15S 174 29 E
Cookeville, *U.S.A.* **77 G3** 36 10N 85 30W
Cookhouse, *S. Africa* **56 E4** 32 44S 25 47 E
Cookshire, *Canada* **79 A13** 45 25N 71 38W
Cookstown, *U.K.* **13 B5** 54 39N 6 45W
Cooksville, *Canada* **78 C5** 43 36N 79 35W
Cooktown, *Australia* **62 B4** 15 30S 145 16 E
Coolabah, *Australia* **63 E4** 31 1S 146 43 E
Cooladdi, *Australia* **63 D4** 26 37S 145 23 E
Coolah, *Australia* **63 E4** 31 48S 149 41 E
Coolamon, *Australia* **63 E4** 34 46S 147 8 E
Coolangatta, *Australia* **63 D5** 28 11S 153 29 E
Coolgardie, *Australia* **61 F3** 30 55S 121 8 E
Coolibah, *Australia* **60 C5** 15 33S 130 56 E
Coolidge, *U.S.A.* **83 K8** 32 59N 111 31W
Coolidge Dam, *U.S.A.* **83 K8** 33 0N 110 20W
Cooma, *Australia* **63 F4** 36 12S 149 8 E
Coon Rapids, *U.S.A.* **80 C8** 45 9N 93 19W
Coonabarabran, *Australia* **63 E4** 31 14S 149 18 E
Coonamble, *Australia* **63 E4** 30 56S 148 27 E
Coonana, *Australia* **61 F3** 31 0S 123 0 E
Coondapoor, *India* **40 N9** 13 42N 74 40 E
Coongie, *Australia* **63 D3** 27 9S 140 8 E
Coongoola, *Australia* **63 D4** 27 43S 145 51 E
Cooninie, L., *Australia* **63 D2** 26 4S 139 59 E
Cooper, *U.S.A.* **81 J7** 33 23N 95 42W
Cooper →, *U.S.A.* **77 J6** 32 50N 79 56W
Cooper Cr. →, *Australia* **63 D2** 28 29S 137 46 E
Cooperstown, *N. Dak., U.S.A.* **80 B5** 47 27N 98 8W
Cooperstown, *N.Y., U.S.A.* **79 D10** 42 42N 74 56W
Coorabie, *Australia* **61 F5** 31 54S 132 18 E
Coorabulka, *Australia* **62 C3** 23 41S 140 20 E
Coorow, *Australia* **61 E2** 29 53S 116 2 E
Cooroy, *Australia* **63 D5** 26 22S 152 54 E
Coos Bay, *U.S.A.* **82 E1** 43 22N 124 13W
Cootamundra, *Australia* **63 E4** 34 36S 148 1 E
Cootehill, *Ireland* **13 B4** 54 4N 7 5W
Cooyar, *Australia* **63 D5** 26 59S 151 51 E
Cooyeana, *Australia* **62 C2** 24 29S 138 45 E
Copahue Paso, *Argentina* **94 D1** 37 49S 71 8W
Copainalá, *Mexico* **87 D6** 17 8N 93 11W
Copán, *Honduras* **88 D2** 14 50N 89 9W
Cope, *U.S.A.* **80 F3** 39 40N 102 51W
Copenhagen = København, *Denmark* **9 J15** 55 41N 12 34 E
Copiapó, *Chile* **94 B1** 27 30S 70 20W
Copiapó →, *Chile* **94 B1** 27 19S 70 56W
Copley, *Australia* **63 E2** 30 36S 138 26 E
Copp L., *Canada* **72 A6** 60 14N 114 40W
Coppename →, *Surinam* **93 B7** 5 48N 55 55W
Copper Cliff, *Canada* **70 C3** 46 28N 81 4W
Copper Harbor, *U.S.A.* **76 B2** 47 28N 87 53W
Copper Queen, *Zimbabwe* **55 F2** 17 29S 29 18 E
Copperbelt □, *Zambia* **55 E2** 13 15S 27 30 E
Coppermine = Kugluktuk, *Canada* **68 B8** 67 50N 115 5W
Coppermine →, *Canada* **68 B8** 67 49N 116 4W
Copperopolis, *U.S.A.* **84 H6** 37 58N 120 38W
Coquet →, *U.K.* **10 B6** 55 20N 1 32W
Coquilhatville = Mbandaka, *Dem. Rep. of the Congo* **52 D3** 0 1N 18 18 E
Coquille, *U.S.A.* **82 E1** 43 11N 124 11W
Coquimbo, *Chile* **94 C1** 30 0S 71 20W
Coquimbo □, *Chile* **94 C1** 31 0S 71 0W
Corabia, *Romania* **17 G13** 43 48N 24 30 E
Coracora, *Peru* **92 G4** 15 5S 73 45W
Coral Gables, *U.S.A.* **77 N5** 25 45N 80 16W
Coral Sea, *Pac. Oc.* **64 J7** 15 0S 150 0 E
Coral Springs, *U.S.A.* **77 M5** 26 16N 80 13W
Coraopolis, *U.S.A.* **78 F4** 40 31N 80 10W
Corato, *Italy* **20 D7** 41 9N 16 25 E
Corbin, *U.S.A.* **76 G3** 36 57N 84 6W
Corby, *U.K.* **11 E7** 52 30N 0 41W
Corcaigh = Cork, *Ireland* **13 E3** 51 54N 8 29W
Corcoran, *U.S.A.* **84 J7** 36 6N 119 33W
Corcubión, *Spain* **19 A1** 42 56N 9 12W
Cordele, *U.S.A.* **77 K4** 31 58N 83 47W
Cordell, *U.S.A.* **81 H5** 35 17N 98 59W
Córdoba, *Argentina* **94 C3** 31 20S 64 10W
Córdoba, *Mexico* **87 D5** 18 50N 97 0W
Córdoba, *Spain* **19 D3** 37 50N 4 50W
Córdoba □, *Argentina* **94 C3** 31 22S 64 15W
Córdoba, Sierra de, *Argentina* **94 C3** 31 10S 64 25W
Cordova, *Ala., U.S.A.* **77 J2** 33 46N 87 11W
Cordova, *Alaska, U.S.A.* **68 B5** 60 33N 145 45W
Corella →, *Australia* **62 B3** 19 34S 140 47 E
Corfield, *Australia* **62 C3** 21 40S 143 21 E
Corfu, Str of, *Greece* **23 A4** 39 34N 20 0 E
Coria, *Spain* **19 C2** 39 58N 6 33W
Corigliano Cálabro, *Italy* **20 E7** 39 36N 16 31 E
Coringa Is., *Australia* **62 B4** 16 58S 149 58 E
Corinna, *Australia* **62 G4** 41 35S 145 10 E
Corinth = Kórinthos, *Greece* **21 F10** 37 56N 22 55 E
Corinth, *Miss., U.S.A.* **77 H1** 34 56N 88 31W
Corinth, *N.Y., U.S.A.* **79 C11** 43 15N 73 49W
Corinth, G. of = Korinthiakós Kólpos, *Greece* **21 E10** 38 16N 22 30 E
Corinto, *Brazil* **93 G10** 18 20S 44 30W
Corinto, *Nic.* **88 D2** 12 30N 87 10W
Cork, *Ireland* **13 E3** 51 54N 8 29W
Cork □, *Ireland* **13 E3** 51 57N 8 40W
Cork Harbour, *Ireland* **13 E3** 51 47N 8 16W
Çorlu, *Turkey* **21 D12** 41 11N 27 49 E
Cormack L., *Canada* **72 A4** 60 56N 121 37W
Cormorant, *Canada* **73 C8** 54 14N 100 35W
Cormorant L., *Canada* **73 C8** 54 15N 100 50W
Corn Is. = Maiz, Is. del, *Nic.* **88 D3** 12 15N 83 4W
Cornélio Procópio, *Brazil* **95 A5** 23 7S 50 40W
Cornell, *U.S.A.* **80 C9** 45 10N 91 9W
Corner Brook, *Canada* **71 C8** 48 57N 57 58W
Cornești, *Moldova* **17 E15** 47 21N 28 1 E
Corning, *Ark., U.S.A.* **81 G9** 36 25N 90 35W
Corning, *Calif., U.S.A.* **82 G2** 39 56N 122 11W
Corning, *Iowa, U.S.A.* **80 E7** 40 59N 94 44W
Corning, *N.Y., U.S.A.* **78 D7** 42 9N 77 3W
Cornwall, *Canada* **70 C5** 45 2N 74 44W
Cornwall □, *U.K.* **11 G3** 50 26N 4 40W
Corny Pt., *Australia* **63 E2** 34 55S 137 0 E
Coro, *Venezuela* **92 A5** 11 25N 69 41W
Coroatá, *Brazil* **93 D10** 4 8S 44 0W
Corocoro, *Bolivia* **92 G5** 17 15S 68 28W
Coroico, *Bolivia* **92 G5** 16 0S 67 50W
Coromandel, *N.Z.* **59 G5** 36 45S 175 31 E
Coromandel Coast, *India* **40 N12** 12 30N 81 0 E
Corona, *Australia* **63 E3** 31 16S 141 24 E
Corona, *Calif., U.S.A.* **85 M9** 33 53N 117 34W
Corona, *N. Mex., U.S.A.* **83 J11** 34 15N 105 36W
Coronado, *U.S.A.* **85 N9** 32 41N 117 11W
Coronado, B. de, *Costa Rica* **88 E3** 9 0N 83 40W
Coronados, Is. los, *U.S.A.* **85 N9** 32 25N 117 15W
Coronation, *Canada* **72 C6** 52 5N 111 27W
Coronation Gulf, *Canada* **68 B9** 68 25N 110 0W
Coronation I., *Antarctica* **5 C18** 60 45S 46 0W
Coronation I., *U.S.A.* **72 B2** 55 52N 134 20W
Coronation Is., *Australia* **60 B3** 14 57S 124 55 E
Coronda, *Argentina* **94 C3** 31 58S 60 56W
Coronel, *Chile* **94 D1** 37 0S 73 10W
Coronel Bogado, *Paraguay* **94 B4** 27 11S 56 18W
Coronel Dorrego, *Argentina* **94 D3** 38 40S 61 10W

Ebetsu

Dounreay, U.K. 12 C5 58 35N 3 44W
Dourada, Serra, Brazil 93 F9 13 10S 48 45W
Dourados, Brazil 95 A5 22 9S 54 50W
Dourados →, Brazil 95 A5 21 58S 54 18W
Douro →, Europe 19 B1 41 8N 8 40W
Dove →, U.K. 10 E6 52 51N 1 36W
Dove Creek, U.S.A. 83 H9 37 46N 108 54W
Dover, Australia 62 G4 43 18S 147 2 E
Dover, U.K. 11 F9 51 7N 1 19 E
Dover, Del., U.S.A. 76 F8 39 10N 75 32W
Dover, N.H., U.S.A. 79 C14 43 12N 70 56W
Dover, N.J., U.S.A. 79 F10 40 53N 74 34W
Dover, Ohio, U.S.A. 78 F3 40 32N 81 29W
Dover, Pt., Australia 61 F4 32 32S 125 32 E
Dover, Str. of, Europe 11 G9 51 0N 1 30 E
Dover-Foxcroft, U.S.A. 71 C6 45 11N 69 13W
Dover Plains, U.S.A. 79 E11 41 43N 73 35W
Dovey = Dyfi →, U.K. 11 E3 52 32N 4 3W
Dovrefjell, Norway 9 E13 62 15N 9 33 E
Dow Rūd, Iran 45 C6 33 28N 49 4 E
Dowa, Malawi 55 E3 13 38S 33 58 E
Dowagiac, U.S.A. 76 E2 41 59N 86 6W
Dowgha'i, Iran 45 B8 36 54N 58 32 E
Dowlatābād, Iran 45 D8 28 20N 56 40 E
Down □, U.K. 13 B5 54 23N 6 2W
Downey, Calif., U.S.A. 85 M8 33 56N 118 7W
Downey, Idaho, U.S.A. 82 E7 42 26N 112 7W
Downham Market, U.K. 11 E8 52 37N 0 23 E
Downieville, U.S.A. 84 F6 39 34N 120 50W
Downpatrick, U.K. 13 B6 54 20N 5 43W
Downpatrick Hd., Ireland 13 B2 54 20N 9 21W
Dowsārī, Iran 45 D8 28 25N 57 59 E
Doyle, U.S.A. 84 E6 40 2N 120 6W
Doylestown, U.S.A. 79 F9 40 21N 75 10W
Drachten, Neths. 15 A6 53 7N 6 5 E
Drăgăşani, Romania 17 F13 44 39N 24 17 E
Dragichyn, Belarus 17 B13 52 15N 25 8 E
Dragoman, Prokhod, Bulgaria 21 C10 42 58N 22 53 E
Draguignan, France 18 E7 43 32N 6 27 E
Drain, U.S.A. 82 E2 43 40N 123 19W
Drake, Australia 63 D5 28 55S 152 25 E
Drake, U.S.A. 80 B4 47 55N 100 23W
Drake Passage, S. Ocean 5 B17 58 0S 68 0W
Drakensberg, S. Africa 57 E4 31 0S 28 0 E
Dráma, Greece 21 D11 41 9N 24 10 E
Drammen, Norway 9 G14 59 42N 10 12 E
Drangajökull, Iceland 8 C2 66 9N 22 15W
Dras, India 43 B6 34 25N 75 48 E
Drau = Drava →, Croatia 21 B8 45 33N 18 55 E
Drava →, Croatia 21 B8 45 33N 18 55 E
Drayton Valley, Canada 72 C6 53 12N 114 58W
Drenthe □, Neths. 15 B6 52 52N 6 40 E
Drepanum, C., Cyprus 23 E11 34 54N 32 19 E
Dresden, Canada 78 D2 42 35N 82 11W
Dresden, Germany 16 C7 51 3N 13 44 E
Dreux, France 18 B4 48 44N 1 23 E
Driffield, U.K. 10 C7 54 0N 0 26W
Driftwood, U.S.A. 78 E6 41 20N 78 8W
Driggs, U.S.A. 82 E8 43 44N 111 6W
Drina →, Bos.-H. 21 B8 44 53N 19 21 E
Drini →, Albania 21 C8 42 1N 19 38 E
Drøbak, Norway 9 G14 59 39N 10 39 E
Drochia, Moldova 17 D14 48 2N 27 48 E
Drogheda, Ireland 13 C5 53 43N 6 22W
Drogichin = Dragichyn, Belarus 17 B13 52 15N 25 8 E
Drogobych = Drohobych, Ukraine 25 E3 49 20N 23 30 E
Drohobych, Ukraine 25 E3 49 20N 23 30 E
Droichead Atha = Drogheda, Ireland 13 C5 53 43N 6 22W
Droichead Nua, Ireland 13 C5 53 11N 6 48W
Droitwich, U.K. 11 E5 52 16N 2 8W
Dromedary, C., Australia 63 F5 36 17S 150 10 E
Dromore, U.K. 13 B4 54 31N 7 28W
Dromore West, Ireland 13 B3 54 15N 8 52W
Dronfield, Australia 62 C3 21 12S 140 3 E
Dronfield, U.K. 10 D6 53 19N 1 27W
Dronten, Neths. 15 B5 52 32N 5 43 E
Drumbo, Canada 78 C4 43 16N 80 35W
Drumheller, Canada 72 C6 51 25N 112 40W
Drummond, U.S.A. 82 C7 46 40N 113 9W
Drummond I., U.S.A. 70 C3 46 1N 83 39W
Drummond Pt., Australia 63 E2 34 9S 135 16 E
Drummond Ra., Australia 62 C4 23 45S 147 10 E
Drummondville, Canada 70 C5 45 55N 72 25W
Drumright, U.S.A. 81 H6 35 59N 96 36W
Druskininkai, Lithuania 9 J20 54 3N 23 58 E
Drut →, Belarus 17 B16 53 8N 30 5 E
Druzhina, Russia 27 C15 68 14N 145 18 E
Dry Tortugas, U.S.A. 88 B3 24 38N 82 55W
Dryden, Canada 73 D10 49 47N 92 50W
Dryden, U.S.A. 81 K3 30 3N 102 7W
Drygalski I., Antarctica 5 C7 66 0S 92 0 E
Drysdale →, Australia 60 B4 13 59S 126 51 E
Drysdale I., Australia 62 A2 11 41S 136 0 E
Du Bois, U.S.A. 78 E6 41 8N 78 46W
Du Quoin, U.S.A. 80 G10 38 1N 89 14W
Duanesburg, U.S.A. 79 D10 42 45N 74 11W
Duaringa, Australia 62 C4 23 42S 149 42 E
Ḍubā, Si. Arabia 44 E2 27 10N 35 40 E
Dubai = Dubayy, U.A.E. 45 E7 25 18N 55 20 E
Dubăsari, Moldova 17 E15 47 15N 29 10 E
Dubăsari Vdkhr., Moldova 17 E15 47 30N 29 0 E
Dubawnt →, Canada 73 A8 64 33N 100 6W
Dubawnt, L., Canada 73 A8 63 4N 101 42W
Dubayy, U.A.E. 45 E7 25 18N 55 20 E
Dubbo, Australia 63 E4 32 11S 148 35 E
Dubele, Dem. Rep. of the Congo 54 B2 2 56N 29 35 E
Dublin, Ireland 13 C5 53 21N 6 15W
Dublin, Ga., U.S.A. 77 J4 32 32N 82 54W
Dublin, Tex., U.S.A. 81 J5 32 5N 98 21W
Dublin □, Ireland 13 C5 53 24N 6 20W
Dubno, Ukraine 17 C13 50 25N 25 45 E
Dubois, U.S.A. 82 D7 44 10N 112 14W
Dubossary = Dubăsari, Moldova 17 E15 47 15N 29 10 E
Dubossary Vdkhr. = Dubăsari Vdkhr., Moldova 17 E15 47 30N 29 0 E
Dubovka, Russia 25 E7 49 5N 44 50 E
Dubrajpur, India 43 H12 23 48N 87 25 E
Dubréka, Guinea 50 G3 9 46N 13 31W
Dubrovitsa = Dubrovytsya, Ukraine 17 C14 51 31N 26 35 E
Dubrovnik, Croatia 21 C8 42 39N 18 6 E
Dubrovytsya, Ukraine 17 C14 51 31N 26 35 E
Dubuque, U.S.A. 80 D9 42 30N 90 41W
Duchesne, U.S.A. 82 F8 40 10N 110 24W
Duchess, Australia 62 C2 21 20S 139 50 E
Ducie I., Pac. Oc. 65 K15 24 40S 124 48W
Duck Cr. →, Australia 60 D2 22 37S 116 53 E
Duck Lake, Canada 73 C7 52 50N 106 16W
Duck Mountain Prov. Park, Canada 73 C8 51 45N 101 0W
Duckwall, Mt., U.S.A. 84 H6 37 58N 120 7W
Dudhi, India 41 G13 24 15N 83 10 E
Dudinka, Russia 27 C9 69 30N 86 13 E
Dudley, U.K. 11 E5 52 31N 2 5W
Duero = Douro →, Europe 19 B1 41 8N 8 40W
Dufftown, U.K. 12 D5 57 27N 3 8W
Dugi Otok, Croatia 16 G8 44 0N 15 3 E
Duifken Pt., Australia 62 A3 12 33S 141 38 E
Duisburg, Germany 16 C4 51 26N 6 45 E
Duiwelskloof, S. Africa 57 C5 23 42S 30 10 E
Dūkdamīn, Iran 45 C8 35 59N 57 43 E
Duke I., U.S.A. 72 C2 54 50N 131 20W
Dukelský Průsmyk, Slovak Rep. 17 D11 49 25N 21 42 E
Dukhān, Qatar 45 E6 25 25N 50 50 E
Duki, Pakistan 40 D6 30 14N 68 25 E
Duku, Nigeria 51 F8 10 43N 10 43 E
Dulce →, Argentina 94 C3 30 32S 62 33W
Dulce, G., Costa Rica 88 E3 8 40N 83 20W
Dulf, Iraq 44 C5 35 7N 45 51 E
Dulit, Banjaran, Malaysia 36 D4 3 15N 114 30 E
Duliu, China 34 E9 39 2N 116 55 E
Dullewala, Pakistan 42 D4 31 50N 71 25 E
Dulq Maghār, Syria 44 B3 36 22N 38 39 E
Dululu, Australia 62 C5 23 48S 150 15 E
Duluth, U.S.A. 80 B8 46 47N 92 6W
Dum Dum, India 43 H13 22 39N 88 33 E
Dum Duma, India 41 F19 27 40N 95 40 E
Dūmā, Syria 47 B5 33 34N 36 24 E
Dumaguete, Phil. 37 C6 9 17N 123 15 E
Dumai, Indonesia 36 D2 1 35N 101 28 E
Dumaran, Phil. 37 B5 10 33N 119 50 E
Dumas, Ark., U.S.A. 81 J9 33 53N 91 29W
Dumas, Tex., U.S.A. 81 H4 35 52N 101 58W
Dumbarton, U.K. 12 F4 55 57N 4 33W
Dumbleyung, Australia 61 F2 33 17S 117 42 E
Dumfries, U.K. 12 F5 55 4N 3 37W
Dumfries & Galloway □, U.K. 12 F5 55 9N 3 58W
Dumka, India 43 G12 24 12N 87 15 E
Dumoine →, Canada 70 C4 46 13N 77 51W
Dumoine L., Canada 70 C4 46 55N 77 55W
Dumraon, India 43 G11 25 33N 84 8 E
Dumyât, Egypt 51 B12 31 24N 31 48 E
Dún Dealgan = Dundalk, Ireland 13 B5 54 1N 6 24W
Dun Laoghaire, Ireland 13 C5 53 17N 6 8W
Duna = Dunărea →, Europe 17 F15 45 20N 29 40 E
Dunaj = Dunărea →, Europe 17 F15 45 20N 29 40 E
Dunakeszi, Hungary 17 E10 47 37N 19 8 E
Dunărea →, Europe 17 F15 45 20N 29 40 E
Dunaújváros, Hungary 17 E10 46 58N 18 57 E
Dunav = Dunărea →, Europe 17 F15 45 20N 29 40 E
Dunay, Russia 30 C6 42 52N 132 22 E
Dunback, N.Z. 59 L3 45 23S 170 36 E
Dunbar, Australia 62 B3 16 0S 142 22 E
Dunbar, U.K. 12 E6 56 0N 2 31W
Dunblane, U.K. 12 E5 56 11N 3 58W
Duncan, Canada 72 D4 48 45N 123 40W
Duncan, Ariz., U.S.A. 83 K9 32 43N 109 6W
Duncan, Okla., U.S.A. 81 H6 34 30N 97 57W
Duncan, L., Canada 70 B4 53 29N 77 58W
Duncan L., Canada 72 A6 62 51N 113 58W
Duncan Town, Bahamas 88 B4 22 15N 75 45W
Duncannon, U.S.A. 78 F7 40 23N 77 2W
Duncansby Head, U.K. 12 C5 58 38N 3 1W
Dundalk, Canada 78 B4 44 10N 80 24W
Dundalk, Ireland 13 B5 54 1N 6 24W
Dundalk Bay, Ireland 13 C5 53 55N 6 15W
Dundas, Canada 70 D4 43 17N 79 59W
Dundas, L., Australia 61 F3 32 35S 121 50 E
Dundas I., Canada 72 C2 54 30N 130 50W
Dundas Str., Australia 60 B5 11 15S 131 35 E
Dundee, S. Africa 57 D5 28 11S 30 15 E
Dundee, U.K. 12 E6 56 28N 2 59W
Dundee City □, U.K. 12 E6 56 30N 2 58W
Dundgovĭ □, Mongolia 34 B4 45 10N 106 0 E
Dundoo, Australia 63 D3 27 40S 144 37 E
Dundrum, U.K. 13 B6 54 16N 5 52W
Dundrum B., U.K. 13 B6 54 13N 5 47W
Dundwara, India 43 F8 27 48N 79 9 E
Dunedin, N.Z. 59 L3 45 50S 170 33 E
Dunedin, U.S.A. 77 L4 28 1N 82 47W
Dunedin →, Canada 72 B4 59 30N 124 5W
Dunfermline, U.K. 12 E5 56 5N 3 27W
Dungannon, Canada 78 C3 43 51N 81 36W
Dungannon, U.K. 13 B5 54 31N 6 46W
Dungarpur, India 42 H5 23 52N 73 45 E
Dungarvan, Ireland 13 D4 52 5N 7 37W
Dungarvan Harbour, Ireland 13 D4 52 4N 7 35W
Dungeness, U.K. 11 G8 50 54N 0 59 E
Dungo, L. do, Angola 56 B2 17 15S 19 0 E
Dungog, Australia 63 E5 32 22S 151 46 E
Dungu, Dem. Rep. of the Congo 54 B2 3 40N 28 32 E
Dungun, Malaysia 39 K4 4 45N 103 25 E
Dunhua, China 35 C15 43 20N 128 14 E
Dunhuang, China 32 B4 40 8N 94 36 E
Dunk I., Australia 62 B4 17 59S 146 29 E
Dunkeld, U.K. 12 E5 56 34N 3 35W
Dunkerque, France 18 A5 51 2N 2 20 E
Dunkery Beacon, U.K. 11 F4 51 9N 3 36W
Dunkirk = Dunkerque, France 18 A5 51 2N 2 20 E
Dunkirk, U.S.A. 78 D5 42 29N 79 20W
Dunlap, U.S.A. 80 E7 41 51N 95 36W
Dúnleary = Dun Laoghaire, Ireland 13 C5 53 17N 6 8W
Dunleer, Ireland 13 C5 53 50N 6 24W
Dunmanus B., Ireland 13 E2 51 31N 9 50W
Dunmanway, Ireland 13 E2 51 43N 9 6W
Dunmara, Australia 62 B1 16 42S 133 25 E
Dunmore, U.S.A. 79 E9 41 25N 75 38W
Dunmore Hd., Ireland 13 D1 52 10N 10 35W
Dunmore Town, Bahamas 88 A4 25 30N 76 39W
Dunn, U.S.A. 77 H6 35 19N 78 37W
Dunnellon, U.S.A. 77 L4 29 3N 82 28W
Dunnet Hd., U.K. 12 C5 58 40N 3 21W
Dunning, U.S.A. 80 E4 41 50N 100 6W
Dunnville, Canada 78 D5 42 54N 79 36W
Dunolly, Australia 63 F3 36 51S 143 44 E
Dunoon, U.K. 12 F4 55 57N 4 56W
Duns, U.K. 12 F6 55 47N 2 20W
Dunseith, U.S.A. 80 A4 48 50N 100 3W
Dunsmuir, U.S.A. 82 F2 41 13N 122 16W
Dunstable, U.K. 11 F7 51 53N 0 32W
Dunstan Mts., N.Z. 59 L2 44 53S 169 35 E
Dunster, Canada 72 C5 53 8N 119 50W
Dunvegan L., Canada 73 A7 60 8N 107 10W
Duolun, China 34 C9 42 12N 116 28 E
Duong Dong, Vietnam 39 G4 10 13N 103 58 E
Dupree, U.S.A. 80 C4 45 4N 101 35W
Dupuyer, U.S.A. 82 B7 48 13N 112 30W
Duque de Caxias, Brazil 95 A7 22 45S 43 19W
Durack →, Australia 60 C4 15 33S 127 52 E
Durack Ra., Australia 60 C4 16 50S 127 40 E
Durance →, France 18 E6 43 55N 4 45 E
Durand, U.S.A. 76 D4 42 55N 83 59W
Durango, Mexico 86 C4 24 3N 104 39W
Durango, U.S.A. 83 H10 37 16N 107 53W
Durango □, Mexico 86 C4 25 0N 105 0W
Duranillin, Australia 61 F2 33 30S 116 45 E
Durant, U.S.A. 81 J6 33 59N 96 25W
Durazno, Uruguay 94 C4 33 25S 56 31W
Durazzo = Durrësi, Albania 21 D8 41 19N 19 28 E
Durban, S. Africa 57 D5 29 49S 31 1 E
Durbuy, Belgium 15 D5 50 21N 5 28 E
Düren, Germany 16 C4 50 48N 6 29 E
Durg, India 41 J12 21 15N 81 22 E
Durgapur, India 43 H12 23 30N 87 20 E
Durham, Canada 78 B4 44 10N 80 49W
Durham, U.K. 10 C6 54 47N 1 34W
Durham, Calif., U.S.A. 84 F5 39 39N 121 48W
Durham, N.C., U.S.A. 77 H6 35 59N 78 54W
Durham □, U.K. 10 C6 54 42N 1 45W
Durham Downs, Australia 63 D4 26 6S 149 5 E
Durmitor, Montenegro, Yug. 21 C8 43 10N 19 0 E
Durness, U.K. 12 C4 58 34N 4 45W
Durrësi, Albania 21 D8 41 19N 19 28 E
Durrie, Australia 62 D3 25 40S 140 15 E
Durrow, Ireland 13 D4 52 51N 7 24W
Dursey I., Ireland 13 E1 51 36N 10 12W
Dursunbey, Turkey 21 E13 39 35N 28 37 E
Duru, Dem. Rep. of the Congo 54 B2 4 14N 28 50 E
Durūz, Jabal ad, Jordan 47 C5 32 35N 36 40 E
D'Urville, Tanjung, Indonesia 37 E9 1 28S 137 54 E
D'Urville I., N.Z. 59 J4 40 50S 173 55 E
Duryea, U.S.A. 79 E9 41 20N 75 45W
Dushak, Turkmenistan 26 F7 37 13N 60 1 E
Dushanbe, Tajikistan 26 F7 38 33N 68 48 E
Dusky Sd., N.Z. 59 L1 45 47S 166 30 E
Dussejour, C., Australia 60 B4 14 45S 128 13 E
Düsseldorf, Germany 16 C4 51 14N 6 47 E
Dutch Harbor, U.S.A. 68 C3 53 53N 166 32W
Dutlwe, Botswana 56 C3 23 58S 23 46 E
Dutton, Canada 78 D3 42 39N 81 30W
Dutton →, Australia 62 C3 20 44S 143 10 E
Duyun, China 32 D5 26 18N 107 29 E
Duzdab = Zāhedān, Iran 45 D9 29 30N 60 50 E
Dvina, Severnaya →, Russia 24 B7 64 32N 40 30 E
Dvinsk = Daugavpils, Latvia 24 C4 55 53N 26 32 E
Dvinskaya Guba, Russia 24 B6 65 0N 39 0 E
Dwarka, India 42 H3 22 18N 69 8 E
Dwellingup, Australia 61 F2 32 43S 116 4 E
Dwight, Canada 78 A5 45 20N 79 1W
Dwight, U.S.A. 76 E1 41 5N 88 26W
Dyatlovo = Dzyatlava, Belarus 17 B13 53 28N 25 28 E
Dyce, U.K. 12 D6 57 13N 2 12W
Dyer, C., Canada 69 B13 66 40N 61 0W
Dyer Plateau, Antarctica 5 D17 70 45S 65 30W
Dyersburg, U.S.A. 81 G10 36 3N 89 23W
Dyfi →, U.K. 11 E3 52 32N 4 3W
Dymer, Ukraine 17 C16 50 47N 30 18 E
Dynevor Downs, Australia 63 D3 28 10S 144 20 E
Dysart, Canada 73 C8 50 57N 104 2W
Dzamin Üüd, Mongolia 34 C6 43 50N 111 58 E
Dzerzhinsk, Russia 24 C7 56 14N 43 30 E
Dzhalinda, Russia 27 D13 53 26N 124 0 E
Dzhambul = Zhambyl, Kazakstan 26 E8 42 54N 71 22 E
Dzhankoy, Ukraine 25 E5 45 40N 34 20 E
Dzhezkazgan = Zhezqazghan, Kazakstan 26 E7 47 44N 67 40 E
Dzhizak = Jizzakh, Uzbekistan 26 E7 40 6N 67 50 E
Dzhugdzur, Khrebet, Russia 27 D14 57 30N 138 0 E
Dzhungarskiye Vorota = Dzungarian Gates, Kazakstan 32 B3 45 0N 82 0 E
Działdowo, Poland 17 B11 53 15N 20 15 E
Dzierżoniów, Poland 17 C9 50 45N 16 39 E
Dzilam de Bravo, Mexico 87 C7 21 24N 88 53W
Dzungaria = Junggar Pendi, China 32 B3 44 30N 86 0 E
Dzungarian Gates, Kazakstan 32 B3 45 0N 82 0 E
Dzuumod, Mongolia 32 B5 47 45N 106 58 E
Dzyarzhynsk, Belarus 24 D4 53 40N 27 1 E
Dzyatlava, Belarus 17 B13 53 28N 25 28 E

E

Eabamet, L., Canada 70 B2 51 30N 87 46W
Eads, U.S.A. 80 F3 38 29N 102 47W
Eagle, U.S.A. 82 G10 39 39N 106 50W
Eagle →, Canada 71 B8 53 36N 57 26W
Eagle Butte, U.S.A. 80 C4 45 0N 101 10W
Eagle Grove, U.S.A. 80 D8 42 40N 93 54W
Eagle L., Calif., U.S.A. 82 F3 40 39N 120 45W
Eagle L., Maine, U.S.A. 71 C6 46 20N 69 22W
Eagle Lake, U.S.A. 81 L6 29 35N 96 20W
Eagle Mountain, U.S.A. 85 M11 33 49N 115 27W
Eagle Nest, U.S.A. 83 H11 36 33N 105 16W
Eagle Pass, U.S.A. 81 L4 28 43N 100 30W
Eagle Pk., U.S.A. 84 G7 38 10N 119 25W
Eagle Pt., Australia 60 C3 16 11S 124 23 E
Eagle River, U.S.A. 80 C10 45 55N 89 15W
Ealing, U.K. 11 F7 51 31N 0 20W
Earaheedy, Australia 61 E3 25 34S 121 29 E
Earl Grey, Canada 73 C8 50 57N 104 43W
Earle, U.S.A. 81 H9 35 16N 90 28W
Earlimart, U.S.A. 85 K7 35 53N 119 16W
Earn →, U.K. 12 E5 56 21N 3 18W
Earn, L., U.K. 12 E4 56 23N 4 13W
Earnslaw, Mt., N.Z. 59 L2 44 32S 168 27 E
Earth, U.S.A. 81 H3 34 14N 102 24W
Easley, U.S.A. 77 H4 34 50N 82 36W
East Angus, Canada 71 C5 45 30N 71 40W
East Aurora, U.S.A. 78 D6 42 46N 78 37W
East Ayrshire □, U.K. 12 F4 55 26N 4 11W
East B., U.S.A. 81 L10 29 0N 89 15W
East Bengal, Bangla. 41 H17 24 0N 90 0 E
East Beskids = Vychodné Beskydy, Europe 17 D11 49 20N 22 0 E
East Brady, U.S.A. 78 F5 40 59N 79 36W
East C., N.Z. 59 G7 37 42S 178 35 E
East Chicago, U.S.A. 76 E2 41 38N 87 27W
East China Sea, Asia 33 D7 30 0N 126 0 E
East Coulee, Canada 72 C6 51 23N 112 27W
East Dereham, U.K. 11 E8 52 41N 0 57 E
East Dunbartonshire □, U.K. 12 F4 55 57N 4 13W
East Falkland, Falk. Is. 96 G5 51 30S 58 30W
East Grand Forks, U.S.A. 80 B6 47 56N 97 1W
East Greenwich, U.S.A. 79 E13 41 40N 71 27W
East Grinstead, U.K. 11 F8 51 7N 0 0 E
East Hartford, U.S.A. 79 E12 41 46N 72 39W
East Helena, U.S.A. 82 C8 46 35N 111 56W
East Indies, Asia 28 K15 0 0 120 0 E
East Jordan, U.S.A. 76 C3 45 10N 85 7W
East Kilbride, U.K. 12 F4 55 47N 4 11W
East Lansing, U.S.A. 76 D3 42 44N 84 29W
East Liverpool, U.S.A. 78 F4 40 37N 80 35W
East London, S. Africa 57 E4 33 0S 27 55 E
East Lothian □, U.K. 12 F6 55 58N 2 44W
East Main = Eastmain, Canada 70 B4 52 10N 78 30W
East Orange, U.S.A. 79 F10 40 46N 74 13W
East Pacific Ridge, Pac. Oc. 65 J17 15 0S 110 0W
East Palestine, U.S.A. 78 F4 40 50N 80 33W
East Pine, Canada 72 B4 55 48N 120 12W
East Point, U.S.A. 77 J3 33 41N 84 27W
East Providence, U.S.A. 79 E13 41 49N 71 23W
East Pt., Canada 71 C7 46 27N 61 58W
East Renfrewshire □, U.K. 12 F4 55 46N 4 21W
East Retford = Retford, U.K. 10 D7 53 19N 0 56W
East Riding of Yorkshire □, U.K. 10 D7 53 55N 0 30W
East St. Louis, U.S.A. 80 F9 38 37N 90 9W
East Schelde → = Oosterschelde, Neths. 15 C4 51 33N 4 0 E
East Siberian Sea, Russia 27 B17 73 0N 160 0 E
East Stroudsburg, U.S.A. 79 E9 41 1N 75 11W
East Sussex □, U.K. 11 G8 50 56N 0 19 E
East Tawas, U.S.A. 76 C4 44 17N 83 29W
East Toorale, Australia 63 E4 30 27S 145 28 E
East Walker →, U.S.A. 84 G7 38 52N 119 10W
Eastbourne, N.Z. 59 J5 41 19S 174 55 E
Eastbourne, U.K. 11 G8 50 46N 0 18 E
Eastend, Canada 73 D7 49 32N 108 50W
Easter Islands = Pascua, I. de, Pac. Oc. 65 K17 27 0S 109 0W
Eastern □, Kenya 54 C4 0 0 38 30 E
Eastern □, Uganda 54 B3 1 50N 33 45 E
Eastern Cape □, S. Africa 56 E4 32 0S 26 0 E
Eastern Cr. →, Australia 62 C3 20 40S 141 35 E
Eastern Ghats, India 40 N11 14 0N 78 50 E
Eastern Group = Lau Group, Fiji 59 C9 17 0S 178 30W
Eastern Group, Australia 61 F3 33 30S 124 30 E
Eastern Transvaal = Mpumalanga □, S. Africa 57 B5 26 0S 30 0 E
Easterville, Canada 73 C9 53 8N 99 49W
Easthampton, U.S.A. 79 D12 42 16N 72 40W
Eastland, U.S.A. 81 J5 32 24N 98 49W
Eastleigh, U.K. 11 G6 50 58N 1 21W
Eastmain, Canada 70 B4 52 10N 78 30W
Eastmain →, Canada 70 B4 52 27N 78 26W
Eastman, Canada 79 A12 45 18N 72 19W
Eastman, U.S.A. 77 J4 32 12N 83 11W
Easton, Md., U.S.A. 76 F7 38 47N 76 5W
Easton, Pa., U.S.A. 79 F9 40 41N 75 13W
Easton, Wash., U.S.A. 84 C5 47 14N 121 11W
Eastport, U.S.A. 71 D6 44 56N 67 0W
Eastsound, U.S.A. 84 B4 48 42N 122 55W
Eaton, U.S.A. 80 E2 40 32N 104 42W
Eatonia, Canada 73 C7 51 13N 109 25W
Eatonton, U.S.A. 77 J4 33 20N 83 23W
Eatontown, U.S.A. 79 F10 40 19N 74 4W
Eatonville, U.S.A. 84 D4 46 52N 122 16W
Eau Claire, U.S.A. 80 C9 44 49N 91 30W
Ebagoola, Australia 62 A3 14 15S 143 12 E
Ebbw Vale, U.K. 11 F4 51 46N 3 12W
Ebeltoft, Denmark 9 H14 56 12N 10 41 E
Ebensburg, U.S.A. 78 F6 40 29N 78 44W
Eberswalde-Finow, Germany 16 B7 52 50N 13 49 E
Ebetsu, Japan 30 C10 43 7N 141 34 E

Fayette

Episkopi, *Cyprus* **23 E11** 34 40N 32 54 E
Episkopi, *Greece* **23 D6** 35 20N 24 20 E
Episkopi Bay, *Cyprus* **23 E11** 34 35N 32 50 E
Epsom, *U.K.* **11 F7** 51 19N 0 16W
Epukiro, *Namibia* **56 C2** 21 40S 19 9 E
Equatorial Guinea ■, *Africa* **52 D1** 2 0N 8 0 E
Er Rahad, *Sudan* **51 F12** 12 45N 30 32 E
Er Rif, *Morocco* **50 A5** 35 1N 4 1W
Erāwadī Myit = Irrawaddy ⟶, *Burma* **41 M19** 15 50N 95 6 E
Erbil = Arbīl, *Iraq* **44 B5** 36 15N 44 5 E
Erciyaş Dağı, *Turkey* **25 G6** 38 30N 35 30 E
Érd, *Hungary* **17 E10** 47 22N 18 56 E
Erdao Jiang ⟶, *China* **35 C14** 43 0N 127 0 E
Erdek, *Turkey* **21 D12** 40 23N 27 47 E
Erdene, *Mongolia* **34 B6** 44 13N 111 10 E
Erebus, Mt., *Antarctica* **5 D11** 77 35S 167 0 E
Erechim, *Brazil* **95 B5** 27 35S 52 15W
Ereğli, *Konya, Turkey* **25 G5** 37 31N 34 4 E
Ereğli, *Zonguldak, Turkey* **25 F5** 41 15N 31 24 E
Erenhot, *China* **34 C7** 43 48N 112 2 E
Eresma ⟶, *Spain* **19 B3** 41 26N 4 45W
Erewadi Myitwanya, *Burma* **41 M19** 15 30N 95 0 E
Erfenisdam, *S. Africa* **56 D4** 28 30S 26 50 E
Erfurt, *Germany* **16 C6** 50 58N 11 2 E
Ergeni Vozvyshennost, *Russia* **25 E7** 47 0N 44 0 E
Ērgli, *Latvia* **9 H21** 56 54N 25 38 E
Eriboll, L., *U.K.* **12 C4** 58 30N 4 42W
Érice, *Italy* **20 E5** 38 2N 12 35 E
Erie, *U.S.A.* **78 D4** 42 8N 80 5W
Erie, L., *N. Amer.* **78 D4** 42 15N 81 0W
Erie Canal, *U.S.A.* **78 C7** 43 5N 78 43W
Erieau, *Canada* **78 D3** 42 16N 81 57W
Erigavo, *Somali Rep.* **46 E4** 10 35N 47 20 E
Erikoúsa, *Greece* **23 A3** 39 53N 19 34 E
Eriksdale, *Canada* **73 C9** 50 52N 98 7W
Erímanthos, *Greece* **21 F9** 37 57N 21 50 E
Erimo-misaki, *Japan* **30 D11** 41 50N 143 15 E
Eriskay, *U.K.* **12 D1** 57 4N 7 18W
Eritrea ■, *Africa* **46 D2** 14 0N 38 30 E
Erlangen, *Germany* **16 D6** 49 36N 11 0 E
Erldunda, *Australia* **62 D1** 25 14S 133 12 E
Ermelo, *Neths.* **15 B5** 52 18N 5 35 E
Ermelo, *S. Africa* **57 D4** 26 31S 29 59 E
Ermones, *Greece* **23 A3** 39 37N 19 46 E
Ernakulam = Cochin, *India* **40 Q10** 9 59N 76 22 E
Erne ⟶, *Ireland* **13 B3** 54 30N 8 16W
Erne, Lower L., *U.K.* **13 B4** 54 28N 7 47W
Erne, Upper L., *U.K.* **13 B4** 54 14N 7 32W
Ernest Giles Ra., *Australia* **61 E3** 27 0S 123 45 E
Erode, *India* **40 P10** 11 24N 77 45 E
Eromanga, *Australia* **63 D3** 26 40S 143 11 E
Erongo, *Namibia* **56 C2** 21 39S 15 58 E
Errabiddy, *Australia* **61 E2** 25 25S 117 5 E
Erramala Hills, *India* **40 M11** 15 30N 78 15 E
Errigal, *Ireland* **13 A3** 55 2N 8 6W
Erris Hd., *Ireland* **13 B1** 54 19N 10 0W
Erskine, *U.S.A.* **80 B7** 47 40N 96 0W
Ertis ⟶ = Irtysh ⟶, *Russia* **26 C7** 61 4N 68 52 E
Erwin, *U.S.A.* **77 G4** 36 9N 82 25W
Erzgebirge, *Germany* **16 C7** 50 27N 12 55 E
Erzin, *Russia* **27 D10** 50 15N 95 10 E
Erzincan, *Turkey* **25 G6** 39 46N 39 30 E
Erzurum, *Turkey* **25 G7** 39 57N 41 15 E
Es Caló, *Spain* **22 C8** 38 40N 1 30 E
Es Caná, *Spain* **22 B8** 39 2N 1 36 E
Es Mercadal, *Spain* **22 B11** 39 59N 4 5 E
Es Sahrâ' Esh Sharqîya, *Egypt* **51 C12** 27 30N 32 30 E
Es Sînâ', *Egypt* **51 C12** 29 0N 34 0 E
Es Vedrà, *Spain* **22 C7** 38 52N 1 12 E
Esambo, *Dem. Rep. of the Congo* **54 C1** 3 48S 23 30 E
Esan-Misaki, *Japan* **30 D10** 41 40N 141 10 E
Esashi, *Hokkaidō, Japan* **30 B11** 44 56N 142 35 E
Esashi, *Hokkaidō, Japan* **30 D10** 41 52N 140 7 E
Esbjerg, *Denmark* **9 J13** 55 29N 8 29 E
Escalante, *U.S.A.* **83 H8** 37 47N 111 36W
Escalante ⟶, *U.S.A.* **83 H8** 37 24N 110 57W
Escalón, *Mexico* **86 B4** 26 46N 104 20W
Escambia ⟶, *U.S.A.* **77 K2** 30 32N 87 11W
Escanaba, *U.S.A.* **76 C2** 45 45N 87 4W
Esch-sur-Alzette, *Lux.* **18 B6** 49 32N 6 0 E
Escondido, *U.S.A.* **85 M9** 33 7N 117 5W
Escuinapa, *Mexico* **86 C3** 22 50N 105 50W
Escuintla, *Guatemala* **88 D1** 14 20N 90 48W
Esenguly, *Turkmenistan* **26 F6** 37 37N 53 59 E
Eşfahān, *Iran* **45 C6** 32 39N 51 43 E
Esfideh, *Iran* **45 C8** 33 39N 59 46 E
Esh Sham = Dimashq, *Syria* **47 B5** 33 30N 36 18 E
Esha Ness, *U.K.* **12 A7** 60 29N 1 38W
Esher, *U.K.* **11 F7** 51 21N 0 20W
Eshowe, *S. Africa* **57 D5** 28 50S 31 30 E
Esil ⟶ = Ishim ⟶, *Russia* **26 D8** 57 45N 71 10 E
Esk ⟶, *Cumb., U.K.* **12 G5** 54 58N 3 2W
Esk ⟶, *N. Yorks., U.K.* **10 C7** 54 30N 0 37W
Eskifjörður, *Iceland* **8 D7** 65 3N 13 55W
Eskilstuna, *Sweden* **9 G17** 59 22N 16 32 E
Eskimo Pt., *Canada* **73 A10** 61 10N 94 15W
Eskişehir, *Turkey* **25 G5** 39 50N 30 30 E
Esla ⟶, *Spain* **19 B2** 41 29N 6 3W
Eslamābād-e Gharb, *Iran* **44 C5** 34 10N 46 30 E
Eşme, *Turkey* **21 E13** 38 23N 28 58 E
Esmeraldas, *Ecuador* **92 C3** 1 0N 79 40W
Espanola, *Canada* **70 C3** 46 15N 81 46W
Esparta, *Costa Rica* **88 E3** 9 59N 84 40W
Esperance, *Australia* **61 F3** 33 45S 121 55 E
Esperance B., *Australia* **61 F3** 33 48S 121 55 E
Esperanza, *Argentina* **94 C3** 31 29S 61 3W
Espichel, C., *Portugal* **19 C1** 38 22N 9 16W
Espigão, Serra do, *Brazil* **95 B5** 26 35S 50 30W
Espinazo, Sierra del = Espinhaço, Serra do, *Brazil* **93 G10** 17 30S 43 30W
Espinhaço, Serra do, *Brazil* **93 G10** 17 30S 43 30W
Espinilho, Serra do, *Brazil* **95 B5** 28 30S 55 0W
Espírito Santo □, *Brazil* **93 H10** 20 0S 40 45W
Espíritu Santo, B. del, *Mexico* **87 D7** 19 15N 87 0W
Espíritu Santo, I., *Mexico* **86 C2** 24 30N 110 23W
Espita, *Mexico* **87 C7** 21 1N 88 19W
Espoo, *Finland* **9 F21** 60 12N 24 40 E
Espungabera, *Mozam.* **57 C5** 20 29S 32 45 E
Esquel, *Argentina* **96 E2** 42 55S 71 20W
Esquina, *Argentina* **94 C4** 30 0S 59 30W
Essaouira, *Morocco* **50 B4** 31 32N 9 42W
Essebie, *Dem. Rep. of the Congo* **54 B3** 2 58N 30 40 E
Essen, *Belgium* **15 C4** 51 28N 4 28 E
Essen, *Germany* **16 C4** 51 28N 7 2 E
Essendon, Mt., *Australia* **61 E3** 25 0S 120 29 E
Essequibo ⟶, *Guyana* **92 B7** 6 50N 58 30W
Essex, *Canada* **78 D2** 42 10N 82 49W
Essex, *Calif., U.S.A.* **85 L11** 34 44N 115 15W
Essex, *N.Y., U.S.A.* **79 B11** 44 19N 73 21W
Essex □, *U.K.* **11 F8** 51 54N 0 27 E
Esslingen, *Germany* **16 D5** 48 44N 9 18 E
Estados, I. de Los, *Argentina* **96 G4** 54 40S 64 30W
Eşţahbānāt, *Iran* **45 D7** 29 8N 54 4 E
Estallenchs, *Spain* **22 B9** 39 39N 2 29 E
Estância, *Brazil* **93 F11** 11 16S 37 26W
Estancia, *U.S.A.* **83 J10** 34 46N 106 4W
Estārm, *Iran* **45 D8** 28 21N 58 21 E
Estcourt, *S. Africa* **57 D4** 29 0S 29 53 E
Estelí, *Nic.* **88 D2** 13 9N 86 22W
Estelline, *S. Dak., U.S.A.* **80 C6** 44 35N 96 54W
Estelline, *Tex., U.S.A.* **81 H4** 34 33N 100 26W
Esterhazy, *Canada* **73 C8** 50 37N 102 5W
Estevan, *Canada* **73 D8** 49 10N 102 59W
Estevan Group, *Canada* **72 C3** 53 3N 129 38W
Estherville, *U.S.A.* **80 D7** 43 24N 94 50W
Eston, *Canada* **73 C7** 51 8N 108 40W
Estonia ■, *Europe* **24 C4** 58 30N 25 30 E
Estreito, *Brazil* **93 E9** 6 32S 47 25W
Estrela, Serra da, *Portugal* **19 B2** 40 10N 7 45W
Estremoz, *Portugal* **19 C2** 38 51N 7 39W
Estrondo, Serra do, *Brazil* **93 E9** 7 20S 48 0W
Esztergom, *Hungary* **17 E10** 47 47N 18 44 E
Etadunna, *Australia* **63 D2** 28 43S 138 38 E
Etah, *India* **43 F8** 27 35N 78 40 E
Étamamu, *Canada* **71 B8** 50 18N 59 59W
Étampes, *France* **18 B5** 48 26N 2 10 E
Etanga, *Namibia* **56 B1** 17 55S 13 0 E
Etawah, *India* **43 F8** 26 48N 79 6 E
Etawah ⟶, *U.S.A.* **77 H3** 34 20N 84 15W
Etawney L., *Canada* **73 B9** 57 50N 96 50W
Ethel, *U.S.A.* **84 D4** 46 32N 122 46W
Ethel Creek, *Australia* **60 D3** 22 55S 120 11 E
Ethelbert, *Canada* **73 C8** 51 32N 100 25W
Ethiopia ■, *Africa* **46 F3** 8 0N 40 0 E
Ethiopian Highlands, *Ethiopia* **28 J7** 10 0N 37 0 E
Etive, L., *U.K.* **12 E3** 56 29N 5 10W
Etna, *Italy* **20 F6** 37 50N 14 55 E
Etoile, *Dem. Rep. of the Congo* **55 E2** 11 33S 27 30 E
Etolin I., *U.S.A.* **72 B2** 56 5N 132 20W
Etosha Pan, *Namibia* **56 B2** 18 40S 16 30 E
Etowah, *U.S.A.* **77 H3** 35 20N 84 32W
Ettelbruck, *Lux.* **15 E6** 49 51N 6 5 E
Ettrick Water ⟶, *U.K.* **12 F6** 55 31N 2 55W
Etuku, *Dem. Rep. of the Congo* **54 C2** 3 42S 25 45 E
Etzatlán, *Mexico* **86 C4** 20 48N 104 5W
Euboea = Évvoia, *Greece* **21 E11** 38 30N 24 0 E
Eucla Motel, *Australia* **61 F4** 31 41S 128 52 E
Euclid, *U.S.A.* **78 E3** 41 34N 81 32W
Eucumbene, L., *Australia* **63 F4** 36 2S 148 40 E
Eudora, *U.S.A.* **81 J9** 33 7N 91 16W
Eufaula, *Ala., U.S.A.* **77 K3** 31 54N 85 9W
Eufaula, *Okla., U.S.A.* **81 H7** 35 17N 95 35W
Eufaula L., *U.S.A.* **81 H7** 35 18N 95 21W
Eugene, *U.S.A.* **82 E2** 44 5N 123 4W
Eugowra, *Australia* **63 E4** 33 22S 148 24 E
Eulo, *Australia* **63 D4** 28 10S 145 3 E
Eunice, *La., U.S.A.* **81 K8** 30 30N 92 25W
Eunice, *N. Mex., U.S.A.* **81 J3** 32 26N 103 10W
Eupen, *Belgium* **15 D6** 50 37N 6 3 E
Euphrates = Furāt, Nahr al ⟶, *Asia* **44 D5** 31 0N 47 25 E
Eureka, *Calif., U.S.A.* **82 F1** 40 47N 124 9W
Eureka, *Kans., U.S.A.* **81 G6** 37 49N 96 17W
Eureka, *Mont., U.S.A.* **82 B6** 48 53N 115 3W
Eureka, *Nev., U.S.A.* **82 G5** 39 31N 115 58W
Eureka, *S. Dak., U.S.A.* **80 C5** 45 46N 99 38W
Eureka, *Utah, U.S.A.* **82 G7** 39 58N 112 7W
Eureka, Mt., *Australia* **61 E3** 26 35S 121 35 E
Euroa, *Australia* **63 F4** 36 44S 145 35 E
Europa, *Île, Ind. Oc.* **53 J8** 22 20S 40 22 E
Europa, Picos de, *Spain* **19 A3** 43 10N 4 49W
Europa, Pta. de, *Gib.* **19 D3** 36 3N 5 21W
Europoort, *Neths.* **15 C4** 51 57N 4 10 E
Eustis, *U.S.A.* **77 L5** 28 51N 81 41W
Eutsuk L., *Canada* **72 C3** 53 20N 126 45W
Eva Downs, *Australia* **62 B1** 18 1S 134 52 E
Evale, *Angola* **56 B2** 16 33S 15 44 E
Evans, *U.S.A.* **80 E2** 40 23N 104 41W
Evans Head, *Australia* **63 D5** 29 7S 153 27 E
Evans L., *Canada* **70 B4** 50 50N 77 0W
Evans Mills, *U.S.A.* **79 B9** 44 6N 75 48W
Evanston, *Ill., U.S.A.* **76 E2** 42 3N 87 41W
Evanston, *Wyo., U.S.A.* **82 F8** 41 16N 110 58W
Evansville, *Ind., U.S.A.* **76 G2** 37 58N 87 35W
Evansville, *Wis., U.S.A.* **80 D10** 42 47N 89 18W
Evaz, *Iran* **45 E7** 27 46N 53 59 E
Eveleth, *U.S.A.* **80 B8** 47 28N 92 32W
Evensk, *Russia* **27 C16** 62 12N 159 30 E
Everard, L., *Australia* **63 E2** 31 30S 135 0 E
Everard Park, *Australia* **61 E5** 27 5S 132 43 E
Everard Ranges, *Australia* **61 E5** 27 5S 132 28 E
Everest, Mt., *Nepal* **43 E12** 28 5N 86 58 E
Everett, *Pa., U.S.A.* **78 F6** 40 1N 78 23W
Everett, *Wash., U.S.A.* **84 C4** 47 59N 122 12W
Everglades, The, *U.S.A.* **77 N5** 25 50N 81 0W
Everglades City, *U.S.A.* **77 N5** 25 52N 81 23W
Everglades National Park, *U.S.A.* **77 N5** 25 30N 81 0W
Evergreen, *U.S.A.* **77 K2** 31 26N 86 57W
Everson, *U.S.A.* **82 B2** 48 57N 122 22W
Evesham, *U.K.* **11 E6** 52 6N 1 56W
Evje, *Norway* **9 G12** 58 36N 7 51 E
Évora, *Portugal* **19 C2** 38 33N 7 57W
Evowghlī, *Iran* **44 B5** 38 43N 45 13 E
Évreux, *France* **18 B4** 49 3N 1 8 E
Évros ⟶, *Bulgaria* **21 D12** 41 40N 26 34 E
Évry, *France* **18 B5** 48 38N 2 27 E
Évvoia, *Greece* **21 E11** 38 30N 24 0 E
Ewe, L., *U.K.* **12 D3** 57 49N 5 38W
Ewing, *U.S.A.* **80 D5** 42 16N 98 21W
Ewo, *Congo* **52 E2** 0 48S 14 45 E
Exaltación, *Bolivia* **92 F5** 13 10S 65 20W
Excelsior Springs, *U.S.A.* **80 F7** 39 20N 94 13W
Exe ⟶, *U.K.* **11 G4** 50 41N 3 29W
Exeter, *Canada* **78 C3** 43 21N 81 29W
Exeter, *U.K.* **11 G4** 50 43N 3 31W
Exeter, *Calif., U.S.A.* **84 J7** 36 18N 119 9W
Exeter, *N.H., U.S.A.* **79 D14** 42 59N 70 57W
Exeter, *Nebr., U.S.A.* **80 E6** 40 39N 97 27W
Exmoor, *U.K.* **11 F4** 51 12N 3 45W
Exmouth, *Australia* **60 D1** 21 54S 114 10 E
Exmouth, *U.K.* **11 G4** 50 37N 3 25W
Exmouth G., *Australia* **60 D1** 22 15S 114 15 E
Expedition Ra., *Australia* **62 C4** 24 30S 149 12 E
Extremadura □, *Spain* **19 C2** 39 30N 6 5W
Exuma Sound, *Bahamas* **88 B4** 24 30N 76 20W
Eyasi, L., *Tanzania* **54 C4** 3 30S 35 0 E
Eye Pen., *U.K.* **12 C2** 58 13N 6 10W
Eyeberry L., *Canada* **73 A8** 63 8N 104 43W
Eyemouth, *U.K.* **12 F6** 55 52N 2 5W
Eyjafjörður, *Iceland* **8 C4** 66 15N 18 30W
Eyre, *Australia* **61 F4** 32 15S 126 18 E
Eyre (North), L., *Australia* **63 D2** 28 30S 137 20 E
Eyre (South), L., *Australia* **63 D2** 29 18S 137 25 E
Eyre Cr. ⟶, *Australia* **63 D2** 26 40S 139 0 E
Eyre Mts., *N.Z.* **59 L2** 45 25S 168 25 E
Eyre Pen., *Australia* **63 E2** 33 30S 136 17 E
Eysturoy, *Fœroe Is.* **8 E9** 62 13N 6 54W
Eyvānkī, *Iran* **45 C6** 35 24N 51 56 E
Ezine, *Turkey* **21 E12** 39 48N 26 20 E
Ezouza ⟶, *Cyprus* **23 E11** 34 44N 32 27 E

F

F.Y.R.O.M. = Macedonia ■, *Europe* **21 D9** 41 53N 21 40 E
Fabens, *U.S.A.* **83 L10** 31 30N 106 10W
Fabriano, *Italy* **20 C5** 43 20N 12 54 E
Fachi, *Niger* **51 E8** 18 6N 11 34 E
Fada, *Chad* **51 E10** 17 13N 21 34 E
Fada-n-Gourma, *Burkina Faso* **50 F6** 12 10N 0 30 E
Faddeyevskiy, Ostrov, *Russia* **27 B15** 76 0N 144 0 E
Fadghāmī, *Syria* **44 C4** 35 53N 40 52 E
Faenza, *Italy* **20 B4** 44 17N 11 53 E
Færoe Is. = Føroyar, *Atl. Oc.* **8 F9** 62 0N 7 0W
Făgăras, *Romania* **17 F13** 45 48N 24 58 E
Fagersta, *Sweden* **9 F16** 60 1N 15 46 E
Fagnano, L., *Argentina* **96 G3** 54 30S 68 0W
Fahlīān, *Iran* **45 D6** 30 11N 51 28 E
Fahraj, *Kermān, Iran* **45 D8** 29 0N 59 0 E
Fahraj, *Yazd, Iran* **45 D7** 31 46N 54 36 E
Faial, *Madeira* **22 D3** 32 47N 16 53W
Fair Hd., *U.K.* **13 A5** 55 14N 6 9W
Fair Oaks, *U.S.A.* **84 G5** 38 39N 121 16W
Fairbank, *U.S.A.* **83 L8** 31 43N 110 11W
Fairbanks, *U.S.A.* **68 B5** 64 51N 147 43W
Fairbury, *U.S.A.* **80 E6** 40 8N 97 11W
Fairfax, *U.S.A.* **81 G6** 36 34N 96 42W
Fairfield, *Ala., U.S.A.* **77 J2** 33 29N 86 55W
Fairfield, *Calif., U.S.A.* **84 G4** 38 15N 122 3W
Fairfield, *Conn., U.S.A.* **79 E11** 41 9N 73 16W
Fairfield, *Idaho, U.S.A.* **82 E6** 43 21N 114 44W
Fairfield, *Ill., U.S.A.* **76 F1** 38 23N 88 22W
Fairfield, *Iowa, U.S.A.* **80 E9** 40 56N 91 57W
Fairfield, *Mont., U.S.A.* **82 C8** 47 37N 111 59W
Fairfield, *Tex., U.S.A.* **81 K7** 31 44N 96 10W
Fairford, *Canada* **73 C9** 51 37N 98 38W
Fairhope, *U.S.A.* **77 K2** 30 31N 87 54W
Fairlie, *N.Z.* **59 L3** 44 5S 170 49 E
Fairmead, *U.S.A.* **84 H6** 37 5N 120 10W
Fairmont, *Minn., U.S.A.* **80 D7** 43 39N 94 28W
Fairmont, *W. Va., U.S.A.* **76 F5** 39 29N 80 9W
Fairmount, *U.S.A.* **85 L8** 34 45N 118 26W
Fairplay, *U.S.A.* **83 G11** 39 15N 106 2W
Fairport, *U.S.A.* **78 C7** 43 6N 77 27W
Fairport Harbor, *U.S.A.* **78 E3** 41 45N 81 17W
Fairview, *Australia* **62 B3** 15 31S 144 17 E
Fairview, *Canada* **72 B5** 56 5N 118 25W
Fairview, *Mont., U.S.A.* **80 B2** 47 51N 104 3W
Fairview, *Okla., U.S.A.* **81 G5** 36 16N 98 29W
Fairview, *Utah, U.S.A.* **82 G8** 39 50N 111 0W
Fairweather, Mt., *U.S.A.* **68 C6** 58 55N 137 32W
Faisalabad, *Pakistan* **42 D5** 31 30N 73 5 E
Faith, *U.S.A.* **80 C3** 45 2N 102 2W
Faizabad, *India* **43 F10** 26 45N 82 10 E
Fajardo, *Puerto Rico* **89 C6** 18 20N 65 39W
Fakenham, *U.K.* **10 E8** 52 51N 0 51 E
Fakfak, *Indonesia* **37 E8** 3 0S 132 15 E
Faku, *China* **35 C12** 42 32N 123 21 E
Falaise, *France* **18 B3** 48 54N 0 12W
Falaise, Mui, *Vietnam* **38 C5** 19 6N 105 45 E
Falam, *Burma* **41 H18** 23 0N 93 45 E
Falcón, C., *Spain* **22 C7** 38 50N 1 23 E
Falcon Dam, *U.S.A.* **81 M5** 26 50N 99 20W
Falconara Marittima, *Italy* **20 C5** 43 37N 13 24 E
Falcone, C. del, *Italy* **20 D3** 40 58N 8 12 E
Falconer, *U.S.A.* **78 D5** 42 7N 79 13W
Faleshty = Făleşti, *Moldova* **17 E14** 47 32N 27 44 E
Făleşti, *Moldova* **17 E14** 47 32N 27 44 E
Falfurrias, *U.S.A.* **81 M5** 27 14N 98 9W
Falher, *Canada* **72 B5** 55 44N 117 15W
Faliraki, *Greece* **23 C10** 36 22N 28 12 E
Falkenberg, *Sweden* **9 H15** 56 54N 12 30 E
Falkirk, *U.K.* **12 F5** 56 0N 3 47W
Falkirk □, *U.K.* **12 F5** 55 58N 3 49W
Falkland, *U.K.* **12 E5** 56 16N 3 12W
Falkland Is. □, *Atl. Oc.* **96 G5** 51 30S 59 0W
Falkland Sd., *Falk. Is.* **96 G5** 52 0S 60 0W
Falköping, *Sweden* **9 G15** 58 12N 13 33 E
Fall River, *U.S.A.* **79 E13** 41 43N 71 10W
Fall River Mills, *U.S.A.* **82 F3** 41 3N 121 26W
Fallbrook, *U.S.A.* **83 K5** 33 25N 117 12W
Fallbrook, *Calif., U.S.A.* **85 M9** 33 23N 117 15W
Fallon, *Mont., U.S.A.* **80 B2** 46 50N 105 8W
Fallon, *Nev., U.S.A.* **82 G4** 39 28N 118 47W
Falls City, *Nebr., U.S.A.* **80 E7** 40 3N 95 36W
Falls City, *Oreg., U.S.A.* **82 D2** 44 52N 123 26W
Falls Creek, *U.S.A.* **78 E6** 41 9N 78 48W
Falmouth, *Jamaica* **88 C4** 18 30N 77 40W
Falmouth, *U.K.* **11 G2** 50 9N 5 5W
Falmouth, *U.S.A.* **76 F3** 38 41N 84 20W
False B., *S. Africa* **56 E2** 34 15S 18 40 E
Falso, C., *Honduras* **88 C3** 15 12N 83 21W
Falster, *Denmark* **9 J14** 54 45N 11 55 E
Falsterbo, *Sweden* **9 J15** 55 23N 12 50 E
Fălticeni, *Romania* **17 E14** 47 21N 26 20 E
Falun, *Sweden* **9 F16** 60 37N 15 37 E
Famagusta, *Cyprus* **23 D12** 35 8N 33 55 E
Famagusta Bay, *Cyprus* **23 D13** 35 15N 34 0 E
Famatina, Sierra de, *Argentina* **94 B2** 27 30S 68 0W
Family L., *Canada* **73 C9** 51 54N 95 27W
Famoso, *U.S.A.* **85 K7** 35 37N 119 12W
Fan Xian, *China* **34 G8** 35 55N 115 38 E
Fanad Hd., *Ireland* **13 A4** 55 17N 7 38W
Fandriana, *Madag.* **57 C8** 20 14S 47 21 E
Fang, *Thailand* **38 C2** 19 55N 99 13 E
Fangcheng, *China* **34 H7** 33 18N 112 59 E
Fangshan, *China* **34 E6** 38 3N 111 25 E
Fangzi, *China* **35 F10** 36 33N 119 10 E
Fanjiatun, *China* **35 C13** 43 40N 125 15 E
Fannich, L., *U.K.* **12 D4** 57 38N 4 59W
Fannūj, *Iran* **45 E8** 26 35N 59 38 E
Fanny Bay, *Canada* **72 D4** 49 37N 124 48W
Fanø, *Denmark* **9 J13** 55 25N 8 25 E
Fano, *Italy* **20 C5** 43 50N 13 1 E
Fanshaw, *U.S.A.* **72 B2** 57 11N 133 30W
Fanshi, *China* **34 E7** 39 12N 113 20 E
Fao = Al Fāw, *Iraq* **45 D6** 30 0N 48 30 E
Faqirwali, *Pakistan* **42 E5** 29 27N 73 0 E
Faradje, *Dem. Rep. of the Congo* **54 B2** 3 50N 29 45 E
Farafangana, *Madag.* **57 C8** 22 49S 47 50 E
Farāh, *Afghan.* **40 C3** 32 20N 62 7 E
Farāh □, *Afghan.* **40 C3** 32 25N 62 10 E
Farahalana, *Madag.* **57 A9** 14 26S 50 10 E
Faranah, *Guinea* **50 F3** 10 3N 10 45W
Farasān, Jazā'ir, *Si. Arabia* **46 D3** 16 45N 41 55 E
Farasan Is. = Farasān, Jazā'ir, *Si. Arabia* **46 D3** 16 45N 41 55 E
Faratsiho, *Madag.* **57 B8** 19 24S 46 57 E
Fareham, *U.K.* **11 G6** 50 51N 1 11W
Farewell, C., *N.Z.* **59 J4** 40 29S 172 43 E
Farewell C. = Farvel, Kap, *Greenland* **66 D15** 59 48N 43 55W
Farghona, *Uzbekistan* **26 E8** 40 23N 71 19 E
Fargo, *U.S.A.* **80 B6** 46 53N 96 48W
Fār'iah, W. al ⟶, *West Bank* **47 C4** 32 12N 35 27 E
Faribault, *U.S.A.* **80 C8** 44 18N 93 16W
Faridkot, *India* **42 D6** 30 44N 74 45 E
Faridpur, *Bangla.* **43 H13** 23 15N 89 55 E
Farīmān, *Iran* **45 C8** 35 40N 59 49 E
Farina, *Australia* **63 E2** 30 3S 138 15 E
Fariones, Pta., *Canary Is.* **22 E6** 29 13N 13 28W
Farmerville, *U.S.A.* **81 J8** 32 47N 92 24W
Farmington, *Calif., U.S.A.* **84 H6** 37 55N 120 59W
Farmington, *N.H., U.S.A.* **79 C13** 43 24N 71 4W
Farmington, *N. Mex., U.S.A.* **83 H9** 36 44N 108 12W
Farmington, *Utah, U.S.A.* **82 F8** 41 0N 111 12W
Farmington ⟶, *U.S.A.* **79 E12** 41 51N 72 38W
Farmville, *U.S.A.* **76 G6** 37 18N 78 24W
Farne Is., *U.K.* **10 B6** 55 38N 1 37W
Farnham, *Canada* **79 A12** 45 17N 72 59W
Faro, *Brazil* **93 D7** 2 10S 56 39W
Faro, *Portugal* **19 D2** 37 2N 7 55W
Fårö, *Sweden* **9 H18** 57 55N 19 5 E
Farquhar, C., *Australia* **61 D1** 23 50S 113 36 E
Farrars Cr. ⟶, *Australia* **62 D3** 25 35S 140 43 E
Farrāshband, *Iran* **45 D7** 28 57N 52 5 E
Farrell, *U.S.A.* **78 E4** 41 13N 80 30W
Farrell Flat, *Australia* **63 E2** 33 48S 138 48 E
Farrokhī, *Iran* **45 C8** 33 50N 59 31 E
Farruch, C., *Spain* **22 B10** 39 47N 3 21 E
Farrukhabad-cum-Fatehgarh, *India* **43 F8** 27 30N 79 32 E
Fārs □, *Iran* **45 D7** 29 30N 55 0 E
Fársala, *Greece* **21 E10** 39 17N 22 23 E
Farsund, *Norway* **9 G12** 58 5N 6 55 E
Fartak, Râs, *Si. Arabia* **44 D2** 28 5N 34 34 E
Fartura, Serra da, *Brazil* **95 B5** 26 21S 52 52W
Fārūj, *Iran* **45 B8** 37 14N 58 14 E
Farvel, Kap, *Greenland* **66 D15** 59 48N 43 55W
Farwell, *U.S.A.* **81 H3** 34 23N 103 2W
Fasā, *Iran* **45 D7** 29 0N 53 39 E
Fasano, *Italy* **20 D7** 40 50N 17 22 E
Fastiv, *Ukraine* **17 C15** 50 7N 29 57 E
Fastov = Fastiv, *Ukraine* **17 C15** 50 7N 29 57 E
Fatagar, Tanjung, *Indonesia* **37 E8** 2 46S 131 57 E
Fatehgarh, *India* **43 F8** 27 25N 79 35 E
Fatehpur, *Raj., India* **42 F6** 28 0N 74 40 E
Fatehpur, *Ut. P., India* **43 G9** 25 56N 81 13 E
Fatima, *Canada* **71 C7** 47 24N 61 53W
Faulkton, *U.S.A.* **80 C5** 45 2N 99 8W
Faure I., *Australia* **61 E1** 25 52S 113 50 E
Fauresmith, *S. Africa* **56 D4** 29 44S 25 17 E
Fauske, *Norway* **8 C16** 67 17N 15 25 E
Favara, *Italy* **20 F5** 37 19N 13 39 E
Favaritx, C., *Spain* **22 B11** 40 0N 4 15 E
Favignana, *Italy* **20 F5** 37 56N 12 20 E
Favourable Lake, *Canada* **70 B1** 52 50N 93 39W
Fawn ⟶, *Canada* **70 A2** 55 20N 87 35W
Fawnskin, *U.S.A.* **85 L10** 34 16N 116 56W
Faxaflói, *Iceland* **8 D2** 64 29N 23 0W
Faya-Largeau, *Chad* **51 E9** 17 58N 19 6 E
Fayd, *Si. Arabia* **44 E4** 27 1N 42 52 E
Fayette, *Ala., U.S.A.* **77 J2** 33 41N 87 50W

Fayette

Fayette, Mo., U.S.A. 80 F8 39 9N 92 41W
Fayetteville, Ark., U.S.A. 81 G7 36 4N 94 10W
Fayetteville, N.C., U.S.A. 77 H6 35 3N 78 53W
Fayetteville, Tenn., U.S.A. 77 H2 35 9N 86 34W
Fazilka, India 42 D6 30 27N 74 2 E
Fazilpur, Pakistan 42 E4 29 18N 70 29 E
Fdérik, Mauritania 50 D3 22 40N 12 45W
Feale →, Ireland 13 D2 52 27N 9 37W
Fear, C., U.S.A. 77 J7 33 50N 77 58W
Feather →, U.S.A. 82 G3 38 47N 121 36W
Feather Falls, U.S.A. 84 F5 39 36N 121 16W
Featherston, N.Z. 59 J5 41 6S 175 20 E
Featherstone, Zimbabwe 55 F3 18 42S 30 55 E
Fécamp, France 18 B4 49 45N 0 22 E
Federación, Argentina 94 C4 31 0S 57 55W
Féderal, Argentina 96 C5 30 57S 58 48W
Fedeshkūh, Iran 45 D7 28 49N 53 50 E
Fehmarn, Germany 16 A6 54 27N 11 7 E
Fehmarn Bælt, Europe 9 J14 54 35N 11 20 E
Fehmarn Belt = Fehmarn Bælt, Europe 9 J14 54 35N 11 20 E
Fei Xian, China 35 G9 35 18N 117 59 E
Feijó, Brazil 92 E4 8 9S 70 21W
Feilding, N.Z. 59 J5 40 13S 175 35 E
Feira de Santana, Brazil 93 F11 12 15S 38 57W
Feixiang, China 34 F8 36 30N 114 45 E
Felanitx, Spain 22 B10 39 28N 3 9 E
Feldkirch, Austria 16 E5 47 15N 9 37 E
Felipe Carrillo Puerto, Mexico 87 D7 19 38N 88 3W
Felixstowe, U.K. 11 F9 51 58N 1 23 E
Felton, U.S.A. 84 H4 37 3N 122 4W
Femer Bælt = Fehmarn Bælt, Europe 9 J14 54 35N 11 20 E
Femunden, Norway 9 E14 62 10N 11 53 E
Fen He →, China 34 G6 35 36N 110 42 E
Fenelon Falls, Canada 78 B6 44 32N 78 45W
Feng Xian, Jiangsu, China 34 G9 34 43N 116 35 E
Feng Xian, Shaanxi, China 34 H4 33 54N 106 40 E
Fengcheng, China 35 D13 40 28N 124 5 E
Fengfeng, China 34 F8 36 28N 114 8 E
Fengjie, China 33 C5 31 5N 109 36 E
Fengning, China 34 D9 41 10N 116 33 E
Fengqiu, China 34 G8 35 2N 114 25 E
Fengrun, China 35 E10 39 48N 118 8 E
Fengtai, China 34 E9 39 50N 116 18 E
Fengxiang, China 34 G4 34 29N 107 25 E
Fengyang, China 35 H9 32 51N 117 29 E
Fengzhen, China 34 D7 40 25N 113 2 E
Fennimore, U.S.A. 80 D9 42 59N 90 39W
Fenoarivo Afovoany, Madag. 57 B8 18 26S 46 34 E
Fenoarivo Atsinanana, Madag. 57 B8 17 22S 49 25 E
Fens, The, U.K. 10 E7 52 38N 0 2W
Fenton, U.S.A. 76 D4 42 48N 83 42W
Fenxi, China 34 F6 36 40N 111 31 E
Fenyang, China 34 F6 37 18N 111 48 E
Feodosiya, Ukraine 25 E6 45 2N 35 16 E
Ferdows, Iran 45 C8 33 58N 58 2 E
Ferfer, Somali Rep. 46 F4 5 4N 45 9 E
Fergana = Farghona, Uzbekistan 26 E8 40 23N 71 19 E
Fergus, Canada 70 D3 43 43N 80 24W
Fergus Falls, U.S.A. 80 B6 46 17N 96 4W
Ferland, Canada 70 B2 50 19N 88 27W
Fermanagh □, U.K. 13 B4 54 21N 7 40W
Fermo, Italy 20 C5 43 9N 13 43 E
Fermoy, Ireland 13 D3 52 9N 8 16W
Fernández, Argentina 94 B3 27 55S 63 50W
Fernandina Beach, U.S.A. 77 K5 30 40N 81 27W
Fernando de Noronha, Brazil 93 D12 4 0S 33 10W
Fernando Póo = Bioko, Eq. Guin. 52 D1 3 30N 8 40 E
Ferndale, Calif., U.S.A. 82 F1 40 35N 124 16W
Ferndale, Wash., U.S.A. 84 B4 48 51N 122 36W
Fernie, Canada 72 D5 49 30N 115 5W
Fernlees, Australia 62 C4 23 51S 148 7 E
Fernley, U.S.A. 82 G4 39 36N 119 15W
Ferozepore = Firozpur, India 42 D6 30 55N 74 40 E
Ferrara, Italy 20 B4 44 50N 11 35 E
Ferreñafe, Peru 92 E3 6 42S 79 50W
Ferrerías, Spain 22 B11 39 59N 4 1 E
Ferret, C., France 18 D3 44 38N 1 15W
Ferriday, U.S.A. 81 K9 31 38N 91 33W
Ferrol, Spain 19 A1 43 29N 8 15W
Ferron, U.S.A. 83 G8 39 5N 111 8W
Ferryland, Canada 71 C9 47 2N 52 53W
Fertile, U.S.A. 80 B6 47 32N 96 17W
Fès, Morocco 50 B5 34 0N 5 0W
Fessenden, U.S.A. 80 B5 47 39N 99 38W
Feteşti, Romania 17 F14 44 22N 27 51 E
Fetlar, U.K. 12 A8 60 36N 0 52W
Feuilles →, Canada 69 C12 58 47N 70 4W
Fezzan, Libya 51 C8 27 0N 13 0 E
Fiambalá, Argentina 94 B2 27 45S 67 37W
Fianarantsoa, Madag. 57 C8 21 26S 47 5 E
Fianarantsoa □, Madag. 57 B8 19 30S 47 0 E
Ficksburg, S. Africa 57 D4 28 51S 27 53 E
Field, Canada 70 C3 46 31N 80 1W
Field →, Australia 62 C2 23 48S 138 0 E
Field I., Australia 60 B5 12 5S 132 23 E
Fieri, Albania 21 D8 40 43N 19 33 E
Fife □, U.K. 12 E5 56 16N 3 1W
Fife Ness, U.K. 12 E6 56 17N 2 35W
Figeac, France 18 D5 44 37N 2 2 E
Figtree, Zimbabwe 55 G2 20 22S 28 20 E
Figueira da Foz, Portugal 19 B1 40 7N 8 54W
Figueres, Spain 19 A7 42 18N 2 58 E
Figuig, Morocco 50 B5 32 5N 1 11W
Fihaonana, Madag. 57 B8 18 36S 47 12 E
Fiherenana, Madag. 57 B8 18 29S 48 24 E
Fiherenana →, Madag. 57 C7 23 19S 43 37 E
Fiji ■, Pac. Oc. 59 C8 17 20S 179 0 E
Filer, U.S.A. 82 E6 42 34N 114 37W
Filey, U.K. 10 C7 54 12N 0 18W
Filey B., U.K. 10 C7 54 12N 0 15W
Filfla, Malta 23 D1 35 47N 14 24 E
Filiatrá, Greece 21 F9 37 9N 21 35 E
Filingué, Niger 50 F6 14 21N 3 22 E
Filipstad, Sweden 9 G16 59 43N 14 9 E
Fillmore, Canada 73 D8 49 50N 103 25W
Fillmore, Calif., U.S.A. 85 L8 34 24N 118 55W
Fillmore, Utah, U.S.A. 83 G7 38 58N 112 20W
Finch, Canada 79 A9 45 11N 75 7W
Findhorn →, U.K. 12 D5 57 38N 3 38W
Findlay, U.S.A. 76 E4 41 2N 83 39W
Finger L., Canada 73 C10 53 33N 93 30W
Fíngoè, Mozam. 55 E3 14 55S 31 50 E
Finisterre, C. = Fisterra, C., Spain 19 A1 42 50N 9 19W
Finke, Australia 62 D1 25 34S 134 35 E
Finke →, Australia 63 D2 27 0S 136 10 E
Finland ■, Europe 24 B4 63 0N 27 0 E
Finland, G. of, Europe 24 C4 60 0N 26 0 E
Finlay →, Canada 72 B3 57 0N 125 10W
Finley, Australia 63 F4 35 38S 145 35 E
Finley, U.S.A. 80 B6 47 31N 97 50W
Finn →, Ireland 13 B4 54 51N 7 28W
Finnigan, Mt., Australia 62 B4 15 49S 145 17 E
Finniss, C., Australia 63 E1 33 8S 134 51 E
Finnmark, Norway 8 B20 69 37N 23 57 E
Finnsnes, Norway 8 B18 69 14N 18 0 E
Finspång, Sweden 9 G16 58 43N 15 47 E
Fiora →, Italy 20 C4 42 20N 11 34 E
Fiq, Syria 47 C4 32 46N 35 41 E
Firat = Furāt, Nahr al →, Asia 44 D5 31 0N 47 25 E
Fire River, Canada 70 C3 48 47N 83 21W
Firebag →, Canada 73 B6 57 45N 111 21W
Firebaugh, U.S.A. 84 J6 36 52N 120 27W
Firedrake L., Canada 73 A8 61 25N 104 30W
Firenze, Italy 20 C4 43 46N 11 15 E
Firk →, Iraq 44 D5 30 59N 44 34 E
Firozabad, India 43 F8 27 10N 78 25 E
Firozpur, India 42 D6 30 55N 74 40 E
Fīrūzābād, Iran 45 D7 28 52N 52 35 E
Fīrūzkūh, Iran 45 C7 35 50N 52 50 E
Firvale, Canada 72 C3 52 27N 126 13W
Fish →, Namibia 56 D2 28 7S 17 10 E
Fish →, S. Africa 56 E3 31 30S 20 16 E
Fisher, Australia 61 F5 30 30S 131 0 E
Fisher B., Canada 73 C9 51 35N 97 13W
Fishguard, U.K. 11 E3 52 0N 4 58W
Fishing L., Canada 73 C9 52 10N 95 24W
Fisterra, C., Spain 19 A1 42 50N 9 19W
Fitchburg, U.S.A. 79 D13 42 35N 71 48W
Fitz Roy, Argentina 96 F3 47 0S 67 0W
Fitzgerald, Canada 72 B6 59 51N 111 36W
Fitzgerald, U.S.A. 77 K4 31 43N 83 15W
Fitzmaurice →, Australia 60 B5 14 45S 130 5 E
Fitzroy →, Queens., Australia 62 C5 23 32S 150 52 E
Fitzroy →, W. Austral., Australia 60 C3 17 31S 123 35 E
Fitzroy, Mte., Argentina 96 F2 49 17S 73 5W
Fitzroy Crossing, Australia 60 C4 18 9S 125 38 E
Fitzwilliam I., Canada 78 A3 45 30N 81 45W
Fiume = Rijeka, Croatia 16 F8 45 20N 14 21 E
Five Points, U.S.A. 84 J6 36 26N 120 6W
Fizi, Dem. Rep. of the Congo 54 C2 4 17S 28 55 E
Flagler, U.S.A. 80 F3 39 18N 103 4W
Flagstaff, U.S.A. 83 J8 35 12N 111 39W
Flaherty I., Canada 70 A4 56 15N 79 15W
Flåm, Norway 9 F12 60 50N 7 7 E
Flambeau →, U.S.A. 80 C9 45 18N 91 14W
Flamborough Hd., U.K. 10 C7 54 7N 0 5W
Flaming Gorge Dam, U.S.A. 82 F9 40 55N 109 25W
Flaming Gorge Reservoir, U.S.A. 82 F9 41 10N 109 25W
Flamingo, Teluk, Indonesia 37 F9 5 30S 138 0 E
Flanders = Flandre, Europe 18 A5 50 50N 2 30 E
Flandre, Europe 18 A5 50 50N 2 30 E
Flandre Occidentale = West-Vlaanderen □, Belgium 15 D2 51 0N 3 0 E
Flandre Orientale = Oost-Vlaanderen □, Belgium 15 C3 51 5N 3 50 E
Flandreau, U.S.A. 80 C6 44 3N 96 36W
Flanigan, U.S.A. 84 E7 40 10N 119 53W
Flannan Is., U.K. 12 C1 58 9N 7 52W
Flåsjön, Sweden 8 D16 64 5N 15 40 E
Flat →, Canada 72 A3 61 33N 125 18W
Flat River, U.S.A. 81 G9 37 51N 90 31W
Flathead L., U.S.A. 82 C7 47 51N 114 8W
Flattery, C., Australia 62 A4 14 58S 145 21 E
Flattery, C., U.S.A. 84 B2 48 23N 124 29W
Flaxton, U.S.A. 80 A3 48 54N 102 24W
Fleetwood, U.K. 10 D4 53 55N 3 1W
Flekkefjord, Norway 9 G12 58 18N 6 39 E
Flemington, U.S.A. 78 E7 41 7N 77 28W
Flensburg, Germany 16 A5 54 47N 9 27 E
Flers, France 18 B3 48 47N 0 33W
Flesherton, Canada 78 B4 44 16N 80 33W
Flesko, Tanjung, Indonesia 37 D6 0 29N 124 30 E
Flevoland □, Neths. 15 B5 52 30N 5 30 E
Flin Flon, Canada 73 C8 54 46N 101 53W
Flinders →, Australia 62 B3 17 36S 140 36 E
Flinders B., Australia 61 F2 34 19S 115 19 E
Flinders Group, Australia 62 A3 14 11S 144 15 E
Flinders I., Australia 62 G4 40 0S 148 0 E
Flinders Ranges, Australia 63 E2 31 30S 138 30 E
Flinders Reefs, Australia 62 B4 17 37S 148 31 E
Flint, U.K. 10 D4 53 15N 3 8W
Flint, U.S.A. 76 D4 43 1N 83 41W
Flint →, U.S.A. 77 K3 30 57N 84 34W
Flint I., Kiribati 65 J12 11 26S 151 48W
Flinton, Australia 63 D4 27 55S 149 32 E
Flintshire □, U.K. 10 D4 53 17N 3 17W
Flodden, U.K. 10 B5 55 37N 2 8W
Floodwood, U.S.A. 80 B8 46 55N 92 55W
Flora, U.S.A. 76 F1 38 40N 88 29W
Florala, U.S.A. 77 K2 31 0N 86 20W
Florence = Firenze, Italy 20 C4 43 46N 11 15 E
Florence, Ala., U.S.A. 77 H2 34 48N 87 41W
Florence, Ariz., U.S.A. 83 K8 33 2N 111 23W
Florence, Colo., U.S.A. 80 F2 38 23N 105 8W
Florence, Oreg., U.S.A. 82 E1 43 58N 124 7W
Florence, S.C., U.S.A. 77 H6 34 12N 79 46W
Florence, L., Australia 63 D2 28 53S 138 9 E
Florencia, Colombia 92 C3 1 36N 75 36W
Florennes, Belgium 15 D4 50 15N 4 35 E
Florenville, Belgium 15 E5 49 40N 5 19 E
Flores, Guatemala 88 C2 16 59N 89 50W
Flores, Indonesia 37 F6 8 35S 121 0 E
Flores I., Canada 72 D3 49 20N 126 10W
Flores Sea, Indonesia 37 F6 6 30S 120 0 E
Floreşti, Moldova 17 E15 47 53N 28 17 E
Floresville, U.S.A. 81 L5 29 8N 98 10W
Floriano, Brazil 93 E10 6 50S 43 0W
Florianópolis, Brazil 95 B6 27 30S 48 30W
Florida, Cuba 88 B4 21 32N 78 14W
Florida, Uruguay 95 C4 34 7S 56 10W
Florida □, U.S.A. 77 L5 28 0N 82 0W
Florida, Straits of, U.S.A. 88 B4 25 0N 80 0W
Florida B., U.S.A. 88 B3 25 0N 80 45W
Florida Keys, U.S.A. 75 F10 24 40N 81 0W
Flórina, Greece 21 D9 40 48N 21 26 E
Florø, Norway 9 F11 61 35N 5 1 E
Flower Station, Canada 79 A8 45 10N 76 41W
Flower's Cove, Canada 71 B8 51 14N 56 46W
Floydada, U.S.A. 81 J4 33 59N 101 20W
Fluk, Indonesia 37 E7 1 42S 127 44 E
Flushing = Vlissingen, Neths. 15 C3 51 26N 3 34 E
Flying Fish, C., Antarctica 5 D15 72 6S 102 29W
Foam Lake, Canada 73 C8 51 40N 103 32W
Foça, Turkey 21 E12 38 39N 26 46 E
Focşani, Romania 17 F14 45 41N 27 15 E
Fóggia, Italy 20 D6 41 27N 15 34 E
Fogo, Canada 71 C9 49 43N 54 17W
Fogo I., Canada 71 C9 49 40N 54 5W
Föhr, Germany 16 A5 54 43N 8 30 E
Foix, France 18 E4 42 58N 1 38 E
Folda, Nord-Trøndelag, Norway 8 D14 64 32N 10 30 E
Folda, Nordland, Norway 8 C16 67 38N 14 50 E
Foleyet, Canada 70 C3 48 15N 82 25W
Folgefonni, Norway 9 F12 60 3N 6 23 E
Foligno, Italy 20 C5 42 57N 12 42 E
Folkestone, U.K. 11 F9 51 5N 1 12 E
Folkston, U.S.A. 77 K5 30 50N 82 0W
Follett, U.S.A. 81 G4 36 26N 100 8W
Folsom Res., U.S.A. 84 G5 38 42N 121 9W
Fond-du-Lac, Canada 73 B7 59 19N 107 12W
Fond du Lac, U.S.A. 80 D10 43 47N 88 27W
Fond-du-Lac →, Canada 73 B7 59 17N 106 0W
Fonda, U.S.A. 79 D10 42 57N 74 22W
Fondi, Italy 20 D5 41 21N 13 25 E
Fonsagrada = A Fonsagrada, Spain 19 A2 43 8N 7 4W
Fonseca, G. de, Cent. Amer. 88 D2 13 10N 87 40W
Fontainebleau, France 18 B5 48 24N 2 40 E
Fontana, U.S.A. 85 L9 34 6N 117 26W
Fontas →, Canada 72 B4 58 14N 121 48W
Fonte Boa, Brazil 92 D5 2 33S 66 0W
Fontenay-le-Comte, France 18 C3 46 28N 0 48W
Fontur, Iceland 8 C6 66 23N 14 32W
Foochow = Fuzhou, China 33 D6 26 5N 119 16 E
Foping, China 34 H5 33 41N 108 0 E
Forbes, Australia 63 E4 33 22S 148 0 E
Forbesganj, India 43 F12 26 17N 87 18 E
Ford City, Calif., U.S.A. 85 K7 35 9N 119 27W
Ford City, Pa., U.S.A. 78 F5 40 46N 79 32W
Førde, Norway 9 F11 61 27N 5 53 E
Ford's Bridge, Australia 63 D4 29 41S 145 29 E
Fordyce, U.S.A. 81 J8 33 49N 92 25W
Forel, Mt., Greenland 66 C16 66 52N 36 55W
Foremost, Canada 72 D6 49 26N 111 34W
Forest, Canada 78 C3 43 6N 82 0W
Forest, U.S.A. 81 J10 32 22N 89 29W
Forest City, Iowa, U.S.A. 80 D8 43 16N 93 39W
Forest City, N.C., U.S.A. 77 H5 35 20N 81 52W
Forest City, Pa., U.S.A. 79 E9 41 39N 75 28W
Forest Grove, U.S.A. 84 E3 45 31N 123 7W
Forestburg, Canada 72 C6 52 35N 112 1W
Foresthill, U.S.A. 84 F6 39 1N 120 49W
Forestier Pen., Australia 62 G4 43 0S 148 0 E
Forestville, Canada 71 C6 48 48N 69 2W
Forestville, Calif., U.S.A. 84 G4 38 28N 122 54W
Forestville, Wis., U.S.A. 76 C2 44 41N 87 29W
Forfar, U.K. 12 E6 56 39N 2 53W
Forks, U.S.A. 84 C2 47 57N 124 23W
Forlì, Italy 20 B5 44 13N 12 3 E
Forman, U.S.A. 80 B6 46 7N 97 38W
Formby Pt., U.K. 10 D4 53 33N 3 6W
Formentera, Spain 22 C7 38 43N 1 27 E
Formentor, C. de, Spain 22 B10 39 58N 3 13 E
Former Yugoslav Republic of Macedonia = Macedonia ■, Europe 21 D9 41 53N 21 40 E
Fórmia, Italy 20 D5 41 15N 13 37 E
Formosa = Taiwan ■, Asia 33 D7 23 30N 121 0 E
Formosa, Argentina 94 B4 26 15S 58 10W
Formosa, Brazil 93 G9 15 32S 47 20W
Formosa □, Argentina 94 B4 25 0S 60 0W
Formosa, Serra, Brazil 93 F8 12 0S 55 0W
Formosa Bay, Kenya 54 C5 2 40S 40 20 E
Fornells, Spain 22 A11 40 3N 4 7 E
Føroyar, Atl. Oc. 8 F9 62 0N 7 0W
Forres, U.K. 12 D5 57 37N 3 37W
Forrest, Vic., Australia 63 F3 38 33S 143 47 E
Forrest, W. Austral., Australia 61 F4 30 51S 128 6 E
Forrest, Mt., Australia 61 D4 24 48S 127 45 E
Forrest City, U.S.A. 81 H9 35 1N 90 47W
Forsayth, Australia 62 B3 18 33S 143 34 E
Forssa, Finland 9 F20 60 49N 23 38 E
Forst, Germany 16 C8 51 45N 14 37 E
Forster, Australia 63 E5 32 12S 152 31 E
Forsyth, Ga., U.S.A. 77 J4 33 2N 83 56W
Forsyth, Mont., U.S.A. 82 C10 46 16N 106 41W
Fort Albany, Canada 70 B3 52 15N 81 35W
Fort Apache, U.S.A. 83 K9 33 50N 110 0W
Fort Assiniboine, Canada 72 C6 54 20N 114 45W
Fort Augustus, U.K. 12 D4 57 9N 4 42W
Fort Beaufort, S. Africa 56 E4 32 46S 26 40 E
Fort Benton, U.S.A. 82 C8 47 49N 110 40W
Fort Bragg, U.S.A. 82 G2 39 26N 123 48W
Fort Bridger, U.S.A. 82 F8 41 19N 110 23W
Fort Chipewyan, Canada 73 B6 58 42N 111 8W
Fort Collins, U.S.A. 80 E2 40 35N 105 5W
Fort-Coulonge, Canada 70 C4 45 50N 76 45W
Fort Davis, U.S.A. 81 K3 30 35N 103 54W
Fort-de-France, Martinique 89 D7 14 36N 61 2W
Fort Defiance, U.S.A. 83 J9 35 45N 109 5W
Fort Dodge, U.S.A. 80 D7 42 30N 94 11W
Fort Edward, U.S.A. 79 C11 43 16N 73 35W
Fort Frances, Canada 73 D10 48 36N 93 24W
Fort Garland, U.S.A. 83 H11 37 26N 105 26W
Fort George = Chisasibi, Canada 70 B4 53 50N 79 0W
Fort Good-Hope, Canada 68 B7 66 14N 128 40W
Fort Hancock, U.S.A. 83 L11 31 18N 105 51W
Fort Hertz = Putao, Burma 41 F20 27 28N 97 30 E
Fort Hope, Canada 70 B2 51 30N 88 0W
Fort Irwin, U.S.A. 85 K10 35 16N 116 34W
Fort Jameson = Chipata, Zambia 55 E3 13 38S 32 28 E
Fort Kent, U.S.A. 71 C6 47 15N 68 36W
Fort Klamath, U.S.A. 82 E3 42 42N 122 0W
Fort-Lamy = Ndjamena, Chad 51 F8 12 10N 14 59 E
Fort Laramie, U.S.A. 80 D2 42 13N 104 31W
Fort Lauderdale, U.S.A. 77 M5 26 7N 80 8W
Fort Liard, Canada 72 A4 60 14N 123 30W
Fort Liberté, Haiti 89 C5 19 42N 71 51W
Fort Lupton, U.S.A. 80 E2 40 5N 104 49W
Fort Mackay, Canada 72 B6 57 12N 111 41W
Fort McKenzie, Canada 71 A6 57 20N 69 0W
Fort Macleod, Canada 72 D6 49 45N 113 30W
Fort McMurray, Canada 72 B6 56 44N 111 7W
Fort McPherson, Canada 68 B6 67 30N 134 55W
Fort Madison, U.S.A. 80 E9 40 38N 91 27W
Fort Meade, U.S.A. 77 M5 27 45N 81 48W
Fort Morgan, U.S.A. 80 E3 40 15N 103 48W
Fort Myers, U.S.A. 77 M5 26 39N 81 52W
Fort Nelson, Canada 72 B4 58 50N 122 44W
Fort Nelson →, Canada 72 B4 59 32N 124 0W
Fort Norman = Tulita, Canada 68 B7 64 57N 125 30W
Fort Payne, U.S.A. 77 H3 34 26N 85 43W
Fort Peck, U.S.A. 82 B10 48 1N 106 27W
Fort Peck Dam, U.S.A. 82 C10 48 0N 106 26W
Fort Peck L., U.S.A. 82 C10 48 0N 106 26W
Fort Pierce, U.S.A. 77 M5 27 27N 80 20W
Fort Pierre, U.S.A. 80 C4 44 21N 100 22W
Fort Plain, U.S.A. 79 D10 42 56N 74 37W
Fort Portal, Uganda 54 B3 0 40N 30 20 E
Fort Providence, Canada 72 A5 61 3N 117 40W
Fort Qu'Appelle, Canada 73 C8 50 45N 103 50W
Fort Resolution, Canada 72 A6 61 10N 113 40W
Fort Rixon, Zimbabwe 55 G2 20 2S 29 17 E
Fort Rosebery = Mansa, Zambia 55 E2 11 13S 28 55 E
Fort Ross, U.S.A. 84 G3 38 32N 123 13W
Fort Rupert = Waskaganish, Canada 70 B4 51 30N 78 40W
Fort St. James, Canada 72 C4 54 30N 124 10W
Fort St. John, Canada 72 B4 56 15N 120 50W
Fort Sandeman = Zhob, Pakistan 42 D3 31 20N 69 31 E
Fort Saskatchewan, Canada 72 C6 53 40N 113 15W
Fort Scott, U.S.A. 81 G7 37 50N 94 42W
Fort Severn, Canada 70 A2 56 0N 87 40W
Fort Shevchenko, Kazakstan 25 F9 44 35N 50 23 E
Fort Simpson, Canada 72 A4 61 45N 121 15W
Fort Smith, Canada 72 B6 60 0N 111 51W
Fort Smith, U.S.A. 81 H7 35 23N 94 25W
Fort Stanton, U.S.A. 83 K11 33 30N 105 31W
Fort Stockton, U.S.A. 81 K3 30 53N 102 53W
Fort Sumner, U.S.A. 81 H2 34 28N 104 15W
Fort Trinquet = Bir Mogreïn, Mauritania 50 C3 25 10N 11 25W
Fort Valley, U.S.A. 77 J4 32 33N 83 53W
Fort Vermilion, Canada 72 B5 58 24N 116 0W
Fort Walton Beach, U.S.A. 77 K2 30 25N 86 36W
Fort Wayne, U.S.A. 76 E3 41 4N 85 9W
Fort William, U.K. 12 E3 56 49N 5 7W
Fort Worth, U.S.A. 81 J6 32 45N 97 18W
Fort Yates, U.S.A. 80 B4 46 5N 100 38W
Fort Yukon, U.S.A. 68 B5 66 34N 145 16W
Fortaleza, Brazil 93 D11 3 45S 38 35W
Forteau, Canada 71 B8 51 28N 56 58W
Forth →, U.K. 12 E5 56 9N 3 50W
Forth, Firth of, U.K. 12 E6 56 5N 2 55W
Fortrose, U.K. 12 D4 57 35N 4 9W
Fortuna, Calif., U.S.A. 82 F1 40 36N 124 9W
Fortuna, N. Dak., U.S.A. 80 A3 48 55N 103 47W
Fortune B., Canada 71 C8 47 30N 55 22W
Foshan, China 33 D6 23 4N 113 5 E
Fosna, Norway 8 E14 63 50N 10 20 E
Fosnavåg, Norway 9 E11 62 22N 5 38 E
Fossano, Italy 18 D7 44 33N 7 43 E
Fossil, U.S.A. 82 D3 45 0N 120 9W
Fossilbrook, Australia 62 B3 17 47S 144 29 E
Fosston, U.S.A. 80 B7 47 35N 95 45W
Foster, Canada 79 A12 45 17N 72 30W
Foster →, Canada 73 B7 55 47N 105 49W
Fosters Ra., Australia 62 C1 21 35S 133 48 E
Fostoria, U.S.A. 76 E4 41 10N 83 25W
Fougères, France 18 B3 48 21N 1 14W
Foul Pt., Sri Lanka 40 Q12 8 35N 81 18 E
Foula, U.K. 12 A6 60 10N 2 5W
Foulness I., U.K. 11 F8 51 36N 0 55 E
Foulpointe, Madag. 57 B8 17 41S 49 31 E
Foumban, Cameroon 52 C2 5 45N 10 50 E
Fountain, Colo., U.S.A. 80 F2 38 41N 104 42W
Fountain, Utah, U.S.A. 82 G8 39 41N 111 37W
Fountain Springs, U.S.A. 85 K8 35 54N 118 51W
Fourchu, Canada 71 C7 45 43N 60 17W
Fouriesburg, S. Africa 56 D4 28 38S 28 14 E
Fouta Djalon, Guinea 50 F3 11 20N 12 10W
Foux, Cap-à-, Haiti 89 C5 19 43N 73 27W
Foveaux Str., N.Z. 59 M2 46 42S 168 10 E
Fowey, U.K. 11 G3 50 20N 4 39W
Fowler, Calif., U.S.A. 84 J7 36 38N 119 41W
Fowler, Colo., U.S.A. 80 F3 38 8N 104 2W
Fowler, Kans., U.S.A. 81 G4 37 23N 100 12W
Fowlers B., Australia 61 F5 31 59S 132 34 E
Fowlerton, U.S.A. 81 L5 28 28N 98 48W
Fox →, Canada 73 B10 56 3N 93 18W
Fox Valley, Canada 73 C7 50 30N 109 25W
Foxe Basin, Canada 69 B12 66 0N 77 0W

Garvie Mts.

Foxe Chan., Canada 69 B12 65 0N 80 0W
Foxe Pen., Canada 69 B12 65 0N 76 0W
Foxpark, U.S.A. 82 F10 41 5N 106 9W
Foxton, N.Z. 59 J5 40 29S 175 18 E
Foyle, Lough, U.K. 13 A4 55 7N 7 4W
Foynes, Ireland 13 D2 52 37N 9 7W
Fóz do Cunene, Angola 56 B1 17 15S 11 48 E
Foz do Iguaçu, Brazil 95 B5 25 30S 54 30W
Frackville, U.S.A. 79 F8 40 47N 76 14W
Framingham, U.S.A. 79 D13 42 17N 71 25W
Franca, Brazil 93 H9 20 33S 47 30W
Francavilla Fontana, Italy 21 D7 40 32N 17 35 E
France ■, Europe 18 C5 47 0N 3 0 E
Frances, Australia 63 F3 36 41S 140 55 E
Frances →, Canada 72 A3 60 16N 129 10W
Frances L., Canada 72 A3 61 23N 129 30W
Francés Viejo, C., Dom. Rep. 89 C6 19 40N 69 55W
Franceville, Gabon 52 E2 1 40S 13 32 E
Franche-Comté, France 18 C6 46 50N 5 55 E
Francisco I. Madero, Coahuila, Mexico 86 B4 25 48N 103 18W
Francisco I. Madero, Durango, Mexico 86 C4 24 32N 104 22W
Francistown, Botswana 57 C4 21 7S 27 33 E
François, Canada 71 C8 47 35N 56 45W
François L., Canada 72 C3 54 0N 125 30W
Franeker, Neths. 15 A5 53 12N 5 33 E
Frankfort, S. Africa 57 D4 27 17S 28 30 E
Frankfort, Ind., U.S.A. 76 E2 40 17N 86 31W
Frankfort, Kans., U.S.A. 80 F6 39 42N 96 25W
Frankfort, Ky., U.S.A. 76 F3 38 12N 84 52W
Frankfort, Mich., U.S.A. 76 C2 44 38N 86 14W
Frankfurt, Brandenburg, Germany 16 B8 52 20N 14 32 E
Frankfurt, Hessen, Germany 16 C5 50 7N 8 41 E
Fränkische Alb, Germany 16 D6 49 10N 11 23 E
Frankland →, Australia 61 G2 35 0S 116 48 E
Franklin, Ky., U.S.A. 77 G2 36 43N 86 35W
Franklin, La., U.S.A. 81 L9 29 48N 91 30W
Franklin, Mass., U.S.A. 79 D13 42 5N 71 24W
Franklin, N.H., U.S.A. 79 C13 43 27N 71 39W
Franklin, Nebr., U.S.A. 80 E5 40 6N 98 57W
Franklin, Pa., U.S.A. 78 E5 41 24N 79 50W
Franklin, Tenn., U.S.A. 77 H2 35 55N 86 52W
Franklin, Va., U.S.A. 77 G7 36 41N 76 56W
Franklin, W. Va., U.S.A. 76 F6 38 39N 79 20W
Franklin B., Canada 68 B7 69 45N 126 0W
Franklin D. Roosevelt L., U.S.A. 82 B4 48 18N 118 9W
Franklin I., Antarctica 5 D11 76 10S 168 30 E
Franklin L., U.S.A. 82 F6 40 25N 115 22W
Franklin Mts., Canada 68 B7 65 0N 125 0W
Franklin Str., Canada 68 A10 72 0N 96 0W
Franklinton, U.S.A. 81 K9 30 51N 90 9W
Franklinville, U.S.A. 78 D6 42 20N 78 27W
Franks Pk., U.S.A. 82 E9 43 58N 109 18W
Frankston, Australia 63 F4 38 8S 145 8 E
Frantsa Iosifa, Zemlya, Russia 26 A6 82 0N 55 0 E
Franz, Canada 70 C3 48 25N 84 30W
Franz Josef Land = Frantsa Iosifa, Zemlya, Russia 26 A6 82 0N 55 0 E
Fraser →, B.C., Canada 72 D4 49 7N 123 11W
Fraser →, Nfld., Canada 71 A7 56 39N 62 10W
Fraser, Mt., Australia 61 E2 25 35S 118 20 E
Fraser I., Australia 63 D5 25 15S 153 10 E
Fraser Lake, Canada 72 C4 54 0N 124 50W
Fraserburg, S. Africa 56 E3 31 55S 21 30 E
Fraserburgh, U.K. 12 D6 57 42N 2 1W
Fraserdale, Canada 70 C3 49 55N 81 37W
Fray Bentos, Uruguay 94 C4 33 10S 58 15W
Frazier Downs, Australia 60 C3 18 48S 121 42 E
Fredericia, Denmark 9 J13 55 34N 9 45 E
Frederick, Md., U.S.A. 76 F7 39 25N 77 25W
Frederick, Okla., U.S.A. 81 H5 34 23N 99 1W
Frederick, S. Dak., U.S.A. 80 C5 45 50N 98 31W
Frederick Sd., U.S.A. 72 B2 57 10N 134 0W
Fredericksburg, Tex., U.S.A. 81 K5 30 16N 98 52W
Fredericksburg, Va., U.S.A. 76 F7 38 18N 77 28W
Fredericktown, U.S.A. 81 G9 37 34N 90 18W
Frederico I. Madero, Presa, Mexico 86 B3 28 7N 105 40W
Fredericton, Canada 71 C6 45 57N 66 40W
Fredericton Junc., Canada 71 C6 45 41N 66 40W
Frederikshavn, Denmark 9 H14 57 28N 10 31 E
Frederiksted, Virgin Is. 89 C7 17 43N 64 53W
Fredonia, Ariz., U.S.A. 83 H7 36 57N 112 32W
Fredonia, Kans., U.S.A. 81 G7 37 32N 95 49W
Fredonia, N.Y., U.S.A. 78 D5 42 26N 79 20W
Fredrikstad, Norway 9 G14 59 13N 10 57 E
Free State □, S. Africa 56 D4 28 30S 27 0 E
Freehold, U.S.A. 79 F10 40 16N 74 17W
Freel Peak, U.S.A. 84 G7 38 52N 119 54W
Freeland, U.S.A. 79 E9 41 1N 75 54W
Freels, C., Canada 71 C9 49 15N 53 30W
Freeman, Calif., U.S.A. 85 K9 35 35N 117 53W
Freeman, S. Dak., U.S.A. 80 D6 43 21N 97 26W
Freeport, Bahamas 88 A4 26 30N 78 47W
Freeport, Canada 71 D6 44 15N 66 20W
Freeport, Ill., U.S.A. 80 D10 42 17N 89 36W
Freeport, N.Y., U.S.A. 79 F11 40 39N 73 35W
Freeport, Tex., U.S.A. 81 L7 28 57N 95 21W
Freetown, S. Leone 50 G3 8 30N 13 17W
Frégate, L., Canada 70 B5 53 15N 74 45W
Fregenal de la Sierra, Spain 19 C2 38 10N 6 39W
Freibourg = Fribourg, Switz. 18 C7 46 49N 7 9 E
Freiburg, Germany 16 E4 47 59N 7 51 E
Freire, Chile 96 D2 38 54S 72 38W
Freirina, Chile 94 B1 28 30S 71 10W
Freising, Germany 16 D6 48 24N 11 45 E
Freistadt, Austria 16 D8 48 30N 14 30 E
Fréjus, France 18 E7 43 25N 6 44 E
Fremantle, Australia 61 F2 32 7S 115 47 E
Fremont, Calif., U.S.A. 84 H4 37 32N 121 57W
Fremont, Mich., U.S.A. 76 D3 43 28N 85 57W
Fremont, Nebr., U.S.A. 80 E6 41 26N 96 30W
Fremont, Ohio, U.S.A. 76 E4 41 21N 83 7W
Fremont →, U.S.A. 83 G8 38 24N 110 42W
Fremont L., U.S.A. 82 E9 42 57N 109 48W
French Camp, U.S.A. 84 H5 37 53N 121 16W
French Creek →, U.S.A. 78 E5 41 24N 79 50W
French Guiana ■, S. Amer. 93 C8 4 0N 53 0W
French Pass, N.Z. 59 J4 40 55S 173 55 E
French Polynesia ■, Pac. Oc. 65 K13 20 0S 145 0W
Frenchglen, U.S.A. 82 E4 42 50N 118 55W
Frenchman Butte, Canada 73 C7 53 35N 109 38W
Frenchman Cr. →, Mont., U.S.A. 82 B10 48 31N 107 10W
Frenchman Cr. →, Nebr., U.S.A. 80 E4 40 14N 100 50W
Fresco →, Brazil 93 E8 7 15S 51 30W
Freshfield, C., Antarctica 5 C10 68 25S 151 10 E
Fresnillo, Mexico 86 C4 23 10N 103 0W
Fresno, U.S.A. 84 J7 36 44N 119 47W
Fresno Reservoir, U.S.A. 82 B9 48 36N 109 57W
Frew →, Australia 62 C2 20 0S 135 38 E
Frewena, Australia 62 B2 19 25S 135 25 E
Freycinet Pen., Australia 62 G4 42 10S 148 25 E
Fria, C., Namibia 56 B1 18 0S 12 0 E
Friant, U.S.A. 84 J7 36 59N 119 43W
Frías, Argentina 94 B2 28 40S 65 5W
Fribourg, Switz. 18 C7 46 49N 7 9 E
Friday Harbor, U.S.A. 84 B3 48 32N 123 1W
Friedrichshafen, Germany 16 E5 47 39N 9 30 E
Friendly Is. = Tonga ■, Pac. Oc. 59 D11 19 50S 174 30W
Friesland □, Neths. 15 A5 53 5N 5 50 E
Frio →, U.S.A. 81 L5 28 26N 98 11W
Frio, C., Brazil 90 F6 22 50S 41 50W
Friona, U.S.A. 81 H3 34 38N 102 43W
Fritch, U.S.A. 81 H4 35 38N 101 36W
Frobisher B., Canada 69 B13 62 30N 66 0W
Frobisher Bay = Iqaluit, Canada 69 B13 63 44N 68 31W
Frobisher L., Canada 73 B7 56 20N 108 15W
Frohavet, Norway 8 E13 64 0N 9 30 E
Froid, U.S.A. 80 A2 48 20N 104 30W
Fromberg, U.S.A. 82 D9 45 24N 108 54W
Frome, U.K. 11 F5 51 14N 2 19W
Frome →, U.K. 11 G5 50 41N 2 6W
Frome, L., Australia 63 E2 30 45S 139 45 E
Frome Downs, Australia 63 E2 31 13S 139 45 E
Front Range, U.S.A. 82 G11 40 25N 105 45W
Front Royal, U.S.A. 76 F6 38 55N 78 12W
Frontera, Canary Is. 22 G2 27 47N 17 59W
Frontera, Mexico 87 D6 18 30N 92 40W
Frosinone, Italy 20 D5 41 38N 13 19 E
Frostburg, U.S.A. 76 F6 39 39N 78 56W
Frostisen, Norway 8 B17 68 14N 17 10 E
Frøya, Norway 8 E13 63 43N 8 40 E
Frunze = Bishkek, Kyrgyzstan 26 E8 42 54N 74 46 E
Frutal, Brazil 93 H9 20 0S 49 0W
Frýdek-Místek, Czech Rep. 17 D10 49 40N 18 20 E
Fu Xian, Liaoning, China 35 E11 39 38N 121 58 E
Fu Xian, Shaanxi, China 34 G5 36 0N 109 20 E
Fucheng, China 34 F9 37 50N 116 10 E
Fuchou = Fuzhou, China 33 D6 26 5N 119 16 E
Fuchū, Japan 31 G6 34 34N 133 14 E
Fuencaliente, Canary Is. 22 F2 28 28N 17 50W
Fuencaliente, Pta., Canary Is. 22 F2 28 27N 17 51W
Fuengirola, Spain 19 D3 36 32N 4 41W
Fuentes de Oñoro, Spain 19 B2 40 33N 6 52W
Fuerte →, Mexico 86 B3 25 50N 109 25W
Fuerte Olimpo, Paraguay 94 A4 21 0S 57 51W
Fuerteventura, Canary Is. 22 F6 28 30N 14 0W
Fufeng, China 34 G5 34 22N 108 0 E
Fugou, China 34 G8 34 3N 114 25 E
Fugu, China 34 E6 39 2N 111 3 E
Fuhai, China 32 B3 47 2N 87 25 E
Fuḥaymī, Iraq 44 C4 34 16N 42 10 E
Fuji, Japan 31 G9 35 9N 138 39 E
Fuji-San, Japan 31 G9 35 22N 138 44 E
Fuji-yoshida, Japan 31 G9 35 30N 138 46 E
Fujian □, China 33 D6 26 0N 118 0 E
Fujinomiya, Japan 31 G9 35 10N 138 40 E
Fujisawa, Japan 31 G9 35 22N 139 29 E
Fukien = Fujian □, China 33 D6 26 0N 118 0 E
Fukuchiyama, Japan 31 G7 35 19N 135 9 E
Fukue-Shima, Japan 31 H4 32 40N 128 45 E
Fukui, Japan 31 F8 36 5N 136 10 E
Fukui □, Japan 31 G8 36 0N 136 12 E
Fukuoka, Japan 31 H5 33 39N 130 21 E
Fukuoka □, Japan 31 H5 33 30N 131 0 E
Fukushima, Japan 30 F10 37 44N 140 28 E
Fukushima □, Japan 30 F10 37 30N 140 15 E
Fukuyama, Japan 31 G6 34 35N 133 20 E
Fulda, Germany 16 C5 50 32N 9 40 E
Fulda →, Germany 16 C5 51 25N 9 39 E
Fullerton, Calif., U.S.A. 85 M9 33 53N 117 56W
Fullerton, Nebr., U.S.A. 80 E6 41 22N 97 58W
Fulongquan, China 35 B13 44 20N 124 42 E
Fulton, Mo., U.S.A. 80 F9 38 52N 91 57W
Fulton, N.Y., U.S.A. 79 C8 43 19N 76 25W
Fulton, Tenn., U.S.A. 77 G1 36 31N 88 53W
Funabashi, Japan 31 G10 35 45N 140 0 E
Funchal, Madeira 22 D3 32 38N 16 54W
Fundación, Colombia 92 A4 10 31N 74 11W
Fundão, Portugal 19 B2 40 8N 7 30W
Fundy, B. of, Canada 71 D6 45 0N 66 0W
Funing, Hebei, China 35 E10 39 53N 119 12 E
Funing, Jiangsu, China 35 H10 33 45N 119 50 E
Funiu Shan, China 34 H7 33 30N 112 20 E
Funtua, Nigeria 50 F7 11 30N 7 18 E
Fuping, Hebei, China 34 E8 38 48N 114 12 E
Fuping, Shaanxi, China 34 G5 34 42N 109 10 E
Furano, Japan 30 C11 43 21N 142 23 E
Furāt, Nahr al →, Asia 44 D5 31 0N 47 25 E
Fūrg, Iran 45 D7 28 18N 55 13 E
Furnás, Spain 22 B8 39 3N 1 32 E
Furnas, Represa de, Brazil 95 A6 20 50S 45 30W
Furneaux Group, Australia 62 G4 40 10S 147 50 E
Furqlus, Syria 47 A6 34 36N 37 8 E
Fürstenwalde, Germany 16 B8 52 22N 14 3 E
Fürth, Germany 16 D6 49 28N 10 59 E
Furukawa, Japan 30 E10 38 34N 140 58 E
Fury and Hecla Str., Canada 69 B11 69 56N 84 0W
Fusagasuga, Colombia 92 C4 4 21N 74 22W
Fushan, Shandong, China 35 F11 37 30N 121 15 E
Fushan, Shanxi, China 34 G6 35 58N 111 51 E
Fushun, China 35 D12 41 50N 123 56 E
Fusong, China 35 C14 42 20N 127 15 E
Futuna, Wall. & F. Is. 59 B8 14 25S 178 20 E
Fuxin, China 35 C11 42 5N 121 48 E
Fuyang, China 34 H8 33 0N 115 48 E
Fuyang He →, China 34 E9 38 12N 117 0 E
Fuyu, China 35 B13 45 12N 124 43 E
Fuzhou, China 33 D6 26 5N 119 16 E
Fylde, U.K. 10 D5 53 50N 2 58W
Fyn, Denmark 9 J14 55 20N 10 30 E
Fyne, L., U.K. 12 F3 55 59N 5 23W

G

Gabela, Angola 52 G2 11 0S 14 24 E
Gabès, Tunisia 51 B8 33 53N 10 2 E
Gabès, G. de, Tunisia 51 B8 34 0N 10 30 E
Gabon ■, Africa 52 E2 0 10S 10 0 E
Gaborone, Botswana 56 C4 24 45S 25 57 E
Gabriels, U.S.A. 79 B10 44 26N 74 12W
Gābrīk, Iran 45 E8 25 44N 58 28 E
Gabrovo, Bulgaria 21 C11 42 52N 25 19 E
Gāch Sār, Iran 45 B6 36 7N 51 19 E
Gachsārān, Iran 45 D6 30 15N 50 45 E
Gadag, India 40 M9 15 30N 75 45 E
Gadap, Pakistan 42 G2 25 5N 67 28 E
Gadarwara, India 43 H8 22 50N 78 50 E
Gadhada, India 42 J4 22 0N 71 35 E
Gadsden, Ala., U.S.A. 77 H3 34 1N 86 1W
Gadsden, Ariz., U.S.A. 83 K6 32 33N 114 47W
Gadwal, India 40 L10 16 10N 77 50 E
Gaffney, U.S.A. 77 H5 35 5N 81 39W
Gafsa, Tunisia 50 B7 34 24N 8 43 E
Gagetown, Canada 71 C6 45 46N 66 10W
Gagnoa, Ivory C. 50 G4 6 56N 5 16W
Gagnon, Canada 71 B6 51 50N 68 5W
Gagnon, L., Canada 73 A6 62 3N 110 27W
Gahini, Rwanda 54 C3 1 50S 30 30 E
Gahmar, India 43 G10 25 27N 83 49 E
Gai Xian, China 35 D12 40 22N 122 20 E
Gaïdhouronísi, Greece 23 E7 34 53N 25 41 E
Gail, U.S.A. 81 J4 32 46N 101 27W
Gaillimh = Galway, Ireland 13 C2 53 17N 9 3W
Gaines, U.S.A. 78 E7 41 46N 77 35W
Gainesville, Fla., U.S.A. 77 L4 29 40N 82 20W
Gainesville, Ga., U.S.A. 77 H4 34 18N 83 50W
Gainesville, Mo., U.S.A. 81 G8 36 36N 92 26W
Gainesville, Tex., U.S.A. 81 J6 33 38N 97 8W
Gainsborough, U.K. 10 D7 53 24N 0 46W
Gairdner, L., Australia 63 E2 31 30S 136 0 E
Gairloch, L., U.K. 12 D3 57 43N 5 45W
Gakuch, Pakistan 43 A5 36 7N 73 45 E
Galán, Cerro, Argentina 94 B2 25 55S 66 52W
Galana →, Kenya 54 C5 3 9S 40 8 E
Galápagos, Pac. Oc. 90 D1 0 0 91 0W
Galashiels, U.K. 12 F6 55 37N 2 49W
Galaţi, Romania 17 F15 45 27N 28 2 E
Galatina, Italy 21 D8 40 10N 18 10 E
Galax, U.S.A. 77 G5 36 40N 80 56W
Galbraith, Australia 62 B3 16 25S 141 30 E
Galcaio, Somali Rep. 46 F4 6 30N 47 30 E
Galdhøpiggen, Norway 9 F12 61 38N 8 18 E
Galeana, Mexico 86 C4 24 50N 100 4W
Galela, Indonesia 37 D7 1 50N 127 49 E
Galera Point, Trin. & Tob. 89 D7 10 8N 61 0W
Galesburg, U.S.A. 80 E9 40 57N 90 22W
Galeton, U.S.A. 78 E7 41 44N 77 39W
Galich, Russia 24 C7 58 22N 42 24 E
Galicia □, Spain 19 A2 42 43N 7 45W
Galilee = Hagalil, Israel 47 C4 32 53N 35 18 E
Galilee, L., Australia 62 C4 22 20S 145 50 E
Galilee, Sea of = Yam Kinneret, Israel 47 C4 32 45N 35 35 E
Galinoporni, Cyprus 23 D13 35 31N 34 18 E
Galion, U.S.A. 78 F2 40 44N 82 47W
Galiuro Mts., U.S.A. 83 K8 32 30N 110 20W
Gallan Hd., U.K. 12 C1 58 15N 7 2W
Gallatin, U.S.A. 77 G2 36 24N 86 27W
Galle, Sri Lanka 40 R12 6 5N 80 10 E
Gállego →, Spain 19 B5 41 39N 0 51W
Gallegos →, Argentina 96 G3 51 35S 69 0W
Galley Hd., Ireland 13 E3 51 32N 8 55W
Gallinas, Pta., Colombia 92 A4 12 28N 71 40W
Gallipoli = Gelibolu, Turkey 21 D12 40 28N 26 43 E
Gallípoli, Italy 21 D8 40 3N 17 58 E
Gallipolis, U.S.A. 76 F4 38 49N 82 12W
Gällivare, Sweden 8 C19 67 9N 20 40 E
Galloway, U.K. 12 F4 55 1N 4 29W
Galloway, Mull of, U.K. 12 G4 54 39N 4 52W
Gallup, U.S.A. 83 J9 35 32N 108 45W
Galong, Australia 63 E4 34 37S 148 34 E
Galoya, Sri Lanka 40 Q12 8 10N 80 55 E
Galt, U.S.A. 84 G5 38 15N 121 18W
Galty Mts., Ireland 13 D3 52 22N 8 10W
Galtymore, Ireland 13 D3 52 21N 8 11W
Galva, U.S.A. 80 E9 41 10N 90 3W
Galveston, U.S.A. 81 L7 29 18N 94 48W
Galveston B., U.S.A. 81 L7 29 36N 94 50W
Gálvez, Argentina 94 C3 32 0S 61 14W
Galway, Ireland 13 C2 53 17N 9 3W
Galway □, Ireland 13 C2 53 22N 9 1W
Galway B., Ireland 13 C2 53 13N 9 10W
Gam →, Vietnam 38 B5 21 55N 105 12 E
Gamagori, Japan 31 G8 34 50N 137 14 E
Gambat, Pakistan 42 F3 27 17N 68 26 E
Gambia ■, W. Afr. 50 F2 13 25N 16 0W
Gambia →, W. Afr. 50 F2 13 28N 16 34W
Gambier, C., Australia 60 B5 11 56S 130 57 E
Gambier Is., Australia 63 F2 35 3S 136 30 E
Gamboli, Pakistan 42 E3 29 53N 68 24 E
Gamboma, Congo 52 E3 1 55S 15 52 E
Gamerco, U.S.A. 83 J9 35 34N 108 46W
Gamlakarleby = Kokkola, Finland 8 E20 63 50N 23 8 E
Gammon →, Canada 73 C9 51 24N 95 44W
Gan Jiang →, China 33 D6 29 15N 116 0 E
Ganado, Ariz., U.S.A. 83 J9 35 43N 109 33W
Ganado, Tex., U.S.A. 81 L6 29 2N 96 31W
Gananoque, Canada 70 D4 44 20N 76 10W
Ganāveh, Iran 45 D6 29 35N 50 35 E
Gäncä, Azerbaijan 25 F8 40 45N 46 20 E
Gancheng, China 38 C7 18 51N 108 37 E
Gand = Gent, Belgium 15 C3 51 2N 3 42 E
Ganda, Angola 53 G2 13 3S 14 35 E
Gandak →, India 43 G11 25 39N 85 13 E
Gandava, Pakistan 42 E2 28 32N 67 32 E
Gander, Canada 71 C9 48 58N 54 35W
Gander L., Canada 71 C9 48 58N 54 35W
Ganderowe Falls, Zimbabwe 55 F2 17 20S 29 10 E
Gandhi Sagar, India 42 G6 24 40N 75 40 E
Gandía, Spain 19 C5 38 58N 0 9W
Gando, Pta., Canary Is. 22 G4 27 55N 15 22W
Ganedidalem = Gani, Indonesia 37 E7 0 48S 128 14 E
Ganga →, India 43 H14 23 20N 90 30 E
Ganganagar, India 42 E5 29 56N 73 56 E
Gangapur, India 42 F7 26 32N 76 49 E
Gangaw, Burma 41 H19 22 5N 94 5 E
Gangdisê Shan, China 41 D12 31 20N 81 0 E
Ganges = Ganga →, India 43 H14 23 20N 90 30 E
Ganges, Mouths of the, India 43 J14 21 30N 90 0 E
Gangoh, India 42 E7 29 46N 77 18 E
Gangtok, India 41 F16 27 20N 88 37 E
Gangu, China 34 G3 34 40N 105 15 E
Gangyao, China 35 B14 44 12N 126 37 E
Gani, Indonesia 37 E7 0 48S 128 14 E
Ganj, India 43 F8 27 45N 78 57 E
Gannett Peak, U.S.A. 82 E9 43 11N 109 39W
Gannvalley, U.S.A. 80 C5 44 2N 98 59W
Ganquan, China 34 F5 36 20N 109 20 E
Gansu □, China 34 G3 36 0N 104 0 E
Ganta, Liberia 50 G4 7 15N 8 59W
Gantheaume, C., Australia 63 F2 36 4S 137 32 E
Gantheaume B., Australia 61 E1 27 40S 114 10 E
Gantsevichi = Hantsavichy, Belarus 17 B14 52 49N 26 30 E
Ganyem = Genyem, Indonesia 37 E10 2 46S 140 12 E
Ganyu, China 35 G10 34 50N 119 8 E
Ganzhou, China 33 D6 25 51N 114 56 E
Gaomi, China 35 F10 36 20N 119 42 E
Gaoping, China 34 G7 35 45N 112 55 E
Gaotang, China 34 F9 36 50N 116 15 E
Gaoua, Burkina Faso 50 F5 10 20N 3 8W
Gaoual, Guinea 50 F3 11 45N 13 25W
Gaoxiong = Kaohsiung, Taiwan 33 D7 22 35N 120 16 E
Gaoyang, China 34 E8 38 40N 115 45 E
Gaoyou Hu, China 35 H10 33 45N 119 20 E
Gaoyuan, China 35 F9 37 8N 117 58 E
Gap, France 18 D7 44 33N 6 5 E
Gar, China 32 C2 32 10N 79 58 E
Garabogazköl Aylagy, Turkmenistan 25 F9 41 0N 53 30 E
Garachico, Canary Is. 22 F3 28 22N 16 46W
Garachiné, Panama 88 E4 8 0N 78 12W
Garafia, Canary Is. 22 F2 28 48N 17 57W
Garajonay, Canary Is. 22 F2 28 7N 17 14W
Garanhuns, Brazil 93 E11 8 50S 36 30W
Garba Tula, Kenya 54 B4 0 30N 38 32 E
Garber, U.S.A. 81 G6 36 26N 97 35W
Garberville, U.S.A. 82 F2 40 6N 123 48W
Garda, L. di, Italy 20 B4 45 40N 10 41 E
Garde L., Canada 73 A7 62 50N 106 13W
Garden City, Kans., U.S.A. 81 G4 37 58N 100 53W
Garden City, Tex., U.S.A. 81 K4 31 52N 101 29W
Garden Grove, U.S.A. 85 M9 33 47N 117 55W
Gardēz, Afghan. 42 C3 33 37N 69 9 E
Gardiner, U.S.A. 82 D8 45 2N 110 22W
Gardiners I., U.S.A. 79 E12 41 6N 72 6W
Gardner, U.S.A. 79 D13 42 34N 71 59W
Gardner Canal, Canada 72 C3 53 27N 128 8W
Gardnerville, U.S.A. 84 G7 38 56N 119 45W
Gardo, Somali Rep. 46 F4 9 30N 49 6 E
Garey, U.S.A. 85 L6 34 53N 120 19W
Garfield, U.S.A. 82 C5 47 1N 117 9W
Garforth, U.K. 10 D6 53 47N 1 24W
Gargano, Mte., Italy 20 D6 41 43N 15 43 E
Garhshankar, India 42 D7 31 13N 76 11 E
Garibaldi Prov. Park, Canada 72 D4 49 50N 122 40W
Garies, S. Africa 56 E2 30 32S 17 59 E
Garigliano →, Italy 20 D5 41 13N 13 45 E
Garissa, Kenya 54 C4 0 25S 39 40 E
Garissa □, Kenya 54 C5 0 20S 40 0 E
Garland, Tex., U.S.A. 81 J6 32 55N 96 38W
Garland, Utah, U.S.A. 82 F7 41 47N 112 10W
Garm, Tajikistan 26 F8 39 0N 70 20 E
Garmāb, Iran 45 C8 35 25N 56 45 E
Garmisch-Partenkirchen, Germany 16 E6 47 30N 11 6 E
Garmsār, Iran 45 C7 35 20N 52 25 E
Garner, U.S.A. 80 D8 43 6N 93 36W
Garnett, U.S.A. 80 F7 38 17N 95 14W
Garo Hills, India 43 G14 25 30N 90 30 E
Garoe, Somali Rep. 46 F4 8 25N 48 33 E
Garonne →, France 18 D3 45 2N 0 36W
Garoua, Cameroon 51 G8 9 19N 13 21 E
Garrison, Mont., U.S.A. 82 C7 46 31N 112 49W
Garrison, N. Dak., U.S.A. 80 B4 47 40N 101 25W
Garrison, Tex., U.S.A. 81 K7 31 49N 94 30W
Garrison Res. = Sakakawea, L., U.S.A. 80 B4 47 30N 101 25W
Garron Pt., U.K. 13 A6 55 3N 5 59W
Garry →, U.K. 12 E5 56 44N 3 47W
Garry, L., Canada 68 B9 65 58N 100 18W
Garsen, Kenya 54 C5 2 20S 40 5 E
Garson L., Canada 73 B6 56 19N 110 2W
Garub, Namibia 56 D2 26 37S 16 0 E
Garut, Indonesia 37 G12 7 14S 107 53 E
Garvie Mts., N.Z. 59 L2 45 30S 168 50 E

Garwa

Garwa = Garoua, Cameroon 51 G8 9 19N 13 21 E
Garwa, India 43 G10 24 11N 83 47 E
Gary, U.S.A. 76 E2 41 36N 87 20W
Garzê, China 32 C5 31 38N 100 1 E
Garzón, Colombia 92 C3 2 10N 75 40W
Gas-San, Japan 30 E10 38 32N 140 1 E
Gasan Kuli = Esenguly, Turkmenistan 26 F6 37 37N 53 59 E
Gascogne, France 18 E4 43 45N 0 20 E
Gascogne, G. de, Europe 18 D2 44 0N 2 0W
Gascony = Gascogne, France 18 E4 43 45N 0 20 E
Gascoyne —►, Australia 61 D1 24 52S 113 37 E
Gascoyne Junc. T.O., Australia 61 E2 25 2S 115 17 E
Gashaka, Nigeria 51 G8 7 20N 11 29 E
Gasherbrum, Pakistan 43 B7 35 40N 76 40 E
Gaspé, Canada 71 C7 48 52N 64 30W
Gaspé, C. de, Canada 71 C7 48 48N 64 7W
Gaspé, Pén. de, Canada 71 C6 48 45N 65 40W
Gaspésie, Parc Prov. de la, Canada 71 C6 48 55N 65 50W
Gassaway, U.S.A. 76 F5 38 41N 80 47W
Gasteiz = Vitoria-Gasteiz, Spain 19 A4 42 50N 2 41W
Gastonia, U.S.A. 77 H5 35 16N 81 11W
Gastre, Argentina 96 E3 42 20S 69 15W
Gata, C., Cyprus 23 E12 34 34N 33 2 E
Gata, C. de, Spain 19 D4 36 41N 2 13W
Gata, Sierra de, Spain 19 B2 40 20N 6 45W
Gataga —►, Canada 72 B3 58 35N 126 59W
Gatehouse of Fleet, U.K. 12 G4 54 53N 4 12W
Gates, U.S.A. 78 C7 43 9N 77 42W
Gateshead, U.K. 10 C6 54 57N 1 35W
Gatesville, U.S.A. 81 K6 31 26N 97 45W
Gaths, Zimbabwe 55 G3 20 2S 30 32 E
Gatico, Chile 94 A1 22 29S 70 20W
Gatineau —►, Canada 70 C4 45 27N 75 42W
Gatineau, Parc de la, Canada 70 C4 45 40N 76 0W
Gatun, L., Panama 88 E4 9 7N 79 56W
Gatyana, S. Africa 57 E4 32 16S 28 31 E
Gau, Fiji 59 D8 18 2S 179 18 E
Gauer L., Canada 73 B9 57 0N 97 50W
Gauhati, India 43 F14 26 10N 91 45 E
Gauja —►, Latvia 9 H21 57 10N 24 16 E
Gaula —►, Norway 8 E14 63 21N 10 14 E
Gausta, Norway 9 G13 59 48N 8 40 E
Gauteng □, S. Africa 57 D4 26 0S 28 0 E
Gāv Koshī, Iran 45 D8 28 38N 57 12 E
Gāvakān, Iran 45 D7 29 37N 53 10 E
Gavāter, Iran 45 E9 25 10N 61 31 E
Gāvbandī, Iran 45 E7 27 12N 53 4 E
Gavdhopoúla, Greece 23 E6 34 56N 24 0 E
Gávdhos, Greece 23 E6 34 50N 24 5 E
Gaviota, U.S.A. 85 L6 34 29N 120 13W
Gävle, Sweden 9 F17 60 40N 17 9 E
Gawachab, Namibia 56 D2 27 4S 17 55 E
Gawilgarh Hills, India 40 J10 21 15N 76 45 E
Gawler, Australia 63 E2 34 30S 138 42 E
Gaxun Nur, China 32 B5 42 22N 100 30 E
Gay, Russia 24 D10 51 27N 58 27 E
Gaya, India 43 G11 24 47N 85 4 E
Gaya, Niger 50 F6 11 52N 3 28 E
Gaylord, U.S.A. 76 C3 45 2N 84 41W
Gayndah, Australia 63 D5 25 35S 151 32 E
Gaysin = Haysyn, Ukraine 17 D15 48 57N 29 25 E
Gayvoron = Hayvoron, Ukraine 17 D15 48 22N 29 52 E
Gaza, Gaza Strip 47 D3 31 30N 34 28 E
Gaza □, Mozam. 57 C5 23 10S 32 45 E
Gaza Strip □, Asia 47 D3 31 29N 34 25 E
Gāzbor, Iran 45 D8 28 5N 58 51 E
Gazi, Dem. Rep. of the Congo 54 B1 1 3N 24 30 E
Gaziantep, Turkey 25 G6 37 6N 37 23 E
Gcuwa, S. Africa 57 E4 32 20S 28 11 E
Gdańsk, Poland 17 A10 54 22N 18 40 E
Gdańska, Zatoka, Poland 17 A10 54 30N 19 20 E
Gdov, Russia 24 C4 58 48N 27 55 E
Gdynia, Poland 17 A10 54 35N 18 33 E
Gebe, Indonesia 37 D7 0 5N 129 25 E
Gebze, Turkey 21 D13 40 47N 29 25 E
Gedaref, Sudan 51 F13 14 2N 35 28 E
Gediz —►, Turkey 21 E12 38 35N 26 48 E
Gedser, Denmark 9 J14 54 35N 11 55 E
Geegully Cr. —►, Australia 60 C3 18 32S 123 41 E
Geel, Belgium 15 C4 51 10N 4 59 E
Geelong, Australia 63 F3 38 10S 144 22 E
Geelvink Chan., Australia 61 E1 28 30S 114 0 E
Geesthacht, Germany 16 B6 53 26N 10 22 E
Geidam, Nigeria 51 F8 12 57N 11 57 E
Geikie —►, Canada 73 B8 57 45N 103 52W
Geita, Tanzania 54 C3 2 48S 32 12 E
Geita □, Tanzania 54 C3 2 50S 32 10 E
Gejiu, China 32 D5 23 20N 103 10 E
Gela, Italy 20 F6 37 4N 14 15 E
Gelderland □, Neths. 15 B6 52 5N 6 10 E
Geldrop, Neths. 15 C5 51 25N 5 32 E
Geleen, Neths. 15 D5 50 57N 5 49 E
Gelibolu, Turkey 21 D12 40 28N 26 43 E
Gelsenkirchen, Germany 16 C4 51 32N 7 6 E
Gemas, Malaysia 39 L4 2 37N 102 36 E
Gembloux, Belgium 15 D4 50 34N 4 43 E
Gemena, Dem. Rep. of the Congo 52 D3 3 13N 19 48 E
Gemlik, Turkey 21 D13 40 26N 29 9 E
General Acha, Argentina 94 D3 37 20S 64 38W
General Alvear, Buenos Aires, Argentina 94 D4 36 0S 60 0W
General Alvear, Mendoza, Argentina 94 D2 35 0S 67 40W
General Artigas, Paraguay 94 B4 26 52S 56 16W
General Belgrano, Argentina 94 D4 36 35S 58 47W
General Cabrera, Argentina 94 C3 32 53S 63 52W
General Cepeda, Mexico 86 B4 25 23N 101 27W
General Guido, Argentina 94 D4 36 40S 57 50W
General Juan Madariaga, Argentina 94 D4 37 0S 57 0W
General La Madrid, Argentina 94 D3 37 17S 61 20W
General MacArthur, Phil. 37 B7 11 18N 125 28 E
General Martin Miguel de Güemes, Argentina 94 A3 24 50S 65 0W
General Paz, Argentina 94 B4 27 45S 57 36W
General Pico, Argentina 94 D3 35 45S 63 50W
General Pinedo, Argentina 94 B3 27 15S 61 20W
General Pinto, Argentina 94 C3 34 45S 61 50W
General Roca, Argentina 96 D3 39 2S 67 35W
General Santos, Phil. 37 C7 6 5N 125 14 E
General Trevino, Mexico 87 B5 26 14N 99 29W
General Trías, Mexico 86 B3 28 21N 106 22W
General Viamonte, Argentina 94 D3 35 1S 61 3W
General Villegas, Argentina 94 D3 35 5S 63 0W
Genesee, Idaho, U.S.A. 82 C5 46 33N 116 56W
Genesee, Pa., U.S.A. 78 E7 41 59N 77 54W
Genesee —►, U.S.A. 78 C7 43 16N 77 36W
Geneseo, Ill., U.S.A. 80 E9 41 27N 90 9W
Geneseo, Kans., U.S.A. 80 F5 38 31N 98 10W
Geneseo, N.Y., U.S.A. 78 D7 42 48N 77 49W
Geneva = Genève, Switz. 18 C7 46 12N 6 9 E
Geneva, Ala., U.S.A. 77 K3 31 2N 85 52W
Geneva, N.Y., U.S.A. 78 D8 42 52N 76 59W
Geneva, Nebr., U.S.A. 80 E6 40 32N 97 36W
Geneva, Ohio, U.S.A. 78 E4 41 48N 80 57W
Geneva, L. = Léman, L., Europe 18 C7 46 26N 6 30 E
Geneva, L., U.S.A. 76 D1 42 38N 88 30W
Genève, Switz. 18 C7 46 12N 6 9 E
Genil —►, Spain 19 D3 37 42N 5 19W
Genk, Belgium 15 D5 50 58N 5 32 E
Gennargentu, Mti. del, Italy 20 D3 40 1N 9 19 E
Genoa = Génova, Italy 18 D8 44 25N 8 57 E
Genoa, Australia 63 F4 37 29S 149 35 E
Genoa, N.Y., U.S.A. 79 D8 42 40N 76 32W
Genoa, Nebr., U.S.A. 80 E6 41 27N 97 44W
Genoa, Nev., U.S.A. 84 F7 39 2N 119 50W
Génova, Italy 18 D8 44 25N 8 57 E
Génova, G. di, Italy 20 C3 44 0N 9 0 E
Genriyetty, Ostrov, Russia 27 B16 77 6N 156 30 E
Gent, Belgium 15 C3 51 2N 3 42 E
Genyem, Indonesia 37 E10 2 46S 140 12 E
Geographe B., Australia 61 F2 33 30S 115 15 E
Geographe Chan., Australia 61 D1 24 30S 113 0 E
Georga, Zemlya, Russia 26 A5 80 30N 49 0 E
George, S. Africa 56 E3 33 58S 22 29 E
George —►, Canada 71 A6 58 49N 66 10W
George, L., N.S.W., Australia 63 F4 35 10S 149 25 E
George, L., S. Austral., Australia 63 F3 37 25S 140 0 E
George, L., W. Austral., Australia 60 D3 22 45S 123 40 E
George, L., Uganda 54 B3 0 5N 30 10 E
George, L., Fla., U.S.A. 77 L5 29 17N 81 36W
George, L., N.Y., U.S.A. 79 C11 43 37N 73 33W
George Gill Ra., Australia 60 D5 24 22S 131 45 E
George River = Kangiqsualujjuaq, Canada 69 C13 58 30N 65 59W
George Sound, N.Z. 59 L1 44 52S 167 25 E
George Town, Bahamas 88 B4 23 33N 75 47W
George Town, Malaysia 39 K3 5 25N 100 15 E
George V Land, Antarctica 5 C10 69 0S 148 0 E
George VI Sound, Antarctica 5 D17 71 0S 68 0W
George West, U.S.A. 81 L5 28 20N 98 7W
Georgetown, Australia 62 B3 18 17S 143 33 E
Georgetown, Ont., Canada 70 D4 43 40N 79 56W
Georgetown, P.E.I., Canada 71 C7 46 13N 62 24W
Georgetown, Cayman Is. 88 C3 19 20N 81 24W
Georgetown, Gambia 50 F3 13 30N 14 47W
Georgetown, Guyana 92 B7 6 50N 58 12W
Georgetown, Calif., U.S.A. 84 G6 38 54N 120 50W
Georgetown, Colo., U.S.A. 82 G11 39 42N 105 42W
Georgetown, Ky., U.S.A. 76 F3 38 13N 84 33W
Georgetown, S.C., U.S.A. 77 J6 33 23N 79 17W
Georgetown, Tex., U.S.A. 81 K6 30 38N 97 41W
Georgia □, U.S.A. 77 K5 32 50N 83 15W
Georgia ■, Asia 25 F7 42 0N 43 0 E
Georgia, Str. of, Canada 72 D4 49 25N 124 0W
Georgian B., Canada 70 C3 45 15N 81 0W
Georgina —►, Australia 62 C2 23 30S 139 47 E
Georgina Downs, Australia 62 C2 21 10S 137 40 E
Georgiu-Dezh = Liski, Russia 25 D6 51 3N 39 30 E
Georgiyevsk, Russia 25 F7 44 12N 43 28 E
Gera, Germany 16 C7 50 53N 12 4 E
Geraardsbergen, Belgium 15 D3 50 45N 3 53 E
Geral, Serra, Brazil 95 B6 26 25S 50 0W
Geral de Goiás, Serra, Brazil 93 F9 12 0S 46 0W
Geraldine, U.S.A. 82 C8 47 36N 110 16W
Geraldton, Australia 61 E1 28 48S 114 32 E
Geraldton, Canada 70 C2 49 44N 86 59W
Gereshk, Afghan. 40 D4 31 47N 64 35 E
Gerik, Malaysia 39 K3 5 50N 101 15 E
Gering, U.S.A. 80 E3 41 50N 103 40W
Gerlach, U.S.A. 82 F4 40 39N 119 21W
Germansen Landing, Canada 72 B4 55 43N 124 40W
Germany ■, Europe 16 C6 51 0N 10 0 E
Germiston, S. Africa 57 D4 26 15S 28 10 E
Gernika-Lumo, Spain 19 A4 43 19N 2 40W
Gero, Japan 31 G8 35 48N 137 14 E
Gerona = Girona, Spain 19 B7 41 58N 2 46 E
Gerrard, Canada 72 C5 50 30N 117 17W
Geser, Indonesia 37 E8 3 50S 130 54 E
Getafe, Spain 19 B4 40 18N 3 44W
Gethsémani, Canada 71 B7 50 13N 60 40W
Gettysburg, Pa., U.S.A. 76 F7 39 50N 77 14W
Gettysburg, S. Dak., U.S.A. 80 C5 45 1N 99 57W
Getxo, Spain 19 A4 43 21N 2 59W
Getz Ice Shelf, Antarctica 5 D14 75 0S 130 0W
Geyser, U.S.A. 82 C8 47 16N 110 30W
Geyserville, U.S.A. 84 G4 38 42N 122 54W
Ghaghara —►, India 43 G11 25 45N 84 40 E
Ghana ■, W. Afr. 50 G5 8 0N 1 0W
Ghansor, India 43 H9 22 39N 80 1 E
Ghanzi, Botswana 56 C3 21 50S 21 34 E
Ghanzi □, Botswana 56 C3 21 50S 21 45 E
Ghardaïa, Algeria 50 B6 32 20N 3 37 E
Gharyān, Libya 51 B8 32 10N 13 0 E
Ghat, Libya 51 D8 24 59N 10 11 E
Ghatal, India 43 H12 22 40N 87 46 E
Ghatampur, India 43 F9 26 8N 80 13 E
Ghaṭṭī, Si. Arabia 44 D3 31 16N 37 31 E
Ghawdex = Gozo, Malta 23 C1 36 3N 14 13 E
Ghazal, Bahr el —►, Chad 51 F9 13 0N 15 47 E
Ghazâl, Bahr el —►, Sudan 51 G12 9 31N 30 25 E
Ghaziabad, India 42 E7 28 42N 77 26 E
Ghazipur, India 43 G10 25 38N 83 35 E
Ghaznī, Afghan. 42 C3 33 30N 68 28 E
Ghaznī □, Afghan. 40 C6 32 10N 68 20 E
Ghent = Gent, Belgium 15 C3 51 2N 3 42 E
Ghizao, Afghan. 42 C1 33 20N 65 44 E
Ghizar —►, Pakistan 43 A5 36 15N 73 43 E
Ghogha, India 42 J5 21 40N 72 20 E
Ghotaru, India 42 F4 27 20N 70 1 E
Ghotki, Pakistan 42 E3 28 5N 69 21 E
Ghowr □, Afghan. 40 C4 34 0N 64 20 E
Ghudaf, W. al —►, Iraq 44 C4 32 56N 43 30 E
Ghudāmis, Libya 49 C4 30 11N 9 29 E
Ghughri, India 43 H9 22 39N 80 41 E
Ghugus, India 40 K11 19 58N 79 12 E
Ghulam Mohammad Barrage, Pakistan 42 G3 25 30N 68 20 E
Ghūrīān, Afghan. 40 B2 34 17N 61 25 E
Gia Dinh, Vietnam 39 G6 10 49N 106 42 E
Gia Lai = Plei Ku, Vietnam 38 F7 13 57N 108 0 E
Gia Nghia, Vietnam 39 G6 11 58N 107 42 E
Gia Ngoc, Vietnam 38 E7 14 50N 108 58 E
Gia Vuc, Vietnam 38 E7 14 42N 108 34 E
Giant Forest, U.S.A. 84 J8 36 36N 118 43W
Giants Causeway, U.K. 13 A5 55 16N 6 29W
Giarabub = Al Jaghbūb, Libya 51 C10 29 42N 24 38 E
Giarre, Italy 20 F6 37 43N 15 11 E
Gibara, Cuba 88 B4 21 9N 76 11W
Gibb River, Australia 60 C4 16 26S 126 26 E
Gibbon, U.S.A. 80 E5 40 45N 98 51W
Gibraltar ■, Europe 19 D3 36 7N 5 22W
Gibraltar, Str. of, Medit. S. 19 E3 35 55N 5 40W
Gibson Desert, Australia 60 D4 24 0S 126 0 E
Gibsons, Canada 72 D4 49 24N 123 32W
Gibsonville, U.S.A. 84 F6 39 46N 120 54W
Giddings, U.S.A. 81 K6 30 11N 96 56W
Giessen, Germany 16 C5 50 34N 8 41 E
Gīfān, Iran 45 B8 37 54N 57 28 E
Gifford Creek, Australia 60 D2 24 3S 116 16 E
Gifu, Japan 31 G8 35 30N 136 45 E
Gifu □, Japan 31 G8 35 40N 137 0 E
Giganta, Sa. de la, Mexico 86 B2 25 30N 111 30W
Gigha, U.K. 12 F3 55 42N 5 44W
Gíglio, Italy 20 C4 42 20N 10 52 E
Gijón, Spain 19 A3 43 32N 5 42W
Gil I., Canada 72 C3 53 12N 129 15W
Gila —►, U.S.A. 83 K6 32 43N 114 33W
Gila Bend, U.S.A. 83 K7 32 57N 112 43W
Gila Bend Mts., U.S.A. 83 K7 33 10N 113 0W
Gīlān □, Iran 45 B6 37 0N 50 0 E
Gilbert —►, Australia 62 B3 16 35S 141 15 E
Gilbert Is., Kiribati 64 G9 1 0N 172 0 E
Gilbert Plains, Canada 73 C8 51 9N 100 28W
Gilbert River, Australia 62 B3 18 9S 142 52 E
Gilberton, Australia 62 B3 19 16S 143 35 E
Gilford I., Canada 72 C3 50 40N 126 30W
Gilgandra, Australia 63 E4 31 43S 148 39 E
Gilgil, Kenya 54 C4 0 30S 36 20 E
Gilgit, India 43 B6 35 50N 74 15 E
Gilgit —►, Pakistan 43 B6 35 44N 74 37 E
Gillam, Canada 73 B10 56 20N 94 40W
Gillen, L., Australia 61 E3 26 11S 124 38 E
Gilles, L., Australia 63 E2 32 50S 136 45 E
Gillette, U.S.A. 80 C2 44 18N 105 30W
Gilliat, Australia 62 C3 20 40S 141 28 E
Gillingham, U.K. 11 F8 51 23N 0 33 E
Gilmer, U.S.A. 81 J7 32 44N 94 57W
Gilmore, Australia 63 F4 35 20S 148 12 E
Gilmore, L., Australia 61 F3 32 29S 121 37 E
Gilmour, Canada 70 D4 44 48N 77 37W
Gilroy, U.S.A. 84 H5 37 1N 121 34W
Gimli, Canada 73 C9 50 40N 97 0W
Gin Gin, Australia 63 D5 25 0S 151 58 E
Gindie, Australia 62 C4 23 44S 148 8 E
Gingin, Australia 61 F2 31 22S 115 54 E
Ginir, Ethiopia 46 F3 7 6N 40 40 E
Gióna, Óros, Greece 21 E10 38 38N 22 14 E
Gir Hills, India 42 J4 21 0N 71 0 E
Girab, India 42 F4 26 2N 70 38 E
Girâfi, W. —►, Egypt 47 F3 29 58N 34 39 E
Girard, Kans., U.S.A. 81 G7 37 31N 94 51W
Girard, Ohio, U.S.A. 78 E4 41 9N 80 42W
Girard, Pa., U.S.A. 78 D4 42 0N 80 19W
Girdle Ness, U.K. 12 D6 57 9N 2 3W
Giresun, Turkey 25 F6 40 55N 38 30 E
Girga, Egypt 51 C12 26 17N 31 55 E
Giridih, India 43 G12 24 10N 86 21 E
Girilambone, Australia 63 E4 31 16S 146 57 E
Girne = Kyrenia, Cyprus 23 D12 35 20N 33 20 E
Girona, Spain 19 B7 41 58N 2 46 E
Gironde —►, France 18 D3 45 32N 1 7W
Giru, Australia 62 B4 19 30S 147 5 E
Girvan, U.K. 12 F4 55 14N 4 51W
Gisborne, N.Z. 59 H7 38 39S 178 5 E
Gisenyi, Rwanda 54 C2 1 41S 29 15 E
Gislaved, Sweden 9 H15 57 19N 13 32 E
Gitega, Burundi 54 C2 3 26S 29 56 E
Giuba —►, Somali Rep. 46 G3 1 30N 42 35 E
Giurgiu, Romania 17 G13 43 52N 25 57 E
Giza = El Gîza, Egypt 51 C12 30 0N 31 10 E
Gizhiga, Russia 27 C17 62 3N 160 30 E
Gizhiginskaya Guba, Russia 27 C16 61 0N 158 0 E
Giżycko, Poland 17 A11 54 2N 21 48 E
Gjirokastra, Albania 21 D9 40 7N 20 10 E
Gjoa Haven, Canada 68 B10 68 20N 96 8W
Gjøvik, Norway 9 F14 60 47N 10 43 E
Glace Bay, Canada 71 C8 46 11N 59 58W
Glacier Bay, U.S.A. 72 B1 58 40N 136 0W
Glacier Nat. Park, Canada 72 C5 51 15N 117 30W
Glacier Park, U.S.A. 82 B7 48 30N 113 18W
Glacier Peak, U.S.A. 82 B3 48 7N 121 7W
Gladewater, U.S.A. 81 J7 32 33N 94 56W
Gladstone, Queens., Australia 62 C5 23 52S 151 16 E
Gladstone, S. Austral., Australia 63 E2 33 15S 138 22 E
Gladstone, W. Austral., Australia 61 E1 25 57S 114 17 E
Gladstone, Canada 73 C9 50 13N 98 57W
Gladstone, U.S.A. 76 C2 45 51N 87 1W
Gladwin, U.S.A. 76 D3 43 59N 84 29W
Gladys L., Canada 72 B2 59 50N 133 0W
Glåma = Glomma —►, Norway 9 G14 59 12N 10 57 E
Gláma, Iceland 8 D2 65 48N 23 0W
Glamis, U.S.A. 85 N11 32 55N 115 5W
Glasco, Kans., U.S.A. 80 F6 39 22N 97 50W
Glasco, N.Y., U.S.A. 79 D11 42 3N 73 57W
Glasgow, U.K. 12 F4 55 51N 4 15W
Glasgow, Ky., U.S.A. 76 G3 37 0N 85 55W
Glasgow, Mont., U.S.A. 82 B10 48 12N 106 38W
Glastonbury, U.K. 11 F5 51 9N 2 43W
Glastonbury, U.S.A. 79 E12 41 43N 72 37W
Glazov, Russia 24 C9 58 9N 52 40 E
Gleiwitz = Gliwice, Poland 17 C10 50 22N 18 41 E
Glen, U.S.A. 79 B13 44 7N 71 11W
Glen Affric, U.K. 12 D3 57 17N 5 1W
Glen Canyon Dam, U.S.A. 83 H8 36 57N 111 29W
Glen Canyon National Recreation Area, U.S.A. 83 H8 37 15N 111 0W
Glen Coe, U.K. 12 E3 56 40N 5 0W
Glen Cove, U.S.A. 79 F11 40 52N 73 38W
Glen Garry, U.K. 12 D3 57 3N 5 7W
Glen Innes, Australia 63 D5 29 44S 151 44 E
Glen Lyon, U.S.A. 79 E8 41 10N 76 5W
Glen Mor, U.K. 12 D4 57 9N 4 37W
Glen Moriston, U.K. 12 D4 57 11N 4 52W
Glen Spean, U.K. 12 E4 56 53N 4 40W
Glen Ullin, U.S.A. 80 B4 46 49N 101 50W
Glenburgh, Australia 61 E2 25 26S 116 6 E
Glencoe, Canada 78 D3 42 45N 81 43W
Glencoe, S. Africa 57 D5 28 11S 30 11 E
Glencoe, U.S.A. 80 C7 44 46N 94 9W
Glendale, Ariz., U.S.A. 83 K7 33 32N 112 11W
Glendale, Calif., U.S.A. 85 L8 34 9N 118 15W
Glendale, Oreg., U.S.A. 82 E2 42 44N 123 26W
Glendale, Zimbabwe 55 F3 17 22S 31 5 E
Glendive, U.S.A. 80 B2 47 7N 104 43W
Glendo, U.S.A. 80 D2 42 30N 105 2W
Glenelg, Australia 63 E2 34 58S 138 31 E
Glenelg —►, Australia 63 F3 38 4S 140 59 E
Glenflorrie, Australia 60 D2 22 55S 115 59 E
Glengarriff, Ireland 13 E2 51 45N 9 34W
Glengyle, Australia 62 C2 24 48S 139 37 E
Glenmora, U.S.A. 81 K8 30 59N 92 35W
Glenmorgan, Australia 63 D4 27 14S 149 42 E
Glenn, U.S.A. 84 F4 39 31N 122 1W
Glennamaddy, Ireland 13 C3 53 37N 8 33W
Glenns Ferry, U.S.A. 82 E6 42 57N 115 18W
Glenorchy, Australia 62 G4 42 49S 147 18 E
Glenore, Australia 62 B3 17 50S 141 12 E
Glenormiston, Australia 62 C2 22 55S 138 50 E
Glenreagh, Australia 63 E5 30 2S 153 1 E
Glenrock, U.S.A. 82 E11 42 52N 105 52W
Glenrothes, U.K. 12 E5 56 12N 3 10W
Glens Falls, U.S.A. 79 C11 43 19N 73 39W
Glenties, Ireland 13 B3 54 49N 8 16W
Glenville, U.S.A. 76 F5 38 56N 80 50W
Glenwood, Alta., Canada 72 D6 49 21N 113 31W
Glenwood, Nfld., Canada 71 C9 49 0N 54 58W
Glenwood, Ark., U.S.A. 81 H8 34 20N 93 33W
Glenwood, Hawaii, U.S.A. 74 J17 19 29N 155 9W
Glenwood, Iowa, U.S.A. 80 E7 41 3N 95 45W
Glenwood, Minn., U.S.A. 80 C7 45 39N 95 23W
Glenwood, Wash., U.S.A. 84 D5 46 1N 121 17W
Glenwood Springs, U.S.A. 82 G10 39 33N 107 19W
Glettinganes, Iceland 8 D7 65 30N 13 37W
Gliwice, Poland 17 C10 50 22N 18 41 E
Globe, U.S.A. 83 K8 33 24N 110 47W
Głogów, Poland 16 C9 51 37N 16 5 E
Glomma —►, Norway 9 G14 59 12N 10 57 E
Glorieuses, Is., Ind. Oc. 57 A8 11 30S 47 20 E
Glossop, U.K. 10 D6 53 27N 1 56W
Gloucester, Australia 63 E5 32 0S 151 59 E
Gloucester, U.K. 11 F5 51 53N 2 15W
Gloucester, U.S.A. 79 D14 42 37N 70 40W
Gloucester I., Australia 62 C4 20 0S 148 30 E
Gloucestershire □, U.K. 11 F5 51 46N 2 15W
Gloversville, U.S.A. 79 C10 43 3N 74 21W
Glovertown, Canada 71 C9 48 40N 54 3W
Glusk, Belarus 17 B15 52 53N 28 41 E
Gmünd, Austria 16 D8 48 45N 15 0 E
Gmunden, Austria 16 E7 47 55N 13 48 E
Gniezno, Poland 17 B9 52 30N 17 35 E
Gnowangerup, Australia 61 F2 33 58S 117 59 E
Go Cong, Vietnam 39 G6 10 22N 106 40 E
Gō-no-ura, Japan 31 H4 33 44N 129 40 E
Goa, India 40 M8 15 33N 73 59 E
Goa □, India 40 M8 15 33N 73 59 E
Goalen Hd., Australia 63 F5 36 33S 150 4 E
Goalpara, India 41 F17 26 10N 90 40 E
Goalundo Ghat, Bangla. 43 H13 23 50N 89 47 E
Goat Fell, U.K. 12 F3 55 38N 5 11W
Goba, Ethiopia 46 F2 7 1N 39 59 E
Goba, Mozam. 57 D5 26 15S 32 13 E
Gobabis, Namibia 56 C2 22 30S 19 0 E
Gobi, Asia 34 C6 44 0N 110 0 E
Gobō, Japan 31 H7 33 53N 135 10 E
Gochas, Namibia 56 C2 24 59S 18 55 E
Godavari —►, India 41 L13 16 25N 82 18 E
Godavari Point, India 41 L13 17 0N 82 20 E
Godbout, Canada 71 C6 49 20N 67 38W
Godda, India 43 G12 24 50N 87 13 E
Goderich, Canada 70 D3 43 45N 81 41W
Godhra, India 42 H5 22 49N 73 40 E
Godoy Cruz, Argentina 94 C2 32 56S 68 52W
Gods —►, Canada 73 B10 56 22N 92 51W
Gods L., Canada 73 C10 54 40N 94 15W
Godthåb = Nuuk, Greenland 69 B14 64 10N 51 35W

Helmand

Haldia, India 41 H16 22 5N 88 3 E
Haldwani, India 43 E8 29 31N 79 30 E
Hale →, Australia 62 C2 24 56S 135 53 E
Haleakala Crater, U.S.A. 74 H16 20 43N 156 16W
Halesowen, U.K. 11 E5 52 27N 2 3W
Haleyville, U.S.A. 77 H2 34 14N 87 37W
Halfway →, Canada 72 B4 56 12N 121 32W
Haliburton, Canada 70 C4 45 3N 78 30W
Halifax, Australia 62 B4 18 32S 146 22 E
Halifax, Canada 71 D7 44 38N 63 35W
Halifax, U.K. 10 D6 53 43N 1 52W
Halifax B., Australia 62 B4 18 50S 147 0 E
Halifax I., Namibia 56 D2 26 38S 15 4 E
Halīl →, Iran 45 E8 27 40N 58 30 E
Halkirk, U.K. 12 C5 58 30N 3 29W
Hall Pt., Australia 60 C3 15 40S 124 23 E
Halland, Sweden 9 H15 57 8N 12 47 E
Halle, Belgium 15 D4 50 44N 4 13 E
Halle, Germany 16 C6 51 30N 11 56 E
Hällefors, Sweden 9 G16 59 47N 14 31 E
Hallett, Australia 63 E2 33 25S 138 55 E
Hallettsville, U.S.A. 81 L6 29 27N 96 57W
Halliday, U.S.A. 80 B3 47 21N 102 20W
Halliday L., Canada 73 A7 61 21N 108 56W
Hallim, S. Korea 35 H14 33 24N 126 15 E
Hallingdalselvi →, Norway 9 F13 60 23N 9 35 E
Hallock, U.S.A. 73 D9 48 47N 96 57W
Halls Creek, Australia 60 C4 18 16S 127 38 E
Hallsberg, Sweden 9 G16 59 5N 15 7 E
Hallstead, U.S.A. 79 E9 41 58N 75 45W
Halmahera, Indonesia 37 D7 0 40N 128 0 E
Halmstad, Sweden 9 H15 56 41N 12 52 E
Hälsingborg = Helsingborg, Sweden 9 H15 56 3N 12 42 E
Hälsingland, Sweden 9 F16 61 40N 16 5 E
Halstad, U.S.A. 80 B6 47 21N 96 50W
Halstead, U.K. 11 F8 51 57N 0 40 E
Halti, Finland 8 B19 69 17N 21 18 E
Halton □, U.K. 10 D5 53 22N 2 45W
Haltwhistle, U.K. 10 C5 54 58N 2 26W
Halul, Qatar 45 E7 25 40N 52 40 E
Ḩalvān, Iran 45 C8 33 57N 56 15 E
Ham Tan, Vietnam 39 G6 10 40N 107 45 E
Ham Yen, Vietnam 38 A5 22 4N 105 3 E
Hamab, Namibia 56 D2 28 7S 19 16 E
Hamada, Japan 31 G6 34 56N 132 4 E
Hamadān, Iran 45 C6 34 52N 48 32 E
Hamadān □, Iran 45 C6 35 0N 49 0 E
Hamāh, Syria 44 C3 35 5N 36 40 E
Hamamatsu, Japan 31 G8 34 45N 137 45 E
Hamar, Norway 9 F14 60 48N 11 7 E
Hambantota, Sri Lanka 40 R12 6 10N 81 10 E
Hamber Prov. Park, Canada 72 C5 52 20N 118 0W
Hamburg, Germany 16 B5 53 33N 9 59 E
Hamburg, Ark., U.S.A. 81 J9 33 14N 91 48W
Hamburg, Iowa, U.S.A. 80 E7 40 36N 95 39W
Hamburg, N.Y., U.S.A. 78 D6 42 43N 78 50W
Hamburg, Pa., U.S.A. 79 F9 40 33N 75 59W
Ḩamḑ, W. al →, Si. Arabia 44 E3 24 55N 36 20 E
Hamden, U.S.A. 79 E12 41 23N 72 54W
Häme, Finland 9 F20 61 38N 25 10 E
Hämeenlinna, Finland 9 F21 61 0N 24 28 E
Hamelin Pool, Australia 61 E1 26 22S 114 20 E
Hameln, Germany 16 B5 52 6N 9 21 E
Hamerkaz □, Israel 47 C3 32 15N 34 55 E
Hamersley Ra., Australia 60 D2 22 0S 117 45 E
Hamhung, N. Korea 35 E14 39 54N 127 30 E
Hami, China 32 B4 42 55N 93 25 E
Hamilton, Australia 63 F3 37 45S 142 2 E
Hamilton, Canada 70 D4 43 15N 79 50W
Hamilton, N.Z. 59 G5 37 47S 175 19 E
Hamilton, U.K. 12 F4 55 46N 4 2W
Hamilton, Mo., U.S.A. 80 F8 39 45N 93 59W
Hamilton, Mont., U.S.A. 82 C6 46 15N 114 10W
Hamilton, N.Y., U.S.A. 79 D9 42 50N 75 33W
Hamilton, Ohio, U.S.A. 76 F3 39 24N 84 34W
Hamilton, Tex., U.S.A. 81 K5 31 42N 98 7W
Hamilton →, Australia 62 C2 23 30S 139 47 E
Hamilton City, U.S.A. 84 F4 39 45N 122 1W
Hamilton Hotel, Australia 62 C3 22 45S 140 40 E
Hamilton Inlet, Canada 71 B8 54 0N 57 30W
Hamina, Finland 9 F22 60 34N 27 12 E
Hamiota, Canada 73 C8 50 11N 100 38W
Hamlet, U.S.A. 77 H6 34 53N 79 42W
Hamley Bridge, Australia 63 E2 34 17S 138 35 E
Hamlin = Hameln, Germany 16 B5 52 6N 9 21 E
Hamlin, N.Y., U.S.A. 78 C7 43 17N 77 55W
Hamlin, Tex., U.S.A. 81 J4 32 53N 100 8W
Hamm, Germany 16 C4 51 40N 7 50 E
Hammerfest, Norway 8 A20 70 39N 23 41 E
Hammond, Ind., U.S.A. 76 E2 41 38N 87 30W
Hammond, La., U.S.A. 81 K9 30 30N 90 28W
Hammonton, U.S.A. 76 F8 39 39N 74 48W
Hampden, N.Z. 59 L3 45 18S 170 50 E
Hampshire □, U.K. 11 F6 51 7N 1 23W
Hampshire Downs, U.K. 11 F6 51 15N 1 10W
Hampton, Ark., U.S.A. 81 J8 33 32N 92 28W
Hampton, Iowa, U.S.A. 80 D8 42 45N 93 13W
Hampton, N.H., U.S.A. 79 D14 42 57N 70 50W
Hampton, S.C., U.S.A. 77 J5 32 52N 81 7W
Hampton, Va., U.S.A. 76 G7 37 2N 76 21W
Hampton Tableland, Australia 61 F4 32 0S 127 0 E
Hamyang, S. Korea 35 G14 35 32N 127 42 E
Han Pijesak, Bos.-H. 21 B8 44 5N 18 57 E
Hana, U.S.A. 74 H17 20 45N 155 59W
Hanak, Si. Arabia 44 E3 25 32N 37 0 E
Hanamaki, Japan 30 E10 39 23N 141 7 E
Hanang, Tanzania 54 C4 4 30S 35 25 E
Hanau, Germany 16 C5 50 7N 8 56 E
Hanbogd, Mongolia 34 C4 43 11N 107 10 E
Hancheng, China 34 G6 35 31N 110 25 E
Hancock, Mich., U.S.A. 80 B10 47 8N 88 35W
Hancock, Minn., U.S.A. 80 C7 45 30N 95 48W
Hancock, N.Y., U.S.A. 79 E9 41 57N 75 17W
Handa, Japan 31 G8 34 53N 136 55 E
Handan, China 34 F8 36 35N 114 28 E
Handeni, Tanzania 54 D4 5 25S 38 2 E
Handeni □, Tanzania 54 D4 5 30S 38 0 E
Handwara, India 43 B6 34 21N 74 20 E
Hanegev, Israel 47 E4 30 50N 35 0 E
Haney, Canada 72 D4 49 12N 122 40W
Hanford, U.S.A. 84 J7 36 20N 119 39W
Hang Chat, Thailand 38 C2 18 20N 99 21 E
Hang Dong, Thailand 38 C2 18 41N 98 55 E
Hangang →, S. Korea 35 F14 37 50N 126 30 E
Hangayn Nuruu, Mongolia 32 B4 47 30N 99 0 E
Hangchou = Hangzhou, China 33 C7 30 18N 120 11 E
Hanggin Houqi, China 34 D4 40 58N 107 4 E
Hanggin Qi, China 34 E5 39 52N 108 50 E
Hangu, China 35 E9 39 18N 117 53 E
Hangzhou, China 33 C7 30 18N 120 11 E
Hangzhou Wan, China 33 C7 30 15N 120 45 E
Hanhongor, Mongolia 34 C3 43 55N 104 28 E
Ḩanīdh, Si. Arabia 45 E6 26 35N 48 38 E
Ḩanīsh, Yemen 46 E3 13 45N 42 46 E
Hankinson, U.S.A. 80 B6 46 4N 96 54W
Hanko, Finland 9 G20 59 50N 22 57 E
Hanksville, U.S.A. 83 G8 38 22N 110 43W
Hanle, India 43 C8 32 42N 79 4 E
Hanmer Springs, N.Z. 59 K4 42 32S 172 50 E
Hann →, Australia 60 C4 17 26S 126 17 E
Hann, Mt., Australia 60 C4 15 45S 126 0 E
Hanna, Canada 72 C6 51 40N 111 54W
Hannaford, U.S.A. 80 B5 47 19N 98 11W
Hannah, U.S.A. 80 A5 48 58N 98 42W
Hannah B., Canada 70 B4 51 40N 80 0W
Hannibal, U.S.A. 80 F9 39 42N 91 22W
Hannover, Germany 16 B5 52 22N 9 46 E
Hanoi, Vietnam 32 D5 21 5N 105 55 E
Hanover = Hannover, Germany 16 B5 52 22N 9 46 E
Hanover, Canada 78 B3 44 9N 81 2W
Hanover, S. Africa 56 E3 31 4S 24 29 E
Hanover, N.H., U.S.A. 79 C12 43 42N 72 17W
Hanover, Ohio, U.S.A. 78 F2 40 4N 82 16W
Hanover, Pa., U.S.A. 76 F7 39 48N 76 59W
Hanover, I., Chile 96 G2 51 0S 74 50W
Hansi, India 42 E6 29 10N 75 57 E
Hanson, L., Australia 63 E2 31 0S 136 15 E
Hantsavichy, Belarus 17 B14 52 49N 26 30 E
Hanzhong, China 34 H4 33 10N 107 1 E
Hanzhuang, China 35 G9 34 33N 117 23 E
Haora, India 43 H13 22 37N 88 20 E
Haparanda, Sweden 8 D21 65 52N 24 8 E
Happy, U.S.A. 81 H4 34 45N 101 52W
Happy Camp, U.S.A. 82 F2 41 48N 123 23W
Happy Valley-Goose Bay, Canada 71 B7 53 15N 60 20W
Hapsu, N. Korea 35 D15 41 13N 128 51 E
Hapur, India 42 E7 28 45N 77 45 E
Ḩaql, Si. Arabia 47 F3 29 10N 34 58 E
Har, Indonesia 37 F8 5 16S 133 14 E
Har-Ayrag, Mongolia 34 B5 45 47N 109 16 E
Har Hu, China 32 C4 38 20N 97 38 E
Har Us Nuur, Mongolia 32 B4 48 0N 92 0 E
Har Yehuda, Israel 47 D3 31 35N 34 57 E
Ḩaraḑ, Si. Arabia 46 C4 24 22N 49 0 E
Haranomachi, Japan 30 F10 37 38N 140 58 E
Harare, Zimbabwe 55 F3 17 43S 31 2 E
Harbin, China 35 B14 45 48N 126 40 E
Harbor Beach, U.S.A. 76 D4 43 51N 82 39W
Harbor Springs, U.S.A. 76 C3 45 26N 85 0W
Harbour Breton, Canada 71 C8 47 29N 55 50W
Harbour Grace, Canada 71 C9 47 40N 53 22W
Harda, India 42 H7 22 27N 77 5 E
Hardangerfjorden, Norway 9 F12 60 5N 6 0 E
Hardangervidda, Norway 9 F12 60 7N 7 20 E
Hardap Dam, Namibia 56 C2 24 32S 17 50 E
Hardenberg, Neths. 15 B6 52 34N 6 37 E
Harderwijk, Neths. 15 B5 52 21N 5 38 E
Hardey →, Australia 60 D2 22 45S 116 8 E
Hardin, U.S.A. 82 D10 45 44N 107 37W
Harding, S. Africa 57 E4 30 35S 29 55 E
Harding Ra., Australia 60 C3 16 17S 124 55 E
Hardisty, Canada 72 C6 52 40N 111 18W
Hardman, U.S.A. 82 D4 45 10N 119 41W
Hardoi, India 43 F9 27 26N 80 6 E
Hardwar = Haridwar, India 42 E8 29 58N 78 9 E
Hardwick, U.S.A. 79 B12 44 30N 72 22W
Hardy, U.S.A. 81 G9 36 19N 91 29W
Hardy, Pen., Chile 96 H3 55 30S 68 20W
Hare B., Canada 71 B8 51 15N 55 45W
Hareid, Norway 9 E12 62 22N 6 1 E
Harer, Ethiopia 46 F3 9 20N 42 8 E
Hargeisa, Somali Rep. 46 F3 9 30N 44 2 E
Hari →, Indonesia 36 E2 1 16S 104 5 E
Haria, Canary Is. 22 E6 29 8N 13 32W
Haridwar, India 42 E8 29 58N 78 9 E
Haringhata →, Bangla. 41 J16 22 0N 89 58 E
Harīrūd →, Asia 40 A2 37 24N 60 38 E
Härjedalen, Sweden 9 E15 62 22N 13 5 E
Harlan, Iowa, U.S.A. 80 E7 41 39N 95 19W
Harlan, Ky., U.S.A. 77 G4 36 51N 83 19W
Harlech, U.K. 10 E3 52 52N 4 6W
Harlem, U.S.A. 82 B9 48 32N 108 47W
Harlingen, Neths. 15 A5 53 11N 5 25 E
Harlingen, U.S.A. 81 M6 26 12N 97 42W
Harlow, U.K. 11 F8 51 46N 0 8 E
Harlowton, U.S.A. 82 C9 46 26N 109 50W
Harney Basin, U.S.A. 82 E4 43 30N 119 0W
Harney L., U.S.A. 82 E4 43 14N 119 8W
Harney Peak, U.S.A. 80 D3 43 52N 103 32W
Härnösand, Sweden 9 E17 62 38N 17 55 E
Haroldswick, U.K. 12 A8 60 48N 0 50W
Harp L., Canada 71 A7 55 5N 61 50W
Harrand, Pakistan 42 E4 29 28N 70 3 E
Harriman, U.S.A. 77 H3 35 56N 84 33W
Harrington Harbour, Canada 71 B8 50 31N 59 30W
Harris, U.K. 12 D2 57 50N 6 55W
Harris, Sd. of, U.K. 12 D1 57 44N 7 6W
Harris L., Australia 63 E2 31 10S 135 10 E
Harrisburg, Ill., U.S.A. 81 G10 37 44N 88 32W
Harrisburg, Nebr., U.S.A. 80 E3 41 33N 103 44W
Harrisburg, Oreg., U.S.A. 82 D2 44 16N 123 10W
Harrisburg, Pa., U.S.A. 78 F8 40 16N 76 53W
Harrismith, S. Africa 57 D4 28 15S 29 8 E
Harrison, Ark., U.S.A. 81 G8 36 14N 93 7W
Harrison, Idaho, U.S.A. 82 C5 47 27N 116 47W
Harrison, Nebr., U.S.A. 80 D3 42 41N 103 53W
Harrison, C., Canada 71 B8 54 55N 57 55W
Harrison L., Canada 72 D4 49 33N 121 50W
Harrisonburg, U.S.A. 76 F6 38 27N 78 52W
Harrisonville, U.S.A. 80 F7 38 39N 94 21W
Harriston, Canada 70 D3 43 57N 80 53W
Harrisville, U.S.A. 78 B1 44 39N 83 17W
Harrogate, U.K. 10 C6 54 0N 1 33W
Harrow, U.K. 11 F7 51 35N 0 21W
Harsīn, Iran 44 C5 34 18N 47 33 E
Harstad, Norway 8 B17 68 48N 16 30 E
Hart, U.S.A. 76 D2 43 42N 86 22W
Hart, L., Australia 63 E2 31 10S 136 25 E
Hartbees →, S. Africa 56 D3 28 45S 20 32 E
Hartford, Conn., U.S.A. 79 E12 41 46N 72 41W
Hartford, Ky., U.S.A. 76 G2 37 27N 86 55W
Hartford, S. Dak., U.S.A. 80 D6 43 38N 96 57W
Hartford, Wis., U.S.A. 80 D10 43 19N 88 22W
Hartford City, U.S.A. 76 E3 40 27N 85 22W
Hartland, Canada 71 C6 46 20N 67 32W
Hartland Pt., U.K. 11 F3 51 1N 4 32W
Hartlepool, U.K. 10 C6 54 42N 1 13W
Hartlepool □, U.K. 10 C6 54 42N 1 17W
Hartley Bay, Canada 72 C3 53 25N 129 15W
Hartmannberge, Namibia 56 B1 17 0S 13 0 E
Hartney, Canada 73 D8 49 30N 100 35W
Harts →, S. Africa 56 D3 28 24S 24 17 E
Hartselle, U.S.A. 77 H2 34 27N 86 56W
Hartshorne, U.S.A. 81 H7 34 51N 95 34W
Hartsville, U.S.A. 77 H5 34 23N 80 4W
Hartwell, U.S.A. 77 H4 34 21N 82 56W
Harunabad, Pakistan 42 E5 29 35N 73 8 E
Harvand, Iran 45 D7 28 25N 55 43 E
Harvey, Australia 61 F2 33 5S 115 54 E
Harvey, Ill., U.S.A. 76 E2 41 36N 87 50W
Harvey, N. Dak., U.S.A. 80 B5 47 47N 99 56W
Harwich, U.K. 11 F9 51 56N 1 17 E
Haryana □, India 42 E7 29 0N 76 10 E
Haryn →, Belarus 17 B14 52 7N 27 17 E
Harz, Germany 16 C6 51 38N 10 44 E
Hasan Kīādeh, Iran 45 B6 37 24N 49 58 E
Ḩasanābād, Iran 45 C7 32 8N 52 44 E
Hasanpur, India 42 E8 28 43N 78 17 E
Hashimoto, Japan 31 G7 34 19N 135 37 E
Hashtjerd, Iran 45 C6 35 52N 50 40 E
Haskell, Okla., U.S.A. 81 H7 35 50N 95 40W
Haskell, Tex., U.S.A. 81 J5 33 10N 99 44W
Haslemere, U.K. 11 F7 51 5N 0 43W
Hasselt, Belgium 15 D5 50 56N 5 21 E
Hassi Messaoud, Algeria 50 B7 31 51N 6 1 E
Hässleholm, Sweden 9 H15 56 10N 13 46 E
Hastings, N.Z. 59 H6 39 39S 176 52 E
Hastings, U.K. 11 G8 50 51N 0 35 E
Hastings, Mich., U.S.A. 76 D3 42 39N 85 17W
Hastings, Minn., U.S.A. 80 C8 44 44N 92 51W
Hastings, Nebr., U.S.A. 80 E5 40 35N 98 23W
Hastings Ra., Australia 63 E5 31 15S 152 14 E
Hat Yai, Thailand 39 J3 7 1N 100 27 E
Hatanbulag, Mongolia 34 C5 43 8N 109 5 E
Hatay = Antalya, Turkey 25 G5 36 52N 30 45 E
Hatch, U.S.A. 83 K10 32 40N 107 9W
Hatches Creek, Australia 62 C2 20 56S 135 12 E
Hatchet L., Canada 73 B8 58 36N 103 40W
Hateruma-Shima, Japan 31 M1 24 3N 123 47 E
Hatfield P.O., Australia 63 E3 33 54S 143 49 E
Hatgal, Mongolia 32 A5 50 26N 100 9 E
Hathras, India 42 F8 27 36N 78 6 E
Hatia, Bangla. 41 H17 22 30N 91 5 E
Hato Mayor, Dom. Rep. 89 C6 18 46N 69 15W
Hattah, Australia 63 E3 34 48S 142 17 E
Hatteras, C., U.S.A. 77 H8 35 14N 75 32W
Hattiesburg, U.S.A. 81 K10 31 20N 89 17W
Hatvan, Hungary 17 E10 47 40N 19 45 E
Hau Duc, Vietnam 38 E7 15 20N 108 13 E
Haugesund, Norway 9 G11 59 23N 5 13 E
Haukipudas, Finland 8 D21 65 12N 25 20 E
Haultain →, Canada 73 B7 55 51N 106 46W
Hauraki G., N.Z. 59 G5 36 35S 175 5 E
Haut Atlas, Morocco 50 B4 32 30N 5 0W
Haut-Zaïre □, Dem. Rep. of the Congo 54 B2 2 20N 26 0 E
Hauterive, Canada 71 C6 49 10N 68 16W
Hautes Fagnes = Hohe Venn, Belgium 15 D6 50 30N 6 5 E
Hauts Plateaux, Algeria 48 C4 35 0N 1 0 E
Havana = La Habana, Cuba 88 B3 23 8N 82 22W
Havana, U.S.A. 80 E9 40 18N 90 4W
Havant, U.K. 11 G7 50 51N 0 58W
Havasu, L., U.S.A. 85 L12 34 18N 114 28W
Havel →, Germany 16 B7 52 50N 12 3 E
Havelian, Pakistan 42 B5 34 2N 73 10 E
Havelock, N.B., Canada 71 C6 46 2N 65 24W
Havelock, Ont., Canada 70 D4 44 26N 77 53W
Havelock, N.Z. 59 J4 41 17S 173 48 E
Haverfordwest, U.K. 11 F3 51 48N 4 58W
Haverhill, U.S.A. 79 D13 42 47N 71 5W
Haverstraw, U.S.A. 79 E11 41 12N 73 58W
Havířov, Czech. 17 D10 49 46N 18 20 E
Havlíčkův Brod, Czech Rep. 16 D8 49 36N 15 33 E
Havre, U.S.A. 82 B9 48 33N 109 41W
Havre-Aubert, Canada 71 C7 47 12N 61 56W
Havre-St.-Pierre, Canada 71 B7 50 18N 63 33W
Haw →, U.S.A. 77 H6 35 36N 79 3W
Hawaii □, U.S.A. 74 H16 19 30N 156 30W
Hawaii I., Pac. Oc. 74 J17 20 0N 155 0W
Hawaiian Is., Pac. Oc. 74 H17 20 30N 156 0W
Hawaiian Ridge, Pac. Oc. 65 E11 24 0N 165 0W
Hawarden, Canada 73 C7 51 25N 106 36W
Hawarden, U.S.A. 80 D6 43 0N 96 29W
Hawea, L., N.Z. 59 L2 44 28S 169 19 E
Hawera, N.Z. 59 H5 39 35S 174 19 E
Hawick, U.K. 12 F6 55 26N 2 47W
Hawk Junction, Canada 70 C3 48 5N 84 38W
Hawke B., N.Z. 59 H6 39 25S 177 20 E
Hawker, Australia 63 E2 31 59S 138 22 E
Hawkesbury, Canada 70 C5 45 37N 74 37W
Hawkesbury I., Canada 72 C3 53 37N 129 3W
Hawkesbury Pt., Australia 62 A1 11 55S 134 5 E
Hawkinsville, U.S.A. 77 J4 32 17N 83 28W
Hawkwood, Australia 63 D5 25 45S 150 50 E
Hawley, U.S.A. 80 B6 46 53N 96 19W
Hawrān, Syria 44 C3 32 45N 36 15 E
Hawsh Mūssá, Lebanon 47 B4 33 45N 35 55 E
Hawthorne, U.S.A. 82 G4 38 32N 118 38W
Haxtun, U.S.A. 80 E3 40 39N 102 38W
Hay, Australia 63 E3 34 30S 144 51 E
Hay →, Australia 62 C2 24 50S 138 0 E
Hay →, Canada 72 A5 60 50N 116 26W
Hay, C., Australia 60 B4 14 5S 129 29 E
Hay L., Canada 72 B5 58 50N 118 50W
Hay Lakes, Canada 72 C6 53 12N 113 2W
Hay-on-Wye, U.K. 11 E4 52 5N 3 8W
Hay River, Canada 72 A5 60 51N 115 44W
Hay Springs, U.S.A. 80 D3 42 41N 102 41W
Haya = Tehoru, Indonesia 37 E7 3 19S 129 37 E
Hayachine-San, Japan 30 E10 39 34N 141 29 E
Hayden, Ariz., U.S.A. 83 K8 33 0N 110 47W
Hayden, Colo., U.S.A. 82 F10 40 30N 107 16W
Haydon, Australia 62 B3 18 0S 141 30 E
Hayes, U.S.A. 80 C4 44 23N 101 1W
Hayes →, Canada 73 B10 57 3N 92 12W
Hayle, U.K. 11 G2 50 11N 5 26W
Hayling I., U.K. 11 G7 50 48N 0 59W
Haynesville, U.S.A. 81 J8 32 58N 93 8W
Hayrabolu, Turkey 21 D12 41 12N 27 5 E
Hays, Canada 72 C6 50 6N 111 48W
Hays, U.S.A. 80 F5 38 53N 99 20W
Haysyn, Ukraine 17 D15 48 57N 29 25 E
Hayvoron, Ukraine 17 D15 48 22N 29 52 E
Hayward, Calif., U.S.A. 84 H4 37 40N 122 5W
Hayward, Wis., U.S.A. 80 B9 46 1N 91 29W
Haywards Heath, U.K. 11 G7 51 0N 0 5W
Hazafon □, Israel 47 C4 32 40N 35 20 E
Hazarām, Kūh-e, Iran 45 D8 29 30N 57 18 E
Hazard, U.S.A. 76 G4 37 15N 83 12W
Hazaribag, India 43 H11 23 58N 85 26 E
Hazaribag Road, India 43 G11 24 12N 85 57 E
Hazelton, Canada 72 B3 55 20N 127 42W
Hazelton, U.S.A. 80 B4 46 29N 100 17W
Hazen, N. Dak., U.S.A. 80 B4 47 18N 101 38W
Hazen, Nev., U.S.A. 82 G4 39 34N 119 3W
Hazlehurst, Ga., U.S.A. 77 K4 31 52N 82 36W
Hazlehurst, Miss., U.S.A. 81 K9 31 52N 90 24W
Hazleton, U.S.A. 79 F9 40 57N 75 59W
Hazlett, L., Australia 60 D4 21 30S 128 48 E
Head of Bight, Australia 61 F5 31 30S 131 25 E
Headlands, Zimbabwe 55 F3 18 15S 32 2 E
Healdsburg, U.S.A. 84 G4 38 37N 122 52W
Healdton, U.S.A. 81 H6 34 14N 97 29W
Healesville, Australia 63 F4 37 35S 145 30 E
Heard I., Ind. Oc. 3 G13 53 0S 74 0 E
Hearne, U.S.A. 81 K6 30 53N 96 36W
Hearne B., Canada 73 A9 60 10N 99 10W
Hearne L., Canada 72 A6 62 20N 113 10W
Hearst, Canada 70 C3 49 40N 83 41W
Heart →, U.S.A. 80 B4 46 46N 100 50W
Heart's Content, Canada 71 C9 47 54N 53 27W
Heath Pt., Canada 71 C7 49 8N 61 40W
Heath Steele, Canada 71 C6 47 17N 66 5W
Heavener, U.S.A. 81 H7 34 53N 94 36W
Hebbronville, U.S.A. 81 M5 27 18N 98 41W
Hebei □, China 34 E9 39 0N 116 0 E
Hebel, Australia 63 D4 28 58S 147 47 E
Heber, U.S.A. 85 N11 32 44N 115 32W
Heber Springs, U.S.A. 81 H9 35 30N 92 2W
Hebert, Canada 73 C7 50 30N 107 10W
Hebgen L., U.S.A. 82 D8 44 52N 111 20W
Hebi, China 34 G8 35 57N 114 7 E
Hebrides, U.K. 6 D4 57 30N 7 0W
Hebron = Al Khalīl, West Bank 47 D4 31 32N 35 6 E
Hebron, Canada 69 C13 58 5N 62 30W
Hebron, N. Dak., U.S.A. 80 B3 46 54N 102 3W
Hebron, Nebr., U.S.A. 80 E6 40 10N 97 35W
Hecate Str., Canada 72 C2 53 10N 130 30W
Hechi, China 32 D5 24 40N 108 2 E
Hechuan, China 32 C5 30 2N 106 12 E
Hecla, U.S.A. 80 C5 45 53N 98 9W
Hecla I., Canada 73 C9 51 10N 96 43W
Hede, Sweden 9 E15 62 23N 13 30 E
Hedemora, Sweden 9 F16 60 18N 15 58 E
Hedley, U.S.A. 81 H4 34 52N 100 39W
Heerde, Neths. 15 B6 52 24N 6 2 E
Heerenveen, Neths. 15 B5 52 57N 5 55 E
Heerhugowaard, Neths. 15 B4 52 40N 4 51 E
Heerlen, Neths. 18 A6 50 55N 5 58 E
Hefa, Israel 47 C4 32 46N 35 0 E
Hefa □, Israel 47 C4 32 40N 35 0 E
Hefei, China 33 C6 31 52N 117 18 E
Hegang, China 33 B8 47 20N 130 19 E
Heichengzhen, China 34 F4 36 24N 106 3 E
Heidelberg, Germany 16 D5 49 24N 8 42 E
Heidelberg, S. Africa 56 E3 34 6S 20 59 E
Heilbron, S. Africa 57 D4 27 16S 27 59 E
Heilbronn, Germany 16 D5 49 9N 9 13 E
Heilongjiang □, China 35 A14 48 0N 126 0 E
Heilunkiang = Heilongjiang □, China 35 A14 48 0N 126 0 E
Heimaey, Iceland 8 E3 63 26N 20 17W
Heinola, Finland 9 F22 61 13N 26 2 E
Heinze Is., Burma 41 M20 14 25N 97 45 E
Heishan, China 35 D12 41 40N 122 5 E
Heishui, China 35 C10 42 8N 119 30 E
Hejaz = Ḩijāz □, Si. Arabia 46 C3 24 0N 40 0 E
Hejian, China 34 E9 38 25N 116 5 E
Hejin, China 34 G6 35 35N 110 42 E
Hekla, Iceland 8 E4 63 56N 19 35W
Hekou, Gansu, China 34 F2 36 10N 103 28 E
Hekou, Yunnan, China 32 D5 22 30N 103 59 E
Helan Shan, China 34 E3 38 30N 105 55 E
Helena, Ark., U.S.A. 81 H9 34 32N 90 36W
Helena, Mont., U.S.A. 82 C7 46 36N 112 2W
Helendale, U.S.A. 85 L9 34 44N 117 19W
Helensburgh, U.K. 12 E4 56 1N 4 43W
Helensville, N.Z. 59 G5 36 41S 174 29 E
Helgeland, Norway 8 C15 66 7N 13 29 E
Helgoland, Germany 16 A4 54 10N 7 53 E
Heligoland = Helgoland, Germany 16 A4 54 10N 7 53 E
Heligoland B. = Deutsche Bucht, Germany 16 A5 54 15N 8 0 E
Hella, Iceland 8 E3 63 50N 20 24W
Hellevoetsluis, Neths. 15 C4 51 50N 4 8 E
Hellín, Spain 19 C5 38 31N 1 40W
Helmand □, Afghan. 40 D4 31 20N 64 0 E

Helmand

Helmand →, Afghan. .. 40 D2 31 12N 61 34 E
Helmond, Neths. .... 15 C5 51 29N 5 41 E
Helmsdale, U.K. 12 C5 58 7N 3 39W
Helmsdale →, U.K. 12 C5 58 7N 3 40W
Helong, China .... 35 C15 42 40N 129 0 E
Helper, U.S.A. 82 G8 39 41N 110 51W
Helsingborg, Sweden ... 9 H15 56 3N 12 42 E
Helsingfors = Helsinki,
Finland .... 9 F21 60 15N 25 3 E
Helsingør, Denmark ..... 9 H15 56 2N 12 35 E
Helsinki, Finland .... 9 F21 60 15N 25 3 E
Helston, U.K. 11 G2 50 6N 5 17W
Helvellyn, U.K. 10 C4 54 32N 3 1W
Hemel Hempstead, U.K. . 11 F7 51 44N 0 28W
Hemet, U.S.A. 85 M10 33 45N 116 58W
Hemingford, U.S.A. 80 D3 42 19N 103 4W
Hemphill, U.S.A. 81 K8 31 20N 93 51W
Hempstead, U.S.A. 81 K6 30 6N 96 5W
Hemse, Sweden .... 9 H18 57 15N 18 22 E
Henan □, China .... 34 H8 34 0N 114 0 E
Henares →, Spain 19 B4 40 24N 3 30W
Henashi-Misaki, Japan .. 30 D9 40 37N 139 51 E
Henderson, Argentina ... 94 D3 36 18S 61 43W
Henderson, Ky., U.S.A. .. 76 G2 37 50N 87 35W
Henderson, N.C., U.S.A. . 77 G6 36 20N 78 25W
Henderson, Nev., U.S.A. . 85 J12 36 2N 114 59W
Henderson, Tenn., U.S.A. 77 H1 35 26N 88 38W
Henderson, Tex., U.S.A. . 81 J7 32 9N 94 48W
Hendersonville, U.S.A. ... 77 H4 35 19N 82 28W
Hendījān, Iran .... 45 D6 30 14N 49 43 E
Hendon, Australia ...... 63 D5 28 5S 151 50 E
Hengcheng, China ...... 34 E4 38 18N 106 28 E
Hengdaohezi, China ..... 35 B15 44 52N 129 0 E
Hengelo, Neths. .... 15 B6 52 16N 6 48 E
Hengshan, China .... 34 F5 37 58N 109 5 E
Hengshui, China .... 34 F8 37 41N 115 40 E
Hengyang, China .... 33 D6 26 52N 112 33 E
Henlopen, C., U.S.A. 76 F8 38 48N 75 6W
Hennenman, S. Africa ... 56 D4 27 59S 27 1 E
Hennessey, U.S.A. 81 G6 36 6N 97 54W
Henrietta, U.S.A. 81 J5 33 49N 98 12W
Henrietta, Ostrov =
Genriyetty, Ostrov,
Russia .... 27 B16 77 6N 156 30 E
Henrietta Maria, C.,
Canada 70 A3 55 9N 82 20W
Henry, U.S.A. 80 E10 41 7N 89 22W
Henryetta, U.S.A. 81 H7 35 27N 95 59W
Hensall, Canada 78 C3 43 26N 81 30W
Hentiyn Nuruu, Mongolia 33 B5 48 30N 108 30 E
Henty, Australia .... 63 F4 35 30S 147 0 E
Henzada, Burma .... 41 L19 17 38N 95 26 E
Heppner, U.S.A. 82 D4 45 21N 119 33W
Hepworth, Canada 78 B3 44 37N 81 9W
Hequ, China .... 34 E6 39 20N 111 15 E
Héraðsflói, Iceland 8 D6 65 42N 14 12W
Héraðsvötn →, Iceland . 8 D4 65 45N 19 25W
Herald Cays, Australia ... 62 B4 16 58S 149 9 E
Herāt, Afghan. .... 40 B3 34 20N 62 7 E
Herāt □, Afghan. .... 40 B3 35 0N 62 0 E
Herbert →, Australia ... 62 B4 18 31S 146 17 E
Herbert Downs, Australia 62 C2 23 7S 139 9 E
Herberton, Australia ... 62 B4 17 20S 145 25 E
Herceg-Novi,
Montenegro, Yug. .... 21 C8 42 30N 18 33 E
Herðubreið, Iceland 8 D5 65 11N 16 21W
Hereford, U.K. 11 E5 52 4N 2 43W
Hereford, U.S.A. 81 H3 34 49N 102 24W
Herefordshire □, U.K. ... 11 E5 52 8N 2 40W
Herentals, Belgium ..... 15 C4 51 12N 4 51 E
Herford, Germany ...... 16 B5 52 7N 8 39 E
Herington, U.S.A. 80 F6 38 40N 96 57W
Herkimer, U.S.A. 79 D10 43 0N 74 59W
Herlong, U.S.A. 84 E6 40 8N 120 8W
Herm, U.K. 11 H5 49 30N 2 28W
Herman, U.S.A. 80 C6 45 49N 96 9W
Hermann, U.S.A. 80 F9 38 42N 91 27W
Hermannsburg Mission,
Australia .... 60 D5 23 57S 132 45 E
Hermanus, S. Africa .... 56 E2 34 27S 19 12 E
Hermidale, Australia .... 63 E4 31 30S 146 42 E
Hermiston, U.S.A. 82 D4 45 51N 119 17W
Hermitage, N.Z. .... 59 K3 43 44S 170 5 E
Hermite, I., Chile 96 H3 55 50S 68 0W
Hermon, Mt. = Ash
Shaykh, J., Lebanon .. 47 B4 33 25N 35 50 E
Hermosillo, Mexico 86 B2 29 10N 111 0W
Hernád →, Hungary .... 17 D11 47 56N 21 8 E
Hernandarias, Paraguay . 95 B5 25 20S 54 40W
Hernandez, U.S.A. 84 J6 36 24N 120 46W
Hernando, Argentina 94 C3 32 28S 63 40W
Hernando, U.S.A. 81 H10 34 50N 90 0W
Herne, Germany .... 15 C7 51 32N 7 14 E
Herne Bay, U.K. .... 11 F9 51 21N 1 8 E
Herning, Denmark ...... 9 H13 56 8N 8 58 E
Heroica = Caborca,
Mexico 86 A2 30 40N 112 10W
Heroica Nogales =
Nogales, Mexico 86 A2 31 20N 110 56W
Heron Bay, Canada 70 C2 48 40N 86 25W
Herradura, Pta. de la,
Canary Is. 22 F5 28 26N 14 8W
Herreid, U.S.A. 80 C4 45 50N 100 4W
Herrick, Australia ...... 62 G4 41 5S 147 55 E
Herrin, U.S.A. 81 G10 37 48N 89 2W
Hersonissos, Greece ... 23 D7 35 18N 25 22 E
Herstal, Belgium .... 15 D5 50 40N 5 38 E
Hertford, U.K. 11 F7 51 48N 0 4W
Hertfordshire □, U.K. 11 F7 51 51N 0 5W
's-Hertogenbosch, Neths. 15 C5 51 42N 5 17 E
Hertzogville, S. Africa .. 56 D4 28 9S 25 30 E
Herzliyya, Israel .... 47 C3 32 10N 34 50 E
Ḥeṣār, Fārs, Iran .... 45 D6 29 52N 50 16 E
Ḥeṣār, Markazī, Iran ..... 45 C6 35 50N 49 12 E
Heshui, China .... 34 G5 36 0N 108 0 E
Heshun, China .... 34 F7 37 22N 113 32 E
Hesperia, U.S.A. 85 L9 34 25N 117 18W
Hesse = Hessen □,
Germany .... 16 C5 50 30N 9 0 E
Hessen □, Germany .... 16 C5 50 30N 9 0 E
Hetch Hetchy Aqueduct,
U.S.A. 84 H5 37 29N 122 19W
Hettinger, U.S.A. 80 C3 46 0N 102 42W
Hexham, U.K. 10 C5 54 58N 2 4W
Hexigten Qi, China ...... 35 C9 43 18N 117 30 E
Ḥeydarābād, Iran .... 45 D7 30 33N 55 38 E
Heyfield, Australia ...... 63 F4 37 59S 146 47 E
Heysham, U.K. 10 C5 54 3N 2 53W
Heywood, Australia ..... 63 F3 38 8S 141 37 E
Heze, China .... 34 G8 35 14N 115 20 E
Hi Vista, U.S.A. 85 L9 34 45N 117 46W
Hialeah, U.S.A. 77 N5 25 50N 80 17W
Hiawatha, Kans., U.S.A. . 80 F7 39 51N 95 32W
Hiawatha, Utah, U.S.A. .. 82 G8 39 29N 111 1W
Hibbing, U.S.A. 80 B8 47 25N 92 56W
Hibbs B., Australia ..... 62 G4 42 35S 145 15 E
Hibernia Reef, Australia . 60 B3 12 0S 123 23 E
Hickory, U.S.A. 77 H5 35 44N 81 21W
Hicks, Pt., Australia ..... 63 F4 37 49S 149 17 E
Hicksville, U.S.A. 79 F11 40 46N 73 32W
Hida-Gawa →, Japan .. 31 G8 35 26N 137 3 E
Hida-Sammyaku, Japan . 31 F8 36 30N 137 40 E
Hidaka-Sammyaku, Japan 30 C11 42 35N 142 45 E
Hidalgo, Mexico 87 C5 24 15N 99 26W
Hidalgo □, Mexico 87 C5 20 30N 99 10W
Hidalgo, Presa M., Mexico 86 B3 26 30N 108 35W
Hidalgo, Pta. del,
Canary Is. 22 F3 28 33N 16 19W
Hidalgo del Parral, Mexico 86 B3 26 58N 105 40W
Hierro, Canary Is. 22 G1 27 44N 18 0W
Higashiajima-San, Japan 30 F10 37 40N 140 10 E
Higashiōsaka, Japan .... 31 G7 34 40N 135 37 E
Higgins, U.S.A. 81 G4 36 7N 100 2W
Higgins Corner, U.S.A. .. 84 F5 39 2N 121 5W
Higginsville, Australia ... 61 F3 31 42S 121 38 E
High Atlas = Haut Atlas,
Morocco 50 B4 32 30N 5 0W
High I., Canada 71 A7 56 40N 61 10W
High Island, U.S.A. 81 L7 29 34N 94 24W
High Level, Canada 72 B5 58 31N 117 8W
High Point, U.S.A. 77 H6 35 57N 80 0W
High Prairie, Canada 72 B5 55 30N 116 30W
High River, Canada 72 C6 50 30N 113 50W
High Springs, U.S.A. 77 L4 29 50N 82 36W
High Tatra = Tatry,
Slovak Rep. .... 17 D11 49 20N 20 0 E
High Veld, Africa .... 48 J6 27 0S 27 0 E
High Wycombe, U.K. 11 F7 51 37N 0 45W
Highbury, Australia ..... 62 B3 16 25S 143 9 E
Highland □, U.K. 12 D4 57 17N 4 21W
Highland Park, U.S.A. ... 76 D2 42 11N 87 48W
Highmore, U.S.A. 80 C5 44 31N 99 27W
Highrock L., Canada 73 B7 57 5N 105 32W
Higüey, Dom. Rep. 89 C6 18 37N 68 42W
Hiiumaa, Estonia ...... 24 C3 58 50N 22 45 E
Ḥijāz □, Si. Arabia ...... 46 C3 24 0N 40 0 E
Hijo = Tagum, Phil. ..... 37 C7 7 33N 125 53 E
Hikari, Japan .... 31 H5 33 58N 131 58 E
Hiko, U.S.A. 84 H11 37 32N 115 14W
Hikone, Japan .... 31 G8 35 15N 136 10 E
Hikurangi, N.Z. .... 59 F5 35 36S 174 17 E
Hikurangi, Mt., N.Z. ..... 59 H6 38 21S 176 52 E
Hildesheim, Germany ... 16 B5 52 9N 9 56 E
Hill →, Australia ...... 61 F2 30 23S 115 3 E
Hill City, Idaho, U.S.A. .. 82 E6 43 18N 115 3W
Hill City, Kans., U.S.A. .. 80 F5 39 22N 99 51W
Hill City, Minn., U.S.A. .. 80 B8 46 59N 93 36W
Hill City, S. Dak., U.S.A. . 80 D3 43 56N 103 35W
Hill Island L., Canada ... 73 A7 60 30N 109 50W
Hillcrest Center, U.S.A. . 85 K8 35 23N 118 57W
Hillegom, Neths. .... 15 B4 52 18N 4 35 E
Hillerød, Denmark ...... 9 J15 55 56N 12 19 E
Hillman, U.S.A. 76 C4 45 4N 83 54W
Hillmond, Canada 73 C7 53 26N 109 41W
Hillsboro, Kans., U.S.A. . 80 F6 38 21N 97 12W
Hillsboro, N. Dak., U.S.A. 80 B6 47 26N 97 3W
Hillsboro, N.H., U.S.A. ... 79 C13 43 7N 71 54W
Hillsboro, N. Mex., U.S.A. 83 K10 32 55N 107 34W
Hillsboro, Oreg., U.S.A. . 84 E4 45 31N 122 59W
Hillsboro, Tex., U.S.A. ... 81 J6 32 1N 97 8W
Hillsborough, Grenada .. 89 D7 12 28N 61 28W
Hillsdale, Mich., U.S.A. . 76 E3 41 56N 84 38W
Hillsdale, N.Y., U.S.A. .. 79 D11 42 11N 73 30W
Hillside, Australia ...... 60 D2 21 45S 119 23 E
Hillsport, Canada 70 C2 49 27N 85 34W
Hillston, Australia ...... 63 E4 33 30S 145 31 E
Hilo, U.S.A. 74 J17 19 44N 155 5W
Hilton, U.S.A. 78 C7 43 17N 77 48W
Hilversum, Neths. ...... 15 B5 52 14N 5 10 E
Himachal Pradesh □, India 42 D7 31 30N 77 0 E
Himalaya, Asia .... 43 E11 29 0N 84 0 E
Himatnagar, India ...... 40 H8 23 37N 72 57 E
Himeji, Japan .... 31 G7 34 50N 134 40 E
Himi, Japan .... 31 F8 36 50N 136 55 E
Ḥimş, Syria .... 47 A5 34 40N 36 45 E
Ḥimş □, Syria .... 47 A6 34 30N 37 0 E
Hinche, Haiti 89 C5 19 9N 72 1W
Hinchinbrook I., Australia 62 B4 18 20S 146 15 E
Hinckley, U.K. 11 E6 52 33N 1 22W
Hinckley, U.S.A. 82 G7 39 20N 112 40W
Hindaun, India .... 42 F7 26 44N 77 5 E
Hindmarsh, L., Australia . 63 F3 36 5S 141 55 E
Hindu Bagh, Pakistan ... 42 D2 30 56N 67 50 E
Hindu Kush, Asia ...... 40 B7 36 0N 71 0 E
Hindubagh, Pakistan .... 40 D5 30 56N 67 57 E
Hindupur, India .... 40 N10 13 49N 77 32 E
Hines Creek, Canada 72 B5 56 20N 118 40W
Hinganghat, India ...... 40 J11 20 30N 78 52 E
Hingham, U.S.A. 82 B8 48 33N 110 25W
Hingoli, India .... 40 K10 19 41N 77 15 E
Hinna = Imi, Ethiopia ... 46 F3 6 28N 42 10 E
Hinnøya, Norway .... 8 B16 68 35N 15 50 E
Hinojosa del Duque, Spain 19 C3 38 30N 5 9W
Hinsdale, U.S.A. 82 B10 48 24N 107 5W
Hinton, Canada 72 C5 53 26N 117 34W
Hinton, U.S.A. 76 G5 37 40N 80 54W
Hirado, Japan .... 31 H4 33 22N 129 33 E
Hirakud Dam, India ..... 41 J13 21 32N 83 45 E
Hiratsuka, Japan .... 31 G9 35 19N 139 21 E
Hiroo, Japan .... 30 C11 42 17N 143 19 E
Hirosaki, Japan .... 30 D10 40 34N 140 28 E
Hiroshima, Japan ...... 31 G6 34 24N 132 30 E
Hiroshima □, Japan .... 31 G6 34 50N 133 0 E
Hisar, India .... 42 E6 29 12N 75 45 E
Hisb →, Iraq .... 44 D5 31 45N 44 17 E
Ḥismá, Si. Arabia ...... 44 D3 28 30N 36 0 E
Hispaniola, W. Indies 89 C5 19 0N 71 0W
Hīt, Iraq .... 44 C4 33 38N 42 49 E
Hita, Japan .... 31 H5 33 20N 130 58 E
Hitachi, Japan .... 31 F10 36 36N 140 39 E
Hitchin, U.K. 11 F7 51 58N 0 16W
Hitoyoshi, Japan .... 31 H5 32 13N 130 45 E
Hitra, Norway .... 8 E13 63 30N 8 45 E
Ḥiyyon, N. →, Israel ... 47 E4 30 25N 35 10 E
Hjalmar L., Canada 73 A7 61 33N 109 25W
Hjälmaren, Sweden ..... 9 G16 59 18N 15 40 E
Hjørring, Denmark ...... 9 H13 57 29N 9 59 E
Hluhluwe, S. Africa ..... 57 D5 28 1S 32 15 E
Hlyboka, Ukraine ...... 17 D13 48 5N 25 56 E
Ho Chi Minh City = Phanh
Bho Ho Chi Minh,
Vietnam .... 39 G6 10 58N 106 40 E
Ho Thuong, Vietnam .... 38 C5 19 32N 105 48 E
Hoa Binh, Vietnam ...... 38 B5 20 50N 105 20 E
Hoa Da, Vietnam .... 39 G7 11 16N 108 40 E
Hoa Hiep, Vietnam ...... 39 G5 11 34N 105 51 E
Hoai Nhon, Vietnam .... 38 E7 14 28N 109 1 E
Hoang Lien Son, Vietnam 38 A4 22 0N 104 0 E
Hobart, Australia .... 62 G4 42 50S 147 21 E
Hobart, U.S.A. 81 H5 35 1N 99 6W
Hobbs, U.S.A. 81 J3 32 42N 103 8W
Hobbs Coast, Antarctica . 5 D14 74 50S 131 0W
Hoboken, U.S.A. 79 F10 40 45N 74 4W
Hobro, Denmark .... 9 H13 56 39N 9 46 E
Hoburgen, Sweden ..... 9 H18 56 55N 18 7 E
Hodaka-Dake, Japan .... 31 F8 36 17N 137 39 E
Hodgson, Canada 73 C9 51 13N 97 36W
Hódmezővásárhely,
Hungary .... 17 E11 46 28N 20 22 E
Hodna, Chott el, Algeria . 50 A6 35 26N 4 43 E
Hodonín, Czech Rep. .... 17 D9 48 50N 17 10 E
Hoeamdong, N. Korea ... 35 C16 42 30N 130 16 E
Hoek van Holland, Neths. 15 C4 52 0N 4 7 E
Hoengsŏng, S. Korea ... 35 F14 37 29N 127 59 E
Hoeryong, N. Korea .... 35 C15 42 30N 129 45 E
Hoeyang, N. Korea ..... 35 E14 38 43N 127 36 E
Hof, Germany .... 16 C6 50 19N 11 55 E
Hofmeyr, S. Africa ..... 56 E4 31 39S 25 50 E
Höfn, Iceland 8 D6 64 15N 15 13W
Hofors, Sweden .... 9 F17 60 31N 16 15 E
Hofsjökull, Iceland 8 D4 64 49N 18 48W
Hōfu, Japan .... 31 G5 34 3N 131 34 E
Hogan Group, Australia . 62 F4 39 13S 147 1 E
Hogansville, U.S.A. 77 J3 33 10N 84 55W
Hogeland, U.S.A. 82 B9 48 51N 108 40W
Hoggar = Ahaggar,
Algeria .... 50 D7 23 0N 6 30 E
Hogsty Reef, Bahamas .. 89 B5 21 41N 73 48W
Hoh →, U.S.A. 84 C2 47 45N 124 29W
Hohe Venn, Belgium .... 15 D6 50 30N 6 5 E
Hohenwald, U.S.A. 77 H2 35 33N 87 33W
Hohhot, China .... 34 D6 40 52N 111 40 E
Hóhlakas, Greece ...... 23 D9 35 57N 27 53 E
Hoi An, Vietnam .... 38 E7 15 30N 108 19 E
Hoi Xuan, Vietnam ..... 38 B5 20 25N 105 9 E
Hoisington, U.S.A. 80 F5 38 31N 98 47W
Hōjō, Japan .... 31 H6 33 58N 132 46 E
Hokianga Harbour, N.Z. . 59 F4 35 31S 173 22 E
Hokitika, N.Z. .... 59 K3 42 42S 171 0 E
Hokkaidō □, Japan ..... 30 C11 43 30N 143 0 E
Holbrook, Australia .... 63 F4 35 42S 147 18 E
Holbrook, U.S.A. 83 J8 34 54N 110 10W
Holden, Canada 72 C6 53 13N 112 11W
Holden, U.S.A. 82 G7 39 6N 112 16W
Holdenville, U.S.A. 81 H6 35 5N 96 24W
Holdfast, Canada 73 C7 50 58N 105 25W
Holdrege, U.S.A. 80 E5 40 26N 99 23W
Holguín, Cuba 88 B4 20 50N 76 20W
Hollams Bird I., Namibia . 56 C1 24 40S 14 30 E
Holland, U.S.A. 76 D2 42 47N 86 7W
Hollandia = Jayapura,
Indonesia .... 37 E10 2 28S 140 38 E
Hollidaysburg, U.S.A. ... 78 F6 40 26N 78 24W
Hollis, U.S.A. 81 H5 34 41N 99 55W
Hollister, Calif., U.S.A. .. 84 J5 36 51N 121 24W
Hollister, Idaho, U.S.A. .. 82 E6 42 21N 114 35W
Holly, U.S.A. 80 F3 38 3N 102 7W
Holly Hill, U.S.A. 77 L5 29 16N 81 3W
Holly Springs, U.S.A. ... 81 H10 34 46N 89 27W
Hollywood, Calif., U.S.A. . 83 J4 34 7N 118 25W
Hollywood, Fla., U.S.A. .. 77 N5 26 1N 80 9W
Holman, Canada 68 A8 70 42N 117 41W
Hólmavík, Iceland 8 D3 65 42N 21 40W
Holmes Reefs, Australia . 62 B4 16 27S 148 0 E
Holmsund, Sweden ..... 8 E19 63 41N 20 20 E
Holroyd →, Australia .. 62 A3 14 10S 141 36 E
Holstebro, Denmark .... 9 H13 56 22N 8 37 E
Holsworthy, U.K. 11 G3 50 48N 4 22W
Holton, Canada 71 B8 54 31N 57 12W
Holton, U.S.A. 80 F7 39 28N 95 44W
Holtville, U.S.A. 85 N11 32 49N 115 23W
Holwerd, Neths. .... 15 A5 53 22N 5 54 E
Holy I., Angl., U.K. 10 D3 53 17N 4 37W
Holy I., Northumb., U.K. . 10 B6 55 40N 1 47W
Holyhead, U.K. 10 D3 53 18N 4 38W
Holyoke, Colo., U.S.A. ... 80 E3 40 35N 102 18W
Holyoke, Mass., U.S.A. .. 79 D12 42 12N 72 37W
Holyrood, Canada 71 C9 47 27N 53 8W
Homa Bay, Kenya ...... 54 C3 0 36S 34 30 E
Homa Bay □, Kenya .... 54 C3 0 50S 34 30 E
Homalin, Burma .... 41 G19 24 55N 95 0 E
Homand, Iran .... 45 C8 32 28N 59 37 E
Hombori, Mali 50 E5 15 20N 1 38W
Home B., Canada 69 B13 68 40N 67 10W
Home Hill, Australia .... 62 B4 19 43S 147 25 E
Homedale, U.S.A. 82 E5 43 37N 116 56W
Homer, Alaska, U.S.A. ... 68 C4 59 39N 151 33W
Homer, La., U.S.A. 81 J8 32 48N 93 4W
Homestead, Australia ... 62 C4 20 20S 145 40 E
Homestead, Fla., U.S.A. . 77 N5 25 28N 80 29W
Homestead, Oreg., U.S.A. 82 D5 45 2N 116 51W
Homewood, U.S.A. 84 F6 39 4N 120 8W
Hominy, U.S.A. 81 G6 36 25N 96 24W
Homoine, Mozam. ...... 57 C6 23 55S 35 8 E
Homs = Ḥimş, Syria ..... 47 A5 34 40N 36 45 E
Homyel, Belarus .... 24 D5 52 28N 31 0 E
Hon Chong, Vietnam .... 39 G5 10 25N 104 30 E
Hon Me, Vietnam ...... 38 C5 19 23N 105 56 E
Honan = Henan □, China 34 H8 34 0N 114 0 E
Honbetsu, Japan .... 30 C11 43 7N 143 37 E
Honcut, U.S.A. 84 F5 39 20N 121 32W
Hondeklipbaai, S. Africa . 56 E2 30 19S 17 17 E
Hondo, Japan .... 31 H5 32 27N 130 12 E
Hondo, U.S.A. 81 L5 29 21N 99 9W
Hondo →, Belize 87 D7 18 25N 88 21W
Honduras ■, Cent. Amer. 88 D2 14 40N 86 30W
Honduras, G. de,
Caribbean 88 C2 16 50N 87 0W
Hønefoss, Norway ..... 9 F14 60 10N 10 18 E
Honesdale, U.S.A. 79 E9 41 34N 75 16W
Honey L., U.S.A. 84 E6 40 15N 120 19W
Honfleur, France ...... 18 B4 49 25N 0 13 E
Hong →, Vietnam ..... 32 D5 22 0N 104 0 E
Hong Gai, Vietnam ..... 38 B6 20 57N 107 5 E
Hong He →, China .... 34 H8 32 25N 115 35 E
Hong Kong, China ..... 33 D6 22 11N 114 14 E
Hongchŏn, S. Korea ... 35 F14 37 44N 127 53 E
Hongjiang, China ...... 33 D5 27 7N 109 59 E
Hongliu He →, China ... 34 F5 38 0N 109 50 E
Hongor, Mongolia ...... 34 B7 45 45N 112 50 E
Hongsa, Laos .... 38 C3 19 43N 101 20 E
Hongshui He →, China . 33 D5 23 48N 109 30 E
Hongsŏng, S. Korea .... 35 F14 36 37N 126 38 E
Hongtong, China ...... 34 F6 36 16N 111 40 E
Honguedo, Détroit d',
Canada 71 C7 49 15N 64 0W
Hongwon, N. Korea ..... 35 E14 40 0N 127 56 E
Hongze Hu, China ..... 35 H10 33 15N 118 35 E
Honiara, Solomon Is. ..... 64 H7 9 27S 159 57 E
Honiton, U.K. 11 G4 50 47N 3 11W
Honjō, Japan .... 30 E10 39 23N 140 3 E
Honningsvåg, Norway .. 8 A21 70 59N 25 59 E
Honolulu, U.S.A. 74 H16 21 19N 157 52W
Honshū, Japan .... 31 G9 36 0N 138 0 E
Hood, Mt., U.S.A. 82 D3 45 23N 121 42W
Hood, Pt., Australia .... 61 F2 34 23S 119 34 E
Hood River, U.S.A. 82 D3 45 43N 121 31W
Hoodsport, U.S.A. 84 C3 47 24N 123 9W
Hoogeveen, Neths. .... 15 B6 52 44N 6 28 E
Hoogezand-Sappemeer,
Neths. .... 15 A6 53 9N 6 45 E
Hooghly → = Hugli →,
India .... 43 J13 21 56N 88 4 E
Hooghly-Chinsura =
Chunchura, India ..... 43 H13 22 53N 88 27 E
Hook Hd., Ireland 13 D5 52 7N 6 56W
Hook I., Australia ..... 62 C4 20 4S 149 0 E
Hook of Holland = Hoek
van Holland, Neths. ... 15 C4 52 0N 4 7 E
Hooker, U.S.A. 81 G4 36 52N 101 13W
Hooker Creek, Australia . 60 C5 18 23S 130 38 E
Hoopeston, U.S.A. 76 E2 40 28N 87 40W
Hoopstad, S. Africa .... 56 D4 27 50S 25 55 E
Hoorn, Neths. .... 15 B5 52 38N 5 4 E
Hoover Dam, U.S.A. 85 K12 36 1N 114 44W
Hooversville, U.S.A. 78 F6 40 9N 78 55W
Hop Bottom, U.S.A. 79 E9 41 42N 75 46W
Hope, Canada 72 D4 49 25N 121 25W
Hope, Ariz., U.S.A. 85 M13 33 43N 113 42W
Hope, Ark., U.S.A. 81 J8 33 40N 93 36W
Hope, N. Dak., U.S.A. ... 80 B6 47 19N 97 43W
Hope, L., Australia ..... 63 D2 28 24S 139 18 E
Hope Town, Bahamas .. 88 A4 26 35N 76 57W
Hopedale, Canada 71 A7 55 28N 60 13W
Hopefield, S. Africa .... 56 E2 33 3S 18 22 E
Hopei = Hebei □, China . 34 E9 39 0N 116 0 E
Hopelchén, Mexico 87 D7 19 46N 89 50W
Hopetoun, Vic., Australia 63 F3 35 42S 142 22 E
Hopetoun, W. Austral.,
Australia .... 61 F3 33 57S 120 7 E
Hopetown, S. Africa .... 56 D3 29 34S 24 3 E
Hopkins, U.S.A. 80 E7 40 33N 94 49W
Hopkins, L., Australia ... 60 D4 24 15S 128 35 E
Hopkinsville, U.S.A. 77 G2 36 52N 87 29W
Hopland, U.S.A. 84 G3 38 58N 123 7W
Hoquiam, U.S.A. 84 D3 46 59N 123 53W
Horden Hills, Australia .. 60 D5 20 15S 130 0 E
Horinger, China .... 34 D6 40 28N 111 48 E
Horlick Mts., Antarctica . 5 E15 84 0S 102 0W
Horlivka, Ukraine ...... 25 E6 48 19N 38 5 E
Hormoz, Iran .... 45 E7 27 35N 55 0 E
Hormoz, Jaz. ye, Iran ... 45 E8 27 8N 56 28 E
Hormuz, Str. of, The Gulf 45 E8 26 30N 56 30 E
Horn, Austria .... 16 D8 48 39N 15 40 E
Horn, Iceland 8 C2 66 28N 22 28W
Horn →, Canada 72 A5 61 30N 118 1W
Horn, Cape = Hornos, C.
de, Chile 96 H3 55 50S 67 30W
Horn Head, Ireland 13 A3 55 14N 8 0W
Horn I., Australia ...... 62 A3 10 37S 142 17 E
Horn I., U.S.A. 77 K1 30 14N 88 39W
Horn Mts., Canada 72 A5 62 15N 119 15W
Hornavan, Sweden ..... 8 C17 66 15N 17 30 E
Hornbeck, U.S.A. 81 K8 31 20N 93 24W
Hornbrook, U.S.A. 82 F2 41 55N 122 33W
Horncastle, U.K. 10 D7 53 13N 0 7W
Hornell, U.S.A. 78 D7 42 20N 77 40W
Hornell L., Canada 72 A5 62 20N 119 25W
Hornepayne, Canada ... 70 C3 49 14N 84 48W
Hornitos, U.S.A. 84 H6 37 30N 120 14W
Hornos, C. de, Chile 96 H3 55 50S 67 30W
Hornsby, Australia ..... 63 E5 33 42S 151 2 E
Hornsea, U.K. 10 D7 53 55N 0 11W
Horobetsu, Japan ..... 30 C10 42 24N 141 6 E
Horodenka, Ukraine .... 17 D13 48 41N 25 29 E
Horodok, Khmelnytskyy,
Ukraine .... 17 D14 49 10N 26 34 E
Horodok, Lviv, Ukraine .. 17 D12 49 46N 23 32 E
Horokhiv, Ukraine ..... 17 C13 50 30N 24 45 E
Horqin Youyi Qianqi,
China .... 35 A12 46 5N 122 3 E
Horqueta, Paraguay 94 A4 23 15S 56 55W
Horse Creek, U.S.A. 80 E3 41 57N 105 10W
Horse Is., Canada 71 B8 50 15N 55 50W
Horsefly L., Canada 72 C4 52 25N 121 0W
Horsens, Denmark ..... 9 J13 55 52N 9 51 E
Horsham, Australia .... 63 F3 36 44S 142 13 E
Horsham, U.K. 11 F7 51 4N 0 20W
Horten, Norway .... 9 G14 59 25N 10 32 E
Horton, U.S.A. 80 F7 39 40N 95 32W
Horton →, Canada 68 B7 69 56N 126 52W
Horwood, L., Canada ... 70 C3 48 5N 82 20W

Jumna

Jacundá →, Brazil 93 D8 1 57S 50 26W
Jadotville = Likasi, Dem. Rep. of the Congo 55 E2 10 55S 26 48 E
Jaén, Peru 92 E3 5 25S 78 40W
Jaén, Spain 19 D4 37 44N 3 43W
Jaffa = Tel Aviv-Yafo, Israel 47 C3 32 4N 34 48 E
Jaffa, C., Australia 63 F2 36 58S 139 40 E
Jaffna, Sri Lanka 40 Q12 9 45N 80 2 E
Jagadhri, India 42 D7 30 10N 77 20 E
Jagadishpur, India 43 G11 25 30N 84 21 E
Jagdalpur, India 41 K13 19 3N 82 0 E
Jagersfontein, S. Africa 56 D4 29 44S 25 27 E
Jagodina, Serbia, Yug. 21 C9 44 5N 21 15 E
Jagraon, India 40 D9 30 50N 75 25 E
Jagtial, India 40 K11 18 50N 79 0 E
Jaguariaíva, Brazil 95 A6 24 10S 49 50W
Jaguaribe →, Brazil 93 D11 4 25S 37 45W
Jagüey Grande, Cuba 88 B3 22 35N 81 7W
Jahangirabad, India 42 E8 28 19N 78 4 E
Jahrom, Iran 45 D7 28 30N 53 31 E
Jailolo, Indonesia 37 D7 1 5N 127 30 E
Jailolo, Selat, Indonesia 37 D7 0 5N 129 5 E
Jaipur, India 42 F6 27 0N 75 50 E
Jājarm, Iran 45 B8 36 58N 56 27 E
Jakarta, Indonesia 37 G12 6 9S 106 49 E
Jakobstad = Pietarsaari, Finland 8 E20 63 40N 22 43 E
Jal, U.S.A. 81 J3 32 7N 103 12W
Jalalabad, Afghan. 42 B4 34 30N 70 29 E
Jalalabad, India 43 F8 27 41N 79 42 E
Jalalpur Jattan, Pakistan 42 C6 32 38N 74 11 E
Jalama, U.S.A. 85 L6 34 29N 120 29W
Jalapa, Guatemala 88 D2 14 39N 89 59W
Jalapa Enríquez, Mexico 87 D5 19 32N 96 55W
Jalasjärvi, Finland 9 E20 62 29N 22 47 E
Jalaun, India 43 F8 26 8N 79 25 E
Jaleswar, Nepal 43 F11 26 38N 85 48 E
Jalgaon, Maharashtra, India 40 J10 21 2N 76 31 E
Jalgaon, Maharashtra, India 40 J9 21 0N 75 42 E
Jalībah, Iraq 44 D5 30 35N 46 32 E
Jalisco □, Mexico 86 D4 20 0N 104 0W
Jalkot, Pakistan 43 B5 35 14N 73 24 E
Jalna, India 40 K9 19 48N 75 38 E
Jalón →, Spain 19 B5 41 47N 1 4W
Jalpa, Mexico 86 C4 21 38N 102 58W
Jalpaiguri, India 41 F16 26 32N 88 46 E
Jaluit I., Pac. Oc. 64 G8 6 0N 169 30 E
Jalūlā, Iraq 44 C5 34 16N 45 10 E
Jamaica ■, W. Indies 88 C4 18 10N 77 30W
Jamalpur, Bangla. 41 G16 24 52N 89 56 E
Jamalpur, India 43 G12 25 18N 86 28 E
Jamalpurganj, India 43 H13 23 2N 88 1 E
Jamanxim →, Brazil 93 D7 4 43S 56 18W
Jambi, Indonesia 36 E2 1 38S 103 30 E
Jambi □, Indonesia 36 E2 1 30S 102 30 E
Jambusar, India 42 H5 22 3N 72 51 E
James →, U.S.A. 80 D6 42 52N 97 18W
James B., Canada 69 C12 54 0N 80 0W
James Ranges, Australia 60 D5 24 10S 132 30 E
James Ross I., Antarctica 5 C18 63 58S 57 50W
Jamestown, Australia 63 E2 33 10S 138 32 E
Jamestown, S. Africa 56 E4 31 6S 26 45 E
Jamestown, Ky., U.S.A. 76 G3 36 59N 85 4W
Jamestown, N. Dak., U.S.A. 80 B5 46 54N 98 42W
Jamestown, N.Y., U.S.A. 78 D5 42 6N 79 14W
Jamestown, Pa., U.S.A. 78 E4 41 29N 80 27W
Jamestown, Tenn., U.S.A. 77 G3 36 26N 84 56W
Jamīlābād, Iran 45 C6 34 24N 48 28 E
Jamiltepec, Mexico 87 D5 16 17N 97 49W
Jamkhandi, India 40 L9 16 30N 75 15 E
Jammu, India 42 C6 32 43N 74 54 E
Jammu & Kashmir □, India 43 B7 34 25N 77 0 E
Jamnagar, India 42 H4 22 30N 70 6 E
Jampur, Pakistan 42 E4 29 39N 70 40 E
Jamrud, Pakistan 42 C4 33 59N 71 24 E
Jämsä, Finland 9 F21 61 53N 25 10 E
Jamshedpur, India 43 H12 22 44N 86 12 E
Jamtara, India 43 H12 23 59N 86 49 E
Jämtland, Sweden 8 E15 63 31N 14 0 E
Jan L., Canada 73 C8 54 56N 102 55W
Janakkala, Finland 9 F21 60 54N 24 36 E
Janaúba, Brazil 93 G10 15 48S 43 19W
Jand, Pakistan 42 C5 33 30N 72 6 E
Jandaq, Iran 45 C7 34 3N 54 22 E
Jandia, Canary Is. 22 F5 28 6N 14 21W
Jandia, Pta. de, Canary Is. 22 F5 28 3N 14 31W
Jandola, Pakistan 42 C4 32 20N 70 9 E
Jandowae, Australia 63 D5 26 45S 151 7 E
Janesville, U.S.A. 80 D10 42 41N 89 1W
Janin, West Bank 47 C4 32 28N 35 18 E
Janos, Mexico 86 A3 30 45N 108 10W
Januária, Brazil 93 G10 15 25S 44 25W
Janubio, Canary Is. 22 F6 28 56N 13 50W
Jaora, India 42 H6 23 40N 75 10 E
Japan ■, Asia 31 G8 36 0N 136 0 E
Japan, Sea of, Asia 30 E7 40 0N 135 0 E
Japan Trench, Pac. Oc. 64 D6 32 0N 142 0 E
Japen = Yapen, Indonesia 37 E9 1 50S 136 0 E
Japurá →, Brazil 92 D5 3 8S 65 46W
Jaqué, Panama 92 B3 7 27N 78 8W
Jarābulus, Syria 44 B3 36 49N 38 1 E
Jarama →, Spain 19 B4 40 24N 3 32W
Jaranwala, Pakistan 42 D5 31 15N 73 26 E
Jarash, Jordan 47 C4 32 17N 35 54 E
Jardim, Brazil 94 A4 21 28S 56 2W
Jardines de la Reina, Is., Cuba 88 B4 20 50N 78 50W
Jargalang, China 35 C12 43 5N 122 55 E
Jargalant = Hovd, Mongolia 32 B4 48 2N 91 37 E
Jari →, Brazil 93 D8 1 9S 51 54W
Jarīr, W. al →, Si. Arabia 44 E4 25 38N 42 30 E
Jarosław, Poland 17 C12 50 2N 22 42 E
Jarrahdale, Australia 61 F2 32 24S 116 5 E
Jarres, Plaine des, Laos 38 C4 19 27N 103 10 E
Jartai, China 34 E3 39 45N 105 48 E
Jarud Qi, China 35 B11 44 28N 120 50 E
Järvenpää, Finland 9 F21 60 29N 25 5 E
Jarvis, Canada 78 D4 42 53N 80 6W
Jarvis I., Pac. Oc. 65 H12 0 15S 159 55W
Jarwa, India 43 F10 27 38N 82 30 E
Jāsimīyah, Iraq 44 C5 33 45N 44 41 E
Jasin, Malaysia 39 L4 2 20N 102 26 E
Jāsk, Iran 45 E8 25 38N 57 45 E
Jasło, Poland 17 D11 49 45N 21 30 E
Jasper, Alta., Canada 72 C5 52 55N 118 5W
Jasper, Ont., Canada 79 B9 44 52N 75 57W
Jasper, Ala., U.S.A. 77 J2 33 50N 87 17W
Jasper, Fla., U.S.A. 77 K4 30 31N 82 57W
Jasper, Minn., U.S.A. 80 D6 43 51N 96 24W
Jasper, Tex., U.S.A. 81 K8 30 56N 94 1W
Jasper Nat. Park, Canada 72 C5 52 50N 118 8W
Jászberény, Hungary 17 E10 47 30N 19 55 E
Jataí, Brazil 93 G8 17 58S 51 48W
Jati, Pakistan 42 G3 24 20N 68 19 E
Jatibarang, Indonesia 37 G13 6 28S 108 18 E
Jatinegara, Indonesia 37 G12 6 13S 106 52 E
Játiva = Xátiva, Spain 19 C5 38 59N 0 32W
Jaú, Brazil 95 A6 22 10S 48 30W
Jauja, Peru 92 F3 11 45S 75 15W
Jaunpur, India 43 G10 25 46N 82 44 E
Java = Jawa, Indonesia 37 G14 7 0S 110 0 E
Java Sea, Indonesia 36 E3 4 35S 107 15 E
Java Trench, Ind. Oc. 64 H2 9 0S 105 0 E
Javhlant = Ulyasutay, Mongolia 32 B4 47 56N 97 28 E
Jawa, Indonesia 37 G14 7 0S 110 0 E
Jay, U.S.A. 81 G7 36 25N 94 48W
Jaya, Puncak, Indonesia 37 E9 3 57S 137 17 E
Jayanti, India 41 F16 26 45N 89 40 E
Jayapura, Indonesia 37 E10 2 28S 140 38 E
Jayawijaya, Pegunungan, Indonesia 37 F9 5 0S 139 0 E
Jaynagar, India 41 F15 26 43N 86 9 E
Jayrūd, Syria 44 C3 33 49N 36 44 E
Jayton, U.S.A. 81 J4 33 15N 100 34W
Jazīreh-ye Shīf, Iran 45 D6 29 4N 50 54 E
Jazminal, Mexico 86 C4 24 56N 101 25W
Jazzīn, Lebanon 47 B4 33 31N 35 35 E
Jean, U.S.A. 85 K11 35 47N 115 20W
Jean Marie River, Canada 72 A4 61 32N 120 38W
Jean Rabel, Haiti 89 C5 19 50N 73 5W
Jeanerette, U.S.A. 81 L9 29 55N 91 40W
Jeanette, Ostrov = Zhannetty, Ostrov, Russia 27 B16 76 43N 158 0 E
Jeannette, U.S.A. 78 F5 40 20N 79 36W
Jebel, Bahr el →, Sudan 51 G12 9 30N 30 25 E
Jedburgh, U.K. 12 F6 55 29N 2 33W
Jedda = Jiddah, Si. Arabia 46 C2 21 29N 39 10 E
Jędrzejów, Poland 17 C11 50 35N 20 15 E
Jedway, Canada 72 C2 52 17N 131 14W
Jefferson, Iowa, U.S.A. 80 D7 42 1N 94 23W
Jefferson, Ohio, U.S.A. 78 E4 41 44N 80 46W
Jefferson, Tex., U.S.A. 81 J7 32 46N 94 21W
Jefferson, Wis., U.S.A. 80 D10 43 0N 88 48W
Jefferson, Mt., Nev., U.S.A. 82 G5 38 51N 117 0W
Jefferson, Mt., Oreg., U.S.A. 82 D3 44 41N 121 48W
Jefferson City, Mo., U.S.A. 80 F8 38 34N 92 10W
Jefferson City, Tenn., U.S.A. 77 G4 36 7N 83 30W
Jeffersonville, U.S.A. 76 F3 38 17N 85 44W
Jega, Nigeria 50 F6 12 15N 4 23 E
Jēkabpils, Latvia 9 H21 56 29N 25 57 E
Jelenia Góra, Poland 16 C8 50 50N 15 45 E
Jelgava, Latvia 24 C3 56 41N 23 49 E
Jellicoe, Canada 70 C2 49 40N 87 30W
Jemaja, Indonesia 39 L5 3 5N 105 45 E
Jemaluang, Malaysia 39 L4 2 16N 103 52 E
Jember, Indonesia 37 H15 8 11S 113 41 E
Jembongan, Malaysia 36 C5 6 45N 117 20 E
Jena, Germany 16 C6 50 54N 11 35 E
Jena, U.S.A. 81 K8 31 41N 92 8W
Jenkins, U.S.A. 76 G4 37 10N 82 38W
Jenner, U.S.A. 84 G3 38 27N 123 7W
Jennings, U.S.A. 81 K8 30 13N 92 40W
Jennings →, Canada 72 B2 59 38N 132 5W
Jeparit, Australia 63 F3 36 8S 142 1 E
Jequié, Brazil 93 F10 13 51S 40 5W
Jequitinhonha, Brazil 93 G10 16 30S 41 0W
Jequitinhonha →, Brazil 93 G11 15 51S 38 53W
Jerantut, Malaysia 39 L4 3 56N 102 22 E
Jérémie, Haiti 89 C5 18 40N 74 10W
Jerez, Punta, Mexico 87 C5 22 58N 97 40W
Jerez de García Salinas, Mexico 86 C4 22 39N 103 0W
Jerez de la Frontera, Spain 19 D2 36 41N 6 7W
Jerez de los Caballeros, Spain 19 C2 38 20N 6 45W
Jericho = El Arīḥā, West Bank 47 D4 31 52N 35 27 E
Jericho, Australia 62 C4 23 38S 146 6 E
Jerilderie, Australia 63 F4 35 20S 145 41 E
Jermyn, U.S.A. 79 E9 41 31N 75 31W
Jerome, U.S.A. 83 J8 34 45N 112 7W
Jersey, U.K. 11 H5 49 11N 2 7W
Jersey City, U.S.A. 79 F10 40 44N 74 4W
Jersey Shore, U.S.A. 78 E7 41 12N 77 15W
Jerseyville, U.S.A. 80 F9 39 7N 90 20W
Jerusalem, Israel 47 D4 31 47N 35 10 E
Jervis B., Australia 63 F5 35 8S 150 46 E
Jesselton = Kota Kinabalu, Malaysia 36 C5 6 0N 116 4 E
Jessore, Bangla. 41 H16 23 10N 89 10 E
Jesup, U.S.A. 77 K5 31 36N 81 53W
Jesús Carranza, Mexico 87 D5 17 28N 95 1W
Jesús María, Argentina 94 C3 30 59S 64 5W
Jetmore, U.S.A. 81 F5 38 4N 99 54W
Jetpur, India 42 J4 21 45N 70 10 E
Jevnaker, Norway 9 F14 60 15N 10 26 E
Jewett, Ohio, U.S.A. 78 F3 40 22N 81 2W
Jewett, Tex., U.S.A. 81 K6 31 22N 96 9W
Jewett City, U.S.A. 79 E13 41 36N 72 0W
Jeyḥūnābād, Iran 45 C6 34 58N 48 59 E
Jeypore, India 41 K13 18 50N 82 38 E
Jhajjar, India 42 E7 28 37N 76 42 E
Jhal Jhao, Pakistan 40 F4 26 20N 65 35 E
Jhalawar, India 42 G7 24 40N 76 10 E
Jhang Maghiana, Pakistan 42 D5 31 15N 72 22 E
Jhansi, India 43 G8 25 30N 78 36 E
Jharia, India 43 H12 23 45N 86 26 E
Jharsuguda, India 41 J14 21 56N 84 5 E
Jhelum, Pakistan 42 C5 33 0N 73 45 E
Jhelum →, Pakistan 42 D5 31 20N 72 10 E
Jhunjhunu, India 42 E6 28 10N 75 30 E
Ji-Paraná, Brazil 92 F6 10 52S 62 57W
Ji Xian, Hebei, China 34 F8 37 35N 115 30 E
Ji Xian, Henan, China 34 G8 35 22N 114 5 E
Ji Xian, Shanxi, China 34 F6 36 7N 110 40 E
Jia Xian, Henan, China 34 H7 33 59N 113 12 E
Jia Xian, Shaanxi, China 34 E6 38 12N 110 28 E
Jiamusi, China 33 B8 46 40N 130 26 E
Ji'an, Jiangxi, China 33 D6 27 6N 114 59 E
Ji'an, Jilin, China 35 D14 41 5N 126 10 E
Jianchang, China 35 D11 40 55N 120 35 E
Jianchangying, China 35 D10 40 10N 118 50 E
Jiangmen, China 33 D6 22 32N 113 0 E
Jiangsu □, China 35 H11 33 0N 120 0 E
Jiangxi □, China 33 D6 27 30N 116 0 E
Jiao Xian, China 35 F11 36 18N 120 1 E
Jiaohe, Hebei, China 34 E9 38 2N 116 20 E
Jiaohe, Jilin, China 35 C14 43 40N 127 22 E
Jiaozhou Wan, China 35 F11 36 5N 120 10 E
Jiaozuo, China 34 G7 35 16N 113 12 E
Jiawang, China 35 G9 34 28N 117 26 E
Jiaxiang, China 34 G9 35 25N 116 20 E
Jiaxing, China 33 C7 30 49N 120 45 E
Jiayi = Chiai, Taiwan 33 D7 23 29N 120 25 E
Jibuti = Djibouti ■, Africa 46 E3 12 0N 43 0 E
Jicarón, I., Panama 88 E3 7 10N 81 50W
Jiddah, Si. Arabia 46 C2 21 29N 39 10 E
Jido, India 41 E19 29 2N 94 58 E
Jieshou, China 34 H8 33 18N 115 22 E
Jiexiu, China 34 F6 37 2N 111 55 E
Jiggalong, Australia 60 D3 23 21S 120 47 E
Jihlava, Czech Rep. 16 D8 49 28N 15 35 E
Jihlava →, Czech Rep. 17 D9 48 55N 16 36 E
Jijiga, Ethiopia 46 F3 9 20N 42 50 E
Jilin, China 35 C14 43 44N 126 30 E
Jilin □, China 35 C14 44 0N 127 0 E
Jilong = Chilung, Taiwan 33 D7 25 3N 121 45 E
Jima, Ethiopia 46 F2 7 40N 36 47 E
Jiménez, Mexico 86 B4 27 10N 104 54W
Jimo, China 35 F11 36 23N 120 30 E
Jin Xian, Hebei, China 34 E8 38 2N 115 2 E
Jin Xian, Liaoning, China 35 E11 38 55N 121 42 E
Jinan, China 34 F9 36 38N 117 1 E
Jincheng, China 34 G7 35 29N 112 50 E
Jind, India 42 E7 29 19N 76 22 E
Jindabyne, Australia 63 F4 36 25S 148 35 E
Jindřichův Hradec, Czech Rep. 16 D8 49 10N 15 2 E
Jing He →, China 34 G5 34 27N 109 4 E
Jingbian, China 34 F5 37 20N 108 30 E
Jingchuan, China 34 G4 35 20N 107 20 E
Jingdezhen, China 33 D6 29 20N 117 11 E
Jinggu, China 32 D5 23 35N 100 41 E
Jinghai, China 34 E9 38 55N 116 55 E
Jingle, China 34 E6 38 20N 111 55 E
Jingning, China 34 G3 35 30N 105 43 E
Jingpo Hu, China 35 C15 43 55N 128 55 E
Jingtai, China 34 F3 37 10N 104 6 E
Jingxing, China 34 E8 38 2N 114 8 E
Jingyang, China 34 G5 34 30N 108 50 E
Jingyu, China 35 C14 42 25N 126 45 E
Jingyuan, China 34 F3 36 30N 104 40 E
Jingziguan, China 34 H6 33 15N 111 0 E
Jinhua, China 33 D6 29 8N 119 38 E
Jining, Nei Mongol Zizhiqu, China 34 D7 41 5N 113 0 E
Jining, Shandong, China 34 G9 35 22N 116 34 E
Jinja, Uganda 54 B3 0 25N 33 12 E
Jinjang, Malaysia 39 L3 3 13N 101 39 E
Jinji, China 34 F4 37 58N 106 8 E
Jinnah Barrage, Pakistan 40 C7 32 58N 71 33 E
Jinotega, Nic. 88 D2 13 6N 85 59W
Jinotepe, Nic. 88 D2 11 50N 86 10W
Jinsha Jiang →, China 32 D5 28 50N 104 36 E
Jinxi, China 35 D11 40 52N 120 50 E
Jinxiang, China 34 G9 35 5N 116 22 E
Jinzhou, China 35 D11 41 5N 121 3 E
Jiparaná →, Brazil 92 E6 8 3S 62 52W
Jipijapa, Ecuador 92 D2 1 0S 80 40W
Jiquilpan, Mexico 86 D4 19 57N 102 42W
Jishan, China 34 G6 35 34N 110 58 E
Jisr ash Shughūr, Syria 44 C3 35 49N 36 18 E
Jitarning, Australia 61 F2 32 48S 117 57 E
Jitra, Malaysia 39 J3 6 16N 100 25 E
Jiu →, Romania 17 F12 43 47N 23 48 E
Jiudengkou, China 34 E4 39 56N 106 40 E
Jiujiang, China 33 D6 29 42N 115 58 E
Jiutai, China 35 B13 44 10N 125 50 E
Jiuxiangcheng, China 34 H8 33 12N 114 50 E
Jiuxincheng, China 34 E8 39 17N 115 59 E
Jixi, China 35 B16 45 20N 130 50 E
Jiyang, China 35 F9 37 0N 117 12 E
Jīzān, Si. Arabia 46 D3 17 0N 42 20 E
Jize, China 34 F8 36 54N 114 56 E
Jizō-Zaki, Japan 31 G6 35 34N 133 20 E
Jizzakh, Uzbekistan 26 E7 40 6N 67 50 E
Joaçaba, Brazil 95 B5 27 5S 51 31W
João Pessoa, Brazil 93 E12 7 10S 34 52W
Joaquín V. González, Argentina 94 B3 25 10S 64 0W
Jodhpur, India 42 F5 26 23N 73 8 E
Joensuu, Finland 24 B4 62 37N 29 49 E
Jofane, Mozam. 57 C5 21 15S 34 18 E
Jõgeva, Estonia 9 G22 58 45N 26 24 E
Joggins, Canada 71 C7 45 42N 64 27W
Jogjakarta = Yogyakarta, Indonesia 37 G14 7 49S 110 22 E
Johannesburg, S. Africa 57 D4 26 10S 28 2 E
Johannesburg, U.S.A. 85 K9 35 22N 117 38W
John Day, U.S.A. 82 D4 44 25N 118 57W
John Day →, U.S.A. 82 D3 45 44N 120 39W
John H. Kerr Reservoir, U.S.A. 77 G6 36 36N 78 18W
John o' Groats, U.K. 12 C5 58 38N 3 4W
Johnnie, U.S.A. 85 J10 36 25N 116 5W
John's Ra., Australia 62 C1 21 55S 133 23 E
Johnson, U.S.A. 81 G4 37 34N 101 45W
Johnson City, N.Y., U.S.A. 79 D9 42 7N 75 58W
Johnson City, Tenn., U.S.A. 77 G4 36 19N 82 21W
Johnson City, Tex., U.S.A. 81 K5 30 17N 98 25W
Johnsonburg, U.S.A. 78 E6 41 29N 78 41W
Johnsondale, U.S.A. 85 K8 35 58N 118 32W
Johnson's Crossing, Canada 72 A2 60 29N 133 18W
Johnston, L., Australia 61 F3 32 25S 120 30 E
Johnston Falls = Mambilima Falls, Zambia 55 E2 10 31S 28 45 E
Johnston I., Pac. Oc. 65 F11 17 10N 169 8W
Johnstone Str., Canada 72 C3 50 28N 126 0W
Johnstown, N.Y., U.S.A. 79 C10 43 0N 74 22W
Johnstown, Pa., U.S.A. 78 F6 40 20N 78 55W
Johor Baharu, Malaysia 39 M4 1 28N 103 46 E
Jõhvi, Estonia 9 G22 59 22N 27 27 E
Joinville, Brazil 95 B6 26 15S 48 55W
Joinville I., Antarctica 5 C18 65 0S 55 30W
Jojutla, Mexico 87 D5 18 37N 99 11W
Jokkmokk, Sweden 8 C18 66 35N 19 50 E
Jökulsá á Bru →, Iceland 8 D6 65 40N 14 16W
Jökulsá á Fjöllum →, Iceland 8 C5 66 10N 16 30W
Jolfā, Āzarbājān-e Sharqī, Iran 44 B5 38 57N 45 38 E
Jolfā, Eşfahan, Iran 45 C6 32 58N 51 37 E
Joliet, U.S.A. 76 E1 41 32N 88 5W
Joliette, Canada 70 C5 46 3N 73 24W
Jolo, Phil. 37 C6 6 0N 121 0 E
Jolon, U.S.A. 84 K5 35 58N 121 9W
Jombang, Indonesia 37 G15 7 33S 112 14 E
Jonava, Lithuania 9 J21 55 8N 24 12 E
Jonesboro, Ark., U.S.A. 81 H9 35 50N 90 42W
Jonesboro, Ill., U.S.A. 81 G10 37 27N 89 16W
Jonesboro, La., U.S.A. 81 J8 32 15N 92 43W
Jonesport, U.S.A. 71 D6 44 32N 67 37W
Joniškis, Lithuania 9 H20 56 13N 23 35 E
Jönköping, Sweden 9 H16 57 45N 14 8 E
Jonquière, Canada 71 C5 48 27N 71 14W
Joplin, U.S.A. 81 G7 37 6N 94 31W
Jordan, U.S.A. 82 C10 47 19N 106 55W
Jordan ■, Asia 47 E5 31 0N 36 0 E
Jordan →, Asia 47 D4 31 48N 35 32 E
Jordan Valley, U.S.A. 82 E5 42 59N 117 3W
Jorhat, India 41 F19 26 45N 94 12 E
Jörn, Sweden 8 D19 65 4N 20 1 E
Jorong, Indonesia 36 E4 3 58S 114 56 E
Jørpeland, Norway 9 G11 59 3N 6 1 E
Jorquera →, Chile 94 B2 28 3S 69 58W
Jos, Nigeria 50 G7 9 53N 8 51 E
José Batlle y Ordóñez, Uruguay 95 C4 33 20S 55 10W
Joseph, U.S.A. 82 D5 45 21N 117 14W
Joseph, L., Nfld., Canada 71 B6 52 45N 65 18W
Joseph, L., Ont., Canada 78 A5 45 10N 79 44W
Joseph Bonaparte G., Australia 60 B4 14 35S 128 50 E
Joseph City, U.S.A. 83 J8 34 57N 110 20W
Joshua Tree, U.S.A. 85 L10 34 8N 116 19W
Joshua Tree National Monument, U.S.A. 85 M10 33 55N 116 0W
Jostedalsbreen, Norway 9 F12 61 40N 6 59 E
Jotunheimen, Norway 9 F13 61 35N 8 25 E
Jourdanton, U.S.A. 81 L5 28 55N 98 33W
Joussard, Canada 72 B5 55 22N 115 50W
Jovellanos, Cuba 88 B3 22 40N 81 10W
Ju Xian, China 35 F10 36 35N 118 20 E
Juan Aldama, Mexico 86 C4 24 20N 103 23W
Juan Bautista Alberdi, Argentina 94 C3 34 26S 61 48W
Juan de Fuca Str., Canada 84 B3 48 15N 124 0W
Juan de Nova, Ind. Oc. 57 B7 17 3S 43 45 E
Juan Fernández, Arch. de, Pac. Oc. 90 G2 33 50S 80 0W
Juan José Castelli, Argentina 94 B3 25 27S 60 57W
Juan L. Lacaze, Uruguay 94 C4 34 26S 57 25W
Juankoski, Finland 8 E23 63 3N 28 19 E
Juárez, Argentina 94 D4 37 40S 59 43W
Juárez, Mexico 85 N11 32 20N 115 57W
Juárez, Sierra de, Mexico 86 A1 32 0N 116 0W
Juàzeiro, Brazil 93 E10 9 30S 40 30W
Juàzeiro do Norte, Brazil 93 E11 7 10S 39 18W
Jubayl, Lebanon 47 A4 34 5N 35 39 E
Jubbah, Si. Arabia 44 D4 28 2N 40 56 E
Jubbulpore = Jabalpur, India 43 H8 23 9N 79 58 E
Jubilee L., Australia 61 E4 29 0S 126 50 E
Juby, C., Morocco 50 C3 28 0N 12 59W
Júcar = Xúquer →, Spain 19 C5 39 5N 0 10W
Júcaro, Cuba 88 B4 21 37N 78 51W
Juchitán, Mexico 87 D5 16 27N 95 5W
Judaea = Har Yehuda, Israel 47 D3 31 35N 34 57 E
Judith →, U.S.A. 82 C9 47 44N 109 39W
Judith, Pt., U.S.A. 79 E13 41 22N 71 29W
Judith Gap, U.S.A. 82 C9 46 41N 109 45W
Jugoslavia = Yugoslavia ■, Europe 21 B9 43 20N 20 0 E
Juigalpa, Nic. 88 D2 12 6N 85 26W
Juiz de Fora, Brazil 95 A7 21 43S 43 19W
Jujuy □, Argentina 94 A2 23 20S 65 40W
Julesburg, U.S.A. 80 E3 40 59N 102 16W
Juli, Peru 92 G5 16 10S 69 25W
Julia Cr. →, Australia 62 C3 20 0S 141 11 E
Julia Creek, Australia 62 C3 20 39S 141 44 E
Juliaca, Peru 92 G4 15 25S 70 10W
Julian, U.S.A. 85 M10 33 4N 116 38W
Julianatop, Surinam 93 C7 3 40N 56 30W
Julimes, Mexico 86 B3 28 25N 105 27W
Jullundur, India 42 D6 31 20N 75 40 E
Julu, China 34 F8 37 15N 115 2 E
Jumbo, Zimbabwe 55 F3 17 30S 30 58 E
Jumbo Pk., U.S.A. 85 J12 36 12N 114 11W
Jumentos Cays, Bahamas 89 B4 23 0N 75 40W
Jumilla, Spain 19 C5 38 28N 1 19W
Jumla, Nepal 43 E10 29 15N 82 13 E
Jumna = Yamuna →, India 43 G9 25 30N 81 53 E

K

Keokuk

Kaolack, *Senegal* **50 F2** 14 5N 16 8W
Kaoshan, *China* **35 B13** 44 38N 124 50 E
Kapadvanj, *India* **42 H5** 23 5N 73 0 E
Kapan, *Armenia* **25 G8** 39 18N 46 27 E
Kapanga, *Dem. Rep. of the Congo* **52 F4** 8 30S 22 40 E
Kapchagai = Qapshaghay, *Kazakstan* **26 E8** 43 51N 77 14 E
Kapela = Velika Kapela, *Croatia* **16 F8** 45 10N 15 5 E
Kapema, *Dem. Rep. of the Congo* **55 E2** 10 45S 28 22 E
Kapfenberg, *Austria* **16 E8** 47 26N 15 18 E
Kapiri Mposhi, *Zambia* **55 E2** 13 59S 28 43 E
Kapiskau →, *Canada* **70 B3** 52 47N 81 55W
Kapit, *Malaysia* **36 D4** 2 0N 112 55 E
Kapiti I., *N.Z.* **59 J5** 40 50S 174 56 E
Kapoe, *Thailand* **39 H2** 9 34N 98 32 E
Kapoeta, *Sudan* **51 H12** 4 50N 33 35 E
Kaposvár, *Hungary* **17 E9** 46 25N 17 47 E
Kapowsin, *U.S.A.* **84 D4** 46 59N 122 13W
Kapps, *Namibia* **56 C2** 22 32S 17 18 E
Kapsan, *N. Korea* **35 D15** 41 4N 128 19 E
Kapsukas = Marijampolė, *Lithuania* **9 J20** 54 33N 23 19 E
Kapuas →, *Indonesia* **36 E3** 0 25S 109 20 E
Kapuas Hulu, Pegunungan, *Malaysia* **36 D4** 1 30N 113 30 E
Kapuas Hulu Ra. = Kapuas Hulu, Pegunungan, *Malaysia* **36 D4** 1 30N 113 30 E
Kapulo, *Dem. Rep. of the Congo* **55 D2** 8 18S 29 15 E
Kapunda, *Australia* **63 E2** 34 20S 138 56 E
Kapuni, *N.Z.* **59 H5** 39 29S 174 8 E
Kapurthala, *India* **42 D6** 31 23N 75 25 E
Kapuskasing, *Canada* **70 C3** 49 25N 82 30W
Kapuskasing →, *Canada* **70 C3** 49 49N 82 0W
Kaputar, *Australia* **63 E5** 30 15S 150 10 E
Kaputir, *Kenya* **54 B4** 2 5N 35 28 E
Kara, *Russia* **26 C7** 69 10N 65 0 E
Kara Bogaz Gol, Zaliv = Garabogazköl Aylagy, *Turkmenistan* **25 F9** 41 0N 53 30 E
Kara Kalpak Republic □ = Karakalpakstan □, *Uzbekistan* **26 E6** 43 0N 58 0 E
Kara Kum, *Turkmenistan* **26 F7** 39 30N 60 0 E
Kara Sea, *Russia* **26 B8** 75 0N 70 0 E
Karabiğa, *Turkey* **21 D12** 40 23N 27 17 E
Karaburun, *Turkey* **21 E12** 38 41N 26 28 E
Karabutak = Qarabutaq, *Kazakstan* **26 E7** 49 59N 60 14 E
Karacabey, *Turkey* **21 D13** 40 12N 28 21 E
Karacasu, *Turkey* **21 F13** 37 43N 28 35 E
Karachi, *Pakistan* **42 G2** 24 53N 67 0 E
Karad, *India* **40 L9** 17 15N 74 10 E
Karaganda = Qaraghandy, *Kazakstan* **26 E8** 49 50N 73 10 E
Karagayly, *Kazakstan* **26 E8** 49 26N 76 0 E
Karaginskiy, Ostrov, *Russia* **27 D17** 58 45N 164 0 E
Karagiye, Vpadina, *Kazakstan* **25 F9** 43 27N 51 45 E
Karagiye Depression = Karagiye, Vpadina, *Kazakstan* **25 F9** 43 27N 51 45 E
Karagwe □, *Tanzania* **54 C3** 2 0S 31 0 E
Karaikal, *India* **40 P11** 10 59N 79 50 E
Karaikkudi, *India* **40 P11** 10 5N 78 45 E
Karaj, *Iran* **45 C6** 35 48N 51 0 E
Karak, *Malaysia* **39 L4** 3 25N 102 2 E
Karakalpakstan □, *Uzbekistan* **26 E6** 43 0N 58 0 E
Karakelong, *Indonesia* **37 D7** 4 35N 126 50 E
Karakitang, *Indonesia* **37 D7** 3 14N 125 28 E
Karaklis = Vanadzor, *Armenia* **25 F7** 40 48N 44 30 E
Karakoram Pass, *Pakistan* **43 B7** 35 33N 77 50 E
Karakoram Ra., *Pakistan* **43 B7** 35 30N 77 0 E
Karalon, *Russia* **27 D12** 57 5N 115 50 E
Karaman, *Turkey* **25 G5** 37 14N 33 13 E
Karamay, *China* **32 B3** 45 30N 84 58 E
Karambu, *Indonesia* **36 E5** 3 53S 116 6 E
Karamea Bight, *N.Z.* **59 J3** 41 22S 171 40 E
Karamsad, *India* **42 H5** 22 35N 72 50 E
Karand, *Iran* **44 C5** 34 16N 46 15 E
Karanganyar, *Indonesia* **37 G13** 7 38S 109 37 E
Karasburg, *Namibia* **56 D2** 28 0S 18 44 E
Karasino, *Russia* **26 C9** 66 50N 86 50 E
Karasjok, *Norway* **8 B21** 69 27N 25 30 E
Karasuk, *Russia* **26 D8** 53 44N 78 2 E
Karasuyama, *Japan* **31 F10** 36 39N 140 9 E
Karatau = Qaratau, *Kazakstan* **26 E8** 43 10N 70 28 E
Karatau, Khrebet, *Kazakstan* **26 E7** 43 30N 69 30 E
Karauli, *India* **42 F7** 26 30N 77 4 E
Karavostasi, *Cyprus* **23 D11** 35 8N 32 50 E
Karawang, *Indonesia* **37 G12** 6 30S 107 15 E
Karawanken, *Europe* **16 E8** 46 30N 14 40 E
Karazhal, *Kazakstan* **26 E8** 48 2N 70 49 E
Karbalā, *Iraq* **44 C5** 32 36N 44 3 E
Karcag, *Hungary* **17 E11** 47 19N 20 57 E
Karcha →, *Pakistan* **43 B7** 34 45N 76 10 E
Kardhítsa, *Greece* **21 E9** 39 23N 21 54 E
Kärdla, *Estonia* **9 G20** 58 50N 22 40 E
Kareeberge, *S. Africa* **56 E3** 30 59S 21 50 E
Karelia □, *Russia* **24 A5** 65 30N 32 30 E
Karelian Republic □ = Karelia □, *Russia* **24 A5** 65 30N 32 30 E
Karevāndar, *Iran* **45 E9** 27 53N 60 44 E
Kargasok, *Russia* **26 D9** 59 3N 80 53 E
Kargat, *Russia* **26 D9** 55 10N 80 15 E
Kargil, *India* **43 B7** 34 32N 76 12 E
Kargopol, *Russia* **24 B6** 61 30N 38 58 E
Karīān, *Iran* **45 E8** 26 57N 57 14 E
Kariba, *Zimbabwe* **55 F2** 16 28S 28 50 E
Kariba, L., *Zimbabwe* **55 F2** 16 40S 28 25 E
Kariba Dam, *Zimbabwe* **55 F2** 16 30S 28 35 E
Kariba Gorge, *Zambia* **55 F2** 16 30S 28 50 E
Karibib, *Namibia* **56 C2** 22 0S 15 56 E
Karimata, Kepulauan, *Indonesia* **36 E3** 1 25S 109 0 E
Karimata, Selat, *Indonesia* **36 E3** 2 0S 108 40 E
Karimata Is. = Karimata, Kepulauan, *Indonesia* **36 E3** 1 25S 109 0 E
Karimnagar, *India* **40 K11** 18 26N 79 10 E
Karimunjawa, Kepulauan, *Indonesia* **36 F4** 5 50S 110 30 E
Karin, *Somali Rep.* **46 E4** 10 50N 45 52 E
Karit, *Iran* **45 C8** 33 29N 56 55 E
Kariya, *Japan* **31 G8** 34 58N 137 1 E
Karkaralinsk = Qarqaraly, *Kazakstan* **26 E8** 49 26N 75 30 E
Karkinitska Zatoka, *Ukraine* **25 E5** 45 56N 33 0 E
Karkinitskiy Zaliv = Karkinitska Zatoka, *Ukraine* **25 E5** 45 56N 33 0 E
Karl-Marx-Stadt = Chemnitz, *Germany* **16 C7** 50 51N 12 54 E
Karlovac, *Croatia* **16 F8** 45 31N 15 36 E
Karlovo, *Bulgaria* **21 C11** 42 38N 24 47 E
Karlovy Vary, *Czech Rep.* **16 C7** 50 13N 12 51 E
Karlsbad = Karlovy Vary, *Czech Rep.* **16 C7** 50 13N 12 51 E
Karlsborg, *Sweden* **9 G16** 58 33N 14 33 E
Karlshamn, *Sweden* **9 H16** 56 10N 14 51 E
Karlskoga, *Sweden* **9 G16** 59 28N 14 33 E
Karlskrona, *Sweden* **9 H16** 56 10N 15 35 E
Karlsruhe, *Germany* **16 D5** 49 0N 8 23 E
Karlstad, *Sweden* **9 G15** 59 23N 13 30 E
Karlstad, *U.S.A.* **80 A6** 48 35N 96 31W
Karnal, *India* **42 E7** 29 42N 77 2 E
Karnali →, *Nepal* **43 E9** 28 45N 81 16 E
Karnaphuli Res., *Bangla.* **41 H18** 22 40N 92 20 E
Karnataka □, *India* **40 N10** 13 15N 77 0 E
Karnes City, *U.S.A.* **81 L6** 28 53N 97 54W
Karnische Alpen, *Europe* **16 E7** 46 36N 13 0 E
Kärnten □, *Austria* **16 E8** 46 52N 13 30 E
Karoi, *Zimbabwe* **55 F2** 16 48S 29 45 E
Karonga, *Malawi* **55 D3** 9 57S 33 55 E
Karoonda, *Australia* **63 F2** 35 1S 139 59 E
Karora, *Sudan* **51 E13** 17 44N 38 15 E
Karpasia □, *Cyprus* **23 D13** 35 32N 34 15 E
Karpinsk, *Russia* **24 C11** 59 45N 60 1 E
Karpogory, *Russia* **24 B7** 64 0N 44 27 E
Karpuz Burnu = Apostolos Andreas, C., *Cyprus* **23 D13** 35 42N 34 35 E
Kars, *Turkey* **25 F7** 40 40N 43 5 E
Karsakpay, *Kazakstan* **26 E7** 47 55N 66 40 E
Karshi = Qarshi, *Uzbekistan* **26 F7** 38 53N 65 48 E
Karsiyang, *India* **43 F13** 26 56N 88 18 E
Karsun, *Russia* **24 D8** 54 14N 46 57 E
Kartaly, *Russia* **26 D7** 53 3N 60 40 E
Kartapur, *India* **42 D6** 31 27N 75 32 E
Karthaus, *U.S.A.* **78 E6** 41 8N 78 9W
Karufa, *Indonesia* **37 E8** 3 50S 133 20 E
Karumba, *Australia* **62 B3** 17 31S 140 50 E
Karumo, *Tanzania* **54 C3** 2 25S 32 50 E
Karumwa, *Tanzania* **54 C3** 3 12S 32 38 E
Karungu, *Kenya* **54 C3** 0 50S 34 10 E
Karviná, *Czech Rep.* **17 D10** 49 53N 18 31 E
Karwar, *India* **40 M9** 14 55N 74 13 E
Karwi, *India* **43 G9** 25 12N 80 57 E
Kasache, *Malawi* **55 E3** 13 25S 34 20 E
Kasai →, *Dem. Rep. of the Congo* **52 E3** 3 30S 16 10 E
Kasai Oriental □, *Dem. Rep. of the Congo* **54 D1** 5 0S 24 30 E
Kasaji, *Dem. Rep. of the Congo* **55 E1** 10 25S 23 27 E
Kasama, *Zambia* **55 E3** 10 16S 31 9 E
Kasan-dong, *N. Korea* **35 D14** 41 18N 126 55 E
Kasane, *Namibia* **56 B3** 17 34S 24 50 E
Kasanga, *Tanzania* **55 D3** 8 30S 31 10 E
Kasaragod, *India* **40 N9** 12 30N 74 58 E
Kasba L., *Canada* **73 A8** 60 20N 102 10W
Kāseh Garān, *Iran* **44 C5** 34 5N 46 2 E
Kasempa, *Zambia* **55 E2** 13 30S 25 44 E
Kasenga, *Dem. Rep. of the Congo* **55 E2** 10 20S 28 45 E
Kasese, *Uganda* **54 B3** 0 13N 30 3 E
Kasewa, *Zambia* **55 E2** 14 28S 28 53 E
Kasganj, *India* **43 F8** 27 48N 78 42 E
Kashabowie, *Canada* **70 C1** 48 40N 90 26W
Kāshān, *Iran* **45 C6** 34 5N 51 30 E
Kashi, *China* **32 C2** 39 30N 76 2 E
Kashimbo, *Dem. Rep. of the Congo* **55 E2** 11 12S 26 19 E
Kashipur, *India* **43 E8** 29 15N 79 0 E
Kashiwazaki, *Japan* **31 F9** 37 22N 138 33 E
Kashk-e Kohneh, *Afghan.* **40 B3** 34 55N 62 30 E
Kāshmar, *Iran* **45 C8** 35 16N 58 26 E
Kashmir, *Asia* **43 C7** 34 0N 76 0 E
Kashmor, *Pakistan* **42 E3** 28 28N 69 32 E
Kashun Noerh = Gaxun Nur, *China* **32 B5** 42 22N 100 30 E
Kasimov, *Russia* **24 D7** 54 55N 41 20 E
Kasinge, *Dem. Rep. of the Congo* **54 D2** 6 15S 26 58 E
Kasiruta, *Indonesia* **37 E7** 0 25S 127 12 E
Kaskaskia →, *U.S.A.* **80 G10** 37 58N 89 57W
Kaskattama →, *Canada* **73 B10** 57 3N 90 4W
Kaskinen, *Finland* **9 E19** 62 22N 21 15 E
Kaslo, *Canada* **72 D5** 49 55N 116 55W
Kasmere L., *Canada* **73 B8** 59 34N 101 10W
Kasongo, *Dem. Rep. of the Congo* **54 C2** 4 30S 26 33 E
Kasongo Lunda, *Dem. Rep. of the Congo* **52 F3** 6 35S 16 49 E
Kásos, *Greece* **21 G12** 35 20N 26 55 E
Kassalâ, *Sudan* **51 E13** 15 30N 36 0 E
Kassel, *Germany* **16 C5** 51 18N 9 26 E
Kassiópi, *Greece* **23 A3** 39 48N 19 53 E
Kastamonu, *Turkey* **25 F5** 41 25N 33 43 E
Kastélli, *Greece* **23 D5** 35 29N 23 38 E
Kastéllion, *Greece* **23 D7** 35 12N 25 20 E
Kasterlee, *Belgium* **15 C4** 51 15N 4 59 E
Kastoría, *Greece* **21 D9** 40 30N 21 19 E
Kasulu, *Tanzania* **54 C3** 4 37S 30 5 E
Kasulu □, *Tanzania* **54 C3** 4 37S 30 5 E
Kasumi, *Japan* **31 G7** 35 38N 134 38 E
Kasungu, *Malawi* **55 E3** 13 0S 33 29 E
Kasur, *Pakistan* **42 D6** 31 5N 74 25 E
Kataba, *Zambia* **55 F2** 16 5S 25 10 E
Katako Kombe, *Dem. Rep. of the Congo* **54 C1** 3 25S 24 20 E
Katale, *Tanzania* **54 C3** 4 52S 31 7 E
Katamatite, *Australia* **63 F4** 36 6S 145 41 E
Katanda, Kivu, *Dem. Rep. of the Congo* **54 C2** 0 55S 29 21 E
Katanda, Shaba, *Dem. Rep. of the Congo* **54 D1** 7 52S 24 13 E
Katanga = Shaba □, *Dem. Rep. of the Congo* **54 D2** 8 0S 25 0 E
Katangi, *India* **40 J11** 21 56N 79 50 E
Katavi Swamp, *Tanzania* **54 D3** 6 50S 31 10 E
Kateríni, *Greece* **21 D10** 40 18N 22 37 E
Katha, *Burma* **41 G20** 24 10N 96 30 E
Katherine, *Australia* **60 B5** 14 27S 132 20 E
Kathiawar, *India* **42 H4** 22 20N 71 0 E
Kathikas, *Cyprus* **23 E11** 34 55N 32 25 E
Katihar, *India* **43 G12** 25 34N 87 36 E
Katima Mulilo, *Zambia* **56 B3** 17 28S 24 13 E
Katimbira, *Malawi* **55 E3** 12 40S 34 0 E
Katingan = Mendawai →, *Indonesia* **36 E4** 3 30S 113 0 E
Katiola, *Ivory C.* **50 G4** 8 10N 5 10W
Katmandu, *Nepal* **43 F11** 27 45N 85 20 E
Káto Arkhánai, *Greece* **23 D7** 35 15N 25 10 E
Káto Khorió, *Greece* **23 D7** 35 3N 25 47 E
Kato Pyrgos, *Cyprus* **23 D11** 35 11N 32 41 E
Katompe, *Dem. Rep. of the Congo* **54 D2** 6 2S 26 23 E
Katonga →, *Uganda* **54 B3** 0 34N 31 50 E
Katoomba, *Australia* **63 E5** 33 41S 150 19 E
Katowice, *Poland* **17 C10** 50 17N 19 5 E
Katrine, L., *U.K.* **12 E4** 56 15N 4 30W
Katrineholm, *Sweden* **9 G17** 59 9N 16 12 E
Katsepe, *Madag.* **57 B8** 15 45S 46 15 E
Katsina, *Nigeria* **50 F7** 13 0N 7 32 E
Katsumoto, *Japan* **31 H4** 33 51N 129 42 E
Katsuura, *Japan* **31 G10** 35 10N 140 20 E
Katsuyama, *Japan* **31 F8** 36 3N 136 30 E
Kattaviá, *Greece* **23 D9** 35 57N 27 46 E
Kattegat, *Denmark* **9 H14** 56 40N 11 20 E
Katumba, *Dem. Rep. of the Congo* **54 D2** 7 40S 25 17 E
Katungu, *Kenya* **54 C5** 2 55S 40 3 E
Katwa, *India* **43 H13** 23 30N 88 5 E
Katwijk, *Neths.* **15 B4** 52 12N 4 24 E
Kauai, *U.S.A.* **74 H15** 22 3N 159 30W
Kauai Channel, *U.S.A.* **74 H15** 21 45N 158 50W
Kaufman, *U.S.A.* **81 J6** 32 35N 96 19W
Kauhajoki, *Finland* **9 E20** 62 25N 22 10 E
Kaukauna, *U.S.A.* **76 C1** 44 17N 88 17W
Kaukauveld, *Namibia* **56 C3** 20 0S 20 15 E
Kaunas, *Lithuania* **24 D3** 54 54N 23 54 E
Kautokeino, *Norway* **8 B20** 69 0N 23 4 E
Kavacha, *Russia* **27 C17** 60 16N 169 51 E
Kavalerovo, *Russia* **30 B7** 44 15N 135 4 E
Kavali, *India* **40 M12** 14 55N 80 1 E
Kaválla, *Greece* **21 D11** 40 57N 24 28 E
Kavār, *Iran* **45 D7** 29 11N 52 44 E
Kavos, *Greece* **23 B4** 39 23N 20 3 E
Kaw, *Fr. Guiana* **93 C8** 4 30N 52 15W
Kawagama L., *Canada* **78 A6** 45 18N 78 45W
Kawagoe, *Japan* **31 G9** 35 55N 139 29 E
Kawaguchi, *Japan* **31 G9** 35 52N 139 45 E
Kawaihae, *U.S.A.* **74 H17** 20 3N 155 50W
Kawambwa, *Zambia* **55 D2** 9 48S 29 3 E
Kawanoe, *Japan* **31 G6** 34 1N 133 34 E
Kawardha, *India* **43 J9** 22 0N 81 17 E
Kawasaki, *Japan* **31 G9** 35 35N 139 42 E
Kawasi, *Indonesia* **37 E7** 1 38S 127 28 E
Kawene, *Canada* **70 C1** 48 45N 91 15W
Kawerau, *N.Z.* **59 H6** 38 7S 176 42 E
Kawhia Harbour, *N.Z.* **59 H5** 38 5S 174 51 E
Kawio, Kepulauan, *Indonesia* **37 D7** 4 30N 125 30 E
Kawnro, *Burma* **41 H21** 22 48N 99 8 E
Kawthaung, *Burma* **39 H2** 10 5N 98 36 E
Kawthoolei = Kawthule □, *Burma* **41 L20** 18 0N 97 30 E
Kawthule □, *Burma* **41 L20** 18 0N 97 30 E
Kaya, *Burkina Faso* **50 F5** 13 4N 1 10W
Kayah □, *Burma* **41 K20** 19 15N 97 15 E
Kayan →, *Indonesia* **36 D5** 2 55N 117 35 E
Kaycee, *U.S.A.* **82 E10** 43 43N 106 38W
Kayeli, *Indonesia* **37 E7** 3 20S 127 10 E
Kayenta, *U.S.A.* **83 H8** 36 44N 110 15W
Kayes, *Mali* **50 F3** 14 25N 11 30W
Kayoa, *Indonesia* **37 D7** 0 1N 127 28 E
Kayomba, *Zambia* **55 E1** 13 11S 24 2 E
Kayrunnera, *Australia* **63 E3** 30 40S 142 30 E
Kayseri, *Turkey* **25 G6** 38 45N 35 30 E
Kaysville, *U.S.A.* **82 F8** 41 2N 111 56W
Kazachye, *Russia* **27 B14** 70 52N 135 58 E
Kazakstan ■, *Asia* **26 E8** 50 0N 70 0 E
Kazan, *Russia* **24 C8** 55 50N 49 10 E
Kazan-Rettō, *Pac. Oc.* **64 E6** 25 0N 141 0 E
Kazanlŭk, *Bulgaria* **21 C11** 42 38N 25 20 E
Kazatin = Kozyatyn, *Ukraine* **17 D15** 49 45N 28 50 E
Kāzerūn, *Iran* **45 D6** 29 38N 51 40 E
Kazuno, *Japan* **30 D10** 40 10N 140 45 E
Kazym →, *Russia* **26 C7** 63 54N 65 50 E
Keady, *U.K.* **13 B5** 54 15N 6 42W
Keams Canyon, *U.S.A.* **83 J8** 35 49N 110 12W
Kearney, *U.S.A.* **80 E5** 40 42N 99 5W
Keban, *Turkey* **25 G6** 38 50N 38 50 E
Kebnekaise, *Sweden* **8 C18** 67 53N 18 33 E
Kebri Dehar, *Ethiopia* **46 F3** 6 45N 44 17 E
Kebumen, *Indonesia* **37 G13** 7 42S 109 40 E
Kechika →, *Canada* **72 B3** 59 41N 127 12W
Kecskemét, *Hungary* **17 E10** 46 57N 19 42 E
Kėdainiai, *Lithuania* **9 J21** 55 15N 24 2 E
Kedgwick, *Canada* **71 C6** 47 40N 67 20W
Kédhros Óros, *Greece* **23 D6** 35 11N 24 37 E
Kedia Hill, *Botswana* **56 C3** 21 28S 24 37 E
Kediri, *Indonesia* **37 G15** 7 51S 112 1 E
Keeler, *U.S.A.* **84 J9** 36 29N 117 52W
Keeley L., *Canada* **73 C7** 54 54N 108 8W
Keeling Is. = Cocos Is., *Ind. Oc.* **64 J1** 12 10S 96 55 E
Keene, *Calif., U.S.A.* **85 K8** 35 13N 118 33W
Keene, *N.H., U.S.A.* **79 D12** 42 56N 72 17W
Keeper Hill, *Ireland* **13 D3** 52 45N 8 16W
Keer-Weer, C., *Australia* **62 A3** 14 0S 141 32 E
Keeseville, *U.S.A.* **79 B11** 44 29N 73 30W
Keetmanshoop, *Namibia* **56 D2** 26 35S 18 8 E
Keewatin, *U.S.A.* **80 B8** 47 24N 93 5W
Keewatin □, *Canada* **73 A10** 63 20N 95 0W
Keewatin →, *Canada* **73 B8** 56 29N 100 46W
Kefallinía, *Greece* **21 E9** 38 20N 20 30 E
Kefamenanu, *Indonesia* **37 F6** 9 28S 124 29 E
Keffi, *Nigeria* **50 G7** 8 55N 7 43 E
Keflavík, *Iceland* **8 D2** 64 2N 22 35W
Keg River, *Canada* **72 B5** 57 54N 117 55W
Kegaska, *Canada* **71 B7** 50 9N 61 18W
Keighley, *U.K.* **10 D6** 53 52N 1 54W
Keila, *Estonia* **9 G21** 59 18N 24 25 E
Keimoes, *S. Africa* **56 D3** 28 41S 20 59 E
Keitele, *Finland* **8 E22** 63 10N 26 20 E
Keith, *Australia* **63 F3** 36 6S 140 20 E
Keith, *U.K.* **12 D6** 57 32N 2 57W
Kekri, *India* **42 G6** 26 0N 75 10 E
Kelan, *China* **34 E6** 38 43N 111 31 E
Kelang, *Malaysia* **39 L3** 3 2N 101 26 E
Kelantan →, *Malaysia* **39 J4** 6 13N 102 14 E
Keller, *U.S.A.* **82 B4** 48 5N 118 41W
Kellerberrin, *Australia* **61 F2** 31 36S 117 38 E
Kelleys I., *U.S.A.* **78 E2** 41 36N 82 42W
Kellogg, *U.S.A.* **82 C5** 47 32N 116 7W
Kells = Ceanannus Mor, *Ireland* **13 C5** 53 44N 6 53W
Kelokedhara, *Cyprus* **23 E11** 34 48N 32 39 E
Kelowna, *Canada* **72 D5** 49 50N 119 25W
Kelsey Bay, *Canada* **72 C3** 50 25N 126 0W
Kelseyville, *U.S.A.* **84 G4** 38 59N 122 50W
Kelso, *N.Z.* **59 L2** 45 54S 169 15 E
Kelso, *U.K.* **12 F6** 55 36N 2 26W
Kelso, *U.S.A.* **84 D4** 46 9N 122 54W
Keluang, *Malaysia* **39 L4** 2 3N 103 18 E
Kelvington, *Canada* **73 C8** 52 10N 103 30W
Kem, *Russia* **24 B5** 65 0N 34 38 E
Kem →, *Russia* **24 B5** 64 57N 34 41 E
Kema, *Indonesia* **37 D7** 1 22N 125 8 E
Kemano, *Canada* **72 C3** 53 35N 128 0W
Kemasik, *Malaysia* **39 K4** 4 25N 103 27 E
Kemerovo, *Russia* **26 D9** 55 20N 86 5 E
Kemi, *Finland* **8 D21** 65 44N 24 34 E
Kemi älv = Kemijoki →, *Finland* **8 D21** 65 47N 24 32 E
Kemijärvi, *Finland* **8 C22** 66 43N 27 22 E
Kemijoki →, *Finland* **8 D21** 65 47N 24 32 E
Kemmerer, *U.S.A.* **82 F8** 41 48N 110 32W
Kemmuna = Comino, *Malta* **23 C1** 36 2N 14 20 E
Kemp, L., *U.S.A.* **81 J5** 33 46N 99 9W
Kemp Land, *Antarctica* **5 C5** 69 0S 55 0 E
Kempsey, *Australia* **63 E5** 31 1S 152 50 E
Kempt, L., *Canada* **70 C5** 47 25N 74 22W
Kempten, *Germany* **16 E6** 47 45N 10 17 E
Kemptville, *Canada* **70 D4** 45 0N 75 38W
Kendal, *Indonesia* **37 G14** 6 56S 110 14 E
Kendal, *U.K.* **10 C5** 54 20N 2 44W
Kendall, *Australia* **63 E5** 31 35S 152 44 E
Kendall →, *Australia* **62 A3** 14 4S 141 35 E
Kendallville, *U.S.A.* **76 E3** 41 27N 85 16W
Kendari, *Indonesia* **37 E6** 3 50S 122 30 E
Kendawangan, *Indonesia* **36 E4** 2 32S 110 17 E
Kendenup, *Australia* **61 F2** 34 30S 117 38 E
Kendrapara, *India* **41 J15** 20 35N 86 30 E
Kendrew, *S. Africa* **56 E3** 32 32S 24 30 E
Kendrick, *U.S.A.* **82 C5** 46 37N 116 39W
Kene Thao, *Laos* **38 D3** 17 44N 101 10 E
Kenedy, *U.S.A.* **81 L6** 28 49N 97 51W
Kenema, *S. Leone* **50 G3** 7 50N 11 14W
Keng Kok, *Laos* **38 D5** 16 26N 105 12 E
Keng Tawng, *Burma* **41 J21** 20 45N 98 18 E
Keng Tung, *Burma* **41 J21** 21 0N 99 30 E
Kengeja, *Tanzania* **54 D4** 5 26S 39 45 E
Kenhardt, *S. Africa* **56 D3** 29 19S 21 12 E
Kenitra, *Morocco* **50 B4** 34 15N 6 40W
Kenli, *China* **35 F10** 37 30N 118 20 E
Kenmare, *Ireland* **13 E2** 51 53N 9 36W
Kenmare, *U.S.A.* **80 A3** 48 41N 102 5W
Kenmare River, *Ireland* **13 E2** 51 48N 9 51W
Kennebec, *U.S.A.* **80 D5** 43 54N 99 52W
Kennedy, *Zimbabwe* **55 F2** 18 52S 27 10 E
Kennedy Ra., *Australia* **61 D2** 24 45S 115 10 E
Kennedy Taungdeik, *Burma* **41 H18** 23 15N 93 45 E
Kenner, *U.S.A.* **81 L9** 29 59N 90 15W
Kennet →, *U.K.* **11 F7** 51 27N 0 57W
Kenneth Ra., *Australia* **60 D2** 23 50S 117 8 E
Kennett, *U.S.A.* **81 G9** 36 14N 90 3W
Kennewick, *U.S.A.* **82 C4** 46 12N 119 7W
Kénogami, *Canada* **71 C5** 48 25N 71 15W
Kenogami →, *Canada* **70 B3** 51 6N 84 28W
Kenora, *Canada* **73 D10** 49 47N 94 29W
Kenosha, *U.S.A.* **76 D2** 42 35N 87 49W
Kensington, *Canada* **71 C7** 46 28N 63 34W
Kensington, *U.S.A.* **80 F5** 39 46N 99 2W
Kensington Downs, *Australia* **62 C3** 22 31S 144 19 E
Kent, *Ohio, U.S.A.* **78 E3** 41 9N 81 22W
Kent, *Oreg., U.S.A.* **82 D3** 45 12N 120 42W
Kent, *Tex., U.S.A.* **81 K2** 31 4N 104 13W
Kent, *Wash., U.S.A.* **84 C4** 47 23N 122 14W
Kent □, *U.K.* **11 F8** 51 12N 0 40 E
Kent Group, *Australia* **62 F4** 39 30S 147 20 E
Kent Pen., *Canada* **68 B9** 68 30N 107 0W
Kentau, *Kazakstan* **26 E7** 43 32N 68 36 E
Kentland, *U.S.A.* **76 E2** 40 46N 87 27W
Kenton, *U.S.A.* **76 E4** 40 39N 83 37W
Kentucky □, *U.S.A.* **76 G3** 37 0N 84 0W
Kentucky →, *U.S.A.* **76 F3** 38 41N 85 11W
Kentucky L., *U.S.A.* **77 G2** 36 25N 88 16W
Kentville, *Canada* **71 C7** 45 6N 64 29W
Kentwood, *U.S.A.* **81 K9** 30 56N 90 31W
Kenya ■, *Africa* **54 B4** 1 0N 38 0 E
Kenya, Mt., *Kenya* **54 C4** 0 10S 37 18 E
Keo Neua, Deo, *Vietnam* **38 C5** 18 23N 105 10 E
Keokuk, *U.S.A.* **80 E9** 40 24N 91 24W

Kep, *Cambodia* **39 G5** 10 29N 104 19 E
Kep, *Vietnam* **38 B6** 21 24N 106 16 E
Kepi, *Indonesia* **37 F9** 6 32S 139 19 E
Kerala □, *India* **40 P10** 11 0N 76 15 E
Kerama-Rettō, *Japan* **31 L3** 26 5N 127 15 E
Keran, *Pakistan* **43 B5** 34 35N 73 59 E
Kerang, *Australia* **63 F3** 35 40S 143 55 E
Keraudren, C., *Australia* **60 C2** 19 58S 119 45 E
Kerava, *Finland* **9 F21** 60 25N 25 5 E
Kerch, *Ukraine* **25 E6** 45 20N 36 20 E
Kerguelen, *Ind. Oc.* **3 G13** 49 15S 69 10 E
Kericho, *Kenya* **54 C4** 0 22S 35 15 E
Kericho □, *Kenya* **54 C4** 0 30S 35 15 E
Kerinci, *Indonesia* **36 E2** 1 40S 101 15 E
Kerki, *Turkmenistan* **26 F7** 37 50N 65 12 E
Kerkrade, *Neths.* **15 D6** 50 53N 6 4 E
Kermadec Is., *Pac. Oc.* **64 L10** 30 0S 178 15W
Kermadec Trench, *Pac. Oc.* **64 L10** 30 30S 176 0W
Kermān, *Iran* **45 D8** 30 15N 57 1 E
Kerman, *U.S.A.* **84 J6** 36 43N 120 4W
Kermān □, *Iran* **45 D8** 30 0N 57 0 E
Kermānshāh = Bākhtarān, *Iran* **44 C5** 34 23N 47 0 E
Kermit, *U.S.A.* **81 K3** 31 52N 103 6W
Kern →, *U.S.A.* **85 K7** 35 16N 119 18W
Kernville, *U.S.A.* **85 K8** 35 45N 118 26W
Keroh, *Malaysia* **39 K3** 5 43N 101 1 E
Kerrera, *U.K.* **12 E3** 56 24N 5 33W
Kerrobert, *Canada* **73 C7** 51 56N 109 8W
Kerrville, *U.S.A.* **81 K5** 30 3N 99 8W
Kerry □, *Ireland* **13 D2** 52 7N 9 35W
Kerry Hd., *Ireland* **13 D2** 52 25N 9 56W
Kerulen →, *Asia* **33 B6** 48 48N 117 0 E
Kerzaz, *Algeria* **50 C5** 29 29N 1 37W
Kesagami →, *Canada* **70 B4** 51 40N 79 45W
Kesagami L., *Canada* **70 B3** 50 23N 80 15W
Keşan, *Turkey* **21 D12** 40 49N 26 38 E
Kesennuma, *Japan* **30 E10** 38 54N 141 35 E
Keshit, *Iran* **45 D8** 29 43N 58 17 E
Kestell, *S. Africa* **57 D4** 28 17S 28 42 E
Kestenga, *Russia* **24 A5** 65 50N 31 45 E
Keswick, *U.K.* **10 C4** 54 36N 3 8W
Ket →, *Russia* **26 D9** 58 55N 81 32 E
Ketapang, *Indonesia* **36 E4** 1 55S 110 0 E
Ketchikan, *U.S.A.* **68 C6** 55 21N 131 39W
Ketchum, *U.S.A.* **82 E6** 43 41N 114 22W
Keti Bandar, *Pakistan* **42 G2** 24 8N 67 27 E
Ketri, *India* **42 E6** 28 1N 75 50 E
Kętrzyn, *Poland* **17 A11** 54 7N 21 22 E
Kettering, *U.K.* **11 E7** 52 24N 0 43W
Kettering, *U.S.A.* **76 F3** 39 41N 84 10W
Kettle →, *Canada* **73 B11** 56 40N 89 34W
Kettle Falls, *U.S.A.* **82 B4** 48 37N 118 3W
Kettleman City, *U.S.A.* **84 J7** 36 1N 119 58W
Keuruu, *Finland* **9 E21** 62 16N 24 41 E
Kevin, *U.S.A.* **82 B8** 48 45N 111 58W
Kewanee, *U.S.A.* **80 E10** 41 14N 89 56W
Kewaunee, *U.S.A.* **76 C2** 44 27N 87 31W
Keweenaw B., *U.S.A.* **76 B1** 47 0N 88 15W
Keweenaw Pen., *U.S.A.* **76 B2** 47 30N 88 0W
Keweenaw Pt., *U.S.A.* **76 B2** 47 25N 87 43W
Key Harbour, *Canada* **70 C3** 45 50N 80 45W
Key West, *U.S.A.* **75 F10** 24 33N 81 48W
Keynsham, *U.K.* **11 F5** 51 24N 2 29W
Keyser, *U.S.A.* **76 F6** 39 26N 78 59W
Keystone, *U.S.A.* **80 D3** 43 54N 103 25W
Kezhma, *Russia* **27 D11** 58 59N 101 9 E
Khabarovsk, *Russia* **27 E14** 48 30N 135 5 E
Khabr, *Iran* **45 D8** 28 51N 56 22 E
Khābūr →, *Syria* **44 C4** 35 17N 40 35 E
Khachrod, *India* **42 H6** 23 25N 75 20 E
Khadro, *Pakistan* **42 F3** 26 11N 68 50 E
Khadzhilyangar, *India* **43 B8** 35 45N 79 20 E
Khagaria, *India* **43 G12** 25 30N 86 32 E
Khaipur, *Bahawalpur, Pakistan* **42 E5** 29 34N 72 17 E
Khaipur, *Hyderabad, Pakistan* **42 F3** 27 32N 68 49 E
Khair, *India* **42 F7** 27 57N 77 46 E
Khairabad, *India* **43 F9** 27 33N 80 47 E
Khairagarh, *India* **43 J9** 21 27N 81 2 E
Khairpur, *Pakistan* **40 F6** 27 32N 68 49 E
Khakassia □, *Russia* **26 D9** 53 0N 90 0 E
Khakhea, *Botswana* **56 C3** 24 48S 23 22 E
Khalafābād, *Iran* **45 D6** 30 54N 49 24 E
Khalilabad, *India* **43 F10** 26 48N 83 5 E
Khalīlī, *Iran* **45 E7** 27 38N 53 17 E
Khalkhāl, *Iran* **45 B6** 37 37N 48 32 E
Khalkís, *Greece* **21 E10** 38 27N 23 42 E
Khalmer-Sede = Tazovskiy, *Russia* **26 C8** 67 30N 78 44 E
Khalmer Yu, *Russia* **24 A12** 67 58N 65 1 E
Khalturin, *Russia* **24 C8** 58 40N 48 50 E
Khalūf, *Oman* **46 C6** 20 30N 58 13 E
Kham Keut, *Laos* **38 C5** 18 15N 104 43 E
Khamas Country, *Botswana* **56 C4** 21 45S 26 30 E
Khambhaliya, *India* **42 H3** 22 14N 69 41 E
Khambhat, *India* **42 H5** 22 23N 72 33 E
Khambhat, G. of, *India* **42 J5** 20 45N 72 30 E
Khamīr, *Iran* **45 E7** 26 57N 55 36 E
Khamir, *Yemen* **46 D3** 16 2N 44 0 E
Khamsa, *Egypt* **47 E1** 30 27N 32 23 E
Khān Abū Shāmat, *Syria* **47 B5** 33 39N 36 53 E
Khān Azād, *Iraq* **44 C5** 33 7N 44 22 E
Khān Mujiddah, *Iraq* **44 C4** 32 21N 43 48 E
Khān Shaykhūn, *Syria* **44 C3** 35 26N 36 38 E
Khān Yūnis, *Gaza Strip* **47 D3** 31 21N 34 18 E
Khānaqīn, *Iraq* **44 C5** 34 23N 45 25 E
Khānbāghī, *Iran* **45 B7** 36 10N 55 25 E
Khandwa, *India* **40 J10** 21 49N 76 22 E
Khandyga, *Russia* **27 C14** 62 42N 135 35 E
Khāneh, *Iran* **44 B5** 36 41N 45 8 E
Khanewal, *Pakistan* **42 D4** 30 20N 71 55 E
Khanh Duong, *Vietnam* **38 F7** 12 44N 108 44 E
Khaniá, *Greece* **23 D6** 35 30N 24 4 E
Khaniá □, *Greece* **23 D6** 35 30N 24 0 E
Khaníon, Kólpos, *Greece* **23 D5** 35 33N 23 55 E
Khanka, L., *Asia* **30 B6** 45 0N 132 24 E
Khankendy = Xankändi, *Azerbaijan* **25 G8** 39 52N 46 49 E
Khanna, *India* **42 D7** 30 42N 76 16 E
Khanpur, *Pakistan* **42 E4** 28 42N 70 35 E
Khanty-Mansiysk, *Russia* **26 C7** 61 0N 69 0 E
Khapalu, *Pakistan* **43 B7** 35 10N 76 20 E
Khapcheranga, *Russia* **27 E12** 49 42N 112 24 E
Kharagpur, *India* **43 H12** 22 20N 87 25 E
Khárakas, *Greece* **23 D7** 35 1N 25 7 E
Kharan Kalat, *Pakistan* **40 E4** 28 34N 65 21 E
Kharānaq, *Iran* **45 C7** 32 20N 54 45 E
Kharda, *India* **40 K9** 18 40N 75 34 E
Khardung La, *India* **43 B7** 34 20N 77 43 E
Khârga, El Wâhât el, *Egypt* **51 C12** 25 10N 30 35 E
Khargon, *India* **40 J9** 21 45N 75 40 E
Khārk, Jazireh, *Iran* **45 D6** 29 15N 50 28 E
Kharkiv, *Ukraine* **25 E6** 49 58N 36 20 E
Kharkov = Kharkiv, *Ukraine* **25 E6** 49 58N 36 20 E
Kharovsk, *Russia* **24 C7** 59 56N 40 13 E
Kharta, *Turkey* **21 D13** 40 55N 29 7 E
Khartoum = El Khartûm, *Sudan* **51 E12** 15 31N 32 35 E
Khasan, *Russia* **30 C5** 42 25N 130 40 E
Khāsh, *Iran* **40 E2** 28 15N 61 15 E
Khashm el Girba, *Sudan* **51 F13** 14 59N 35 58 E
Khaskovo, *Bulgaria* **21 D11** 41 56N 25 30 E
Khatanga, *Russia* **27 B11** 72 0N 102 20 E
Khatanga →, *Russia* **27 B11** 72 55N 106 0 E
Khatauli, *India* **42 E7** 29 17N 77 43 E
Khātūnābād, *Iran* **45 C6** 35 30N 51 40 E
Khatyrka, *Russia* **27 C18** 62 3N 175 15 E
Khaybar, Harrat, *Si. Arabia* **44 E4** 25 45N 40 0 E
Khāzimiyah, *Iraq* **44 C4** 34 46N 43 37 E
Khe Bo, *Vietnam* **38 C5** 19 8N 104 41 E
Khe Long, *Vietnam* **38 B5** 21 29N 104 46 E
Khed Brahma, *India* **40 G8** 24 7N 73 5 E
Khekra, *India* **42 E7** 28 52N 77 20 E
Khemarak Phouminville, *Cambodia* **39 G4** 11 37N 102 59 E
Khemmarat, *Thailand* **38 D5** 16 10N 105 15 E
Khenāmān, *Iran* **45 D8** 30 27N 56 29 E
Khenchela, *Algeria* **50 A7** 35 28N 7 11 E
Kherson, *Ukraine* **25 E5** 46 35N 32 35 E
Khersónisos Akrotíri, *Greece* **23 D6** 35 30N 24 10 E
Kheta →, *Russia* **27 B11** 71 54N 102 6 E
Khilok, *Russia* **27 D12** 51 30N 110 45 E
Khiuma = Hiiumaa, *Estonia* **24 C3** 58 50N 22 45 E
Khiva, *Uzbekistan* **26 E7** 41 30N 60 18 E
Khīyāv, *Iran* **44 B5** 38 30N 47 45 E
Khlong Khlung, *Thailand* **38 D2** 16 12N 99 43 E
Khmelnik, *Ukraine* **17 D14** 49 33N 27 58 E
Khmelnitskiy = Khmelnytskyy, *Ukraine* **25 E4** 49 23N 27 0 E
Khmelnytskyy, *Ukraine* **25 E4** 49 23N 27 0 E
Khmer Rep. = Cambodia ■, *Asia* **38 F5** 12 15N 105 0 E
Khoai, Hon, *Vietnam* **39 H5** 8 26N 104 50 E
Khodoriv, *Ukraine* **17 D13** 49 24N 24 19 E
Khodzent = Khudzhand, *Tajikistan* **26 E7** 40 17N 69 37 E
Khojak Pass, *Afghan.* **40 D5** 30 55N 66 30 E
Khok Kloi, *Thailand* **39 H2** 8 17N 98 19 E
Khok Pho, *Thailand* **39 J3** 6 43N 101 6 E
Kholm, *Russia* **24 C5** 57 10N 31 15 E
Kholmsk, *Russia* **27 E15** 47 40N 142 5 E
Khomas Hochland, *Namibia* **56 C2** 22 40S 16 0 E
Khomeyn, *Iran* **45 C6** 33 40N 50 7 E
Khon Kaen, *Thailand* **38 D4** 16 30N 102 47 E
Khong →, *Cambodia* **38 F5** 13 32N 105 58 E
Khong Sedone, *Laos* **38 E5** 15 34N 105 49 E
Khonuu, *Russia* **27 C15** 66 30N 143 12 E
Khóra Sfakíon, *Greece* **23 D6** 35 15N 24 9 E
Khorāsān □, *Iran* **45 C8** 34 0N 58 0 E
Khorat = Nakhon Ratchasima, *Thailand* **38 E4** 14 59N 102 12 E
Khorat, Cao Nguyen, *Thailand* **38 E4** 15 30N 102 50 E
Khorixas, *Namibia* **56 C1** 20 16S 14 59 E
Khorramābād, *Khorāsān, Iran* **45 C8** 35 6N 57 57 E
Khorramābād, *Lorestān, Iran* **45 C6** 33 30N 48 25 E
Khorrāmshahr, *Iran* **45 D6** 30 29N 48 15 E
Khorugh, *Tajikistan* **26 F8** 37 30N 71 36 E
Khosravī, *Iran* **45 D6** 30 48N 51 28 E
Khosrowābād, *Khuzestān, Iran* **45 D6** 30 10N 48 25 E
Khosrowābād, *Kordestān, Iran* **44 C5** 35 31N 47 38 E
Khosūyeh, *Iran* **45 D7** 28 32N 54 26 E
Khotyn, *Ukraine* **17 D14** 48 31N 26 27 E
Khouribga, *Morocco* **50 B4** 32 58N 6 57W
Khowai, *Bangla.* **41 G17** 24 5N 91 40 E
Khoyniki, *Belarus* **17 C15** 51 54N 29 55 E
Khrysokhou B., *Cyprus* **23 D11** 35 6N 32 25 E
Khu Khan, *Thailand* **38 E5** 14 42N 104 12 E
Khudzhand, *Tajikistan* **26 E7** 40 17N 69 37 E
Khuff, *Si. Arabia* **44 E5** 24 55N 44 53 E
Khūgīānī, *Afghan.* **42 D1** 31 28N 65 14 E
Khulna, *Bangla.* **41 H16** 22 45N 89 34 E
Khulna □, *Bangla.* **41 H16** 22 25N 89 35 E
Khumago, *Botswana* **56 C3** 20 26S 24 32 E
Khūnsorkh, *Iran* **45 E8** 27 9N 56 7 E
Khūr, *Iran* **45 C8** 32 55N 58 18 E
Khurai, *India* **42 G8** 24 3N 78 23 E
Khurayş, *Si. Arabia* **45 E6** 25 6N 48 2 E
Khurīyā Murīyā, Jazā 'ir, *Oman* **46 D6** 17 30N 55 58 E
Khurja, *India* **42 E7** 28 15N 77 58 E
Khūsf, *Iran* **45 C8** 32 46N 58 53 E
Khush, *Afghan.* **40 C3** 32 55N 62 10 E
Khushab, *Pakistan* **42 C5** 32 20N 72 20 E
Khust, *Ukraine* **17 D12** 48 10N 23 18 E
Khuzdar, *Pakistan* **42 F2** 27 52N 66 30 E
Khūzestān □, *Iran* **45 D6** 31 0N 49 0 E
Khvājeh, *Iran* **44 B5** 38 9N 46 35 E
Khvānsār, *Iran* **45 D7** 29 56N 54 8 E
Khvor, *Iran* **45 C7** 33 45N 55 0 E
Khvorgū, *Iran* **45 E8** 27 34N 56 27 E
Khvormūj, *Iran* **45 D6** 28 40N 51 30 E
Khvoy, *Iran* **44 B5** 38 35N 45 0 E
Khyber Pass, *Afghan.* **42 B4** 34 10N 71 8 E
Kiabukwa, *Dem. Rep. of the Congo* **55 D1** 8 40S 24 48 E
Kiama, *Australia* **63 E5** 34 40S 150 50 E
Kiamba, *Phil.* **37 C6** 6 2N 124 46 E
Kiambi, *Dem. Rep. of the Congo* **54 D2** 7 15S 28 0 E
Kiambu, *Kenya* **54 C4** 1 8S 36 50 E
Kiangsi = Jiangxi □, *China* **33 D6** 27 30N 116 0 E
Kiangsu = Jiangsu □, *China* **35 H11** 33 0N 120 0 E
Kibanga Port, *Uganda* **54 B3** 0 10N 32 58 E
Kibara, *Tanzania* **54 C3** 2 8S 33 30 E
Kibare, Mts., *Dem. Rep. of the Congo* **54 D2** 8 25S 27 10 E
Kibombo, *Dem. Rep. of the Congo* **54 C2** 3 57S 25 53 E
Kibondo, *Tanzania* **54 C3** 3 35S 30 45 E
Kibondo □, *Tanzania* **54 C3** 4 0S 30 55 E
Kibumbu, *Burundi* **54 C2** 3 32S 29 45 E
Kibungo, *Rwanda* **54 C3** 2 10S 30 32 E
Kibuye, *Burundi* **54 C2** 3 39S 29 59 E
Kibuye, *Rwanda* **54 C2** 2 3S 29 21 E
Kibwesa, *Tanzania* **54 D2** 6 30S 29 58 E
Kibwezi, *Kenya* **54 C4** 2 27S 37 57 E
Kicking Horse Pass, *Canada* **72 C5** 51 28N 116 16W
Kidal, *Mali* **50 E6** 18 26N 1 22 E
Kidderminster, *U.K.* **11 E5** 52 24N 2 15W
Kidete, *Tanzania* **54 D4** 6 25S 37 17 E
Kidnappers, C., *N.Z.* **59 H6** 39 38S 177 5 E
Kidsgrove, *U.K.* **10 D5** 53 5N 2 14W
Kidston, *Australia* **62 B3** 18 52S 144 8 E
Kidugallo, *Tanzania* **54 D4** 6 49S 38 15 E
Kiel, *Germany* **16 A6** 54 19N 10 8 E
Kiel Canal = Nord-Ostsee-Kanal →, *Germany* **16 A5** 54 12N 9 32 E
Kielce, *Poland* **17 C11** 50 52N 20 42 E
Kielder Water, *U.K.* **10 B5** 55 11N 2 31W
Kieler Bucht, *Germany* **16 A6** 54 35N 10 25 E
Kien Binh, *Vietnam* **39 H5** 9 55N 105 19 E
Kien Tan, *Vietnam* **39 G5** 10 7N 105 17 E
Kienge, *Dem. Rep. of the Congo* **55 E2** 10 30S 27 30 E
Kiev = Kyyiv, *Ukraine* **25 D5** 50 30N 30 28 E
Kiffa, *Mauritania* **50 E3** 16 37N 11 24W
Kifrī, *Iraq* **44 C5** 34 45N 45 0 E
Kigali, *Rwanda* **54 C3** 1 59S 30 4 E
Kigarama, *Tanzania* **54 C3** 1 1S 31 50 E
Kigoma □, *Tanzania* **54 D3** 5 0S 30 0 E
Kigoma-Ujiji, *Tanzania* **54 C2** 4 55S 29 36 E
Kigomasha, Ras, *Tanzania* **54 C4** 4 58S 38 58 E
Kihee, *Australia* **63 D3** 27 23S 142 37 E
Kihnu, *Estonia* **9 G21** 58 9N 24 1 E
Kii-Sanchi, *Japan* **31 G8** 34 20N 136 0 E
Kii-Suidō, *Japan* **31 H7** 33 40N 134 45 E
Kikaiga-Shima, *Japan* **31 K4** 28 19N 129 59 E
Kikinda, *Serbia, Yug.* **21 B9** 45 50N 20 30 E
Kikládhes, *Greece* **21 F11** 37 0N 24 30 E
Kikwit, *Dem. Rep. of the Congo* **52 F3** 5 0S 18 45 E
Kilauea Crater, *U.S.A.* **74 J17** 19 25N 155 17W
Kilbrannan Sd., *U.K.* **12 F3** 55 37N 5 26W
Kilchu, *N. Korea* **35 D15** 40 57N 129 25 E
Kilcoy, *Australia* **63 D5** 26 59S 152 30 E
Kildare, *Ireland* **13 C5** 53 9N 6 55W
Kildare □, *Ireland* **13 C5** 53 10N 6 50W
Kilfinnane, *Ireland* **13 D3** 52 21N 8 28W
Kilgore, *U.S.A.* **81 J7** 32 23N 94 53W
Kilifi, *Kenya* **54 C4** 3 40S 39 48 E
Kilifi □, *Kenya* **54 C4** 3 30S 39 40 E
Kilimanjaro, *Tanzania* **54 C4** 3 7S 37 20 E
Kilimanjaro □, *Tanzania* **54 C4** 4 0S 38 0 E
Kilindini, *Kenya* **54 C4** 4 4S 39 40 E
Kiliya, *Ukraine* **17 F15** 45 28N 29 16 E
Kilkee, *Ireland* **13 D2** 52 41N 9 39W
Kilkeel, *U.K.* **13 B5** 54 4N 6 0W
Kilkenny, *Ireland* **13 D4** 52 39N 7 15W
Kilkenny □, *Ireland* **13 D4** 52 35N 7 15W
Kilkieran B., *Ireland* **13 C2** 53 20N 9 41W
Kilkís, *Greece* **21 D10** 40 58N 22 57 E
Killala, *Ireland* **13 B2** 54 13N 9 12W
Killala B., *Ireland* **13 B2** 54 16N 9 8W
Killaloe, *Ireland* **13 D3** 52 48N 8 28W
Killaloe Sta., *Canada* **78 A7** 45 33N 77 25W
Killam, *Canada* **72 C6** 52 47N 111 51W
Killarney, *Australia* **63 D5** 28 20S 152 18 E
Killarney, *Canada* **70 C3** 45 55N 81 30W
Killarney, *Ireland* **13 D2** 52 4N 9 30W
Killary Harbour, *Ireland* **13 C2** 53 38N 9 52W
Killdeer, *Canada* **73 D7** 49 6N 106 22W
Killdeer, *U.S.A.* **80 B3** 47 26N 102 48W
Killeen, *U.S.A.* **81 K6** 31 7N 97 44W
Killin, *U.K.* **12 E4** 56 28N 4 19W
Killíni, *Greece* **21 F10** 37 54N 22 25 E
Killorglin, *Ireland* **13 D2** 52 6N 9 47W
Killybegs, *Ireland* **13 B3** 54 38N 8 26W
Kilmarnock, *U.K.* **12 F4** 55 37N 4 29W
Kilmore, *Australia* **63 F3** 37 25S 144 53 E
Kilondo, *Tanzania* **55 D3** 9 45S 34 20 E
Kilosa, *Tanzania* **54 D4** 6 48S 37 0 E
Kilosa □, *Tanzania* **54 D4** 6 48S 37 0 E
Kilrush, *Ireland* **13 D2** 52 38N 9 29W
Kilwa □, *Tanzania* **55 D4** 9 0S 39 0 E
Kilwa Kisiwani, *Tanzania* **55 D4** 8 58S 39 32 E
Kilwa Kivinje, *Tanzania* **55 D4** 8 45S 39 25 E
Kilwa Masoko, *Tanzania* **55 D4** 8 55S 39 30 E
Kilwinning, *U.K.* **12 F4** 55 39N 4 43W
Kim, *U.S.A.* **81 G3** 37 15N 103 21W
Kimaam, *Indonesia* **37 F9** 7 58S 138 53 E
Kimamba, *Tanzania* **54 D4** 6 45S 37 10 E
Kimba, *Australia* **63 E2** 33 8S 136 23 E
Kimball, *Nebr., U.S.A.* **80 E3** 41 14N 103 40W
Kimball, *S. Dak., U.S.A.* **80 D5** 43 45N 98 57W
Kimberley, *Canada* **72 D5** 49 40N 115 59W
Kimberley, *S. Africa* **56 D3** 28 43S 24 46 E
Kimberley Downs, *Australia* **60 C3** 17 24S 124 22 E
Kimberly, *U.S.A.* **82 E6** 42 32N 114 22W
Kimchaek, *N. Korea* **35 D15** 40 40N 129 10 E
Kimchŏn, *S. Korea* **35 F15** 36 11N 128 4 E
Kimje, *S. Korea* **35 G14** 35 48N 126 45 E
Kimmirut, *Canada* **69 B13** 62 50N 69 50W
Kimry, *Russia* **24 C6** 56 55N 37 15 E
Kimsquit, *Canada* **72 C3** 52 45N 126 57W
Kinabalu, Gunong, *Malaysia* **36 C5** 6 3N 116 14 E
Kinaskan L., *Canada* **72 B2** 57 38N 130 8W
Kinbasket L., *Canada* **72 C5** 52 0N 118 10W
Kincaid, *Canada* **73 D7** 49 40N 107 0W
Kincardine, *Canada* **70 D3** 44 10N 81 40W
Kinda, *Dem. Rep. of the Congo* **55 D2** 9 18S 25 4 E
Kinder Scout, *U.K.* **10 D6** 53 24N 1 52W
Kindersley, *Canada* **73 C7** 51 30N 109 10W
Kindia, *Guinea* **50 F3** 10 0N 12 52W
Kindu, *Dem. Rep. of the Congo* **54 C2** 2 55S 25 50 E
Kineshma, *Russia* **24 C7** 57 30N 42 5 E
Kinesi, *Tanzania* **54 C3** 1 25S 33 50 E
King, L., *Australia* **61 F2** 33 10S 119 35 E
King, Mt., *Australia* **62 D4** 25 10S 147 30 E
King City, *U.S.A.* **84 J5** 36 13N 121 8W
King Cr. →, *Australia* **62 C2** 24 35S 139 30 E
King Edward →, *Australia* **60 B4** 14 14S 126 35 E
King George B., *Falk. Is.* **96 G4** 51 30S 60 30W
King George I., *Antarctica* **5 C18** 60 0S 60 0W
King George Is., *Canada* **69 C11** 57 20N 80 30W
King I. = Kadan Kyun, *Burma* **38 F2** 12 30N 98 20 E
King I., *Australia* **62 F3** 39 50S 144 0 E
King I., *Canada* **72 C3** 52 10N 127 40W
King Leopold Ranges, *Australia* **60 C4** 17 30S 125 45 E
King Sd., *Australia* **60 C3** 16 50S 123 20 E
King William I., *Canada* **68 B10** 69 10N 97 25W
King William's Town, *S. Africa* **56 E4** 32 51S 27 22 E
Kingaroy, *Australia* **63 D5** 26 32S 151 51 E
Kingfisher, *U.S.A.* **81 H6** 35 52N 97 56W
Kingirbān, *Iraq* **44 C5** 34 40N 44 54 E
Kingisepp = Kuressaare, *Estonia* **9 G20** 58 15N 22 30 E
Kingman, *Ariz., U.S.A.* **85 K12** 35 12N 114 4W
Kingman, *Kans., U.S.A.* **81 G5** 37 39N 98 7W
Kingoonya, *Australia* **63 E2** 30 55S 135 19 E
Kings →, *U.S.A.* **84 J7** 36 3N 119 50W
Kings Canyon National Park, *U.S.A.* **84 J8** 36 50N 118 40W
King's Lynn, *U.K.* **10 E8** 52 45N 0 24 E
Kings Mountain, *U.S.A.* **77 H5** 35 15N 81 20W
King's Peak, *U.S.A.* **82 F8** 40 46N 110 27W
Kingsbridge, *U.K.* **11 G4** 50 17N 3 47W
Kingsburg, *U.S.A.* **84 J7** 36 31N 119 33W
Kingscote, *Australia* **63 F2** 35 40S 137 38 E
Kingscourt, *Ireland* **13 C5** 53 55N 6 48W
Kingsley, *U.S.A.* **80 D7** 42 35N 95 58W
Kingsport, *U.S.A.* **77 G4** 36 33N 82 33W
Kingston, *Canada* **70 D4** 44 14N 76 30W
Kingston, *Jamaica* **88 C4** 18 0N 76 50W
Kingston, *N.Z.* **59 L2** 45 20S 168 43 E
Kingston, *N.Y., U.S.A.* **79 E11** 41 56N 73 59W
Kingston, *Pa., U.S.A.* **79 E9** 41 16N 75 54W
Kingston, *R.I., U.S.A.* **79 E13** 41 29N 71 30W
Kingston Pk., *U.S.A.* **85 K11** 35 45N 115 54W
Kingston South East, *Australia* **63 F2** 36 51S 139 55 E
Kingston upon Hull, *U.K.* **10 D7** 53 45N 0 21W
Kingston upon Hull □, *U.K.* **10 D7** 53 45N 0 21W
Kingston-upon-Thames, *U.K.* **11 F7** 51 24N 0 17W
Kingstown, *St. Vincent* **89 D7** 13 10N 61 10W
Kingstree, *U.S.A.* **77 J6** 33 40N 79 50W
Kingsville, *Canada* **70 D3** 42 2N 82 45W
Kingsville, *U.S.A.* **81 M6** 27 31N 97 52W
Kingussie, *U.K.* **12 D4** 57 6N 4 2W
Kınık, *Turkey* **21 E12** 39 6N 27 24 E
Kinistino, *Canada* **73 C7** 52 57N 105 2W
Kinkala, *Congo* **52 E2** 4 18S 14 49 E
Kinki □, *Japan* **31 H8** 33 45N 136 0 E
Kinleith, *N.Z.* **59 H5** 38 20S 175 56 E
Kinmount, *Canada* **78 B6** 44 48N 78 45W
Kinna, *Sweden* **9 H15** 57 32N 12 42 E
Kinnaird, *Canada* **72 D5** 49 17N 117 39W
Kinnairds Hd., *U.K.* **12 D6** 57 43N 2 1W
Kinnarodden, *Norway* **6 A11** 71 8N 27 40 E
Kino, *Mexico* **86 B2** 28 45N 111 59W
Kinoje →, *Canada* **70 B3** 52 8N 81 25W
Kinomoto, *Japan* **31 G8** 35 30N 136 13 E
Kinoni, *Uganda* **54 C3** 0 41S 30 28 E
Kinross, *U.K.* **12 E5** 56 13N 3 25W
Kinsale, *Ireland* **13 E3** 51 42N 8 31W
Kinsale, Old Hd. of, *Ireland* **13 E3** 51 37N 8 33W
Kinsha = Chang Jiang →, *China* **33 C7** 31 48N 121 10 E
Kinshasa, *Dem. Rep. of the Congo* **52 E3** 4 20S 15 15 E
Kinsley, *U.S.A.* **81 G5** 37 55N 99 25W
Kinston, *U.S.A.* **77 H7** 35 16N 77 35W
Kintore Ra., *Australia* **60 D4** 23 15S 128 47 E
Kintyre, *U.K.* **12 F3** 55 30N 5 35W
Kintyre, Mull of, *U.K.* **12 F3** 55 17N 5 47W
Kinushseo →, *Canada* **70 A3** 55 15N 83 45W
Kinuso, *Canada* **72 B5** 55 20N 115 25W
Kinyangiri, *Tanzania* **54 C3** 4 25S 34 37 E
Kinzua, *U.S.A.* **78 E6** 41 52N 78 58W
Kinzua Dam, *U.S.A.* **78 E6** 41 53N 79 0W
Kiosk, *Canada* **70 C4** 46 6N 78 53W
Kiowa, *Kans., U.S.A.* **81 G5** 37 1N 98 29W
Kiowa, *Okla., U.S.A.* **81 H7** 34 43N 95 54W
Kipahigan L., *Canada* **73 B8** 55 20N 101 55W
Kipanga, *Tanzania* **54 D4** 6 15S 35 20 E
Kiparissía, *Greece* **21 F9** 37 15N 21 40 E
Kiparissiakós Kólpos, *Greece* **21 F9** 37 25N 21 25 E
Kipembawe, *Tanzania* **54 D3** 7 38S 33 27 E
Kipengere Ra., *Tanzania* **55 D3** 9 12S 34 15 E
Kipili, *Tanzania* **54 D3** 7 28S 30 32 E
Kipini, *Kenya* **54 C5** 2 30S 40 32 E
Kipling, *Canada* **73 C8** 50 6N 102 38W
Kippure, *Ireland* **13 C5** 53 11N 6 21W
Kipushi, *Dem. Rep. of the Congo* **55 E2** 11 48S 27 12 E
Kiratpur, *India* **42 E8** 29 32N 78 12 E

K'oshih

Kirensk, Russia 27 D11 57 50N 107 55 E
Kirgella Rocks, Australia 61 F3 30 5S 122 50 E
Kirghizia = Kyrgyzstan ■, Asia 26 E8 42 0N 75 0 E
Kirghizstan = Kyrgyzstan ■, Asia 26 E8 42 0N 75 0 E
Kirgiziya Steppe, Eurasia 25 E10 50 0N 55 0 E
Kiribati ■, Pac. Oc. 64 H10 5 0S 180 0 E
Kırıkkale, Turkey 25 G5 39 51N 33 32 E
Kirillov, Russia 24 C6 59 49N 38 24 E
Kirin = Jilin, China 35 C14 43 44N 126 30 E
Kiritimati, Kiribati 65 G12 1 58N 157 27W
Kirkby, U.K. 10 D5 53 30N 2 54W
Kirkby Lonsdale, U.K. 10 C5 54 12N 2 36W
Kirkcaldy, U.K. 12 E5 56 7N 3 9W
Kirkcudbright, U.K. 12 G4 54 50N 4 2W
Kirkee, India 40 K8 18 34N 73 56 E
Kirkenes, Norway 8 B23 69 40N 30 5 E
Kirkjubæjarklaustur, Iceland 8 E4 63 47N 18 4W
Kirkkonummi, Finland 9 F21 60 8N 24 26 E
Kirkland, U.S.A. 83 J7 34 25N 112 43W
Kirkland Lake, Canada 70 C3 48 9N 80 2W
Kırklareli, Turkey 21 D12 41 44N 27 15 E
Kirksville, U.S.A. 80 E8 40 12N 92 35W
Kirkūk, Iraq 44 C5 35 30N 44 21 E
Kirkwall, U.K. 12 C6 58 59N 2 58W
Kirkwood, S. Africa 56 E4 33 22S 25 15 E
Kirov, Russia 24 C8 58 35N 49 40 E
Kirovabad = Gäncä, Azerbaijan 25 F8 40 45N 46 20 E
Kirovakan = Vanadzor, Armenia 25 F7 40 48N 44 30 E
Kirovograd = Kirovohrad, Ukraine 25 E5 48 35N 32 20 E
Kirovohrad, Ukraine 25 E5 48 35N 32 20 E
Kirovsk = Babadayhan, Turkmenistan 26 F7 37 42N 60 23 E
Kirovsk, Russia 24 A5 67 32N 33 41 E
Kirovskiy, Kamchatka, Russia 27 D16 54 27N 155 42 E
Kirovskiy, Primorsk, Russia 30 B6 45 7N 133 30 E
Kirriemuir, U.K. 12 E5 56 41N 3 1W
Kirsanov, Russia 24 D7 52 35N 42 40 E
Kırşehir, Turkey 25 G5 39 14N 34 5 E
Kirthar Range, Pakistan 42 F2 27 0N 67 0 E
Kiruna, Sweden 8 C19 67 52N 20 15 E
Kirundu, Dem. Rep. of the Congo 54 C2 0 50S 25 35 E
Kirup, Australia 61 F2 33 40S 115 50 E
Kiryū, Japan 31 F9 36 24N 139 20 E
Kisaga, Tanzania 54 C3 4 30S 34 23 E
Kisalaya, Nic. 88 D3 14 40N 84 3W
Kisámou, Kólpos, Greece 23 D5 35 30N 23 38 E
Kisanga, Dem. Rep. of the Congo 54 B2 2 30N 26 35 E
Kisangani, Dem. Rep. of the Congo 54 B2 0 35N 25 15 E
Kisar, Indonesia 37 F7 8 5S 127 10 E
Kisarawe, Tanzania 54 D4 6 53S 39 0 E
Kisarawe □, Tanzania 54 D4 7 3S 39 0 E
Kisarazu, Japan 31 G9 35 23N 139 55 E
Kishanganga →, Pakistan 43 B5 34 18N 73 28 E
Kishanganj, India 43 F13 26 3N 88 14 E
Kishangarh, India 42 F4 27 50N 70 30 E
Kishinev = Chişinău, Moldova 25 E4 47 2N 28 50 E
Kishiwada, Japan 31 G7 34 28N 135 22 E
Kishtwar, India 43 C6 33 20N 75 48 E
Kisii, Kenya 54 C3 0 40S 34 45 E
Kisii □, Kenya 54 C3 0 40S 34 45 E
Kisiju, Tanzania 54 D4 7 23S 39 19 E
Kisizi, Uganda 54 C2 1 0S 29 58 E
Kiskatinaw →, Canada 72 B4 56 8N 120 10W
Kiskittogisu L., Canada 73 C9 54 13N 98 20W
Kiskőrös, Hungary 17 E10 46 37N 19 20 E
Kiskunfélegyháza, Hungary 17 E10 46 42N 19 53 E
Kiskunhalas, Hungary 17 E10 46 28N 19 37 E
Kislovodsk, Russia 25 F7 43 50N 42 45 E
Kismayu = Chisimaio, Somali Rep. 49 G8 0 22S 42 32 E
Kiso-Gawa →, Japan 31 G8 35 20N 136 45 E
Kiso-Sammyaku, Japan 31 G8 35 45N 137 45 E
Kisofukushima, Japan 31 G8 35 52N 137 43 E
Kisoro, Uganda 54 C2 1 17S 29 48 E
Kissidougou, Guinea 50 G3 9 5N 10 5W
Kissimmee, U.S.A. 77 L5 28 18N 81 24W
Kissimmee →, U.S.A. 77 M5 27 9N 80 52W
Kississing L., Canada 73 B8 55 10N 101 20W
Kissónerga, Cyprus 23 E11 34 49N 32 24 E
Kisumu, Kenya 54 C3 0 3S 34 45 E
Kiswani, Tanzania 54 C4 4 5S 37 57 E
Kiswere, Tanzania 55 D4 9 27S 39 30 E
Kit Carson, U.S.A. 80 F3 38 46N 102 48W
Kita, Mali 50 F4 13 5N 9 25W
Kitaibaraki, Japan 31 F10 36 50N 140 45 E
Kitakami, Japan 30 E10 39 20N 141 10 E
Kitakami-Gawa →, Japan 30 E10 38 25N 141 19 E
Kitakami-Sammyaku, Japan 30 E10 39 30N 141 30 E
Kitakata, Japan 30 F9 37 39N 139 52 E
Kitakyūshū, Japan 31 H5 33 50N 130 50 E
Kitale, Kenya 54 B4 1 0N 35 0 E
Kitami, Japan 30 C11 43 48N 143 54 E
Kitami-Sammyaku, Japan 30 B11 44 22N 142 43 E
Kitangiri, L., Tanzania 54 C3 4 5S 34 20 E
Kitaya, Tanzania 55 E5 10 38S 40 8 E
Kitchener, Australia 61 F3 30 55S 124 8 E
Kitchener, Canada 70 D3 43 27N 80 29W
Kitega = Gitega, Burundi 54 C2 3 26S 29 56 E
Kitengo, Dem. Rep. of the Congo 54 D1 7 26S 24 8 E
Kiteto □, Tanzania 54 D4 5 0S 37 0 E
Kitgum, Uganda 54 B3 3 17N 32 52 E
Kíthira, Greece 21 F10 36 8N 23 0 E
Kíthnos, Greece 21 F11 37 26N 24 27 E
Kiti, Cyprus 23 E12 34 50N 33 34 E
Kiti, C., Cyprus 23 E12 34 48N 33 36 E
Kitimat, Canada 72 C3 54 3N 128 38W
Kitinen →, Finland 8 C22 67 14N 27 27 E
Kitsuki, Japan 31 H5 33 25N 131 37 E
Kittakittaooloo, L., Australia 63 D2 28 3S 138 14 E
Kittanning, U.S.A. 78 F5 40 49N 79 31W
Kittatinny Mts., U.S.A. 79 F10 41 0N 75 0W
Kittery, U.S.A. 77 D10 43 5N 70 45W
Kittilä, Finland 8 C21 67 40N 24 51 E
Kitui, Kenya 54 C4 1 17S 38 0 E
Kitui □, Kenya 54 C4 1 30S 38 25 E
Kitwe, Zambia 55 E2 12 54S 28 13 E
Kivarli, India 42 G5 24 33N 72 46 E
Kivertsi, Ukraine 17 C13 50 50N 25 28 E
Kividhes, Cyprus 23 E11 34 46N 32 51 E
Kivu □, Dem. Rep. of the Congo 54 C2 3 10S 27 0 E
Kivu, L., Dem. Rep. of the Congo 54 C2 1 48S 29 0 E
Kiyev = Kyyiv, Ukraine 25 D5 50 30N 30 28 E
Kiyevskoye Vdkhr. = Kyyivske Vdskh., Ukraine 25 D5 51 0N 30 25 E
Kizel, Russia 24 C10 59 3N 57 40 E
Kiziguru, Rwanda 54 C3 1 46S 30 23 E
Kızıl Irmak →, Turkey 25 F6 41 44N 35 58 E
Kizil Jilga, India 43 B8 35 26N 78 50 E
Kizimkazi, Tanzania 54 D4 6 28S 39 30 E
Kizlyar, Russia 25 F8 43 51N 46 40 E
Kizyl-Arvat = Gyzylarbat, Turkmenistan 26 F6 39 4N 56 23 E
Kjölur, Iceland 8 D4 64 50N 19 25W
Kladno, Czech Rep. 16 C8 50 10N 14 7 E
Klaeng, Thailand 38 F3 12 47N 101 39 E
Klagenfurt, Austria 16 E8 46 38N 14 20 E
Klaipeda, Lithuania 24 C3 55 43N 21 10 E
Klaksvík, Færoe Is. 8 E9 62 14N 6 35W
Klamath →, U.S.A. 82 F1 41 33N 124 5W
Klamath Falls, U.S.A. 82 E3 42 13N 121 46W
Klamath Mts., U.S.A. 82 F2 41 20N 123 0W
Klappan →, Canada 72 B3 58 0N 129 43W
Klarälven →, Sweden 9 G15 59 23N 13 32 E
Klatovy, Czech Rep. 16 D7 49 23N 13 18 E
Klawer, S. Africa 56 E2 31 44S 18 36 E
Klawock, U.S.A. 72 B2 55 33N 133 6W
Klazienaveen, Neths. 15 B6 52 44N 7 0 E
Kleena Kleene, Canada 72 C4 52 0N 124 59W
Klein, U.S.A. 82 C9 46 24N 108 33W
Klein-Karas, Namibia 56 D2 27 33S 18 7 E
Klerksdorp, S. Africa 56 D4 26 53S 26 38 E
Kletsk = Klyetsk, Belarus 17 B14 53 5N 26 45 E
Kletskiy, Russia 26 E5 49 16N 43 11 E
Klickitat, U.S.A. 82 D3 45 49N 121 9W
Klickitat →, U.S.A. 84 E5 45 42N 121 17W
Klidhes, Cyprus 23 D13 35 42N 34 36 E
Klinaklini →, Canada 72 C3 51 21N 125 40W
Klipdale, S. Africa 56 E2 34 19S 19 57 E
Klipplaat, S. Africa 56 E3 33 1S 24 22 E
Kłodzko, Poland 17 C9 50 28N 16 38 E
Klouto, Togo 50 G6 6 57N 0 44 E
Kluane L., Canada 68 B6 61 15N 138 40W
Kluczbork, Poland 17 C10 50 58N 18 12 E
Klyetsk, Belarus 17 B14 53 5N 26 45 E
Klyuchevskaya, Gora, Russia 27 D17 55 50N 160 30 E
Knaresborough, U.K. 10 C6 54 1N 1 28W
Knee L., Man., Canada 73 B10 55 3N 94 45W
Knee L., Sask., Canada 73 B7 55 51N 107 0W
Knight Inlet, Canada 72 C3 50 45N 125 40W
Knighton, U.K. 11 E4 52 21N 3 3W
Knights Ferry, U.S.A. 84 H6 37 50N 120 40W
Knights Landing, U.S.A. 84 G5 38 48N 121 43W
Knob, C., Australia 61 F2 34 32S 119 16 E
Knock, Ireland 13 C3 53 48N 8 55W
Knockmealdown Mts., Ireland 13 D4 52 14N 7 56W
Knokke-Heist, Belgium 15 C3 51 21N 3 17 E
Knossós, Greece 23 D7 35 16N 25 10 E
Knox, U.S.A. 76 E2 41 18N 86 37W
Knox, C., Canada 72 C2 54 11N 133 5W
Knox City, U.S.A. 81 J5 33 25N 99 49W
Knox Coast, Antarctica 5 C8 66 30S 108 0 E
Knoxville, Iowa, U.S.A. 80 E8 41 19N 93 6W
Knoxville, Tenn., U.S.A. 77 H4 35 58N 83 55W
Knysna, S. Africa 56 E3 34 2S 23 2 E
Ko Kha, Thailand 38 C2 18 11N 99 24 E
Koartac = Quaqtaq, Canada 69 B13 60 55N 69 40W
Koba, Indonesia 37 F8 6 37S 134 37 E
Kobarid, Slovenia 16 E7 46 15N 13 30 E
Kobayashi, Japan 31 J5 31 56N 130 59 E
Kobdo = Hovd, Mongolia 32 B4 48 2N 91 37 E
Kōbe, Japan 31 G7 34 45N 135 10 E
København, Denmark 9 J15 55 41N 12 34 E
Kōbi-Sho, Japan 31 M1 25 56N 123 41 E
Koblenz, Germany 16 C4 50 21N 7 36 E
Kobryn, Belarus 17 B13 52 15N 24 22 E
Kocaeli, Turkey 25 F4 40 45N 29 50 E
Kočani, Macedonia 21 D10 41 55N 22 25 E
Koch Bihar, India 41 F16 26 22N 89 29 E
Kochang, S. Korea 35 G14 35 41N 127 55 E
Kochas, India 43 G10 25 15N 83 56 E
Kōchi, Japan 31 H6 33 30N 133 35 E
Kōchi □, Japan 31 H6 33 40N 133 30 E
Kochiu = Gejiu, China 32 D5 23 20N 103 10 E
Kodiak, U.S.A. 68 C4 57 47N 152 24W
Kodiak I., U.S.A. 68 C4 57 30N 152 45W
Kodinar, India 42 J4 20 46N 70 46 E
Koes, Namibia 56 D2 26 0S 19 15 E
Koffiefontein, S. Africa 56 D4 29 30S 25 0 E
Kofiau, Indonesia 37 E7 1 11S 129 50 E
Koforidua, Ghana 50 G5 6 3N 0 17W
Kōfu, Japan 31 G9 35 40N 138 30 E
Koga, Japan 31 F9 36 11N 139 43 E
Kogaluk →, Canada 71 A7 56 12N 61 44W
Kogan, Australia 63 D5 27 2S 150 40 E
Køge, Denmark 9 J15 55 27N 12 11 E
Koh-i-Bābā, Afghan. 40 B5 34 30N 67 0 E
Koh-i-Khurd, Afghan. 42 C1 33 30N 65 59 E
Kohat, Pakistan 42 C4 33 40N 71 29 E
Kohima, India 41 G19 25 35N 94 10 E
Kohkīlūyeh va Būyer Aḩmadi □, Iran 45 D6 31 30N 50 30 E
Kohler Ra., Antarctica 5 D15 77 0S 110 0W
Kohtla-Järve, Estonia 9 G22 59 20N 27 20 E
Koillismaa, Finland 8 D23 65 44N 28 36 E
Koin-dong, N. Korea 35 D14 40 28N 126 18 E
Kojŏ, N. Korea 35 E14 38 58N 127 58 E
Kojonup, Australia 61 F2 33 48S 117 10 E
Kojūr, Iran 45 B6 36 23N 51 43 E
Kokand = Qŭqon, Uzbekistan 26 E8 40 30N 70 57 E
Kokanee Glacier Prov. Park, Canada 72 D5 49 47N 117 10W
Kokas, Indonesia 37 E8 2 42S 132 26 E
Kokchetav = Kökshetaū, Kazakstan 26 D7 53 20N 69 25 E
Kokemäenjoki →, Finland 9 F19 61 32N 21 44 E
Kokkola, Finland 8 E20 63 50N 23 8 E
Koko Kyunzu, Burma 41 M18 14 10N 93 25 E
Kokomo, U.S.A. 76 E2 40 29N 86 8W
Koksan, N. Korea 35 E14 38 46N 126 40 E
Kökshetaū, Kazakstan 26 D7 53 20N 69 25 E
Koksoak →, Canada 69 C13 58 30N 68 10W
Kokstad, S. Africa 57 E4 30 32S 29 29 E
Kokubu, Japan 31 J5 31 44N 130 46 E
Kola, Indonesia 37 F8 5 35S 134 30 E
Kola, Russia 24 A5 68 45N 33 8 E
Kola Pen. = Kolskiy Poluostrov, Russia 24 A6 67 30N 38 0 E
Kolahoi, India 43 B6 34 12N 75 22 E
Kolaka, Indonesia 37 E6 4 3S 121 46 E
Kolar, India 40 N11 13 12N 78 15 E
Kolar Gold Fields, India 40 N11 12 58N 78 16 E
Kolari, Finland 8 C20 67 20N 23 48 E
Kolayat, India 40 F8 27 50N 72 50 E
Kolchugino = Leninsk-Kuznetskiy, Russia 26 D9 54 44N 86 10 E
Kolding, Denmark 9 J13 55 30N 9 29 E
Kolepom = Dolak, Pulau, Indonesia 37 F9 8 0S 138 30 E
Kolguyev, Ostrov, Russia 24 A8 69 20N 48 30 E
Kolhapur, India 40 L9 16 43N 74 15 E
Kolín, Czech Rep. 16 C8 50 2N 15 9 E
Kolkas rags, Latvia 9 H20 57 46N 22 37 E
Kollum, Neths. 15 A6 53 17N 6 10 E
Kolmanskop, Namibia 56 D2 26 45S 15 14 E
Köln, Germany 16 C4 50 56N 6 57 E
Koło, Poland 17 B10 52 14N 18 40 E
Kołobrzeg, Poland 16 A8 54 10N 15 35 E
Kolomna, Russia 24 C6 55 8N 38 45 E
Kolomyya, Ukraine 25 E4 48 31N 25 2 E
Kolonodale, Indonesia 37 E6 2 3S 121 25 E
Kolosib, India 41 G18 24 15N 92 45 E
Kolpashevo, Russia 26 D9 58 20N 83 5 E
Kolpino, Russia 24 C5 59 44N 30 39 E
Kolskiy Poluostrov, Russia 24 A6 67 30N 38 0 E
Kolskiy Zaliv, Russia 24 A5 69 23N 34 0 E
Kolwezi, Dem. Rep. of the Congo 55 E2 10 40S 25 25 E
Kolyma →, Russia 27 C17 69 30N 161 0 E
Kolymskoye Nagorye, Russia 27 C16 63 0N 157 0 E
Komandorskiye Is. = Komandorskiye Ostrova, Russia 27 D17 55 0N 167 0 E
Komandorskiye Ostrova, Russia 27 D17 55 0N 167 0 E
Komárno, Slovak Rep. 17 E10 47 49N 18 5 E
Komatipoort, S. Africa 57 D5 25 25S 31 55 E
Komatou Yialou, Cyprus 23 D13 35 25N 34 8 E
Komatsu, Japan 31 F8 36 25N 136 30 E
Komatsujima, Japan 31 H7 34 0N 134 35 E
Komi □, Russia 24 B10 64 0N 55 0 E
Kommunarsk = Alchevsk, Ukraine 25 E6 48 30N 38 45 E
Kommunizma, Pik, Tajikistan 26 F8 39 0N 72 2 E
Komodo, Indonesia 37 F5 8 37S 119 20 E
Komoran, Pulau, Indonesia 37 F9 8 18S 138 45 E
Komoro, Japan 31 F9 36 19N 138 26 E
Komotini, Greece 21 D11 41 9N 25 26 E
Kompasberg, S. Africa 56 E3 31 45S 24 32 E
Kompong Bang, Cambodia 39 F5 12 24N 104 40 E
Kompong Cham, Cambodia 39 G5 12 0N 105 30 E
Kompong Chhnang = Kampang Chhnang, Cambodia 39 F5 12 20N 104 35 E
Kompong Chikreng, Cambodia 38 F5 13 5N 104 18 E
Kompong Kleang, Cambodia 38 F5 13 6N 104 8 E
Kompong Luong, Cambodia 39 G5 11 49N 104 48 E
Kompong Pranak, Cambodia 38 F5 13 35N 104 55 E
Kompong Som = Kampong Saom, Cambodia 39 G4 10 38N 103 30 E
Kompong Som, Chhung = Kampong Saom, Chaak, Cambodia 39 G4 10 50N 103 32 E
Kompong Speu, Cambodia 39 G5 11 26N 104 32 E
Kompong Sralao, Cambodia 38 E5 14 5N 105 46 E
Kompong Thom, Cambodia 38 F5 12 35N 104 51 E
Kompong Trabeck, Cambodia 38 F5 13 6N 105 14 E
Kompong Trabeck, Cambodia 39 G5 11 9N 105 28 E
Kompong Trach, Cambodia 39 G5 11 25N 105 48 E
Kompong Tralach, Cambodia 39 G5 11 54N 104 47 E
Komrat = Comrat, Moldova 17 E15 46 18N 28 40 E
Komsberg, S. Africa 56 E3 32 40S 20 45 E
Komsomolets, Ostrov, Russia 27 A10 80 30N 95 0 E
Komsomolsk, Russia 27 D14 50 30N 137 0 E
Kon Tum, Vietnam 38 E7 14 24N 108 0 E
Kon Tum, Plateau du, Vietnam 38 E7 14 30N 108 30 E
Konarhá □, Afghan. 40 B7 35 30N 71 3 E
Konārī, Iran 45 D6 28 13N 51 36 E
Konawa, U.S.A. 81 H6 34 58N 96 45W
Konch, India 43 G8 26 0N 79 10 E
Konde, Tanzania 54 C4 4 57S 39 45 E
Kondinin, Australia 61 F2 32 34S 118 8 E
Kondoa, Tanzania 54 C4 4 55S 35 50 E
Kondoa □, Tanzania 54 D4 5 0S 36 0 E
Kondókali, Greece 23 A3 39 38N 19 51 E
Kondopaga, Russia 24 B5 62 12N 34 17 E
Kondratyevo, Russia 27 D10 57 22N 98 15 E
Köneürgench, Turkmenistan 26 E6 42 19N 59 10 E
Konevo, Russia 24 B6 62 8N 39 20 E
Kong, Ivory C. 50 G5 8 54N 4 36W
Kong → = Khong →, Cambodia 38 F5 13 32N 105 58 E
Kong, Koh, Cambodia 39 G4 11 20N 103 0 E
Kongju, S. Korea 35 F14 36 30N 127 0 E
Konglu, Burma 41 F20 27 13N 97 57 E
Kongolo, Kasai Or., Dem. Rep. of the Congo 54 D1 5 26S 24 49 E
Kongolo, Shaba, Dem. Rep. of the Congo 54 D2 5 22S 27 0 E
Kongsberg, Norway 9 G13 59 39N 9 39 E
Kongsvinger, Norway 9 F15 60 12N 12 2 E
Kongwa, Tanzania 54 D4 6 11S 36 26 E
Koni, Dem. Rep. of the Congo 55 E2 10 40S 27 11 E
Koni, Mts., Dem. Rep. of the Congo 55 E2 10 36S 27 10 E
Königsberg = Kaliningrad, Russia 24 D3 54 42N 20 32 E
Konin, Poland 17 B10 52 12N 18 15 E
Konjic, Bos.-H. 21 C7 43 42N 17 58 E
Konkiep, Namibia 56 D2 26 49S 17 15 E
Konosha, Russia 24 B7 61 0N 40 5 E
Kōnosu, Japan 31 F9 36 3N 139 31 E
Konotop, Ukraine 25 D5 51 12N 33 7 E
Końskie, Poland 17 C11 51 15N 20 23 E
Konstanz, Germany 16 E5 47 40N 9 10 E
Kont, Iran 45 E9 26 55N 61 50 E
Kontagora, Nigeria 50 F7 10 23N 5 27 E
Konya, Turkey 25 G5 37 52N 32 35 E
Konza, Kenya 54 C4 1 45S 37 7 E
Kookynie, Australia 61 E3 29 17S 121 22 E
Kooline, Australia 60 D2 22 57S 116 20 E
Kooloonong, Australia 63 E3 34 48S 143 10 E
Koolyanobbing, Australia 61 F2 30 48S 119 36 E
Koondrook, Australia 63 F3 35 33S 144 8 E
Koonibba, Australia 63 E1 31 54S 133 25 E
Koorawatha, Australia 63 E4 34 2S 148 33 E
Koorda, Australia 61 F2 30 48S 117 35 E
Kooskia, U.S.A. 82 C6 46 9N 115 59W
Kootenai →, Canada 82 B5 49 15N 117 39W
Kootenay L., Canada 72 D5 49 45N 116 50W
Kootenay Nat. Park, Canada 72 C5 51 0N 116 0W
Kootjieskolk, S. Africa 56 E3 31 15S 20 21 E
Kopaonik, Serbia, Yug. 21 C9 43 10N 20 50 E
Kópavogur, Iceland 8 D3 64 6N 21 55W
Koper, Slovenia 16 F7 45 31N 13 44 E
Kopervik, Norway 9 G11 59 17N 5 17 E
Kopi, Australia 63 E2 33 24S 135 40 E
Köping, Sweden 9 G17 59 31N 16 3 E
Koppeh Dāgh, Asia 45 B8 38 0N 58 0 E
Koppies, S. Africa 57 D4 27 20S 27 30 E
Koprivnica, Croatia 20 A7 46 12N 16 45 E
Kopychyntsi, Ukraine 17 D13 49 7N 25 58 E
Korab, Macedonia 21 D9 41 44N 20 40 E
Korakiána, Greece 23 A3 39 42N 19 45 E
Korba, India 43 H10 22 20N 82 45 E
Korbu, G., Malaysia 39 K3 4 41N 101 18 E
Korça, Albania 21 D9 40 37N 20 50 E
Korce = Korça, Albania 21 D9 40 37N 20 50 E
Korčula, Croatia 20 C7 42 56N 16 57 E
Kord Kūy, Iran 45 B7 36 48N 54 7 E
Kord Sheykh, Iran 45 D7 28 31N 52 53 E
Kordestān □, Iran 44 C5 36 0N 47 0 E
Kordofân, Sudan 51 F11 13 0N 29 0 E
Korea, North ■, Asia 35 E14 40 0N 127 0 E
Korea, South ■, Asia 35 G15 36 0N 128 0 E
Korea Bay, Korea 35 E13 39 0N 124 0 E
Korea Strait, Asia 35 H15 34 0N 129 30 E
Korets, Ukraine 17 C14 50 40N 27 5 E
Korhogo, Ivory C. 50 G4 9 29N 5 28W
Korinthiakós Kólpos, Greece 21 E10 38 16N 22 30 E
Kórinthos, Greece 21 F10 37 56N 22 55 E
Koríssa, Límni, Greece 23 B3 39 27N 19 53 E
Kōriyama, Japan 30 F10 37 24N 140 23 E
Korla, China 32 B3 41 45N 86 4 E
Kormakiti, C., Cyprus 23 D11 35 23N 32 56 E
Korneshty = Corneşti, Moldova 17 E15 47 21N 28 1 E
Koro, Fiji 59 C8 17 19S 179 23 E
Koro, Ivory C. 50 G4 8 32N 7 30W
Koro Sea, Fiji 59 C9 17 30S 179 45W
Korogwe, Tanzania 54 D4 5 5S 38 25 E
Korogwe □, Tanzania 54 D4 5 0S 38 20 E
Koroit, Australia 63 F3 38 18S 142 24 E
Koror, Pac. Oc. 37 C8 7 20N 134 28 E
Körös →, Hungary 17 E11 46 43N 20 12 E
Korosten, Ukraine 17 C15 50 54N 28 36 E
Korostyshev, Ukraine 17 C15 50 19N 29 4 E
Korraraika, Helodranon' i, Madag. 57 B7 17 45S 43 57 E
Korsakov, Russia 27 E15 46 36N 142 42 E
Korshunovo, Russia 27 D12 58 37N 110 10 E
Korsør, Denmark 9 J14 55 20N 11 9 E
Kortrijk, Belgium 15 D3 50 50N 3 17 E
Korwai, India 42 G8 24 7N 78 5 E
Koryakskoye Nagorye, Russia 27 C18 61 0N 171 0 E
Koryŏng, S. Korea 35 G15 35 44N 128 15 E
Koschagyl, Kazakstan 25 E9 46 40N 54 0 E
Kościan, Poland 17 B9 52 5N 16 40 E
Kosciusko, U.S.A. 81 J10 33 4N 89 35W
Kosciusko I., U.S.A. 72 B2 56 0N 133 40W
Kosciuszko, Mt., Australia 63 F4 36 27S 148 16 E
Kosha, Sudan 51 D12 20 50N 30 30 E
K'oshih = Kashi, China 32 C2 39 30N 76 2 E

Koshiki-Rettō

Koshiki-Rettō, *Japan* .... **31 J4** 31 45N 129 49 E
Kosi, *India* .... **42 F7** 27 48N 77 29 E
Košice, *Slovak Rep.* .... **17 D11** 48 42N 21 15 E
Koskhinoú, *Greece* .... **23 C10** 36 23N 28 13 E
Koslan, *Russia* .... **24 B8** 63 34N 49 14 E
Kosŏng, *N. Korea* .... **35 E15** 38 40N 128 22 E
Kosovo □, *Serbia, Yug.* .. **21 C9** 42 30N 21 0 E
Kosovska Mitrovica, *Serbia, Yug.* .... **21 C9** 42 54N 20 52 E
Kostamuksa, *Russia* .... **24 B5** 62 34N 32 44 E
Koster, *S. Africa* .... **56 D4** 25 52S 26 54 E
Kôstî, *Sudan* .... **51 F12** 13 8N 32 43 E
Kostopil, *Ukraine* .... **17 C14** 50 51N 26 22 E
Kostroma, *Russia* .... **24 C7** 57 50N 40 58 E
Kostrzyn, *Poland* .... **16 B8** 52 35N 14 39 E
Koszalin, *Poland* .... **16 A9** 54 11N 16 8 E
Kot Addu, *Pakistan* .... **42 D4** 30 30N 71 0 E
Kot Moman, *Pakistan* ... **42 C5** 32 13N 73 0 E
Kota, *India* .... **42 G6** 25 14N 75 49 E
Kota Baharu, *Malaysia* .. **39 J4** 6 7N 102 14 E
Kota Belud, *Malaysia* .... **36 C5** 6 21N 116 26 E
Kota Kinabalu, *Malaysia* . **36 C5** 6 0N 116 4 E
Kota Kubu Baharu, *Malaysia* .... **39 L3** 3 34N 101 39 E
Kota Tinggi, *Malaysia* ... **39 M4** 1 44N 103 53 E
Kotaagung, *Indonesia* ... **36 F2** 5 38S 104 29 E
Kotabaru, *Indonesia* .... **36 E5** 3 20S 116 20 E
Kotabumi, *Indonesia* .... **36 E2** 4 49S 104 54 E
Kotamobagu, *Indonesia* . **37 D6** 0 57N 124 31 E
Kotaneelee →, *Canada* . **72 A4** 60 11N 123 42W
Kotcho L., *Canada* **72 B4** 59 7N 121 12W
Kotelnich, *Russia* .... **24 C8** 58 22N 48 24 E
Kotelnikovo, *Russia* .... **26 E5** 47 38N 43 8 E
Kotelnyy, Ostrov, *Russia* . **27 B14** 75 10N 139 0 E
Kothi, *India* .... **43 G9** 24 45N 80 40 E
Kotiro, *Pakistan* .... **42 F2** 26 17N 67 13 E
Kotka, *Finland* .... **9 F22** 60 28N 26 58 E
Kotlas, *Russia* .... **24 B8** 61 17N 46 43 E
Kotli, *Pakistan* .... **42 C5** 33 30N 73 55 E
Kotmul, *Pakistan* .... **43 B6** 35 32N 75 10 E
Kotor, *Montenegro, Yug.* . **21 C8** 42 25N 18 47 E
Kotovsk, *Ukraine* .... **17 E15** 47 45N 29 35 E
Kotputli, *India* .... **42 F7** 27 43N 76 12 E
Kotri, *Pakistan* .... **42 G3** 25 22N 68 22 E
Kottayam, *India* .... **40 Q10** 9 35N 76 33 E
Kotturu, *India* .... **40 M10** 14 45N 76 10 E
Kotuy →, *Russia* .... **27 B11** 71 54N 102 6 E
Kotzebue, *U.S.A.* **68 B3** 66 53N 162 39W
Koudougou, *Burkina Faso* **50 F5** 12 10N 2 20W
Koufonísi, *Greece* .... **23 E8** 34 56N 26 8 E
Kougaberge, *S. Africa* .... **56 E3** 33 48S 23 50 E
Kouilou →, *Congo* .... **52 E2** 4 10S 12 5 E
Koula Moutou, *Gabon* ... **52 E2** 1 15S 12 25 E
Koulen = Kulen, *Cambodia* .... **38 F5** 13 50N 104 40 E
Kouloúra, *Greece* .... **23 A3** 39 42N 19 54 E
Koúm-bournoú, Ákra, *Greece* .... **23 C10** 36 15N 28 11 E
Koumala, *Australia* .... **62 C4** 21 38S 149 15 E
Koumra, *Chad* .... **51 G9** 8 50N 17 35 E
Kounradskiy, *Kazakstan* . **26 E8** 46 59N 75 0 E
Kountze, *U.S.A.* **81 K7** 30 22N 94 19W
Kouris →, *Cyprus* .... **23 E11** 34 38N 32 54 E
Kourou, *Fr. Guiana* **93 B8** 5 9N 52 39W
Kousseri, *Cameroon* .... **51 F8** 12 0N 14 55 E
Kouvola, *Finland* .... **9 F22** 60 52N 26 43 E
Kovdor, *Russia* .... **24 A5** 67 34N 30 24 E
Kovel, *Ukraine* .... **24 D3** 51 11N 24 38 E
Kovrov, *Russia* .... **24 C7** 56 25N 41 25 E
Kowanyama, *Australia* .. **62 B3** 15 29S 141 44 E
Kowkash, *Canada* **70 B2** 50 20N 87 12W
Kowŏn, *N. Korea* .... **35 E14** 39 26N 127 14 E
Köyceğiz, *Turkey* .... **21 F13** 36 57N 28 40 E
Koza, *Japan* .... **31 L3** 26 19N 127 46 E
Kozáni, *Greece* .... **21 D9** 40 19N 21 47 E
Kozhikode = Calicut, *India* **40 P9** 11 15N 75 43 E
Kozhva, *Russia* .... **24 A10** 65 10N 57 0 E
Kozyatyn, *Ukraine* .... **17 D15** 49 45N 28 50 E
Kra, Isthmus of = Kra, Kho Khot, *Thailand* ... **39 G2** 10 15N 99 30 E
Kra, Kho Khot, *Thailand* .. **39 G2** 10 15N 99 30 E
Kra Buri, *Thailand* .... **39 G2** 10 22N 98 46 E
Krabi, *Thailand* .... **39 H2** 8 4N 98 55 E
Kracheh, *Cambodia* .... **38 F6** 12 32N 106 10 E
Kragan, *Indonesia* .... **37 G14** 6 43S 111 38 E
Kragerø, *Norway* .... **9 G13** 58 52N 9 25 E
Kragujevac, *Serbia, Yug.* . **21 B9** 44 2N 20 56 E
Krajina, *Bos.-H.* .... **20 B7** 44 45N 16 35 E
Krakatau = Rakata, Pulau, *Indonesia* .... **36 F3** 6 10S 105 20 E
Krakor, *Cambodia* .... **38 F5** 12 32N 104 12 E
Kraków, *Poland* .... **17 C10** 50 4N 19 57 E
Kralanh, *Cambodia* .... **38 F4** 13 35N 103 25 E
Kraljevo, *Serbia, Yug.* ... **21 C9** 43 44N 20 41 E
Kramatorsk, *Ukraine* .... **25 E6** 48 50N 37 30 E
Kramfors, *Sweden* .... **9 E17** 62 55N 17 48 E
Kranj, *Slovenia* .... **16 E8** 46 16N 14 22 E
Krankskop, *S. Africa* .... **57 D5** 28 0S 30 47 E
Krasavino, *Russia* .... **24 B8** 60 58N 46 29 E
Kraskino, *Russia* .... **30 C5** 42 44N 130 48 E
Kraśnik, *Poland* .... **17 C12** 50 55N 22 15 E
Krasnoarmeysk, *Russia* .. **26 D5** 51 0N 45 42 E
Krasnodar, *Russia* .... **25 E6** 45 5N 39 0 E
Krasnokamsk, *Russia* .... **24 C10** 58 4N 55 48 E
Krasnoperekopsk, *Ukraine* **25 E5** 46 0N 33 54 E
Krasnorechenskiy, *Russia* **30 B7** 44 41N 135 14 E
Krasnoselkup, *Russia* ... **26 C9** 65 20N 82 10 E
Krasnoturinsk, *Russia* ... **24 C11** 59 46N 60 12 E
Krasnoufimsk, *Russia* ... **24 C10** 56 36N 57 38 E
Krasnouralsk, *Russia* ... **24 C11** 58 21N 60 3 E
Krasnovishersk, *Russia* .. **24 B10** 60 23N 57 3 E
Krasnovodsk = Türkmenbashi, *Turkmenistan* .... **25 G9** 40 5N 53 5 E
Krasnoyarsk, *Russia* .... **27 D10** 56 8N 93 0 E
Krasnyy Luch, *Ukraine* .. **25 E6** 48 13N 39 0 E
Krasnyy Yar, *Russia* .... **25 E8** 46 43N 48 23 E
Kratie = Kracheh, *Cambodia* .... **38 F6** 12 32N 106 10 E
Krau, *Indonesia* .... **37 E10** 3 19S 140 5 E
Kravanh, Chuor Phnum, *Cambodia* .... **39 G4** 12 0N 103 32 E
Krefeld, *Germany* .... **16 C4** 51 20N 6 33 E
Kremen, *Croatia* .... **16 F8** 44 28N 15 53 E
Kremenchug = Kremenchuk, *Ukraine* . **25 E5** 49 5N 33 25 E
Kremenchuk, *Ukraine* ... **25 E5** 49 5N 33 25 E
Kremenchuksk Vdskh., *Ukraine* .... **25 E5** 49 20N 32 30 E
Kremenets, *Ukraine* .... **17 C13** 50 8N 25 43 E
Kremmling, *U.S.A.* **82 F10** 40 4N 106 24W
Krems, *Austria* .... **16 D8** 48 25N 15 36 E
Kretinga, *Lithuania* .... **9 J19** 55 53N 21 15 E
Kribi, *Cameroon* .... **52 D1** 2 57N 9 56 E
Krichev = Krychaw, *Belarus* .... **17 B16** 53 40N 31 41 E
Kriós, Ákra, *Greece* .... **23 D5** 35 13N 23 34 E
Krishna →, *India* .... **41 M12** 15 57N 80 59 E
Krishnanagar, *India* .... **43 H13** 23 24N 88 33 E
Kristiansand, *Norway* ... **9 G13** 58 8N 8 1 E
Kristianstad, *Sweden* ... **9 H16** 56 2N 14 9 E
Kristiansund, *Norway* ... **8 E12** 63 7N 7 45 E
Kristiinankaupunki, *Finland* .... **9 E19** 62 16N 21 21 E
Kristinehamn, *Sweden* .. **9 G16** 59 18N 14 7 E
Kristinestad = Kristiinankaupunki, *Finland* .... **9 E19** 62 16N 21 21 E
Kríti, *Greece* .... **23 D7** 35 15N 25 0 E
Kritsá, *Greece* .... **23 D7** 35 10N 25 41 E
Krivoy Rog = Kryvyy Rih, *Ukraine* .... **25 E5** 47 51N 33 20 E
Krk, *Croatia* .... **16 F8** 45 8N 14 40 E
Krokodil →, *Mozam.* ... **57 D5** 25 14S 32 18 E
Kronprins Olav Kyst, *Antarctica* .... **5 C5** 69 0S 42 0 E
Kronshtadt, *Russia* .... **24 B4** 59 57N 29 51 E
Kroonstad, *S. Africa* .... **56 D4** 27 43S 27 19 E
Kropotkin, *Russia* .... **25 E7** 45 28N 40 28 E
Krosno, *Poland* .... **17 D11** 49 42N 21 46 E
Krotoszyn, *Poland* .... **17 C9** 51 42N 17 23 E
Kroussón, *Greece* .... **23 D6** 35 13N 24 59 E
Kruger Nat. Park, *S. Africa* **57 C5** 23 30S 31 40 E
Krugersdorp, *S. Africa* ... **57 D4** 26 5S 27 46 E
Kruisfontein, *S. Africa* ... **56 E3** 33 59S 24 43 E
Krung Thep = Bangkok, *Thailand* .... **38 F3** 13 45N 100 35 E
Krupki, *Belarus* .... **17 A15** 54 19N 29 8 E
Kruševac, *Serbia, Yug.* .. **21 C9** 43 35N 21 28 E
Kruzof I., *U.S.A.* **72 B1** 57 10N 135 40W
Krychaw, *Belarus* .... **17 B16** 53 40N 31 41 E
Krymskiy Poluostrov = Krymskyy Pivostriv, *Ukraine* .... **25 F5** 45 0N 34 0 E
Krymskyy Pivostriv, *Ukraine* .... **25 F5** 45 0N 34 0 E
Kryvyy Rih, *Ukraine* .... **25 E5** 47 51N 33 20 E
Ksar el Kebir, *Morocco* .. **50 B4** 35 0N 6 0W
Ksar es Souk = Ar Rachidiya, *Morocco* ... **50 B5** 31 58N 4 20W
Kuala Berang, *Malaysia* . **39 K4** 5 5N 103 1 E
Kuala Dungun = Dungun, *Malaysia* .... **39 K4** 4 45N 103 25 E
Kuala Kangsar, *Malaysia* . **39 K3** 4 46N 100 56 E
Kuala Kelawang, *Malaysia* **39 L4** 2 56N 102 5 E
Kuala Kerai, *Malaysia* ... **39 K4** 5 30N 102 12 E
Kuala Lipis, *Malaysia* ... **39 K4** 4 10N 102 3 E
Kuala Lumpur, *Malaysia* . **39 L3** 3 9N 101 41 E
Kuala Nerang, *Malaysia* . **39 J3** 6 16N 100 37 E
Kuala Pilah, *Malaysia* ... **39 L4** 2 45N 102 15 E
Kuala Rompin, *Malaysia* . **39 L4** 2 49N 103 29 E
Kuala Selangor, *Malaysia* **39 L3** 3 20N 101 15 E
Kuala Sepetang, *Malaysia* **39 K3** 4 50N 100 38 E
Kuala Terengganu, *Malaysia* .... **39 K4** 5 20N 103 8 E
Kualajelai, *Indonesia* .... **36 E4** 2 58S 110 46 E
Kualakapuas, *Indonesia* .. **36 E4** 2 55S 114 20 E
Kualakurun, *Indonesia* ... **36 E4** 1 10S 113 50 E
Kualapembuang, *Indonesia* .... **36 E4** 3 14S 112 38 E
Kualasimpang, *Indonesia* **36 D1** 4 17N 98 3 E
Kuancheng, *China* .... **35 D10** 40 37N 118 30 E
Kuandang, *Indonesia* .... **37 D6** 0 56N 123 1 E
Kuandian, *China* .... **35 D13** 40 45N 124 45 E
Kuangchou = Guangzhou, *China* .... **33 D6** 23 5N 113 10 E
Kuantan, *Malaysia* .... **39 L4** 3 49N 103 20 E
Kuba = Quba, *Azerbaijan* **25 F8** 41 21N 48 32 E
Kuban →, *Russia* .... **25 E6** 45 20N 37 30 E
Kubokawa, *Japan* .... **31 H6** 33 12N 133 8 E
Kucha Gompa, *India* .... **43 B7** 34 25N 76 56 E
Kuchaman, *India* .... **42 F6** 27 13N 74 47 E
Kuching, *Malaysia* .... **36 D4** 1 33N 110 25 E
Kuchino-eruba-Jima, *Japan* .... **31 J5** 30 28N 130 12 E
Kuchino-Shima, *Japan* ... **31 K4** 29 57N 129 55 E
Kuchinotsu, *Japan* .... **31 H5** 32 36N 130 11 E
Kucing = Kuching, *Malaysia* .... **36 D4** 1 33N 110 25 E
Kud →, *Pakistan* .... **42 F2** 26 5N 66 20 E
Kuda, *India* .... **40 H7** 23 10N 71 15 E
Kudat, *Malaysia* .... **36 C5** 6 55N 116 55 E
Kudus, *Indonesia* .... **37 G14** 6 48S 110 51 E
Kudymkar, *Russia* .... **26 D6** 59 1N 54 39 E
Kueiyang = Guiyang, *China* .... **32 D5** 26 32N 106 40 E
Kufra Oasis = Al Kufrah, *Libya* .... **51 D10** 24 17N 23 15 E
Kufstein, *Austria* .... **16 E7** 47 35N 12 11 E
Kugluktuk, *Canada* **68 B8** 67 50N 115 5W
Kugong I., *Canada* **70 A4** 56 18N 79 50W
Kūh-e-Hazārān, *Iran* .... **45 D8** 29 35N 57 20 E
Kūhak, *Iran* .... **40 F3** 27 12N 63 10 E
Kūhbonān, *Iran* .... **45 D8** 31 23N 56 19 E
Kūhestak, *Iran* .... **45 E8** 26 47N 57 2 E
Kūhīn, *Iran* .... **45 C6** 35 13N 48 25 E
Kūhīrī, *Iran* .... **45 E9** 26 55N 61 2 E
Kūhpāyeh, *Eşfahan, Iran* . **45 C7** 32 44N 52 20 E
Kūhpāyeh, *Kermān, Iran* . **45 D8** 30 35N 57 15 E
Kui Buri, *Thailand* .... **39 F2** 12 3N 99 52 E
Kuito, *Angola* .... **53 G3** 12 22S 16 55 E
Kujang, *N. Korea* .... **35 E14** 39 57N 126 1 E
Kuji, *Japan* .... **30 D10** 40 11N 141 46 E
Kujū-San, *Japan* .... **31 H5** 33 5N 131 15 E
Kukerin, *Australia* .... **61 F2** 33 13S 118 0 E
Kukësi, *Albania* .... **21 C9** 42 5N 20 27 E
Kukup, *Malaysia* .... **39 M4** 1 20N 103 27 E
Kula, *Turkey* .... **21 E13** 38 32N 28 40 E
Kulai, *Malaysia* .... **39 M4** 1 44N 103 35 E
Kulal, Mt., *Kenya* .... **54 B4** 2 42N 36 57 E
Kulasekarappattinam, *India* .... **40 Q11** 8 20N 78 5 E
Kuldīga, *Latvia* .... **9 H19** 56 58N 21 59 E
Kuldja = Yining, *China* .. **26 E9** 43 58N 81 10 E
Kulen, *Cambodia* .... **38 F5** 13 50N 104 40 E
Kulgam, *India* .... **43 C6** 33 36N 75 2 E
Kulim, *Malaysia* .... **39 K3** 5 22N 100 34 E
Kulin, *Australia* .... **61 F2** 32 40S 118 2 E
Kulja, *Australia* .... **61 F2** 30 28S 117 18 E
Kulm, *U.S.A.* **80 B5** 46 18N 98 57W
Kŭlob, *Tajikistan* .... **26 F7** 37 55N 69 50 E
Kulsary, *Kazakstan* .... **25 E9** 46 59N 54 1 E
Kulti, *India* .... **43 H12** 23 43N 86 50 E
Kulumbura, *Australia* ... **60 B4** 13 55S 126 35 E
Kulunda, *Russia* .... **26 D8** 52 35N 78 57 E
Kulungar, *Afghan.* .... **42 C3** 34 0N 69 2 E
Kūlvand, *Iran* .... **45 D7** 31 21N 54 35 E
Kulwin, *Australia* .... **63 F3** 35 0S 142 42 E
Kulyab = Kŭlob, *Tajikistan* **26 F7** 37 55N 69 50 E
Kuma →, *Russia* .... **25 F8** 44 55N 47 0 E
Kumagaya, *Japan* .... **31 F9** 36 9N 139 22 E
Kumai, *Indonesia* .... **36 E4** 2 44S 111 43 E
Kumamba, Kepulauan, *Indonesia* .... **37 E9** 1 36S 138 45 E
Kumamoto, *Japan* .... **31 H5** 32 45N 130 45 E
Kumamoto □, *Japan* .... **31 H5** 32 55N 130 55 E
Kumanovo, *Macedonia* .. **21 C9** 42 9N 21 42 E
Kumara, *N.Z.* .... **59 K3** 42 37S 171 12 E
Kumarl, *Australia* .... **61 F3** 32 47S 121 33 E
Kumasi, *Ghana* **50 G5** 6 41N 1 38W
Kumayri = Gyumri, *Armenia* .... **25 F7** 40 47N 43 50 E
Kumba, *Cameroon* .... **52 D1** 4 36N 9 24 E
Kumbakonam, *India* .... **40 P11** 10 58N 79 25 E
Kumbarilla, *Australia* .... **63 D5** 27 15S 150 55 E
Kŭmchŏn, *N. Korea* .... **35 E14** 38 10N 126 29 E
Kumdok, *India* .... **43 C8** 33 32N 78 10 E
Kume-Shima, *Japan* .... **31 L3** 26 20N 126 47 E
Kumertau, *Russia* .... **24 D10** 52 45N 55 57 E
Kŭmhwa, *S. Korea* .... **35 E14** 38 17N 127 28 E
Kumi, *Uganda* .... **54 B3** 1 30N 33 58 E
Kumla, *Sweden* .... **9 G16** 59 8N 15 10 E
Kumo, *Nigeria* .... **51 F8** 10 1N 11 12 E
Kumon Bum, *Burma* .... **41 F20** 26 30N 97 15 E
Kunama, *Australia* .... **63 F4** 35 35S 148 4 E
Kunashir, Ostrov, *Russia* . **27 E15** 44 0N 146 0 E
Kunda, *Estonia* .... **9 G22** 59 30N 26 34 E
Kundla, *India* .... **42 J4** 21 21N 71 25 E
Kungala, *Australia* .... **63 D5** 29 58S 153 7 E
Kunghit I., *Canada* **72 C2** 52 6N 131 3W
Kungrad = Qŭnghirot, *Uzbekistan* .... **26 E6** 43 6N 58 54 E
Kungsbacka, *Sweden* .... **9 H15** 57 30N 12 5 E
Kungur, *Russia* .... **24 C10** 57 25N 56 57 E
Kungurri, *Australia* .... **62 C4** 21 3S 148 46 E
Kunhar →, *Pakistan* .... **43 B5** 34 20N 73 30 E
Kuningan, *Indonesia* .... **37 G13** 6 59S 108 29 E
Kunlong, *Burma* .... **41 H21** 23 20N 98 50 E
Kunlun Shan, *Asia* .... **32 C3** 36 0N 86 30 E
Kunming, *China* .... **32 D5** 25 1N 102 41 E
Kunsan, *S. Korea* .... **35 G14** 35 59N 126 45 E
Kununurra, *Australia* .... **60 C4** 15 40S 128 50 E
Kunwarara, *Australia* .... **62 C5** 22 55S 150 9 E
Kunya-Urgench = Köneürgench, *Turkmenistan* .... **26 E6** 42 19N 59 10 E
Kuopio, *Finland* .... **8 E22** 62 53N 27 35 E
Kupa →, *Croatia* .... **16 F9** 45 28N 16 24 E
Kupang, *Indonesia* .... **37 F6** 10 19S 123 39 E
Kuqa, *China* .... **32 B3** 41 35N 82 30 E
Kür →, *Azerbaijan* .... **25 G8** 39 29N 49 15 E
Kura = Kür →, *Azerbaijan* .... **25 G8** 39 29N 49 15 E
Kuranda, *Australia* .... **62 B4** 16 48S 145 35 E
Kurashiki, *Japan* .... **31 G6** 34 40N 133 50 E
Kurayoshi, *Japan* .... **31 G6** 35 26N 133 50 E
Kŭrdzhali, *Bulgaria* .... **21 D11** 41 38N 25 21 E
Kure, *Japan* .... **31 G6** 34 14N 132 32 E
Kuressaare, *Estonia* .... **9 G20** 58 15N 22 30 E
Kurgan, *Russia* .... **26 D7** 55 26N 65 18 E
Kuria Maria Is. = Khurīyā Murīyā, Jazā 'ir, *Oman* **46 D6** 17 30N 55 58 E
Kuridala, *Australia* .... **62 C3** 21 16S 140 29 E
Kurigram, *Bangla.* .... **41 G16** 25 49N 89 39 E
Kurikka, *Finland* .... **9 E20** 62 36N 22 24 E
Kuril Is. = Kurilskiye Ostrova, *Russia* .... **27 E16** 45 0N 150 0 E
Kuril Trench, *Pac. Oc.* .... **64 C7** 44 0N 153 0 E
Kurilsk, *Russia* .... **27 E15** 45 14N 147 53 E
Kurilskiye Ostrova, *Russia* **27 E16** 45 0N 150 0 E
Kurino, *Japan* .... **31 J5** 31 57N 130 43 E
Kurnool, *India* .... **40 M11** 15 45N 78 0 E
Kuro-Shima, *Kagoshima, Japan* .... **31 J4** 30 50N 129 57 E
Kuro-Shima, *Okinawa, Japan* .... **31 M2** 24 14N 124 1 E
Kurow, *N.Z.* .... **59 L3** 44 44S 170 29 E
Kurrajong, *Australia* .... **63 E5** 33 33S 150 42 E
Kurram →, *Pakistan* .... **42 C4** 32 36N 71 20 E
Kurri Kurri, *Australia* .... **63 E5** 32 50S 151 28 E
Kurshskiy Zaliv, *Russia* .. **9 J19** 55 9N 21 6 E
Kursk, *Russia* .... **24 D6** 51 42N 36 11 E
Kuruktag, *China* .... **32 B3** 41 0N 89 0 E
Kuruman, *S. Africa* .... **56 D3** 27 28S 23 28 E
Kuruman →, *S. Africa* .. **56 D3** 26 56S 20 39 E
Kurume, *Japan* .... **31 H5** 33 15N 130 30 E
Kurunegala, *Sri Lanka* ... **40 R12** 7 30N 80 23 E
Kus Gölü, *Turkey* .... **21 D12** 40 10N 27 55 E
Kuşadası, *Turkey* .... **21 F12** 37 52N 27 15 E
Kusatsu, *Japan* .... **31 F9** 36 37N 138 36 E
Kusawa L., *Canada* **72 A1** 60 20N 136 13W
Kushikino, *Japan* .... **31 J5** 31 44N 130 16 E
Kushima, *Japan* .... **31 J5** 31 29N 131 14 E
Kushimoto, *Japan* .... **31 H7** 33 28N 135 47 E
Kushiro, *Japan* .... **30 C12** 43 0N 144 25 E
Kushiro →, *Japan* .... **30 C12** 42 59N 144 23 E
Kūshk, *Iran* .... **45 D8** 28 46N 56 51 E
Kushka = Gushgy, *Turkmenistan* .... **26 F7** 35 20N 62 18 E
Kūshkī, *Īlām, Iran* .... **44 C5** 33 31N 47 13 E
Kūshkī, *Khorāsān, Iran* .. **45 B8** 37 2N 57 26 E
Kūshkū, *Iran* .... **45 E7** 27 19N 53 28 E
Kushol, *India* .... **43 C7** 33 40N 76 36 E
Kushtia, *Bangla.* .... **41 H16** 23 55N 89 5 E
Kushva, *Russia* .... **24 C10** 58 18N 59 45 E
Kuskokwim B., *U.S.A.* **68 C3** 59 45N 162 25W
Kussharo-Ko, *Japan* .... **30 C12** 43 38N 144 21 E
Kustanay = Qostanay, *Kazakstan* .... **26 D7** 53 10N 63 35 E
Kut, Ko, *Thailand* .... **39 G4** 11 40N 102 35 E
Kütahya, *Turkey* .... **25 G5** 39 30N 30 2 E
Kutaisi, *Georgia* .... **25 F7** 42 19N 42 40 E
Kutaraja = Banda Aceh, *Indonesia* .... **36 C1** 5 35N 95 20 E
Kutch, Gulf of = Kachchh, Gulf of, *India* .... **42 H3** 22 50N 69 15 E
Kutch, Rann of = Kachchh, Rann of, *India* **42 H4** 24 0N 70 0 E
Kutiyana, *India* .... **42 J4** 21 36N 70 2 E
Kutno, *Poland* .... **17 B10** 52 15N 19 23 E
Kuttabul, *Australia* .... **62 C4** 21 5S 148 48 E
Kutu, *Dem. Rep. of the Congo* **52 E3** 2 40S 18 11 E
Kutum, *Sudan* .... **51 F10** 14 10N 24 40 E
Kuujjuaq, *Canada* **69 C13** 58 6N 68 15W
Kuŭp-tong, *N. Korea* .... **35 D14** 40 45N 126 1 E
Kuusamo, *Finland* .... **8 D23** 65 57N 29 8 E
Kuusankoski, *Finland* ... **9 F22** 60 55N 26 38 E
Kuwait = Al Kuwayt, *Kuwait* .... **44 D5** 29 30N 48 0 E
Kuwait ■, *Asia* .... **44 D5** 29 30N 47 30 E
Kuwana, *Japan* .... **31 G8** 35 5N 136 43 E
Kuybyshev = Samara, *Russia* .... **24 D9** 53 8N 50 6 E
Kuybyshev, *Russia* .... **26 D8** 55 27N 78 19 E
Kuybyshevskoye Vdkhr., *Russia* .... **24 C8** 55 2N 49 30 E
Kuye He →, *China* .... **34 E6** 38 23N 110 46 E
Kūyeh, *Iran* .... **44 B5** 38 45N 47 57 E
Kūysanjaq, *Iraq* .... **44 B5** 36 5N 44 38 E
Kuyto, Ozero, *Russia* .... **24 B5** 65 6N 31 20 E
Kuyumba, *Russia* .... **27 C10** 60 58N 96 59 E
Kuzey Anadolu Dağları, *Turkey* .... **25 F6** 41 30N 35 0 E
Kuznetsk, *Russia* .... **24 D8** 53 12N 46 40 E
Kuzomen, *Russia* .... **24 A6** 66 22N 36 50 E
Kvænangen, *Norway* .... **8 A19** 70 5N 21 15 E
Kvaløy, *Norway* .... **8 B18** 69 40N 18 30 E
Kvarner, *Croatia* .... **16 F8** 44 50N 14 10 E
Kvarnerič, *Croatia* .... **16 F8** 44 43N 14 37 E
Kwabhaca, *S. Africa* .... **57 E4** 30 51S 29 0 E
Kwadacha →, *Canada* . **72 B3** 57 28N 125 38W
Kwakhanai, *Botswana* .... **56 C3** 21 39S 21 16 E
Kwakoegron, *Surinam* **93 B7** 5 12N 55 25W
Kwale, *Kenya* .... **54 C4** 4 15S 39 31 E
Kwale □, *Kenya* .... **54 C4** 4 15S 39 10 E
KwaMashu, *S. Africa* .... **57 D5** 29 45S 30 58 E
Kwando →, *Africa* .... **56 B3** 18 27S 23 32 E
Kwangdaeri, *N. Korea* ... **35 D14** 40 31N 127 32 E
Kwangju, *S. Korea* .... **35 G14** 35 9N 126 54 E
Kwango →, *Dem. Rep. of the Congo* **49 G5** 3 14S 17 22 E
Kwangsi-Chuang = Guangxi Zhuangzu Zizhiqu □, *China* .... **33 D5** 24 0N 109 0 E
Kwangtung = Guangdong □, *China* .. **33 D6** 23 0N 113 0 E
Kwataboahegan →, *Canada* **70 B3** 51 9N 80 50W
Kwatisore, *Indonesia* .... **37 E8** 3 18S 134 50 E
KwaZulu Natal □, *S. Africa* **57 D5** 29 0S 30 0 E
Kweichow = Guizhou □, *China* .... **32 D5** 27 0N 107 0 E
Kwekwe, *Zimbabwe* .... **55 F2** 18 58S 29 48 E
Kwidzyn, *Poland* .... **17 B10** 53 44N 18 55 E
Kwimba □, *Tanzania* .... **54 C3** 3 0S 33 0 E
Kwinana New Town, *Australia* .... **61 F2** 32 15S 115 47 E
Kwoka, *Indonesia* .... **37 E8** 0 31S 132 27 E
Kyabra Cr. →, *Australia* **63 D3** 25 36S 142 55 E
Kyabram, *Australia* .... **63 F4** 36 19S 145 4 E
Kyaikto, *Burma* .... **38 D1** 17 20N 97 3 E
Kyakhta, *Russia* .... **27 D11** 50 30N 106 25 E
Kyancutta, *Australia* .... **63 E2** 33 8S 135 33 E
Kyangin, *Burma* .... **41 K19** 18 20N 95 20 E
Kyaukpadaung, *Burma* ... **41 J19** 20 52N 95 8 E
Kyaukpyu, *Burma* .... **41 K18** 19 28N 93 30 E
Kyaukse, *Burma* .... **41 J20** 21 36N 96 10 E
Kyburz, *U.S.A.* **84 G6** 38 47N 120 18W
Kyenjojo, *Uganda* .... **54 B3** 0 40N 30 37 E
Kyle Dam, *Zimbabwe* .... **55 G3** 20 15S 31 0 E
Kyle of Lochalsh, *U.K.* ... **12 D3** 57 17N 5 44W
Kymijoki →, *Finland* .... **9 F22** 60 30N 26 55 E
Kyneton, *Australia* .... **63 F3** 37 10S 144 29 E
Kynuna, *Australia* .... **62 C3** 21 37S 141 55 E
Kyō-ga-Saki, *Japan* .... **31 G7** 35 45N 135 15 E
Kyoga, L., *Uganda* .... **54 B3** 1 35N 33 0 E
Kyogle, *Australia* .... **63 D5** 28 40S 153 0 E
Kyongju, *S. Korea* .... **35 G15** 35 51N 129 14 E
Kyongpyaw, *Burma* .... **41 L19** 17 12N 95 10 E
Kyŏngsŏng, *N. Korea* .... **35 D15** 41 35N 129 36 E
Kyōto, *Japan* .... **31 G7** 35 0N 135 45 E
Kyōto □, *Japan* .... **31 G7** 35 15N 135 45 E
Kyparissovouno, *Cyprus* . **23 D12** 35 19N 33 10 E
Kyperounda, *Cyprus* .... **23 E11** 34 56N 32 58 E
Kyrenia, *Cyprus* .... **23 D12** 35 20N 33 20 E
Kyrgyzstan ■, *Asia* .... **26 E8** 42 0N 75 0 E
Kyrönjoki →, *Finland* ... **8 E19** 63 14N 21 45 E
Kystatyam, *Russia* .... **27 C13** 67 20N 123 10 E
Kythréa, *Cyprus* .... **23 D12** 35 15N 33 29 E
Kyunhla, *Burma* .... **41 H19** 23 25N 95 15 E
Kyuquot, *Canada* **72 C3** 50 3N 127 25W
Kyūshū, *Japan* .... **31 H5** 33 0N 131 0 E
Kyūshū □, *Japan* .... **31 H5** 33 0N 131 0 E
Kyūshū-Sanchi, *Japan* ... **31 H5** 32 35N 131 17 E
Kyustendil, *Bulgaria* .... **21 C10** 42 16N 22 41 E
Kyusyur, *Russia* .... **27 B13** 70 19N 127 30 E
Kywong, *Australia* .... **63 E4** 34 58S 146 44 E

Lardhos, Ákra

Kyyiv, Ukraine 25 D5 50 30N 30 28 E
Kyyivske Vdskh., Ukraine 25 D5 51 0N 30 25 E
Kyzyl, Russia 27 D10 51 50N 94 30 E
Kyzyl Kum, Uzbekistan 26 E7 42 30N 65 0 E
Kyzyl-Kyya, Kyrgyzstan 26 E8 40 16N 72 8 E
Kzyl-Orda = Qyzylorda, Kazakstan 26 E7 44 48N 65 28 E

L

La Alcarria, Spain 19 B4 40 31N 2 45W
La Asunción, Venezuela 92 A6 11 2N 63 53W
La Banda, Argentina 94 B3 27 45S 64 10W
La Barca, Mexico 86 C4 20 20N 102 40W
La Barge, U.S.A. 82 E8 42 16N 110 12W
La Belle, U.S.A. 77 M5 26 46N 81 26W
La Biche —►, Canada 72 B4 59 57N 123 50W
La Bomba, Mexico 86 A1 31 53N 115 2W
La Calera, Chile 94 C1 32 50S 71 10W
La Canal, Spain 22 C7 38 51N 1 23 E
La Carlota, Argentina 94 C3 33 30S 63 20W
La Ceiba, Honduras 88 C2 15 40N 86 50W
La Chaux-de-Fonds, Switz. 18 C7 47 7N 6 50 E
La Cocha, Argentina 94 B2 27 50S 65 40W
La Concordia, Mexico 87 D6 16 8N 92 38W
La Conner, U.S.A. 82 B2 48 23N 122 30W
La Coruña = A Coruña, Spain 19 A1 43 20N 8 25W
La Crete, Canada 72 B5 58 11N 116 24W
La Crosse, Kans., U.S.A. 80 F5 38 32N 99 18W
La Crosse, Wis., U.S.A. 80 D9 43 48N 91 15W
La Cruz, Costa Rica 88 D2 11 4N 85 39W
La Cruz, Mexico 86 C3 23 55N 106 54W
La Escondida, Mexico 86 C5 24 6N 99 55W
La Esmeralda, Paraguay 94 A3 22 16S 62 33W
La Esperanza, Cuba 88 B3 22 46N 83 44W
La Esperanza, Honduras 88 D2 14 15N 88 10W
La Estrada = A Estrada, Spain 19 A1 42 43N 8 27W
La Fayette, U.S.A. 77 H3 34 42N 85 17W
La Fé, Cuba 88 B3 22 2N 84 15W
La Follette, U.S.A. 77 G3 36 23N 84 7W
La Grande, U.S.A. 82 D4 45 20N 118 5W
La Grange, Calif., U.S.A. 84 H6 37 42N 120 27W
La Grange, Ga., U.S.A. 77 J3 33 2N 85 2W
La Grange, Ky., U.S.A. 76 F3 38 25N 85 23W
La Grange, Tex., U.S.A. 81 L6 29 54N 96 52W
La Guaira, Venezuela 92 A5 10 36N 66 56W
La Habana, Cuba 88 B3 23 8N 82 22W
La Harpe, U.S.A. 80 E9 40 35N 90 58W
La Independencia, Mexico 87 D6 16 31N 91 47W
La Isabela, Dom. Rep. 89 C5 19 58N 71 2W
La Jara, U.S.A. 83 H11 37 16N 105 58W
La Junta, U.S.A. 81 F3 37 59N 103 33W
La Laguna, Canary Is. 22 F3 28 28N 16 18W
La Libertad, Guatemala 88 C1 16 47N 90 7W
La Libertad, Mexico 86 B2 29 55N 112 41W
La Ligua, Chile 94 C1 32 30S 71 16W
La Línea de la Concepción, Spain 19 D3 36 15N 5 23W
La Loche, Canada 73 B7 56 29N 109 26W
La Louvière, Belgium 15 D4 50 27N 4 10 E
La Malbaie, Canada 71 C5 47 40N 70 10W
La Mancha, Spain 19 C4 39 10N 2 54W
La Mesa, Calif., U.S.A. 85 N9 32 46N 117 3W
La Mesa, N. Mex., U.S.A. 83 K10 32 7N 106 42W
La Misión, Mexico 86 A1 32 5N 116 50W
La Moure, U.S.A. 80 B5 46 21N 98 18W
La Negra, Chile 94 A1 23 46S 70 18W
La Oliva, Canary Is. 22 F6 28 36N 13 57W
La Orotava, Canary Is. 22 F3 28 22N 16 31W
La Oroya, Peru 92 F3 11 32S 75 54W
La Palma, Canary Is. 22 F2 28 40N 17 50W
La Palma, Panama 88 E4 8 15N 78 0W
La Palma del Condado, Spain 19 D2 37 21N 6 38W
La Paloma, Chile 94 C1 30 35S 71 0W
La Pampa □, Argentina 94 D2 36 50S 66 0W
La Paragua, Venezuela 92 B6 6 50N 63 20W
La Paz, Entre Ríos, Argentina 94 C4 30 50S 59 45W
La Paz, San Luis, Argentina 94 C2 33 30S 67 20W
La Paz, Bolivia 92 G5 16 20S 68 10W
La Paz, Honduras 88 D2 14 20N 87 47W
La Paz, Mexico 86 C2 24 10N 110 20W
La Paz Centro, Nic. 88 D2 12 20N 86 41W
La Pedrera, Colombia 92 D5 1 18S 69 43W
La Perouse Str., Asia 30 B11 45 40N 142 0 E
La Pesca, Mexico 87 C5 23 46N 97 47W
La Piedad, Mexico 86 C4 20 20N 102 1W
La Pine, U.S.A. 82 E3 43 40N 121 30W
La Plant, U.S.A. 80 C4 45 9N 100 39W
La Plata, Argentina 94 D4 35 0S 57 55W
La Porte, U.S.A. 76 E2 41 36N 86 43W
La Purísima, Mexico 86 B2 26 10N 112 4W
La Push, U.S.A. 84 C2 47 55N 124 38W
La Quiaca, Argentina 94 A2 22 5S 65 35W
La Reine, Canada 70 C4 48 50N 79 30W
La Restinga, Canary Is. 22 G2 27 38N 17 59W
La Rioja, Argentina 94 B2 29 20S 67 0W
La Rioja □, Argentina 94 B2 29 30S 67 0W
La Rioja □, Spain 19 A4 42 20N 2 20W
La Robla, Spain 19 A3 42 50N 5 41W
La Roche-en-Ardenne, Belgium 15 D5 50 11N 5 35 E
La Roche-sur-Yon, France 18 C3 46 40N 1 25W
La Rochelle, France 18 C3 46 10N 1 9W
La Roda, Spain 19 C4 39 13N 2 15W
La Romana, Dom. Rep. 89 C6 18 27N 68 57W
La Ronge, Canada 73 B7 55 5N 105 20W
La Rumorosa, Mexico 85 N10 32 33N 116 4W
La Sabina, Spain 22 C7 38 44N 1 25 E
La Salle, U.S.A. 80 E10 41 20N 89 6W
La Santa, Canary Is. 22 E6 29 5N 13 40W
La Sarre, Canada 70 C4 48 45N 79 15W
La Scie, Canada 71 C8 49 57N 55 36W
La Selva Beach, U.S.A. 84 J5 36 56N 121 51W
La Serena, Chile 94 B1 29 55S 71 10W
La Seu d'Urgell, Spain 19 A6 42 22N 1 23 E
La Seyne-sur-Mer, France 18 E6 43 7N 5 52 E
La Spézia, Italy 18 D8 44 7N 9 50 E
La Tagua, Colombia 92 C4 0 3N 74 40W
La Tortuga, Venezuela 89 D6 11 0N 65 22W
La Tuque, Canada 70 C5 47 30N 72 50W
La Unión, Chile 96 E2 40 10S 73 0W
La Unión, El Salv. 88 D2 13 20N 87 50W
La Unión, Mexico 86 D4 17 58N 101 49W
La Urbana, Venezuela 92 B5 7 8N 66 56W
La Vall d'Uixó, Spain 19 C5 39 49N 0 15W
La Vega, Dom. Rep. 89 C5 19 20N 70 30W
La Vela, Venezuela 92 A5 11 27N 69 34W
La Venta, Mexico 87 D6 18 8N 94 3W
La Ventura, Mexico 86 C4 24 38N 100 54W
Labe = Elbe —►, Europe 16 B5 53 50N 9 0 E
Labé, Guinea 50 F3 11 24N 12 16W
Laberge, L., Canada 72 A1 61 11N 135 12W
Labis, Malaysia 39 L4 2 22N 103 2 E
Laboulaye, Argentina 94 C3 34 10S 63 30W
Labrador, Canada 71 B7 53 20N 61 0W
Labrador City, Canada 71 B6 52 57N 66 55W
Lábrea, Brazil 92 E6 7 15S 64 51W
Labuan, Malaysia 36 C5 5 20N 115 14 E
Labuan, Pulau, Malaysia 36 C5 5 21N 115 13 E
Labuha, Indonesia 37 E7 0 30S 127 30 E
Labuhan, Indonesia 37 G11 6 22S 105 50 E
Labuhanbajo, Indonesia 37 F6 8 28S 120 1 E
Labuk, Telok, Malaysia 36 C5 6 10N 117 50 E
Labyrinth, L., Australia 63 E2 30 40S 135 11 E
Labytnangi, Russia 24 A12 66 39N 66 21 E
Lac Allard, Canada 71 B7 50 33N 63 24W
Lac Bouchette, Canada 71 C5 48 16N 72 11W
Lac du Flambeau, U.S.A. 80 B10 45 58N 89 53W
Lac Édouard, Canada 70 C5 47 40N 72 16W
Lac La Biche, Canada 72 C6 54 45N 111 58W
Lac la Martre = Wha Ti, Canada 68 B8 63 8N 117 16W
Lac-Mégantic, Canada 71 C5 45 35N 70 53W
Lac Seul, Res., Canada 70 B1 50 25N 92 30W
Lac Thien, Vietnam 38 F7 12 25N 108 11 E
Lacanau, France 18 D3 44 58N 1 5W
Lacantúm —►, Mexico 87 D6 16 36N 90 40W
Laccadive Is. = Lakshadweep Is., Ind. Oc. 28 H11 10 0N 72 30 E
Lacepede B., Australia 63 F2 36 40S 139 40 E
Lacepede Is., Australia 60 C3 16 55S 122 0 E
Lacerdónia, Mozam. 55 F4 18 3S 35 35 E
Lacey, U.S.A. 84 C4 47 7N 122 49W
Lachhmangarh, India 42 F6 27 50N 75 4 E
Lachi, Pakistan 42 C4 33 25N 71 20 E
Lachine, Canada 70 C5 45 30N 73 40W
Lachlan —►, Australia 63 E3 34 22S 143 55 E
Lachute, Canada 70 C5 45 39N 74 21W
Lackawanna, U.S.A. 78 D6 42 50N 78 50W
Lacolle, Canada 79 A11 45 5N 73 22W
Lacombe, Canada 72 C6 52 30N 113 44W
Lacona, U.S.A. 79 C8 43 39N 76 10W
Laconia, U.S.A. 79 C13 43 32N 71 28W
Lacrosse, U.S.A. 82 C5 46 51N 117 58W
Ladakh Ra., India 43 C8 34 0N 78 0 E
Ladismith, S. Africa 56 E3 33 28S 21 15 E
Lādīz, Iran 45 D9 28 55N 61 15 E
Ladnun, India 42 F6 27 38N 74 25 E
Ladoga, L. = Ladozhskoye Ozero, Russia 24 B5 61 15N 30 30 E
Ladozhskoye Ozero, Russia 24 B5 61 15N 30 30 E
Lady Grey, S. Africa 56 E4 30 43S 27 13 E
Ladybrand, S. Africa 56 D4 29 9S 27 29 E
Ladysmith, Canada 72 D4 49 0N 123 49W
Ladysmith, S. Africa 57 D4 28 32S 29 46 E
Ladysmith, U.S.A. 80 C9 45 28N 91 12W
Lae, Papua N. G. 64 H6 6 40S 147 2 E
Laem Ngop, Thailand 39 F4 12 10N 102 26 E
Laem Pho, Thailand 39 J3 6 55N 101 19 E
Læsø, Denmark 9 H14 57 15N 11 5 E
Lafayette, Colo., U.S.A. 80 F2 39 58N 105 12W
Lafayette, Ind., U.S.A. 76 E2 40 25N 86 54W
Lafayette, La., U.S.A. 81 K9 30 14N 92 1W
Lafayette, Tenn., U.S.A. 77 G3 36 31N 86 2W
Laferte —►, Canada 72 A5 61 53N 117 44W
Lafia, Nigeria 50 G7 8 30N 8 34 E
Lafleche, Canada 73 D7 49 45N 106 40W
Lagan —►, U.K. 13 B6 54 36N 5 55W
Lagarfljót —►, Iceland 8 D6 65 40N 14 18W
Lågen —►, Oppland, Norway 9 F14 61 8N 10 25 E
Lågen —►, Vestfold, Norway 9 G14 59 3N 10 3 E
Laghouat, Algeria 50 B6 33 50N 2 59 E
Lagonoy G., Phil. 37 B6 13 50N 123 50 E
Lagos, Nigeria 50 G6 6 25N 3 27 E
Lagos, Portugal 19 D1 37 5N 8 41W
Lagos de Moreno, Mexico 86 C4 21 21N 101 55W
Lagrange, Australia 60 C3 18 45S 121 43 E
Lagrange B., Australia 60 C3 18 38S 121 42 E
Laguna, Brazil 95 B6 28 30S 48 50W
Laguna, U.S.A. 83 J10 35 2N 107 25W
Laguna Beach, U.S.A. 85 M9 33 33N 117 47W
Laguna Limpia, Argentina 94 B4 26 32S 59 45W
Laguna Madre, U.S.A. 87 B5 27 0N 97 20W
Lagunas, Chile 94 A2 21 0S 69 45W
Lahad Datu, Malaysia 37 D5 5 0N 118 20 E
Lahad Datu, Teluk, Malaysia 37 D5 4 50N 118 20 E
Lahan Sai, Thailand 38 E4 14 25N 102 52 E
Lahanam, Laos 38 D5 16 16N 105 16 E
Laharpur, India 43 F9 27 43N 80 56 E
Lahat, Indonesia 36 E2 3 45S 103 30 E
Lahewa, Indonesia 36 D1 1 22N 97 12 E
Lāhījān, Iran 45 B6 37 10N 50 6 E
Lahn —►, Germany 16 C4 50 19N 7 37 E
Laholm, Sweden 9 H15 56 30N 13 2 E
Lahontan Reservoir, U.S.A. 82 G4 39 28N 119 4W
Lahore, Pakistan 42 D6 31 32N 74 22 E
Lahti, Finland 9 F21 60 58N 25 40 E
Lahtis = Lahti, Finland 9 F21 60 58N 25 40 E
Laï, Chad 51 G9 9 25N 16 18 E
Lai Chau, Vietnam 38 A4 22 5N 103 3 E
Laidley, Australia 63 D5 27 39S 152 20 E
Laikipia □, Kenya 54 B4 0 30N 36 30 E
Laingsburg, S. Africa 56 E3 33 9S 20 52 E
Lainio älv —►, Sweden 8 C20 67 35N 22 40 E
Lairg, U.K. 12 C4 58 2N 4 24W
Laishui, China 34 E8 39 23N 115 45 E
Laiwu, China 35 F9 36 15N 117 40 E
Laixi, China 35 F11 36 50N 120 31 E
Laiyang, China 35 F11 36 59N 120 45 E
Laiyuan, China 34 E8 39 20N 114 40 E
Laizhou Wan, China 35 F10 37 30N 119 30 E
Laja —►, Mexico 86 C4 20 55N 100 46W
Lajes, Brazil 95 B5 27 48S 50 20W
Lak Sao, Laos 38 C5 18 11N 104 59 E
Lakaband, Pakistan 42 D3 31 2N 69 15 E
Lake Alpine, U.S.A. 84 G7 38 29N 120 0W
Lake Andes, U.S.A. 80 D5 43 9N 98 32W
Lake Anse, U.S.A. 76 B1 46 42N 88 25W
Lake Arthur, U.S.A. 81 K8 30 5N 92 41W
Lake Cargelligo, Australia 63 E4 33 15S 146 22 E
Lake Charles, U.S.A. 81 K8 30 14N 93 13W
Lake City, Colo., U.S.A. 83 G10 38 2N 107 19W
Lake City, Fla., U.S.A. 77 K4 30 11N 82 38W
Lake City, Iowa, U.S.A. 80 D7 42 16N 94 44W
Lake City, Mich., U.S.A. 76 C3 44 20N 85 13W
Lake City, Minn., U.S.A. 80 C8 44 27N 92 16W
Lake City, Pa., U.S.A. 78 D4 42 1N 80 21W
Lake City, S.C., U.S.A. 77 J6 33 52N 79 45W
Lake George, U.S.A. 79 C11 43 26N 73 43W
Lake Grace, Australia 61 F2 33 7S 118 28 E
Lake Harbour = Kimmirut, Canada 69 B13 62 50N 69 50W
Lake Havasu City, U.S.A. 85 L12 34 27N 114 22W
Lake Hughes, U.S.A. 85 L8 34 41N 118 26W
Lake Isabella, U.S.A. 85 K8 35 38N 118 28W
Lake King, Australia 61 F2 33 5S 119 45 E
Lake Lenore, Canada 73 C8 52 24N 104 59W
Lake Louise, Canada 72 C5 51 30N 116 10W
Lake Mead National Recreation Area, U.S.A. 85 K12 36 15N 114 30W
Lake Mills, U.S.A. 80 D8 43 25N 93 32W
Lake Nash, Australia 62 C2 20 57S 138 0 E
Lake Providence, U.S.A. 81 J9 32 48N 91 10W
Lake River, Canada 70 B3 54 30N 82 31W
Lake Superior Prov. Park, Canada 70 C3 47 45N 84 45W
Lake Village, U.S.A. 81 J9 33 20N 91 17W
Lake Wales, U.S.A. 77 M5 27 54N 81 35W
Lake Worth, U.S.A. 77 M5 26 37N 80 3W
Lakefield, Canada 70 D4 44 25N 78 16W
Lakeland, Australia 62 B3 15 49S 144 57 E
Lakeland, U.S.A. 77 M5 28 3N 81 57W
Lakemba, Fiji 59 D9 18 13S 178 47W
Lakeport, U.S.A. 84 F4 39 3N 122 55W
Lakes Entrance, Australia 63 F4 37 50S 148 0 E
Lakeside, Ariz., U.S.A. 83 J9 34 9N 109 58W
Lakeside, Calif., U.S.A. 85 N10 32 52N 116 55W
Lakeside, Nebr., U.S.A. 80 D3 42 3N 102 26W
Lakeview, U.S.A. 82 E3 42 11N 120 21W
Lakewood, Colo., U.S.A. 80 F2 39 44N 105 5W
Lakewood, N.J., U.S.A. 79 F10 40 6N 74 13W
Lakewood, Ohio, U.S.A. 78 E3 41 29N 81 48W
Lakewood Center, U.S.A. 84 C4 47 11N 122 32W
Lakhaniá, Greece 23 D9 35 58N 27 54 E
Lakhonpheng, Laos 38 E5 15 54N 105 34 E
Lakhpat, India 42 H3 23 48N 68 47 E
Lakin, U.S.A. 81 G4 37 57N 101 15W
Lakitusaki —►, Canada 70 B3 54 21N 82 25W
Lákkoi, Greece 23 D5 35 24N 23 57 E
Lakonikós Kólpos, Greece 21 F10 36 40N 22 40 E
Lakor, Indonesia 37 F7 8 15S 128 17 E
Lakota, Ivory C. 50 G4 5 50N 5 30W
Lakota, U.S.A. 80 A5 48 2N 98 21W
Laksefjorden, Norway 8 A22 70 45N 26 50 E
Lakselv, Norway 8 A21 70 2N 25 0 E
Lakshadweep Is., Ind. Oc. 28 H11 10 0N 72 30 E
Lakshmikantapur, India 43 H13 22 5N 88 20 E
Lala Ghat, India 41 G18 24 30N 92 40 E
Lala Musa, Pakistan 42 C5 32 40N 73 57 E
Lalago, Tanzania 54 C3 3 28S 33 58 E
Lalapanzi, Zimbabwe 55 F3 19 20S 30 15 E
L'Albufera, Spain 19 C5 39 20N 0 27W
Lalganj, India 43 G11 25 52N 85 13 E
Lalibela, Ethiopia 46 E2 12 2N 39 2 E
Lalin, China 35 B14 45 12N 127 0 E
Lalín, Spain 19 A1 42 40N 8 5W
Lalin He —►, China 35 B13 45 32N 125 40 E
Lalitapur = Patan, Nepal 41 F14 27 40N 85 20 E
Lalitpur, India 43 G8 24 42N 78 28 E
Lam, Vietnam 38 B6 21 21N 106 31 E
Lam Pao Res., Thailand 38 D4 16 50N 103 15 E
Lamaing, Burma 41 M20 15 25N 97 53 E
Lamar, Colo., U.S.A. 80 F3 38 5N 102 37W
Lamar, Mo., U.S.A. 81 G7 37 30N 94 16W
Lamas, Peru 92 E3 6 28S 76 31W
Lambaréné, Gabon 52 E2 0 41S 10 12 E
Lambasa, Fiji 59 C8 16 30S 179 10 E
Lambay I., Ireland 13 C5 53 29N 6 1W
Lambert, U.S.A. 80 B2 47 41N 104 37W
Lambert Glacier, Antarctica 5 D6 71 0S 70 0 E
Lamberts Bay, S. Africa 56 E2 32 5S 18 17 E
Lambi Kyun, Burma 39 G2 10 50N 98 20 E
Lame Deer, U.S.A. 82 D10 45 37N 106 40W
Lamego, Portugal 19 B2 41 5N 7 52W
Lamèque, Canada 71 C7 47 45N 64 38W
Lameroo, Australia 63 F3 35 19S 140 33 E
Lamesa, U.S.A. 81 J4 32 44N 101 58W
Lamía, Greece 21 E10 38 55N 22 26 E
Lammermuir Hills, U.K. 12 F6 55 50N 2 40W
Lamon B., Phil. 37 B6 14 30N 122 20 E
Lamont, Canada 72 C6 53 46N 112 50W
Lamont, U.S.A. 85 K8 35 15N 118 55W
Lampa, Peru 92 G4 15 22S 70 22W
Lampang, Thailand 38 C2 18 16N 99 32 E
Lampasas, U.S.A. 81 K5 31 4N 98 11W
Lampazos de Naranjo, Mexico 86 B4 27 2N 100 32W
Lampedusa, Medit. S. 20 G5 35 36N 12 40 E
Lampeter, U.K. 11 E3 52 7N 4 4W
Lampione, Medit. S. 20 G5 35 33N 12 20 E
Lampman, Canada 73 D8 49 25N 102 50W
Lamprey, Canada 73 B10 58 33N 94 8W
Lampung □, Indonesia 36 F2 5 30S 104 30 E
Lamu, Kenya 54 C5 2 16S 40 55 E
Lamu □, Kenya 54 C5 2 0S 40 45 E
Lamy, U.S.A. 83 J11 35 29N 105 53W
Lan Xian, China 34 E6 38 15N 111 35 E
Lanai, U.S.A. 74 H16 20 50N 156 55W
Lanak La, India 43 B8 34 27N 79 32 E
Lanak'o Shank'ou = Lanak La, India 43 B8 34 27N 79 32 E
Lanark, Canada 79 A8 45 1N 76 22W
Lanark, U.K. 12 F5 55 40N 3 47W
Lancang Jiang —►, China 32 D5 21 40N 101 10 E
Lancashire □, U.K. 10 D5 53 50N 2 48W
Lancaster, Canada 79 A10 45 10N 74 30W
Lancaster, U.K. 10 C5 54 3N 2 48W
Lancaster, Calif., U.S.A. 85 L8 34 42N 118 8W
Lancaster, Ky., U.S.A. 76 G3 37 37N 84 35W
Lancaster, N.H., U.S.A. 79 B13 44 29N 71 34W
Lancaster, N.Y., U.S.A. 78 D6 42 54N 78 40W
Lancaster, Pa., U.S.A. 79 F8 40 2N 76 19W
Lancaster, S.C., U.S.A. 77 H5 34 43N 80 46W
Lancaster, Wis., U.S.A. 80 D9 42 51N 90 43W
Lancaster Sd., Canada 69 A11 74 13N 84 0W
Lancer, Canada 73 C7 50 48N 108 53W
Lanchow = Lanzhou, China 34 F2 36 1N 103 52 E
Lanciano, Italy 20 C6 42 14N 14 23 E
Lancun, China 35 F11 36 25N 120 10 E
Landeck, Austria 16 E6 47 9N 10 34 E
Lander, U.S.A. 82 E9 42 50N 108 44W
Lander —►, Australia 60 D5 22 0S 132 0 E
Landes, France 18 D3 44 0N 1 0W
Landi Kotal, Pakistan 42 B4 34 7N 71 6 E
Landor, Australia 61 E2 25 10S 116 54 E
Land's End, U.K. 11 G2 50 4N 5 44W
Landsborough Cr. —►, Australia 62 C3 22 28S 144 35 E
Landshut, Germany 16 D7 48 34N 12 8 E
Landskrona, Sweden 9 J15 55 53N 12 50 E
Lanesboro, U.S.A. 79 E9 41 57N 75 34W
Lanett, U.S.A. 77 J3 32 52N 85 12W
Lang Bay, Canada 72 D4 49 45N 124 21W
Lang Qua, Vietnam 38 A5 22 16N 104 27 E
Lang Shan, China 34 D4 41 0N 106 30 E
Lang Son, Vietnam 38 B6 21 52N 106 42 E
Lang Suan, Thailand 39 H2 9 57N 99 4 E
La'nga Co, China 41 D12 30 45N 81 15 E
Langar, Iran 45 C9 35 23N 60 25 E
Langara I., Canada 72 C2 54 14N 133 1W
Langdon, U.S.A. 80 A5 48 45N 98 22W
Langeberg, S. Africa 56 E3 33 55S 21 0 E
Langeberge, S. Africa 56 D3 28 15S 22 33 E
Langeland, Denmark 9 J14 54 56N 10 48 E
Langenburg, Canada 73 C8 50 51N 101 43W
Langholm, U.K. 12 F5 55 9N 3 0W
Langjökull, Iceland 8 D3 64 39N 20 12W
Langkawi, Pulau, Malaysia 39 J2 6 25N 99 45 E
Langklip, S. Africa 56 D3 28 12S 20 20 E
Langkon, Malaysia 36 C5 6 30N 116 40 E
Langlade, St- P. & M. 71 C8 46 50N 56 20W
Langlois, U.S.A. 82 E1 42 56N 124 27W
Langøya, Norway 8 B16 68 45N 14 50 E
Langreo, Spain 19 A3 43 18N 5 40W
Langres, France 18 C6 47 52N 5 20 E
Langres, Plateau de, France 18 C6 47 45N 5 3 E
Langsa, Indonesia 36 D1 4 30N 97 57 E
Langtry, U.S.A. 81 L4 29 49N 101 34W
Langu, Thailand 39 J2 6 53N 99 47 E
Languedoc, France 18 E5 43 58N 3 55 E
Langxiangzhen, China 34 E9 39 43N 116 8 E
Lanigan, Canada 73 C7 51 51N 105 2W
Lankao, China 34 G8 34 48N 114 50 E
Länkäran, Azerbaijan 25 G8 38 48N 48 52 E
Lannion, France 18 B2 48 46N 3 29W
L'Annonciation, Canada 70 C5 46 25N 74 55W
Lansdale, U.S.A. 79 F9 40 14N 75 17W
Lansdowne, Australia 63 E5 31 48S 152 30 E
Lansdowne, Canada 79 B8 44 24N 76 1W
Lansdowne House, Canada 70 B2 52 14N 87 53W
L'Anse, U.S.A. 70 C2 46 45N 88 27W
L'Anse au Loup, Canada 71 B8 51 32N 56 50W
Lansford, U.S.A. 79 F9 40 50N 75 53W
Lansing, U.S.A. 76 D3 42 44N 84 33W
Lanta Yai, Ko, Thailand 39 J2 7 35N 99 3 E
Lantian, China 34 G5 34 11N 109 20 E
Lanus, Argentina 94 C4 34 44S 58 27W
Lanusei, Italy 20 E3 39 52N 9 34 E
Lanzarote, Canary Is. 22 F6 29 0N 13 40W
Lanzhou, China 34 F2 36 1N 103 52 E
Lao Bao, Laos 38 D6 16 35N 106 30 E
Lao Cai, Vietnam 38 A4 22 30N 103 57 E
Laoag, Phil. 37 A6 18 7N 120 34 E
Laoang, Phil. 37 B7 12 32N 125 8 E
Laoha He —►, China 35 C11 43 25N 120 35 E
Laois □, Ireland 13 D4 52 57N 7 36W
Laon, France 18 B5 49 33N 3 35 E
Laona, U.S.A. 76 C1 45 34N 88 40W
Laos ■, Asia 38 D5 17 45N 105 0 E
Lapa, Brazil 95 B6 25 46S 49 44W
Lapeer, U.S.A. 76 D4 43 3N 83 19W
Lapithos, Cyprus 23 D12 35 21N 33 11 E
Lapland = Lappland, Europe 8 B21 68 7N 24 0 E
Laporte, U.S.A. 79 E8 41 25N 76 30W
Lappeenranta, Finland 9 F23 61 3N 28 12 E
Lappland, Europe 8 B21 68 7N 24 0 E
Laprida, Argentina 94 D3 37 34S 60 45W
Lapseki, Turkey 21 D12 40 20N 26 41 E
Laptev Sea, Russia 27 B13 76 0N 125 0 E
Lapua, Finland 8 E20 62 58N 23 0 E
L'Áquila, Italy 20 C5 42 22N 13 22 E
Lār, Āzarbājān-e Sharqī, Iran 44 B5 38 30N 47 52 E
Lār, Fārs, Iran 45 E7 27 40N 54 14 E
Laramie, U.S.A. 80 E2 41 19N 105 35W
Laramie Mts., U.S.A. 80 E2 42 0N 105 30W
Laranjeiras do Sul, Brazil 95 B5 25 23S 52 23W
Larantuka, Indonesia 37 F6 8 21S 122 55 E
Larat, Indonesia 37 F8 7 0S 132 0 E
Larde, Mozam. 55 F4 16 28S 39 43 E
Larder Lake, Canada 70 C4 48 5N 79 40W
Lardhos, Ákra = Líndhos, Ákra, Greece 23 C10 36 4N 28 10 E

Malyn

McGehee, U.S.A. 81 J9 33 38N 91 24W
McGill, U.S.A. 82 G6 39 23N 114 47W
Macgillycuddy's Reeks, Ireland 13 E2 51 58N 9 45W
MacGregor, Canada 73 D9 49 57N 98 48W
McGregor, U.S.A. 80 D9 43 1N 91 11W
McGregor →, Canada 72 B4 55 10N 122 0W
McGregor Ra., Australia 63 D3 27 0S 142 45 E
Mach, Pakistan 40 E5 29 50N 67 20 E
Māch Kowr, Iran 45 E9 25 48N 61 28 E
Machado = Jiparaná →, Brazil 92 E6 8 3S 62 52W
Machagai, Argentina 94 B3 26 56S 60 2W
Machakos, Kenya 54 C4 1 30S 37 15 E
Machakos □, Kenya 54 C4 1 30S 37 15 E
Machala, Ecuador 92 D3 3 20S 79 57W
Machanga, Mozam. 57 C6 20 59S 35 0 E
Machattie, L., Australia 62 C2 24 50S 139 48 E
Machava, Mozam. 57 D5 25 54S 32 28 E
Machece, Mozam. 55 F4 19 15S 35 32 E
Machias, U.S.A. 71 D6 44 43N 67 28W
Machichi →, Canada 73 B10 57 3N 92 6W
Machico, Madeira 22 D3 32 43N 16 44W
Machilipatnam, India 41 L12 16 12N 81 8 E
Machiques, Venezuela 92 A4 10 4N 72 34W
Machupicchu, Peru 92 F4 13 8S 72 30W
Machynlleth, U.K. 11 E4 52 35N 3 50W
McIlwraith Ra., Australia 62 A3 13 50S 143 20 E
McIntosh, U.S.A. 80 C4 45 55N 101 21W
McIntosh L., Canada 73 B8 55 45N 105 0W
Macintosh Ra., Australia 61 E4 27 39S 125 32 E
Macintyre →, Australia 63 D5 28 37S 150 47 E
Mackay, Australia 62 C4 21 8S 149 11 E
Mackay, U.S.A. 82 E7 43 55N 113 37W
MacKay →, Canada 72 B6 57 10N 111 38W
Mackay, L., Australia 60 D4 22 30S 129 0 E
McKay Ra., Australia 60 D3 23 0S 122 30 E
McKeesport, U.S.A. 78 F5 40 21N 79 52W
McKenna, U.S.A. 84 D4 46 56N 122 33W
Mackenzie, Canada 72 B4 55 20N 123 5W
McKenzie, U.S.A. 77 G1 36 8N 88 31W
Mackenzie →, Australia 62 C4 23 38S 149 46 E
Mackenzie →, Canada 68 B6 69 10N 134 20W
McKenzie →, U.S.A. 82 D2 44 7N 123 6W
Mackenzie City = Linden, Guyana 92 B7 6 0N 58 10W
Mackenzie Highway, Canada 72 B5 58 0N 117 15W
Mackenzie Mts., Canada 68 B7 64 0N 130 0W
Mackinaw City, U.S.A. 76 C3 45 47N 84 44W
McKinlay, Australia 62 C3 21 16S 141 18 E
McKinlay →, Australia 62 C3 20 50S 141 28 E
McKinley, Mt., U.S.A. 68 B4 63 4N 151 0W
McKinney, U.S.A. 81 J6 33 12N 96 37W
Mackinnon Road, Kenya 54 C4 3 40S 39 1 E
Macksville, Australia 63 E5 30 40S 152 56 E
McLaughlin, U.S.A. 80 C4 45 49N 100 49W
Maclean, Australia 63 D5 29 26S 153 16 E
McLean, U.S.A. 81 H4 35 14N 100 36W
McLeansboro, U.S.A. 80 F10 38 6N 88 32W
Maclear, S. Africa 57 E4 31 2S 28 23 E
Macleay →, Australia 63 E5 30 56S 153 0 E
McLennan, Canada 72 B5 55 42N 116 50W
McLeod, B., Canada 73 A7 62 53N 110 0W
McLeod, L., Australia 61 D1 24 9S 113 47 E
MacLeod Lake, Canada 72 C4 54 58N 123 0W
McLoughlin, Mt., U.S.A. 82 E2 42 27N 122 19W
McLure, Canada 72 C4 51 2N 120 13W
McMechen, U.S.A. 78 G4 39 57N 80 44W
McMillan, L., U.S.A. 81 J2 32 36N 104 21W
McMinnville, Oreg., U.S.A. 82 D2 45 13N 123 12W
McMinnville, Tenn., U.S.A. 77 H3 35 41N 85 46W
McMorran, Canada 73 C7 51 19N 108 42W
McMurdo Sd., Antarctica 5 D11 77 0S 170 0 E
McMurray = Fort McMurray, Canada 72 B6 56 44N 111 7W
McMurray, U.S.A. 84 B4 48 19N 122 14W
McNary, U.S.A. 83 J9 34 4N 109 51W
MacNutt, Canada 73 C8 51 5N 101 36W
Macodoene, Mozam. 57 C6 23 32S 35 5 E
Macomb, U.S.A. 80 E9 40 27N 90 40W
Mâcon, France 18 C6 46 19N 4 50 E
Macon, Ga., U.S.A. 77 J4 32 51N 83 38W
Macon, Miss., U.S.A. 77 J1 33 7N 88 34W
Macon, Mo., U.S.A. 80 F8 39 44N 92 28W
Macossa, Mozam. 55 F3 17 55S 33 56 E
Macoun L., Canada 73 B8 56 32N 103 40W
Macovane, Mozam. 57 C6 21 30S 35 2 E
McPherson, U.S.A. 80 F6 38 22N 97 40W
McPherson Pk., U.S.A. 85 L7 34 53N 119 53W
McPherson Ra., Australia 63 D5 28 15S 153 15 E
Macquarie Harbour, Australia 62 G4 42 15S 145 23 E
Macquarie Is., Pac. Oc. 64 N7 54 36S 158 55 E
MacRobertson Land, Antarctica 5 D6 71 0S 64 0 E
Macroom, Ireland 13 E3 51 54N 8 57W
Macroy, Australia 60 D2 20 53S 118 2 E
MacTier, Canada 78 A5 45 9N 79 46W
Macubela, Mozam. 55 F4 16 53S 37 49 E
Macuiza, Mozam. 55 F3 18 7S 34 29 E
Macusani, Peru 92 F4 14 4S 70 29W
Macuse, Mozam. 55 F4 17 45S 37 10 E
Macuspana, Mexico 87 D6 17 46N 92 36W
Macusse, Angola 56 B3 17 48S 20 23 E
McVille, U.S.A. 80 B5 47 46N 98 11W
Madadeni, S. Africa 57 D5 27 43S 30 3 E
Madagascar ■, Africa 57 C8 20 0S 47 0 E
Madā'in Sālih, Si. Arabia 44 E3 26 46N 37 57 E
Madama, Niger 51 D8 22 0N 13 40 E
Madame I., Canada 71 C7 45 30N 60 58W
Madaripur, Bangla. 41 H17 23 19N 90 15 E
Madauk, Burma 41 L20 17 56N 96 52 E
Madawaska, Canada 78 A7 45 30N 78 0W
Madawaska →, Canada 78 A8 45 27N 76 21W
Madaya, Burma 41 H20 22 12N 96 10 E
Maddalena, Italy 20 D3 41 16N 9 23 E
Madeira, Atl. Oc. 22 D3 32 50N 17 0W
Madeira →, Brazil 92 D7 3 22S 58 45W
Madeleine, Is. de la, Canada 71 C7 47 30N 61 40W
Madera, U.S.A. 84 J6 36 57N 120 3W
Madha, India 40 L9 18 0N 75 30 E
Madhubani, India 43 F12 26 21N 86 7 E
Madhya Pradesh □, India 42 J8 22 50N 78 0 E
Madidi →, Bolivia 92 F5 12 32S 66 52W
Madikeri, India 40 N9 12 30N 75 45 E
Madill, U.S.A. 81 H6 34 6N 96 46W
Madimba, Dem. Rep. of the Congo 52 E3 4 58S 15 5 E
Ma'din, Syria 44 C3 35 45N 39 36 E
Madingou, Congo 52 E2 4 10S 13 33 E
Madirovalo, Madag. 57 B8 16 26S 46 32 E
Madison, Calif., U.S.A. 84 G5 38 41N 121 59W
Madison, Fla., U.S.A. 77 K4 30 28N 83 25W
Madison, Ind., U.S.A. 76 F3 38 44N 85 23W
Madison, Nebr., U.S.A. 80 E6 41 50N 97 27W
Madison, Ohio, U.S.A. 78 E3 41 46N 81 3W
Madison, S. Dak., U.S.A. 80 D6 44 0N 97 7W
Madison, Wis., U.S.A. 80 D10 43 4N 89 24W
Madison →, U.S.A. 82 D8 45 56N 111 31W
Madisonville, Ky., U.S.A. 76 G2 37 20N 87 30W
Madisonville, Tex., U.S.A. 81 K7 30 57N 95 55W
Madista, Botswana 56 C4 21 15S 25 6 E
Madiun, Indonesia 37 G14 7 38S 111 32 E
Madona, Latvia 9 H22 56 53N 26 5 E
Madras = Chennai, India 40 N12 13 8N 80 19 E
Madras = Tamil Nadu □, India 40 P10 11 0N 77 0 E
Madras, U.S.A. 82 D3 44 38N 121 8W
Madre, L., Mexico 87 C5 25 0N 97 30W
Madre, Laguna, U.S.A. 81 M6 27 0N 97 30W
Madre, Sierra, Phil. 37 A6 17 0N 122 0 E
Madre de Dios →, Bolivia 92 F5 10 59S 66 8W
Madre de Dios, I., Chile 96 G1 50 20S 75 10W
Madre del Sur, Sierra, Mexico 87 D5 17 30N 100 0W
Madre Occidental, Sierra, Mexico 86 B3 27 0N 107 0W
Madre Oriental, Sierra, Mexico 86 C5 25 0N 100 0W
Madri, India 42 G5 24 16N 73 32 E
Madrid, Spain 19 B4 40 25N 3 45W
Madura, Selat, Indonesia 37 G15 7 30S 113 20 E
Madura Motel, Australia 61 F4 31 55S 127 0 E
Madurai, India 40 Q11 9 55N 78 10 E
Madurantakam, India 40 N11 12 30N 79 50 E
Mae Chan, Thailand 38 B2 20 9N 99 52 E
Mae Hong Son, Thailand 38 C2 19 16N 97 56 E
Mae Khlong →, Thailand 38 F3 13 24N 100 0 E
Mae Phrik, Thailand 38 D2 17 27N 99 7 E
Mae Ramat, Thailand 38 D2 16 58N 98 31 E
Mae Rim, Thailand 38 C2 18 54N 98 57 E
Mae Sot, Thailand 38 D2 16 43N 98 34 E
Mae Suai, Thailand 38 C2 19 39N 99 33 E
Mae Tha, Thailand 38 C2 18 28N 99 8 E
Maebashi, Japan 31 F9 36 24N 139 4 E
Maesteg, U.K. 11 F4 51 36N 3 40W
Maestra, Sierra, Cuba 88 B4 20 15N 77 0W
Maestrazgo, El, Spain 19 B5 40 30N 0 25W
Maevatanana, Madag. 57 B8 16 56S 46 49 E
Mafeking = Mafikeng, S. Africa 56 D4 25 50S 25 38 E
Mafeking, Canada 73 C8 52 40N 101 10W
Mafeteng, Lesotho 56 D4 29 51S 27 15 E
Maffra, Australia 63 F4 37 53S 146 58 E
Mafia I., Tanzania 54 D4 7 45S 39 50 E
Mafikeng, S. Africa 56 D4 25 50S 25 38 E
Mafra, Brazil 95 B6 26 10S 49 55W
Mafra, Portugal 19 C1 38 55N 9 20W
Mafungabusi Plateau, Zimbabwe 55 F2 18 30S 29 8 E
Magadan, Russia 27 D16 59 38N 150 50 E
Magadi, Kenya 54 C4 1 54S 36 19 E
Magadi, L., Kenya 54 C4 1 54S 36 19 E
Magaliesburg, S. Africa 57 D4 26 0S 27 32 E
Magallanes, Estrecho de, Chile 96 G2 52 30S 75 0W
Magangué, Colombia 92 B4 9 14N 74 45W
Magdalen Is. = Madeleine, Is. de la, Canada 71 C7 47 30N 61 40W
Magdalena, Argentina 94 D4 35 5S 57 30W
Magdalena, Bolivia 92 F6 13 13S 63 57W
Magdalena, Mexico 86 A2 30 50N 112 0W
Magdalena, U.S.A. 83 J10 34 7N 107 15W
Magdalena →, Colombia 92 A4 11 6N 74 51W
Magdalena →, Mexico 86 A2 30 40N 112 25W
Magdalena, B., Mexico 86 C2 24 30N 112 10W
Magdalena, Llano de la, Mexico 86 C2 25 0N 111 30W
Magdeburg, Germany 16 B6 52 7N 11 38 E
Magdelaine Cays, Australia 62 B5 16 33S 150 18 E
Magee, U.S.A. 81 K10 31 52N 89 44W
Magelang, Indonesia 37 G14 7 29S 110 13 E
Magellan's Str. = Magallanes, Estrecho de, Chile 96 G2 52 30S 75 0W
Magenta, L., Australia 61 F2 33 30S 119 2 E
Magerøya, Norway 8 A21 71 3N 25 40 E
Maggiore, L., Italy 18 D8 45 57N 8 39 E
Magherafelt, U.K. 13 B5 54 45N 6 37W
Magistralnyy, Russia 27 D11 56 16N 107 36 E
Magnetic Pole (South) = South Magnetic Pole, Antarctica 5 C9 64 8S 138 8 E
Magnitogorsk, Russia 24 D10 53 27N 59 4 E
Magnolia, Ark., U.S.A. 81 J8 33 16N 93 14W
Magnolia, Miss., U.S.A. 81 K9 31 9N 90 28W
Magog, Canada 71 C5 45 18N 72 9W
Magoro, Uganda 54 B3 1 45N 34 12 E
Magosa = Famagusta, Cyprus 23 D12 35 8N 33 55 E
Magouládhes, Greece 23 A3 39 45N 19 42 E
Magoye, Zambia 55 F2 16 1S 27 30 E
Magpie L., Canada 71 B7 51 0N 64 41W
Magrath, Canada 72 D6 49 25N 112 50W
Magu □, Tanzania 54 C3 2 31S 33 28 E
Maguarinho, C., Brazil 93 D9 0 15S 48 30W
Mağusa = Famagusta, Cyprus 23 D12 35 8N 33 55 E
Maguse L., Canada 73 A9 61 40N 95 10W
Maguse Pt., Canada 73 A10 61 20N 93 50W
Magwe, Burma 41 J19 20 10N 95 0 E
Maha Sarakham, Thailand 38 D4 16 12N 103 16 E
Mahābād, Iran 44 B5 36 50N 45 45 E
Mahabharat Lekh, Nepal 43 E10 28 30N 82 0 E
Mahabo, Madag. 57 C7 20 23S 44 40 E
Mahadeo Hills, India 42 H8 22 20N 78 30 E
Mahagi, Dem. Rep. of the Congo 54 B3 2 20N 31 0 E
Mahajamba →, Madag. 57 B8 15 33S 47 8 E
Mahajamba, Helodranon' i, Madag. 57 B8 15 24S 47 5 E
Mahajan, India 42 E5 28 48N 73 56 E
Mahajanga, Madag. 57 B8 15 40S 46 25 E
Mahajanga □, Madag. 57 B8 17 0S 47 0 E
Mahajilo →, Madag. 57 B8 19 42S 45 22 E
Mahakam →, Indonesia 36 E5 0 35S 117 17 E
Mahalapye, Botswana 56 C4 23 1S 26 51 E
Maḩallāt, Iran 45 C6 33 55N 50 30 E
Māhān, Iran 45 D8 30 5N 57 18 E
Mahanadi →, India 41 J15 20 20N 86 25 E
Mahanoro, Madag. 57 B8 19 54S 48 48 E
Mahanoy City, U.S.A. 79 F8 40 49N 76 9W
Maharashtra □, India 40 J9 20 30N 75 30 E
Mahari Mts., Tanzania 54 D3 6 20S 30 0 E
Mahasham, W. →, Egypt 47 E3 30 15N 34 10 E
Mahasolo, Madag. 57 B8 19 7S 46 22 E
Mahattat ash Shīdīyah, Jordan 47 F4 29 55N 35 55 E
Mahattat 'Unayzah, Jordan 47 E4 30 30N 35 47 E
Mahaxay, Laos 38 D5 17 22N 105 12 E
Mahbubnagar, India 40 L10 16 45N 77 59 E
Maḩḑah, Oman 45 E7 24 24N 55 59 E
Mahdia, Tunisia 51 A8 35 28N 11 0 E
Mahe, India 43 C8 33 10N 78 32 E
Mahenge, Tanzania 55 D4 8 45S 36 41 E
Maheno, N.Z. 59 L3 45 10S 170 50 E
Mahesana, India 42 H5 23 39N 72 26 E
Mahia Pen., N.Z. 59 H6 39 9S 177 55 E
Mahilyow, Belarus 24 D5 53 55N 30 18 E
Mahmud Kot, Pakistan 42 D4 30 16N 71 0 E
Mahnomen, U.S.A. 80 B7 47 19N 95 58W
Mahoba, India 43 G8 25 15N 79 55 E
Mahón = Maó, Spain 22 B11 39 53N 4 16 E
Mahone Bay, Canada 71 D7 44 30N 64 20W
Mai-Ndombe, L., Dem. Rep. of the Congo 52 E3 2 0S 18 20 E
Mai-Sai, Thailand 38 B2 20 20N 99 55 E
Maicurú →, Brazil 93 D8 2 14S 54 17W
Maidan Khula, Afghan. 42 C3 33 36N 69 50 E
Maidenhead, U.K. 11 F7 51 31N 0 42W
Maidstone, Canada 73 C7 53 5N 109 20W
Maidstone, U.K. 11 F8 51 16N 0 32 E
Maiduguri, Nigeria 51 F8 12 0N 13 20 E
Maijdi, Bangla. 41 H17 22 48N 91 10 E
Maikala Ra., India 41 J12 22 0N 81 0 E
Mailsi, Pakistan 42 E5 29 48N 72 15 E
Main →, Germany 16 C5 50 0N 8 18 E
Main →, U.K. 13 B5 54 48N 6 18W
Main Centre, Canada 73 C7 50 35N 107 21W
Maine, France 18 C3 48 20N 0 15W
Maine □, U.S.A. 71 C6 45 20N 69 0W
Maine →, Ireland 13 D2 52 9N 9 45W
Maingkwan, Burma 41 F20 26 15N 96 37 E
Mainit, L., Phil. 37 C7 9 31N 125 30 E
Mainland, Orkney, U.K. 12 C5 58 59N 3 8W
Mainland, Shet., U.K. 12 A7 60 15N 1 22W
Mainpuri, India 43 F8 27 18N 79 4 E
Maintirano, Madag. 57 B7 18 3S 44 1 E
Mainz, Germany 16 C5 50 1N 8 14 E
Maipú, Argentina 94 D4 36 52S 57 50W
Maiquetía, Venezuela 92 A5 10 36N 66 57W
Mairabari, India 41 F18 26 30N 92 22 E
Maisí, Cuba 89 B5 20 17N 74 9W
Maisi, Pta. de, Cuba 89 B5 20 10N 74 10W
Maitland, N.S.W., Australia 63 E5 32 33S 151 36 E
Maitland, S. Austral., Australia 63 E2 34 23S 137 40 E
Maitland →, Canada 78 C3 43 45N 81 43W
Maiz, Is. del, Nic. 88 D3 12 15N 83 4W
Maizuru, Japan 31 G7 35 25N 135 22 E
Majalengka, Indonesia 37 G13 6 50S 108 13 E
Majene, Indonesia 37 E5 3 38S 118 57 E
Major, Canada 73 C7 51 52N 109 37W
Majorca = Mallorca, Spain 22 B10 39 30N 3 0 E
Makale, Indonesia 37 E5 3 6S 119 51 E
Makamba, Burundi 54 C2 4 8S 29 49 E
Makarikari = Makgadikgadi Salt Pans, Botswana 56 C4 20 40S 25 45 E
Makarovo, Russia 27 D11 57 40N 107 45 E
Makasar = Ujung Pandang, Indonesia 37 F5 5 10S 119 20 E
Makasar, Selat, Indonesia 37 E5 1 0S 118 20 E
Makasar, Str. of = Makasar, Selat, Indonesia 37 E5 1 0S 118 20 E
Makat, Kazakstan 25 E9 47 39N 53 19 E
Makedhonía □, Greece 21 D10 40 39N 22 0 E
Makedonija = Macedonia ■, Europe 21 D9 41 53N 21 40 E
Makena, U.S.A. 74 H16 20 39N 156 27W
Makeyevka = Makiyivka, Ukraine 25 E6 48 0N 38 0 E
Makgadikgadi Salt Pans, Botswana 56 C4 20 40S 25 45 E
Makhachkala, Russia 25 F8 43 0N 47 30 E
Makhmūr, Iraq 44 C4 35 46N 43 35 E
Makian, Indonesia 37 D7 0 20N 127 20 E
Makindu, Kenya 54 C4 2 18S 37 50 E
Makinsk, Kazakstan 26 D8 52 37N 70 26 E
Makiyivka, Ukraine 25 E6 48 0N 38 0 E
Makkah, Si. Arabia 46 C2 21 30N 39 54 E
Makkovik, Canada 71 A8 55 10N 59 10W
Makó, Hungary 17 E11 46 14N 20 33 E
Makokou, Gabon 52 D2 0 40N 12 50 E
Makongo, Dem. Rep. of the Congo 54 B2 3 25N 26 17 E
Makoro, Dem. Rep. of the Congo 54 B2 3 10N 29 59 E
Makrai, India 40 H10 22 2N 77 0 E
Makran Coast Range, Pakistan 40 G4 25 40N 64 0 E
Makrana, India 42 F6 27 2N 74 46 E
Makriyialos, Greece 23 D7 35 2N 25 59 E
Mākū, Iran 44 B5 39 15N 44 31 E
Makunda, Botswana 56 C3 22 30S 20 7 E
Makurazaki, Japan 31 J5 31 15N 130 20 E
Makurdi, Nigeria 50 G7 7 43N 8 35 E
Makūyeh, Iran 45 D7 28 7N 53 9 E
Makwassie, S. Africa 56 D4 27 17S 26 0 E
Mal B., Ireland 13 D2 52 50N 9 30W
Mala, Pta., Panama 88 E3 7 28N 80 2W
Malabar Coast, India 40 P9 11 0N 75 0 E
Malabo = Rey Malabo, Eq. Guin. 52 D1 3 45N 8 50 E
Malacca, Str. of, Indonesia 39 L3 3 0N 101 0 E
Malad City, U.S.A. 82 E7 42 12N 112 15W
Maladzyechna, Belarus 17 A14 54 20N 26 50 E
Málaga, Spain 19 D3 36 43N 4 23W
Malaga, U.S.A. 81 J2 32 14N 104 4W
Malagarasi, Tanzania 54 D3 5 5S 30 50 E
Malagarasi →, Tanzania 54 D2 5 12S 29 47 E
Malahide, Ireland 13 C5 53 26N 6 9W
Malaimbandy, Madag. 57 C8 20 20S 45 36 E
Malakâl, Sudan 51 G12 9 33N 31 40 E
Malakand, Pakistan 42 B4 34 40N 71 55 E
Malakoff, U.S.A. 81 J7 32 10N 96 1W
Malang, Indonesia 37 G15 7 59S 112 45 E
Malangen, Norway 8 B18 69 24N 18 37 E
Malanje, Angola 52 F3 9 36S 16 17 E
Mälaren, Sweden 9 G17 59 30N 17 10 E
Malargüe, Argentina 94 D2 35 32S 69 30W
Malartic, Canada 70 C4 48 9N 78 9W
Malaryta, Belarus 17 C13 51 50N 24 3 E
Malatya, Turkey 25 G6 38 25N 38 20 E
Malawi ■, Africa 55 E3 11 55S 34 0 E
Malawi, L. = Nyasa, L., Africa 55 E3 12 30S 34 30 E
Malay Pen., Asia 39 J3 7 25N 100 0 E
Malaybalay, Phil. 37 C7 8 5N 125 7 E
Malāyer, Iran 45 C6 34 19N 48 51 E
Malaysia ■, Asia 36 D4 5 0N 110 0 E
Malazgirt, Turkey 25 G7 39 10N 42 33 E
Malbon, Australia 62 C3 21 5S 140 17 E
Malbooma, Australia 63 E1 30 41S 134 11 E
Malbork, Poland 17 B10 54 3N 19 1 E
Malcolm, Australia 61 E3 28 51S 121 25 E
Malcolm, Pt., Australia 61 F3 33 48S 123 45 E
Maldegem, Belgium 15 C3 51 14N 3 26 E
Malden, Mass., U.S.A. 79 D13 42 26N 71 4W
Malden, Mo., U.S.A. 81 G10 36 34N 89 57W
Malden I., Kiribati 65 H12 4 3S 155 1W
Maldives ■, Ind. Oc. 29 J11 5 0N 73 0 E
Maldonado, Uruguay 95 C5 34 59S 55 0W
Maldonado, Punta, Mexico 87 D5 16 19N 98 35W
Malé Karpaty, Slovak Rep. 17 D9 48 30N 17 20 E
Maléa, Ákra, Greece 21 F10 36 28N 23 7 E
Malegaon, India 40 J9 20 30N 74 38 E
Malei, Mozam. 55 F4 17 12S 36 58 E
Malek Kandī, Iran 44 B5 37 9N 46 6 E
Malela, Dem. Rep. of the Congo 54 C2 4 22S 26 8 E
Malema, Mozam. 55 E4 14 57S 37 20 E
Máleme, Greece 23 D5 35 31N 23 49 E
Malerkotla, India 42 D6 30 32N 75 58 E
Máles, Greece 23 D7 35 6N 25 35 E
Malgomaj, Sweden 8 D17 64 40N 16 30 E
Malha, Sudan 51 E11 15 8N 25 10 E
Malheur →, U.S.A. 82 D5 44 4N 116 59W
Malheur L., U.S.A. 82 E4 43 20N 118 48W
Mali ■, Africa 50 E5 17 0N 3 0W
Mali →, Burma 41 G20 25 40N 97 40 E
Mali Kyun, Burma 38 F2 13 0N 98 20 E
Malibu, U.S.A. 85 L8 34 2N 118 41W
Maliku, Indonesia 37 E6 0 39S 123 16 E
Malili, Indonesia 37 E6 2 42S 121 6 E
Malimba, Mts., Dem. Rep. of the Congo 54 D2 7 30S 29 30 E
Malin Hd., Ireland 13 A4 55 23N 7 23W
Malin Pen., Ireland 13 A4 55 20N 7 17W
Malindi, Kenya 54 C5 3 12S 40 5 E
Malines = Mechelen, Belgium 15 C4 51 2N 4 29 E
Malino, Indonesia 37 D6 1 0N 121 0 E
Malinyi, Tanzania 55 D4 8 56S 36 0 E
Malita, Phil. 37 C7 6 19N 125 39 E
Malkara, Turkey 21 D12 40 53N 26 53 E
Mallacoota, Australia 63 F4 37 40S 149 40 E
Mallacoota Inlet, Australia 63 F4 37 34S 149 40 E
Mallaig, U.K. 12 D3 57 0N 5 50W
Mallawan, India 43 F9 27 4N 80 12 E
Mallawi, Egypt 51 C12 27 44N 30 44 E
Mállia, Greece 23 D7 35 17N 25 32 E
Mallión, Kólpos, Greece 23 D7 35 19N 25 27 E
Mallorca, Spain 22 B10 39 30N 3 0 E
Mallorytown, Canada 79 B9 44 29N 75 53W
Mallow, Ireland 13 D3 52 8N 8 39W
Malmberget, Sweden 8 C19 67 11N 20 40 E
Malmédy, Belgium 15 D6 50 25N 6 2 E
Malmesbury, S. Africa 56 E2 33 28S 18 41 E
Malmö, Sweden 9 J15 55 36N 12 59 E
Malolos, Phil. 37 B6 14 50N 120 49 E
Malombe L., Malawi 55 E4 14 40S 35 15 E
Malone, U.S.A. 79 B10 44 51N 74 18W
Måløy, Norway 9 F11 61 57N 5 6 E
Malozemelskaya Tundra, Russia 24 A9 67 0N 50 0 E
Malpaso, Canary Is. 22 G1 27 43N 18 3W
Malpelo, Colombia 92 C2 4 3N 81 35W
Malta, Idaho, U.S.A. 82 E7 42 18N 113 22W
Malta, Mont., U.S.A. 82 B10 48 21N 107 52W
Malta ■, Europe 23 D2 35 50N 14 30 E
Maltahöhe, Namibia 56 C2 24 55S 17 0 E
Malton, Canada 78 C5 43 42N 79 38W
Malton, U.K. 10 C7 54 8N 0 49W
Maluku, Indonesia 37 E7 1 0S 127 0 E
Maluku □, Indonesia 37 E7 3 0S 128 0 E
Maluku Sea = Molucca Sea, Indonesia 37 E6 2 0S 124 0 E
Malvan, India 40 L8 16 2N 73 30 E
Malvern, U.S.A. 81 H8 34 22N 92 49W
Malvern Hills, U.K. 11 E5 52 0N 2 19W
Malvinas, Is. = Falkland Is. □, Atl. Oc. 96 G5 51 30S 59 0W
Malya, Tanzania 54 C3 3 5S 33 38 E
Malyn, Ukraine 17 C15 50 46N 29 3 E

Melchor Ocampo

Melchor Ocampo, *Mexico* **86 C4** 24 52N 101 40W
Mélèzes →, *Canada* **69 C12** 57 30N 71 0W
Melfort, *Canada* **73 C8** 52 50N 104 37W
Melfort, *Zimbabwe* **55 F3** 18 0S 31 25 E
Melhus, *Norway* **8 E14** 63 17N 10 18 E
Melilla, *N. Afr.* **19 E4** 35 21N 2 57W
Melipilla, *Chile* **94 C1** 33 42S 71 15W
Mélissa, Ákra, *Greece* **23 D6** 35 6N 24 33 E
Melita, *Canada* **73 D8** 49 15N 101 0W
Melitopol, *Ukraine* **25 E6** 46 50N 35 22 E
Melk, *Austria* **16 D8** 48 13N 15 20 E
Mellansel, *Sweden* **8 E18** 63 25N 18 17 E
Mellen, *U.S.A.* **80 B9** 46 20N 90 40W
Mellerud, *Sweden* **9 G15** 58 41N 12 28 E
Mellette, *U.S.A.* **80 C5** 45 9N 98 30W
Mellieha, *Malta* **23 D1** 35 57N 14 21 E
Melo, *Uruguay* **95 C5** 32 20S 54 10W
Melolo, *Indonesia* **37 F6** 9 53S 120 40 E
Melouprey, *Cambodia* **38 F5** 13 48N 105 16 E
Melrose, *N.S.W., Australia* **63 E4** 32 42S 146 57 E
Melrose, *W. Austral., Australia* **61 E3** 27 50S 121 15 E
Melrose, *U.K.* **12 F6** 55 36N 2 43W
Melrose, *U.S.A.* **81 H3** 34 26N 103 38W
Melstone, *U.S.A.* **82 C10** 46 36N 107 52W
Melton Mowbray, *U.K.* **10 E7** 52 47N 0 54W
Melun, *France* **18 B5** 48 32N 2 39 E
Melville, *Canada* **73 C8** 50 55N 102 50W
Melville, C., *Australia* **62 A3** 14 11S 144 30 E
Melville, L., *Canada* **71 B8** 53 30N 60 0W
Melville B., *Australia* **62 A2** 12 0S 136 45 E
Melville I., *Australia* **60 B5** 11 30S 131 0 E
Melville I., *Canada* **66 B8** 75 30N 112 0W
Melville Pen., *Canada* **69 B11** 68 0N 84 0W
Melvin →, *Canada* **72 B5** 59 11N 117 31W
Memba, *Mozam.* **55 E5** 14 11S 40 30 E
Memboro, *Indonesia* **37 F5** 9 30S 119 30 E
Memel = Klaipėda, *Lithuania* **24 C3** 55 43N 21 10 E
Memel, *S. Africa* **57 D4** 27 38S 29 36 E
Memmingen, *Germany* **16 E6** 47 58N 10 10 E
Mempawah, *Indonesia* **36 D3** 0 30N 109 5 E
Memphis, *Tenn., U.S.A.* **81 H10** 35 8N 90 3W
Memphis, *Tex., U.S.A.* **81 H4** 34 44N 100 33W
Mena, *U.S.A.* **81 H7** 34 35N 94 15W
Menai Strait, *U.K.* **10 D3** 53 11N 4 13W
Ménaka, *Mali* **50 E6** 15 59N 2 18 E
Menan = Chao Phraya →, *Thailand* **38 F3** 13 32N 100 36 E
Menarandra →, *Madag.* **57 D7** 25 17S 44 30 E
Menard, *U.S.A.* **81 K5** 30 55N 99 47W
Menasha, *U.S.A.* **76 C1** 44 13N 88 26W
Mendawai →, *Indonesia* **36 E4** 3 30S 113 0 E
Mende, *France* **18 D5** 44 31N 3 30 E
Mendez, *Mexico* **87 B5** 25 7N 98 34W
Mendhar, *India* **43 C6** 33 35N 74 10 E
Mendip Hills, *U.K.* **11 F5** 51 17N 2 40W
Mendocino, *U.S.A.* **82 G2** 39 19N 123 48W
Mendocino, C., *U.S.A.* **82 F1** 40 26N 124 25W
Mendota, *Calif., U.S.A.* **84 J6** 36 45N 120 23W
Mendota, *Ill., U.S.A.* **80 E10** 41 33N 89 7W
Mendoza, *Argentina* **94 C2** 32 50S 68 52W
Mendoza □, *Argentina* **94 C2** 33 0S 69 0W
Mene Grande, *Venezuela* **92 B4** 9 49N 70 56W
Menemen, *Turkey* **21 E12** 38 34N 27 3 E
Menen, *Belgium* **15 D3** 50 47N 3 7 E
Menggala, *Indonesia* **36 E3** 4 30S 105 15 E
Mengjin, *China* **34 G7** 34 55N 112 45 E
Mengyin, *China* **35 G9** 35 40N 117 58 E
Mengzi, *China* **32 D5** 23 20N 103 22 E
Menihek L., *Canada* **71 B6** 54 0N 67 0W
Menin = Menen, *Belgium* **15 D3** 50 47N 3 7 E
Menindee, *Australia* **63 E3** 32 20S 142 25 E
Menindee L., *Australia* **63 E3** 32 20S 142 25 E
Meningie, *Australia* **63 F2** 35 50S 139 18 E
Menlo Park, *U.S.A.* **84 H4** 37 27N 122 12W
Menominee, *U.S.A.* **76 C2** 45 6N 87 37W
Menominee →, *U.S.A.* **76 C2** 45 6N 87 36W
Menomonie, *U.S.A.* **80 C9** 44 53N 91 55W
Menongue, *Angola* **53 G3** 14 48S 17 52 E
Menorca, *Spain* **22 B11** 40 0N 4 0 E
Mentakab, *Malaysia* **39 L4** 3 29N 102 21 E
Mentawai, Kepulauan, *Indonesia* **36 E1** 2 0S 99 0 E
Menton, *France* **18 E7** 43 50N 7 29 E
Mentor, *U.S.A.* **78 E3** 41 40N 81 21W
Menzelinsk, *Russia* **24 C9** 55 47N 53 11 E
Menzies, *Australia* **61 E3** 29 40S 121 2 E
Me'ona, *Israel* **47 B4** 33 1N 35 15 E
Meoqui, *Mexico* **86 B3** 28 17N 105 29W
Mepaco, *Mozam.* **55 F3** 15 57S 30 48 E
Meppel, *Neths.* **15 B6** 52 42N 6 12 E
Mer Rouge, *U.S.A.* **81 J9** 32 47N 91 48W
Merabéllou, Kólpos, *Greece* **23 D7** 35 10N 25 50 E
Meramangye, L., *Australia* **61 E5** 28 25S 132 13 E
Meran = Merano, *Italy* **20 A4** 46 40N 11 9 E
Merano, *Italy* **20 A4** 46 40N 11 9 E
Merauke, *Indonesia* **37 F10** 8 29S 140 24 E
Merbein, *Australia* **63 E3** 34 10S 142 2 E
Merca, *Somali Rep.* **46 G3** 1 48N 44 50 E
Merced, *U.S.A.* **84 H6** 37 18N 120 29W
Merced Pk., *U.S.A.* **84 H7** 37 36N 119 24W
Mercedes, *Buenos Aires, Argentina* **94 C4** 34 40S 59 30W
Mercedes, *Corrientes, Argentina* **94 B4** 29 10S 58 5W
Mercedes, *San Luis, Argentina* **94 C2** 33 40S 65 21W
Mercedes, *Uruguay* **94 C4** 33 12S 58 0W
Merceditas, *Chile* **94 B1** 28 20S 70 35W
Mercer, *N.Z.* **59 G5** 37 16S 175 5 E
Mercer, *U.S.A.* **78 E4** 41 14N 80 15W
Mercury, *U.S.A.* **85 J11** 36 40N 115 58W
Mercy C., *Canada* **69 B13** 65 0N 63 30W
Mere, *U.K.* **11 F5** 51 6N 2 16W
Meredith, C., *Falk. Is.* **96 G4** 52 15S 60 40W
Meredith, L., *U.S.A.* **81 H4** 35 43N 101 33W
Mergui, *Burma* **38 F2** 12 26N 98 34 E
Mergui Arch. = Myeik Kyunzu, *Burma* **39 G1** 11 30N 97 30 E
Mérida, *Mexico* **87 C7** 20 58N 89 37W
Mérida, *Spain* **19 C2** 38 55N 6 25W
Mérida, *Venezuela* **92 B4** 8 24N 71 8W
Mérida, Cord. de, *Venezuela* **90 C3** 9 0N 71 0W
Meriden, *U.K.* **11 E6** 52 26N 1 38W
Meriden, *U.S.A.* **79 E12** 41 32N 72 48W
Meridian, *Calif., U.S.A.* **84 F5** 39 9N 121 55W
Meridian, *Idaho, U.S.A.* **82 E5** 43 37N 116 24W
Meridian, *Miss., U.S.A.* **77 J1** 32 22N 88 42W
Meridian, *Tex., U.S.A.* **81 K6** 31 56N 97 39W
Meriruma, *Brazil* **93 C8** 1 15N 54 50W
Merkel, *U.S.A.* **81 J5** 32 28N 100 1W
Mermaid Reef, *Australia* **60 C2** 17 6S 119 36 E
Merredin, *Australia* **61 F2** 31 28S 118 18 E
Merrick, *U.K.* **12 F4** 55 8N 4 28W
Merrickville, *Canada* **79 B9** 44 55N 75 50W
Merrill, *Oreg., U.S.A.* **82 E3** 42 1N 121 36W
Merrill, *Wis., U.S.A.* **80 C10** 45 11N 89 41W
Merriman, *U.S.A.* **80 D4** 42 55N 101 42W
Merritt, *Canada* **72 C4** 50 10N 120 45W
Merriwa, *Australia* **63 E5** 32 6S 150 22 E
Merriwagga, *Australia* **63 E4** 33 47S 145 43 E
Merry I., *Canada* **70 A4** 55 29N 77 31W
Merrygoen, *Australia* **63 E4** 31 51S 149 12 E
Merryville, *U.S.A.* **81 K8** 30 45N 93 33W
Mersch, *Lux.* **15 E6** 49 44N 6 7 E
Mersea I., *U.K.* **11 F8** 51 47N 0 58 E
Merseburg, *Germany* **16 C6** 51 22N 11 59 E
Mersey →, *U.K.* **10 D4** 53 25N 3 1W
Merseyside □, *U.K.* **10 D4** 53 31N 3 2W
Mersin, *Turkey* **25 G5** 36 51N 34 36 E
Mersing, *Malaysia* **39 L4** 2 25N 103 50 E
Merta, *India* **42 F6** 26 39N 74 4 E
Merthyr Tydfil, *U.K.* **11 F4** 51 45N 3 22W
Merthyr Tydfil □, *U.K.* **11 F4** 51 46N 3 21W
Mértola, *Portugal* **19 D2** 37 40N 7 40W
Mertzon, *U.S.A.* **81 K4** 31 16N 100 49W
Meru, *Kenya* **54 B4** 0 3N 37 40 E
Meru, *Tanzania* **54 C4** 3 15S 36 46 E
Meru □, *Kenya* **54 B4** 0 3N 37 46 E
Mesa, *U.S.A.* **83 K8** 33 25N 111 50W
Mesanagrós, *Greece* **23 C9** 36 1N 27 49 E
Mesaoría □, *Cyprus* **23 D12** 35 12N 33 14 E
Mesarás, Kólpos, *Greece* **23 D6** 35 6N 24 47 E
Mesgouez, L., *Canada* **70 B5** 51 20N 75 0W
Meshed = Mashhad, *Iran* **45 B8** 36 20N 59 35 E
Meshoppen, *U.S.A.* **79 E8** 41 36N 76 3W
Mesick, *U.S.A.* **76 C3** 44 24N 85 43W
Mesilinka →, *Canada* **72 B4** 56 6N 124 30W
Mesilla, *U.S.A.* **83 K10** 32 16N 106 48W
Mesolóngion, *Greece* **21 E9** 38 21N 21 28 E
Mesopotamia = Al Jazirah, *Iraq* **44 C5** 33 30N 44 0 E
Mesquite, *U.S.A.* **83 H6** 36 47N 114 6W
Mess Cr. →, *Canada* **72 B2** 57 55N 131 14W
Messalo →, *Mozam.* **55 E4** 12 25S 39 15 E
Messina, *Italy* **20 E6** 38 11N 15 34 E
Messina, *S. Africa* **57 C5** 22 20S 30 5 E
Messina, Str. di, *Italy* **20 F6** 38 15N 15 35 E
Messíni, *Greece* **21 F10** 37 4N 22 1 E
Messiniakós Kólpos, *Greece* **21 F10** 36 45N 22 5 E
Messonghi, *Greece* **23 B3** 39 29N 19 56 E
Mesta →, *Bulgaria* **21 D11** 40 54N 24 49 E
Meta →, *S. Amer.* **92 B5** 6 12N 67 28W
Metairie, *U.S.A.* **81 L9** 29 58N 90 10W
Metaline Falls, *U.S.A.* **82 B5** 48 52N 117 22W
Metán, *Argentina* **94 B3** 25 30S 65 0W
Metangula, *Mozam.* **55 E3** 12 40S 34 50 E
Metengobalame, *Mozam.* **55 E3** 14 49S 34 30 E
Methven, *N.Z.* **59 K3** 43 38S 171 40 E
Methy L., *Canada* **73 B7** 56 28N 109 30W
Metil, *Mozam.* **55 F4** 16 24S 39 0 E
Metlakatla, *U.S.A.* **72 B2** 55 8N 131 35W
Metropolis, *U.S.A.* **81 G10** 37 9N 88 44W
Mettur Dam, *India* **40 P10** 11 45N 77 45 E
Metz, *France* **18 B7** 49 8N 6 10 E
Meulaboh, *Indonesia* **36 D1** 4 11N 96 3 E
Meureudu, *Indonesia* **36 C1** 5 19N 96 10 E
Meuse →, *Europe* **18 A6** 50 45N 5 41 E
Mexia, *U.S.A.* **81 K6** 31 41N 96 29W
Mexiana, I., *Brazil* **93 D9** 0 0 49 30W
Mexicali, *Mexico* **86 A1** 32 40N 115 30W
Mexican Plateau, *Mexico* **66 G9** 25 0N 104 0W
México, *Mexico* **87 D5** 19 20N 99 10W
Mexico, *Maine, U.S.A.* **79 B14** 44 34N 70 33W
Mexico, *Mo., U.S.A.* **80 F9** 39 10N 91 53W
México □, *Mexico* **86 D5** 19 20N 99 10W
Mexico ■, *Cent. Amer.* **86 C4** 25 0N 105 0W
Mexico, G. of, *Cent. Amer.* **87 C7** 25 0N 90 0W
Meymaneh, *Afghan.* **40 B4** 35 53N 64 38 E
Mezen, *Russia* **24 A7** 65 50N 44 20 E
Mezen →, *Russia* **24 A7** 65 44N 44 22 E
Mézenc, Mt., *France* **18 D6** 44 54N 4 11 E
Mezőkövesd, *Hungary* **17 E11** 47 49N 20 35 E
Mezőtúr, *Hungary* **17 E11** 47 1N 20 41 E
Mezquital, *Mexico* **86 C4** 23 29N 104 23W
Mgeta, *Tanzania* **55 D4** 8 22S 36 6 E
Mhlaba Hills, *Zimbabwe* **55 F3** 18 30S 30 30 E
Mhow, *India* **42 H6** 22 33N 75 50 E
Miahuatlán, *Mexico* **87 D5** 16 21N 96 36W
Miallo, *Australia* **62 B4** 16 28S 145 22 E
Miami, *Ariz., U.S.A.* **83 K8** 33 24N 110 52W
Miami, *Fla., U.S.A.* **77 N5** 25 47N 80 11W
Miami, *Tex., U.S.A.* **81 H4** 35 42N 100 38W
Miami →, *U.S.A.* **76 F3** 39 20N 84 40W
Miami Beach, *U.S.A.* **77 N5** 25 47N 80 8W
Mian Xian, *China* **34 H4** 33 10N 106 32 E
Mianchi, *China* **34 G6** 34 48N 111 48 E
Mīāndowāb, *Iran* **44 B5** 37 0N 46 5 E
Miandrivazo, *Madag.* **57 B8** 19 31S 45 29 E
Mīāneh, *Iran* **44 B5** 37 30N 47 40 E
Mianwali, *Pakistan* **42 C4** 32 38N 71 28 E
Miarinarivo, *Madag.* **57 B8** 18 57S 46 55 E
Miass, *Russia* **24 D11** 54 59N 60 6 E
Michalovce, *Slovak Rep.* **17 D11** 48 47N 21 58 E
Michigan □, *U.S.A.* **76 C3** 44 0N 85 0W
Michigan, L., *U.S.A.* **76 D2** 44 0N 87 0W
Michigan City, *U.S.A.* **76 E2** 41 43N 86 54W
Michikamau L., *Canada* **71 B7** 54 20N 63 10W
Michipicoten, *Canada* **70 C3** 47 55N 84 55W
Michipicoten I., *Canada* **70 C2** 47 40N 85 40W
Michoacan □, *Mexico* **86 D4** 19 0N 102 0W
Michurin, *Bulgaria* **21 C12** 42 9N 27 51 E
Michurinsk, *Russia* **24 D7** 52 58N 40 27 E
Miclere, *Australia* **62 C4** 22 34S 147 32 E
Mico, Pta., *Nic.* **88 D3** 12 0N 83 30W
Micronesia, Federated States of ■, *Pac. Oc.* **64 G7** 9 0N 150 0 E
Midai, *Indonesia* **39 L6** 3 0N 107 47 E
Midale, *Canada* **73 D8** 49 25N 103 20W
Middelburg, *Neths.* **15 C3** 51 30N 3 36 E
Middelburg, *Eastern Cape, S. Africa* **56 E4** 31 30S 25 0 E
Middelburg, *Mpumalanga, S. Africa* **57 D4** 25 49S 29 28 E
Middelwit, *S. Africa* **56 C4** 24 51S 27 3 E
Middle Alkali L., *U.S.A.* **82 F3** 41 27N 120 5W
Middle Fork Feather →, *U.S.A.* **84 F5** 38 33N 121 30W
Middle I., *Australia* **61 F3** 34 6S 123 11 E
Middle Loup →, *U.S.A.* **80 E5** 41 17N 98 24W
Middleboro, *U.S.A.* **79 E14** 41 54N 70 55W
Middleburg, *N.Y., U.S.A.* **79 D10** 42 36N 74 20W
Middleburg, *Pa., U.S.A.* **78 F7** 40 47N 77 3W
Middlebury, *U.S.A.* **79 B11** 44 1N 73 10W
Middleport, *U.S.A.* **76 F4** 39 0N 82 3W
Middlesboro, *U.S.A.* **77 G4** 36 36N 83 43W
Middlesbrough, *U.K.* **10 C6** 54 35N 1 13W
Middlesbrough □, *U.K.* **10 C6** 54 28N 1 13W
Middlesex, *Belize* **88 C2** 17 2N 88 31W
Middlesex, *U.S.A.* **79 F10** 40 36N 74 30W
Middleton, *Australia* **62 C3** 22 22S 141 32 E
Middleton, *Canada* **71 D6** 44 57N 65 4W
Middletown, *U.K.* **13 B5** 54 17N 6 51W
Middletown, *Calif., U.S.A.* **84 G4** 38 45N 122 37W
Middletown, *Conn., U.S.A.* **79 E12** 41 34N 72 39W
Middletown, *N.Y., U.S.A.* **79 E10** 41 27N 74 25W
Middletown, *Ohio, U.S.A.* **76 F3** 39 31N 84 24W
Middletown, *Pa., U.S.A.* **79 F8** 40 12N 76 44W
Midhurst, *U.K.* **11 G7** 50 59N 0 44W
Midi, Canal du →, *France* **18 E4** 43 45N 1 21 E
Midland, *Canada* **70 D4** 44 45N 79 50W
Midland, *Calif., U.S.A.* **85 M12** 33 52N 114 48W
Midland, *Mich., U.S.A.* **76 D3** 43 37N 84 14W
Midland, *Pa., U.S.A.* **78 F4** 40 39N 80 27W
Midland, *Tex., U.S.A.* **81 K3** 32 0N 102 3W
Midlands □, *Zimbabwe* **55 F2** 19 40S 29 0 E
Midleton, *Ireland* **13 E3** 51 55N 8 10W
Midlothian, *U.S.A.* **81 J6** 32 30N 97 0W
Midlothian □, *U.K.* **12 F5** 55 51N 3 5W
Midongy, Tangorombohitr' i, *Madag.* **57 C8** 23 30S 47 0 E
Midongy Atsimo, *Madag.* **57 C8** 23 35S 47 1 E
Midway Is., *Pac. Oc.* **64 E10** 28 13N 177 22W
Midway Wells, *U.S.A.* **85 N11** 32 41N 115 7W
Midwest, *U.S.A.* **75 B9** 42 0N 90 0W
Midwest, *Wyo., U.S.A.* **82 E10** 43 25N 106 16W
Midwest City, *U.S.A.* **81 H6** 35 27N 97 24W
Midzŏr, *Bulgaria* **21 C10** 43 24N 22 40 E
Mie □, *Japan* **31 G8** 34 30N 136 10 E
Międzychód, *Poland* **16 B8** 52 35N 15 53 E
Międzyrzec Podlaski, *Poland* **17 C12** 51 58N 22 45 E
Mielec, *Poland* **17 C11** 50 15N 21 25 E
Mienga, *Angola* **56 B2** 17 12S 19 48 E
Miercurea-Ciuc, *Romania* **17 E13** 46 21N 25 48 E
Mieres, *Spain* **19 A3** 43 18N 5 48W
Mifflintown, *U.S.A.* **78 F7** 40 34N 77 24W
Mifraz Hefa, *Israel* **47 C4** 32 52N 35 0 E
Miguel Alemán, Presa, *Mexico* **87 D5** 18 15N 96 40W
Mihara, *Japan* **31 G6** 34 24N 133 5 E
Mikese, *Tanzania* **54 D4** 6 48S 37 55 E
Mikhaylovgrad = Montana, *Bulgaria* **21 C10** 43 27N 23 16 E
Mikkeli, *Finland* **9 F22** 61 43N 27 15 E
Mikkwa →, *Canada* **72 B6** 58 25N 114 46W
Mikumi, *Tanzania* **54 D4** 7 26S 37 0 E
Mikun, *Russia* **24 B9** 62 20N 50 0 E
Milaca, *U.S.A.* **80 C8** 45 45N 93 39W
Milagro, *Ecuador* **92 D3** 2 11S 79 36W
Milan = Milano, *Italy* **18 D8** 45 28N 9 12 E
Milan, *Mo., U.S.A.* **80 E8** 40 12N 93 7W
Milan, *Tenn., U.S.A.* **77 H1** 35 55N 88 46W
Milang, *Australia* **63 E2** 32 2S 139 10 E
Milange, *Mozam.* **55 F4** 16 3S 35 45 E
Milano, *Italy* **18 D8** 45 28N 9 12 E
Milâs, *Turkey* **25 G4** 37 20N 27 50 E
Milatos, *Greece* **23 D7** 35 18N 25 34 E
Milazzo, *Italy* **20 E6** 38 13N 15 15 E
Milbank, *U.S.A.* **80 C6** 45 13N 96 38W
Milden, *Canada* **73 C7** 51 29N 107 32W
Mildenhall, *U.K.* **11 E8** 52 21N 0 32 E
Mildmay, *Canada* **78 B3** 44 3N 81 7W
Mildura, *Australia* **63 E3** 34 13S 142 9 E
Miles, *Australia* **63 D5** 26 40S 150 9 E
Miles, *U.S.A.* **81 K4** 31 36N 100 11W
Miles City, *U.S.A.* **80 B2** 46 25N 105 51W
Milestone, *Canada* **73 D8** 49 59N 104 31W
Miletus, *Turkey* **21 F12** 37 30N 27 18 E
Mileura, *Australia* **61 E2** 26 22S 117 20 E
Milford, *Calif., U.S.A.* **84 E6** 40 10N 120 22W
Milford, *Conn., U.S.A.* **79 E11** 41 14N 73 3W
Milford, *Del., U.S.A.* **76 F8** 38 55N 75 26W
Milford, *Mass., U.S.A.* **79 D13** 42 8N 71 31W
Milford, *Pa., U.S.A.* **79 E10** 41 19N 74 48W
Milford, *Utah, U.S.A.* **83 G7** 38 24N 113 1W
Milford Haven, *U.K.* **11 F2** 51 42N 5 7W
Milford Sd., *N.Z.* **59 L1** 44 41S 167 47 E
Milgun, *Australia* **61 D2** 24 56S 118 18 E
Milḩ, Baḩr al, *Iraq* **44 C4** 32 40N 43 35 E
Miling, *Australia* **61 F2** 30 30S 116 17 E
Milk →, *U.S.A.* **82 B10** 48 4N 106 19W
Milk River, *Canada* **72 D6** 49 10N 112 5W
Mill City, *U.S.A.* **82 D2** 44 45N 122 29W
Mill I., *Antarctica* **5 C8** 66 0S 101 30 E
Mill Valley, *U.S.A.* **84 H4** 37 54N 122 32W
Millau, *France* **18 D5** 44 8N 3 4 E
Millbridge, *Canada* **78 B7** 44 41N 77 36W
Millbrook, *Canada* **78 B6** 44 10N 78 29W
Mille Lacs, L. des, *Canada* **70 C1** 48 45N 90 35W
Mille Lacs L., *U.S.A.* **80 B8** 46 15N 93 39W
Milledgeville, *U.S.A.* **77 J4** 33 5N 83 14W
Millen, *U.S.A.* **77 J5** 32 48N 81 57W
Miller, *U.S.A.* **80 C5** 44 31N 98 59W
Millersburg, *Ohio, U.S.A.* **78 F3** 40 33N 81 55W
Millersburg, *Pa., U.S.A.* **78 F8** 40 32N 76 58W
Millerton, *U.S.A.* **79 E11** 41 57N 73 31W
Millerton L., *U.S.A.* **84 J7** 37 1N 119 41W
Millicent, *Australia* **63 F3** 37 34S 140 21 E
Millinocket, *U.S.A.* **71 C6** 45 39N 68 43W
Millmerran, *Australia* **63 D5** 27 53S 151 16 E
Millom, *U.K.* **10 C4** 54 13N 3 16W
Mills L., *Canada* **72 A5** 61 30N 118 20W
Millsboro, *U.S.A.* **78 G5** 40 0N 80 0W
Milltown Malbay, *Ireland* **13 D2** 52 52N 9 24W
Millville, *U.S.A.* **76 F8** 39 24N 75 2W
Millwood L., *U.S.A.* **81 J8** 33 42N 93 58W
Milne →, *Australia* **62 C2** 21 10S 137 33 E
Milnor, *U.S.A.* **80 B6** 46 16N 97 27W
Milo, *Canada* **72 C6** 50 34N 112 53W
Mílos, *Greece* **21 F11** 36 44N 24 25 E
Milparinka P.O., *Australia* **63 D3** 29 46S 141 57 E
Milton, *Canada* **78 C5** 43 31N 79 53W
Milton, *N.Z.* **59 M2** 46 7S 169 59 E
Milton, *Calif., U.S.A.* **84 G6** 38 3N 120 51W
Milton, *Fla., U.S.A.* **77 K2** 30 38N 87 3W
Milton, *Pa., U.S.A.* **78 F8** 41 1N 76 51W
Milton-Freewater, *U.S.A.* **82 D4** 45 56N 118 23W
Milton Keynes, *U.K.* **11 E7** 52 1N 0 44W
Milton Keynes □, *U.K.* **11 E7** 52 1N 0 44W
Milverton, *Canada* **78 C4** 43 34N 80 55W
Milwaukee, *U.S.A.* **76 D2** 43 2N 87 55W
Milwaukee Deep, *Atl. Oc.* **89 C6** 19 50N 68 0W
Milwaukie, *U.S.A.* **84 E4** 45 27N 122 38W
Min Jiang →, *Fujian, China* **33 D6** 26 0N 119 35 E
Min Jiang →, *Sichuan, China* **32 D5** 28 45N 104 40 E
Min Xian, *China* **34 G3** 34 25N 104 5 E
Mina, *U.S.A.* **83 G4** 38 24N 118 7W
Mina Pirquitas, *Argentina* **94 A2** 22 40S 66 30W
Mīnā Su'ud, *Si. Arabia* **45 D6** 28 45N 48 28 E
Mīnā'al Aḩmadī, *Kuwait* **45 D6** 29 5N 48 10 E
Mīnāb, *Iran* **45 E8** 27 10N 57 1 E
Minago →, *Canada* **73 C9** 54 33N 98 59W
Minaki, *Canada* **73 D10** 49 59N 94 40W
Minamata, *Japan* **31 H5** 32 10N 130 30 E
Minami-Tori-Shima, *Pac. Oc.* **64 E7** 24 0N 153 45 E
Minas, *Uruguay* **95 C4** 34 20S 55 10W
Minas, Sierra de las, *Guatemala* **88 C2** 15 9N 89 31W
Minas Basin, *Canada* **71 C7** 45 20N 64 12W
Minas Gerais □, *Brazil* **93 G9** 18 50S 46 0W
Minatitlán, *Mexico* **87 D6** 17 59N 94 31W
Minbu, *Burma* **41 J19** 20 10N 94 52 E
Mindanao, *Phil.* **37 C7** 8 0N 125 0 E
Mindanao Sea = Bohol Sea, *Phil.* **37 C6** 9 0N 124 0 E
Mindanao Trench, *Pac. Oc.* **37 B7** 12 0N 126 6 E
Minden, *Canada* **78 B6** 44 55N 78 43W
Minden, *Germany* **16 B5** 52 17N 8 55 E
Minden, *La., U.S.A.* **81 J8** 32 37N 93 17W
Minden, *Nev., U.S.A.* **84 G7** 38 57N 119 46W
Mindiptana, *Indonesia* **37 F10** 5 55S 140 22 E
Mindoro, *Phil.* **37 B6** 13 0N 121 0 E
Mindoro Str., *Phil.* **37 B6** 12 30N 120 30 E
Mine, *Japan* **31 G5** 34 12N 131 7 E
Minehead, *U.K.* **11 F4** 51 12N 3 29W
Mineola, *U.S.A.* **81 J7** 32 40N 95 29W
Mineral King, *U.S.A.* **84 J8** 36 27N 118 36W
Mineral Wells, *U.S.A.* **81 J5** 32 48N 98 7W
Minersville, *Pa., U.S.A.* **79 F8** 40 41N 76 16W
Minersville, *Utah, U.S.A.* **83 G7** 38 13N 112 56W
Minerva, *U.S.A.* **78 F3** 40 44N 81 6W
Minetto, *U.S.A.* **79 C8** 43 24N 76 28W
Mingäçevir Su Anbarı, *Azerbaijan* **25 F8** 40 57N 46 50 E
Mingan, *Canada* **71 B7** 50 20N 64 0W
Mingechaurskoye Vdkhr. = Mingäçevir Su Anbarı, *Azerbaijan* **25 F8** 40 57N 46 50 E
Mingela, *Australia* **62 B4** 19 52S 146 38 E
Mingenew, *Australia* **61 E2** 29 12S 115 21 E
Mingera Cr. →, *Australia* **62 C2** 20 38S 137 45 E
Mingin, *Burma* **41 H19** 22 50N 94 30 E
Mingt'iehkaitafan = Mintaka Pass, *Pakistan* **43 A6** 37 0N 74 58 E
Mingyuegue, *China* **35 C15** 43 2N 128 50 E
Minho = Miño →, *Spain* **19 A2** 41 52N 8 40W
Minho, *Portugal* **19 B1** 41 25N 8 20W
Minidoka, *U.S.A.* **82 E7** 42 45N 113 29W
Minigwal, L., *Australia* **61 E3** 29 31S 123 14 E
Minilya, *Australia* **61 D1** 23 55S 114 0 E
Minilya →, *Australia* **61 D1** 23 45S 114 0 E
Minipi, L., *Canada* **71 B7** 52 25N 60 45W
Mink L., *Canada* **72 A5** 61 54N 117 40W
Minna, *Nigeria* **50 G7** 9 37N 6 30 E
Minneapolis, *Kans., U.S.A.* **80 F6** 39 8N 97 42W
Minneapolis, *Minn., U.S.A.* **80 C8** 44 59N 93 16W
Minnedosa, *Canada* **73 C9** 50 14N 99 50W
Minnesota □, *U.S.A.* **80 B8** 46 0N 94 15W
Minnie Creek, *Australia* **61 D2** 24 3S 115 42 E
Minnipa, *Australia* **63 E2** 32 51S 135 9 E
Minnitaki L., *Canada* **70 C1** 49 57N 92 10W
Mino, *Japan* **31 G8** 35 32N 136 55 E
Miño →, *Spain* **19 A2** 41 52N 8 40W
Minorca = Menorca, *Spain* **22 B11** 40 0N 4 0 E
Minore, *Australia* **63 E4** 32 14S 148 27 E
Minot, *U.S.A.* **80 A4** 48 14N 101 18W
Minqin, *China* **34 E2** 38 38N 103 20 E
Minsk, *Belarus* **24 D4** 53 52N 27 30 E
Mińsk Mazowiecki, *Poland* **17 B11** 52 10N 21 33 E
Mintaka Pass, *Pakistan* **43 A6** 37 0N 74 58 E
Minton, *Canada* **73 D8** 49 10N 104 35W
Minturn, *U.S.A.* **82 G10** 39 35N 106 26W
Minusinsk, *Russia* **27 D10** 53 43N 91 20 E
Minutang, *India* **41 E20** 28 15N 96 30 E
Mīr Kūh, *Iran* **45 E8** 26 22N 58 55 E
Mīr Shahdād, *Iran* **45 E8** 26 15N 58 29 E
Mira, *Italy* **20 B5** 45 26N 12 8 E
Mira por vos Cay, *Bahamas* **89 B5** 22 9N 74 30W
Miraj, *India* **40 L9** 16 50N 74 45 E
Miram Shah, *Pakistan* **42 C4** 33 0N 70 2 E
Miramar, *Argentina* **94 D4** 38 15S 57 50W

Moores Res.

Miramar, Mozam. 57 C6 23 50S 35 35 E
Miramichi B., Canada 71 C7 47 15N 65 0W
Miranda, Brazil 93 H7 20 10S 56 15W
Miranda →, Brazil 92 G7 19 25S 57 20W
Miranda de Ebro, Spain 19 A4 42 41N 2 57W
Miranda do Douro, Portugal 19 B2 41 30N 6 16W
Mirando City, U.S.A. 81 M5 27 26N 99 0W
Mirandópolis, Brazil 95 A5 21 9S 51 6W
Mirango, Malawi 55 E3 13 32S 34 58 E
Mirani, Australia 62 C4 21 9S 148 53 E
Mirassol, Brazil 95 A6 20 46S 49 28W
Mirbāţ, Oman 46 D5 17 0N 54 45 E
Miri, Malaysia 36 D4 4 23N 113 59 E
Miriam Vale, Australia 62 C5 24 20S 151 33 E
Mirim, L., S. Amer. 95 C5 32 45S 52 50W
Mirnyy, Russia 27 C12 62 33N 113 53 E
Mirond L., Canada 73 B8 55 6N 102 47W
Mirpur, Pakistan 43 C5 33 32N 73 56 E
Mirpur Bibiwari, Pakistan 42 E2 28 33N 67 44 E
Mirpur Khas, Pakistan 42 G3 25 30N 69 0 E
Mirpur Sakro, Pakistan 42 G2 24 33N 67 41 E
Mirror, Canada 72 C6 52 30N 113 7W
Miryang, S. Korea 35 G15 35 31N 128 44 E
Mirzapur, India 43 G10 25 10N 82 34 E
Mirzapur-cum-Vindhyachal = Mirzapur, India 43 G10 25 10N 82 34 E
Misantla, Mexico 87 D5 19 56N 96 50W
Misawa, Japan 30 D10 40 41N 141 24 E
Miscou I., Canada 71 C7 47 57N 64 31W
Mish'āb, Ra'as al, Si. Arabia 45 D6 28 15N 48 43 E
Mishan, China 33 B8 45 37N 131 48 E
Mishawaka, U.S.A. 76 E2 41 40N 86 11W
Mishima, Japan 31 G9 35 10N 138 52 E
Misión, Mexico 85 N10 32 6N 116 53W
Misiones □, Argentina 95 B5 27 0S 55 0W
Misiones □, Paraguay 94 B4 27 0S 56 0W
Miskah, Si. Arabia 44 E4 24 49N 42 56 E
Miskitos, Cayos, Nic. 88 D3 14 26N 82 50W
Miskolc, Hungary 17 D11 48 7N 20 50 E
Misoke, Dem. Rep. of the Congo 54 C2 0 42S 28 2 E
Misool, Indonesia 37 E8 1 52S 130 10 E
Misrātah, Libya 51 B9 32 24N 15 3 E
Missanabie, Canada 70 C3 48 20N 84 6W
Missinaibi →, Canada 70 B3 50 43N 81 29W
Missinaibi L., Canada 70 C3 48 23N 83 40W
Mission, S. Dak., U.S.A. 80 D4 43 18N 100 39W
Mission, Tex., U.S.A. 81 M5 26 13N 98 20W
Mission City, Canada 72 D4 49 10N 122 15W
Mission Viejo, U.S.A. 85 M9 33 36N 117 40W
Missisa L., Canada 70 B2 52 20N 85 7W
Mississagi →, Canada 70 C3 46 15N 83 9W
Mississippi □, U.S.A. 81 J10 33 0N 90 0W
Mississippi →, U.S.A. 81 L10 29 9N 89 15W
Mississippi L., Canada 79 A8 45 5N 76 10W
Mississippi River Delta, U.S.A. 81 L9 29 10N 89 15W
Mississippi Sd., U.S.A. 81 K10 30 20N 89 0W
Missoula, U.S.A. 82 C7 46 52N 114 1W
Missouri □, U.S.A. 80 F8 38 25N 92 30W
Missouri →, U.S.A. 80 F9 38 49N 90 7W
Missouri Valley, U.S.A. 80 E7 41 34N 95 53W
Mist, U.S.A. 84 E3 45 59N 123 15W
Mistake B., Canada 73 A10 62 8N 93 0W
Mistassini →, Canada 71 C5 48 42N 72 20W
Mistassini L., Canada 70 B5 51 0N 73 30W
Mistastin L., Canada 71 A7 55 57N 63 20W
Mistatim, Canada 73 C8 52 52N 103 22W
Misty L., Canada 73 B8 58 53N 101 40W
Misurata = Misrātah, Libya 51 B9 32 24N 15 3 E
Mitchell, Australia 63 D4 26 29S 147 58 E
Mitchell, Canada 78 C3 43 28N 81 12W
Mitchell, Ind., U.S.A. 76 F2 38 44N 86 28W
Mitchell, Nebr., U.S.A. 80 E3 41 57N 103 49W
Mitchell, Oreg., U.S.A. 82 D3 44 34N 120 9W
Mitchell, S. Dak., U.S.A. 80 D6 43 43N 98 2W
Mitchell →, Australia 62 B3 15 12S 141 35 E
Mitchell, Mt., U.S.A. 77 H4 35 46N 82 16W
Mitchell Ranges, Australia 62 A2 12 49S 135 36 E
Mitchelstown, Ireland 13 D3 52 15N 8 16W
Mitha Tiwana, Pakistan 42 C5 32 13N 72 6 E
Mitilíni, Greece 21 E12 39 6N 26 35 E
Mito, Japan 31 F10 36 20N 140 30 E
Mitrovica = Kosovska Mitrovica, Serbia, Yug. 21 C9 42 54N 20 52 E
Mitsinjo, Madag. 57 B8 16 1S 45 52 E
Mitsiwa, Eritrea 46 D2 15 35N 39 25 E
Mitsukaidō, Japan 31 F9 36 1N 139 59 E
Mittagong, Australia 63 E5 34 28S 150 29 E
Mitú, Colombia 92 C4 1 8N 70 3W
Mitumba, Tanzania 54 D3 7 8S 31 2 E
Mitumba, Mts., Dem. Rep. of the Congo 54 D2 7 0S 27 30 E
Mitwaba, Dem. Rep. of the Congo 55 D2 8 2S 27 17 E
Mityana, Uganda 54 B3 0 23N 32 2 E
Mixteco →, Mexico 87 D5 18 11N 98 30W
Miyagi □, Japan 30 E10 38 15N 140 45 E
Miyah, W. el →, Syria 44 C3 34 44N 39 57 E
Miyake-Jima, Japan 31 G9 34 5N 139 30 E
Miyako, Japan 30 E10 39 40N 141 59 E
Miyako-Jima, Japan 31 M2 24 45N 125 20 E
Miyako-Rettō, Japan 31 M2 24 24N 125 0 E
Miyakonojō, Japan 31 J5 31 40N 131 5 E
Miyanoura-Dake, Japan 31 J5 30 20N 130 31 E
Miyazaki, Japan 31 J5 31 56N 131 30 E
Miyazaki □, Japan 31 H5 32 30N 131 30 E
Miyazu, Japan 31 G7 35 35N 135 10 E
Miyet, Bahr el = Dead Sea, Asia 47 D4 31 30N 35 30 E
Miyoshi, Japan 31 G6 34 48N 132 51 E
Miyun, China 34 D9 40 28N 116 50 E
Miyun Shuiku, China 35 D9 40 30N 117 0 E
Mizdah, Libya 51 B8 31 30N 13 0 E
Mizen Hd., Cork, Ireland 13 E2 51 27N 9 50W
Mizen Hd., Wick., Ireland 13 D5 52 51N 6 4W
Mizhi, China 34 F6 37 47N 110 12 E
Mizoram □, India 41 H18 23 30N 92 40 E
Mizpe Ramon, Israel 47 E3 30 34N 34 49 E
Mizusawa, Japan 30 E10 39 8N 141 8 E
Mjölby, Sweden 9 G16 58 20N 15 10 E
Mjøsa, Norway 9 F14 60 40N 11 0 E
Mkata, Tanzania 54 D4 5 45S 38 20 E
Mkokotoni, Tanzania 54 D4 5 55S 39 15 E
Mkomazi, Tanzania 54 C4 4 40S 38 7 E
Mkomazi →, S. Africa 57 E5 30 12S 30 50 E
Mkulwe, Tanzania 55 D3 8 37S 32 20 E
Mkumbi, Ras, Tanzania 54 D4 7 38S 39 55 E
Mkushi, Zambia 55 E2 14 25S 29 15 E
Mkushi River, Zambia 55 E2 13 32S 29 45 E
Mkuze, S. Africa 57 D5 27 10S 32 0 E
Mladá Boleslav, Czech Rep. 16 C8 50 27N 14 53 E
Mlala Hills, Tanzania 54 D3 6 50S 31 40 E
Mlange = Mulanje, Malawi 55 F4 16 2S 35 33 E
Mława, Poland 17 B11 53 9N 20 25 E
Mljet, Croatia 20 C7 42 43N 17 30 E
Mmabatho, S. Africa 56 D4 25 49S 25 30 E
Mo i Rana, Norway 8 C16 66 20N 14 7 E
Moa, Indonesia 37 F7 8 0S 128 0 E
Moab, U.S.A. 83 G9 38 35N 109 33W
Moala, Fiji 59 D8 18 36S 179 53 E
Moalie Park, Australia 63 D3 29 42S 143 3 E
Moate, Ireland 13 C4 53 24N 7 44W
Moba, Dem. Rep. of the Congo 54 D2 7 0S 29 48 E
Mobārakābād, Iran 45 D7 28 24N 53 20 E
Mobārakīyeh, Iran 45 C6 32 23N 51 37 E
Mobaye, C.A.R. 52 D4 4 25N 21 5 E
Mobayi, Dem. Rep. of the Congo 52 D4 4 15N 21 8 E
Moberly, U.S.A. 80 F8 39 25N 92 26W
Moberly →, Canada 72 B4 56 12N 120 55W
Mobile, U.S.A. 77 K1 30 41N 88 3W
Mobile B., U.S.A. 77 K2 30 30N 88 0W
Mobridge, U.S.A. 80 C4 45 32N 100 26W
Mobutu Sese Seko, L. = Albert L., Africa 54 B3 1 30N 31 0 E
Moc Chau, Vietnam 38 B5 20 50N 104 38 E
Moc Hoa, Vietnam 39 G5 10 46N 105 56 E
Mocabe Kasari, Dem. Rep. of the Congo 55 D2 9 58S 26 12 E
Moçambique, Mozam. 55 F5 15 3S 40 42 E
Moçâmedes = Namibe, Angola 53 H2 15 7S 12 11 E
Mochudi, Botswana 56 C4 24 27S 26 7 E
Mocimboa da Praia, Mozam. 55 E5 11 25S 40 20 E
Moclips, U.S.A. 84 C2 47 14N 124 13W
Mocoa, Colombia 92 C3 1 7N 76 35W
Mococa, Brazil 95 A6 21 28S 47 0W
Mocorito, Mexico 86 B3 25 30N 107 53W
Moctezuma, Mexico 86 B3 29 50N 109 0W
Moctezuma →, Mexico 87 C5 21 59N 98 34W
Mocuba, Mozam. 55 F4 16 54S 36 57 E
Mocúzari, Presa, Mexico 86 B3 27 10N 109 10W
Modane, France 18 D7 45 12N 6 40 E
Modasa, India 42 H5 23 30N 73 21 E
Modder →, S. Africa 56 D3 29 2S 24 37 E
Modderrivier, S. Africa 56 D3 29 2S 24 38 E
Módena, Italy 20 B4 44 40N 10 55 E
Modena, U.S.A. 83 H7 37 48N 113 56W
Modesto, U.S.A. 84 H6 37 39N 121 0W
Módica, Italy 20 F6 36 52N 14 46 E
Moe, Australia 63 F4 38 12S 146 19 E
Moebase, Mozam. 55 F4 17 3S 38 41 E
Moengo, Surinam 93 B8 5 45N 54 20W
Moffat, U.K. 12 F5 55 21N 3 27W
Moga, India 42 D6 30 48N 75 8 E
Mogadishu = Muqdisho, Somali Rep. 46 G4 2 2N 45 25 E
Mogador = Essaouira, Morocco 50 B4 31 32N 9 42W
Mogalakwena →, S. Africa 57 C4 22 38S 28 40 E
Mogami →, Japan 30 E10 38 45N 140 0 E
Mogán, Canary Is. 22 G4 27 53N 15 43W
Mogaung, Burma 41 G20 25 20N 97 0 E
Mogi das Cruzes, Brazil 95 A6 23 31S 46 11W
Mogi-Guaçu →, Brazil 95 A6 20 53S 48 10W
Mogi-Mirim, Brazil 95 A6 22 29S 47 0W
Mogilev = Mahilyow, Belarus 24 D5 53 55N 30 18 E
Mogilev-Podolskiy = Mohyliv-Podilskyy, Ukraine 25 E4 48 26N 27 48 E
Mogincual, Mozam. 55 F5 15 35S 40 25 E
Mogocha, Russia 27 D12 53 40N 119 50 E
Mogok, Burma 41 H20 23 0N 96 40 E
Mogumber, Australia 61 F2 31 2S 116 3 E
Mohács, Hungary 17 F10 45 58N 18 41 E
Mohales Hoek, Lesotho 56 E4 30 7S 27 26 E
Mohall, U.S.A. 80 A4 48 46N 101 31W
Moḩammadābād, Iran 45 B8 37 52N 59 5 E
Mohave, L., U.S.A. 85 K12 35 12N 114 34W
Mohawk →, U.S.A. 79 D11 42 47N 73 41W
Mohoro, Tanzania 54 D4 8 6S 39 8 E
Mohyliv-Podilskyy, Ukraine 25 E4 48 26N 27 48 E
Moidart, L., U.K. 12 E3 56 47N 5 52W
Moires, Greece 23 D6 35 4N 24 56 E
Moisaküla, Estonia 9 G21 58 3N 25 12 E
Moisie, Canada 71 B6 50 12N 66 1W
Moisie →, Canada 71 B6 50 14N 66 5W
Mojave, U.S.A. 85 K8 35 3N 118 10W
Mojave Desert, U.S.A. 85 L10 35 0N 116 30W
Mojo, Bolivia 94 A2 21 48S 65 33W
Mojokerto, Indonesia 37 G15 7 28S 112 26 E
Mokai, N.Z. 59 H5 38 32S 175 56 E
Mokambo, Dem. Rep. of the Congo 55 E2 12 25S 28 20 E
Mokameh, India 43 G11 25 24N 85 55 E
Mokelumne →, U.S.A. 84 G5 38 13N 121 28W
Mokelumne Hill, U.S.A. 84 G6 38 18N 120 43W
Mokhós, Greece 23 D7 35 16N 25 27 E
Mokhotlong, Lesotho 57 D4 29 22S 29 2 E
Mokokchung, India 41 F19 26 15N 94 30 E
Mokpo, S. Korea 35 G14 34 50N 126 25 E
Mokra Gora, Serbia, Yug. 21 C9 42 50N 20 30 E
Mol, Belgium 15 C5 51 11N 5 5 E
Molchanovo, Russia 26 D9 57 40N 83 50 E
Mold, U.K. 10 D4 53 9N 3 8W
Moldavia = Moldova ■, Europe 25 E4 47 0N 28 0 E
Molde, Norway 8 E12 62 45N 7 9 E
Moldova ■, Europe 25 E4 47 0N 28 0 E
Moldoveana, Vf., Romania 17 F13 45 36N 24 45 E
Mole →, U.K. 11 F7 51 24N 0 21W
Molepolole, Botswana 56 C4 24 28S 25 28 E
Molfetta, Italy 20 D7 41 12N 16 36 E
Moline, U.S.A. 80 E9 41 30N 90 31W
Molinos, Argentina 94 B2 25 28S 66 15W
Moliro, Dem. Rep. of the Congo 54 D3 8 12S 30 30 E
Mollahat, Bangla. 43 H13 22 56N 89 48 E
Mollendo, Peru 92 G4 17 0S 72 0W
Mollerin, L., Australia 61 F2 30 30S 117 35 E
Molodechno = Maladzyechna, Belarus 17 A14 54 20N 26 50 E
Molokai, U.S.A. 74 H16 21 8N 157 0W
Molong, Australia 63 E4 33 5S 148 54 E
Molopo →, Africa 56 D3 27 30S 20 13 E
Molotov = Perm, Russia 24 C10 58 0N 56 10 E
Molson L., Canada 73 C9 54 22N 96 40W
Molteno, S. Africa 56 E4 31 22S 26 22 E
Molu, Indonesia 37 F8 6 45S 131 40 E
Molucca Sea, Indonesia 37 E6 2 0S 124 0 E
Moluccas = Maluku, Indonesia 37 E7 1 0S 127 0 E
Moma, Dem. Rep. of the Congo 54 C1 1 35S 23 52 E
Moma, Mozam. 55 F4 16 47S 39 4 E
Mombasa, Kenya 54 C4 4 2S 39 43 E
Mombetsu, Japan 30 B11 44 21N 143 22 E
Momchilgrad, Bulgaria 21 D11 41 33N 25 23 E
Momi, Dem. Rep. of the Congo 54 C2 1 42S 27 0 E
Mompós, Colombia 92 B4 9 14N 74 26W
Møn, Denmark 9 J15 54 57N 12 20 E
Mon →, Burma 41 J19 20 25N 94 30 E
Mona, Canal de la, W. Indies 89 C6 18 30N 67 45W
Mona, Isla, Puerto Rico 89 C6 18 5N 67 54W
Mona, Pta., Costa Rica 88 E3 9 37N 82 36W
Monaco ■, Europe 18 E7 43 46N 7 23 E
Monadhliath Mts., U.K. 12 D4 57 10N 4 4W
Monaghan, Ireland 13 B5 54 15N 6 57W
Monaghan □, Ireland 13 B5 54 11N 6 56W
Monahans, U.S.A. 81 K3 31 36N 102 54W
Monapo, Mozam. 55 E5 14 56S 40 19 E
Monar, L., U.K. 12 D3 57 26N 5 8W
Monarch Mt., Canada 72 C3 51 55N 125 57W
Monasterevin, Ireland 13 C4 53 8N 7 4W
Monastir = Bitola, Macedonia 21 D9 41 1N 21 20 E
Moncayo, Sierra del, Spain 19 B5 41 48N 1 50W
Monchegorsk, Russia 24 A5 67 54N 32 58 E
Mönchengladbach, Germany 16 C4 51 11N 6 27 E
Monchique, Portugal 19 D1 37 19N 8 38W
Monclova, Mexico 86 B4 26 50N 101 30W
Moncton, Canada 71 C7 46 7N 64 51W
Mondego →, Portugal 19 B1 40 9N 8 52W
Mondeodo, Indonesia 37 E6 3 34S 122 9 E
Mondovì, Italy 18 D7 44 23N 7 49 E
Mondovi, U.S.A. 80 C9 44 34N 91 40W
Mondrain I., Australia 61 F3 34 9S 122 14 E
Monduli □, Tanzania 54 C4 3 0S 36 0 E
Monessen, U.S.A. 78 F5 40 9N 79 54W
Monett, U.S.A. 81 G8 36 55N 93 55W
Moneymore, U.K. 13 B5 54 41N 6 40W
Monforte de Lemos, Spain 19 A2 42 31N 7 33W
Mong Hsu, Burma 41 J21 21 54N 98 30 E
Mong Kung, Burma 41 J20 21 35N 97 35 E
Mong Nai, Burma 41 J20 20 32N 97 46 E
Mong Pawk, Burma 41 H21 22 4N 99 16 E
Mong Ton, Burma 41 J21 20 17N 98 45 E
Mong Wa, Burma 41 J22 21 26N 100 27 E
Mong Yai, Burma 41 H21 22 21N 98 3 E
Mongalla, Sudan 51 G12 5 8N 31 42 E
Mongers, L., Australia 61 E2 29 25S 117 5 E
Monghyr = Munger, India 43 G12 25 23N 86 30 E
Mongibello = Etna, Italy 20 F6 37 50N 14 55 E
Mongo, Chad 51 F9 12 14N 18 43 E
Mongolia ■, Asia 27 E10 47 0N 103 0 E
Mongu, Zambia 53 H4 15 16S 23 12 E
Môngua, Angola 56 B2 16 43S 15 20 E
Monifieth, U.K. 12 E6 56 30N 2 48W
Monkey Bay, Malawi 55 E4 14 7S 35 1 E
Monkey River, Belize 87 D7 16 22N 88 29W
Monkira, Australia 62 C3 24 46S 140 30 E
Monkoto, Dem. Rep. of the Congo 52 E4 1 38S 20 35 E
Monmouth, U.K. 11 F5 51 48N 2 42W
Monmouth, U.S.A. 80 E9 40 55N 90 39W
Monmouthshire □, U.K. 11 F5 51 48N 2 54W
Mono L., U.S.A. 84 H7 38 1N 119 1W
Monolith, U.S.A. 85 K8 35 7N 118 22W
Monólithos, Greece 23 C9 36 7N 27 45 E
Monongahela, U.S.A. 78 F5 40 12N 79 56W
Monópoli, Italy 20 D7 40 57N 17 18 E
Monroe, Ga., U.S.A. 77 J4 33 47N 83 43W
Monroe, La., U.S.A. 81 J8 32 30N 92 7W
Monroe, Mich., U.S.A. 76 E4 41 55N 83 24W
Monroe, N.C., U.S.A. 77 H5 34 59N 80 33W
Monroe, N.Y., U.S.A. 79 E10 41 20N 74 11W
Monroe, Utah, U.S.A. 83 G7 38 38N 112 7W
Monroe, Wash., U.S.A. 84 C5 47 51N 121 58W
Monroe, Wis., U.S.A. 80 D10 42 36N 89 38W
Monroe City, U.S.A. 80 F9 39 39N 91 44W
Monroeville, Ala., U.S.A. 77 K2 31 31N 87 20W
Monroeville, Pa., U.S.A. 78 F5 40 26N 79 45W
Monrovia, Liberia 50 G3 6 18N 10 47W
Mons, Belgium 15 D3 50 27N 3 58 E
Monse, Indonesia 37 E6 4 0S 123 10 E
Mont-de-Marsan, France 18 E3 43 54N 0 31W
Mont-Joli, Canada 71 C6 48 37N 68 10W
Mont-Laurier, Canada 70 C4 46 35N 75 30W
Mont-St-Michel, Le = Le Mont-St-Michel, France 18 B3 48 40N 1 30W
Mont Tremblant Prov. Park, Canada 70 C5 46 30N 74 30W
Montagu, S. Africa 56 E3 33 45S 20 8 E
Montagu I., Antarctica 5 B1 58 25S 26 20W
Montague, Canada 71 C7 46 10N 62 39W
Montague, U.S.A. 82 F2 41 44N 122 32W
Montague, I., Mexico 86 A2 31 40N 114 56W
Montague Ra., Australia 61 E2 27 15S 119 30 E
Montague Sd., Australia 60 B4 14 28S 125 20 E
Montalbán, Spain 19 B5 40 50N 0 45W
Montalvo, U.S.A. 85 L7 34 15N 119 12W
Montana, Bulgaria 21 C10 43 27N 23 16 E
Montaña, Peru 92 E4 6 0S 73 0W
Montana □, U.S.A. 82 C9 47 0N 110 0W
Montaña Clara, I., Canary Is. 22 E6 29 17N 13 33W
Montargis, France 18 C5 47 59N 2 43 E
Montauban, France 18 D4 44 2N 1 21 E
Montauk, U.S.A. 79 E13 41 3N 71 57W
Montauk Pt., U.S.A. 79 E13 41 4N 71 52W
Montbéliard, France 18 C7 47 31N 6 48 E
Montceau-les-Mines, France 18 C6 46 40N 4 23 E
Montclair, U.S.A. 79 F10 40 49N 74 13W
Monte Albán, Mexico 87 D5 17 2N 96 45W
Monte Alegre, Brazil 93 D8 2 0S 54 0W
Monte Azul, Brazil 93 G10 15 9S 42 53W
Monte Bello Is., Australia 60 D2 20 30S 115 45 E
Monte-Carlo, Monaco 18 E7 43 46N 7 23 E
Monte Caseros, Argentina 94 C4 30 10S 57 50W
Monte Comán, Argentina 94 C2 34 40S 67 53W
Monte Cristi, Dom. Rep. 89 C5 19 52N 71 39W
Monte Lindo →, Paraguay 94 A4 23 56S 57 12W
Monte Quemado, Argentina 94 B3 25 53S 62 41W
Monte Rio, U.S.A. 84 G4 38 28N 123 0W
Monte Santu, C. di, Italy 20 D3 40 5N 9 44 E
Monte Vista, U.S.A. 83 H10 37 35N 106 9W
Monteagudo, Argentina 95 B5 27 14S 54 8W
Montebello, Canada 70 C5 45 40N 74 55W
Montecito, U.S.A. 85 L7 34 26N 119 40W
Montecristo, Italy 20 C4 42 20N 10 19 E
Montego Bay, Jamaica 88 C4 18 30N 78 0W
Montejinnie, Australia 60 C5 16 40S 131 38 E
Montélimar, France 18 D6 44 33N 4 45 E
Montello, U.S.A. 80 D10 43 48N 89 20W
Montemorelos, Mexico 87 B5 25 11N 99 42W
Montenegro, Brazil 95 B5 29 39S 51 29W
Montenegro □, Yugoslavia 21 C8 42 40N 19 20 E
Montepuez, Mozam. 55 E4 13 8S 38 59 E
Montepuez →, Mozam. 55 E5 12 32S 40 27 E
Monterey, U.S.A. 84 J5 36 37N 121 55W
Monterey B., U.S.A. 84 J5 36 45N 122 0W
Montería, Colombia 92 B3 8 46N 75 53W
Monteros, Argentina 94 B2 27 11S 65 30W
Monterrey, Mexico 86 B4 25 40N 100 30W
Montes Claros, Brazil 93 G10 16 30S 43 50W
Montesano, U.S.A. 84 D3 46 59N 123 36W
Montesilvano, Italy 20 C6 42 29N 14 8 E
Montevideo, Uruguay 95 C4 34 50S 56 11W
Montevideo, U.S.A. 80 C7 44 57N 95 43W
Montezuma, U.S.A. 80 E8 41 35N 92 32W
Montgomery = Sahiwal, Pakistan 42 D5 30 45N 73 8 E
Montgomery, U.K. 11 E4 52 34N 3 8W
Montgomery, Ala., U.S.A. 77 J2 32 23N 86 19W
Montgomery, W. Va., U.S.A. 76 F5 38 11N 81 19W
Monticello, Ark., U.S.A. 81 J9 33 38N 91 47W
Monticello, Fla., U.S.A. 77 K4 30 33N 83 52W
Monticello, Ind., U.S.A. 76 E2 40 45N 86 46W
Monticello, Iowa, U.S.A. 80 D9 42 15N 91 12W
Monticello, Ky., U.S.A. 77 G3 36 50N 84 51W
Monticello, Minn., U.S.A. 80 C8 45 18N 93 48W
Monticello, Miss., U.S.A. 81 K9 31 33N 90 7W
Monticello, N.Y., U.S.A. 79 E10 41 39N 74 42W
Monticello, Utah, U.S.A. 83 H9 37 52N 109 21W
Montijo, Portugal 19 C1 38 41N 8 54W
Montilla, Spain 19 D3 37 36N 4 40W
Montluçon, France 18 C5 46 22N 2 36 E
Montmagny, Canada 71 C5 46 58N 70 34W
Montmartre, Canada 73 C8 50 14N 103 27W
Montmorency, Canada 71 C5 46 53N 71 11W
Montmorillon, France 18 C4 46 26N 0 50 E
Monto, Australia 62 C5 24 52S 151 6 E
Montoro, Spain 19 C3 38 1N 4 27W
Montour Falls, U.S.A. 78 D8 42 21N 76 51W
Montpelier, Idaho, U.S.A. 82 E8 42 19N 111 18W
Montpelier, Ohio, U.S.A. 76 E3 41 35N 84 37W
Montpelier, Vt., U.S.A. 79 B12 44 16N 72 35W
Montpellier, France 18 E5 43 37N 3 52 E
Montréal, Canada 70 C5 45 31N 73 34W
Montreal L., Canada 73 C7 54 20N 105 45W
Montreal Lake, Canada 73 C7 54 3N 105 46W
Montreux, Switz. 18 C7 46 26N 6 55 E
Montrose, U.K. 12 E6 56 44N 2 27W
Montrose, Colo., U.S.A. 83 G10 38 29N 107 53W
Montrose, Pa., U.S.A. 79 E9 41 50N 75 53W
Monts, Pte. des, Canada 71 C6 49 20N 67 12W
Montserrat ■, W. Indies 89 C7 16 40N 62 10W
Montuiri, Spain 22 B9 39 34N 2 59 E
Monywa, Burma 41 H19 22 7N 95 11 E
Monza, Italy 18 D8 45 35N 9 16 E
Monze, Zambia 55 F2 16 17S 27 29 E
Monze, C., Pakistan 42 G2 24 47N 66 37 E
Monzón, Spain 19 B6 41 52N 0 10 E
Mooi River, S. Africa 57 D4 29 13S 29 50 E
Moolawatana, Australia 63 D2 29 55S 139 45 E
Mooliabeenee, Australia 61 F2 31 20S 116 2 E
Mooloogool, Australia 61 E2 26 2S 119 5 E
Moomin Cr. →, Australia 63 D4 29 44S 149 20 E
Moonah →, Australia 62 C2 22 3S 138 33 E
Moonbeam, Canada 70 C3 49 20N 82 10W
Moonda, L., Australia 62 D3 25 52S 140 25 E
Moonie, Australia 63 D5 27 46S 150 20 E
Moonie →, Australia 63 D4 29 19S 148 43 E
Moonta, Australia 63 E2 34 6S 137 32 E
Moora, Australia 61 F2 30 37S 115 58 E
Mooraberree, Australia 62 D3 25 13S 140 54 E
Moorarie, Australia 61 E2 25 56S 117 35 E
Moorcroft, U.S.A. 80 C2 44 16N 104 57W
Moore →, Australia 61 F2 31 22S 115 30 E
Moore, L., Australia 61 E2 29 50S 117 35 E
Moore Reefs, Australia 62 B4 16 0S 149 5 E
Moorefield, U.S.A. 76 F6 39 5N 78 59W
Moores Res., U.S.A. 79 B13 44 45N 71 50W

Nanam

Mulligan →, Australia 62 D2 25 0S 139 0 E
Mullin, U.S.A. 81 K5 31 33N 98 40W
Mullingar, Ireland 13 C4 53 31N 7 21W
Mullins, U.S.A. 77 H6 34 12N 79 15W
Mullumbimby, Australia 63 D5 28 30S 153 30 E
Mulobezi, Zambia 55 F2 16 45S 25 7 E
Mulroy B., Ireland 13 A4 55 15N 7 46W
Multan, Pakistan 42 D4 30 15N 71 36 E
Mulumbe, Mts.,
Dem. Rep. of the Congo 55 D2 8 40S 27 30 E
Mulungushi Dam, Zambia 55 E2 14 48S 28 48 E
Mulvane, U.S.A. 81 G6 37 29N 97 15W
Mulwala, Australia 63 F4 35 59S 146 0 E
Mumbai, India 40 K8 18 55N 72 50 E
Mumbwa, Zambia 55 F2 15 0S 27 0 E
Mun →, Thailand 38 E5 15 19N 105 30 E
Muna, Indonesia 37 F6 5 0S 122 30 E
Munamagi, Estonia 9 H22 57 43N 27 4 E
München, Germany 16 D6 48 8N 11 34 E
Munchen-Gladbach =
Mönchengladbach,
Germany 16 C4 51 11N 6 27 E
Muncho Lake, Canada 72 B3 59 0N 125 50W
Munchŏn, N. Korea 35 E14 39 14N 127 19 E
Muncie, U.S.A. 76 E3 40 12N 85 23W
Muncoonie, L., Australia 62 D2 25 12S 138 40 E
Mundare, Canada 72 C6 53 35N 112 20W
Munday, U.S.A. 81 J5 33 27N 99 38W
Münden, Germany 16 C5 51 25N 9 38 E
Mundiwindi, Australia 60 D3 23 47S 120 9 E
Mundo Novo, Brazil 93 F10 11 50S 40 29W
Mundra, India 42 H3 22 54N 69 48 E
Mundrabilla, Australia 61 F4 31 52S 127 51 E
Mungallala, Australia 63 D4 26 28S 147 34 E
Mungallala Cr. →,
Australia 63 D4 28 53S 147 5 E
Mungana, Australia 62 B3 17 8S 144 27 E
Mungaoli, India 42 G8 24 24N 78 7 E
Mungari, Mozam. 55 F3 17 12S 33 30 E
Mungbere,
Dem. Rep. of the Congo 54 B2 2 36N 28 28 E
Munger, India 43 G12 25 23N 86 30 E
Mungindi, Australia 63 D4 28 58S 149 1 E
Munich = München,
Germany 16 D6 48 8N 11 34 E
Munising, U.S.A. 76 B2 46 25N 86 40W
Munku-Sardyk, Russia 27 D11 51 45N 100 20 E
Muñoz Gamero, Pen.,
Chile 96 G2 52 30S 73 5W
Munroe L., Canada 73 B9 59 13N 98 35W
Munsan, S. Korea 35 F14 37 51N 126 48 E
Münster, Germany 16 C4 51 58N 7 37 E
Munster □, Ireland 13 D3 52 18N 8 44W
Muntadgin, Australia 61 F2 31 45S 118 33 E
Muntok, Indonesia 36 E3 2 5S 105 10 E
Munyama, Zambia 55 F2 16 5S 28 31 E
Muong Beng, Laos 38 B3 20 23N 101 46 E
Muong Boum, Vietnam 38 A4 22 24N 102 49 E
Muong Et, Laos 38 B5 20 49N 104 1 E
Muong Hai, Laos 38 B3 21 3N 101 49 E
Muong Hiem, Laos 38 B4 20 5N 103 22 E
Muong Houn, Laos 38 B3 20 8N 101 23 E
Muong Hung, Vietnam 38 B4 20 56N 103 53 E
Muong Kau, Laos 38 E5 15 6N 105 47 E
Muong Khao, Laos 38 C4 19 38N 103 32 E
Muong Khoua, Laos 38 B4 21 5N 102 31 E
Muong Liep, Laos 38 C3 18 29N 101 40 E
Muong May, Laos 38 E6 14 49N 106 56 E
Muong Ngeun, Laos 38 B3 20 36N 101 3 E
Muong Ngoi, Laos 38 B4 20 43N 102 41 E
Muong Nhie, Vietnam 38 A4 22 12N 102 28 E
Muong Nong, Laos 38 D6 16 22N 106 30 E
Muong Ou Tay, Laos 38 A3 22 7N 101 48 E
Muong Oua, Laos 38 C3 18 18N 101 20 E
Muong Peun, Laos 38 B4 20 13N 103 52 E
Muong Phalane, Laos 38 D5 16 39N 105 34 E
Muong Phieng, Laos 38 C3 19 6N 101 32 E
Muong Phine, Laos 38 D6 16 32N 106 2 E
Muong Sai, Laos 38 B3 20 42N 101 59 E
Muong Saiapoun, Laos 38 C3 18 24N 101 31 E
Muong Sen, Vietnam 38 C5 19 24N 104 8 E
Muong Sing, Laos 38 B3 21 11N 101 9 E
Muong Son, Laos 38 B4 20 27N 103 19 E
Muong Soui, Laos 38 C4 19 33N 102 52 E
Muong Va, Laos 38 B4 21 53N 102 19 E
Muong Xia, Vietnam 38 B5 20 19N 104 50 E
Muonio, Finland 8 C20 67 57N 23 40 E
Muonionjoki →, Finland 8 C20 67 11N 23 34 E
Muping, China 35 F11 37 22N 121 36 E
Muqdisho, Somali Rep. 46 G4 2 2N 45 25 E
Mur →, Austria 17 E9 46 18N 16 52 E
Murakami, Japan 30 E9 38 14N 139 29 E
Murallón, Cerro, Chile 96 F2 49 48S 73 30W
Muranda, Rwanda 54 C2 1 52S 29 20 E
Murang'a, Kenya 54 C4 0 45S 37 9 E
Murashi, Russia 24 C8 59 30N 49 0 E
Muratlı, Turkey 21 D12 41 10N 27 29 E
Murayama, Japan 30 E10 38 30N 140 25 E
Murban, U.A.E. 45 F7 23 50N 53 45 E
Murchison →, Australia 61 E1 27 45S 114 0 E
Murchison, Mt., Antarctica 5 D11 73 0S 168 0 E
Murchison Falls, Uganda 54 B3 2 15N 31 30 E
Murchison House,
Australia 61 E1 27 39S 114 14 E
Murchison Ra., Australia 62 C1 20 0S 134 10 E
Murchison Rapids, Malawi 55 F3 15 55S 34 35 E
Murcia, Spain 19 D5 38 5N 1 10W
Murcia □, Spain 19 D5 37 50N 1 30W
Murdo, U.S.A. 80 D4 43 53N 100 43W
Murdoch Pt., Australia 62 A3 14 37S 144 55 E
Mureş →, Romania 17 E11 46 15N 20 13 E
Mureşul = Mureş →,
Romania 17 E11 46 15N 20 13 E
Murfreesboro, U.S.A. 77 H2 35 51N 86 24W
Murgab = Murghob,
Tajikistan 26 F8 38 10N 74 2 E
Murghob, Tajikistan 26 F8 38 10N 74 2 E
Murgon, Australia 63 D5 26 15S 151 54 E
Murgoo, Australia 61 E2 27 24S 116 28 E
Muria, Indonesia 37 G14 6 36S 110 53 E
Muriaé, Brazil 95 A7 21 8S 42 23W
Muriel Mine, Zimbabwe 55 F3 17 14S 30 40 E
Müritz, Germany 16 B7 53 25N 12 42 E
Murka, Kenya 54 C4 3 27S 38 0 E
Murmansk, Russia 24 A5 68 57N 33 10 E
Muro, Spain 22 B10 39 44N 3 3 E
Murom, Russia 24 C7 55 35N 42 3 E
Muroran, Japan 30 C10 42 25N 141 0 E
Muroto, Japan 31 H7 33 18N 134 9 E
Muroto-Misaki, Japan 31 H7 33 15N 134 10 E
Murphy, U.S.A. 82 E5 43 13N 116 33W
Murphys, U.S.A. 84 G6 38 8N 120 28W
Murphysboro, U.S.A. 81 G10 37 46N 89 20W
Murray, Ky., U.S.A. 77 G1 36 37N 88 19W
Murray, Utah, U.S.A. 82 F8 40 40N 111 53W
Murray →, Australia 63 F2 35 20S 139 22 E
Murray →, Canada 72 B4 56 11N 120 45W
Murray, L., U.S.A. 77 H5 34 3N 81 13W
Murray Bridge, Australia 63 F2 35 6S 139 14 E
Murray Downs, Australia 62 C1 21 4S 134 40 E
Murray Harbour, Canada 71 C7 46 0N 62 28W
Murraysburg, S. Africa 56 E3 31 58S 23 47 E
Murree, Pakistan 42 C5 33 56N 73 28 E
Murrieta, U.S.A. 85 M9 33 33N 117 13W
Murrin Murrin, Australia 61 E3 28 58S 121 33 E
Murrumbidgee →,
Australia 63 E3 34 43S 143 12 E
Murrumburrah, Australia 63 E4 34 32S 148 22 E
Murrurundi, Australia 63 E5 31 42S 150 51 E
Murshidabad, India 43 G13 24 11N 88 19 E
Murtle L., Canada 72 C5 52 8N 119 38W
Murtoa, Australia 63 F3 36 35S 142 28 E
Murungu, Tanzania 54 C3 4 12S 31 10 E
Murwara, India 43 H9 23 46N 80 28 E
Murwillumbah, Australia 63 D5 28 18S 153 27 E
Mürzzuschlag, Austria 16 E8 47 36N 15 41 E
Muş, Turkey 25 G7 38 45N 41 30 E
Mûsa, Gebel, Egypt 51 C12 28 33N 33 59 E
Musa Khel, Pakistan 42 D3 30 59N 69 52 E
Mūsá Qal'eh, Afghan. 40 C4 32 20N 64 50 E
Musaffargarh, Pakistan 40 D7 30 10N 71 10 E
Musala, Bulgaria 21 C10 42 13N 23 37 E
Musala, Indonesia 36 D1 1 41N 98 28 E
Musan, N. Korea 35 C15 42 12N 129 12 E
Musangu,
Dem. Rep. of the Congo 55 E1 10 28S 23 55 E
Musasa, Tanzania 54 C3 3 25S 31 30 E
Musay'id, Qatar 45 E6 25 0N 51 33 E
Muscat = Masqat, Oman 46 C6 23 37N 58 36 E
Muscat & Oman =
Oman ■, Asia 46 C6 23 0N 58 0 E
Muscatine, U.S.A. 80 E9 41 25N 91 3W
Musgrave, Australia 62 A3 14 47S 143 30 E
Musgrave Ranges,
Australia 61 E5 26 0S 132 0 E
Mushie,
Dem. Rep. of the Congo 52 E3 2 56S 16 55 E
Musi →, Indonesia 36 E2 2 20S 104 56 E
Muskeg →, Canada 72 A4 60 20N 123 20W
Muskegon, U.S.A. 76 D2 43 14N 86 16W
Muskegon →, U.S.A. 76 D2 43 14N 86 21W
Muskegon Heights, U.S.A. 76 D2 43 12N 86 16W
Muskogee, U.S.A. 81 H7 35 45N 95 22W
Muskwa →, Canada 72 B4 58 47N 122 48W
Muslīmiyah, Syria 44 B3 36 19N 37 12 E
Musofu, Zambia 55 E2 13 30S 29 0 E
Musoma, Tanzania 54 C3 1 30S 33 48 E
Musoma □, Tanzania 54 C3 1 50S 34 30 E
Musquaro, L., Canada 71 B7 50 38N 61 5W
Musquodoboit Harbour,
Canada 71 D7 44 50N 63 9W
Musselburgh, U.K. 12 F5 55 57N 3 2W
Musselshell →, U.S.A. 82 C10 47 21N 107 57W
Mussoorie, India 42 D8 30 27N 78 6 E
Mussuco, Angola 56 B2 17 2S 19 3 E
Mustafakemalpaşa, Turkey 21 D13 40 2N 28 24 E
Mustang, Nepal 43 E10 29 10N 83 55 E
Musters, L., Argentina 96 F3 45 20S 69 25W
Musudan, N. Korea 35 D15 40 50N 129 43 E
Muswellbrook, Australia 63 E5 32 16S 150 56 E
Mût, Egypt 51 C11 25 28N 28 58 E
Mutanda, Mozam. 57 C5 21 0S 33 34 E
Mutanda, Zambia 55 E2 12 24S 26 13 E
Mutare, Zimbabwe 55 F3 18 58S 32 38 E
Muting, Indonesia 37 F10 7 23S 140 20 E
Mutoray, Russia 27 C11 60 56N 101 0 E
Mutshatsha,
Dem. Rep. of the Congo 55 E1 10 35S 24 20 E
Mutsu, Japan 30 D10 41 5N 140 55 E
Mutsu-Wan, Japan 30 D10 41 5N 140 55 E
Muttaburra, Australia 62 C3 22 38S 144 29 E
Mutton I., Ireland 13 D2 52 49N 9 32W
Mutuáli, Mozam. 55 E4 14 55S 37 0 E
Muweilih, Egypt 47 E3 30 42N 34 19 E
Muy Muy, Nic. 88 D2 12 39N 85 36W
Muyinga, Burundi 54 C3 3 14S 30 33 E
Muynak, Uzbekistan 26 E6 43 44N 59 10 E
Muzaffarabad, Pakistan 43 B5 34 25N 73 30 E
Muzaffargarh, Pakistan 42 D4 30 5N 71 14 E
Muzaffarnagar, India 42 E7 29 26N 77 40 E
Muzaffarpur, India 43 F11 26 7N 85 23 E
Muzhi, Russia 26 C7 65 25N 64 40 E
Muzon, C., U.S.A. 72 C2 54 40N 132 42W
Mvuma, Zimbabwe 55 F3 19 16S 30 30 E
Mvurwi, Zimbabwe 55 F3 17 0S 30 57 E
Mwadui, Tanzania 54 C3 3 26S 33 32 E
Mwambo, Tanzania 55 E5 10 30S 40 22 E
Mwandi, Zambia 55 F1 17 30S 24 51 E
Mwanza,
Dem. Rep. of the Congo 54 D2 7 55S 26 43 E
Mwanza, Tanzania 54 C3 2 30S 32 58 E
Mwanza, Zambia 55 F1 16 58S 24 28 E
Mwanza □, Tanzania 54 C3 2 0S 33 0 E
Mwaya, Tanzania 55 D3 9 32S 33 55 E
Mweelrea, Ireland 13 C2 53 39N 9 49W
Mweka,
Dem. Rep. of the Congo 52 E4 4 50S 21 34 E
Mwenezi, Zimbabwe 55 G3 21 15S 30 48 E
Mwenezi →, Mozam. 55 G3 22 40S 31 50 E
Mwenga,
Dem. Rep. of the Congo 54 C2 3 1S 28 28 E
Mweru, L., Zambia 55 D2 9 0S 28 40 E
Mweza Range, Zimbabwe 55 G3 21 0S 30 0 E
Mwilambwe,
Dem. Rep. of the Congo 54 D2 8 7S 25 5 E
Mwimbi, Tanzania 55 D3 8 38S 31 39 E
Mwinilunga, Zambia 55 E1 11 43S 24 25 E
My Tho, Vietnam 39 G6 10 29N 106 23 E
Myajlar, India 42 F4 26 15N 70 20 E
Myanaung, Burma 41 K19 18 18N 95 22 E
Myanmar = Burma ■,
Asia 41 J20 21 0N 96 30 E
Myaungmya, Burma 41 L19 16 30N 94 40 E
Mycenæ, Greece 21 F10 37 39N 22 52 E
Myeik Kyunzu, Burma 39 G1 11 30N 97 30 E
Myerstown, U.S.A. 79 F8 40 22N 76 19W
Myingyan, Burma 41 J19 21 30N 95 20 E
Myitkyina, Burma 41 G20 25 24N 97 26 E
Mykines, Færoe Is. 8 E9 62 7N 7 35W
Mykolayiv, Ukraine 25 E5 46 58N 32 0 E
Mymensingh, Bangla. 41 G17 24 45N 90 24 E
Mynydd Du, U.K. 11 F4 51 52N 3 50W
Mýrdalsjökull, Iceland 8 E4 63 40N 19 6W
Myroodah, Australia 60 C3 18 7S 124 16 E
Myrtle Beach, U.S.A. 77 J6 33 42N 78 53W
Myrtle Creek, U.S.A. 82 E2 43 1N 123 17W
Myrtle Point, U.S.A. 82 E1 43 4N 124 8W
Myrtou, Cyprus 23 D12 35 18N 33 4 E
Mysia, Turkey 21 E12 39 50N 27 0 E
Mysore = Karnataka □,
India 40 N10 13 15N 77 0 E
Mysore, India 40 N10 12 17N 76 41 E
Mystic, U.S.A. 79 E13 41 21N 71 58W
Myszków, Poland 17 C10 50 45N 19 22 E
Mytishchi, Russia 24 C6 55 50N 37 50 E
Myton, U.S.A. 82 F8 40 12N 110 4W
Mývatn, Iceland 8 D5 65 36N 17 0W
Mzimba, Malawi 55 E3 11 55S 33 39 E
Mzimkulu →, S. Africa 57 E5 30 44S 30 28 E
Mzimvubu →, S. Africa 57 E4 31 38S 29 33 E
Mzuzu, Malawi 55 E3 11 30S 33 55 E

N

Na Hearadh = Harris, U.K. 12 D2 57 50N 6 55W
Na Noi, Thailand 38 C3 18 19N 100 43 E
Na Phao, Laos 38 D5 17 35N 105 44 E
Na Sam, Vietnam 38 A6 22 3N 106 37 E
Na San, Vietnam 38 B5 21 12N 104 2 E
Naab →, Germany 16 D6 49 1N 12 2 E
Naantali, Finland 9 F19 60 29N 22 2 E
Naas, Ireland 13 C5 53 12N 6 40W
Nababiep, S. Africa 56 D2 29 36S 17 46 E
Nabadwip = Navadwip,
India 43 H13 23 34N 88 20 E
Nabari, Japan 31 G8 34 37N 136 5 E
Nabawa, Australia 61 E1 28 30S 114 48 E
Nabberu, L., Australia 61 E3 25 50S 120 30 E
Naberezhnyye Chelny,
Russia 24 C9 55 42N 52 19 E
Nabeul, Tunisia 51 A8 36 30N 10 44 E
Nabha, India 42 D7 30 26N 76 14 E
Nabīd, Iran 45 D8 29 40N 57 38 E
Nabire, Indonesia 37 E9 3 15S 135 26 E
Nabisar, Pakistan 42 G3 25 8N 69 40 E
Nabisipi →, Canada 71 B7 50 14N 62 13W
Nabiswera, Uganda 54 B3 1 27N 32 15 E
Nablus = Nābulus,
West Bank 47 C4 32 14N 35 15 E
Naboomspruit, S. Africa 57 C4 24 32S 28 40 E
Nābulus, West Bank 47 C4 32 14N 35 15 E
Nacala, Mozam. 55 E5 14 31S 40 34 E
Nacala-Velha, Mozam. 55 E5 14 32S 40 34 E
Nacaome, Honduras 88 D2 13 31N 87 30W
Nacaroa, Mozam. 55 E4 14 22S 39 56 E
Naches, U.S.A. 82 C3 46 44N 120 42W
Naches →, U.S.A. 84 D6 46 38N 120 31W
Nachingwea, Tanzania 55 E4 10 23S 38 49 E
Nachingwea □, Tanzania 55 E4 10 30S 38 30 E
Nachna, India 42 F4 27 34N 71 41 E
Nacimiento Reservoir,
U.S.A. 84 K6 35 46N 120 53W
Nackara, Australia 63 E2 32 48S 139 12 E
Naco, Mexico 86 A3 31 20N 109 56W
Naco, U.S.A. 83 L9 31 20N 109 57W
Nacogdoches, U.S.A. 81 K7 31 36N 94 39W
Nácori Chico, Mexico 86 B3 29 39N 109 1W
Nacozari, Mexico 86 A3 30 24N 109 39W
Nadiad, India 42 H5 22 41N 72 56 E
Nadur, Malta 23 C1 36 2N 14 17 E
Nadūshan, Iran 45 C7 32 2N 53 35 E
Nadvirna, Ukraine 17 D13 48 37N 24 30 E
Nadvoitsy, Russia 24 B5 63 52N 34 14 E
Nadvornaya = Nadvirna,
Ukraine 17 D13 48 37N 24 30 E
Nadym, Russia 26 C8 65 35N 72 42 E
Nadym →, Russia 26 C8 66 12N 72 0 E
Nærbø, Norway 9 G11 58 40N 5 39 E
Næstved, Denmark 9 J14 55 13N 11 44 E
Naftshahr, Iran 44 C5 34 0N 45 30 E
Nafud Desert = An Nafūd,
Si. Arabia 44 D4 28 15N 41 0 E
Naga, Phil. 37 B6 13 38N 123 15 E
Nagagami →, Canada 70 C3 49 40N 84 40W
Nagahama, Japan 31 G8 35 23N 136 16 E
Nagai, Japan 30 E10 38 6N 140 2 E
Nagaland □, India 41 G19 26 0N 94 30 E
Nagano, Japan 31 F9 36 40N 138 10 E
Nagano □, Japan 31 F9 36 15N 138 0 E
Nagaoka, Japan 31 F9 37 27N 138 51 E
Nagappattinam, India 40 P11 10 46N 79 51 E
Nagar Parkar, Pakistan 42 G4 24 28N 70 46 E
Nagasaki, Japan 31 H4 32 47N 129 50 E
Nagasaki □, Japan 31 H4 32 50N 129 40 E
Nagato, Japan 31 G5 34 19N 131 5 E
Nagaur, India 42 F5 27 15N 73 45 E
Nagercoil, India 40 Q10 8 12N 77 26 E
Nagina, India 43 E8 29 30N 78 30 E
Nagīneh, Iran 45 C8 34 20N 57 15 E
Nagir, Pakistan 43 A6 36 12N 74 42 E
Nagoorin, Australia 62 C5 24 17S 151 15 E
Nagornyy, Russia 27 D13 55 58N 124 57 E
Nagoya, Japan 31 G8 35 10N 136 50 E
Nagpur, India 40 J11 21 8N 79 10 E
Nagua, Dom. Rep. 89 C6 19 23N 69 50W
Nagykanizsa, Hungary 17 E9 46 28N 17 0 E
Nagykőrös, Hungary 17 E10 47 5N 19 48 E
Naha, Japan 31 L3 26 13N 127 42 E
Nahanni Butte, Canada 72 A4 61 2N 123 31W
Nahanni Nat. Park, Canada 72 A4 61 15N 125 0W
Nahariyya, Israel 44 C2 33 1N 35 5 E
Nahāvand, Iran 45 C6 34 10N 48 22 E
Nahlin, Canada 72 B2 58 55N 131 38W
Naicá, Mexico 86 B3 27 53N 105 31W
Naicam, Canada 73 C8 52 30N 104 30W
Nain, Canada 71 A7 56 34N 61 40W
Nā'īn, Iran 45 C7 32 54N 53 0 E
Naini Tal, India 43 E8 29 30N 79 30 E
Nainpur, India 40 H12 22 30N 80 10 E
Nairn, U.K. 12 D5 57 35N 3 53W
Nairobi, Kenya 54 C4 1 17S 36 48 E
Naissaar, Estonia 9 G21 59 34N 24 29 E
Naivasha, Kenya 54 C4 0 40S 36 30 E
Naivasha, L., Kenya 54 C4 0 48S 36 20 E
Najafābād, Iran 45 C6 32 40N 51 15 E
Najibabad, India 42 E8 29 40N 78 20 E
Najin, N. Korea 35 C16 42 12N 130 15 E
Najmah, Si. Arabia 45 E6 26 42N 50 6 E
Naju, S. Korea 35 G14 35 3N 126 43 E
Nakadōri-Shima, Japan 31 H4 32 57N 129 4 E
Nakalagba,
Dem. Rep. of the Congo 54 B2 2 50N 27 58 E
Nakaminato, Japan 31 F10 36 21N 140 36 E
Nakamura, Japan 31 H6 32 59N 132 56 E
Nakano, Japan 31 F9 36 45N 138 22 E
Nakano-Shima, Japan 31 K4 29 51N 129 52 E
Nakashibetsu, Japan 30 C12 43 33N 144 59 E
Nakfa, Eritrea 46 D2 16 40N 38 32 E
Nakhichevan = Naxçıvan,
Azerbaijan 25 G8 39 12N 45 15 E
Nakhichevan Republic □
= Naxçıvan □,
Azerbaijan 25 G8 39 25N 45 26 E
Nakhl, Egypt 47 F2 29 55N 33 43 E
Nakhl-e Taqī, Iran 45 E7 27 28N 52 36 E
Nakhodka, Russia 30 C6 42 53N 132 54 E
Nakhon Nayok, Thailand 38 E3 14 12N 101 13 E
Nakhon Pathom, Thailand 38 F3 13 49N 100 3 E
Nakhon Phanom, Thailand 38 D5 17 23N 104 43 E
Nakhon Ratchasima,
Thailand 38 E4 14 59N 102 12 E
Nakhon Sawan, Thailand 38 E3 15 35N 100 10 E
Nakhon Si Thammarat,
Thailand 39 H3 8 29N 100 0 E
Nakhon Thai, Thailand 38 D3 17 5N 100 44 E
Nakina, B.C., Canada 72 B2 59 12N 132 52W
Nakina, Ont., Canada 70 B2 50 10N 86 40W
Nakodar, India 42 D6 31 8N 75 31 E
Nakskov, Denmark 9 J14 54 50N 11 8 E
Naktong →, S. Korea 35 G15 35 7N 128 57 E
Nakuru, Kenya 54 C4 0 15S 36 4 E
Nakuru □, Kenya 54 C4 0 15S 35 5 E
Nakuru, L., Kenya 54 C4 0 23S 36 5 E
Nakusp, Canada 72 C5 50 20N 117 45W
Nal →, Pakistan 42 G1 25 20N 65 30 E
Nalchik, Russia 25 F7 43 30N 43 33 E
Nalgonda, India 40 L11 17 6N 79 15 E
Nalhati, India 43 G12 24 17N 87 52 E
Nallamalai Hills, India 40 M11 15 30N 78 50 E
Nam Can, Vietnam 39 H5 8 46N 104 59 E
Nam Co, China 32 C4 30 30N 90 45 E
Nam Dinh, Vietnam 38 B6 20 25N 106 5 E
Nam Du, Hon, Vietnam 39 H5 9 41N 104 21 E
Nam Ngum Dam, Laos 38 C4 18 35N 102 34 E
Nam-Phan = Cochin
China, Vietnam 39 G6 10 30N 106 0 E
Nam Phong, Thailand 38 D4 16 42N 102 52 E
Nam Tha, Laos 38 B3 20 58N 101 30 E
Nam Tok, Thailand 38 E2 14 21N 99 4 E
Namacunde, Angola 56 B2 17 18S 15 50 E
Namacurra, Mozam. 57 B6 17 30S 36 50 E
Namak, Daryācheh-ye,
Iran 45 C7 34 30N 52 0 E
Namak, Kavir-e, Iran 45 C8 34 30N 57 30 E
Namaland, Namibia 56 C2 26 0S 17 0 E
Namangan, Uzbekistan 26 E8 41 0N 71 40 E
Namapa, Mozam. 55 E4 13 43S 39 50 E
Namaqualand, S. Africa 56 E2 30 0S 17 25 E
Namasagali, Uganda 54 B3 1 2N 33 0 E
Namber, Indonesia 37 E8 1 2S 134 49 E
Nambour, Australia 63 D5 26 32S 152 58 E
Nambucca Heads,
Australia 63 E5 30 37S 153 0 E
Namcha Barwa, China 32 D4 29 40N 95 10 E
Namche Bazar, Nepal 43 F12 27 51N 86 47 E
Namchonjŏm, N. Korea 35 E14 38 15N 126 26 E
Namecunda, Mozam. 55 E4 14 54S 37 37 E
Nameponda, Mozam. 55 F4 15 50S 39 50 E
Nametil, Mozam. 55 F4 15 40S 39 21 E
Namew L., Canada 73 C8 54 14N 101 56W
Namib Desert =
Namibwoestyn, Namibia 56 C2 22 30S 15 0 E
Namibe, Angola 53 H2 15 7S 12 11 E
Namibe □, Angola 56 B1 16 35S 12 30 E
Namibia ■, Africa 56 C2 22 0S 18 9 E
Namibwoestyn, Namibia 56 C2 22 30S 15 0 E
Namlea, Indonesia 37 E7 3 18S 127 5 E
Namoi →, Australia 63 E4 30 12S 149 30 E
Nampa, U.S.A. 82 E5 43 34N 116 34W
Nampo, N. Korea 35 E13 38 52N 125 10 E
Nampō-Shotō, Japan 31 J10 32 0N 140 0 E
Nampula, Mozam. 55 F4 15 6S 39 15 E
Namrole, Indonesia 37 E7 3 46S 126 46 E
Namse Shankou, China 41 E13 30 0N 82 25 E
Namsen →, Norway 8 D14 64 28N 11 37 E
Namsos, Norway 8 D14 64 29N 11 30 E
Namtsy, Russia 27 C13 62 43N 129 37 E
Namtu, Burma 41 H20 23 5N 97 28 E
Namtumbo, Tanzania 55 E4 10 30S 36 4 E
Namu, Canada 72 C3 51 52N 127 50W
Namur, Belgium 15 D4 50 27N 4 52 E
Namur □, Belgium 15 D4 50 17N 5 0 E
Namutoni, Namibia 56 B2 18 49S 16 55 E
Namwala, Zambia 55 F2 15 44S 26 30 E
Namwŏn, S. Korea 35 G14 35 23N 127 23 E
Nan, Thailand 38 C3 18 48N 100 46 E
Nan →, Thailand 38 E3 15 42N 100 9 E
Nanaimo, Canada 72 D4 49 10N 124 0W
Nanam, N. Korea 35 D15 41 44N 129 40 E

North Rhine Westphalia

Newberry, *S.C., U.S.A.* .. **77 H5** 34 17N 81 37W
Newberry Springs, *U.S.A.* **85 L10** 34 50N 116 41W
Newbridge = Droichead Nua, *Ireland* **13 C5** 53 11N 6 48W
Newbrook, *Canada* **72 C6** 54 24N 112 57W
Newburgh, *U.S.A.* **79 E10** 41 30N 74 1W
Newbury, *U.K.* **11 F6** 51 24N 1 20W
Newbury, *U.S.A.* **79 B12** 43 19N 72 3W
Newburyport, *U.S.A.* **79 D14** 42 49N 70 53W
Newcastle, *Australia* .... **63 E5** 33 0S 151 46 E
Newcastle, *Canada* **71 C6** 47 1N 65 38W
Newcastle, *S. Africa* .... **57 D4** 27 45S 29 58 E
Newcastle, *U.K.* **13 B6** 54 13N 5 54W
Newcastle, *Calif., U.S.A.* . **84 G5** 38 53N 121 8W
Newcastle, *Wyo., U.S.A.* . **80 D2** 43 50N 104 11W
Newcastle Emlyn, *U.K.* .. **11 E3** 52 2N 4 28W
Newcastle Ra., *Australia* . **60 C5** 15 45S 130 15 E
Newcastle-under-Lyme, *U.K.* **10 D5** 53 1N 2 14W
Newcastle-upon-Tyne, *U.K.* **10 C6** 54 58N 1 36W
Newcastle Waters, *Australia* .... **62 B1** 17 30S 133 28 E
Newcastle West, *Ireland* . **13 D2** 52 27N 9 3W
Newdegate, *Australia* ... **61 F2** 33 6S 119 0 E
Newell, *U.S.A.* **80 C3** 44 43N 103 25W
Newfoundland □, *Canada* **71 B8** 53 0N 58 0W
Newfoundland I., *N. Amer.* **66 E14** 49 0N 55 0W
Newhalem, *U.S.A.* **72 D4** 48 40N 121 15W
Newhall, *U.S.A.* **85 L8** 34 23N 118 32W
Newhaven, *U.K.* .... **11 G8** 50 47N 0 3 E
Newkirk, *U.S.A.* **81 G6** 36 53N 97 3W
Newlyn, *U.K.* **11 G2** 50 6N 5 34W
Newman, *Australia* ..... **60 D2** 23 18S 119 45 E
Newman, *U.S.A.* **84 H5** 37 19N 121 1W
Newmarket, *Canada* **78 B5** 44 3N 79 28W
Newmarket, *Ireland* **13 D2** 52 13N 9 0W
Newmarket, *U.K.* .... **11 E8** 52 15N 0 25 E
Newmarket, *U.S.A.* **79 C14** 43 5N 70 56W
Newnan, *U.S.A.* **77 J3** 33 23N 84 48W
Newport, *Ireland* **13 C2** 53 53N 9 33W
Newport, *I. of W., U.K.* .. **11 G6** 50 42N 1 17W
Newport, *Newp., U.K.* ... **11 F5** 51 35N 3 0W
Newport, *Ark., U.S.A.* ... **81 H9** 35 37N 91 16W
Newport, *Ky., U.S.A.* **76 F3** 39 5N 84 30W
Newport, *N.H., U.S.A.* ... **79 C12** 43 22N 72 10W
Newport, *Oreg., U.S.A.* .. **82 D1** 44 39N 124 3W
Newport, *Pa., U.S.A.* **78 F7** 40 29N 77 8W
Newport, *R.I., U.S.A.* **79 E13** 41 29N 71 19W
Newport, *Tenn., U.S.A.* .. **77 H4** 35 58N 83 11W
Newport, *Vt., U.S.A.* **79 B12** 44 56N 72 13W
Newport, *Wash., U.S.A.* . **82 B5** 48 11N 117 3W
Newport □, *U.K.* **11 F4** 51 33N 3 1W
Newport Beach, *U.S.A.* .. **85 M9** 33 37N 117 56W
Newport News, *U.S.A.* .. **76 G7** 36 59N 76 25W
Newport Pagnell, *U.K.* ... **11 E7** 52 5N 0 43W
Newquay, *U.K.* **11 G2** 50 25N 5 6W
Newry, *U.K.* **13 B5** 54 11N 6 21W
Newton, *Iowa, U.S.A.* ... **80 E8** 41 42N 93 3W
Newton, *Mass., U.S.A.* .. **79 D13** 42 21N 71 12W
Newton, *Miss., U.S.A.* ... **81 J10** 32 19N 89 10W
Newton, *N.C., U.S.A.* **77 H5** 35 40N 81 13W
Newton, *N.J., U.S.A.* **79 E10** 41 3N 74 45W
Newton, *Tex., U.S.A.* **81 K8** 30 51N 93 46W
Newton Abbot, *U.K.* **11 G4** 50 32N 3 37W
Newton Aycliffe, *U.K.* ... **10 C6** 54 37N 1 34W
Newton Boyd, *Australia* . **63 D5** 29 45S 152 16 E
Newton Stewart, *U.K.* ... **12 G4** 54 57N 4 30W
Newtonmore, *U.K.* **12 D4** 57 4N 4 8W
Newtown, *U.K.* **11 E4** 52 31N 3 19W
Newtownabbey, *U.K.* **13 B6** 54 40N 5 56W
Newtownards, *U.K.* **13 B6** 54 36N 5 42W
Newtownbarry = Bunclody, *Ireland* **13 D5** 52 39N 6 40W
Newtownstewart, *U.K.* .. **13 B4** 54 43N 7 23W
Newville, *U.S.A.* **78 F7** 40 10N 77 24W
Neya, *Russia* .... **24 C7** 58 21N 43 49 E
Neyrīz, *Iran* .... **45 D7** 29 15N 54 19 E
Neyshābūr, *Iran* .... **45 B8** 36 10N 58 50 E
Nezhin = Nizhyn, *Ukraine* **25 D5** 51 5N 31 55 E
Nezperce, *U.S.A.* **82 C5** 46 14N 116 14W
Ngabang, *Indonesia* .... **36 D3** 0 23N 109 55 E
Ngabordamlu, Tanjung, *Indonesia* .... **37 F8** 6 56S 134 11 E
Ngami Depression, *Botswana* .... **56 C3** 20 30S 22 46 E
Ngamo, *Zimbabwe* ..... **55 F2** 19 3S 27 32 E
Nganglong Kangri, *China* **41 C12** 33 0N 81 0 E
Ngao, *Thailand* .... **38 C2** 18 46N 99 59 E
Ngaoundéré, *Cameroon* . **52 C2** 7 15N 13 35 E
Ngapara, *N.Z.* .... **59 L3** 44 57S 170 46 E
Ngara, *Tanzania* .... **54 C3** 2 29S 30 40 E
Ngara □, *Tanzania* ...... **54 C3** 2 29S 30 40 E
Ngawi, *Indonesia* ...... **37 G14** 7 24S 111 26 E
Nghia Lo, *Vietnam* ...... **38 B5** 21 33N 104 28 E
Ngoma, *Malawi* .... **55 E3** 13 8S 33 45 E
Ngomahura, *Zimbabwe* . **55 G3** 20 26S 30 43 E
Ngomba, *Tanzania* ..... **55 D3** 8 20S 32 53 E
Ngoring Hu, *China* ...... **32 C4** 34 55N 97 5 E
Ngorongoro, *Tanzania* .. **54 C4** 3 11S 35 32 E
Ngozi, *Burundi* .... **54 C2** 2 54S 29 50 E
Ngudu, *Tanzania* .... **54 C3** 2 58S 33 25 E
Nguigmi, *Niger* .... **51 F8** 14 20N 13 20 E
Ngukurr, *Australia* ..... **62 A1** 14 44S 134 44 E
Ngunga, *Tanzania* ...... **54 C3** 3 37S 33 37 E
Nguru, *Nigeria* .... **51 F8** 12 56N 10 29 E
Nguru Mts., *Tanzania* ... **54 D4** 6 0S 37 30 E
Nguyen Binh, *Vietnam* .. **38 A5** 22 39N 105 56 E
Nha Trang, *Vietnam* .... **39 F7** 12 16N 109 10 E
Nhacoongo, *Mozam.* .... **57 C6** 24 18S 35 14 E
Nhamaabué, *Mozam.* .... **55 F4** 17 25S 35 5 E
Nhamundá →, *Brazil* ... **93 D7** 2 12S 56 41W
Nhangutazi, L., *Mozam.* . **57 C5** 24 0S 34 30 E
Nhill, *Australia* .... **63 F3** 36 18S 141 40 E
Nho Quan, *Vietnam* ..... **38 B5** 20 18N 105 45 E
Nhulunbuy, *Australia* ... **62 A2** 12 10S 137 20 E
Nia-nia, *Dem. Rep. of the Congo* **54 B2** 1 30N 27 40 E
Niagara, *U.S.A.* **76 C2** 45 45N 88 0W
Niagara Falls, *Canada* .. **70 D4** 43 7N 79 5W
Niagara Falls, *U.S.A.* **78 C6** 43 5N 79 4W
Niagara-on-the-Lake, *Canada* **78 C5** 43 15N 79 4W
Niah, *Malaysia* .... **36 D4** 3 58N 113 46 E
Niamey, *Niger* .... **50 F6** 13 27N 2 6 E
Niangara, *Dem. Rep. of the Congo* **54 B2** 3 42N 27 50 E
Nias, *Indonesia* .... **36 D1** 1 0N 97 30 E
Niassa □, *Mozam.* ...... **55 E4** 13 30S 36 0 E
Nicaragua ■, *Cent. Amer.* **88 D2** 11 40N 85 30W
Nicaragua, L. de, *Nic.* ... **88 D2** 12 0N 85 30W
Nicastro, *Italy* .... **20 E7** 38 59N 16 19 E
Nice, *France* .... **18 E7** 43 42N 7 14 E
Niceville, *U.S.A.* **77 K2** 30 31N 86 30W
Nichinan, *Japan* .... **31 J5** 31 38N 131 23 E
Nicholás, Canal, *W. Indies* **88 B3** 23 30N 80 5W
Nicholasville, *U.S.A.* **76 G3** 37 53N 84 34W
Nichols, *U.S.A.* **79 D8** 42 1N 76 22W
Nicholson, *Australia* .... **60 C4** 18 2S 128 54 E
Nicholson, *U.S.A.* **79 E9** 41 37N 75 47W
Nicholson →, *Australia* . **62 B2** 17 31S 139 36 E
Nicholson Ra., *Australia* . **61 E2** 27 15S 116 45 E
Nicobar Is., *Ind. Oc.* .... **28 J13** 9 0N 93 0 E
Nicola, *Canada* **72 C4** 50 12N 120 40W
Nicolet, *Canada* **70 C5** 46 17N 72 35W
Nicolls Town, *Bahamas* . **88 A4** 25 8N 78 0W
Nicosia, *Cyprus* .... **23 D12** 35 10N 33 25 E
Nicoya, *Costa Rica* **88 D2** 10 9N 85 27W
Nicoya, G. de, *Costa Rica* **88 E3** 10 0N 85 0W
Nicoya, Pen. de, *Costa Rica* **88 E2** 9 45N 85 40W
Nidd →, *U.K.* **10 D6** 53 59N 1 23W
Niedersachsen □, *Germany* .... **16 B5** 52 50N 9 0 E
Niekerkshoop, *S. Africa* .. **56 D3** 29 19S 22 51 E
Niemba, *Dem. Rep. of the Congo* **54 D2** 5 58S 28 24 E
Niemen = Neman →, *Lithuania* .... **24 C3** 55 25N 21 10 E
Nienburg, *Germany* ..... **16 B5** 52 39N 9 13 E
Nieu Bethesda, *S. Africa* . **56 E3** 31 51S 24 34 E
Nieuw Amsterdam, *Surinam* **93 B7** 5 53N 55 5W
Nieuw Nickerie, *Surinam* **93 B7** 6 0N 56 59W
Nieuwoudtville, *S. Africa* **56 E2** 31 23S 19 7 E
Nieuwpoort, *Belgium* ... **15 C2** 51 8N 2 45 E
Nieves, Pico de las, *Canary Is.* **22 G4** 27 57N 15 35W
Niğde, *Turkey* .... **25 G5** 37 58N 34 40 E
Nigel, *S. Africa* .... **57 D4** 26 27S 28 25 E
Niger ■, *W. Afr.* .... **50 E7** 17 30N 10 0 E
Niger →, *W. Afr.* .... **50 G7** 5 33N 6 33 E
Nigeria ■, *W. Afr.* .... **50 G7** 8 30N 8 0 E
Nightcaps, *N.Z.* .... **59 L2** 45 57S 168 2 E
Nihtaur, *India* .... **43 E8** 29 20N 78 23 E
Nii-Jima, *Japan* .... **31 G9** 34 20N 139 15 E
Niigata, *Japan* .... **30 F9** 37 58N 139 0 E
Niigata □, *Japan* .... **31 F9** 37 15N 138 45 E
Niihama, *Japan* .... **31 H6** 33 55N 133 16 E
Niihau, *U.S.A.* **74 H14** 21 54N 160 9W
Niimi, *Japan* .... **31 G6** 34 59N 133 28 E
Niitsu, *Japan* .... **30 F9** 37 48N 139 7 E
Nijil, *Jordan* .... **47 E4** 30 32N 35 33 E
Nijkerk, *Neths.* .... **15 B5** 52 13N 5 30 E
Nijmegen, *Neths.* .... **15 C5** 51 50N 5 52 E
Nijverdal, *Neths.* .... **15 B6** 52 22N 6 28 E
Nīk Pey, *Iran* .... **45 B6** 36 50N 48 10 E
Nikiniki, *Indonesia* ...... **37 F6** 9 49S 124 30 E
Nikkō, *Japan* .... **31 F9** 36 45N 139 35 E
Nikolayev = Mykolayiv, *Ukraine* .... **25 E5** 46 58N 32 0 E
Nikolayevsk, *Russia* ..... **25 E8** 50 0N 45 35 E
Nikolayevsk-na-Amur, *Russia* .... **27 D15** 53 8N 140 44 E
Nikolskoye, *Russia* ...... **27 D17** 55 12N 166 0 E
Nikopol, *Ukraine* .... **25 E5** 47 35N 34 25 E
Nīkshahr, *Iran* .... **45 E9** 26 15N 60 10 E
Nikšić, *Montenegro, Yug.* **21 C8** 42 50N 18 57 E
Nîl, Nahr en →, *Africa* .. **51 B12** 30 10N 31 6 E
Nîl el Abyad →, *Sudan* .. **51 E12** 15 38N 32 31 E
Nîl el Azraq →, *Sudan* .. **51 E12** 15 38N 32 31 E
Niland, *U.S.A.* **85 M11** 33 14N 115 31W
Nile = Nîl, Nahr en →, *Africa* .... **51 B12** 30 10N 31 6 E
Niles, *U.S.A.* **78 E4** 41 11N 80 46W
Nimach, *India* .... **42 G6** 24 30N 74 56 E
Nimbahera, *India* .... **42 G6** 24 37N 74 45 E
Nîmes, *France* .... **18 E6** 43 50N 4 23 E
Nimfaíon, Ákra = Pínnes, Ákra, *Greece* .... **21 D11** 40 5N 24 20 E
Nimmitabel, *Australia* ... **63 F4** 36 29S 149 15 E
Nīnawá, *Iraq* .... **44 B4** 36 25N 43 10 E
Nindigully, *Australia* .... **63 D4** 28 21S 148 50 E
Ninemile, *U.S.A.* **72 B2** 56 0N 130 7W
Nineveh = Nīnawá, *Iraq* . **44 B4** 36 25N 43 10 E
Ning Xian, *China* .... **34 G4** 35 30N 107 58 E
Ningaloo, *Australia* ..... **60 D1** 22 41S 113 41 E
Ning'an, *China* .... **35 B15** 44 22N 129 20 E
Ningbo, *China* .... **33 D7** 29 51N 121 28 E
Ningcheng, *China* .... **35 D10** 41 32N 119 53 E
Ningjin, *China* .... **34 F8** 37 35N 114 57 E
Ningjing Shan, *China* .... **32 D4** 30 0N 98 20 E
Ningling, *China* .... **34 G8** 34 25N 115 22 E
Ningpo = Ningbo, *China* . **33 D7** 29 51N 121 28 E
Ningqiang, *China* .... **34 H4** 32 47N 106 15 E
Ningshan, *China* .... **34 H5** 33 21N 108 21 E
Ningsia Hui A.R. = Ningxia Huizu Zizhiqu □, *China* ...... **34 F4** 38 0N 106 0 E
Ningwu, *China* .... **34 E7** 39 0N 112 18 E
Ningxia Huizu Zizhiqu □, *China* .... **34 F4** 38 0N 106 0 E
Ningyang, *China* .... **34 G9** 35 47N 116 45 E
Ninh Binh, *Vietnam* ..... **38 B5** 20 15N 105 55 E
Ninh Giang, *Vietnam* .... **38 B6** 20 44N 106 24 E
Ninh Hoa, *Vietnam* ..... **38 F7** 12 30N 109 7 E
Ninh Ma, *Vietnam* ...... **38 F7** 12 48N 109 21 E
Ninove, *Belgium* .... **15 D4** 50 51N 4 2 E
Nioaque, *Brazil* **95 A4** 21 5S 55 50W
Niobrara, *U.S.A.* **80 D6** 42 45N 98 2W
Niobrara →, *U.S.A.* **80 D6** 42 46N 98 3W
Nioro du Sahel, *Mali* **50 E4** 15 15N 9 30W
Niort, *France* **18 C3** 46 19N 0 29W
Nipawin, *Canada* **73 C8** 53 20N 104 0W
Nipawin Prov. Park, *Canada* **73 C8** 54 0N 104 37W
Nipigon, *Canada* **70 C2** 49 0N 88 17W
Nipigon, L., *Canada* **70 C2** 49 50N 88 30W
Nipin →, *Canada* **73 B7** 55 46N 108 35W
Nipishish L., *Canada* **71 B7** 54 12N 60 45W
Nipissing L., *Canada* **70 C4** 46 20N 80 0W
Nipomo, *U.S.A.* **85 K6** 35 3N 120 29W
Nipton, *U.S.A.* **85 K11** 35 28N 115 16W
Niquelândia, *Brazil* **93 F9** 14 33S 48 23W
Nīr, *Iran* .... **44 B5** 38 2N 47 59 E
Nirasaki, *Japan* .... **31 G9** 35 42N 138 27 E
Nirmal, *India* .... **40 K11** 19 3N 78 20 E
Nirmali, *India* .... **43 F12** 26 20N 86 35 E
Niš, *Serbia, Yug.* .... **21 C9** 43 19N 21 58 E
Nişāb, *Si. Arabia* .... **44 D5** 29 11N 44 43 E
Nişāb, *Yemen* .... **46 E4** 14 25N 46 29 E
Nishinomiya, *Japan* ..... **31 G7** 34 45N 135 20 E
Nishino'omote, *Japan* ... **31 J5** 30 43N 130 59 E
Nishiwaki, *Japan* .... **31 G7** 34 59N 134 58 E
Niskibi →, *Canada* **70 A2** 56 29N 88 9W
Nisqually →, *U.S.A.* **84 C4** 47 6N 122 42W
Nissáki, *Greece* .... **23 A3** 39 43N 19 52 E
Nissum Bredning, *Denmark* .... **9 H13** 56 40N 8 20 E
Nistru = Dnister →, *Europe* .... **25 E5** 46 18N 30 17 E
Nisutlin →, *Canada* **72 A2** 60 14N 132 34W
Nitchequon, *Canada* **71 B5** 53 10N 70 58W
Niterói, *Brazil* **95 A7** 22 52S 43 0W
Nith →, *U.K.* **12 F5** 55 14N 3 33W
Nitra, *Slovak Rep.* ...... **17 D10** 48 19N 18 4 E
Nitra →, *Slovak Rep.* ... **17 E10** 47 46N 18 10 E
Niuafo'ou, *Tonga* **59 B11** 15 30S 175 58W
Niue, *Cook Is.* **65 J11** 19 2S 169 54W
Niut, *Indonesia* .... **36 D4** 0 55N 110 6 E
Niuzhuang, *China* .... **35 D12** 40 58N 122 28 E
Nivala, *Finland* .... **8 E21** 63 56N 24 57 E
Nivelles, *Belgium* .... **15 D4** 50 35N 4 20 E
Nivernais, *France* .... **18 C5** 47 15N 3 30 E
Nixon, *U.S.A.* **81 L6** 29 16N 97 46W
Nizamabad, *India* .... **40 K11** 18 45N 78 7 E
Nizamghat, *India* .... **41 E19** 28 20N 95 45 E
Nizhne Kolymsk, *Russia* . **27 C17** 68 34N 160 55 E
Nizhnekamsk, *Russia* ... **24 C9** 55 38N 51 49 E
Nizhneudinsk, *Russia* ... **27 D10** 54 54N 99 3 E
Nizhnevartovsk, *Russia* .. **26 C8** 60 56N 76 38 E
Nizhniy Novgorod, *Russia* **24 C7** 56 20N 44 0 E
Nizhniy Tagil, *Russia* .... **24 C10** 57 55N 59 57 E
Nizhyn, *Ukraine* .... **25 D5** 51 5N 31 55 E
Nízké Tatry, *Slovak Rep.* . **17 D10** 48 55N 19 30 E
Njakwa, *Malawi* .... **55 E3** 11 1S 33 56 E
Njanji, *Zambia* .... **55 E3** 14 25S 31 46 E
Njinjo, *Tanzania* .... **55 D4** 8 48S 38 54 E
Njombe, *Tanzania* .... **55 D3** 9 20S 34 50 E
Njombe □, *Tanzania* ..... **55 D3** 9 20S 34 49 E
Njombe →, *Tanzania* ... **54 D4** 6 56S 35 6 E
Nkana, *Zambia* .... **55 E2** 12 50S 28 8 E
Nkayi, *Zimbabwe* .... **55 F2** 19 41S 29 20 E
Nkhotakota, *Malawi* ..... **55 E3** 12 56S 34 15 E
Nkongsamba, *Cameroon* . **52 D1** 4 55N 9 55 E
Nkurenkuru, *Namibia* ... **56 B2** 17 42S 18 32 E
Nmai →, *Burma* .... **41 G20** 25 30N 97 25 E
Noakhali = Maijdi, *Bangla.* **41 H17** 22 48N 91 10 E
Nobel, *Canada* **78 A4** 45 25N 80 6W
Nobeoka, *Japan* .... **31 H5** 32 36N 131 41 E
Noblesville, *U.S.A.* **76 E3** 40 3N 86 1W
Nocera Inferiore, *Italy* ... **20 D6** 40 44N 14 38 E
Nockatunga, *Australia* ... **63 D3** 27 42S 142 42 E
Nocona, *U.S.A.* **81 J6** 33 47N 97 44W
Noda, *Japan* .... **31 G9** 35 56N 139 52 E
Noel, *U.S.A.* **81 G7** 36 33N 94 29W
Nogales, *Mexico* **86 A2** 31 20N 110 56W
Nogales, *U.S.A.* **83 L8** 31 20N 110 56W
Nōgata, *Japan* .... **31 H5** 33 48N 130 44 E
Noggerup, *Australia* .... **61 F2** 33 32S 116 5 E
Noginsk, *Russia* .... **27 C10** 64 30N 90 50 E
Nogoa →, *Australia* .... **62 C4** 23 40S 147 55 E
Nogoyá, *Argentina* **94 C4** 32 24S 59 48W
Nohar, *India* .... **42 E6** 29 11N 74 49 E
Noire, Mts., *France* **18 B2** 48 7N 3 28W
Noirmoutier, Î. de, *France* **18 C2** 46 58N 2 10W
Nojane, *Botswana* .... **56 C3** 23 15S 20 14 E
Nojima-Zaki, *Japan* ..... **31 G9** 34 54N 139 53 E
Nok Kundi, *Pakistan* .... **40 E3** 28 50N 62 45 E
Nokaneng, *Botswana* .... **56 B3** 19 40S 22 17 E
Nokia, *Finland* .... **9 F20** 61 30N 23 30 E
Nokomis, *Canada* **73 C8** 51 35N 105 0W
Nokomis L., *Canada* **73 B8** 57 0N 103 0W
Nola, *C.A.R.* .... **52 D3** 3 35N 16 4 E
Noma Omuramba →, *Namibia* .... **56 B3** 18 52S 20 53 E
Noman L., *Canada* **73 A7** 62 15N 108 55W
Nombre de Dios, *Panama* **88 E4** 9 34N 79 28W
Nome, *U.S.A.* **68 B3** 64 30N 165 25W
Nomo-Zaki, *Japan* ...... **31 H4** 32 35N 129 44 E
Nonacho L., *Canada* **73 A7** 61 42N 109 40W
Nonda, *Australia* .... **62 C3** 20 40S 142 28 E
Nong Chang, *Thailand* ... **38 E2** 15 23N 99 51 E
Nong Het, *Laos* .... **38 C4** 19 29N 103 59 E
Nong Khai, *Thailand* .... **38 D4** 17 50N 102 46 E
Nong'an, *China* .... **35 B13** 44 25N 125 5 E
Nongoma, *S. Africa* ..... **57 D5** 27 58S 31 35 E
Nonoava, *Mexico* **86 B3** 27 28N 106 44W
Nonthaburi, *Thailand* ... **38 F3** 13 51N 100 34 E
Noonamah, *Australia* ... **60 B5** 12 40S 131 4 E
Noonan, *U.S.A.* **80 A3** 48 54N 103 1W
Noondoo, *Australia* ..... **63 D4** 28 35S 148 30 E
Noonkanbah, *Australia* .. **60 C3** 18 30S 124 50 E
Noord Brabant □, *Neths.* **15 C5** 51 40N 5 0 E
Noord Holland □, *Neths.* . **15 B4** 52 30N 4 45 E
Noordbeveland, *Neths.* .. **15 C3** 51 35N 3 50 E
Noordoostpolder, *Neths.* . **15 B5** 52 45N 5 45 E
Noordwijk, *Neths.* ...... **15 B4** 52 14N 4 26 E
Nootka, *Canada* **72 D3** 49 38N 126 38W
Nootka I., *Canada* **72 D3** 49 32N 126 42W
Noranda = Rouyn-Noranda, *Canada* **70 C4** 48 20N 79 0W
Norco, *U.S.A.* **85 M9** 33 56N 117 33W
Nord-Ostsee-Kanal →, *Germany* .... **16 A5** 54 12N 9 32 E
Nordegg, *Canada* **72 C5** 52 29N 116 5W
Norderney, *Germany* .... **16 B4** 53 42N 7 9 E
Norderstedt, *Germany* .. **16 B5** 53 42N 10 1 E
Nordfjord, *Norway* ...... **9 F11** 61 55N 5 30 E
Nordfriesische Inseln, *Germany* .... **16 A5** 54 40N 8 20 E
Nordhausen, *Germany* .. **16 C6** 51 30N 10 47 E
Norðoyar, *Færoe Is.* **8 E9** 62 17N 6 35W
Nordkapp, *Norway* ..... **8 A21** 71 10N 25 50 E
Nordkinn = Kinnarodden, *Norway* .... **6 A11** 71 8N 27 40 E
Nordkinn-halvøya, *Norway* **8 A22** 70 55N 27 40 E
Nordrhein-Westfalen □, *Germany* .... **16 C4** 51 45N 7 30 E
Nordvik, *Russia* .... **27 B12** 74 2N 111 32 E
Nore →, *Ireland* **13 D4** 52 25N 6 58W
Norembega, *Canada* **70 C3** 48 59N 80 43W
Norfolk, *Nebr., U.S.A.* ... **80 D6** 42 2N 97 25W
Norfolk, *Va., U.S.A.* **76 G7** 36 51N 76 17W
Norfolk □, *U.K.* .... **11 E8** 52 39N 0 54 E
Norfolk I., *Pac. Oc.* ..... **64 K8** 28 58S 168 3 E
Norfork Res., *U.S.A.* **81 G8** 36 13N 92 15W
Norilsk, *Russia* .... **27 C9** 69 20N 88 6 E
Norley, *Australia* .... **63 D3** 27 45S 143 48 E
Norma, Mt., *Australia* ... **62 C3** 20 55S 140 42 E
Normal, *U.S.A.* **80 E10** 40 31N 88 59W
Norman, *U.S.A.* **81 H6** 35 13N 97 26W
Norman →, *Australia* ... **62 B3** 19 18S 141 51 E
Norman Wells, *Canada* .. **68 B7** 65 17N 126 51W
Normanby →, *Australia* **62 A3** 14 23S 144 10 E
Normandie, *France* ..... **18 B4** 48 45N 0 10 E
Normandin, *Canada* **70 C5** 48 49N 72 31W
Normandy = Normandie, *France* .... **18 B4** 48 45N 0 10 E
Normanhurst, Mt., *Australia* .... **61 E3** 25 4S 122 30 E
Normanton, *Australia* ... **62 B3** 17 40S 141 10 E
Norquay, *Canada* **73 C8** 51 53N 102 5W
Norquinco, *Argentina* ... **96 E2** 41 51S 70 55W
Norrbotten □, *Sweden* .. **8 C19** 66 30N 22 30 E
Norris, *U.S.A.* **82 D8** 45 34N 111 41W
Norristown, *U.S.A.* **79 F9** 40 7N 75 21W
Norrköping, *Sweden* .... **9 G17** 58 37N 16 11 E
Norrland, *Sweden* ...... **9 E16** 62 15N 15 45 E
Norrtälje, *Sweden* ...... **9 G18** 59 46N 18 42 E
Norseman, *Australia* .... **61 F3** 32 8S 121 43 E
Norsk, *Russia* .... **27 D14** 52 30N 130 5 E
Norte, Pta. del, *Canary Is.* **22 G2** 27 51N 17 57W
Norte, Serra do, *Brazil* ... **92 F7** 11 20S 59 0W
North Adams, *U.S.A.* **79 D11** 42 42N 73 7W
North Ayrshire □, *U.K.* .. **12 F4** 55 45N 4 44W
North Battleford, *Canada* **73 C7** 52 50N 108 17W
North Bay, *Canada* **70 C4** 46 20N 79 30W
North Belcher Is., *Canada* **70 A4** 56 50N 79 50W
North Bend, *Canada* **72 D4** 49 50N 121 27W
North Bend, *Oreg., U.S.A.* **82 E1** 43 24N 124 14W
North Bend, *Pa., U.S.A.* .. **78 E7** 41 20N 77 42W
North Bend, *Wash., U.S.A.* **84 C5** 47 30N 121 47W
North Berwick, *U.K.* **12 E6** 56 4N 2 42W
North Berwick, *U.S.A.* ... **79 C14** 43 18N 70 44W
North C., *Canada* **71 C7** 47 2N 60 20W
North C., *N.Z.* .... **59 F4** 34 23S 173 4 E
North Canadian →, *U.S.A.* **81 H7** 35 16N 95 31W
North Cape = Nordkapp, *Norway* .... **8 A21** 71 10N 25 50 E
North Caribou L., *Canada* **70 B1** 52 50N 90 40W
North Carolina □, *U.S.A.* **77 H6** 35 30N 80 0W
North Channel, *Canada* .. **70 C3** 46 0N 83 0W
North Channel, *U.K.* **12 F3** 55 13N 5 52W
North Charleston, *U.S.A.* **77 J6** 32 53N 79 58W
North Chicago, *U.S.A.* ... **76 D2** 42 19N 87 51W
North Dakota □, *U.S.A.* .. **80 B5** 47 30N 100 15W
North Dandalup, *Australia* **61 F2** 32 30S 115 57 E
North Downs, *U.K.* ...... **11 F8** 51 19N 0 21 E
North East, *U.S.A.* **78 D5** 42 13N 79 50W
North East Frontier Agency = Arunachal Pradesh □, *India* ...... **41 F19** 28 0N 95 0 E
North East Lincolnshire □, *U.K.* **10 D7** 53 34N 0 2W
North East Providence Chan., *W. Indies* **88 A4** 26 0N 76 0W
North Eastern □, *Kenya* . **54 B5** 1 30N 40 0 E
North Esk →, *U.K.* **12 E6** 56 46N 2 24W
North European Plain, *Europe* .... **6 E10** 55 0N 25 0 E
North Foreland, *U.K.* .... **11 F9** 51 22N 1 28 E
North Fork, *U.S.A.* **84 H7** 37 14N 119 21W
North Fork American →, *U.S.A.* **84 G5** 38 57N 120 59W
North Fork Feather →, *U.S.A.* **84 F5** 38 33N 121 30W
North Frisian Is. = Nordfriesische Inseln, *Germany* .... **16 A5** 54 40N 8 20 E
North Henik L., *Canada* .. **73 A9** 61 45N 97 40W
North Highlands, *U.S.A.* . **84 G5** 38 40N 121 23W
North Horr, *Kenya* ...... **54 B4** 3 20N 37 8 E
North I., *Kenya* .... **54 B4** 4 5N 36 5 E
North I., *N.Z.* .... **59 H5** 38 0S 175 0 E
North Kingsville, *U.S.A.* . **78 E4** 41 54N 80 42W
North Knife →, *Canada* . **73 B10** 58 53N 94 45W
North Koel →, *India* .... **43 G10** 24 45N 83 50 E
North Korea ■, *Asia* .... **35 E14** 40 0N 127 0 E
North Lakhimpur, *India* .. **41 F19** 27 14N 94 7 E
North Lanarkshire □, *U.K.* **12 F5** 55 52N 3 56W
North Las Vegas, *U.S.A.* . **85 J11** 36 12N 115 7W
North Lincolnshire □, *U.K.* **10 D7** 53 36N 0 30W
North Little Rock, *U.S.A.* . **81 H8** 34 45N 92 16W
North Loup →, *U.S.A.* ... **80 E5** 41 17N 98 24W
North Minch, *U.K.* **12 C3** 58 5N 5 55W
North Nahanni →, *Canada* **72 A4** 62 15N 123 20W
North Olmsted, *U.S.A.* .. **78 E3** 41 25N 81 56W
North Ossetia □, *Russia* . **25 F7** 43 30N 44 30 E
North Pagai, I. = Pagai Utara, Pulau, *Indonesia* **36 E2** 2 35S 100 0 E
North Palisade, *U.S.A.* .. **84 H8** 37 6N 118 31W
North Platte, *U.S.A.* **80 E4** 41 8N 100 46W
North Platte →, *U.S.A.* .. **80 E4** 41 7N 100 42W
North Portal, *Canada* ... **73 D8** 49 0N 102 33W
North Powder, *U.S.A.* ... **82 D5** 45 2N 117 55W
North Pt., *Canada* **71 C7** 47 5N 64 0W
North Rhine Westphalia □ = Nordrhein-Westfalen □, *Germany* **16 C4** 51 45N 7 30 E

O

Óssa, Óros

Ogowe = Ogooué →, Gabon 52 E1 1 0S 9 0 E
Ogre, Latvia 9 H21 56 49N 24 36 E
Ohai, N.Z. 59 L2 45 55S 168 0 E
Ohakune, N.Z. 59 H5 39 24S 175 24 E
Ohata, Japan 30 D10 41 24N 141 10 E
Ohau, L., N.Z. 59 L2 44 15S 169 53 E
Ohio □, U.S.A. 76 E3 40 15N 82 45W
Ohio →, U.S.A. 76 G1 36 59N 89 8W
Ohře →, Czech Rep. 16 C8 50 30N 14 10 E
Ohrid, Macedonia 21 D9 41 8N 20 52 E
Ohridsko Jezero, Macedonia 21 D9 41 8N 20 52 E
Ohrigstad, S. Africa 57 C5 24 39S 30 36 E
Oiapoque, Brazil 93 C8 3 50N 51 50W
Oikou, China 35 E9 38 35N 117 42 E
Oil City, U.S.A. 78 E5 41 26N 79 42W
Oildale, U.S.A. 85 K7 35 25N 119 1W
Oise →, France 18 B5 49 0N 2 4 E
Ōita, Japan 31 H5 33 14N 131 36 E
Ōita □, Japan 31 H5 33 15N 131 30 E
Oiticica, Brazil 93 E10 5 3S 41 5W
Ojai, U.S.A. 85 L7 34 27N 119 15W
Ojinaga, Mexico 86 B4 29 34N 104 25W
Ojiya, Japan 31 F9 37 18N 138 48 E
Ojos del Salado, Cerro, Argentina 94 B2 27 0S 68 40W
Oka →, Russia 26 D5 56 20N 43 59 E
Okaba, Indonesia 37 F9 8 6S 139 42 E
Okahandja, Namibia 56 C2 22 0S 16 59 E
Okahukura, N.Z. 59 H5 38 48S 175 14 E
Okanagan L., Canada 72 D5 50 0N 119 30W
Okanogan, U.S.A. 82 B4 48 22N 119 35W
Okanogan →, U.S.A. 82 B4 48 6N 119 44W
Okaputa, Namibia 56 C2 20 5S 17 0 E
Okara, Pakistan 42 D5 30 50N 73 31 E
Okarito, N.Z. 59 K3 43 15S 170 9 E
Okaukuejo, Namibia 56 B2 19 10S 16 0 E
Okavango Swamps, Botswana 56 B3 18 45S 22 45 E
Okaya, Japan 31 F9 36 5N 138 10 E
Okayama, Japan 31 G6 34 40N 133 54 E
Okayama □, Japan 31 G6 35 0N 133 50 E
Okazaki, Japan 31 G8 34 57N 137 10 E
Okeechobee, U.S.A. 77 M5 27 15N 80 50W
Okeechobee, L., U.S.A. 77 M5 27 0N 80 50W
Okefenokee Swamp, U.S.A. 77 K4 30 40N 82 20W
Okehampton, U.K. 11 G4 50 44N 4 0W
Okha, Russia 27 D15 53 40N 143 0 E
Okhotsk, Russia 27 D15 59 20N 143 10 E
Okhotsk, Sea of, Asia 27 D15 55 0N 145 0 E
Okhotskiy Perevoz, Russia 27 C14 61 52N 135 35 E
Oki-Shotō, Japan 31 F6 36 5N 133 15 E
Okiep, S. Africa 56 D2 29 39S 17 53 E
Okinawa □, Japan 31 L4 26 40N 128 0 E
Okinawa-Guntō, Japan 31 L4 26 40N 128 0 E
Okinawa-Jima, Japan 31 L4 26 32N 128 0 E
Okino-erabu-Shima, Japan 31 L4 27 21N 128 33 E
Oklahoma □, U.S.A. 81 H6 35 20N 97 30W
Oklahoma City, U.S.A. 81 H6 35 30N 97 30W
Okmulgee, U.S.A. 81 H7 35 37N 95 58W
Oknitsa = Ocniţa, Moldova 17 D14 48 25N 27 30 E
Okolo, Uganda 54 B3 2 37N 31 8 E
Okolona, U.S.A. 81 J10 34 0N 88 45W
Oksibil, Indonesia 37 E10 4 59S 140 35 E
Oksovskiy, Russia 24 B6 62 33N 39 57 E
Oktabrsk = Oktyabrsk, Kazakstan 25 E10 49 28N 57 25 E
Oktyabrsk, Kazakstan 25 E10 49 28N 57 25 E
Oktyabrskiy = Aktsyabrski, Belarus 17 B15 52 38N 28 53 E
Oktyabrskiy, Russia 24 D9 54 28N 53 28 E
Oktyabrskoy Revolyutsii, Ostrov, Russia 27 B10 79 30N 97 0 E
Okuru, N.Z. 59 K2 43 55S 168 55 E
Okushiri-Tō, Japan 30 C9 42 15N 139 30 E
Okwa →, Botswana 56 C3 22 30S 23 0 E
Ola, U.S.A. 81 H8 35 2N 93 13W
Ólafsfjörður, Iceland 8 C4 66 4N 18 39W
Ólafsvík, Iceland 8 D2 64 53N 23 43W
Olancha, U.S.A. 85 J8 36 17N 118 1W
Olancha Pk., U.S.A. 85 J8 36 15N 118 7W
Olanchito, Honduras 88 C2 15 30N 86 30W
Öland, Sweden 9 H17 56 45N 16 38 E
Olary, Australia 63 E3 32 18S 140 19 E
Olascoaga, Argentina 94 D3 35 15S 60 39W
Olathe, U.S.A. 80 F7 38 53N 94 49W
Olavarría, Argentina 94 D3 36 55S 60 20W
Oława, Poland 17 C9 50 57N 17 20 E
Ólbia, Italy 20 D3 40 55N 9 31 E
Old Bahama Chan. = Bahama, Canal Viejo de, W. Indies 88 B4 22 10N 77 30W
Old Baldy Pk. = San Antonio, Mt., U.S.A. 85 L9 34 17N 117 38W
Old Cork, Australia 62 C3 22 57S 141 52 E
Old Crow, Canada 68 B6 67 30N 139 55W
Old Dale, U.S.A. 85 L11 34 8N 115 47W
Old Forge, N.Y., U.S.A. 79 C10 43 43N 74 58W
Old Forge, Pa., U.S.A. 79 E9 41 22N 75 45W
Old Fort →, Canada 73 B6 58 36N 110 24W
Old Shinyanga, Tanzania 54 C3 3 33S 33 27 E
Old Speck Mt., U.S.A. 79 B14 44 34N 70 57W
Old Town, U.S.A. 71 D6 44 56N 68 39W
Old Wives L., Canada 73 C7 50 5N 106 0W
Oldbury, U.K. 11 F5 51 38N 2 33W
Oldcastle, Ireland 13 C4 53 46N 7 10W
Oldeani, Tanzania 54 C4 3 22S 35 35 E
Oldenburg, Germany 16 B5 53 9N 8 13 E
Oldenzaal, Neths. 15 B6 52 19N 6 53 E
Oldham, U.K. 10 D5 53 33N 2 7W
Oldman →, Canada 72 D6 49 57N 111 42W
Oldmeldrum, U.K. 12 D6 57 20N 2 19W
Olds, Canada 72 C6 51 50N 114 10W
Olean, U.S.A. 78 D6 42 5N 78 26W
Olekma →, Russia 27 C13 60 22N 120 42 E
Olekminsk, Russia 27 C13 60 25N 120 30 E
Oleksandriya, Ukraine 17 C14 50 37N 26 19 E
Olema, U.S.A. 84 G4 38 3N 122 47W
Olenegorsk, Russia 24 A5 68 9N 33 18 E
Olenek, Russia 27 C12 68 28N 112 18 E
Olenek →, Russia 27 B13 73 0N 120 10 E
Oléron, Î. d', France 18 D3 45 55N 1 15W
Oleśnica, Poland 17 C9 51 13N 17 22 E
Olevsk, Ukraine 17 C14 51 12N 27 39 E
Olga, Russia 27 E14 43 50N 135 14 E
Olga, L., Canada 70 C4 49 47N 77 15W
Olga, Mt., Australia 61 E5 25 20S 130 50 E
Olhão, Portugal 19 D2 37 3N 7 48W
Olifants →, Africa 57 C5 23 57S 31 58 E
Olifantshoek, S. Africa 56 D3 27 57S 22 42 E
Ólimbos, Óros, Greece 21 D10 40 6N 22 23 E
Olímpia, Brazil 95 A6 20 44S 48 54W
Olinda, Brazil 93 E12 8 1S 34 51W
Oliva, Argentina 94 C3 32 0S 63 38W
Olivehurst, U.S.A. 84 F5 39 6N 121 34W
Olivenza, Spain 19 C2 38 41N 7 9W
Oliver, Canada 72 D5 49 13N 119 37W
Oliver L., Canada 73 B8 56 56N 103 22W
Ollagüe, Chile 94 A2 21 15S 68 10W
Olney, Ill., U.S.A. 76 F1 38 44N 88 5W
Olney, Tex., U.S.A. 81 J5 33 22N 98 45W
Olomane →, Canada 71 B7 50 14N 60 37W
Olomouc, Czech Rep. 17 D9 49 38N 17 12 E
Olonets, Russia 24 B5 61 0N 32 54 E
Olongapo, Phil. 37 B6 14 50N 120 18 E
Olot, Spain 19 A7 42 11N 2 30 E
Olovyannaya, Russia 27 D12 50 58N 115 35 E
Oloy →, Russia 27 C16 66 29N 159 29 E
Olsztyn, Poland 17 B11 53 48N 20 29 E
Olt →, Romania 17 G13 43 43N 24 51 E
Olteniţa, Romania 17 F14 44 7N 26 42 E
Olton, U.S.A. 81 H3 34 11N 102 8W
Olymbos, Cyprus 23 D12 35 21N 33 45 E
Olympia, Greece 21 F9 37 39N 21 39 E
Olympia, U.S.A. 84 D4 47 3N 122 53W
Olympic Mts., U.S.A. 84 C3 47 55N 123 45W
Olympic Nat. Park, U.S.A. 84 C3 47 48N 123 30W
Olympus, Cyprus 23 E11 34 56N 32 52 E
Olympus, Mt. = Ólimbos, Óros, Greece 21 D10 40 6N 22 23 E
Olympus, Mt. = Uludağ, Turkey 21 D13 40 4N 29 13 E
Olympus, Mt., U.S.A. 84 C3 47 48N 123 43W
Olyphant, U.S.A. 79 E9 41 27N 75 36W
Om →, Russia 26 D8 54 59N 73 22 E
Om Koi, Thailand 38 D2 17 48N 98 22 E
Ōma, Japan 30 D10 41 45N 141 5 E
Ōmachi, Japan 31 F8 36 30N 137 50 E
Omae-Zaki, Japan 31 G9 34 36N 138 14 E
Ōmagari, Japan 30 E10 39 27N 140 29 E
Omagh, U.K. 13 B4 54 36N 7 19W
Omagh □, U.K. 13 B4 54 35N 7 15W
Omaha, U.S.A. 80 E7 41 17N 95 58W
Omak, U.S.A. 82 B4 48 25N 119 31W
Omalos, Greece 23 D5 35 19N 23 55 E
Oman ■, Asia 46 C6 23 0N 58 0 E
Oman, G. of, Asia 45 E8 24 30N 58 30 E
Omaruru, Namibia 56 C2 21 26S 16 0 E
Omaruru →, Namibia 56 C1 22 7S 14 15 E
Omate, Peru 92 G4 16 45S 71 0W
Ombai, Selat, Indonesia 37 F6 8 30S 124 50 E
Omboué, Gabon 52 E1 1 35S 9 15 E
Ombrone →, Italy 20 C4 42 42N 11 5 E
Omdurmân, Sudan 51 E12 15 40N 32 28 E
Omeonga, Dem. Rep. of the Congo 54 C1 3 40S 24 22 E
Ometepe, I. de, Nic. 88 D2 11 32N 85 35W
Ometepec, Mexico 87 D5 16 39N 98 23W
Ominato, Japan 30 D10 41 17N 141 10 E
Omineca →, Canada 72 B4 56 3N 124 16W
Omitara, Namibia 56 C2 22 16S 18 2 E
Ōmiya, Japan 31 G9 35 54N 139 38 E
Ommen, Neths. 15 B6 52 31N 6 26 E
Ömnögovĭ □, Mongolia 34 C3 43 15N 104 0 E
Omo →, Ethiopia 46 F2 6 25N 36 10 E
Omodhos, Cyprus 23 E11 34 51N 32 48 E
Omolon →, Russia 27 C16 68 42N 158 36 E
Omono-Gawa →, Japan 30 E10 39 46N 140 3 E
Omsk, Russia 26 D8 55 0N 73 12 E
Omsukchan, Russia 27 C16 62 32N 155 48 E
Ōmu, Japan 30 B11 44 34N 142 58 E
Omul, Vf., Romania 17 F13 45 27N 25 29 E
Ōmura, Japan 31 H4 32 56N 129 57 E
Omuramba Omatako →, Namibia 53 H4 17 45S 20 25 E
Ōmuta, Japan 31 H5 33 5N 130 26 E
Onaga, U.S.A. 80 F6 39 29N 96 10W
Onalaska, U.S.A. 80 D9 43 53N 91 14W
Onamia, U.S.A. 80 B8 46 4N 93 40W
Onancock, U.S.A. 76 G8 37 43N 75 45W
Onang, Indonesia 37 E5 3 2S 118 49 E
Onaping L., Canada 70 C3 47 3N 81 30W
Onavas, Mexico 86 B3 28 28N 109 30W
Onawa, U.S.A. 80 D6 42 2N 96 6W
Onaway, U.S.A. 76 C3 45 21N 84 14W
Oncócua, Angola 56 B1 16 30S 13 25 E
Onda, Spain 19 C5 39 55N 0 17W
Ondaejin, N. Korea 35 D15 41 34N 129 40 E
Ondangua, Namibia 56 B2 17 57S 16 4 E
Ondjiva, Angola 56 B2 16 48S 15 50 E
Öndörshil, Mongolia 34 B5 45 13N 108 5 E
Öndverðarnes, Iceland 8 D1 64 52N 24 0W
Onega, Russia 24 B6 64 0N 38 10 E
Onega →, Russia 24 B6 63 58N 38 2 E
Onega, G. of = Onezhskaya Guba, Russia 24 B6 64 24N 36 38 E
Onega, L. = Onezhskoye Ozero, Russia 24 B6 61 44N 35 22 E
Onehunga, N.Z. 59 G5 36 55S 174 48 E
Oneida, U.S.A. 79 C9 43 6N 75 39W
Oneida L., U.S.A. 79 C9 43 12N 75 54W
O'Neill, U.S.A. 80 D5 42 27N 98 39W
Onekotan, Ostrov, Russia 27 E16 49 25N 154 45 E
Onema, Dem. Rep. of the Congo 54 C1 4 35S 24 30 E
Oneonta, Ala., U.S.A. 77 J2 33 57N 86 28W
Oneonta, N.Y., U.S.A. 79 D9 42 27N 75 4W
Oneşti, Romania 17 E14 46 15N 26 45 E
Onezhskaya Guba, Russia 24 B6 64 24N 36 38 E
Onezhskoye Ozero, Russia 24 B6 61 44N 35 22 E
Ongarue, N.Z. 59 H5 38 42S 175 19 E
Ongerup, Australia 61 F2 33 58S 118 28 E
Ongjin, N. Korea 35 F13 37 56N 125 21 E
Ongkharak, Thailand 38 E3 14 8N 101 1 E
Ongniud Qi, China 35 C10 43 0N 118 38 E
Ongoka, Dem. Rep. of the Congo 54 C2 1 20S 26 0 E
Ongole, India 40 M12 15 33N 80 2 E
Ongon, Mongolia 34 B7 45 41N 113 5 E
Onida, U.S.A. 80 C4 44 42N 100 4W
Onilahy →, Madag. 57 C7 23 34S 43 45 E
Onitsha, Nigeria 50 G7 6 6N 6 42 E
Onoda, Japan 31 G5 34 2N 131 25 E
Onpyŏng-ni, S. Korea 35 H14 33 25N 126 55 E
Onslow, Australia 60 D2 21 40S 115 12 E
Onslow B., U.S.A. 77 H7 34 20N 77 15W
Ontake-San, Japan 31 G8 35 53N 137 29 E
Ontario, Calif., U.S.A. 85 L9 34 4N 117 39W
Ontario, Oreg., U.S.A. 82 D5 44 2N 116 58W
Ontario □, Canada 70 B2 48 0N 83 0W
Ontario, L., U.S.A. 70 D4 43 20N 78 0W
Ontonagon, U.S.A. 80 B10 46 52N 89 19W
Onyx, U.S.A. 85 K8 35 41N 118 14W
Oodnadatta, Australia 63 D2 27 33S 135 30 E
Ooldea, Australia 61 F5 30 27S 131 50 E
Oombulgurri, Australia 60 C4 15 15S 127 45 E
Oona River, Canada 72 C2 53 57N 130 16W
Oorindi, Australia 62 C3 20 40S 141 1 E
Oost-Vlaanderen □, Belgium 15 C3 51 5N 3 50 E
Oostende, Belgium 15 C2 51 15N 2 54 E
Oosterhout, Neths. 15 C4 51 39N 4 47 E
Oosterschelde, Neths. 15 C4 51 33N 4 0 E
Oosterwolde, Neths. 15 B6 53 0N 6 17 E
Ootacamund = Udagamandalam, India 40 P10 11 30N 76 44 E
Ootsa L., Canada 72 C3 53 50N 126 2W
Opala, Dem. Rep. of the Congo 54 C1 0 40S 24 20 E
Opanake, Sri Lanka 40 R12 6 35N 80 40 E
Opasatika, Canada 70 C3 49 30N 82 50W
Opasquia, Canada 73 C10 53 16N 93 34W
Opava, Czech Rep. 17 D9 49 57N 17 58 E
Opelousas, U.S.A. 81 K8 30 32N 92 5W
Opémisca, L., Canada 70 C5 49 56N 74 52W
Opheim, U.S.A. 82 B10 48 51N 106 24W
Ophthalmia Ra., Australia 60 D2 23 15S 119 30 E
Opinaca →, Canada 70 B4 52 15N 78 2W
Opinaca L., Canada 70 B4 52 39N 76 20W
Opiskotish, L., Canada 71 B6 53 10N 67 50W
Opole, Poland 17 C9 50 42N 17 58 E
Oporto = Porto, Portugal 19 B1 41 8N 8 40W
Opotiki, N.Z. 59 H6 38 1S 177 19 E
Opp, U.S.A. 77 K2 31 17N 86 16W
Oppdal, Norway 9 E13 62 35N 9 41 E
Opua, N.Z. 59 F5 35 19S 174 9 E
Opunake, N.Z. 59 H4 39 26S 173 52 E
Ora, Cyprus 23 E12 34 51N 33 12 E
Ora Banda, Australia 61 F3 30 20S 121 0 E
Oracle, U.S.A. 83 K8 32 37N 110 46W
Oradea, Romania 17 E11 47 2N 21 58 E
Öræfajökull, Iceland 8 D5 64 2N 16 39W
Orai, India 43 G8 25 58N 79 30 E
Oral = Zhayyq →, Kazakstan 25 E9 47 0N 51 48 E
Oral, Kazakstan 24 D9 51 20N 51 20 E
Oran, Algeria 50 A5 35 45N 0 39W
Oran, Argentina 94 A3 23 10S 64 20W
Orange, Australia 63 E4 33 15S 149 7 E
Orange, France 18 D6 44 8N 4 47 E
Orange, Calif., U.S.A. 85 M9 33 47N 117 51W
Orange, Mass., U.S.A. 79 D12 42 35N 72 19W
Orange, Tex., U.S.A. 81 K8 30 6N 93 44W
Orange, Va., U.S.A. 76 F6 38 15N 78 7W
Orange →, S. Africa 56 D2 28 41S 16 28 E
Orange, C., Brazil 93 C8 4 20N 51 30W
Orange Cove, U.S.A. 84 J7 36 38N 119 19W
Orange Free State □ = Free State □, S. Africa 56 D4 28 30S 27 0 E
Orange Grove, U.S.A. 81 M6 27 58N 97 56W
Orange Walk, Belize 87 D7 18 6N 88 33W
Orangeburg, U.S.A. 77 J5 33 30N 80 52W
Orangeville, Canada 70 D3 43 55N 80 5W
Oranienburg, Germany 16 B7 52 45N 13 14 E
Oranje = Orange →, S. Africa 56 D2 28 41S 16 28 E
Oranje Vrystaat □ = Free State □, S. Africa 56 D4 28 30S 27 0 E
Oranjemund, Namibia 56 D2 28 38S 16 29 E
Oranjerivier, S. Africa 56 D3 29 40S 24 12 E
Oras, Phil. 37 B7 12 9N 125 28 E
Oraşul Stalin = Braşov, Romania 17 F13 45 38N 25 35 E
Orbetello, Italy 20 C4 42 27N 11 13 E
Orbost, Australia 63 F4 37 40S 148 29 E
Orchila, I., Venezuela 92 A5 11 48N 66 10W
Orcutt, U.S.A. 85 L6 34 52N 120 27W
Ord →, Australia 60 C4 15 33S 128 15 E
Ord, Mt., Australia 60 C4 17 20S 125 34 E
Orderville, U.S.A. 83 H7 37 17N 112 38W
Ordos = Mu Us Shamo, China 34 E5 39 0N 109 0 E
Ordway, U.S.A. 80 F3 38 13N 103 46W
Ordzhonikidze = Vladikavkaz, Russia 25 F7 43 0N 44 35 E
Ore, Dem. Rep. of the Congo 54 B2 3 17N 29 30 E
Ore Mts. = Erzgebirge, Germany 16 C7 50 27N 12 55 E
Örebro, Sweden 9 G16 59 20N 15 18 E
Oregon, U.S.A. 80 D10 42 1N 89 20W
Oregon □, U.S.A. 82 E3 44 0N 121 0W
Oregon City, U.S.A. 84 E4 45 21N 122 36W
Orekhovo-Zuyevo, Russia 24 C6 55 50N 38 55 E
Orel, Russia 24 D6 52 57N 36 3 E
Orem, U.S.A. 82 F8 40 19N 111 42W
Ören, Turkey 21 F12 37 3N 27 57 E
Orenburg, Russia 24 D10 51 45N 55 6 E
Orense = Ourense, Spain 19 A2 42 19N 7 55W
Orepuki, N.Z. 59 M1 46 19S 167 46 E
Orestiás, Greece 21 D12 41 30N 26 33 E
Orford Ness, U.K. 11 E9 52 5N 1 35 E
Organos, Pta. de los, Canary Is. 22 F2 28 12N 17 17W
Orgaz, Spain 19 C4 39 39N 3 53W
Orgeyev = Orhei, Moldova 17 E15 47 24N 28 50 E
Orhaneli, Turkey 21 E13 39 54N 28 59 E
Orhangazi, Turkey 21 D13 40 29N 29 18 E
Orhei, Moldova 17 E15 47 24N 28 50 E
Orhon Gol →, Mongolia 32 A5 50 21N 106 0 E
Orient, Australia 63 D3 28 7S 142 50 E
Oriental, Cordillera, Colombia 92 B4 6 0N 73 0W
Oriente, Argentina 94 D3 38 44S 60 37W
Orihuela, Spain 19 C5 38 7N 0 55W
Orinoco →, Venezuela 92 B6 9 15N 61 30W
Orissa □, India 41 K14 20 0N 84 0 E
Orissaare, Estonia 9 G20 58 34N 23 5 E
Oristano, Italy 20 E3 39 54N 8 36 E
Oristano, G. di, Italy 20 E3 39 50N 8 29 E
Orizaba, Mexico 87 D5 18 51N 97 6W
Orkanger, Norway 8 E13 63 18N 9 52 E
Orkla →, Norway 8 E13 63 18N 9 51 E
Orkney, S. Africa 56 D4 26 58S 26 40 E
Orkney □, U.K. 12 B5 59 2N 3 13W
Orkney Is., U.K. 12 B6 59 0N 3 0W
Orland, U.S.A. 84 F4 39 45N 122 12W
Orlando, U.S.A. 77 L5 28 33N 81 23W
Orléanais, France 18 C5 48 0N 2 0 E
Orléans, France 18 C4 47 54N 1 52 E
Orleans, U.S.A. 79 B12 44 49N 72 12W
Orléans, I. d', Canada 71 C5 46 54N 70 58W
Ormara, Pakistan 40 G4 25 16N 64 33 E
Ormoc, Phil. 37 B6 11 0N 124 37 E
Ormond, N.Z. 59 H6 38 33S 177 56 E
Ormond Beach, U.S.A. 77 L5 29 17N 81 3W
Ormskirk, U.K. 10 D5 53 35N 2 54W
Ormstown, Canada 79 A11 45 8N 74 0W
Örnsköldsvik, Sweden 8 E18 63 17N 18 40 E
Oro, N. Korea 35 D14 40 1N 127 27 E
Oro →, Mexico 86 B3 25 35N 105 2W
Oro Grande, U.S.A. 85 L9 34 36N 117 20W
Orocué, Colombia 92 C4 4 48N 71 20W
Orogrande, U.S.A. 83 K10 32 24N 106 5W
Orol Dengizi = Aral Sea, Asia 26 E7 44 30N 60 0 E
Oromocto, Canada 71 C6 45 54N 66 29W
Orono, Canada 78 C6 43 59N 78 37W
Oronsay, U.K. 12 E2 56 1N 6 15W
Oroqen Zizhiqi, China 33 A7 50 34N 123 43 E
Oroquieta, Phil. 37 C6 8 32N 123 44 E
Orosháza, Hungary 17 E11 46 32N 20 42 E
Orotukan, Russia 27 C16 62 16N 151 42 E
Oroville, Calif., U.S.A. 84 F5 39 31N 121 33W
Oroville, Wash., U.S.A. 82 B4 48 56N 119 26W
Oroville, L., U.S.A. 84 F5 39 33N 121 29W
Orroroo, Australia 63 E2 32 43S 138 38 E
Orrville, U.S.A. 78 F3 40 50N 81 46W
Orsha, Belarus 24 D5 54 30N 30 25 E
Orsk, Russia 24 D10 51 12N 58 34 E
Orşova, Romania 17 F12 44 41N 22 25 E
Ortaca, Turkey 21 F13 36 49N 28 45 E
Ortegal, C., Spain 19 A2 43 43N 7 52W
Orthez, France 18 E3 43 29N 0 48W
Ortigueira, Spain 19 A2 43 40N 7 50W
Orting, U.S.A. 84 C4 47 6N 122 12W
Ortles, Italy 18 C9 46 31N 10 33 E
Ortón →, Bolivia 92 F5 10 50S 67 0W
Orūmīyeh, Iran 44 B5 37 40N 45 0 E
Orūmīyeh, Daryācheh-ye, Iran 44 B5 37 50N 45 30 E
Oruro, Bolivia 92 G5 18 0S 67 9W
Orust, Sweden 9 G14 58 10N 11 40 E
Oruzgān □, Afghan. 40 C5 33 30N 66 0 E
Orvieto, Italy 20 C5 42 43N 12 7 E
Orwell, U.S.A. 78 E4 41 32N 80 52W
Orwell →, U.K. 11 F9 51 59N 1 18 E
Oryakhovo, Bulgaria 21 C10 43 40N 23 57 E
Osa, Russia 24 C10 57 17N 55 26 E
Osa, Pen. de, Costa Rica 88 E3 8 0N 84 0W
Osage, Iowa, U.S.A. 80 D8 43 17N 92 49W
Osage, Wyo., U.S.A. 80 D2 43 59N 104 25W
Osage →, U.S.A. 80 F9 38 35N 91 57W
Osage City, U.S.A. 80 F7 38 38N 95 50W
Ōsaka, Japan 31 G7 34 40N 135 30 E
Osan, S. Korea 35 F14 37 11N 127 4 E
Osawatomie, U.S.A. 80 F7 38 31N 94 57W
Osborne, U.S.A. 80 F5 39 26N 98 42W
Osceola, Ark., U.S.A. 81 H10 35 42N 89 58W
Osceola, Iowa, U.S.A. 80 E8 41 2N 93 46W
Oscoda, U.S.A. 78 B1 44 26N 83 20W
Ösel = Saaremaa, Estonia 24 C3 58 30N 22 30 E
Osh, Kyrgyzstan 26 E8 40 37N 72 49 E
Oshawa, Canada 70 D4 43 50N 78 50W
Oshkosh, Nebr., U.S.A. 80 E3 41 24N 102 21W
Oshkosh, Wis., U.S.A. 80 C10 44 1N 88 33W
Oshmyany = Ashmyany, Belarus 9 J21 54 26N 25 52 E
Oshnovīyeh, Iran 44 B5 37 2N 45 6 E
Oshogbo, Nigeria 50 G6 7 48N 4 37 E
Oshtorīnān, Iran 45 C6 34 1N 48 38 E
Oshwe, Dem. Rep. of the Congo 52 E3 3 25S 19 28 E
Osijek, Croatia 21 B8 45 34N 18 41 E
Osipenko = Berdyansk, Ukraine 25 E6 46 45N 36 50 E
Osipovichi = Asipovichy, Belarus 17 B15 53 19N 28 33 E
Osizweni, S. Africa 57 D5 27 49S 30 7 E
Oskaloosa, U.S.A. 80 E8 41 18N 92 39W
Oskarshamn, Sweden 9 H17 57 15N 16 27 E
Oskélanéo, Canada 70 C4 48 5N 75 15W
Öskemen, Kazakstan 26 E9 50 0N 82 36 E
Oslo, Norway 9 G14 59 55N 10 45 E
Oslofjorden, Norway 9 G14 59 20N 10 35 E
Osmanabad, India 40 K10 18 5N 76 10 E
Osmaniye, Turkey 25 G6 37 5N 36 10 E
Osnabrück, Germany 16 B5 52 17N 8 3 E
Osorio, Brazil 95 B5 29 53S 50 17W
Osorno, Chile 96 E2 40 25S 73 0W
Osoyoos, Canada 72 D5 49 0N 119 30W
Osøyro, Norway 9 F11 60 9N 5 30 E
Ospika →, Canada 72 B4 56 20N 124 0W
Osprey Reef, Australia 62 A4 13 52S 146 36 E
Oss, Neths. 15 C5 51 46N 5 32 E
Ossa, Mt., Australia 62 G4 41 52S 146 3 E
Óssa, Óros, Greece 21 E10 39 47N 22 42 E

Ossabaw I.

Ossabaw I., *U.S.A.* **77 K5** 31 50N 81 5W
Ossining, *U.S.A.* **79 E11** 41 10N 73 55W
Ossipee, *U.S.A.* **79 C13** 43 41N 71 7W
Ossokmanuan L., *Canada* **71 B7** 53 25N 65 0W
Ossora, *Russia* **27 D17** 59 20N 163 13 E
Ostend = Oostende, *Belgium* **15 C2** 51 15N 2 54 E
Oster, *Ukraine* **17 C16** 50 57N 30 53 E
Österdalälven, *Sweden* **9 F16** 61 30N 13 45 E
Østerdalen, *Norway* **9 F14** 61 40N 10 50 E
Östersund, *Sweden* **8 E16** 63 10N 14 38 E
Ostfriesische Inseln, *Germany* **16 B4** 53 42N 7 0 E
Ostrava, *Czech Rep.* **17 D10** 49 51N 18 18 E
Ostróda, *Poland* **17 B10** 53 42N 19 58 E
Ostroh, *Ukraine* **17 C14** 50 20N 26 30 E
Ostrołęka, *Poland* **17 B11** 53 4N 21 32 E
Ostrów Mazowiecka, *Poland* **17 B11** 52 50N 21 51 E
Ostrów Wielkopolski, *Poland* **17 C9** 51 36N 17 44 E
Ostrowiec-Świętokrzyski, *Poland* **17 C11** 50 55N 21 22 E
Ostuni, *Italy* **21 D7** 40 44N 17 35 E
Ōsumi-Kaikyō, *Japan* **31 J5** 30 55N 131 0 E
Ōsumi-Shotō, *Japan* **31 J5** 30 30N 130 0 E
Osuna, *Spain* **19 D3** 37 14N 5 8W
Oswego, *U.S.A.* **79 C8** 43 27N 76 31W
Oswestry, *U.K.* **10 E4** 52 52N 3 3W
Oświęcim, *Poland* **17 C10** 50 2N 19 11 E
Otago □, *N.Z.* **59 L2** 45 15S 170 0 E
Otago Harbour, *N.Z.* **59 L3** 45 47S 170 42 E
Ōtake, *Japan* **31 G6** 34 12N 132 13 E
Otaki, *N.Z.* **59 J5** 40 45S 175 10 E
Otaru, *Japan* **30 C10** 43 10N 141 0 E
Otaru-Wan = Ishikari-Wan, *Japan* **30 C10** 43 25N 141 1 E
Otavalo, *Ecuador* **92 C3** 0 13N 78 20W
Otavi, *Namibia* **56 B2** 19 40S 17 24 E
Otchinjau, *Angola* **56 B1** 16 30S 13 56 E
Othello, *U.S.A.* **82 C4** 46 50N 119 10W
Otira Gorge, *N.Z.* **59 K3** 42 53S 171 33 E
Otis, *U.S.A.* **80 E3** 40 9N 102 58W
Otjiwarongo, *Namibia* **56 C2** 20 30S 16 33 E
Otoineppu, *Japan* **30 B11** 44 44N 142 16 E
Otorohanga, *N.Z.* **59 H5** 38 12S 175 14 E
Otoskwin →, *Canada* **70 B2** 52 13N 88 6W
Otosquen, *Canada* **73 C8** 53 17N 102 1W
Otra →, *Norway* **9 G13** 58 9N 8 1 E
Otranto, *Italy* **21 D8** 40 9N 18 28 E
Otranto, C. d', *Italy* **21 D8** 40 7N 18 30 E
Otranto, Str. of, *Italy* **21 D8** 40 15N 18 40 E
Otse, *S. Africa* **56 D4** 25 2S 25 45 E
Ōtsu, *Japan* **31 G7** 35 0N 135 50 E
Ōtsuki, *Japan* **31 G9** 35 36N 138 57 E
Ottawa = Outaouais →, *Canada* **70 C5** 45 27N 74 8W
Ottawa, *Canada* **70 C4** 45 27N 75 42W
Ottawa, *Ill., U.S.A.* **80 E10** 41 21N 88 51W
Ottawa, *Kans., U.S.A.* **80 F7** 38 37N 95 16W
Ottawa Is., *Canada* **69 C11** 59 35N 80 10W
Otter L., *Canada* **73 B8** 55 35N 104 39W
Otter Rapids, *Ont., Canada* **70 B3** 50 11N 81 39W
Otter Rapids, *Sask., Canada* **73 B8** 55 38N 104 44W
Otterville, *Canada* **78 D4** 42 55N 80 36W
Ottery St. Mary, *U.K.* **11 G4** 50 44N 3 17W
Otto Beit Bridge, *Zimbabwe* **55 F2** 15 59S 28 56 E
Ottosdal, *S. Africa* **56 D4** 26 46S 25 59 E
Ottumwa, *U.S.A.* **80 E8** 41 1N 92 25W
Oturkpo, *Nigeria* **50 G7** 7 16N 8 8 E
Otway, B., *Chile* **96 G2** 53 30S 74 0W
Otway, C., *Australia* **63 F3** 38 52S 143 30 E
Otwock, *Poland* **17 B11** 52 5N 21 20 E
Ou →, *Laos* **38 B4** 20 4N 102 13 E
Ou Neua, *Laos* **38 A3** 22 18N 101 48 E
Ou-Sammyaku, *Japan* **30 E10** 39 20N 140 35 E
Ouachita →, *U.S.A.* **81 K9** 31 38N 91 49W
Ouachita, L., *U.S.A.* **81 H8** 34 34N 93 12W
Ouachita Mts., *U.S.A.* **81 H7** 34 40N 94 25W
Ouagadougou, *Burkina Faso* **50 F5** 12 25N 1 30W
Ouahran = Oran, *Algeria* **50 A5** 35 45N 0 39W
Ouallene, *Algeria* **50 D6** 24 41N 1 11 E
Ouargla, *Algeria* **50 B7** 31 59N 5 16 E
Ouarzazate, *Morocco* **50 B4** 30 55N 6 50W
Oubangi →, *Dem. Rep. of the Congo* **52 E3** 0 30S 17 50 E
Ouddorp, *Neths.* **15 C3** 51 50N 3 57 E
Oude Rijn →, *Neths.* **15 B4** 52 12N 4 24 E
Oudenaarde, *Belgium* **15 D3** 50 50N 3 37 E
Oudtshoorn, *S. Africa* **56 E3** 33 35S 22 14 E
Ouessant, Î. d', *France* **18 B1** 48 28N 5 6W
Ouesso, *Congo* **52 D3** 1 37N 16 5 E
Ouest, Pte., *Canada* **71 C7** 49 52N 64 40W
Ouezzane, *Morocco* **50 B4** 34 51N 5 35W
Oughterard, *Ireland* **13 C2** 53 26N 9 18W
Oujda, *Morocco* **50 B5** 34 41N 1 55W
Oulainen, *Finland* **8 D21** 64 17N 24 47 E
Oulu, *Finland* **8 D21** 65 1N 25 29 E
Oulujärvi, *Finland* **8 D22** 64 25N 27 15 E
Oulujoki →, *Finland* **8 D21** 65 1N 25 30 E
Oum Chalouba, *Chad* **51 E10** 15 48N 20 46 E
Oum Hadjer, *Chad* **51 F9** 13 18N 19 41 E
Ounasjoki →, *Finland* **8 C21** 66 31N 25 40 E
Ounguati, *Namibia* **56 C2** 22 0S 15 46 E
Ounianga Sérir, *Chad* **51 E10** 18 54N 20 51 E
Our →, *Lux.* **15 E6** 49 55N 6 5 E
Ouray, *U.S.A.* **83 G10** 38 1N 107 40W
Ourense, *Spain* **19 A2** 42 19N 7 55W
Ouricuri, *Brazil* **93 E10** 7 53S 40 5W
Ourinhos, *Brazil* **95 A6** 23 0S 49 54W
Ouro Fino, *Brazil* **95 A6** 22 16S 46 25W
Ouro Prêto, *Brazil* **95 A7** 20 20S 43 30W
Ourthe →, *Belgium* **15 D5** 50 29N 5 35 E
Ouse, *Australia* **62 G4** 42 38S 146 42 E
Ouse →, *E. Susx., U.K.* **11 G8** 50 47N 0 4 E
Ouse →, *N. Yorks., U.K.* **10 D7** 53 44N 0 55W
Outaouais →, *Canada* **70 C5** 45 27N 74 8W
Outardes →, *Canada* **71 C6** 49 24N 69 30W
Outer Hebrides, *U.K.* **12 D1** 57 30N 7 40W
Outer I., *Canada* **71 B8** 51 10N 58 35W
Outjo, *Namibia* **56 C2** 20 5S 16 7 E
Outlook, *Canada* **73 C7** 51 30N 107 0W
Outlook, *U.S.A.* **80 A2** 48 53N 104 47W
Outokumpu, *Finland* **8 E23** 62 43N 29 1 E
Ouyen, *Australia* **63 F3** 35 1S 142 22 E
Ovalau, *Fiji* **59 C8** 17 40S 178 48 E
Ovalle, *Chile* **94 C1** 30 33S 71 18W
Ovamboland, *Namibia* **56 B2** 18 30S 16 0 E
Overflakkee, *Neths.* **15 C4** 51 44N 4 10 E
Overijssel □, *Neths.* **15 B6** 52 25N 6 35 E
Overland Park, *U.S.A.* **80 F7** 38 55N 94 50W
Overton, *U.S.A.* **85 J12** 36 33N 114 27W
Övertorneå, *Sweden* **8 C20** 66 23N 23 38 E
Ovid, *U.S.A.* **80 E3** 40 58N 102 23W
Oviedo, *Spain* **19 A3** 43 25N 5 50W
Oviši, *Latvia* **9 H19** 57 33N 21 44 E
Övör Hangay □, *Mongolia* **34 B2** 45 0N 102 30 E
Øvre Årdal, *Norway* **9 F12** 61 19N 7 48 E
Ovruch, *Ukraine* **17 C15** 51 25N 28 45 E
Owaka, *N.Z.* **59 M2** 46 27S 169 40 E
Owambo = Ovamboland, *Namibia* **56 B2** 18 30S 16 0 E
Owase, *Japan* **31 G8** 34 7N 136 12 E
Owatonna, *U.S.A.* **80 C8** 44 5N 93 14W
Owbeh, *Afghan.* **40 B3** 34 28N 63 10 E
Owego, *U.S.A.* **79 D8** 42 6N 76 16W
Owen Falls Dam, *Uganda* **54 B3** 0 30N 33 5 E
Owen Sound, *Canada* **70 D3** 44 35N 80 55W
Owens →, *U.S.A.* **84 J9** 36 32N 117 59W
Owens L., *U.S.A.* **85 J9** 36 26N 117 57W
Owensboro, *U.S.A.* **76 G2** 37 46N 87 7W
Owensville, *U.S.A.* **80 F9** 38 21N 91 30W
Owl →, *Canada* **73 B10** 57 51N 92 44W
Owo, *Nigeria* **50 G7** 7 10N 5 39 E
Owosso, *U.S.A.* **76 D3** 43 0N 84 10W
Owyhee, *U.S.A.* **82 F5** 41 57N 116 6W
Owyhee →, *U.S.A.* **82 E5** 43 49N 117 2W
Owyhee, L., *U.S.A.* **82 E5** 43 38N 117 14W
Ox Mts. = Slieve Gamph, *Ireland* **13 B3** 54 6N 9 0W
Öxarfjörður, *Iceland* **8 C5** 66 15N 16 45W
Oxelösund, *Sweden* **9 G17** 58 43N 17 5 E
Oxford, *N.Z.* **59 K4** 43 18S 172 11 E
Oxford, *U.K.* **11 F6** 51 46N 1 15W
Oxford, *Miss., U.S.A.* **81 H10** 34 22N 89 31W
Oxford, *N.C., U.S.A.* **77 G6** 36 19N 78 35W
Oxford, *Ohio, U.S.A.* **76 F3** 39 31N 84 45W
Oxford L., *Canada* **73 C9** 54 51N 95 37W
Oxfordshire □, *U.K.* **11 F6** 51 48N 1 16W
Oxley, *Australia* **63 E3** 34 11S 144 6 E
Oxnard, *U.S.A.* **85 L7** 34 12N 119 11W
Oxus = Amudarya →, *Uzbekistan* **26 E6** 43 58N 59 34 E
Oya, *Malaysia* **36 D4** 2 55N 111 55 E
Oyama, *Japan* **31 F9** 36 18N 139 48 E
Oyem, *Gabon* **52 D2** 1 34N 11 31 E
Oyen, *Canada* **73 C6** 51 22N 110 28W
Oykel →, *U.K.* **12 D4** 57 56N 4 26W
Oymyakon, *Russia* **27 C15** 63 25N 142 44 E
Oyo, *Nigeria* **50 G6** 7 46N 3 56 E
Oyster Bay, *U.S.A.* **79 F11** 40 52N 73 32W
Ōyūbari, *Japan* **30 C11** 43 1N 142 5 E
Ozamiz, *Phil.* **37 C6** 8 15N 123 50 E
Ozark, *Ala., U.S.A.* **77 K3** 31 28N 85 39W
Ozark, *Ark., U.S.A.* **81 H8** 35 29N 93 50W
Ozark, *Mo., U.S.A.* **81 G8** 37 1N 93 12W
Ozark Plateau, *U.S.A.* **81 G9** 37 20N 91 40W
Ozarks, L. of the, *U.S.A.* **80 F8** 38 12N 92 38W
Ózd, *Hungary* **17 D11** 48 14N 20 15 E
Ozette L., *U.S.A.* **84 B2** 48 6N 124 38W
Ozona, *U.S.A.* **81 K4** 30 43N 101 12W
Ozuluama, *Mexico* **87 C5** 21 40N 97 50W

P

Pa-an, *Burma* **41 L20** 16 51N 97 40 E
Pa Mong Dam, *Thailand* **38 D4** 18 0N 102 22 E
Paarl, *S. Africa* **56 E2** 33 45S 18 56 E
Paauilo, *U.S.A.* **74 H17** 20 2N 155 22W
Pab Hills, *Pakistan* **42 F2** 26 30N 66 45 E
Pabbay, *U.K.* **12 D1** 57 46N 7 14W
Pabianice, *Poland* **17 C10** 51 40N 19 20 E
Pabna, *Bangla.* **41 G16** 24 1N 89 18 E
Pabo, *Uganda* **54 B3** 3 1N 32 10 E
Pacaja →, *Brazil* **93 D8** 1 56S 50 50W
Pacaraima, Sierra, *Venezuela* **90 C4** 4 0N 62 30W
Pacasmayo, *Peru* **92 E3** 7 20S 79 35W
Pachhar, *India* **42 G7** 24 40N 77 42 E
Pachitea →, *Peru* **92 E4** 8 46S 74 33W
Pachpadra, *India* **40 G8** 25 58N 72 10 E
Pachuca, *Mexico* **87 C5** 20 10N 98 40W
Pacific, *Canada* **72 C3** 54 48N 128 28W
Pacific-Antarctic Ridge, *Pac. Oc.* **65 M16** 43 0S 115 0W
Pacific Grove, *U.S.A.* **84 J5** 36 38N 121 56W
Pacific Ocean, *Pac. Oc.* **65 G14** 10 0N 140 0W
Pacifica, *U.S.A.* **84 H4** 37 36N 122 30W
Pacitan, *Indonesia* **37 H14** 8 12S 111 7 E
Packwood, *U.S.A.* **84 D5** 46 36N 121 40W
Padaido, Kepulauan, *Indonesia* **37 E9** 1 5S 138 0 E
Padang, *Indonesia* **36 E2** 1 0S 100 20 E
Padang Endau, *Malaysia* **39 L4** 2 40N 103 38 E
Padangpanjang, *Indonesia* **36 E2** 0 40S 100 20 E
Padangsidempuan, *Indonesia* **36 D1** 1 30N 99 15 E
Paddockwood, *Canada* **73 C7** 53 30N 105 30W
Paderborn, *Germany* **16 C5** 51 42N 8 45 E
Pádova, *Italy* **20 B4** 45 25N 11 53 E
Padra, *India* **42 H5** 22 15N 73 7 E
Padrauna, *India* **43 F10** 26 54N 83 59 E
Padre I., *U.S.A.* **81 M6** 27 10N 97 25W
Padstow, *U.K.* **11 G3** 50 33N 4 58W
Padua = Pádova, *Italy* **20 B4** 45 25N 11 53 E
Paducah, *Ky., U.S.A.* **76 G1** 37 5N 88 37W
Paducah, *Tex., U.S.A.* **81 H4** 34 1N 100 18W
Paengnyong-do, *S. Korea* **35 F13** 37 57N 124 40 E
Paeroa, *N.Z.* **59 G5** 37 23S 175 41 E
Pafúri, *Mozam.* **57 C5** 22 28S 31 17 E
Pag, *Croatia* **16 F8** 44 25N 15 3 E
Pagadian, *Phil.* **37 C6** 7 55N 123 30 E
Pagai Selatan, Pulau, *Indonesia* **36 E2** 3 0S 100 15 E
Pagai Utara, Pulau, *Indonesia* **36 E2** 2 35S 100 0 E
Pagalu = Annobón, *Atl. Oc.* **49 G4** 1 25S 5 36 E
Pagastikós Kólpos, *Greece* **21 E10** 39 15N 23 0 E
Pagatan, *Indonesia* **36 E5** 3 33S 115 59 E
Page, *Ariz., U.S.A.* **83 H8** 36 57N 111 27W
Page, *N. Dak., U.S.A.* **80 B6** 47 10N 97 34W
Pago Pago, *Amer. Samoa* **59 B13** 14 16S 170 43W
Pagosa Springs, *U.S.A.* **83 H10** 37 16N 107 1W
Pagwa River, *Canada* **70 B2** 50 2N 85 14W
Pahala, *U.S.A.* **74 J17** 19 12N 155 29W
Pahang →, *Malaysia* **39 L4** 3 30N 103 9 E
Pahiatua, *N.Z.* **59 J5** 40 27S 175 50 E
Pahokee, *U.S.A.* **77 M5** 26 50N 80 40W
Pahrump, *U.S.A.* **85 J11** 36 12N 115 59W
Pahute Mesa, *U.S.A.* **84 H10** 37 20N 116 45W
Pai, *Thailand* **38 C2** 19 19N 98 27 E
Paia, *U.S.A.* **74 H16** 20 54N 156 22W
Paicines, *U.S.A.* **84 J5** 36 44N 121 17W
Paide, *Estonia* **9 G21** 58 57N 25 31 E
Paignton, *U.K.* **11 G4** 50 26N 3 35W
Päijänne, *Finland* **9 F21** 61 30N 25 30 E
Pailin, *Cambodia* **38 F4** 12 46N 102 36 E
Painan, *Indonesia* **36 E2** 1 21S 100 34 E
Painesville, *U.S.A.* **78 E3** 41 43N 81 15W
Paint Hills = Wemindji, *Canada* **70 B4** 53 0N 78 49W
Paint L., *Canada* **73 B9** 55 28N 97 57W
Paint Rock, *U.S.A.* **81 K5** 31 31N 99 55W
Painted Desert, *U.S.A.* **83 J8** 36 0N 111 0W
Paintsville, *U.S.A.* **76 G4** 37 49N 82 48W
País Vasco □, *Spain* **19 A4** 42 50N 2 45W
Paisley, *Canada* **78 B3** 44 18N 81 16W
Paisley, *U.K.* **12 F4** 55 50N 4 25W
Paisley, *U.S.A.* **82 E3** 42 42N 120 32W
Paita, *Peru* **92 E2** 5 11S 81 9W
Pajares, Puerto de, *Spain* **19 A3** 42 58N 5 46W
Pak Lay, *Laos* **38 C3** 18 15N 101 27 E
Pak Phanang, *Thailand* **39 H3** 8 21N 100 12 E
Pak Sane, *Laos* **38 C4** 18 22N 103 39 E
Pak Song, *Laos* **38 E6** 15 11N 106 14 E
Pak Suong, *Laos* **38 C4** 19 58N 102 15 E
Pákhnes, *Greece* **23 D6** 35 16N 24 4 E
Pakistan ■, *Asia* **42 E4** 30 0N 70 0 E
Pakkading, *Laos* **38 C4** 18 19N 103 59 E
Pakokku, *Burma* **41 J19** 21 20N 95 0 E
Pakpattan, *Pakistan* **42 D5** 30 25N 73 27 E
Paktīā □, *Afghan.* **40 C6** 33 0N 69 15 E
Pakwach, *Uganda* **54 B3** 2 28N 31 27 E
Pakxe, *Laos* **38 E5** 15 5N 105 52 E
Pala, *Chad* **51 G9** 9 25N 15 5 E
Pala, *Dem. Rep. of the Congo* **54 D2** 6 45S 29 30 E
Pala, *U.S.A.* **85 M9** 33 22N 117 5W
Palabek, *Uganda* **54 B3** 3 22N 32 33 E
Palacios, *U.S.A.* **81 L6** 28 42N 96 13W
Palagruža, *Croatia* **20 C7** 42 24N 16 15 E
Palaiókastron, *Greece* **23 D8** 35 12N 26 15 E
Palaiokhóra, *Greece* **23 D5** 35 16N 23 39 E
Palam, *India* **40 K10** 19 0N 77 0 E
Palampur, *India* **42 C7** 32 10N 76 30 E
Palana, *Australia* **62 F4** 39 45S 147 55 E
Palana, *Russia* **27 D16** 59 10N 159 59 E
Palanan, *Phil.* **37 A6** 17 8N 122 29 E
Palanan Pt., *Phil.* **37 A6** 17 17N 122 30 E
Palandri, *Pakistan* **43 C5** 33 42N 73 40 E
Palanga, *Lithuania* **9 J19** 55 58N 21 3 E
Palangkaraya, *Indonesia* **36 E4** 2 16S 113 56 E
Palani Hills, *India* **40 P10** 10 14N 77 33 E
Palanpur, *India* **42 G5** 24 10N 72 25 E
Palapye, *Botswana* **56 C4** 22 30S 27 7 E
Palas, *Pakistan* **43 B5** 35 4N 73 14 E
Palatka, *Russia* **27 C16** 60 6N 150 54 E
Palatka, *U.S.A.* **77 L5** 29 39N 81 38W
Palau ■, *Pac. Oc.* **64 G5** 7 30N 134 30 E
Palauk, *Burma* **38 F2** 13 10N 98 40 E
Palawan, *Phil.* **36 C5** 9 30N 118 30 E
Palayankottai, *India* **40 Q10** 8 45N 77 45 E
Paldiski, *Estonia* **9 G21** 59 23N 24 9 E
Paleleh, *Indonesia* **37 D6** 1 10N 121 50 E
Palembang, *Indonesia* **36 E2** 3 0S 104 50 E
Palencia, *Spain* **19 A3** 42 1N 4 34W
Paleokastrítsa, *Greece* **23 A3** 39 40N 19 41 E
Paleometokho, *Cyprus* **23 D12** 35 7N 33 11 E
Palermo, *Italy* **20 E5** 38 7N 13 22 E
Palermo, *U.S.A.* **82 G3** 39 26N 121 33W
Palestina, *Chile* **96 A3** 23 50S 69 47W
Palestine, *Asia* **47 D4** 32 0N 35 0 E
Palestine, *U.S.A.* **81 K7** 31 46N 95 38W
Paletwa, *Burma* **41 J18** 21 10N 92 50 E
Palghat, *India* **40 P10** 10 46N 76 42 E
Palgrave, Mt., *Australia* **60 D2** 23 22S 115 58 E
Pali, *India* **42 G5** 25 50N 73 20 E
Palioúrion, Ákra, *Greece* **21 E10** 39 57N 23 45 E
Palisade, *U.S.A.* **80 E4** 40 21N 101 7W
Paliseul, *Belgium* **15 E5** 49 54N 5 8 E
Palitana, *India* **42 J4** 21 32N 71 49 E
Palizada, *Mexico* **87 D6** 18 18N 92 8W
Palk Bay, *Asia* **40 Q11** 9 30N 79 15 E
Palk Strait, *Asia* **40 Q11** 10 0N 79 45 E
Palkānah, *Iraq* **44 C5** 35 49N 44 26 E
Palla Road = Dinokwe, *Botswana* **56 C4** 23 29S 26 37 E
Pallanza = Verbánia, *Italy* **18 D8** 45 56N 8 33 E
Pallisa, *Uganda* **54 B3** 1 12N 33 43 E
Pallu, *India* **42 E6** 28 59N 74 14 E
Palm Bay, *U.S.A.* **77 L5** 28 2N 80 35W
Palm Beach, *U.S.A.* **77 M6** 26 43N 80 2W
Palm Desert, *U.S.A.* **85 M10** 33 43N 116 22W
Palm Is., *Australia* **62 B4** 18 40S 146 35 E
Palm Springs, *U.S.A.* **85 M10** 33 50N 116 33W
Palma, *Mozam.* **55 E5** 10 46S 40 29 E
Palma, B. de, *Spain* **22 B9** 39 30N 2 39 E
Palma de Mallorca, *Spain* **22 B9** 39 35N 2 39 E
Palma Soriano, *Cuba* **88 B4** 20 15N 76 0W
Palmares, *Brazil* **93 E11** 8 41S 35 28W
Palmas, *Brazil* **95 B5** 26 29S 52 0W
Palmas, C., *Liberia* **50 H4** 4 27N 7 46W
Pálmas, G. di, *Italy* **20 E3** 39 0N 8 30 E
Palmdale, *U.S.A.* **85 L8** 34 35N 118 7W
Palmeira dos Índios, *Brazil* **93 E11** 9 25S 36 37W
Palmer, *U.S.A.* **68 B5** 61 36N 149 7W
Palmer →, *Australia* **62 B3** 16 0S 142 26 E
Palmer Arch., *Antarctica* **5 C17** 64 15S 65 0W
Palmer Lake, *U.S.A.* **80 F2** 39 7N 104 55W
Palmer Land, *Antarctica* **5 D18** 73 0S 63 0W
Palmerston, *Canada* **78 C4** 43 50N 80 51W
Palmerston, *N.Z.* **59 L3** 45 29S 170 43 E
Palmerston North, *N.Z.* **59 J5** 40 21S 175 39 E
Palmerton, *U.S.A.* **79 F9** 40 48N 75 37W
Palmetto, *U.S.A.* **77 M4** 27 31N 82 34W
Palmi, *Italy* **20 E6** 38 21N 15 51 E
Palmira, *Argentina* **94 C2** 32 59S 68 34W
Palmira, *Colombia* **92 C3** 3 32N 76 16W
Palmyra = Tudmur, *Syria* **44 C3** 34 36N 38 15 E
Palmyra, *Mo., U.S.A.* **80 F9** 39 48N 91 32W
Palmyra, *N.Y., U.S.A.* **78 C7** 43 5N 77 18W
Palmyra Is., *Pac. Oc.* **65 G11** 5 52N 162 5W
Palo Alto, *U.S.A.* **84 H4** 37 27N 122 10W
Palo Verde, *U.S.A.* **85 M12** 33 26N 114 44W
Palopo, *Indonesia* **37 E6** 3 0S 120 16 E
Palos, C. de, *Spain* **19 D5** 37 38N 0 40W
Palos Verdes, *U.S.A.* **85 M8** 33 48N 118 23W
Palos Verdes, Pt., *U.S.A.* **85 M8** 33 43N 118 26W
Palouse, *U.S.A.* **82 C5** 46 55N 117 4W
Palparara, *Australia* **62 C3** 24 47S 141 28 E
Palu, *Indonesia* **37 E5** 1 0S 119 52 E
Palu, *Turkey* **25 G7** 38 45N 40 0 E
Palwal, *India* **42 E7** 28 8N 77 19 E
Pamanukan, *Indonesia* **37 G12** 6 16S 107 49 E
Pamiers, *France* **18 E4** 43 7N 1 39 E
Pamir, *Tajikistan* **26 F8** 37 40N 73 0 E
Pamlico →, *U.S.A.* **77 H7** 35 20N 76 28W
Pamlico Sd., *U.S.A.* **77 H8** 35 20N 76 0W
Pampa, *U.S.A.* **81 H4** 35 32N 100 58W
Pampa de las Salinas, *Argentina* **94 C2** 32 1S 66 58W
Pampanua, *Indonesia* **37 E6** 4 16S 120 8 E
Pampas, *Argentina* **94 D3** 35 0S 63 0W
Pampas, *Peru* **92 F4** 12 20S 74 50W
Pamplona, *Colombia* **92 B4** 7 23N 72 39W
Pamplona, *Spain* **19 A5** 42 48N 1 38W
Pampoenpoort, *S. Africa* **56 E3** 31 3S 22 40 E
Pana, *U.S.A.* **80 F10** 39 23N 89 5W
Panaca, *U.S.A.* **83 H6** 37 47N 114 23W
Panaitan, *Indonesia* **37 G11** 6 36S 105 12 E
Panaji, *India* **40 M8** 15 25N 73 50 E
Panamá, *Panama* **88 E4** 9 0N 79 25W
Panama ■, *Cent. Amer.* **88 E4** 8 48N 79 55W
Panamá, G. de, *Panama* **88 E4** 8 4N 79 20W
Panama Canal, *Panama* **88 E4** 9 10N 79 37W
Panama City, *U.S.A.* **77 K3** 30 10N 85 40W
Panamint Range, *U.S.A.* **85 J9** 36 20N 117 20W
Panamint Springs, *U.S.A.* **85 J9** 36 20N 117 28W
Panão, *Peru* **92 E3** 9 55S 75 55W
Panare, *Thailand* **39 J3** 6 51N 101 30 E
Panay, *Phil.* **37 B6** 11 10N 122 30 E
Panay, G., *Phil.* **37 B6** 11 0N 122 30 E
Pancake Range, *U.S.A.* **83 G6** 38 30N 115 50W
Pančevo, *Serbia, Yug.* **21 B9** 44 52N 20 41 E
Pandan, *Phil.* **37 B6** 11 45N 122 10 E
Pandegelang, *Indonesia* **37 G12** 6 25S 106 5 E
Pandharpur, *India* **40 L9** 17 41N 75 20 E
Pando, *Uruguay* **95 C4** 34 44S 56 0W
Pando, L. = Hope, L., *Australia* **63 D2** 28 24S 139 18 E
Pandokrátor, *Greece* **23 A3** 39 45N 19 50 E
Pandora, *Costa Rica* **88 E3** 9 43N 83 3W
Panevėžys, *Lithuania* **24 C3** 55 42N 24 25 E
Panfilov, *Kazakstan* **26 E9** 44 10N 80 0 E
Pang-Long, *Burma* **41 H21** 23 11N 98 45 E
Pang-Yang, *Burma* **41 H21** 22 7N 98 48 E
Panga, *Dem. Rep. of the Congo* **54 B2** 1 52N 26 18 E
Pangalanes, Canal des, *Madag.* **57 C8** 22 48S 47 50 E
Pangani, *Tanzania* **54 D4** 5 25S 38 58 E
Pangani □, *Tanzania* **54 D4** 5 25S 39 0 E
Pangani →, *Tanzania* **54 D4** 5 26S 38 58 E
Pangfou = Bengbu, *China* **35 H9** 32 58N 117 20 E
Pangil, *Dem. Rep. of the Congo* **54 C2** 3 10S 26 35 E
Pangkah, Tanjung, *Indonesia* **37 G15** 6 51S 112 33 E
Pangkajene, *Indonesia* **37 E5** 4 46S 119 34 E
Pangkalanbrandan, *Indonesia* **36 D1** 4 1N 98 20 E
Pangkalanbuun, *Indonesia* **36 E4** 2 41S 111 37 E
Pangkalpinang, *Indonesia* **36 E3** 2 0S 106 0 E
Pangnirtung, *Canada* **69 B13** 66 8N 65 54W
Panguitch, *U.S.A.* **83 H7** 37 50N 112 26W
Pangutaran Group, *Phil.* **37 C6** 6 18N 120 34 E
Panhandle, *U.S.A.* **81 H4** 35 21N 101 23W
Pani Mines, *India* **42 H5** 22 29N 73 50 E
Pania-Mutombo, *Dem. Rep. of the Congo* **54 D1** 5 11S 23 51 E
Panipat, *India* **42 E7** 29 25N 77 2 E
Panjal Range, *India* **42 C7** 32 30N 76 50 E
Panjgur, *Pakistan* **40 F4** 27 0N 64 5 E
Panjim = Panaji, *India* **40 M8** 15 25N 73 50 E
Panjinad Barrage, *Pakistan* **40 E7** 29 22N 71 15 E
Panjwai, *Afghan.* **42 D1** 31 26N 65 27 E
Panmunjŏm, *N. Korea* **35 F14** 37 59N 126 38 E
Panna, *India* **43 G9** 24 40N 80 15 E
Panna Hills, *India* **43 G9** 24 40N 81 15 E
Pano Lefkara, *Cyprus* **23 E12** 34 53N 33 20 E
Pano Panayia, *Cyprus* **23 E11** 34 55N 32 38 E
Panorama, *Brazil* **95 A5** 21 21S 51 51W
Pánormon, *Greece* **23 D6** 35 25N 24 41 E
Panshan, *China* **35 D12** 41 3N 122 2 E
Panshi, *China* **35 C14** 42 58N 126 5 E
Pantanal, *Brazil* **92 H7** 17 30S 57 40W
Pantar, *Indonesia* **37 F6** 8 28S 124 10 E
Pante Macassar, *Indonesia* **37 F6** 9 30S 123 58 E
Pantelleria, *Italy* **20 F4** 36 50N 11 57 E
Pánuco, *Mexico* **87 C5** 22 0N 98 15W
Paola, *Malta* **23 D2** 35 52N 14 30 E
Paola, *U.S.A.* **80 F7** 38 35N 94 53W
Paonia, *U.S.A.* **83 G10** 38 52N 107 36W
Paoting = Baoding, *China* **34 E8** 38 50N 115 28 E
Paot'ou = Baotou, *China* **34 D6** 40 32N 110 2 E

Rebun-Tō

Qinhuangdao, China 35 E10 39 56N 119 30 E
Qinling Shandi, China 34 H5 33 50N 108 10 E
Qinshui, China 34 G7 35 40N 112 8 E
Qinyang, China 34 G7 35 7N 112 57 E
Qinyuan, China 34 F7 36 29N 112 20 E
Qinzhou, China 32 D5 21 58N 108 38 E
Qionghai, China 38 C8 19 15N 110 26 E
Qiongzhou Haixia, China 38 B8 20 10N 110 15 E
Qiqihar, China 27 E13 47 26N 124 0 E
Qiraîya, W. →, Egypt 47 E3 30 27N 34 0 E
Qiryat Ata, Israel 47 C4 32 47N 35 6 E
Qiryat Gat, Israel 47 D3 31 32N 34 46 E
Qiryat Mal'akhi, Israel 47 D3 31 44N 34 44 E
Qiryat Shemona, Israel 47 B4 33 13N 35 35 E
Qiryat Yam, Israel 47 C4 32 51N 35 4 E
Qishan, China 34 G4 34 25N 107 38 E
Qitai, China 32 B3 44 2N 89 35 E
Qixia, China 35 F11 37 17N 120 52 E
Qojūr, Iran 44 B5 36 12N 47 55 E
Qom, Iran 45 C6 34 40N 51 0 E
Qomsheh, Iran 45 D6 32 0N 51 55 E
Qostanay, Kazakstan 26 D7 53 10N 63 35 E
Quairading, Australia 61 F2 32 0S 117 21 E
Quakertown, U.S.A. 79 F9 40 26N 75 21W
Qualeup, Australia 61 F2 33 48S 116 48 E
Quambatook, Australia 63 F3 35 49S 143 34 E
Quambone, Australia 63 E4 30 57S 147 53 E
Quamby, Australia 62 C3 20 22S 140 17 E
Quan Long = Ca Mau, Vietnam 39 H5 9 7N 105 8 E
Quanah, U.S.A. 81 H5 34 18N 99 44W
Quandialla, Australia 63 E4 34 1S 147 47 E
Quang Ngai, Vietnam 38 E7 15 13N 108 58 E
Quang Tri, Vietnam 38 D6 16 45N 107 13 E
Quang Yen, Vietnam 38 B6 20 56N 106 52 E
Quantock Hills, U.K. 11 F4 51 8N 3 10W
Quanzhou, China 33 D6 24 55N 118 34 E
Quaqtaq, Canada 69 B13 60 55N 69 40W
Quaraí, Brazil 94 C4 30 15S 56 20W
Quartu Sant'Élena, Italy 20 E3 39 15N 9 10 E
Quartzsite, U.S.A. 85 M12 33 40N 114 13W
Quatsino, Canada 72 C3 50 30N 127 40W
Quatsino Sd., Canada 72 C3 50 25N 127 58W
Quba, Azerbaijan 25 F8 41 21N 48 32 E
Qūchān, Iran 45 B8 37 10N 58 27 E
Queanbeyan, Australia 63 F4 35 17S 149 14 E
Québec, Canada 71 C5 46 52N 71 13W
Québec □, Canada 71 C6 48 0N 74 0W
Queen Alexandra Ra., Antarctica 5 E11 85 0S 170 0 E
Queen Charlotte, Canada 72 C2 53 15N 132 2W
Queen Charlotte Is., Canada 72 C2 53 20N 132 10W
Queen Charlotte Sd., Canada 72 C3 51 0N 128 0W
Queen Elizabeth Is., Canada 66 B10 76 0N 95 0W
Queen Elizabeth Nat. Park, Uganda 54 C3 0 0 30 0 E
Queen Mary Land, Antarctica 5 D7 70 0S 95 0 E
Queen Maud G., Canada 68 B9 68 15N 102 30W
Queen Maud Land, Antarctica 5 D3 72 30S 12 0 E
Queen Maud Mts., Antarctica 5 E13 86 0S 160 0W
Queens Chan., Australia 60 C4 15 0S 129 30 E
Queenscliff, Australia 63 F3 38 16S 144 39 E
Queensland □, Australia 62 C3 22 0S 142 0 E
Queenstown, Australia 62 G4 42 4S 145 35 E
Queenstown, N.Z. 59 L2 45 1S 168 40 E
Queenstown, S. Africa 56 E4 31 52S 26 52 E
Queets, U.S.A. 84 C2 47 32N 124 20W
Queguay Grande →, Uruguay 94 C4 32 9S 58 9W
Queimadas, Brazil 93 F11 11 0S 39 38W
Quelimane, Mozam. 55 F4 17 53S 36 58 E
Quellón, Chile 96 E2 43 7S 73 37W
Quelpart = Cheju Do, S. Korea 35 H14 33 29N 126 34 E
Quemado, N. Mex., U.S.A. 83 J9 34 20N 108 30W
Quemado, Tex., U.S.A. 81 L4 28 58N 100 35W
Quemú-Quemú, Argentina 94 D3 36 3S 63 36W
Quequén, Argentina 94 D4 38 30S 58 30W
Querétaro, Mexico 86 C4 20 36N 100 23W
Querétaro □, Mexico 86 C5 20 30N 100 0W
Queshan, China 34 H8 32 55N 114 2 E
Quesnel, Canada 72 C4 53 0N 122 30W
Quesnel →, Canada 72 C4 52 58N 122 29W
Quesnel L., Canada 72 C4 52 30N 121 20W
Questa, U.S.A. 83 H11 36 42N 105 36W
Quetico Prov. Park, Canada 70 C1 48 30N 91 45W
Quetta, Pakistan 42 D2 30 15N 66 55 E
Quezaltenango, Guatemala 88 D1 14 50N 91 30W
Quezon City, Phil. 37 B6 14 38N 121 0 E
Qufār, Si. Arabia 44 E4 27 26N 41 37 E
Qui Nhon, Vietnam 38 F7 13 40N 109 13 E
Quibaxe, Angola 52 F2 8 24S 14 27 E
Quibdo, Colombia 92 B3 5 42N 76 40W
Quiberon, France 18 C2 47 29N 3 9W
Quick, Canada 72 C3 54 36N 126 54W
Quiet L., Canada 72 A2 61 5N 133 5W
Quiindy, Paraguay 94 B4 25 58S 57 14W
Quila, Mexico 86 C3 24 23N 107 13W
Quilán, C., Chile 96 E2 43 15S 74 30W
Quilcene, U.S.A. 84 C4 47 49N 122 53W
Quilimarí, Chile 94 C1 32 5S 71 30W
Quilino, Argentina 94 C3 30 14S 64 29W
Quillabamba, Peru 92 F4 12 50S 72 50W
Quillagua, Chile 94 A2 21 40S 69 40W
Quillaicillo, Chile 94 C1 31 17S 71 40W
Quillota, Chile 94 C1 32 54S 71 16W
Quilmes, Argentina 94 C4 34 43S 58 15W
Quilon, India 40 Q10 8 50N 76 38 E
Quilpie, Australia 63 D3 26 35S 144 11 E
Quilpué, Chile 94 C1 33 5S 71 33W
Quilua, Mozam. 55 F4 16 17S 39 54 E
Quimilí, Argentina 94 B3 27 40S 62 30W
Quimper, France 18 B1 48 0N 4 9W
Quimperlé, France 18 C2 47 53N 3 33W
Quinault →, U.S.A. 84 C2 47 21N 124 18W
Quincy, Calif., U.S.A. 84 F6 39 56N 120 57W
Quincy, Fla., U.S.A. 77 K3 30 35N 84 34W
Quincy, Ill., U.S.A. 80 F9 39 56N 91 23W
Quincy, Mass., U.S.A. 79 D14 42 15N 71 0W
Quincy, Wash., U.S.A. 82 C4 47 22N 119 56W
Quines, Argentina 94 C2 32 13S 65 48W
Quinga, Mozam. 55 F5 15 49S 40 15 E
Quintana Roo □, Mexico 87 D7 19 0N 88 0W
Quintanar de la Orden, Spain 19 C4 39 36N 3 5W
Quintero, Chile 94 C1 32 45S 71 30W
Quinyambie, Australia 63 E3 30 15S 141 0 E
Quirihue, Chile 94 D1 36 15S 72 35W
Quirindi, Australia 63 E5 31 28S 150 40 E
Quirinópolis, Brazil 93 G8 18 32S 50 30W
Quissanga, Mozam. 55 E5 12 24S 40 28 E
Quitilipi, Argentina 94 B3 26 50S 60 13W
Quitman, Ga., U.S.A. 77 K4 30 47N 83 34W
Quitman, Miss., U.S.A. 77 J1 32 2N 88 44W
Quitman, Tex., U.S.A. 81 J7 32 48N 95 27W
Quito, Ecuador 92 D3 0 15S 78 35W
Quixadá, Brazil 93 D11 4 55S 39 0W
Quixaxe, Mozam. 55 F5 15 17S 40 4 E
Qumbu, S. Africa 57 E4 31 10S 28 48 E
Quneitra, Syria 47 B4 33 7N 35 48 E
Qŭnghirot, Uzbekistan 26 E6 43 6N 58 54 E
Quoin I., Australia 60 B4 14 54S 129 32 E
Quoin Pt., S. Africa 56 E2 34 46S 19 37 E
Quondong, Australia 63 E3 33 6S 140 18 E
Quorn, Australia 63 E2 32 25S 138 5 E
Qŭqon, Uzbekistan 26 E8 40 30N 70 57 E
Qurnat as Sawdā', Lebanon 47 A5 34 18N 36 6 E
Qusaybah, Iraq 44 C4 34 24N 40 59 E
Quseir, Egypt 51 C12 26 7N 34 16 E
Qūshchī, Iran 44 B5 37 59N 45 3 E
Quthing, Lesotho 57 E4 30 25S 27 36 E
Qūṭīābād, Iran 45 C6 35 47N 48 30 E
Quwo, China 34 G6 35 38N 111 25 E
Quyang, China 34 E8 38 35N 114 40 E
Quynh Nhai, Vietnam 38 B4 21 49N 103 33 E
Quzi, China 34 F4 36 20N 107 20 E
Qyzylorda, Kazakstan 26 E7 44 48N 65 28 E

R

Ra, Ko, Thailand 39 H2 9 13N 98 16 E
Raahe, Finland 8 D21 64 40N 24 28 E
Raalte, Neths. 15 B6 52 23N 6 16 E
Raasay, U.K. 12 D2 57 25N 6 4W
Raasay, Sd. of, U.K. 12 D2 57 30N 6 8W
Raba, Indonesia 37 F5 8 36S 118 55 E
Rába →, Hungary 17 E9 47 38N 17 38 E
Rabai, Kenya 54 C4 3 50S 39 31 E
Rabat, Malta 23 D1 35 53N 14 25 E
Rabat, Morocco 50 B4 34 2N 6 48W
Rabaul, Papua N. G. 64 H7 4 24S 152 18 E
Rabbit →, Canada 72 B3 59 41N 127 12W
Rabbit Lake, Canada 73 C7 53 8N 107 46W
Rabbitskin →, Canada 72 A4 61 47N 120 42W
Râbniţa, Moldova 17 E15 47 45N 29 0 E
Rābor, Iran 45 D8 29 17N 56 55 E
Race, C., Canada 71 C9 46 40N 53 5W
Rach Gia, Vietnam 39 G5 10 5N 105 5 E
Racibórz, Poland 17 C10 50 7N 18 18 E
Racine, U.S.A. 76 D2 42 41N 87 51W
Rackerby, U.S.A. 84 F5 39 26N 121 22W
Radama, Nosy, Madag. 57 A8 14 0S 47 47 E
Radama, Saikanosy, Madag. 57 A8 14 16S 47 53 E
Rădăuţi, Romania 17 E13 47 50N 25 59 E
Radekhiv, Ukraine 17 C13 50 25N 24 32 E
Radekhov = Radekhiv, Ukraine 17 C13 50 25N 24 32 E
Radford, U.S.A. 76 G5 37 8N 80 34W
Radhanpur, India 42 H4 23 50N 71 38 E
Radisson, Canada 73 C7 52 30N 107 20W
Radium Hot Springs, Canada 72 C5 50 35N 116 2W
Radnor Forest, U.K. 11 E4 52 17N 3 10W
Radom, Poland 17 C11 51 23N 21 12 E
Radomsko, Poland 17 C10 51 5N 19 28 E
Radomyshl, Ukraine 17 C15 50 30N 29 12 E
Radstock, C., Australia 63 E1 33 12S 134 20 E
Radviliškis, Lithuania 9 J20 55 49N 23 33 E
Radville, Canada 73 D8 49 30N 104 15W
Rae, Canada 72 A5 62 50N 116 3W
Rae Bareli, India 43 F9 26 18N 81 20 E
Rae Isthmus, Canada 69 B11 66 40N 87 30W
Raeren, Belgium 15 D6 50 41N 6 7 E
Raeside, L., Australia 61 E3 29 20S 122 0 E
Raetihi, N.Z. 59 H5 39 25S 175 17 E
Rafaela, Argentina 94 C3 31 10S 61 30W
Rafah, Gaza Strip 47 D3 31 18N 34 14 E
Rafai, C.A.R. 54 B1 4 59N 23 58 E
Rafḥā, Si. Arabia 44 D4 29 35N 43 35 E
Rafsanjān, Iran 45 D8 30 30N 56 5 E
Raft Pt., Australia 60 C3 16 4S 124 26 E
Ragachow, Belarus 17 B16 53 8N 30 5 E
Ragama, Sri Lanka 40 R11 7 0N 79 50 E
Ragged, Mt., Australia 61 F3 33 27S 123 25 E
Raglan, Australia 62 C5 23 42S 150 49 E
Raglan, N.Z. 59 G5 37 55S 174 55 E
Ragusa, Italy 20 F6 36 55N 14 44 E
Raha, Indonesia 37 E6 4 55S 123 0 E
Rahaeng = Tak, Thailand 38 D2 16 52N 99 8 E
Raḥimah, Si. Arabia 45 E6 26 42N 50 4 E
Rahimyar Khan, Pakistan 42 E4 28 30N 70 25 E
Rāhjerd, Iran 45 C6 34 22N 50 22 E
Raichur, India 40 L10 16 10N 77 20 E
Raiganj, India 43 G13 25 37N 88 10 E
Raigarh, India 41 J13 21 56N 83 25 E
Raijua, Indonesia 37 F6 10 37S 121 36 E
Railton, Australia 62 G4 41 25S 146 28 E
Rainbow Lake, Canada 72 B5 58 30N 119 23W
Rainier, U.S.A. 84 D4 46 53N 122 41W
Rainier, Mt., U.S.A. 84 D5 46 52N 121 46W
Rainy L., Canada 73 D10 48 42N 93 10W
Rainy River, Canada 73 D10 48 43N 94 29W
Raippaluoto, Finland 8 E19 63 13N 21 14 E
Raipur, India 41 J12 21 17N 81 45 E
Raisio, Finland 9 F20 60 28N 22 11 E
Raj Nandgaon, India 41 J12 21 5N 81 5 E
Raja, Ujung, Indonesia 36 D1 3 40N 96 25 E
Raja Ampat, Kepulauan, Indonesia 37 E8 0 30S 130 0 E
Rajahmundry, India 41 L12 17 1N 81 48 E
Rajang →, Malaysia 36 D4 2 30N 112 0 E
Rajapalaiyam, India 40 Q10 9 25N 77 35 E
Rajasthan □, India 42 F5 26 45N 73 30 E
Rajasthan Canal, India 42 F5 28 0N 72 0 E
Rajauri, India 43 C6 33 25N 74 21 E
Rajgarh, Mad. P., India 42 G7 24 2N 76 45 E
Rajgarh, Raj., India 42 E6 28 40N 75 25 E
Rajkot, India 42 H4 22 15N 70 56 E
Rajmahal Hills, India 43 G12 24 30N 87 30 E
Rajpipla, India 40 J8 21 50N 73 30 E
Rajpura, India 42 D7 30 25N 76 32 E
Rajshahi, Bangla. 41 G16 24 22N 88 39 E
Rajshahi □, Bangla. 43 G13 25 0N 89 0 E
Rakaia, N.Z. 59 K4 43 45S 172 1 E
Rakaia →, N.Z. 59 K4 43 36S 172 15 E
Rakan, Ra's, Qatar 45 E6 26 10N 51 20 E
Rakaposhi, Pakistan 43 A6 36 10N 74 25 E
Rakata, Pulau, Indonesia 36 F3 6 10S 105 20 E
Rakhiv, Ukraine 17 D13 48 3N 24 12 E
Rakhni, Pakistan 42 D3 30 4N 69 56 E
Rakitnoye, Russia 30 B7 45 36N 134 17 E
Rakops, Botswana 56 C3 21 1S 24 28 E
Rakvere, Estonia 9 G22 59 20N 26 25 E
Raleigh, U.S.A. 77 H6 35 47N 78 39W
Raleigh B., U.S.A. 77 H7 34 50N 76 15W
Ralls, U.S.A. 81 J4 33 41N 101 24W
Ram →, Canada 72 A4 62 1N 123 41W
Rām Allāh, West Bank 47 D4 31 55N 35 10 E
Ram Hd., Australia 63 F4 37 47S 149 30 E
Rama, Nic. 88 D3 12 9N 84 15W
Raman, Thailand 39 J3 6 29N 101 18 E
Ramanathapuram, India 40 Q11 9 25N 78 55 E
Ramanetaka, B. de, Madag. 57 A8 14 13S 47 52 E
Ramat Gan, Israel 47 C3 32 4N 34 48 E
Ramatlhabama, S. Africa 56 D4 25 37S 25 33 E
Ramban, India 43 C6 33 14N 75 12 E
Rambipuji, Indonesia 37 H15 8 12S 113 37 E
Ramea, Canada 71 C8 47 31N 57 23W
Ramechhap, Nepal 43 F12 27 25N 86 10 E
Ramgarh, Bihar, India 43 H11 23 40N 85 35 E
Ramgarh, Raj., India 42 F6 27 16N 75 14 E
Ramgarh, Raj., India 42 F4 27 30N 70 36 E
Rāmhormoz, Iran 45 D6 31 15N 49 35 E
Ramiān, Iran 45 B7 37 3N 55 16 E
Ramingining, Australia 62 A2 12 19S 135 3 E
Ramla, Israel 47 D3 31 55N 34 52 E
Ramnad = Ramanathapuram, India 40 Q11 9 25N 78 55 E
Ramnagar, India 43 C6 32 47N 75 18 E
Râmnicu Sărat, Romania 17 F14 45 26N 27 3 E
Râmnicu Vâlcea, Romania 17 F13 45 9N 24 21 E
Ramona, U.S.A. 85 M10 33 2N 116 52W
Ramore, Canada 70 C3 48 30N 80 25W
Ramotswa, Botswana 56 C4 24 50S 25 52 E
Rampur, H.P., India 42 D7 31 26N 77 43 E
Rampur, Mad. P., India 42 H5 23 25N 73 53 E
Rampur, Ut. P., India 43 E8 28 50N 79 5 E
Rampur Hat, India 43 G12 24 10N 87 50 E
Rampura, India 42 G6 24 30N 75 27 E
Ramree I. = Ramree Kyun, Burma 41 K19 19 0N 94 0 E
Ramree Kyun, Burma 41 K19 19 0N 94 0 E
Rāmsar, Iran 45 B6 36 53N 50 41 E
Ramsey, Canada 70 C3 47 25N 82 20W
Ramsey, U.K. 10 C3 54 20N 4 22W
Ramsgate, U.K. 11 F9 51 20N 1 25 E
Ramtek, India 40 J11 21 20N 79 15 E
Ranaghat, India 43 H13 23 15N 88 35 E
Ranahu, Pakistan 42 G3 25 55N 69 45 E
Ranau, Malaysia 36 C5 6 2N 116 40 E
Rancagua, Chile 94 C1 34 10S 70 50W
Rancheria →, Canada 72 A3 60 13N 129 7W
Ranchester, U.S.A. 82 D10 44 54N 107 10W
Ranchi, India 43 H11 23 19N 85 27 E
Rancho Cucamonga, U.S.A. 85 L9 34 10N 117 30W
Randalstown, U.K. 13 B5 54 45N 6 19W
Randers, Denmark 9 H14 56 29N 10 1 E
Randfontein, S. Africa 57 D4 26 8S 27 45 E
Randle, U.S.A. 84 D5 46 32N 121 57W
Randolph, Mass., U.S.A. 79 D13 42 10N 71 2W
Randolph, N.Y., U.S.A. 78 D6 42 10N 78 59W
Randolph, Utah, U.S.A. 82 F8 41 40N 111 11W
Randolph, Vt., U.S.A. 79 C12 43 55N 72 40W
Råne älv →, Sweden 8 D20 65 50N 22 20 E
Rangae, Thailand 39 J3 6 19N 101 44 E
Rangaunu B., N.Z. 59 F4 34 51S 173 15 E
Rangeley, U.S.A. 79 B14 44 58N 70 39W
Rangely, U.S.A. 82 F9 40 5N 108 48W
Ranger, U.S.A. 81 J5 32 28N 98 41W
Rangia, India 41 F17 26 28N 91 38 E
Rangiora, N.Z. 59 K4 43 19S 172 36 E
Rangitaiki →, N.Z. 59 G6 37 54S 176 49 E
Rangitata →, N.Z. 59 K3 43 45S 171 15 E
Rangkasbitung, Indonesia 37 G12 6 21S 106 15 E
Rangon →, Burma 41 L20 16 28N 96 40 E
Rangoon, Burma 41 L20 16 45N 96 20 E
Rangpur, Bangla. 41 G16 25 42N 89 22 E
Rangsit, Thailand 38 F3 13 59N 100 37 E
Ranibennur, India 40 M9 14 35N 75 30 E
Raniganj, India 43 H12 23 40N 87 5 E
Raniwara, India 40 G8 24 50N 72 10 E
Rāniyah, Iraq 44 B5 36 15N 44 53 E
Ranken →, Australia 62 C2 20 31S 137 36 E
Rankin, U.S.A. 81 K4 31 13N 101 56W
Rankin Inlet, Canada 68 B10 62 30N 93 0W
Rankins Springs, Australia 63 E4 33 49S 146 14 E
Rannoch, L., U.K. 12 E4 56 41N 4 20W
Rannoch Moor, U.K. 12 E4 56 38N 4 48W
Ranobe, Helodranon' i, Madag. 57 C7 23 3S 43 33 E
Ranohira, Madag. 57 C8 22 29S 45 24 E
Ranomafana, Toamasina, Madag. 57 B8 18 57S 48 50 E
Ranomafana, Toliara, Madag. 57 C8 24 34S 47 0 E
Ranong, Thailand 39 H2 9 56N 98 40 E
Rānsa, Iran 45 C6 33 39N 48 18 E
Ransiki, Indonesia 37 E8 1 30S 134 10 E
Rantauprapat, Indonesia 36 D1 2 15N 99 50 E
Rantemario, Indonesia 37 E5 3 15S 119 57 E
Rantoul, U.S.A. 76 E1 40 19N 88 9W
Raoyang, China 34 E8 38 15N 115 45 E
Rapa, Pac. Oc. 65 K13 27 35S 144 20W
Rapallo, Italy 18 D8 44 21N 9 14 E
Rāpch, Iran 45 E8 25 40N 59 15 E
Rapid →, Canada 72 B3 59 15N 129 5W
Rapid City, U.S.A. 80 D3 44 5N 103 14W
Rapid River, U.S.A. 76 C2 45 55N 86 58W
Rapides des Joachims, Canada 70 C4 46 13N 77 43W
Rapla, Estonia 9 G21 59 1N 24 52 E
Rarotonga, Cook Is. 65 K12 21 30S 160 0W
Ra's al 'Ayn, Syria 44 B4 36 45N 40 12 E
Ra's al Khaymah, U.A.E. 45 E8 25 50N 56 5 E
Ra's an Naqb, Jordan 47 F4 30 0N 35 29 E
Ras Dashen, Ethiopia 46 E2 13 8N 38 26 E
Râs Timirist, Mauritania 50 E2 19 21N 16 30W
Rasca, Pta. de la, Canary Is. 22 G3 27 59N 16 41W
Raseiniai, Lithuania 9 J20 55 25N 23 5 E
Rasht, Iran 45 B6 37 20N 49 40 E
Rasi Salai, Thailand 38 E5 15 20N 104 9 E
Rason L., Australia 61 E3 28 45S 124 25 E
Rasra, India 43 G10 25 50N 83 50 E
Rat Buri, Thailand 38 F2 13 30N 99 54 E
Rat Islands, U.S.A. 68 C1 52 0N 178 0 E
Rat River, Canada 72 A6 61 7N 112 36W
Ratangarh, India 42 E6 28 5N 74 35 E
Raṭāwī, Iraq 44 D5 30 38N 47 13 E
Rath, India 43 G8 25 36N 79 37 E
Rath Luirc, Ireland 13 D3 52 21N 8 40W
Rathdrum, Ireland 13 D5 52 56N 6 14W
Rathenow, Germany 16 B7 52 37N 12 19 E
Rathkeale, Ireland 13 D3 52 32N 8 56W
Rathlin I., U.K. 13 A5 55 18N 6 14W
Rathmelton, Ireland 13 A4 55 2N 7 38W
Ratibor = Racibórz, Poland 17 C10 50 7N 18 18 E
Ratlam, India 42 H6 23 20N 75 0 E
Ratnagiri, India 40 L8 16 57N 73 18 E
Raton, U.S.A. 81 G2 36 54N 104 24W
Rattaphum, Thailand 39 J3 7 8N 100 16 E
Rattray Hd., U.K. 12 D7 57 38N 1 50W
Ratz, Mt., Canada 72 B2 57 23N 132 12W
Raub, Malaysia 39 L3 3 47N 101 52 E
Rauch, Argentina 94 D4 36 45S 59 5W
Raufarhöfn, Iceland 8 C6 66 27N 15 57W
Raufoss, Norway 9 F14 60 44N 10 37 E
Raukumara Ra., N.Z. 59 H6 38 5S 177 55 E
Rauma, Finland 9 F19 61 10N 21 30 E
Raurkela, India 43 H11 22 14N 84 50 E
Rausu-Dake, Japan 30 B12 44 4N 145 7 E
Rava-Ruska, Poland 17 C12 50 15N 23 42 E
Rava Russkaya = Rava-Ruska, Poland 17 C12 50 15N 23 42 E
Ravānsar, Iran 44 C5 34 43N 46 40 E
Rāvar, Iran 45 D8 31 20N 56 51 E
Ravena, U.S.A. 79 D11 42 28N 73 49W
Ravenna, Italy 20 B5 44 25N 12 12 E
Ravenna, Nebr., U.S.A. 80 E5 41 1N 98 55W
Ravenna, Ohio, U.S.A. 78 E3 41 9N 81 15W
Ravensburg, Germany 16 E5 47 46N 9 36 E
Ravenshoe, Australia 62 B4 17 37S 145 29 E
Ravensthorpe, Australia 61 F3 33 35S 120 2 E
Ravenswood, Australia 62 C4 20 6S 146 54 E
Ravenswood, U.S.A. 76 F5 38 57N 81 46W
Ravi →, Pakistan 42 D4 30 35N 71 49 E
Rawalpindi, Pakistan 42 C5 33 38N 73 8 E
Rawāndūz, Iraq 44 B5 36 40N 44 30 E
Rawang, Malaysia 39 L3 3 20N 101 35 E
Rawdon, Canada 70 C5 46 3N 73 40W
Rawene, N.Z. 59 F4 35 25S 173 32 E
Rawlinna, Australia 61 F4 30 58S 125 28 E
Rawlins, U.S.A. 82 F10 41 47N 107 14W
Rawlinson Ra., Australia 61 D4 24 40S 128 30 E
Rawson, Argentina 96 E3 43 15S 65 5W
Ray, U.S.A. 80 A3 48 21N 103 10W
Ray, C., Canada 71 C8 47 33N 59 15W
Rayadurg, India 40 M10 14 40N 76 50 E
Rayagada, India 41 K13 19 15N 83 20 E
Raychikhinsk, Russia 27 E13 49 46N 129 25 E
Rāyen, Iran 45 D8 29 34N 57 26 E
Rayleigh, U.K. 11 F8 51 36N 0 37 E
Raymond, Canada 72 D6 49 30N 112 35W
Raymond, Calif., U.S.A. 84 H7 37 13N 119 54W
Raymond, Wash., U.S.A. 84 D3 46 41N 123 44W
Raymondville, U.S.A. 81 M6 26 29N 97 47W
Raymore, Canada 73 C8 51 25N 104 31W
Rayne, U.S.A. 81 K8 30 14N 92 16W
Rayón, Mexico 86 B2 29 43N 110 35W
Rayong, Thailand 38 F3 12 40N 101 20 E
Rayville, U.S.A. 81 J9 32 29N 91 46W
Raz, Pte. du, France 18 C1 48 2N 4 47W
Razan, Iran 45 C6 35 23N 49 2 E
Razdel'naya = Rozdilna, Ukraine 17 E16 46 50N 30 2 E
Razdolnoye, Russia 30 C5 43 30N 131 52 E
Razeh, Iran 45 C6 32 47N 48 9 E
Razgrad, Bulgaria 21 C12 43 33N 26 34 E
Razim, Lacul, Romania 17 F15 44 50N 29 0 E
Razmak, Pakistan 42 C3 32 45N 69 50 E
Ré, I. de, France 18 C3 46 12N 1 30W
Reading, U.K. 11 F7 51 27N 0 58W
Reading, U.S.A. 79 F9 40 20N 75 56W
Reading □, U.K. 11 F7 51 27N 0 58W
Realicó, Argentina 94 D3 35 0S 64 15W
Ream, Cambodia 39 G4 10 34N 103 39 E
Reata, Mexico 86 B4 26 8N 101 5W
Reay Forest, U.K. 12 C4 58 22N 4 55W
Rebecca, L., Australia 61 F3 30 0S 122 15 E
Rebi, Indonesia 37 F8 6 23S 134 7 E
Rebiana, Libya 51 D10 24 12N 22 10 E
Rebun-Tō, Japan 30 B10 45 23N 141 2 E

Sadimi

Rockwell City, U.S.A. 80 D7 42 24N 94 38W
Rockwood, U.S.A. 77 H3 35 52N 84 41W
Rocky Ford, U.S.A. 80 F3 38 3N 103 43W
Rocky Gully, Australia 61 F2 34 30S 116 57 E
Rocky Lane, Canada 72 B5 58 31N 116 22W
Rocky Mount, U.S.A. 77 H7 35 57N 77 48W
Rocky Mountain House, Canada 72 C6 52 22N 114 55W
Rocky Mts., N. Amer. 72 C4 55 0N 121 0W
Rockyford, Canada 72 C6 51 14N 113 10W
Rod, Pakistan 40 E3 28 10N 63 5 E
Rødbyhavn, Denmark 9 J14 54 39N 11 22 E
Roddickton, Canada 71 B8 50 51N 56 8W
Roderick I., Canada 72 C3 52 38N 128 22W
Rodez, France 18 D5 44 21N 2 33 E
Rodhopoú, Greece 23 D5 35 34N 23 45 E
Ródhos, Greece 23 C10 36 15N 28 10 E
Rodney, Canada 78 D3 42 34N 81 41W
Rodney, C., N.Z. 59 G5 36 17S 174 50 E
Rodriguez, Ind. Oc. 3 E13 19 45S 63 20 E
Roe →, U.K. 13 A5 55 6N 6 59W
Roebling, U.S.A. 79 F10 40 7N 74 47W
Roebourne, Australia 60 D2 20 44S 117 9 E
Roebuck B., Australia 60 C3 18 5S 122 20 E
Roebuck Plains, Australia 60 C3 17 56S 122 28 E
Roermond, Neths. 15 C6 51 12N 6 0 E
Roes Welcome Sd., Canada 69 B11 65 0N 87 0W
Roeselare, Belgium 15 D3 50 57N 3 7 E
Rogachev = Ragachow, Belarus 17 B16 53 8N 30 5 E
Rogagua, L., Bolivia 92 F5 13 43S 66 50W
Rogatyn, Ukraine 17 D13 49 24N 24 36 E
Rogdhia, Greece 23 D7 35 22N 25 1 E
Rogers, U.S.A. 81 G7 36 20N 94 7W
Rogers City, U.S.A. 76 C4 45 25N 83 49W
Rogerson, U.S.A. 82 E6 42 13N 114 36W
Rogersville, U.S.A. 77 G4 36 24N 83 1W
Roggan River, Canada 70 B4 54 25N 79 32W
Roggeveldberge, S. Africa 56 E3 32 10S 20 10 E
Rogoaguado, L., Bolivia 92 F5 13 0S 65 30W
Rogue →, U.S.A. 82 E1 42 26N 124 26W
Róhda, Greece 23 A3 39 48N 19 46 E
Rohnert Park, U.S.A. 84 G4 38 16N 122 40W
Rohri, Pakistan 42 F3 27 45N 68 51 E
Rohri Canal, Pakistan 42 F3 26 15N 68 27 E
Rohtak, India 42 E7 28 55N 76 43 E
Roi Et, Thailand 38 D4 16 4N 103 40 E
Roja, Latvia 9 H20 57 29N 22 43 E
Rojas, Argentina 94 C3 34 10S 60 45W
Rojo, C., Mexico 87 C5 21 33N 97 20W
Rokan →, Indonesia 36 D2 2 0N 100 50 E
Rokeby, Australia 62 A3 13 39S 142 40 E
Rokiškis, Lithuania 9 J21 55 55N 25 35 E
Rolândia, Brazil 95 A5 23 18S 51 23W
Rolette, U.S.A. 80 A5 48 40N 99 51W
Rolla, Kans., U.S.A. 81 G4 37 7N 101 38W
Rolla, Mo., U.S.A. 81 G9 37 57N 91 46W
Rolla, N. Dak., U.S.A. 80 A5 48 52N 99 37W
Rolleston, Australia 62 C4 24 28S 148 35 E
Rollingstone, Australia 62 B4 19 2S 146 24 E
Roma, Australia 63 D4 26 32S 148 49 E
Roma, Italy 20 D5 41 54N 12 29 E
Roma, Sweden 9 H18 57 32N 18 26 E
Roman, Romania 17 E14 46 57N 26 55 E
Romang, Indonesia 37 F7 7 30S 127 20 E
Români, Egypt 47 E1 30 59N 32 38 E
Romania ■, Europe 17 F12 46 0N 25 0 E
Romano, Cayo, Cuba 88 B4 22 0N 77 30W
Romanovka = Basarabeasca, Moldova 17 E15 46 21N 28 58 E
Romans-sur-Isère, France 18 D6 45 3N 5 3 E
Romblon, Phil. 37 B6 12 33N 122 17 E
Rombo □, Tanzania 54 C4 3 10S 37 30 E
Rome = Roma, Italy 20 D5 41 54N 12 29 E
Rome, Ga., U.S.A. 77 H3 34 15N 85 10W
Rome, N.Y., U.S.A. 79 C9 43 13N 75 27W
Romney, U.S.A. 76 F6 39 21N 78 45W
Romney Marsh, U.K. 11 F8 51 2N 0 54 E
Rømø, Denmark 9 J13 55 10N 8 30 E
Romorantin-Lanthenay, France 18 C4 47 21N 1 45 E
Romsdalen, Norway 9 E12 62 25N 7 52 E
Romsey, U.K. 11 G6 51 0N 1 29W
Ron, Vietnam 38 D6 17 53N 106 27 E
Rona, U.K. 12 D3 57 34N 5 59W
Ronan, U.S.A. 82 C6 47 32N 114 6W
Roncador, Cayos, Caribbean 88 D3 13 32N 80 4W
Roncador, Serra do, Brazil 93 F8 12 30S 52 30W
Ronceverte, U.S.A. 76 G5 37 45N 80 28W
Ronda, Spain 19 D3 36 46N 5 12W
Rondane, Norway 9 F13 61 57N 9 50 E
Rondônia □, Brazil 92 F6 11 0S 63 0W
Rondonópolis, Brazil 93 G8 16 28S 54 38W
Ronge, L. la, Canada 73 B7 55 6N 105 17W
Rønne, Denmark 9 J16 55 6N 14 43 E
Ronne Ice Shelf, Antarctica 5 D18 78 0S 60 0W
Ronsard, C., Australia 61 D1 24 46S 113 10 E
Ronse, Belgium 15 D3 50 45N 3 35 E
Roodepoort, S. Africa 57 D4 26 11S 27 54 E
Roof Butte, U.S.A. 83 H9 36 28N 109 5W
Roorkee, India 42 E7 29 52N 77 59 E
Roosendaal, Neths. 15 C4 51 32N 4 29 E
Roosevelt, Minn., U.S.A. 80 A7 48 48N 95 6W
Roosevelt, Utah, U.S.A. 82 F8 40 18N 109 59W
Roosevelt →, Brazil 92 E6 7 35S 60 20W
Roosevelt, Mt., Canada 72 B3 58 26N 125 20W
Roosevelt I., Antarctica 5 D12 79 30S 162 0W
Roosevelt Res., U.S.A. 83 K8 33 46N 111 0W
Roper →, Australia 62 A2 14 43S 135 27 E
Ropesville, U.S.A. 81 J3 33 26N 102 9W
Roque Pérez, Argentina 94 D4 35 25S 59 24W
Roquetas de Mar, Spain 19 D4 36 46N 2 36W
Roraima □, Brazil 92 C6 2 0N 61 30W
Roraima, Mt., Venezuela 92 B6 5 10N 60 40W
Rorketon, Canada 73 C9 51 24N 99 35W
Røros, Norway 9 E14 62 35N 11 23 E
Rosa, Zambia 55 D3 9 33S 31 15 E
Rosa, Monte, Europe 18 D7 45 57N 7 53 E
Rosalia, U.S.A. 82 C5 47 14N 117 22W
Rosamond, U.S.A. 85 L8 34 52N 118 10W
Rosario, Argentina 94 C3 33 0S 60 40W
Rosário, Brazil 93 D10 3 0S 44 15W
Rosario, Baja Calif., Mexico 86 B1 30 0N 115 50W
Rosario, Sinaloa, Mexico 86 C3 23 0N 105 52W
Rosario, Paraguay 94 A4 24 30S 57 35W
Rosario de la Frontera, Argentina 94 B3 25 50S 65 0W
Rosario de Lerma, Argentina 94 A2 24 59S 65 35W
Rosario del Tala, Argentina 94 C4 32 20S 59 10W
Rosário do Sul, Brazil 95 C5 30 15S 54 55W
Rosarito, Mexico 85 N9 32 18N 117 4W
Roscoe, U.S.A. 80 C5 45 27N 99 20W
Roscommon, Ireland 13 C3 53 38N 8 11W
Roscommon, U.S.A. 76 C3 44 30N 84 35W
Roscommon □, Ireland 13 C3 53 49N 8 23W
Roscrea, Ireland 13 D4 52 57N 7 49W
Rose →, Australia 62 A2 14 16S 135 45 E
Rose Blanche, Canada 71 C8 47 38N 58 45W
Rose Harbour, Canada 72 C2 52 15N 131 10W
Rose Pt., Canada 72 C2 54 11N 131 39W
Rose Valley, Canada 73 C8 52 19N 103 49W
Roseau, Domin. 89 C7 15 20N 61 24W
Roseau, U.S.A. 80 A7 48 51N 95 46W
Rosebery, Australia 62 G4 41 46S 145 33 E
Rosebud, U.S.A. 81 K6 31 4N 96 59W
Roseburg, U.S.A. 82 E2 43 13N 123 20W
Rosedale, Australia 62 C5 24 38S 151 53 E
Rosedale, U.S.A. 81 J9 33 51N 91 2W
Roseland, U.S.A. 84 G4 38 25N 122 43W
Rosemary, Canada 72 C6 50 46N 112 5W
Rosenberg, U.S.A. 81 L7 29 34N 95 49W
Rosenheim, Germany 16 E7 47 51N 12 7 E
Roses, G. de, Spain 19 A7 42 10N 3 15 E
Rosetown, Canada 73 C7 51 35N 107 59W
Roseville, U.S.A. 84 G5 38 45N 121 17W
Rosewood, N. Terr., Australia 60 C4 16 28S 128 58 E
Rosewood, Queens., Australia 63 D5 27 38S 152 36 E
Roshkhvār, Iran 45 C8 34 58N 59 37 E
Rosignano Marittimo, Italy 20 C4 43 24N 10 28 E
Rosignol, Guyana 92 B7 6 15N 57 30W
Roşiori-de-Vede, Romania 17 F13 44 7N 24 59 E
Roskilde, Denmark 9 J15 55 38N 12 3 E
Roslavl, Russia 24 D5 53 57N 32 55 E
Roslyn, Australia 63 E4 34 29S 149 37 E
Rosmead, S. Africa 56 E4 31 29S 25 8 E
Ross, Australia 62 G4 42 2S 147 30 E
Ross, N.Z. 59 K3 42 53S 170 49 E
Ross I., Antarctica 5 D11 77 30S 168 0 E
Ross Ice Shelf, Antarctica 5 E12 80 0S 180 0 E
Ross L., U.S.A. 82 B3 48 44N 121 4W
Ross-on-Wye, U.K. 11 F5 51 54N 2 34W
Ross Sea, Antarctica 5 D11 74 0S 178 0 E
Rossall Pt., U.K. 10 D4 53 55N 3 3W
Rossan Pt., Ireland 13 B3 54 42N 8 47W
Rossano, Italy 20 E7 39 36N 16 39 E
Rossburn, Canada 73 C8 50 40N 100 49W
Rosseau, Canada 78 A5 45 16N 79 39W
Rosses, The, Ireland 13 A3 55 2N 8 20W
Rossignol, L., Canada 70 B5 52 43N 73 40W
Rossignol Res., Canada 71 D6 44 12N 65 10W
Rossland, Canada 72 D5 49 6N 117 50W
Rosslare, Ireland 13 D5 52 17N 6 24W
Rosso, Mauritania 50 E2 16 40N 15 45W
Rossosh, Russia 25 D6 50 15N 39 28 E
Rossport, Canada 70 C2 48 50N 87 30W
Røssvatnet, Norway 8 D16 65 45N 14 5 E
Rossville, Australia 62 B4 15 48S 145 15 E
Røst, Norway 8 C15 67 32N 12 0 E
Rosthern, Canada 73 C7 52 40N 106 20W
Rostock, Germany 16 A7 54 5N 12 8 E
Rostov, Don, Russia 25 E6 47 15N 39 45 E
Rostov, Yaroslavl, Russia 24 C6 57 14N 39 25 E
Roswell, Ga., U.S.A. 77 H3 34 2N 84 22W
Roswell, N. Mex., U.S.A. 81 J2 33 24N 104 32W
Rotan, U.S.A. 81 J4 32 51N 100 28W
Rother →, U.K. 11 G8 50 59N 0 45 E
Rotherham, U.K. 10 D6 53 26N 1 20W
Rothes, U.K. 12 D5 57 32N 3 13W
Rothesay, Canada 71 C6 45 23N 66 0W
Rothesay, U.K. 12 F3 55 50N 5 3W
Roti, Indonesia 37 F6 10 50S 123 0 E
Roto, Australia 63 E4 33 0S 145 30 E
Rotondo Mte., France 18 E8 42 14N 9 8 E
Rotoroa, L., N.Z. 59 J4 41 55S 172 39 E
Rotorua, N.Z. 59 H6 38 9S 176 16 E
Rotorua, L., N.Z. 59 H6 38 5S 176 18 E
Rotterdam, Neths. 15 C4 51 55N 4 30 E
Rottnest I., Australia 61 F2 32 0S 115 27 E
Rottumeroog, Neths. 15 A6 53 33N 6 34 E
Rottweil, Germany 16 D5 48 9N 8 37 E
Rotuma, Fiji 64 J9 12 25S 177 5 E
Roubaix, France 18 A5 50 40N 3 10 E
Rouen, France 18 B4 49 27N 1 4 E
Rouleau, Canada 73 C8 50 10N 104 56W
Round Mountain, U.S.A. 82 G5 38 43N 117 4W
Round Mt., Australia 63 E5 30 26S 152 16 E
Roundup, U.S.A. 82 C9 46 27N 108 33W
Rousay, U.K. 12 B5 59 10N 3 2W
Rouses Point, U.S.A. 79 B11 44 59N 73 22W
Roussillon, France 18 E5 42 30N 2 35 E
Rouxville, S. Africa 56 E4 30 25S 26 50 E
Rouyn-Noranda, Canada 70 C4 48 20N 79 0W
Rovaniemi, Finland 8 C21 66 29N 25 41 E
Rovereto, Italy 20 B4 45 53N 11 3 E
Rovigo, Italy 20 B4 45 4N 11 47 E
Rovinj, Croatia 16 F7 45 5N 13 40 E
Rovno = Rivne, Ukraine 25 D4 50 40N 26 10 E
Rovuma = Ruvuma →, Tanzania 55 E5 10 29S 40 28 E
Row'ān, Iran 45 C6 35 8N 48 51 E
Rowena, Australia 63 D4 29 48S 148 55 E
Rowley Shoals, Australia 60 C2 17 30S 119 0 E
Roxas, Phil. 37 B6 11 36N 122 49 E
Roxboro, U.S.A. 77 G6 36 24N 78 59W
Roxborough Downs, Australia 62 C2 22 30S 138 45 E
Roxburgh, N.Z. 59 L2 45 33S 169 19 E
Roy, Mont., U.S.A. 82 C9 47 20N 108 58W
Roy, N. Mex., U.S.A. 81 H2 35 57N 104 12W
Roy Hill, Australia 60 D2 22 37S 119 58 E
Royal Canal, Ireland 13 C4 53 30N 7 13W
Royal Leamington Spa, U.K. 11 E6 52 18N 1 31W
Royal Tunbridge Wells, U.K. 11 F8 51 7N 0 16 E
Royan, France 18 D3 45 37N 1 2W
Royston, U.K. 11 E7 52 3N 0 0 E
Rozdilna, Ukraine 17 E16 46 50N 30 2 E
Rozhyshche, Ukraine 17 C13 50 54N 25 15 E
Rtishchevo, Russia 24 C7 52 18N 43 46 E
Ruacaná, Angola 56 B1 17 20S 14 12 E
Ruahine Ra., N.Z. 59 H6 39 55S 176 2 E
Ruapehu, N.Z. 59 H5 39 17S 175 35 E
Ruapuke I., N.Z. 59 M2 46 46S 168 31 E
Ruâq, W. →, Egypt 47 F2 30 0N 33 49 E
Rub' al Khālī, Si. Arabia 46 D4 18 0N 48 0 E
Rubeho Mts., Tanzania 54 D4 6 50S 36 25 E
Rubh a' Mhail, U.K. 12 F2 55 56N 6 8W
Rubha Hunish, U.K. 12 D2 57 42N 6 20W
Rubha Robhanais = Lewis, Butt of, U.K. 12 C2 58 31N 6 16W
Rubicon →, U.S.A. 84 G5 38 53N 121 4W
Rubio, Venezuela 92 B4 7 43N 72 22W
Rubtsovsk, Russia 26 D9 51 30N 81 10 E
Ruby L., U.S.A. 82 F6 40 10N 115 28W
Ruby Mts., U.S.A. 82 F6 40 30N 115 20W
Rūd Sar, Iran 45 B6 37 8N 50 18 E
Rudall, Australia 63 E2 33 43S 136 17 E
Rudall →, Australia 60 D3 22 34S 122 13 E
Rudewa, Tanzania 55 E3 10 7S 34 40 E
Rudnichnyy, Russia 24 C9 59 38N 52 26 E
Rudnyy, Kazakstan 26 D7 52 57N 63 7 E
Rudolfa, Ostrov, Russia 26 A6 81 45N 58 30 E
Rudyard, U.S.A. 76 B3 46 14N 84 36W
Rufiji □, Tanzania 54 D4 8 0S 38 30 E
Rufiji →, Tanzania 54 D4 7 50S 39 15 E
Rufino, Argentina 94 C3 34 20S 62 50W
Rufunsa, Zambia 55 F2 15 4S 29 34 E
Rugby, U.K. 11 E6 52 23N 1 16W
Rugby, U.S.A. 80 A5 48 22N 100 0W
Rügen, Germany 16 A7 54 22N 13 24 E
Ruhengeri, Rwanda 54 C2 1 30S 29 36 E
Ruhnu, Estonia 9 H20 57 48N 23 15 E
Ruhr →, Germany 16 C4 51 27N 6 43 E
Ruhuhu →, Tanzania 55 E3 10 31S 34 34 E
Ruidosa, U.S.A. 81 L2 29 59N 104 41W
Ruidoso, U.S.A. 83 K11 33 20N 105 41W
Ruivo, Pico, Madeira 22 D3 32 45N 16 56W
Rujm Tal'at al Jamā'ah, Jordan 47 E4 30 24N 35 30 E
Ruk, Pakistan 42 F3 27 50N 68 42 E
Rukwa □, Tanzania 54 D3 7 0S 31 30 E
Rukwa, L., Tanzania 54 D3 8 0S 32 20 E
Rulhieres, C., Australia 60 B4 13 56S 127 22 E
Rum = Rhum, U.K. 12 E2 57 0N 6 20W
Rum Cay, Bahamas 89 B5 23 40N 74 58W
Rum Jungle, Australia 60 B5 13 0S 130 59 E
Rumāḥ, Si. Arabia 44 E5 25 29N 47 10 E
Rumania = Romania ■, Europe 17 F12 46 0N 25 0 E
Rumaylah, Iraq 44 D5 30 47N 47 37 E
Rumbalara, Australia 62 D1 25 20S 134 29 E
Rumbêk, Sudan 51 G11 6 54N 29 37 E
Rumford, U.S.A. 79 B14 44 33N 70 33W
Rumia, Poland 17 A10 54 37N 18 25 E
Rumoi, Japan 30 C10 43 56N 141 39 E
Rumonge, Burundi 54 C2 3 59S 29 26 E
Rumsey, Canada 72 C6 51 51N 112 48W
Rumula, Australia 62 B4 16 35S 145 20 E
Rumuruti, Kenya 54 B4 0 17N 36 32 E
Runan, China 34 H8 33 0N 114 30 E
Runanga, N.Z. 59 K3 42 25S 171 15 E
Runaway, C., N.Z. 59 G6 37 32S 177 59 E
Runcorn, U.K. 10 D5 53 21N 2 44W
Rungwa, Tanzania 54 D3 6 55S 33 32 E
Rungwa →, Tanzania 54 D3 7 36S 31 50 E
Rungwe, Tanzania 55 D3 9 11S 33 32 E
Rungwe □, Tanzania 55 D3 9 25S 33 32 E
Runton Ra., Australia 60 D3 23 31S 123 6 E
Ruoqiang, China 32 C3 38 55N 88 10 E
Rupa, India 41 F18 27 15N 92 21 E
Rupar, India 42 D7 31 2N 76 38 E
Rupat, Indonesia 36 D2 1 45N 101 40 E
Rupert →, Canada 70 B4 51 29N 78 45W
Rupert House = Waskaganish, Canada 70 B4 51 30N 78 40W
Rurrenabaque, Bolivia 92 F5 14 30S 67 32W
Rusambo, Zimbabwe 55 F3 16 30S 32 4 E
Rusape, Zimbabwe 55 F3 18 35S 32 8 E
Ruschuk = Ruse, Bulgaria 21 C12 43 48N 25 59 E
Ruse, Bulgaria 21 C12 43 48N 25 59 E
Rush, Ireland 13 C5 53 31N 6 6W
Rushan, China 35 F11 36 56N 121 30 E
Rushden, U.K. 11 E7 52 18N 0 35W
Rushford, U.S.A. 80 D9 43 49N 91 46W
Rushville, Ill., U.S.A. 80 E9 40 7N 90 34W
Rushville, Ind., U.S.A. 76 F3 39 37N 85 27W
Rushville, Nebr., U.S.A. 80 D3 42 43N 102 28W
Rushworth, Australia 63 F4 36 32S 145 1 E
Russas, Brazil 93 D11 4 55S 37 50W
Russell, Canada 73 C8 50 50N 101 20W
Russell, U.S.A. 80 F5 38 54N 98 52W
Russell L., Man., Canada 73 B8 56 15N 101 30W
Russell L., N.W.T., Canada 72 A5 63 5N 115 44W
Russellkonda, India 41 K14 19 57N 84 42 E
Russellville, Ala., U.S.A. 77 H2 34 30N 87 44W
Russellville, Ark., U.S.A. 81 H8 35 17N 93 8W
Russellville, Ky., U.S.A. 77 G2 36 51N 86 53W
Russia ■, Eurasia 27 C11 62 0N 105 0 E
Russian →, U.S.A. 84 G3 38 27N 123 8W
Rustam, Pakistan 42 B5 34 25N 72 13 E
Rustam Shahr, Pakistan 42 F2 26 58N 66 6 E
Rustavi, Georgia 25 F8 41 30N 45 0 E
Rustenburg, S. Africa 56 D4 25 41S 27 14 E
Ruston, U.S.A. 81 J8 32 32N 92 38W
Rutana, Burundi 54 C3 3 55S 30 0 E
Ruteng, Indonesia 37 F6 8 35S 120 30 E
Ruth, Mich., U.S.A. 78 C2 43 42N 82 45W
Ruth, Nev., U.S.A. 82 G6 39 17N 114 59W
Rutherford, U.S.A. 84 G4 38 26N 122 24W
Rutland □, U.K. 11 E7 52 38N 0 40W
Rutland Plains, Australia 62 B3 15 38S 141 43 E
Rutland Water, U.K. 11 E7 52 39N 0 38W
Rutledge →, Canada 73 A6 61 4N 112 0W
Rutledge L., Canada 73 A6 61 33N 110 47W
Rutshuru, Dem. Rep. of the Congo 54 C2 1 13S 29 25 E
Ruvu, Tanzania 54 D4 6 49S 38 43 E
Ruvu →, Tanzania 54 D4 6 23S 38 52 E
Ruvuma □, Tanzania 55 E4 10 20S 36 0 E
Ruvuma →, Tanzania 55 E5 10 29S 40 28 E
Ruwais, U.A.E. 45 E7 24 5N 52 50 E
Ruwenzori, Africa 54 B2 0 30N 29 55 E
Ruyigi, Burundi 54 C3 3 29S 30 15 E
Ružomberok, Slovak Rep. 17 D10 49 3N 19 17 E
Rwanda ■, Africa 54 C3 2 0S 30 0 E
Ryan, L., U.K. 12 G3 55 0N 5 2W
Ryazan, Russia 24 D6 54 40N 39 40 E
Ryazhsk, Russia 24 D7 53 45N 40 3 E
Rybache = Rybachye, Kazakstan 26 E9 46 40N 81 20 E
Rybachiy Poluostrov, Russia 24 A5 69 43N 32 0 E
Rybachye = Ysyk-Köl, Kyrgyzstan 28 E11 42 26N 76 12 E
Rybachye, Kazakstan 26 E9 46 40N 81 20 E
Rybinsk, Russia 24 C6 58 5N 38 50 E
Rybinskoye Vdkhr., Russia 24 C6 58 30N 38 25 E
Rybnitsa = Râbniţa, Moldova 17 E15 47 45N 29 0 E
Ryde, U.K. 11 G6 50 43N 1 9W
Ryderwood, U.S.A. 84 D3 46 23N 123 3W
Rye, U.K. 11 G8 50 57N 0 45 E
Rye →, U.K. 10 C7 54 11N 0 44W
Rye Bay, U.K. 11 G8 50 52N 0 49 E
Rye Patch Reservoir, U.S.A. 82 F4 40 28N 118 19W
Ryegate, U.S.A. 82 C9 46 18N 109 15W
Rylstone, Australia 63 E4 32 46S 149 58 E
Ryōthu, Japan 30 E9 38 5N 138 26 E
Rypin, Poland 17 B10 53 3N 19 25 E
Ryūgasaki, Japan 31 G10 35 54N 140 11 E
Ryūkyū Is. = Ryūkyū-rettō, Japan 31 M3 26 0N 126 0 E
Ryūkyū-rettō, Japan 31 M3 26 0N 126 0 E
Rzeszów, Poland 17 C11 50 5N 21 58 E
Rzhev, Russia 24 C5 56 20N 34 20 E

S

Sa, Thailand 38 C3 18 34N 100 45 E
Sa Conillera, Spain 22 C7 38 59N 1 13 E
Sa Dec, Vietnam 39 G5 10 20N 105 46 E
Sa Dragonera, , Spain 22 B9 39 35N 2 19 E
Sa'ādatābād, Fārs, Iran 45 D7 30 10N 53 5 E
Sa'ādatābād, Kermān, Iran 45 D7 28 3N 55 53 E
Saale →, Germany 16 C6 51 56N 11 54 E
Saalfeld, Germany 16 C6 50 38N 11 21 E
Saar →, Europe 18 B7 49 41N 6 32 E
Saarbrücken, Germany 16 D4 49 14N 6 59 E
Saaremaa, Estonia 24 C3 58 30N 22 30 E
Saarijärvi, Finland 9 E21 62 43N 25 16 E
Saariselkä, Finland 8 B23 68 16N 28 15 E
Sab 'Ābar, Syria 44 C3 33 46N 37 41 E
Saba, W. Indies 89 C7 17 42N 63 26W
Šabac, Serbia, Yug. 21 B8 44 48N 19 42 E
Sabadell, Spain 19 B7 41 28N 2 7 E
Sabah □, Malaysia 36 C5 6 0N 117 0 E
Sabak Bernam, Malaysia 39 L3 3 46N 100 58 E
Sabalana, Kepulauan, Indonesia 37 F5 6 45S 118 50 E
Sábana de la Mar, Dom. Rep. 89 C6 19 7N 69 24W
Sábanalarga, Colombia 92 A4 10 38N 74 55W
Sabang, Indonesia 36 C1 5 50N 95 15 E
Sabará, Brazil 93 G10 19 55S 43 46W
Sabattis, U.S.A. 79 B10 44 6N 74 40W
Saberania, Indonesia 37 E9 2 5S 138 18 E
Sabhah, Libya 51 C8 27 9N 14 29 E
Sabie, S. Africa 57 D5 25 10S 30 48 E
Sabinal, Mexico 86 A3 30 58N 107 25W
Sabinal, U.S.A. 81 L5 29 19N 99 28W
Sabinas, Mexico 86 B4 27 50N 101 10W
Sabinas →, Mexico 86 B4 27 37N 100 42W
Sabinas Hidalgo, Mexico 86 B4 26 33N 100 10W
Sabine →, U.S.A. 81 L8 29 59N 93 47W
Sabine L., U.S.A. 81 L8 29 53N 93 51W
Sabine Pass, U.S.A. 81 L8 29 44N 93 54W
Sabkhet el Bardawîl, Egypt 47 D2 31 10N 33 15 E
Sablayan, Phil. 37 B6 12 50N 120 50 E
Sable, C., Canada 71 D6 43 29N 65 38W
Sable, C., U.S.A. 75 E10 25 9N 81 8W
Sable I., Canada 71 D8 44 0N 60 0W
Sabrina Coast, Antarctica 5 C9 68 0S 120 0 E
Sabulubbek, Indonesia 36 E1 1 36S 98 40 E
Sabzevār, Iran 45 B8 36 15N 57 40 E
Sabzvārān, Iran 45 D8 28 45N 57 50 E
Sac City, U.S.A. 80 D7 42 25N 95 0W
Săcele, Romania 17 F13 45 37N 25 41 E
Sachigo →, Canada 70 A2 55 6N 88 58W
Sachigo, L., Canada 70 B1 53 50N 92 12W
Sachsen □, Germany 16 C7 50 55N 13 10 E
Sachsen-Anhalt □, Germany 16 C7 52 0N 12 0 E
Sackets Harbor, U.S.A. 79 C8 43 57N 76 7W
Saco, Maine, U.S.A. 77 D10 43 30N 70 27W
Saco, Mont., U.S.A. 82 B10 48 28N 107 21W
Sacramento, U.S.A. 84 G5 38 35N 121 29W
Sacramento →, U.S.A. 84 G5 38 3N 121 56W
Sacramento Mts., U.S.A. 83 K11 32 30N 105 30W
Sacramento Valley, U.S.A. 84 G5 39 30N 122 0W
Sadani, Tanzania 54 D4 5 58S 38 35 E
Sadao, Thailand 39 J3 6 38N 100 26 E
Sadd el Aali, Egypt 51 D12 23 54N 32 54 E
Saddle Mt., U.S.A. 84 E3 45 58N 123 41W
Sadimi, Dem. Rep. of the Congo 55 D1 9 25S 23 32 E

Soto la Marina

Sintang, Indonesia 36 D4 0 5N 111 35 E
Sinton, U.S.A. 81 L6 28 2N 97 31W
Sintra, Portugal 19 C1 38 47N 9 25W
Sinŭiju, N. Korea 35 D13 40 5N 124 24 E
Siocon, Phil. 37 C6 7 40N 122 10 E
Siófok, Hungary 17 E10 46 54N 18 3 E
Sioma, Zambia 56 B3 16 25S 23 28 E
Sion, Switz. 18 C7 46 14N 7 20 E
Sion Mills, U.K. 13 B4 54 48N 7 29W
Sioux City, U.S.A. 80 D6 42 30N 96 24W
Sioux Falls, U.S.A. 80 D6 43 33N 96 44W
Sioux Lookout, Canada 70 B1 50 10N 91 50W
Siping, China 35 C13 43 8N 124 21 E
Sipiwesk L., Canada 73 B9 55 5N 97 35W
Sipura, Indonesia 36 E1 2 18S 99 40 E
Siquia →, Nic. 88 D3 12 10N 84 20W
Siquijor, Phil. 37 C6 9 12N 123 35 E
Siquirres, Costa Rica 88 D3 10 6N 83 30W
Sir Edward Pellew Group, Australia 62 B2 15 40S 137 10 E
Sir Graham Moore Is., Australia 60 B4 13 53S 126 34 E
Sira →, Norway 9 G12 58 23N 6 34 E
Siracusa, Italy 20 F6 37 4N 15 17 E
Sirajganj, Bangla. 43 G13 24 25N 89 47 E
Sīrdān, Iran 45 B6 36 39N 49 12 E
Sirdaryo = Syrdarya →, Kazakstan 26 E7 46 3N 61 0 E
Sirer, Spain 22 C7 38 56N 1 22 E
Siret →, Romania 17 F14 45 24N 28 1 E
Sirohi, India 42 G5 24 52N 72 53 E
Sironj, India 42 G7 24 5N 77 39 E
Sirretta Pk., U.S.A. 85 K8 35 56N 118 19W
Sirsa, India 42 E6 29 33N 75 4 E
Sisak, Croatia 16 F9 45 30N 16 21 E
Sisaket, Thailand 38 E5 15 8N 104 23 E
Sishen, S. Africa 56 D3 27 47S 22 59 E
Sishui, Henan, China 34 G7 34 48N 113 15 E
Sishui, Shandong, China 35 G9 35 42N 117 18 E
Sisipuk L., Canada 73 B8 55 45N 101 50W
Sisophon, Cambodia 38 F4 13 38N 102 59 E
Sisseton, U.S.A. 80 C6 45 40N 97 3W
Sīstān va Balūchestān □, Iran 45 E9 27 0N 62 0 E
Sisters, U.S.A. 82 D3 44 18N 121 33W
Sitamarhi, India 43 F11 26 37N 85 30 E
Sitapur, India 43 F9 27 38N 80 45 E
Siteki, Swaziland 57 D5 26 32S 31 58 E
Sitges, Spain 19 B6 41 17N 1 47 E
Sitia, Greece 23 D8 35 13N 26 6 E
Sitka, U.S.A. 68 C6 57 3N 135 20W
Sitoti, Botswana 56 C3 23 15S 23 40 E
Sittang Myit →, Burma 41 L20 17 20N 96 45 E
Sittard, Neths. 15 C5 51 0N 5 52 E
Sittingbourne, U.K. 11 F8 51 21N 0 45 E
Sittwe, Burma 41 J18 20 18N 92 45 E
Siuna, Nic. 88 D3 13 37N 84 45W
Siuri, India 43 H12 23 50N 87 34 E
Sivana, India 42 E8 28 37N 78 6 E
Sīvand, Iran 45 D7 30 5N 52 55 E
Sivas, Turkey 25 G6 39 43N 36 58 E
Sivomaskinskiy, Russia 24 A11 66 40N 62 35 E
Sivrihisar, Turkey 25 G5 39 30N 31 35 E
Sîwa, Egypt 51 C11 29 11N 25 31 E
Sīwa Oasis, Egypt 48 D6 29 10N 25 30 E
Siwalik Range, Nepal 43 F10 28 0N 83 0 E
Siwan, India 43 F11 26 13N 84 21 E
Sixmilebridge, Ireland 13 D3 52 44N 8 46W
Siziwang Qi, China 34 D6 41 25N 111 40 E
Sjælland, Denmark 9 J14 55 30N 11 30 E
Sjumen = Shumen, Bulgaria 21 C12 43 18N 26 55 E
Skadarsko Jezero, Montenegro, Yug. 21 C8 42 10N 19 20 E
Skaftafell, Iceland 8 D5 64 1N 17 0W
Skagafjörður, Iceland 8 D4 65 54N 19 35W
Skagastølstindane, Norway 9 F12 61 28N 7 52 E
Skagaströnd, Iceland 8 D3 65 50N 20 19W
Skagen, Denmark 9 H14 57 43N 10 35 E
Skagerrak, Denmark 9 H13 57 30N 9 0 E
Skagit →, U.S.A. 84 B4 48 23N 122 22W
Skagway, U.S.A. 72 B1 59 28N 135 19W
Skala-Podilska, Ukraine 17 D14 48 50N 26 15 E
Skala Podolskaya = Skala-Podilska, Ukraine 17 D14 48 50N 26 15 E
Skalat, Ukraine 17 D13 49 23N 25 55 E
Skåne, Sweden 9 J15 55 59N 13 30 E
Skara, Sweden 9 G15 58 25N 13 30 E
Skardu, Pakistan 43 B6 35 20N 75 44 E
Skarżysko-Kamienna, Poland 17 C11 51 7N 20 52 E
Skeena →, Canada 72 C2 54 9N 130 5W
Skeena Mts., Canada 72 B3 56 40N 128 30W
Skegness, U.K. 10 D8 53 9N 0 20 E
Skeldon, Guyana 92 B7 5 55N 57 20W
Skellefte älv →, Sweden 8 D19 64 45N 21 10 E
Skellefteå, Sweden 8 D19 64 45N 20 50 E
Skelleftehamn, Sweden 8 D19 64 40N 21 9 E
Skerries, The, U.K. 10 D3 53 25N 4 36W
Ski, Norway 9 G14 59 43N 10 52 E
Skíathos, Greece 21 E10 39 12N 23 30 E
Skibbereen, Ireland 13 E2 51 33N 9 16W
Skiddaw, U.K. 10 C4 54 39N 3 9W
Skien, Norway 9 G13 59 12N 9 35 E
Skierniewice, Poland 17 C11 51 58N 20 10 E
Skikda, Algeria 50 A7 36 50N 6 58 E
Skilloura, Cyprus 23 D12 35 14N 33 10 E
Skipton, Australia 63 F3 37 39S 143 40 E
Skipton, U.K. 10 D5 53 58N 2 3W
Skirmish Pt., Australia 62 A1 11 59S 134 17 E
Skive, Denmark 9 H13 56 33N 9 2 E
Skjálfandafljót →, Iceland 8 D5 65 59N 17 25W
Skjálfandi, Iceland 8 C5 66 5N 17 30W
Skoghall, Sweden 9 G15 59 20N 13 30 E
Skole, Ukraine 17 D12 49 3N 23 30 E
Skopí, Greece 23 D8 35 11N 26 2 E
Skopje, Macedonia 21 C9 42 1N 21 26 E
Skövde, Sweden 9 G15 58 24N 13 50 E
Skovorodino, Russia 27 D13 54 0N 124 0 E
Skowhegan, U.S.A. 71 D6 44 46N 69 43W
Skownan, Canada 73 C9 51 58N 99 35W
Skull, Ireland 13 E2 51 32N 9 34W
Skunk →, U.S.A. 80 E9 40 42N 91 7W
Skuodas, Lithuania 9 H19 56 16N 21 33 E
Skvyra, Ukraine 17 D15 49 44N 29 40 E
Skye, U.K. 12 D2 57 15N 6 10W
Skykomish, U.S.A. 82 C3 47 42N 121 22W
Slættaratindur, Færoe Is. 8 E9 62 18N 7 1W
Slagelse, Denmark 9 J14 55 23N 11 19 E
Slamet, Indonesia 37 G13 7 16S 109 8 E
Slaney →, Ireland 13 D5 52 26N 6 33W
Śląsk, Poland 16 C9 51 0N 16 30 E
Slate Is., Canada 70 C2 48 40N 87 0W
Slatina, Romania 17 F13 44 28N 24 22 E
Slaton, U.S.A. 81 J4 33 26N 101 39W
Slave →, Canada 72 A6 61 18N 113 39W
Slave Coast, W. Afr. 48 F4 6 0N 2 30 E
Slave Lake, Canada 72 B6 55 17N 114 43W
Slave Pt., Canada 72 A5 61 11N 115 56W
Slavgorod, Russia 26 D8 53 1N 78 37 E
Slavonski Brod, Croatia 21 B8 45 11N 18 1 E
Slavuta, Ukraine 17 C14 50 15N 27 2 E
Slavyanka, Russia 30 C5 42 53N 131 21 E
Slavyansk = Slovyansk, Ukraine 25 E6 48 55N 37 36 E
Slawharad, Belarus 17 B16 53 27N 31 0 E
Sleaford, U.K. 10 D7 53 0N 0 24W
Sleaford B., Australia 63 E2 34 55S 135 45 E
Sleat, Sd. of, U.K. 12 D3 57 5N 5 47W
Sleeper Is., Canada 69 C11 58 30N 81 0W
Sleepy Eye, U.S.A. 80 C7 44 18N 94 43W
Slemon L., Canada 72 A5 63 13N 116 4W
Slidell, U.S.A. 81 K10 30 17N 89 47W
Sliema, Malta 23 D2 35 54N 14 30 E
Slieve Aughty, Ireland 13 C3 53 4N 8 30W
Slieve Bloom, Ireland 13 C4 53 4N 7 40W
Slieve Donard, U.K. 13 B6 54 11N 5 55W
Slieve Gamph, Ireland 13 B3 54 6N 9 0W
Slieve Gullion, U.K. 13 B5 54 7N 6 26W
Slieve Mish, Ireland 13 D2 52 12N 9 50W
Slievenamon, Ireland 13 D4 52 25N 7 34W
Sligeach = Sligo, Ireland 13 B3 54 16N 8 28W
Sligo, Ireland 13 B3 54 16N 8 28W
Sligo □, Ireland 13 B3 54 8N 8 42W
Sligo B., Ireland 13 B3 54 18N 8 40W
Slite, Sweden 9 H18 57 42N 18 48 E
Sliven, Bulgaria 21 C12 42 42N 26 19 E
Sloan, U.S.A. 85 K11 35 57N 115 13W
Sloansville, U.S.A. 79 D10 42 45N 74 22W
Slobodskoy, Russia 24 C9 58 40N 50 6 E
Slobozia, Romania 17 F14 44 34N 27 23 E
Slocan, Canada 72 D5 49 48N 117 28W
Slonim, Belarus 17 B13 53 4N 25 19 E
Slough, U.K. 11 F7 51 30N 0 36W
Slough □, U.K. 11 F7 51 30N 0 36W
Sloughhouse, U.S.A. 84 G5 38 26N 121 12W
Slovak Rep. ■, Europe 17 D10 48 30N 20 0 E
Slovakia = Slovak Rep. ■, Europe 17 D10 48 30N 20 0 E
Slovakian Ore Mts. = Slovenské Rudohorie, Slovak Rep. 17 D10 48 45N 20 0 E
Slovenia ■, Europe 16 F8 45 58N 14 30 E
Slovenija = Slovenia ■, Europe 16 F8 45 58N 14 30 E
Slovenské Rudohorie, Slovak Rep. 17 D10 48 45N 20 0 E
Slovyansk, Ukraine 25 E6 48 55N 37 36 E
Sluch →, Ukraine 17 C14 51 37N 26 38 E
Sluis, Neths. 15 C3 51 18N 3 23 E
Słupsk, Poland 17 A9 54 30N 17 3 E
Slurry, S. Africa 56 D4 25 49S 25 42 E
Slutsk, Belarus 17 B14 53 2N 27 31 E
Slyne Hd., Ireland 13 C1 53 25N 10 10W
Slyudyanka, Russia 27 D11 51 40N 103 40 E
Småland, Sweden 9 H16 57 15N 15 25 E
Smalltree L., Canada 73 A8 61 0N 105 0W
Smallwood Res., Canada 71 B7 54 0N 64 0W
Smara, Morocco 50 B4 32 9N 8 16W
Smarhon, Belarus 17 A14 54 20N 26 24 E
Smartt Syndicate Dam, S. Africa 56 E3 30 45S 23 10 E
Smartville, U.S.A. 84 F5 39 13N 121 18W
Smeaton, Canada 73 C8 53 30N 104 49W
Smederevo, Serbia, Yug. 21 B9 44 40N 20 57 E
Smerwick Harbour, Ireland 13 D1 52 12N 10 23W
Smethport, U.S.A. 78 E6 41 49N 78 27W
Smidovich, Russia 27 E14 48 36N 133 49 E
Smiley, Canada 73 C7 51 38N 109 29W
Smith, Canada 72 B6 55 10N 114 0W
Smith →, Canada 72 B3 59 34N 126 30W
Smith Center, U.S.A. 80 F5 39 47N 98 47W
Smithburne →, Australia 62 B3 17 3S 140 57 E
Smithers, Canada 72 C3 54 45N 127 10W
Smithfield, S. Africa 57 E4 30 9S 26 30 E
Smithfield, N.C., U.S.A. 77 H6 35 31N 78 21W
Smithfield, Utah, U.S.A. 82 F8 41 50N 111 50W
Smiths Falls, Canada 70 D4 44 55N 76 0W
Smithton, Australia 62 G4 40 53S 145 6 E
Smithtown, Australia 63 E5 30 58S 152 48 E
Smithville, Canada 78 C5 43 6N 79 33W
Smithville, U.S.A. 81 K6 30 1N 97 10W
Smoky →, Canada 72 B5 56 10N 117 21W
Smoky Bay, Australia 63 E1 32 22S 134 13 E
Smoky Falls, Canada 70 B3 50 4N 82 10W
Smoky Hill →, U.S.A. 80 F6 39 4N 96 48W
Smoky Lake, Canada 72 C6 54 10N 112 30W
Smøla, Norway 8 E13 63 23N 8 3 E
Smolensk, Russia 24 D5 54 45N 32 5 E
Smolikas, Óros, Greece 21 D9 40 9N 20 58 E
Smolyan, Bulgaria 21 D11 41 36N 24 38 E
Smooth Rock Falls, Canada 70 C3 49 17N 81 37W
Smoothstone L., Canada 73 C7 54 40N 106 50W
Smorgon = Smarhon, Belarus 17 A14 54 20N 26 24 E
Smyrna = İzmir, Turkey 25 G4 38 25N 27 8 E
Snæfell, Iceland 8 D6 64 48N 15 34W
Snaefell, U.K. 10 C3 54 16N 4 27W
Snæfellsjökull, Iceland 8 D2 64 49N 23 46W
Snake →, U.S.A. 82 C4 46 12N 119 2W
Snake I., Australia 63 F4 38 47S 146 33 E
Snake L., Canada 73 B7 55 32N 106 35W
Snake Range, U.S.A. 82 G6 39 0N 114 20W
Snake River Plain, U.S.A. 82 E7 42 50N 114 0W
Snåsavatnet, Norway 8 D14 64 12N 12 0 E
Sneek, Neths. 15 A5 53 2N 5 40 E
Sneeuberge, S. Africa 56 E3 31 46S 24 20 E
Snelling, U.S.A. 84 H6 37 31N 120 26W
Sněžka, Europe 16 C8 50 41N 15 50 E
Snizort, L., U.K. 12 D2 57 33N 6 28W
Snøhetta, Norway 9 E13 62 19N 9 16 E
Snohomish, U.S.A. 84 C4 47 55N 122 6W
Snoul, Cambodia 39 F6 12 4N 106 26 E
Snow Hill, U.S.A. 76 F8 38 11N 75 24W
Snow Lake, Canada 73 C8 54 52N 100 3W
Snow Mt., U.S.A. 84 F4 39 23N 122 45W
Snowbird L., Canada 73 A8 60 45N 103 0W
Snowdon, U.K. 10 D3 53 4N 4 5W
Snowdrift →, Canada 73 A6 62 24N 110 44W
Snowflake, U.S.A. 83 J8 34 30N 110 5W
Snowshoe Pk., U.S.A. 82 B6 48 13N 115 41W
Snowtown, Australia 63 E2 33 46S 138 14 E
Snowville, U.S.A. 82 F7 41 58N 112 43W
Snowy →, Australia 63 F4 37 46S 148 30 E
Snowy Mts., Australia 63 F4 36 30S 148 20 E
Snug Corner, Bahamas 89 B5 22 33N 73 52W
Snyatyn, Ukraine 17 D13 48 27N 25 38 E
Snyder, Okla., U.S.A. 81 H5 34 40N 98 57W
Snyder, Tex., U.S.A. 81 J4 32 44N 100 55W
Soahanina, Madag. 57 B7 18 42S 44 13 E
Soalala, Madag. 57 B8 16 6S 45 20 E
Soan →, Pakistan 42 C4 33 1N 71 44 E
Soanierana-Ivongo, Madag. 57 B8 16 55S 49 35 E
Soap Lake, U.S.A. 82 C4 47 23N 119 29W
Sobat, Nahr →, Sudan 51 G12 9 22N 31 33 E
Sobhapur, India 42 H8 22 47N 78 17 E
Sobradinho, Reprêsa de, Brazil 93 E10 9 30S 42 0 E
Sobral, Brazil 93 D10 3 50S 40 20W
Soc Giang, Vietnam 38 A6 22 54N 106 1 E
Soc Trang, Vietnam 39 H5 9 37N 105 50 E
Soch'e = Shache, China 32 C2 38 20N 77 10 E
Sochi, Russia 25 F6 43 35N 39 40 E
Société, Is. de la, Pac. Oc. 65 J12 17 0S 151 0W
Society Is. = Société, Is. de la, Pac. Oc. 65 J12 17 0S 151 0W
Socompa, Portezuelo de, Chile 94 A2 24 27S 68 18W
Socorro, U.S.A. 83 J10 34 4N 106 54W
Socorro, I., Mexico 86 D2 18 45N 110 58W
Socotra, Ind. Oc. 46 E5 12 30N 54 0 E
Soda L., U.S.A. 83 J5 35 10N 116 4W
Soda Plains, India 43 B8 35 30N 79 0 E
Soda Springs, U.S.A. 82 E8 42 39N 111 36W
Sodankylä, Finland 8 C22 67 29N 26 40 E
Söderhamn, Sweden 9 F17 61 18N 17 10 E
Söderköping, Sweden 9 G17 58 31N 16 20 E
Södermanland, Sweden 9 G17 58 56N 16 55 E
Södertälje, Sweden 9 G17 59 12N 17 39 E
Sodiri, Sudan 51 F11 14 27N 29 0 E
Sodus, U.S.A. 78 C7 43 14N 77 4W
Soekmekaar, S. Africa 57 C4 23 30S 29 55 E
Soest, Neths. 15 B5 52 9N 5 19 E
Sofia = Sofiya, Bulgaria 21 C10 42 45N 23 20 E
Sofia →, Madag. 57 B8 15 27S 47 23 E
Sofiya, Bulgaria 21 C10 42 45N 23 20 E
Sōfu-Gan, Japan 31 K10 29 49N 140 21 E
Sogamoso, Colombia 92 B4 5 43N 72 56W
Sogār, Iran 45 E8 25 53N 58 6 E
Sogndalsfjøra, Norway 9 F12 61 14N 7 5 E
Søgne, Norway 9 G12 58 5N 7 48 E
Sognefjorden, Norway 9 F11 61 10N 5 50 E
Sŏgwi-po, S. Korea 35 H14 33 13N 126 34 E
Soh, Iran 45 C6 33 26N 51 27 E
Sohâg, Egypt 51 C12 26 33N 31 43 E
Sŏhori, N. Korea 35 D15 40 7N 128 23 E
Soignies, Belgium 15 D4 50 35N 4 5 E
Soissons, France 18 B5 49 25N 3 19 E
Sōja, Japan 31 G6 34 40N 133 45 E
Sojat, India 42 G5 25 55N 73 45 E
Sokal, Ukraine 17 C13 50 31N 24 15 E
Söke, Turkey 21 F12 37 48N 27 28 E
Sokelo, Dem. Rep. of the Congo 55 D1 9 55S 24 36 E
Sokhumi, Georgia 25 F7 43 0N 41 0 E
Sokodé, Togo 50 G6 9 0N 1 11 E
Sokol, Russia 24 C7 59 30N 40 5 E
Sokółka, Poland 17 B12 53 25N 23 30 E
Sokolów Podlaski, Poland 17 B12 52 25N 22 15 E
Sokoto, Nigeria 50 F7 13 2N 5 16 E
Sol Iletsk, Russia 24 D10 51 10N 55 0 E
Solai, Kenya 54 B4 0 2N 36 12 E
Solano, Phil. 37 A6 16 31N 121 15 E
Solapur, India 40 L9 17 43N 75 56 E
Soléa □, Cyprus 23 D12 35 5N 33 4 E
Soledad, Colombia 92 A4 10 55N 74 46W
Soledad, U.S.A. 84 J5 36 26N 121 20W
Soledad, Venezuela 92 B6 8 10N 63 34W
Solent, The, U.K. 11 G6 50 45N 1 25W
Solfonn, Norway 9 F12 60 2N 6 57 E
Soligalich, Russia 24 C7 59 5N 42 10 E
Soligorsk = Salihorsk, Belarus 17 B14 52 51N 27 27 E
Solihull, U.K. 11 E6 52 26N 1 47W
Solikamsk, Russia 24 C10 59 38N 56 50 E
Solila, Madag. 57 C8 21 25S 46 37 E
Solimões = Amazonas →, S. Amer. 93 D9 0 5S 50 0W
Solingen, Germany 16 C4 51 10N 7 5 E
Sollefteå, Sweden 8 E17 63 12N 17 20 E
Sóller, Spain 22 B9 39 46N 2 43 E
Sologne, France 18 C4 47 40N 1 45 E
Solok, Indonesia 36 E2 0 45S 100 40 E
Sololá, Guatemala 88 D1 14 49N 91 10W
Solomon, N. Fork →, U.S.A. 80 F5 39 29N 98 26W
Solomon, S. Fork →, U.S.A. 80 F5 39 25N 99 12W
Solomon Is. ■, Pac. Oc. 64 H7 6 0S 155 0 E
Solon, China 33 B7 46 32N 121 10 E
Solon Springs, U.S.A. 80 B9 46 22N 91 49W
Solor, Indonesia 37 F6 8 27S 123 0 E
Solothurn, Switz. 18 C7 47 13N 7 32 E
Šolta, Croatia 20 C7 43 24N 16 15 E
Solṭānābād, Khorāsān, Iran 45 C8 34 13N 59 58 E
Solṭānābād, Khorāsān, Iran 45 B8 36 29N 58 5 E
Solṭānābād, Markazī, Iran 45 C6 35 31N 51 10 E
Solunska Glava, Macedonia 21 D9 41 44N 21 31 E
Solvang, U.S.A. 85 L6 34 36N 120 8W
Solvay, U.S.A. 79 C8 43 3N 76 13W
Sölvesborg, Sweden 9 H16 56 5N 14 35 E
Solvychegodsk, Russia 24 B8 61 21N 46 56 E
Solway Firth, U.K. 10 C4 54 49N 3 35W
Solwezi, Zambia 55 E2 12 11S 26 21 E
Sōma, Japan 30 F10 37 40N 140 50 E
Soma, Turkey 21 E12 39 10N 27 35 E
Somali Pen., Africa 48 F8 7 0N 46 0 E
Somali Rep. ■, Africa 46 F4 7 0N 47 0 E
Somalia = Somali Rep. ■, Africa 46 F4 7 0N 47 0 E
Sombor, Serbia, Yug. 21 B8 45 46N 19 9 E
Sombra, Canada 78 D2 42 43N 82 29W
Sombrerete, Mexico 86 C4 23 40N 103 40W
Sombrero, Anguilla 89 C7 18 37N 63 30W
Somers, U.S.A. 82 B6 48 5N 114 13W
Somerset, Canada 73 D9 49 25N 98 39W
Somerset, Colo., U.S.A. 83 G10 38 56N 107 28W
Somerset, Ky., U.S.A. 76 G3 37 5N 84 36W
Somerset, Mass., U.S.A. 79 E13 41 47N 71 8W
Somerset, Pa., U.S.A. 78 F5 40 1N 79 5W
Somerset □, U.K. 11 F5 51 9N 3 0W
Somerset East, S. Africa 56 E4 32 42S 25 35 E
Somerset I., Canada 68 A10 73 30N 93 0W
Somerset West, S. Africa 56 E2 34 8S 18 50 E
Somerton, U.S.A. 83 K6 32 36N 114 43W
Somerville, U.S.A. 79 F10 40 35N 74 38W
Someş →, Romania 17 D12 47 49N 22 43 E
Sommariva, Australia 63 D4 26 24S 146 36 E
Somme →, France 18 A4 50 11N 1 38 E
Somosierra, Puerto de, Spain 19 B4 41 4N 3 35W
Somoto, Nic. 88 D2 13 28N 86 37W
Somport, Puerto de, Spain 18 E3 42 48N 0 31W
Son Ha, Vietnam 38 E7 15 3N 108 34 E
Son Hoa, Vietnam 38 F7 13 2N 108 58 E
Son La, Vietnam 38 B4 21 20N 103 50 E
Son Tay, Vietnam 38 B5 21 8N 105 30 E
Soná, Panama 88 E3 8 0N 81 20W
Sonamarg, India 43 B6 34 18N 75 21 E
Sonamukhi, India 43 H12 23 18N 87 27 E
Sŏnchŏn, N. Korea 35 E13 39 48N 124 55 E
Sondags →, S. Africa 56 E4 33 44S 25 51 E
Sondar, India 43 C6 33 28N 75 56 E
Sønderborg, Denmark 9 J13 54 55N 9 49 E
Sóndrio, Italy 18 C8 46 10N 9 52 E
Sone, Mozam. 55 F3 17 23S 34 55 E
Sonepur, India 41 J13 20 55N 83 50 E
Song, Thailand 38 C3 18 28N 100 11 E
Song Cau, Vietnam 38 F7 13 27N 109 18 E
Song Xian, China 34 G7 34 12N 112 8 E
Songchŏn, N. Korea 35 E14 39 12N 126 15 E
Songea, Tanzania 55 E4 10 40S 35 40 E
Songea □, Tanzania 55 E4 10 30S 36 0 E
Songhua Hu, China 35 C14 43 35N 126 50 E
Songhua Jiang →, China 33 B8 47 45N 132 30 E
Songjin, N. Korea 35 D15 40 40N 129 10 E
Songjŏng-ni, S. Korea 35 G14 35 8N 126 47 E
Songkhla, Thailand 39 J3 7 13N 100 37 E
Songnim, N. Korea 35 E13 38 45N 125 39 E
Songpan, China 32 C5 32 40N 103 30 E
Songwe, Dem. Rep. of the Congo 54 C2 3 20S 26 16 E
Songwe →, Africa 55 D3 9 44S 33 58 E
Sonid Youqi, China 34 C7 42 45N 112 48 E
Sonipat, India 42 E7 29 0N 77 5 E
Sonmiani, Pakistan 42 G2 25 25N 66 40 E
Sonora, Calif., U.S.A. 84 H6 37 59N 120 23W
Sonora, Tex., U.S.A. 81 K4 30 34N 100 39W
Sonora □, Mexico 86 B2 29 0N 111 0W
Sonora →, Mexico 86 B2 28 50N 111 33W
Sonora Desert, U.S.A. 85 L12 33 40N 114 15W
Sonoyta, Mexico 86 A2 31 51N 112 50W
Sŏnsan, S. Korea 35 F15 36 14N 128 17 E
Sonsonate, El Salv. 88 D2 13 43N 89 44W
Soochow = Suzhou, China 33 C7 31 19N 120 38 E
Sop Hao, Laos 38 B5 20 33N 104 27 E
Sop Prap, Thailand 38 D2 17 53N 99 20 E
Sopi, Indonesia 37 D7 2 34N 128 28 E
Sopot, Poland 17 A10 54 27N 18 31 E
Sopron, Hungary 17 E9 47 45N 16 32 E
Sop's Arm, Canada 71 C8 49 46N 56 56W
Sopur, India 43 B6 34 18N 74 27 E
Sør-Rondane, Antarctica 5 D4 72 0S 25 0 E
Sorah, Pakistan 42 F3 27 13N 68 56 E
Sorel, Canada 70 C5 46 0N 73 10W
Sórgono, Italy 20 D3 40 1N 9 6 E
Soria, Spain 19 B4 41 43N 2 32W
Soriano, Uruguay 94 C4 33 24S 58 19W
Sorkh, Kuh-e, Iran 45 C8 35 40N 58 30 E
Soroca, Moldova 17 D15 48 8N 28 12 E
Sorocaba, Brazil 95 A6 23 31S 47 27W
Sorochinsk, Russia 24 D9 52 26N 53 10 E
Soroki = Soroca, Moldova 17 D15 48 8N 28 12 E
Soron, India 43 F8 27 55N 78 45 E
Sorong, Indonesia 37 E8 0 55S 131 15 E
Soroní, Greece 23 C10 36 21N 28 1 E
Soroti, Uganda 54 B3 1 43N 33 35 E
Sørøya, Norway 8 A20 70 40N 22 30 E
Sørøysundet, Norway 8 A20 70 25N 23 0 E
Sorrento, Australia 63 F3 38 22S 144 47 E
Sorsele, Sweden 8 D17 65 31N 17 30 E
Sorsogon, Phil. 37 B6 13 0N 124 0 E
Sortavala, Russia 24 B5 61 42N 30 41 E
Sortland, Norway 8 B16 68 42N 15 25 E
Sŏsan, S. Korea 35 F14 36 47N 126 27 E
Soscumica, L., Canada 70 B4 50 15N 77 27W
Sosnogorsk, Russia 24 B9 63 37N 53 51 E
Sosnowiec, Poland 17 C10 50 20N 19 10 E
Sŏsura, N. Korea 35 C16 42 16N 130 36 E
Sosva, Russia 24 C11 59 10N 61 50 E
Sotkamo, Finland 8 D23 64 8N 28 23 E
Soto la Marina →, Mexico 87 C5 23 40N 97 40W

Szombathely

Storm Lake, U.S.A. 80 D7 42 39N 95 13W
Stormberge, S. Africa 56 E4 31 16S 26 17 E
Stormsrivier, S. Africa 56 E3 33 59S 23 52 E
Stornoway, U.K. 12 C2 58 13N 6 23W
Storozhinets = Storozhynets, Ukraine 17 D13 48 14N 25 45 E
Storozhynets, Ukraine 17 D13 48 14N 25 45 E
Storsjön, Sweden 8 E16 63 9N 14 30 E
Storuman, Sweden 8 D17 65 5N 17 10 E
Storuman, sjö, Sweden 8 D17 65 13N 16 50 E
Stoughton, Canada 73 D8 49 40N 103 0W
Stour →, Dorset, U.K. 11 G6 50 43N 1 47W
Stour →, Kent, U.K. 11 F9 51 18N 1 22 E
Stour →, Suffolk, U.K. 11 F9 51 57N 1 4 E
Stourbridge, U.K. 11 E5 52 28N 2 8W
Stout, L., Canada 73 C10 52 0N 94 40W
Stove Pipe Wells Village, U.S.A. 85 J9 36 35N 117 11W
Stowbtsy, Belarus 17 B14 53 30N 26 43 E
Stowmarket, U.K. 11 E9 52 12N 1 0 E
Strabane, U.K. 13 B4 54 50N 7 27W
Strahan, Australia 62 G4 42 9S 145 20 E
Stralsund, Germany 16 A7 54 18N 13 4 E
Strand, S. Africa 56 E2 34 9S 18 48 E
Stranda, Møre og Romsdal, Norway 9 E12 62 19N 6 58 E
Stranda, Nord-Trøndelag, Norway 8 E14 63 33N 10 14 E
Strangford L., U.K. 13 B6 54 30N 5 37W
Strangsville, U.S.A. 78 E3 41 19N 81 50W
Stranraer, U.K. 12 G3 54 54N 5 1W
Strasbourg, Canada 73 C8 51 4N 104 55W
Strasbourg, France 18 B7 48 35N 7 42 E
Strasburg, U.S.A. 80 B4 46 8N 100 10W
Stratford, Canada 70 D3 43 23N 81 0W
Stratford, N.Z. 59 H5 39 20S 174 19 E
Stratford, Calif., U.S.A. 84 J7 36 11N 119 49W
Stratford, Conn., U.S.A. 79 E11 41 12N 73 8W
Stratford, Tex., U.S.A. 81 G3 36 20N 102 4W
Stratford-upon-Avon, U.K. 11 E6 52 12N 1 42W
Strath Spey, U.K. 12 D5 57 9N 3 49W
Strathalbyn, Australia 63 F2 35 13S 138 53 E
Strathaven, U.K. 12 F4 55 40N 4 5W
Strathcona Prov. Park, Canada 72 D3 49 38N 125 40W
Strathmore, Australia 62 B3 17 50S 142 35 E
Strathmore, Canada 72 C6 51 5N 113 18W
Strathmore, U.K. 12 E5 56 37N 3 7W
Strathmore, U.S.A. 84 J7 36 9N 119 4W
Strathnaver, Canada 72 C4 53 20N 122 33W
Strathpeffer, U.K. 12 D4 57 35N 4 32W
Strathroy, Canada 70 D3 42 58N 81 38W
Strathy Pt., U.K. 12 C4 58 36N 4 1W
Stratton, U.S.A. 80 F3 39 19N 102 36W
Straubing, Germany 16 D7 48 52N 12 34 E
Straumnes, Iceland 8 C2 66 26N 23 8W
Strawberry Reservoir, U.S.A. 82 F8 40 8N 111 9W
Strawn, U.S.A. 81 J5 32 33N 98 30W
Streaky B., Australia 63 E1 32 48S 134 13 E
Streaky Bay, Australia 63 E1 32 51S 134 18 E
Streator, U.S.A. 80 E10 41 8N 88 50W
Streeter, U.S.A. 80 B5 46 39N 99 21W
Streetsville, Canada 78 C5 43 35N 79 42W
Strelka, Russia 27 D10 58 5N 93 3 E
Streng →, Cambodia 38 F4 13 12N 103 37 E
Streymoy, Færoe Is. 8 E9 62 8N 7 5W
Strezhevoy, Russia 26 C8 60 42N 77 34 E
Strimón →, Greece 21 D10 40 46N 23 51 E
Strimonikós Kólpos, Greece 21 D11 40 33N 24 0 E
Stroma, U.K. 12 C5 58 41N 3 7W
Strómboli, Italy 20 E6 38 47N 15 13 E
Stromeferry, U.K. 12 D3 57 21N 5 33W
Stromness, U.K. 12 C5 58 58N 3 17W
Stromsburg, U.S.A. 80 E6 41 7N 97 36W
Strömstad, Sweden 9 G14 58 56N 11 10 E
Strömsund, Sweden 8 E16 63 51N 15 33 E
Stronsay, U.K. 12 B6 59 7N 2 35W
Stroud, U.K. 11 F5 51 45N 2 13W
Stroud Road, Australia 63 E5 32 18S 151 57 E
Stroudsburg, U.S.A. 79 F9 40 59N 75 12W
Stroumbi, Cyprus 23 E11 34 53N 32 29 E
Struer, Denmark 9 H13 56 30N 8 35 E
Strumica, Macedonia 21 D10 41 28N 22 41 E
Struthers, Canada 70 C2 48 41N 85 51W
Struthers, U.S.A. 78 E4 41 4N 80 39W
Stryker, U.S.A. 82 B6 48 41N 114 46W
Stryy, Ukraine 17 D12 49 16N 23 48 E
Strzelecki Cr. →, Australia 63 D2 29 37S 139 59 E
Stuart, Fla., U.S.A. 77 M5 27 12N 80 15W
Stuart, Nebr., U.S.A. 80 D5 42 36N 99 8W
Stuart →, Canada 72 C4 54 0N 123 35W
Stuart Bluff Ra., Australia 60 D5 22 50S 131 52 E
Stuart L., Canada 72 C4 54 30N 124 30W
Stuart Ra., Australia 63 D1 29 10S 134 56 E
Stull, L., Canada 70 B1 54 24N 92 34W
Stung Treng = Stoeng Treng, Cambodia 38 F5 13 31N 105 58 E
Stupart →, Canada 73 B10 56 0N 93 25W
Sturgeon B., Canada 73 C9 52 0N 97 50W
Sturgeon Bay, U.S.A. 76 C2 44 50N 87 23W
Sturgeon Falls, Canada 70 C4 46 25N 79 57W
Sturgeon L., Alta., Canada 72 B5 55 6N 117 32W
Sturgeon L., Ont., Canada 70 C1 50 0N 90 45W
Sturgeon L., Ont., Canada 78 B6 44 28N 78 43W
Sturgis, Mich., U.S.A. 76 E3 41 48N 85 25W
Sturgis, S. Dak., U.S.A. 80 C3 44 25N 103 31W
Sturt Cr. →, Australia 60 C4 19 8S 127 50 E
Sturt Creek, Australia 60 C4 19 12S 128 8 E
Stutterheim, S. Africa 56 E4 32 33S 27 28 E
Stuttgart, Germany 16 D5 48 48N 9 11 E
Stuttgart, U.S.A. 81 H9 34 30N 91 33W
Stuyvesant, U.S.A. 79 D11 42 23N 73 45W
Stykkishólmur, Iceland 8 D2 65 2N 22 40W
Styria = Steiermark □, Austria 16 E8 47 26N 15 0 E
Su Xian, China 34 H9 33 41N 116 59 E
Suakin, Sudan 51 E13 19 8N 37 20 E
Suan, N. Korea 35 E14 38 42N 126 22 E
Suaqui, Mexico 86 B3 29 12N 109 41W
Subang, Indonesia 37 G12 6 34S 107 45 E
Subansiri →, India 41 F18 26 48N 93 50 E
Subayhah, Si. Arabia 44 D3 30 2N 38 50 E
Subi, Indonesia 39 L7 2 58N 108 50 E
Subotica, Serbia, Yug. 21 A8 46 6N 19 39 E
Success, Canada 73 C7 50 28N 108 6W
Suceava, Romania 17 E14 47 38N 26 16 E
Suchan, Russia 30 C6 43 8N 133 9 E
Suchitoto, El Salv. 88 D2 13 56N 89 0W
Suchou = Suzhou, China 33 C7 31 19N 120 38 E
Süchow = Xuzhou, China 35 G9 34 18N 117 10 E
Suck →, Ireland 13 C3 53 17N 8 3W
Sucre, Bolivia 92 G5 19 0S 65 15W
Sucuriú →, Brazil 93 H8 20 47S 51 38W
Sud, Pte., Canada 71 C7 49 3N 62 14W
Sud-Ouest, Pte. du, Canada 71 C7 49 23N 63 36W
Sudan, U.S.A. 81 H3 34 4N 102 32W
Sudan ■, Africa 51 E11 15 0N 30 0 E
Sudbury, Canada 70 C3 46 30N 81 0W
Sudbury, U.K. 11 E8 52 2N 0 45 E
Sûdd, Sudan 51 G12 8 20N 30 0 E
Sudeten Mts. = Sudety, Europe 17 C9 50 20N 16 45 E
Sudety, Europe 17 C9 50 20N 16 45 E
Suðuroy, Færoe Is. 8 F9 61 32N 6 50W
Sudi, Tanzania 55 E4 10 11S 39 57 E
Sudirman, Pegunungan, Indonesia 37 E9 4 30S 137 0 E
Sueca, Spain 19 C5 39 12N 0 21W
Suez = El Suweis, Egypt 51 C12 29 58N 32 31 E
Suez, G. of = Suweis, Khalîg el, Egypt 51 C12 28 40N 33 0 E
Suffield, Canada 73 C6 50 12N 111 10W
Suffolk, U.S.A. 76 G7 36 44N 76 35W
Suffolk □, U.K. 11 E9 52 16N 1 0 E
Sugar City, U.S.A. 80 F3 38 14N 103 40W
Sugluk = Salluit, Canada 69 B12 62 14N 75 38W
Şuḩār, Oman 45 E8 24 20N 56 40 E
Sühbaatar □, Mongolia 34 B8 45 30N 114 0 E
Suhl, Germany 16 C6 50 36N 10 42 E
Sui Xian, China 34 G8 34 25N 115 2 E
Suide, China 34 F6 37 30N 110 12 E
Suifenhe, China 35 B16 44 25N 131 10 E
Suihua, China 33 B7 46 32N 126 55 E
Suining, China 35 H9 33 56N 117 58 E
Suiping, China 34 H7 33 10N 113 59 E
Suir →, Ireland 13 D4 52 16N 7 9W
Suiyang, China 35 B16 44 30N 130 56 E
Suizhong, China 35 D11 40 21N 120 20 E
Sujangarh, India 42 F6 27 42N 74 31 E
Sukabumi, Indonesia 37 G12 6 56S 106 50 E
Sukadana, Indonesia 36 E4 1 10S 110 0 E
Sukagawa, Japan 31 F10 37 17N 140 23 E
Sukaraja, Indonesia 36 E4 2 28S 110 25 E
Sukarnapura = Jayapura, Indonesia 37 E10 2 28S 140 38 E
Sukchŏn, N. Korea 35 E13 39 22N 125 35 E
Sukhona →, Russia 24 C6 61 15N 46 39 E
Sukhothai, Thailand 38 D2 17 1N 99 49 E
Sukhumi = Sokhumi, Georgia 25 F7 43 0N 41 0 E
Sukkur, Pakistan 42 F3 27 42N 68 54 E
Sukkur Barrage, Pakistan 42 F3 27 40N 68 50 E
Sukumo, Japan 31 H6 32 56N 132 44 E
Sukunka →, Canada 72 B4 55 45N 121 15W
Sula, Kepulauan, Indonesia 37 E7 1 45S 125 0 E
Sulaco →, Honduras 88 C2 15 2N 87 44W
Sulaiman Range, Pakistan 42 D3 30 30N 69 50 E
Sūlār, Iran 45 D6 31 53N 51 54 E
Sulawesi □, Indonesia 37 E6 2 0S 120 0 E
Sulawesi Sea = Celebes Sea, Indonesia 37 D6 3 0N 123 0 E
Sulima, S. Leone 50 G3 6 58N 11 32W
Sulina, Romania 17 F15 45 10N 29 40 E
Sulitjelma, Norway 8 C17 67 9N 16 3 E
Sullana, Peru 92 D2 4 52S 80 39W
Sullivan, Ill., U.S.A. 80 F10 39 36N 88 37W
Sullivan, Ind., U.S.A. 76 F2 39 6N 87 24W
Sullivan, Mo., U.S.A. 80 F9 38 13N 91 10W
Sullivan Bay, Canada 72 C3 50 55N 126 50W
Sullivan I. = Lambi Kyun, Burma 39 G2 10 50N 98 20 E
Sulphur, La., U.S.A. 81 K8 30 14N 93 23W
Sulphur, Okla., U.S.A. 81 H6 34 31N 96 58W
Sulphur Pt., Canada 72 A6 60 56N 114 48W
Sulphur Springs, U.S.A. 81 J7 33 8N 95 36W
Sulphur Springs Draw →, U.S.A. 81 J4 32 12N 101 36W
Sultan, Canada 70 C3 47 36N 82 47W
Sultan, U.S.A. 84 C5 47 52N 121 49W
Sultanpur, India 43 F10 26 18N 82 4 E
Sultsa, Russia 24 B8 63 27N 46 2 E
Sulu Arch., Phil. 37 C6 6 0N 121 0 E
Sulu Sea, E. Indies 37 C6 8 0N 120 0 E
Suluq, Libya 51 B10 31 44N 20 14 E
Sulzberger Ice Shelf, Antarctica 5 D10 78 0S 150 0 E
Sumalata, Indonesia 37 D6 1 0N 122 31 E
Sumampa, Argentina 94 B3 29 25S 63 29W
Sumatera □, Indonesia 36 D2 0 40N 100 20 E
Sumatra = Sumatera □, Indonesia 36 D2 0 40N 100 20 E
Sumatra, U.S.A. 82 C10 46 37N 107 33W
Sumba, Indonesia 37 F5 9 45S 119 35 E
Sumba, Selat, Indonesia 37 F5 9 0S 118 40 E
Sumbawa, Indonesia 36 F5 8 26S 117 30 E
Sumbawa Besar, Indonesia 36 F5 8 30S 117 26 E
Sumbawanga □, Tanzania 54 D3 8 0S 31 30 E
Sumbe, Angola 52 G2 11 10S 13 48 E
Sumburgh Hd., U.K. 12 B7 59 52N 1 17W
Sumdo, India 43 B8 35 6N 78 41 E
Sumedang, Indonesia 37 G12 6 52S 107 55 E
Šumen = Shumen, Bulgaria 21 C12 43 18N 26 55 E
Sumenep, Indonesia 37 G15 7 1S 113 52 E
Sumgait = Sumqayıt, Azerbaijan 25 F8 40 34N 49 38 E
Summer L., U.S.A. 82 E3 42 50N 120 45W
Summerland, Canada 72 D5 49 32N 119 41W
Summerside, Canada 71 C7 46 24N 63 47W
Summerville, Ga., U.S.A. 77 H3 34 29N 85 21W
Summerville, S.C., U.S.A. 77 J5 33 1N 80 11W
Summit Lake, Canada 72 C4 54 20N 122 40W
Summit Peak, U.S.A. 83 H10 37 21N 106 42W
Sumner, Iowa, U.S.A. 80 D8 42 51N 92 6W
Sumner, Wash., U.S.A. 84 C4 47 12N 122 14W
Sumoto, Japan 31 G7 34 21N 134 54 E
Šumperk, Czech Rep. 17 D9 49 59N 16 59 E
Sumqayıt, Azerbaijan 25 F8 40 34N 49 38 E
Sumter, U.S.A. 77 J5 33 55N 80 21W
Sumy, Ukraine 25 D5 50 57N 34 50 E
Sun City, Ariz., U.S.A. 83 K7 33 36N 112 17W
Sun City, Calif., U.S.A. 85 M9 33 42N 117 11W
Sunagawa, Japan 30 C10 43 29N 141 55 E
Sunan, N. Korea 35 E13 39 15N 125 40 E
Sunart, L., U.K. 12 E3 56 42N 5 43W
Sunburst, U.S.A. 82 B8 48 53N 111 55W
Sunbury, Australia 63 F3 37 35S 144 44 E
Sunbury, U.S.A. 79 F8 40 52N 76 48W
Sunchales, Argentina 94 C3 30 58S 61 35W
Suncho Corral, Argentina 94 B3 27 55S 63 27W
Sunchon, S. Korea 35 G14 34 52N 127 31 E
Suncook, U.S.A. 79 C13 43 8N 71 27W
Sunda, Selat, Indonesia 36 F3 6 20S 105 30 E
Sunda Is., Indonesia 64 H2 5 0S 105 0 E
Sunda Str. = Sunda, Selat, Indonesia 36 F3 6 20S 105 30 E
Sundance, U.S.A. 80 C2 44 24N 104 23W
Sundarbans, The, Asia 41 J16 22 0N 89 0 E
Sundargarh, India 41 H14 22 4N 84 5 E
Sundays = Sondags →, S. Africa 56 E4 33 44S 25 51 E
Sunderland, Canada 78 B5 44 16N 79 4W
Sunderland, U.K. 10 C6 54 55N 1 23W
Sundre, Canada 72 C6 51 49N 114 38W
Sundridge, Canada 70 C4 45 45N 79 25W
Sundsvall, Sweden 9 E17 62 23N 17 17 E
Sung Hei, Vietnam 39 G6 10 20N 106 2 E
Sungai Kolok, Thailand 39 J3 6 2N 101 58 E
Sungai Lembing, Malaysia 39 L4 3 55N 103 3 E
Sungai Petani, Malaysia 39 K3 5 37N 100 30 E
Sungaigerong, Indonesia 36 E2 2 59S 104 52 E
Sungailiat, Indonesia 36 E3 1 51S 106 8 E
Sungaipenuh, Indonesia 36 E2 2 1S 101 20 E
Sungari = Songhua Jiang →, China 33 B8 47 45N 132 30 E
Sunghua Chiang = Songhua Jiang →, China 33 B8 47 45N 132 30 E
Sunndalsøra, Norway 9 E13 62 40N 8 33 E
Sunnyside, Utah, U.S.A. 82 G8 39 34N 110 23W
Sunnyside, Wash., U.S.A. 82 C3 46 20N 120 0W
Sunnyvale, U.S.A. 84 H4 37 23N 122 2W
Sunray, U.S.A. 81 G4 36 1N 101 49W
Suntar, Russia 27 C12 62 15N 117 30 E
Suomenselkä, Finland 8 E21 62 52N 24 0 E
Suomussalmi, Finland 8 D23 64 54N 29 10 E
Suoyarvi, Russia 24 B5 62 3N 32 20 E
Supai, U.S.A. 83 H7 36 15N 112 41W
Supaul, India 43 F12 26 10N 86 40 E
Superior, Ariz., U.S.A. 83 K8 33 18N 111 6W
Superior, Mont., U.S.A. 82 C6 47 12N 114 53W
Superior, Nebr., U.S.A. 80 E5 40 1N 98 4W
Superior, Wis., U.S.A. 80 B8 46 44N 92 6W
Superior, L., U.S.A. 70 C2 47 0N 87 0W
Suphan Buri, Thailand 38 E3 14 14N 100 10 E
Supiori, Indonesia 37 E9 1 0S 136 0 E
Supung Shuiku, China 35 D13 40 35N 124 50 E
Sūq Suwayq, Si. Arabia 44 E3 24 23N 38 27 E
Suqian, China 35 H10 33 54N 118 8 E
Sūr, Lebanon 47 B4 33 19N 35 16 E
Sur, Pt., U.S.A. 84 J5 36 18N 121 54W
Sura →, Russia 24 C8 56 6N 46 0 E
Surab, Pakistan 42 E2 28 25N 66 15 E
Surabaja = Surabaya, Indonesia 37 G15 7 17S 112 45 E
Surabaya, Indonesia 37 G15 7 17S 112 45 E
Surakarta, Indonesia 37 G14 7 35S 110 48 E
Surat, Australia 63 D4 27 10S 149 6 E
Surat, India 40 J8 21 12N 72 55 E
Surat Thani, Thailand 39 H2 9 6N 99 20 E
Suratgarh, India 42 E5 29 18N 73 55 E
Surendranagar, India 42 H4 22 45N 71 40 E
Surf, U.S.A. 85 L6 34 41N 120 36W
Surgut, Russia 26 C8 61 14N 73 20 E
Suriapet, India 40 L11 17 10N 79 40 E
Surigao, Phil. 37 C7 9 47N 125 29 E
Surin, Thailand 38 E4 14 50N 103 34 E
Surin Nua, Ko, Thailand 39 H1 9 30N 97 55 E
Surinam ■, S. Amer. 93 C7 4 0N 56 0W
Suriname = Surinam ■, S. Amer. 93 C7 4 0N 56 0W
Suriname →, Surinam 93 B7 5 50N 55 15W
Sūrmaq, Iran 45 D7 31 3N 52 48 E
Surprise L., Canada 72 B2 59 40N 133 15W
Surrey □, U.K. 11 F7 51 15N 0 31W
Surt, Libya 51 B9 31 11N 16 39 E
Surt, Khalīj, Libya 51 B9 31 40N 18 30 E
Surtsey, Iceland 8 E3 63 20N 20 30W
Suruga-Wan, Japan 31 G9 34 45N 138 30 E
Susaki, Japan 31 H6 33 22N 133 17 E
Süsangerd, Iran 45 D6 31 35N 48 6 E
Susanville, U.S.A. 82 F3 40 25N 120 39W
Susquehanna →, U.S.A. 79 G8 39 33N 76 5W
Susquehanna Depot, U.S.A. 79 E9 41 57N 75 36W
Susques, Argentina 94 A2 23 35S 66 25W
Sussex, Canada 71 C6 45 45N 65 37W
Sussex, U.S.A. 79 E10 41 13N 74 37W
Sussex, E. □, U.K. 11 G8 51 0N 0 20 E
Sussex, W. □, U.K. 11 G7 51 0N 0 30W
Sustut →, Canada 72 B3 56 20N 127 30W
Susuman, Russia 27 C15 62 47N 148 10 E
Susunu, Indonesia 37 E8 3 20S 133 25 E
Susurluk, Turkey 21 E13 39 54N 28 8 E
Sutherland, S. Africa 56 E3 32 24S 20 40 E
Sutherland, U.S.A. 80 E4 41 10N 101 8W
Sutherland Falls, N.Z. 59 L1 44 48S 167 46 E
Sutherlin, U.S.A. 82 E2 43 23N 123 19W
Sutlej →, Pakistan 42 E4 29 23N 71 3 E
Sutter, U.S.A. 84 F5 39 10N 121 45W
Sutter Creek, U.S.A. 84 G6 38 24N 120 48W
Sutton, Canada 79 A12 45 6N 72 37W
Sutton, U.S.A. 80 E6 40 36N 97 52W
Sutton →, Canada 70 A3 55 15N 83 45W
Sutton Coldfield, U.K. 11 E6 52 35N 1 49W
Sutton in Ashfield, U.K. 10 D6 53 8N 1 16W
Suttor →, Australia 62 C4 21 36S 147 2 E
Suttsu, Japan 30 C10 42 48N 140 14 E
Suva, Fiji 59 D8 18 6S 178 30 E
Suva Planina, Serbia, Yug. 21 C10 43 10N 22 5 E
Suvorov Is. = Suwarrow Is., Cook Is. 65 J11 15 0S 163 0W
Suwałki, Poland 17 A12 54 8N 22 59 E
Suwannaphum, Thailand 38 E4 15 33N 103 47 E
Suwannee →, U.S.A. 77 L4 29 17N 83 10W
Suwanose-Jima, Japan 31 K4 29 38N 129 43 E
Suwarrow Is., Cook Is. 65 J11 15 0S 163 0W
Suwayq aş Şuqban, Iraq 44 D5 31 32N 46 7 E
Suweis, Khalîg el, Egypt 51 C12 28 40N 33 0 E
Suwŏn, S. Korea 35 F14 37 17N 127 1 E
Suzdal, Russia 24 C7 56 29N 40 26 E
Suzhou, China 33 C7 31 19N 120 38 E
Suzu, Japan 31 F8 37 25N 137 17 E
Suzu-Misaki, Japan 31 F8 37 31N 137 21 E
Suzuka, Japan 31 G8 34 55N 136 36 E
Svalbard, Arctic 3 A10 78 0N 17 0 E
Svappavaara, Sweden 8 C19 67 40N 21 3 E
Svartisen, Norway 8 C15 66 40N 13 50 E
Svay Chek, Cambodia 38 F4 13 48N 102 58 E
Svay Rieng, Cambodia 39 G5 11 5N 105 48 E
Svealand □, Sweden 9 G16 60 20N 15 0 E
Sveg, Sweden 9 E16 62 2N 14 21 E
Svendborg, Denmark 9 J14 55 4N 10 35 E
Sverdlovsk = Yekaterinburg, Russia 24 C11 56 50N 60 30 E
Sverdrup Is., Canada 66 B10 79 0N 97 0W
Svetlaya, Russia 30 A9 46 33N 138 18 E
Svetlogorsk = Svyetlahorsk, Belarus 17 B15 52 38N 29 46 E
Svir →, Russia 24 B5 60 30N 32 48 E
Svishtov, Bulgaria 21 C11 43 36N 25 23 E
Svislach, Belarus 17 B13 53 3N 24 2 E
Svobodnyy, Russia 27 D13 51 20N 128 0 E
Svolvær, Norway 8 B16 68 15N 14 34 E
Svyetlahorsk, Belarus 17 B15 52 38N 29 46 E
Swabian Alps = Schwäbische Alb, Germany 16 D5 48 20N 9 30 E
Swainsboro, U.S.A. 77 J4 32 36N 82 20W
Swakopmund, Namibia 56 C1 22 37S 14 30 E
Swale →, U.K. 10 C6 54 5N 1 20W
Swan Hill, Australia 63 F3 35 20S 143 33 E
Swan Hills, Canada 72 C5 54 42N 115 24W
Swan Is., W. Indies 88 C3 17 22N 83 57W
Swan L., Canada 73 C8 52 30N 100 40W
Swan River, Canada 73 C8 52 10N 101 16W
Swanage, U.K. 11 G6 50 36N 1 58W
Swansea, Australia 63 E5 33 3S 151 35 E
Swansea, U.K. 11 F4 51 37N 3 57W
Swansea □, U.K. 11 F3 51 38N 4 3W
Swar →, Pakistan 43 B5 34 40N 72 5 E
Swartberge, S. Africa 56 E3 33 20S 22 0 E
Swartmodder, S. Africa 56 D3 28 1S 20 32 E
Swartruggens, S. Africa 56 D4 25 39S 26 42 E
Swastika, Canada 70 C3 48 7N 80 6W
Swatow = Shantou, China 33 D6 23 18N 116 40 E
Swaziland ■, Africa 57 D5 26 30S 31 30 E
Sweden ■, Europe 9 G16 57 0N 15 0 E
Sweet Home, U.S.A. 82 D2 44 24N 122 44W
Sweetwater, Nev., U.S.A. 84 G7 38 27N 119 9W
Sweetwater, Tex., U.S.A. 81 J4 32 28N 100 25W
Sweetwater →, U.S.A. 82 E10 42 31N 107 2W
Swellendam, S. Africa 56 E3 34 1S 20 26 E
Świdnica, Poland 17 C9 50 50N 16 30 E
Świdnik, Poland 17 C12 51 13N 22 39 E
Świebodzin, Poland 16 B8 52 15N 15 31 E
Świecie, Poland 17 B10 53 25N 18 30 E
Swift Current, Canada 73 C7 50 20N 107 45W
Swiftcurrent →, Canada 73 C7 50 38N 107 44W
Swilly, L., Ireland 13 A4 55 12N 7 33W
Swindle, I., Canada 72 C3 52 30N 128 35W
Swindon, U.K. 11 F6 51 34N 1 46W
Swindon □, U.K. 11 F6 51 34N 1 46W
Swinemünde = Świnoujście, Poland 16 B8 53 54N 14 16 E
Swinford, Ireland 13 C3 53 57N 8 58W
Świnoujście, Poland 16 B8 53 54N 14 16 E
Switzerland ■, Europe 18 C8 46 30N 8 0 E
Swords, Ireland 13 C5 53 28N 6 13W
Sydney, Australia 63 E5 33 53S 151 10 E
Sydney, Canada 71 C7 46 7N 60 7W
Sydney Mines, Canada 71 C7 46 18N 60 15W
Sydra, G. of = Surt, Khalīj, Libya 51 B9 31 40N 18 30 E
Syktyvkar, Russia 24 B9 61 45N 50 40 E
Sylacauga, U.S.A. 77 J2 33 10N 86 15W
Sylarna, Sweden 8 E15 63 2N 12 13 E
Sylhet, Bangla. 41 G17 24 54N 91 52 E
Sylt, Germany 16 A5 54 54N 8 22 E
Sylvan Lake, Canada 72 C6 52 20N 114 3W
Sylvania, U.S.A. 77 J5 32 45N 81 38W
Sylvester, U.S.A. 77 K4 31 32N 83 50W
Sym, Russia 26 C9 60 20N 88 18 E
Symón, Mexico 86 C4 24 42N 102 35W
Synnott Ra., Australia 60 C4 16 30S 125 20 E
Syracuse, Kans., U.S.A. 81 G4 37 59N 101 45W
Syracuse, N.Y., U.S.A. 79 C8 43 3N 76 9W
Syrdarya →, Kazakstan 26 E7 46 3N 61 0 E
Syria ■, Asia 44 C3 35 0N 38 0 E
Syrian Desert = Ash Shām, Bādiyat, Asia 28 F7 32 0N 40 0 E
Syzran, Russia 24 D8 53 12N 48 30 E
Szczecin, Poland 16 B8 53 27N 14 27 E
Szczecinek, Poland 17 B9 53 43N 16 41 E
Szczeciński, Zalew = Stettiner Haff, Germany 16 B8 53 47N 14 15 E
Szczytno, Poland 17 B11 53 33N 21 0 E
Szechwan = Sichuan □, China 32 C5 30 30N 103 0 E
Szeged, Hungary 17 E11 46 16N 20 10 E
Székesfehérvár, Hungary 17 E10 47 15N 18 25 E
Szekszárd, Hungary 17 E10 46 22N 18 42 E
Szentes, Hungary 17 E11 46 39N 20 21 E
Szolnok, Hungary 17 E11 46 10N 20 15 E
Szombathely, Hungary 17 E9 47 14N 16 38 E

Ta Khli Khok

T

Ta Khli Khok, *Thailand* **38 E3** 15 18N 100 20 E
Ta Lai, *Vietnam* **39 G6** 11 24N 107 23 E
Tabacal, *Argentina* **94 A3** 23 15S 64 15W
Tabaco, *Phil.* **37 B6** 13 22N 123 44 E
Ţābah, *Si. Arabia* **44 E4** 26 55N 42 38 E
Ţabas, *Khorāsān, Iran* **45 C9** 32 48N 60 12 E
Ţabas, *Khorāsān, Iran* **45 C8** 33 35N 56 55 E
Tabasará, Serranía de, *Panama* **88 E3** 8 35N 81 40W
Tabasco □, *Mexico* **87 D6** 17 45N 93 30W
Tabatinga, Serra da, *Brazil* **93 F10** 10 30S 44 0W
Tabāzīn, *Iran* **45 D8** 31 12N 57 54 E
Taber, *Canada* **72 D6** 49 47N 112 8W
Tablas, *Phil.* **37 B6** 12 25N 122 2 E
Table B. = Tafelbaai, *S. Africa* **56 E2** 33 35S 18 25 E
Table B., *Canada* **71 B8** 53 40N 56 25W
Table Mt., *S. Africa* **56 E2** 34 0S 18 22 E
Tableland, *Australia* **60 C4** 17 16S 126 51 E
Tabletop, Mt., *Australia* **62 C4** 23 24S 147 11 E
Tábor, *Czech Rep.* **16 D8** 49 25N 14 39 E
Tabora, *Tanzania* **54 D3** 5 2S 32 50 E
Tabora □, *Tanzania* **54 D3** 5 0S 33 0 E
Tabou, *Ivory C.* **50 H4** 4 30N 7 20W
Tabrīz, *Iran* **44 B5** 38 7N 46 20 E
Tabuaeran, *Pac. Oc.* **65 G12** 3 51N 159 22W
Tabūk, *Si. Arabia* **44 D3** 28 23N 36 36 E
Tacámbaro de Codallos, *Mexico* **86 D4** 19 14N 101 28W
Tacheng, *China* **32 B3** 46 40N 82 58 E
Tach'ing Shan = Daqing Shan, *China* **34 D6** 40 40N 111 0 E
Tacloban, *Phil.* **37 B6** 11 15N 124 58 E
Tacna, *Peru* **92 G4** 18 0S 70 20W
Tacoma, *U.S.A.* **84 C4** 47 14N 122 26W
Tacuarembó, *Uruguay* **95 C4** 31 45S 56 0W
Tademaït, Plateau du, *Algeria* **50 C6** 28 30N 2 30 E
Tadjoura, *Djibouti* **46 E3** 11 50N 42 55 E
Tadmor, *N.Z.* **59 J4** 41 27S 172 45 E
Tadoule, L., *Canada* **73 B9** 58 36N 98 20W
Tadoussac, *Canada* **71 C6** 48 11N 69 42W
Tadzhikistan = Tajikistan ■, *Asia* **26 F8** 38 30N 70 0 E
Taechŏn-ni, *S. Korea* **35 F14** 36 21N 126 36 E
Taegu, *S. Korea* **35 G15** 35 50N 128 37 E
Taegwan, *N. Korea* **35 D13** 40 13N 125 12 E
Taejŏn, *S. Korea* **35 F14** 36 20N 127 28 E
Tafalla, *Spain* **19 A5** 42 30N 1 41W
Tafelbaai, *S. Africa* **56 E2** 33 35S 18 25 E
Tafermaar, *Indonesia* **37 F8** 6 47S 134 10 E
Tafí Viejo, *Argentina* **94 B2** 26 43S 65 17W
Tafīhān, *Iran* **45 D7** 29 25N 52 39 E
Taft, *Iran* **45 D7** 31 45N 54 14 E
Taft, *Phil.* **37 B7** 11 57N 125 30 E
Taft, *Calif., U.S.A.* **85 K7** 35 8N 119 28W
Taft, *Tex., U.S.A.* **81 M6** 27 59N 97 24W
Taga Dzong, *Bhutan* **41 F16** 27 5N 89 55 E
Taganrog, *Russia* **25 E6** 47 12N 38 50 E
Tagbilaran, *Phil.* **37 C6** 9 39N 123 51 E
Tagish, *Canada* **72 A2** 60 19N 134 16W
Tagish L., *Canada* **72 A2** 60 10N 134 20W
Tagliamento →, *Italy* **20 B5** 45 38N 13 6 E
Tagomago, *Spain* **22 B8** 39 2N 1 39 E
Taguatinga, *Brazil* **93 F10** 12 16S 42 26W
Tagum, *Phil.* **37 C7** 7 33N 125 53 E
Tagus = Tejo →, *Europe* **19 C1** 38 40N 9 24W
Tahakopa, *N.Z.* **59 M2** 46 30S 169 23 E
Tahan, Gunong, *Malaysia* **39 K4** 4 34N 102 17 E
Tahat, *Algeria* **50 D7** 23 18N 5 33 E
Tāherī, *Iran* **45 E7** 27 43N 52 20 E
Tahiti, *Pac. Oc.* **65 J13** 17 37S 149 27W
Tahoe, L., *U.S.A.* **84 G6** 39 6N 120 2W
Tahoe City, *U.S.A.* **84 F6** 39 10N 120 9W
Taholah, *U.S.A.* **84 C2** 47 21N 124 17W
Tahoua, *Niger* **50 F7** 14 57N 5 16 E
Tahta, *Egypt* **51 C12** 26 44N 31 32 E
Tahulandang, *Indonesia* **37 D7** 2 27N 125 23 E
Tahuna, *Indonesia* **37 D7** 3 38N 125 30 E
Tai Shan, *China* **35 F9** 36 25N 117 20 E
Tai'an, *China* **35 F9** 36 12N 117 8 E
Taibei = T'aipei, *Taiwan* **33 D7** 25 2N 121 30 E
Taibique, *Canary Is.* **22 G2** 27 42N 17 58W
Taibus Qi, *China* **34 D8** 41 54N 115 22 E
T'aichung, *Taiwan* **33 D7** 24 9N 120 37 E
Taieri →, *N.Z.* **59 M3** 46 3S 170 12 E
Taigu, *China* **34 F7** 37 28N 112 30 E
Taihang Shan, *China* **34 G7** 36 0N 113 30 E
Taihape, *N.Z.* **59 H5** 39 41S 175 48 E
Taihe, *China* **34 H8** 33 20N 115 42 E
Taikang, *China* **34 G8** 34 5N 114 50 E
Tailem Bend, *Australia* **63 F2** 35 12S 139 29 E
Taimyr Peninsula = Taymyr, Poluostrov, *Russia* **27 B11** 75 0N 100 0 E
Tain, *U.K.* **12 D4** 57 49N 4 4W
T'ainan, *Taiwan* **33 D7** 23 0N 120 10 E
Taínaron, Ákra, *Greece* **21 F10** 36 22N 22 27 E
T'aipei, *Taiwan* **33 D7** 25 2N 121 30 E
Taiping, *Malaysia* **39 K3** 4 51N 100 44 E
Taipingzhen, *China* **34 H6** 33 35N 111 42 E
Tairbeart = Tarbert, *U.K.* **12 D2** 57 54N 6 49W
Taita □, *Kenya* **54 C4** 4 0S 38 30 E
Taita Hills, *Kenya* **54 C4** 3 25S 38 15 E
Taitao, Pen. de, *Chile* **96 F2** 46 30S 75 0W
T'aitung, *Taiwan* **33 D7** 22 43N 121 4 E
Taivalkoski, *Finland* **8 D23** 65 33N 28 12 E
Taiwan ■, *Asia* **33 D7** 23 30N 121 0 E
Taïyetos Óros, *Greece* **21 F10** 37 0N 22 23 E
Taiyiba, *Israel* **47 C4** 32 36N 35 27 E
Taiyuan, *China* **34 F7** 37 52N 112 33 E
Taizhong = T'aichung, *Taiwan* **33 D7** 24 9N 120 37 E
Ta'izz, *Yemen* **46 E3** 13 35N 44 2 E
Tājābād, *Iran* **45 D7** 30 2N 54 24 E
Tajikistan ■, *Asia* **26 F8** 38 30N 70 0 E
Tajima, *Japan* **31 F9** 37 12N 139 46 E
Tajo = Tejo →, *Europe* **19 C1** 38 40N 9 24W
Tajrīsh, *Iran* **45 C6** 35 48N 51 25 E
Tak, *Thailand* **38 D2** 16 52N 99 8 E
Takāb, *Iran* **44 B5** 36 24N 47 7 E
Takachiho, *Japan* **31 H5** 32 42N 131 18 E
Takada, *Japan* **31 F9** 37 7N 138 15 E
Takahagi, *Japan* **31 F10** 36 43N 140 45 E
Takaka, *N.Z.* **59 J4** 40 51S 172 50 E
Takamatsu, *Japan* **31 G7** 34 20N 134 5 E
Takaoka, *Japan* **31 F8** 36 47N 137 0 E
Takapuna, *N.Z.* **59 G5** 36 47S 174 47 E
Takasaki, *Japan* **31 F9** 36 20N 139 0 E
Takatsuki, *Japan* **31 G7** 34 51N 135 37 E
Takaungu, *Kenya* **54 C4** 3 38S 39 52 E
Takayama, *Japan* **31 F8** 36 18N 137 11 E
Take-Shima, *Japan* **31 J5** 30 49N 130 26 E
Takefu, *Japan* **31 G8** 35 50N 136 10 E
Takengon, *Indonesia* **36 D1** 4 45N 96 50 E
Takeo, *Japan* **31 H5** 33 12N 130 1 E
Tākestān, *Iran* **45 C6** 36 0N 49 40 E
Taketa, *Japan* **31 H5** 32 58N 131 24 E
Takev, *Cambodia* **39 G5** 10 59N 104 47 E
Takh, *India* **43 C7** 33 6N 77 32 E
Takikawa, *Japan* **30 C10** 43 33N 141 54 E
Takla L., *Canada* **72 B3** 55 15N 125 45W
Takla Landing, *Canada* **72 B3** 55 30N 125 50W
Takla Makan = Taklamakan Shamo, *China* **32 C3** 38 0N 83 0 E
Taklamakan Shamo, *China* **32 C3** 38 0N 83 0 E
Taku →, *Canada* **72 B2** 58 30N 133 50W
Tal Halāl, *Iran* **45 D7** 28 54N 55 1 E
Tala, *Uruguay* **95 C4** 34 21S 55 46W
Talagante, *Chile* **94 C1** 33 40S 70 50W
Talamanca, Cordillera de, *Cent. Amer.* **88 E3** 9 20N 83 20W
Talara, *Peru* **92 D2** 4 38S 81 18W
Talas, *Kyrgyzstan* **26 E8** 42 30N 72 13 E
Talâta, *Egypt* **47 E1** 30 36N 32 20 E
Talaud, Kepulauan, *Indonesia* **37 D7** 4 30N 127 10 E
Talaud Is. = Talaud, Kepulauan, *Indonesia* **37 D7** 4 30N 127 10 E
Talavera de la Reina, *Spain* **19 C3** 39 55N 4 46W
Talawana, *Australia* **60 D3** 22 51S 121 9 E
Talayan, *Phil.* **37 C6** 6 52N 124 24 E
Talbot, C., *Australia* **60 B4** 13 48S 126 43 E
Talbragar →, *Australia* **63 E4** 32 12S 148 37 E
Talca, *Chile* **94 D1** 35 28S 71 40W
Talca □, *Chile* **94 D1** 35 20S 71 46W
Talcahuano, *Chile* **94 D1** 36 40S 73 10W
Talcher, *India* **41 J14** 21 0N 85 18 E
Taldy Kurgan = Taldyqorghan, *Kazakstan* **26 E8** 45 10N 78 45 E
Taldyqorghan, *Kazakstan* **26 E8** 45 10N 78 45 E
Tālesh, *Iran* **45 B6** 37 58N 48 58 E
Ţalesh, Kūhhā-ye, *Iran* **45 B6** 37 42N 48 55 E
Tali Post, *Sudan* **51 G12** 5 55N 30 44 E
Talibon, *Phil.* **37 B6** 10 9N 124 20 E
Talibong, Ko, *Thailand* **39 J2** 7 15N 99 23 E
Talihina, *U.S.A.* **81 H7** 34 45N 95 3W
Taliwang, *Indonesia* **36 F5** 8 50S 116 55 E
Tall Kalakh, *Syria* **47 A5** 34 41N 36 15 E
Talladega, *U.S.A.* **77 J2** 33 26N 86 6W
Tallahassee, *U.S.A.* **77 K3** 30 27N 84 17W
Tallangatta, *Australia* **63 F4** 36 15S 147 19 E
Tallarook, *Australia* **63 F4** 37 5S 145 6 E
Tallering Pk., *Australia* **61 E2** 28 6S 115 37 E
Tallinn, *Estonia* **24 C3** 59 22N 24 48 E
Tallulah, *U.S.A.* **81 J9** 32 25N 91 11W
Taloyoak, *Canada* **68 B10** 69 32N 93 32W
Talpa de Allende, *Mexico* **86 C4** 20 23N 104 51W
Talsi, *Latvia* **9 H20** 57 10N 22 30 E
Taltal, *Chile* **94 B1** 25 23S 70 33W
Taltson →, *Canada* **72 A6** 61 24N 112 46W
Talwood, *Australia* **63 D4** 28 29S 149 29 E
Talyawalka Cr. →, *Australia* **63 E3** 32 28S 142 22 E
Tam Chau, *Vietnam* **39 G5** 10 48N 105 12 E
Tam Ky, *Vietnam* **38 E7** 15 34N 108 29 E
Tam Quan, *Vietnam* **38 E7** 14 35N 109 3 E
Tama, *U.S.A.* **80 E8** 41 58N 92 35W
Tamala, *Australia* **61 E1** 26 42S 113 47 E
Tamale, *Ghana* **50 G5** 9 22N 0 50W
Tamano, *Japan* **31 G6** 34 29N 133 59 E
Tamanrasset, *Algeria* **50 D7** 22 50N 5 30 E
Tamaqua, *U.S.A.* **79 F9** 40 48N 75 58W
Tamar →, *U.K.* **11 G3** 50 27N 4 15W
Tamarang, *Australia* **63 E5** 31 27S 150 5 E
Tamarinda, *Spain* **22 B10** 39 55N 3 49 E
Tamashima, *Japan* **31 G6** 34 32N 133 40 E
Tamaulipas □, *Mexico* **87 C5** 24 0N 99 0W
Tamaulipas, Sierra de, *Mexico* **87 C5** 23 30N 98 20W
Tamazula, *Mexico* **86 C3** 24 55N 106 58W
Tamazunchale, *Mexico* **87 C5** 21 16N 98 47W
Tambacounda, *Senegal* **50 F3** 13 45N 13 40W
Tambelan, Kepulauan, *Indonesia* **36 D3** 1 0N 107 30 E
Tambellup, *Australia* **61 F2** 34 4S 117 37 E
Tambo, *Australia* **62 C4** 24 54S 146 14 E
Tambo de Mora, *Peru* **92 F3** 13 30S 76 8W
Tambohorano, *Madag.* **57 B7** 17 30S 43 58 E
Tambora, *Indonesia* **36 F5** 8 12S 118 5 E
Tambov, *Russia* **24 D7** 52 45N 41 28 E
Tambuku, *Indonesia* **37 G15** 7 8S 113 40 E
Tâmega →, *Portugal* **19 B1** 41 5N 8 21W
Tamenglong, *India* **41 G18** 25 0N 93 35 E
Tamiahua, L. de, *Mexico* **87 C5** 21 30N 97 30W
Tamil Nadu □, *India* **40 P10** 11 0N 77 0 E
Tamluk, *India* **43 H12** 22 18N 87 58 E
Tammerfors = Tampere, *Finland* **9 F20** 61 30N 23 50 E
Tammisaari, *Finland* **9 F20** 60 0N 23 26 E
Tamo Abu, Pegunungan, *Malaysia* **36 D5** 3 10N 115 5 E
Tampa, *U.S.A.* **77 M4** 27 57N 82 27W
Tampa B., *U.S.A.* **77 M4** 27 50N 82 30W
Tampere, *Finland* **9 F20** 61 30N 23 50 E
Tampico, *Mexico* **87 C5** 22 20N 97 50W
Tampin, *Malaysia* **39 L4** 2 28N 102 13 E
Tamu, *Burma* **41 G19** 24 13N 94 12 E
Tamworth, *Australia* **63 E5** 31 7S 150 58 E
Tamworth, *U.K.* **11 E6** 52 39N 1 41W
Tamyang, *S. Korea* **35 G14** 35 19N 126 59 E
Tan An, *Vietnam* **39 G6** 10 32N 106 25 E
Tana →, *Kenya* **54 C5** 2 32S 40 31 E
Tana →, *Norway* **8 A23** 70 30N 28 14 E
Tana, L., *Ethiopia* **46 E2** 13 5N 37 30 E
Tana River, *Kenya* **54 C4** 2 0S 39 30 E
Tanabe, *Japan* **31 H7** 33 44N 135 22 E
Tanafjorden, *Norway* **8 A23** 70 45N 28 25 E
Tanaga, Pta., *Canary Is.* **22 G1** 27 42N 18 10W
Tanahbala, *Indonesia* **36 E1** 0 30S 98 30 E
Tanahgrogot, *Indonesia* **36 E5** 1 55S 116 15 E
Tanahjampea, *Indonesia* **37 F6** 7 10S 120 35 E
Tanahmasa, *Indonesia* **36 E1** 0 12S 98 39 E
Tanahmerah, *Indonesia* **37 F10** 6 5S 140 16 E
Tanakura, *Japan* **31 F10** 37 10N 140 20 E
Tanami, *Australia* **60 C4** 19 59S 129 43 E
Tanami Desert, *Australia* **60 C5** 18 50S 132 0 E
Tanana →, *U.S.A.* **68 B4** 65 10N 151 58W
Tananarive = Antananarivo, *Madag.* **57 B8** 18 55S 47 31 E
Tánaro →, *Italy* **18 D8** 44 55N 8 40 E
Tanbar, *Australia* **62 D3** 25 51S 141 55 E
Tancheng, *China* **35 G10** 34 25N 118 20 E
Tanchŏn, *N. Korea* **35 D15** 40 27N 128 54 E
Tanda, *Ut. P., India* **43 F10** 26 33N 82 35 E
Tanda, *Ut. P., India* **43 E8** 28 57N 78 56 E
Tandag, *Phil.* **37 C7** 9 4N 126 9 E
Tandaia, *Tanzania* **55 D3** 9 25S 34 15 E
Tandaué, *Angola* **56 B2** 16 58S 18 5 E
Tandil, *Argentina* **94 D4** 37 15S 59 6W
Tandil, Sa. del, *Argentina* **94 D4** 37 30S 59 0W
Tandlianwala, *Pakistan* **42 D5** 31 3N 73 9 E
Tando Adam, *Pakistan* **42 G3** 25 45N 68 40 E
Tandou L., *Australia* **63 E3** 32 40S 142 5 E
Tandragee, *U.K.* **13 B5** 54 21N 6 24W
Tane-ga-Shima, *Japan* **31 J5** 30 30N 131 0 E
Taneatua, *N.Z.* **59 H6** 38 4S 177 1 E
Tanen Tong Dan, *Burma* **41 L21** 16 30N 98 30 E
Tanezrouft, *Algeria* **50 D6** 23 9N 0 11 E
Tang, Koh, *Cambodia* **39 G4** 10 16N 103 7 E
Tang Krasang, *Cambodia* **38 F5** 12 34N 105 3 E
Tanga, *Tanzania* **54 D4** 5 5S 39 2 E
Tanga □, *Tanzania* **54 D4** 5 20S 38 0 E
Tanganyika, L., *Africa* **54 D3** 6 40S 30 0 E
Tanger = Tangier, *Morocco* **50 A4** 35 50N 5 49W
Tangerang, *Indonesia* **37 G12** 6 11S 106 37 E
Tanggu, *China* **35 E9** 39 2N 117 40 E
Tanggula Shan, *China* **32 C4** 32 40N 92 10 E
Tanghe, *China* **34 H7** 32 47N 112 50 E
Tangier, *Morocco* **50 A4** 35 50N 5 49W
Tangorin P.O., *Australia* **62 C3** 21 47S 144 12 E
Tangshan, *China* **35 E10** 39 38N 118 10 E
Tangtou, *China* **35 G10** 35 28N 118 30 E
Tanimbar, Kepulauan, *Indonesia* **37 F8** 7 30S 131 30 E
Tanimbar Is. = Tanimbar, Kepulauan, *Indonesia* **37 F8** 7 30S 131 30 E
Taninthari, *Burma* **39 F2** 12 6N 99 3 E
Tanjay, *Phil.* **37 C6** 9 30N 123 5 E
Tanjong Malim, *Malaysia* **39 L3** 3 42N 101 31 E
Tanjore = Thanjavur, *India* **40 P11** 10 48N 79 12 E
Tanjung, *Indonesia* **36 E5** 2 10S 115 25 E
Tanjungbalai, *Indonesia* **36 D1** 2 55N 99 44 E
Tanjungbatu, *Indonesia* **36 D5** 2 23N 118 3 E
Tanjungkarang Telukbetung, *Indonesia* **36 F3** 5 20S 105 10 E
Tanjungpandan, *Indonesia* **36 E3** 2 43S 107 38 E
Tanjungpinang, *Indonesia* **36 D2** 1 5N 104 30 E
Tanjungredeb, *Indonesia* **36 D5** 2 9N 117 29 E
Tanjungselor, *Indonesia* **36 D5** 2 55N 117 25 E
Tank, *Pakistan* **42 C4** 32 14N 70 25 E
Tannu-Ola, *Russia* **27 D10** 51 0N 94 0 E
Tanout, *Niger* **50 F7** 14 50N 8 55 E
Tanta, *Egypt* **51 B12** 30 45N 30 57 E
Tantoyuca, *Mexico* **87 C5** 21 21N 98 10W
Tantung = Dandong, *China* **35 D13** 40 10N 124 20 E
Tanunda, *Australia* **63 E2** 34 30S 139 0 E
Tanzania ■, *Africa* **54 D3** 6 0S 34 0 E
Tanzilla →, *Canada* **72 B2** 58 8N 130 43W
Tao, Ko, *Thailand* **39 G2** 10 5N 99 52 E
Tao'an, *China* **35 B12** 45 22N 122 40 E
Tao'er He →, *China* **35 B13** 45 45N 124 5 E
Taolanaro, *Madag.* **57 D8** 25 2S 47 0 E
Taole, *China* **34 E4** 38 48N 106 40 E
Taos, *U.S.A.* **83 H11** 36 24N 105 35W
Taoudenni, *Mali* **50 D5** 22 40N 3 55W
Tapa, *Estonia* **9 G21** 59 15N 25 50 E
Tapa Shan = Daba Shan, *China* **33 C5** 32 0N 109 0 E
Tapachula, *Mexico* **87 E6** 14 54N 92 17W
Tapah, *Malaysia* **39 K3** 4 12N 101 15 E
Tapajós →, *Brazil* **93 D8** 2 24S 54 41W
Tapaktuan, *Indonesia* **36 D1** 3 15N 97 10 E
Tapanahoni →, *Surinam* **93 C8** 4 20N 54 25W
Tapanui, *N.Z.* **59 L2** 45 56S 169 18 E
Tapauá →, *Brazil* **92 E6** 5 40S 64 21W
Tapeta, *Liberia* **50 G4** 6 29N 8 52W
Taphan Hin, *Thailand* **38 D3** 16 13N 100 26 E
Tapi →, *India* **40 J8** 21 8N 72 41 E
Tapirapecó, Serra, *Venezuela* **92 C6** 1 10N 65 0W
Tappahannock, *U.S.A.* **76 G7** 37 56N 76 52W
Tapuaenuku, Mt., *N.Z.* **59 K4** 42 0S 173 39 E
Tapul Group, *Phil.* **37 C6** 5 35N 120 50 E
Tapurucuará, *Brazil* **92 D5** 0 24S 65 2W
Taqīābād, *Iran* **45 C8** 35 33N 59 11 E
Ţaqţaq, *Iraq* **44 C5** 35 53N 44 35 E
Taquara, *Brazil* **95 B5** 29 36S 50 46W
Taquari →, *Brazil* **92 G7** 19 15S 57 17W
Tara, *Australia* **63 D5** 27 17S 150 31 E
Tara, *Canada* **78 B3** 44 28N 81 9W
Tara, *Russia* **26 D8** 56 55N 74 24 E
Tara, *Zambia* **55 F2** 16 58S 26 45 E
Tara →, *Montenegro, Yug.* **21 C8** 43 21N 18 51 E
Tarabagatay, Khrebet, *Kazakstan* **26 E9** 48 0N 83 0 E
Tarābulus, *Lebanon* **47 A4** 34 31N 35 50 E
Tarābulus, *Libya* **51 B8** 32 49N 13 7 E
Tarajalejo, *Canary Is.* **22 F5** 28 12N 14 7W
Tarakan, *Indonesia* **36 D5** 3 20N 117 35 E
Tarakit, Mt., *Kenya* **54 B4** 2 2N 35 10 E
Taralga, *Australia* **63 E4** 34 26S 149 52 E
Tarama-Jima, *Japan* **31 M2** 24 39N 124 42 E
Taran, Mys, *Russia* **9 J18** 54 56N 19 59 E
Taranagar, *India* **42 E6** 28 43N 74 50 E
Taranaki □, *N.Z.* **59 H5** 39 25S 174 30 E
Tarancón, *Spain* **19 B4** 40 1N 3 0W
Taranga, *India* **42 H5** 23 56N 72 43 E
Taranga Hill, *India* **42 H5** 24 0N 72 40 E
Taransay, *U.K.* **12 D1** 57 54N 7 0W
Táranto, *Italy* **20 D7** 40 28N 17 14 E
Táranto, G. di, *Italy* **20 D7** 40 8N 17 20 E
Tarapacá, *Colombia* **92 D5** 2 56S 69 46W
Tarapacá □, *Chile* **94 A2** 20 45S 69 30W
Tarapoto, *Peru* **92 E3** 6 30S 76 20W
Tararua Ra., *N.Z.* **59 J5** 40 45S 175 25 E
Tarashcha, *Ukraine* **17 D16** 49 30N 30 31 E
Tarauacá, *Brazil* **92 E4** 8 6S 70 48W
Tarauacá →, *Brazil* **92 E5** 6 42S 69 48W
Tarawera, *N.Z.* **59 H6** 39 2S 176 36 E
Tarawera L., *N.Z.* **59 H6** 38 13S 176 27 E
Tarazona, *Spain* **19 B5** 41 55N 1 43W
Tarbat Ness, *U.K.* **12 D5** 57 52N 3 47W
Tarbela Dam, *Pakistan* **42 B5** 34 8N 72 52 E
Tarbert, *Arg. & Bute, U.K.* **12 F3** 55 52N 5 25W
Tarbert, *W. Isles, U.K.* **12 D2** 57 54N 6 49W
Tarbes, *France* **18 E4** 43 15N 0 3 E
Tarboro, *U.S.A.* **77 H7** 35 54N 77 32W
Tarbrax, *Australia* **62 C3** 21 7S 142 26 E
Tarcoola, *Australia* **63 E1** 30 44S 134 36 E
Tarcoon, *Australia* **63 E4** 30 15S 146 43 E
Taree, *Australia* **63 E5** 31 50S 152 30 E
Tarfaya, *Morocco* **50 C3** 27 55N 12 55W
Târgovişte, *Romania* **17 F13** 44 55N 25 27 E
Târgu-Jiu, *Romania* **17 F12** 45 5N 23 19 E
Târgu Mureş, *Romania* **17 E13** 46 31N 24 38 E
Tarifa, *Spain* **19 D3** 36 1N 5 36W
Tarija, *Bolivia* **94 A3** 21 30S 64 40W
Tarija □, *Bolivia* **94 A3** 21 30S 63 30W
Tariku →, *Indonesia* **37 E9** 2 55S 138 26 E
Tarim Basin = Tarim Pendi, *China* **32 B3** 40 0N 84 0 E
Tarim He →, *China* **32 C3** 39 30N 88 30 E
Tarim Pendi, *China* **32 B3** 40 0N 84 0 E
Tarime □, *Tanzania* **54 C3** 1 15S 34 0 E
Taritatu →, *Indonesia* **37 E9** 2 54S 138 27 E
Tarka →, *S. Africa* **56 E4** 32 10S 26 0 E
Tarkastad, *S. Africa* **56 E4** 32 0S 26 16 E
Tarkhankut, Mys, *Ukraine* **25 E5** 45 25N 32 30 E
Tarko Sale, *Russia* **26 C8** 64 55N 77 50 E
Tarkwa, *Ghana* **50 G5** 5 20N 2 0W
Tarlac, *Phil.* **37 A6** 15 29N 120 35 E
Tarlton Downs, *Australia* **62 C2** 22 40S 136 45 E
Tarma, *Peru* **92 F3** 11 25S 75 45W
Tarn →, *France* **18 E4** 44 5N 1 6 E
Târnăveni, *Romania* **17 E13** 46 19N 24 13 E
Tarnobrzeg, *Poland* **17 C11** 50 35N 21 41 E
Tarnów, *Poland* **17 C11** 50 3N 21 0 E
Tarnowskie Góry, *Poland* **17 C10** 50 27N 18 54 E
Taroom, *Australia* **63 D4** 25 36S 149 48 E
Taroudannt, *Morocco* **50 B4** 30 30N 8 52W
Tarpon Springs, *U.S.A.* **77 L4** 28 9N 82 45W
Tarragona, *Spain* **19 B6** 41 5N 1 17 E
Tarrasa = Terrassa, *Spain* **19 B7** 41 34N 2 1 E
Tarrytown, *U.S.A.* **79 E11** 41 4N 73 52W
Tarshiha = Me'ona, *Israel* **47 B4** 33 1N 35 15 E
Tarso Emissi, *Chad* **51 D9** 21 27N 18 36 E
Tarsus, *Turkey* **25 G5** 36 58N 34 55 E
Tartagal, *Argentina* **94 A3** 22 30S 63 50W
Tartu, *Estonia* **24 C4** 58 20N 26 44 E
Ţarţūs, *Syria* **44 C2** 34 55N 35 55 E
Tarumizu, *Japan* **31 J5** 31 29N 130 42 E
Tarutao, Ko, *Thailand* **39 J2** 6 33N 99 40 E
Tarutung, *Indonesia* **36 D1** 2 0N 98 54 E
Taschereau, *Canada* **70 C4** 48 40N 78 40W
Taseko →, *Canada* **72 C4** 52 8N 123 45W
Tash-Kömür, *Kyrgyzstan* **26 E8** 41 40N 72 10 E
Tash-Kumyr = Tash-Kömür, *Kyrgyzstan* **26 E8** 41 40N 72 10 E
Tashauz = Dashhowuz, *Turkmenistan* **26 E6** 41 49N 59 58 E
Tashi Chho Dzong = Thimphu, *Bhutan* **41 F16** 27 31N 89 45 E
Tashkent = Toshkent, *Uzbekistan* **26 E7** 41 20N 69 10 E
Tashtagol, *Russia* **26 D9** 52 47N 87 53 E
Tasikmalaya, *Indonesia* **37 G13** 7 18S 108 12 E
Tåsjön, *Sweden* **8 D16** 64 15N 15 40 E
Taskan, *Russia* **27 C16** 62 59N 150 20 E
Tasman B., *N.Z.* **59 J4** 40 59S 173 25 E
Tasman Mts., *N.Z.* **59 J4** 41 3S 172 25 E
Tasman Pen., *Australia* **62 G4** 43 10S 148 0 E
Tasman Sea, *Pac. Oc.* **64 L8** 36 0S 160 0 E
Tasmania □, *Australia* **62 G4** 42 0S 146 30 E
Tassili n'Ajjer, *Algeria* **48 D4** 25 47N 8 1 E
Tasu Sd., *Canada* **72 C2** 52 47N 132 2W
Tatabánya, *Hungary* **17 E10** 47 32N 18 25 E
Tatar Republic □ = Tatarstan □, *Russia* **24 C9** 55 30N 51 30 E
Tatarbunary, *Ukraine* **17 F15** 45 50N 29 39 E
Tatarsk, *Russia* **26 D8** 55 14N 76 0 E
Tatarstan □, *Russia* **24 C9** 55 30N 51 30 E
Tateyama, *Japan* **31 G9** 35 0N 139 50 E
Tathlina L., *Canada* **72 A5** 60 33N 117 39W
Tathra, *Australia* **63 F4** 36 44S 149 59 E
Tatinnai L., *Canada* **73 A9** 60 55N 97 40W
Tatnam, C., *Canada* **73 B10** 57 16N 91 0W
Tatra = Tatry, *Slovak Rep.* **17 D11** 49 20N 20 0 E
Tatry, *Slovak Rep.* **17 D11** 49 20N 20 0 E
Tatsuno, *Japan* **31 G7** 34 52N 134 33 E
Tatta, *Pakistan* **42 G2** 24 42N 67 55 E
Tatuī, *Brazil* **95 A6** 23 25S 47 53W
Tatum, *U.S.A.* **81 J3** 33 16N 103 19W
Tat'ung = Datong, *China* **34 D7** 40 6N 113 18 E
Tatvan, *Turkey* **25 G7** 38 31N 42 15 E
Taubaté, *Brazil* **95 A6** 23 0S 45 36W
Tauern, *Austria* **16 E7** 47 15N 12 40 E
Taumarunui, *N.Z.* **59 H5** 38 53S 175 15 E

Thrace

Thrace, Turkey 21 D12 41 0N 27 0 E
Three Forks, U.S.A. 82 D8 45 54N 111 33W
Three Hills, Canada 72 C6 51 43N 113 15W
Three Hummock I., Australia 62 G3 40 25S 144 55 E
Three Lakes, U.S.A. 80 C10 45 48N 89 10W
Three Points, C., Ghana 50 H5 4 42N 2 6W
Three Rivers, Australia 61 E2 25 10S 119 5 E
Three Rivers, Calif., U.S.A. 84 J8 36 26N 118 54W
Three Rivers, Tex., U.S.A. 81 L5 28 28N 98 11W
Three Sisters, U.S.A. 82 D3 44 4N 121 51W
Throssell, L., Australia 61 E3 27 33S 124 10 E
Throssell Ra., Australia 60 D3 22 3S 121 43 E
Thuan Hoa, Vietnam 39 H5 8 58N 105 30 E
Thubun Lakes, Canada 73 A6 61 30N 112 0W
Thuin, Belgium 15 D4 50 20N 4 17 E
Thun, Switz. 18 C7 46 45N 7 38 E
Thundelarra, Australia 61 E2 28 53S 117 7 E
Thunder B., U.S.A. 78 B1 45 0N 83 20W
Thunder Bay, Canada 70 C2 48 20N 89 15W
Thung Song, Thailand 39 H2 8 10N 99 40 E
Thunkar, Bhutan 41 F17 27 55N 91 0 E
Thuong Tra, Vietnam 38 D6 16 2N 107 42 E
Thüringer Wald, Germany 16 C6 50 35N 11 0 E
Thurles, Ireland 13 D4 52 41N 7 49W
Thurloo Downs, Australia 63 D3 29 15S 143 30 E
Thurrock □, U.K. 11 F8 51 31N 0 23 E
Thursday I., Australia 62 A3 10 30S 142 3 E
Thurso, Canada 70 C4 45 36N 75 15W
Thurso, U.K. 12 C5 58 36N 3 32W
Thurso →, U.K. 12 C5 58 36N 3 32W
Thurston I., Antarctica 5 D16 72 0S 100 0W
Thutade L., Canada 72 B3 57 0N 126 55W
Thylungra, Australia 63 D3 26 4S 143 28 E
Thyolo, Malawi 55 F4 16 7S 35 5 E
Thysville = Mbanza Ngungu, Dem. Rep. of the Congo 52 F2 5 12S 14 53 E
Tia, Australia 63 E5 31 10S 151 50 E
Tian Shan, Asia 32 B3 42 0N 76 0 E
Tianjin, China 35 E9 39 8N 117 10 E
Tianshui, China 34 G3 34 32N 105 40 E
Tianzhen, China 34 D8 40 24N 114 5 E
Tianzhuangtai, China 35 D12 40 43N 122 5 E
Tiaret, Algeria 50 A6 35 20N 1 21 E
Tibagi, Brazil 95 A5 24 30S 50 24W
Tibagi →, Brazil 95 A5 22 47S 51 1W
Tiber = Tevere →, Italy 20 D5 41 44N 12 14 E
Tiber Reservoir, U.S.A. 82 B8 48 19N 111 6W
Tiberias = Teverya, Israel 47 C4 32 47N 35 32 E
Tiberias, L. = Yam Kinneret, Israel 47 C4 32 45N 35 35 E
Tibesti, Chad 51 D9 21 0N 17 30 E
Tibet = Xizang Zizhiqu □, China 32 C3 32 0N 88 0 E
Tibet, Plateau of, Asia 28 F12 32 0N 86 0 E
Tibnī, Syria 44 C3 35 36N 39 50 E
Tibooburra, Australia 63 D3 29 26S 142 1 E
Tiburón, Mexico 86 B2 29 0N 112 30W
Ticino →, Italy 18 D8 45 9N 9 14 E
Ticonderoga, U.S.A. 79 C11 43 51N 73 26W
Ticul, Mexico 87 C7 20 20N 89 31W
Tidaholm, Sweden 9 G15 58 12N 13 58 E
Tiddim, Burma 41 H18 23 28N 93 45 E
Tidjikja, Mauritania 50 E3 18 29N 11 35W
Tidore, Indonesia 37 D7 0 40N 127 25 E
Tiel, Neths. 15 C5 51 53N 5 26 E
Tieling, China 35 C12 42 20N 123 55 E
Tielt, Belgium 15 C3 51 0N 3 20 E
Tien Shan = Tian Shan, Asia 32 B3 42 0N 76 0 E
Tien-tsin = Tianjin, China 35 E9 39 8N 117 10 E
Tien Yen, Vietnam 38 B6 21 20N 107 24 E
T'ienching = Tianjin, China 35 E9 39 8N 117 10 E
Tienen, Belgium 15 D4 50 48N 4 57 E
Tientsin = Tianjin, China 35 E9 39 8N 117 10 E
Tierra Amarilla, Chile 94 B1 27 28S 70 18W
Tierra Amarilla, U.S.A. 83 H10 36 42N 106 33W
Tierra Colorada, Mexico 87 D5 17 10N 99 35W
Tierra de Campos, Spain 19 A3 42 10N 4 50W
Tierra del Fuego, I. Gr. de, Argentina 96 G3 54 0S 69 0W
Tiétar →, Spain 19 C3 39 50N 6 1W
Tieté →, Brazil 95 A5 20 40S 51 35W
Tieyon, Australia 63 D1 26 12S 133 52 E
Tiffin, U.S.A. 76 E4 41 7N 83 11W
Tiflis = Tbilisi, Georgia 25 F7 41 43N 44 50 E
Tifton, U.S.A. 77 K4 31 27N 83 31W
Tifu, Indonesia 37 E7 3 39S 126 24 E
Tighina, Moldova 25 E4 46 50N 29 30 E
Tigil, Russia 27 D16 57 49N 158 40 E
Tignish, Canada 71 C7 46 58N 64 2W
Tigre →, Peru 92 D4 4 30S 74 10W
Tigre →, Venezuela 92 B6 9 20N 62 30W
Tigris = Dijlah, Nahr →, Asia 44 D5 31 0N 47 25 E
Tigyaing, Burma 41 H20 23 45N 96 10 E
Tijuana, Mexico 85 N9 32 30N 117 10W
Tikal, Guatemala 88 C2 17 13N 89 24W
Tikamgarh, India 43 G8 24 44N 78 50 E
Tikhoretsk, Russia 25 E7 45 56N 40 5 E
Tikrīt, Iraq 44 C4 34 35N 43 37 E
Tiksi, Russia 27 B13 71 40N 128 45 E
Tilamuta, Indonesia 37 D6 0 32N 122 23 E
Tilburg, Neths. 15 C5 51 31N 5 6 E
Tilbury, Canada 70 D3 42 17N 82 23W
Tilbury, U.K. 11 F8 51 27N 0 22 E
Tilcara, Argentina 94 A2 23 36S 65 23W
Tilden, Nebr., U.S.A. 80 D6 42 3N 97 50W
Tilden, Tex., U.S.A. 81 L5 28 28N 98 33W
Tilhar, India 43 F8 28 0N 79 45 E
Tilichiki, Russia 27 C17 60 27N 166 5 E
Tílissos, Greece 23 D7 35 20N 25 1 E
Till →, U.K. 10 B5 55 41N 2 13W
Tillamook, U.S.A. 82 D2 45 27N 123 51W
Tillsonburg, Canada 70 D3 42 53N 80 44W
Tillyeria □, Cyprus 23 D11 35 6N 32 40 E
Tílos, Greece 21 F12 36 27N 27 27 E
Tilpa, Australia 63 E3 30 57S 144 24 E
Tilsit = Sovetsk, Russia 24 C3 55 6N 21 50 E
Tilt →, U.K. 12 E5 56 46N 3 51W
Tilton, U.S.A. 79 C13 43 27N 71 36W
Timagami L., Canada 70 C3 47 0N 80 10W
Timanskiy Kryazh, Russia 24 A9 65 58N 50 5 E
Timaru, N.Z. 59 L3 44 23S 171 14 E
Timau, Kenya 54 B4 0 4N 37 15 E
Timbákion, Greece 23 D6 35 4N 24 45 E
Timber Lake, U.S.A. 80 C4 45 26N 101 5W
Timber Mt., U.S.A. 84 H10 37 6N 116 28W
Timboon, Australia 63 F3 38 30S 142 58 E
Timbuktu = Tombouctou, Mali 50 E5 16 50N 3 0W
Timi, Cyprus 23 E11 34 44N 32 31 E
Timimoun, Algeria 50 C6 29 14N 0 16 E
Timişoara, Romania 17 F11 45 43N 21 15 E
Timmins, Canada 70 C3 48 28N 81 25W
Timok →, Serbia, Yug. 21 B10 44 10N 22 40 E
Timor, Indonesia 37 F7 9 0S 125 0 E
Timor Sea, Ind. Oc. 60 B4 12 0S 127 0 E
Timor Timur □, Indonesia 37 F7 9 0S 125 0 E
Tin Mt., U.S.A. 84 J9 36 50N 117 10W
Tinaca Pt., Phil. 37 C7 5 30N 125 25 E
Tinajo, Canary Is. 22 E6 29 4N 13 42W
Tindouf, Algeria 50 C4 27 42N 8 10W
Tinggi, Pulau, Malaysia 39 L5 2 18N 104 7 E
Tingo Maria, Peru 92 E3 9 10S 75 54W
Tinh Bien, Vietnam 39 G5 10 36N 104 57 E
Tinkurrin, Australia 61 F2 32 59S 117 46 E
Tinnevelly = Tirunelveli, India 40 Q10 8 45N 77 45 E
Tinogasta, Argentina 94 B2 28 5S 67 32W
Tintina, Argentina 94 B3 27 2S 62 45W
Tintinara, Australia 63 F3 35 48S 140 2 E
Tioga, U.S.A. 78 E7 41 55N 77 8W
Tioman, Pulau, Malaysia 39 L5 2 50N 104 10 E
Tionesta, U.S.A. 78 E5 41 30N 79 28W
Tipongpani, India 41 F19 27 20N 95 55 E
Tipperary, Ireland 13 D3 52 28N 8 10W
Tipperary □, Ireland 13 D4 52 37N 7 55W
Tipton, Calif., U.S.A. 84 J7 36 4N 119 19W
Tipton, Ind., U.S.A. 76 E2 40 17N 86 2W
Tipton, Iowa, U.S.A. 80 E9 41 46N 91 8W
Tipton Mt., U.S.A. 85 K12 35 32N 114 12W
Tiptonville, U.S.A. 81 G10 36 23N 89 29W
Tīrān, Iran 45 C6 32 45N 51 8 E
Tirana, Albania 21 D8 41 18N 19 49 E
Tiranë = Tirana, Albania 21 D8 41 18N 19 49 E
Tiraspol, Moldova 25 E4 46 55N 29 35 E
Tire, Turkey 21 E12 38 5N 27 45 E
Tirebolu, Turkey 25 F6 40 58N 38 45 E
Tiree, U.K. 12 E2 56 31N 6 55W
Tiree, Passage of, U.K. 12 E2 56 30N 6 30W
Tîrgovişte = Târgovişte, Romania 17 F13 44 55N 25 27 E
Tîrgu-Jiu = Târgu-Jiu, Romania 17 F12 45 5N 23 19 E
Tîrgu Mureş = Târgu Mureş, Romania 17 E13 46 31N 24 38 E
Tirich Mir, Pakistan 40 A7 36 15N 71 55 E
Tírnavos, Greece 21 E10 39 45N 22 18 E
Tirodi, India 40 J11 21 40N 79 44 E
Tirol □, Austria 16 E6 47 3N 10 43 E
Tirso →, Italy 20 E3 39 53N 8 32 E
Tiruchchirappalli, India 40 P11 10 45N 78 45 E
Tirunelveli, India 40 Q10 8 45N 77 45 E
Tirupati, India 40 N11 13 39N 79 25 E
Tiruppur, India 40 P10 11 5N 77 22 E
Tiruvannamalai, India 40 N11 12 15N 79 5 E
Tisa →, Serbia, Yug. 21 B9 45 15N 20 17 E
Tisdale, Canada 73 C8 52 50N 104 0W
Tishomingo, U.S.A. 81 H6 34 14N 96 41W
Tisza = Tisa →, Serbia, Yug. 21 B9 45 15N 20 17 E
Tit-Ary, Russia 27 B13 71 55N 127 2 E
Tithwal, Pakistan 43 B5 34 21N 73 50 E
Titicaca, L., S. Amer. 92 G5 15 30S 69 30W
Titograd = Podgorica, Montenegro, Yug. 21 C8 42 30N 19 19 E
Titule, Dem. Rep. of the Congo 54 B2 3 15N 25 31 E
Titusville, Fla., U.S.A. 77 L5 28 37N 80 49W
Titusville, Pa., U.S.A. 78 E5 41 38N 79 41W
Tivaouane, Senegal 50 F2 14 56N 16 45W
Tiverton, U.K. 11 G4 50 54N 3 29W
Tívoli, Italy 20 D5 41 58N 12 45 E
Tizi-Ouzou, Algeria 50 A6 36 42N 4 3 E
Tizimín, Mexico 87 C7 21 0N 88 1W
Tjeggelvas, Sweden 8 C17 66 37N 17 45 E
Tjirebon = Cirebon, Indonesia 37 G13 6 45S 108 32 E
Tjörn, Sweden 9 G14 58 0N 11 35 E
Tlacotalpan, Mexico 87 D5 18 37N 95 40W
Tlahualilo, Mexico 86 B4 26 20N 103 30W
Tlaquepaque, Mexico 86 C4 20 39N 103 19W
Tlaxcala, Mexico 87 D5 19 20N 98 14W
Tlaxcala □, Mexico 87 D5 19 30N 98 20W
Tlaxiaco, Mexico 87 D5 17 18N 97 40W
Tlell, Canada 72 C2 53 34N 131 56W
Tlemcen, Algeria 50 B5 34 52N 1 21W
To Bong, Vietnam 38 F7 12 45N 109 16 E
Toad →, Canada 72 B4 59 25N 124 57W
Toamasina, Madag. 57 B8 18 10S 49 25 E
Toamasina □, Madag. 57 B8 18 0S 49 0 E
Toay, Argentina 94 D3 36 43S 64 38W
Toba, Japan 31 G8 34 30N 136 51 E
Toba, Danau, Indonesia 36 D1 2 30N 97 30 E
Toba Kakar, Pakistan 42 D3 31 30N 69 0 E
Toba Tek Singh, Pakistan 42 D5 30 55N 72 25 E
Tobago, W. Indies 89 D7 11 10N 60 30W
Tobelo, Indonesia 37 D7 1 45N 127 56 E
Tobermorey, Australia 62 C2 22 12S 138 0 E
Tobermory, Canada 70 C3 45 12N 81 40W
Tobermory, U.K. 12 E2 56 38N 6 5W
Tobin, U.S.A. 84 F5 39 55N 121 19W
Tobin, L., Australia 60 D4 21 45S 125 49 E
Tobin L., Canada 73 C8 53 35N 103 30W
Toboali, Indonesia 36 E3 3 0S 106 25 E
Tobol →, Russia 26 D7 58 10N 68 12 E
Toboli, Indonesia 37 E6 0 38S 120 5 E
Tobolsk, Russia 26 D7 58 15N 68 10 E
Tobruk = Tubruq, Libya 51 B10 32 7N 23 55 E
Tobyhanna, U.S.A. 79 E9 41 11N 75 25W
Tobyl = Tobol →, Russia 26 D7 58 10N 68 12 E
Tocantinópolis, Brazil 93 E9 6 20S 47 25W
Tocantins □, Brazil 93 F9 10 0S 48 0W
Tocantins →, Brazil 93 D9 1 45S 49 10W
Toccoa, U.S.A. 77 H4 34 35N 83 19W
Tochigi, Japan 31 F9 36 25N 139 45 E
Tochigi □, Japan 31 F9 36 45N 139 45 E
Tocopilla, Chile 94 A1 22 5S 70 10W
Tocumwal, Australia 63 F4 35 51S 145 31 E
Tocuyo →, Venezuela 92 A5 11 3N 68 23W
Todd →, Australia 62 C2 24 52S 135 48 E
Todeli, Indonesia 37 E6 1 38S 124 34 E
Todenyang, Kenya 54 B4 4 35N 35 56 E
Todos os Santos, B. de, Brazil 93 F11 12 48S 38 38W
Todos Santos, Mexico 86 C2 23 27N 110 13W
Toe Hd., U.K. 12 D1 57 50N 7 8W
Tofield, Canada 72 C6 53 25N 112 40W
Tofino, Canada 72 D3 49 11N 125 55W
Tofua, Tonga 59 D11 19 45S 175 5W
Tōgane, Japan 31 G10 35 33N 140 22 E
Togian, Kepulauan, Indonesia 37 E6 0 20S 121 50 E
Togliatti, Russia 24 D8 53 32N 49 24 E
Togo ■, W. Afr. 50 G6 8 30N 1 35 E
Togtoh, China 34 D6 40 15N 111 10 E
Tōhoku □, Japan 30 E10 39 50N 141 45 E
Toinya, Sudan 51 G11 6 17N 29 46 E
Tojikiston = Tajikistan ■, Asia 26 F8 38 30N 70 0 E
Tojo, Indonesia 37 E6 1 20S 121 15 E
Tōjō, Japan 31 G6 34 53N 133 16 E
Tokachi-Dake, Japan 30 C11 43 17N 142 5 E
Tokachi-Gawa →, Japan 30 C11 42 44N 143 42 E
Tokala, Indonesia 37 E6 1 30S 121 40 E
Tōkamachi, Japan 31 F9 37 8N 138 43 E
Tokanui, N.Z. 59 M2 46 34S 168 56 E
Tokara-Rettō, Japan 31 K4 29 37N 129 43 E
Tokarahi, N.Z. 59 L3 44 56S 170 39 E
Tokashiki-Shima, Japan 31 L3 26 11N 127 21 E
Tŏkchŏn, N. Korea 35 E14 39 45N 126 18 E
Tokeland, U.S.A. 84 D3 46 42N 123 59W
Tokelau Is., Pac. Oc. 64 H10 9 0S 171 45W
Tokmak, Kyrgyzstan 26 E8 42 49N 75 15 E
Toko Ra., Australia 62 C2 23 5S 138 20 E
Tokoro-Gawa →, Japan 30 B12 44 7N 144 5 E
Tokuno-Shima, Japan 31 L4 27 56N 128 55 E
Tokushima, Japan 31 G7 34 4N 134 34 E
Tokushima □, Japan 31 H7 33 55N 134 0 E
Tokuyama, Japan 31 G5 34 3N 131 50 E
Tōkyō, Japan 31 G9 35 45N 139 45 E
Tolaga Bay, N.Z. 59 H7 38 21S 178 20 E
Tolbukhin = Dobrich, Bulgaria 21 C12 43 37N 27 49 E
Toledo, Spain 19 C3 39 50N 4 2W
Toledo, Ohio, U.S.A. 76 E4 41 39N 83 33W
Toledo, Oreg., U.S.A. 82 D2 44 37N 123 56W
Toledo, Wash., U.S.A. 82 C2 46 26N 122 51W
Toledo, Montes de, Spain 19 C3 39 33N 4 20W
Toliara, Madag. 57 C7 23 21S 43 40 E
Toliara □, Madag. 57 C8 21 0S 45 0 E
Tolima, Colombia 92 C3 4 40N 75 19W
Tolitoli, Indonesia 37 D6 1 5N 120 50 E
Tollhouse, U.S.A. 84 H7 37 1N 119 24W
Tolo, Teluk, Indonesia 37 E6 2 20S 122 10 E
Toluca, Mexico 87 D5 19 20N 99 40W
Tom Burke, S. Africa 57 C4 23 5S 28 0 E
Tom Price, Australia 60 D2 22 40S 117 48 E
Tomah, U.S.A. 80 D9 43 59N 90 30W
Tomahawk, U.S.A. 80 C10 45 28N 89 44W
Tomakomai, Japan 30 C10 42 38N 141 36 E
Tomales, U.S.A. 84 G4 38 15N 122 53W
Tomales B., U.S.A. 84 G3 38 15N 123 58W
Tomar, Portugal 19 C1 39 36N 8 25W
Tomaszów Mazowiecki, Poland 17 C10 51 30N 20 2 E
Tomatlán, Mexico 86 D3 19 56N 105 15W
Tombador, Serra do, Brazil 92 F7 12 0S 58 0W
Tombigbee →, U.S.A. 77 K2 31 8N 87 57W
Tombouctou, Mali 50 E5 16 50N 3 0W
Tombstone, U.S.A. 83 L8 31 43N 110 4W
Tombua, Angola 56 B1 15 55S 11 55 E
Tomé, Chile 94 D1 36 36S 72 57W
Tomelloso, Spain 19 C4 39 10N 3 2W
Tomingley, Australia 63 E4 32 26S 148 16 E
Tomini, Indonesia 37 D6 0 30N 120 30 E
Tomini, Teluk, Indonesia 37 E6 0 10S 122 0 E
Tomintoul, U.K. 12 D5 57 15N 3 23W
Tomkinson Ranges, Australia 61 E4 26 11S 129 5 E
Tommot, Russia 27 D13 59 4N 126 20 E
Tomnop Ta Suos, Cambodia 39 G5 11 20N 104 15 E
Tomo →, Colombia 92 B5 5 20N 67 48W
Toms Place, U.S.A. 84 H8 37 34N 118 41W
Toms River, U.S.A. 79 G10 39 58N 74 12W
Tomsk, Russia 26 D9 56 30N 85 5 E
Tonalá, Mexico 87 D6 16 8N 93 41W
Tonalea, U.S.A. 83 H8 36 19N 110 56W
Tonantins, Brazil 92 D5 2 45S 67 45W
Tonasket, U.S.A. 82 B4 48 42N 119 26W
Tonawanda, U.S.A. 78 D6 43 1N 78 53W
Tonbridge, U.K. 11 F8 51 11N 0 17 E
Tondano, Indonesia 37 D6 1 35N 124 54 E
Tonekābon, Iran 45 B6 36 45N 51 12 E
Tong Xian, China 34 E9 39 55N 116 35 E
Tonga ■, Pac. Oc. 59 D11 19 50S 174 30W
Tonga Trench, Pac. Oc. 64 J10 18 0S 173 0W
Tongaat, S. Africa 57 D5 29 33S 31 9 E
Tongareva, Cook Is. 65 H12 9 0S 158 0W
Tongatapu, Tonga 59 E12 21 10S 174 0W
Tongchŏn-ni, N. Korea 35 E14 39 50N 127 25 E
Tongchuan, China 34 G5 35 6N 109 3 E
Tongeren, Belgium 15 D5 50 47N 5 28 E
Tongguan, China 34 G6 34 40N 110 25 E
Tonghua, China 35 D13 41 42N 125 58 E
Tongjosŏn Man, N. Korea 35 E15 39 30N 128 0 E
Tongking, G. of = Tonkin, G. of, Asia 32 E5 20 0N 108 0 E
Tongliao, China 35 C12 43 38N 122 18 E
Tongnae, S. Korea 35 G15 35 12N 129 5 E
Tongobory, Madag. 57 C7 23 32S 44 20 E
Tongoy, Chile 94 C1 30 16S 71 31W
Tongres = Tongeren, Belgium 15 D5 50 47N 5 28 E
Tongsa Dzong, Bhutan 41 F17 27 31N 90 31 E
Tongue, U.K. 12 C4 58 29N 4 25W
Tongue →, U.S.A. 80 B2 46 25N 105 52W
Tongwei, China 34 G3 35 0N 105 5 E
Tongxin, China 34 F3 36 59N 105 58 E
Tongyang, N. Korea 35 E14 39 9N 126 53 E
Tongyu, China 35 B12 44 45N 123 4 E
Tonk, India 42 F6 26 6N 75 54 E
Tonkawa, U.S.A. 81 G6 36 41N 97 18W
Tonkin = Bac Phan, Vietnam 38 B5 22 0N 105 0 E
Tonkin, G. of, Asia 32 E5 20 0N 108 0 E
Tonle Sap, Cambodia 38 F5 13 0N 104 0 E
Tono, Japan 30 E10 39 19N 141 32 E
Tonopah, U.S.A. 83 G5 38 4N 117 14W
Tonosí, Panama 88 E3 7 20N 80 20W
Tønsberg, Norway 9 G14 59 19N 10 25 E
Tooele, U.S.A. 82 F7 40 32N 112 18W
Toompine, Australia 63 D3 27 15S 144 19 E
Toonpan, Australia 62 B4 19 28S 146 48 E
Toora, Australia 63 F4 38 39S 146 23 E
Toora-Khem, Russia 27 D10 52 28N 96 17 E
Toowoomba, Australia 63 D5 27 32S 151 56 E
Top-ozero, Russia 24 A5 65 35N 32 0 E
Topaz, U.S.A. 84 G7 38 41N 119 30W
Topeka, U.S.A. 80 F7 39 3N 95 40W
Topley, Canada 72 C3 54 49N 126 18W
Topocalma, Pta., Chile 94 C1 34 10S 72 2W
Topock, U.S.A. 85 L12 34 46N 114 29W
Topol'čany, Slovak Rep. 17 D10 48 35N 18 12 E
Topolobampo, Mexico 86 B3 25 40N 109 4W
Toppenish, U.S.A. 82 C3 46 23N 120 19W
Toraka Vestale, Madag. 57 B7 16 20S 43 58 E
Torata, Peru 92 G4 17 23S 70 1W
Torbalı, Turkey 21 E12 38 10N 27 21 E
Torbay, Canada 71 C9 47 40N 52 42W
Torbay □, U.K. 11 G4 50 26N 3 31W
Tordesillas, Spain 19 B3 41 30N 5 0W
Torfaen □, U.K. 11 F4 51 43N 3 3W
Torgau, Germany 16 C7 51 34N 13 0 E
Torhout, Belgium 15 C3 51 5N 3 7 E
Tori-Shima, Japan 31 J10 30 29N 140 19 E
Torin, Mexico 86 B2 27 33N 110 15W
Torino, Italy 18 D7 45 3N 7 40 E
Torit, Sudan 51 H12 4 27N 32 31 E
Tormes →, Spain 19 B2 41 18N 6 29W
Tornado Mt., Canada 72 D6 49 55N 114 40W
Torne älv →, Sweden 8 D21 65 50N 24 12 E
Torneå = Tornio, Finland 8 D21 65 50N 24 12 E
Torneträsk, Sweden 8 B18 68 24N 19 15 E
Tornio, Finland 8 D21 65 50N 24 12 E
Tornionjoki →, Finland 8 D21 65 50N 24 12 E
Tornquist, Argentina 94 D3 38 8S 62 15W
Toro, Spain 22 B11 39 59N 4 8 E
Toro, Cerro del, Chile 94 B2 29 10S 69 50W
Toro Pk., U.S.A. 85 M10 33 34N 116 24W
Toroníios Kólpos, Greece 21 D10 40 5N 23 30 E
Toronto, Australia 63 E5 33 0S 151 30 E
Toronto, Canada 70 D4 43 39N 79 20W
Toronto, U.S.A. 78 F4 40 28N 80 36W
Toropets, Russia 24 C5 56 30N 31 40 E
Tororo, Uganda 54 B3 0 45N 34 12 E
Toros Dağları, Turkey 25 G5 37 0N 32 30 E
Torquay, Canada 73 D8 49 9N 103 30W
Torquay, U.K. 11 G4 50 27N 3 32W
Torrance, U.S.A. 85 M8 33 50N 118 19W
Torre de Moncorvo, Portugal 19 B2 41 12N 7 8W
Torre del Greco, Italy 20 D6 40 47N 14 22 E
Torrejón de Ardoz, Spain 19 B4 40 27N 3 29W
Torrelavega, Spain 19 A3 43 20N 4 5W
Torremolinos, Spain 19 D3 36 38N 4 30W
Torrens, L., Australia 63 E2 31 0S 137 50 E
Torrens Cr. →, Australia 62 C4 22 23S 145 9 E
Torrens Creek, Australia 62 C4 20 48S 145 3 E
Torrent, Spain 19 C5 39 27N 0 28W
Torreón, Mexico 86 B4 25 33N 103 26W
Torres, Mexico 86 B2 28 46N 110 47W
Torres Strait, Australia 64 H6 9 50S 142 20 E
Torres Vedras, Portugal 19 C1 39 5N 9 15W
Torrevieja, Spain 19 D5 37 59N 0 42W
Torrey, U.S.A. 83 G8 38 18N 111 25W
Torridge →, U.K. 11 G3 51 0N 4 13W
Torridon, L., U.K. 12 D3 57 35N 5 50W
Torrington, Conn., U.S.A. 79 E11 41 48N 73 7W
Torrington, Wyo., U.S.A. 80 D2 42 4N 104 11W
Tórshavn, Færoe Is. 8 E9 62 5N 6 56W
Tortola, Virgin Is. 89 C7 18 19N 64 45W
Tortosa, Spain 19 B6 40 49N 0 31 E
Tortosa, C., Spain 19 B6 40 41N 0 52 E
Tortue, I. de la, Haiti 89 B5 20 5N 72 57W
Torūd, Iran 45 C7 35 25N 55 5 E
Toruń, Poland 17 B10 53 2N 18 39 E
Tory I., Ireland 13 A3 55 16N 8 14W
Tosa, Japan 31 H6 33 24N 133 23 E
Tosa-Shimizu, Japan 31 H6 32 52N 132 58 E
Tosa-Wan, Japan 31 H6 33 15N 133 30 E
Toscana □, Italy 20 C4 43 25N 11 0 E
Toshkent, Uzbekistan 26 E7 41 20N 69 10 E
Tostado, Argentina 94 B3 29 15S 61 50W
Tostón, Pta. de, Canary Is. 22 F5 28 42N 14 2W
Tosu, Japan 31 H5 33 22N 130 31 E
Toteng, Botswana 56 C3 20 22S 22 58 E
Totma, Russia 24 C7 60 0N 42 40 E
Totnes, U.K. 11 G4 50 26N 3 42W
Totness, Surinam 93 B7 5 53N 56 19W
Totonicapán, Guatemala 88 D1 14 58N 91 12W
Totten Glacier, Antarctica 5 C8 66 45S 116 10 E
Tottenham, Australia 63 E4 32 14S 147 21 E
Tottenham, Canada 78 B5 44 1N 79 49W
Tottori, Japan 31 G7 35 30N 134 15 E
Tottori □, Japan 31 G7 35 30N 134 12 E
Toubkal, Djebel, Morocco 50 B4 31 0N 8 0W
Tougan, Burkina Faso 50 F5 13 11N 2 58W
Touggourt, Algeria 50 B7 33 6N 6 4 E
Toul, France 18 B6 48 40N 5 53 E
Toulon, France 18 E6 43 10N 5 55 E
Toulouse, France 18 E4 43 37N 1 27 E
Toummo, Niger 51 D8 22 45N 14 8 E

Tursāq

W

Westmeath

Wanapitei L., *Canada* ... **70 C3** 46 45N 80 40W
Wanbi, *Australia* .... **63 E3** 34 46S 140 17 E
Wandarrie, *Australia* ... **61 E2** 27 50S 117 52 E
Wanderer, *Zimbabwe* ... **55 F3** 19 36S 30 1 E
Wandoan, *Australia* .... **63 D4** 26 5S 149 55 E
Wanfu, *China* .... **35 D12** 40 8N 122 38 E
Wang →, *Thailand* .... **38 D2** 17 8N 99 2 E
Wang Noi, *Thailand* .... **38 E3** 14 13N 100 44 E
Wang Saphung, *Thailand* **38 D3** 17 18N 101 46 E
Wang Thong, *Thailand* .. **38 D3** 16 50N 100 26 E
Wanga,
Dem. Rep. of the Congo **54 B2** 2 58N 29 12 E
Wangal, *Indonesia* ...... **37 F8** 6 8S 134 9 E
Wanganella, *Australia* ... **63 F3** 35 6S 144 49 E
Wanganui, *N.Z.* .... **59 H5** 39 56S 175 3 E
Wangaratta, *Australia* ... **63 F4** 36 21S 146 19 E
Wangary, *Australia* ..... **63 E2** 34 35S 135 29 E
Wangdu, *China* .... **34 E8** 38 40N 115 7 E
Wangerooge, *Germany* .. **16 B4** 53 47N 7 54 E
Wangi, *Kenya* .... **54 C5** 1 58S 40 58 E
Wangiwangi, *Indonesia* .. **37 F6** 5 22S 123 37 E
Wangqing, *China* .... **35 C15** 43 12N 129 42 E
Wankaner, *India* .... **42 H4** 22 35N 71 0 E
Wanless, *Canada* **73 C8** 54 11N 101 21W
Wanning, *Taiwan* .... **38 C8** 23 15N 121 17 E
Wanon Niwat, *Thailand* .. **38 D4** 17 38N 103 46 E
Wanquan, *China* .... **34 D8** 40 50N 114 40 E
Wanrong, *China* .... **34 G6** 35 25N 110 50 E
Wantage, *U.K.* **11 F6** 51 35N 1 25W
Wanxian, *China* .... **33 C5** 30 42N 108 20 E
Wapakoneta, *U.S.A.* **76 E3** 40 34N 84 12W
Wapato, *U.S.A.* **82 C3** 46 27N 120 25W
Wapawekka L., *Canada* .. **73 C8** 54 55N 104 40W
Wapikopa L., *Canada* **70 B2** 52 56N 87 53W
Wappingers Falls, *U.S.A.* **79 E11** 41 36N 73 55W
Wapsipinicon →, *U.S.A.* **80 E9** 41 44N 90 19W
Warangal, *India* .... **40 L11** 17 58N 79 35 E
Waratah, *Australia* ...... **62 G4** 41 30S 145 30 E
Waratah B., *Australia* ... **63 F4** 38 54S 146 5 E
Warburton, *Vic., Australia* **63 F4** 37 47S 145 42 E
Warburton, *W. Austral., Australia* .... **61 E4** 26 8S 126 35 E
Warburton Ra., *Australia* **61 E4** 25 55S 126 28 E
Ward, *N.Z.* .... **59 J5** 41 49S 174 11 E
Ward →, *Australia* .... **63 D4** 26 28S 146 6 E
Ward Cove, *U.S.A.* **72 B2** 55 25N 132 43W
Ward Mt., *U.S.A.* **84 H8** 37 12N 118 54W
Warden, *S. Africa* .... **57 D4** 27 50S 29 0 E
Wardha, *India* .... **40 J11** 20 45N 78 39 E
Wardha →, *India* ...... **40 K11** 19 57N 79 11 E
Wardlow, *Canada* **72 C6** 50 56N 111 31W
Ware, *Canada* **72 B3** 57 26N 125 41W
Ware, *U.S.A.* **79 D12** 42 16N 72 14W
Waregem, *Belgium* ...... **15 D3** 50 53N 3 27 E
Wareham, *U.S.A.* **79 E14** 41 46N 70 43W
Waremme, *Belgium* ..... **15 D5** 50 43N 5 15 E
Warialda, *Australia* ..... **63 D5** 29 29S 150 33 E
Wariap, *Indonesia* ...... **37 E8** 1 30S 134 5 E
Warin Chamrap, *Thailand* **38 E5** 15 12N 104 53 E
Warkopi, *Indonesia* ..... **37 E8** 1 12S 134 9 E
Warm Springs, *U.S.A.* ... **83 G5** 38 10N 116 20W
Warman, *Canada* **73 C7** 52 19N 106 30W
Warmbad, *Namibia* ..... **56 D2** 28 25S 18 42 E
Warmbad, *S. Africa* ..... **57 C4** 24 51S 28 19 E
Warminster, *U.K.* **11 F5** 51 12N 2 10W
Warnambool Downs, *Australia* .... **62 C3** 22 48S 142 52 E
Warner, *Canada* **72 D6** 49 17N 112 12W
Warner Mts., *U.S.A.* **82 F3** 41 40N 120 15W
Warner Robins, *U.S.A.* .. **77 J4** 32 37N 83 36W
Waroona, *Australia* ..... **61 F2** 32 50S 115 58 E
Warracknabeal, *Australia* **63 F3** 36 9S 142 26 E
Warragul, *Australia* ..... **63 F4** 38 10S 145 58 E
Warrawagine, *Australia* .. **60 D3** 20 51S 120 42 E
Warrego →, *Australia* .. **63 E4** 30 24S 145 21 E
Warrego Ra., *Australia* .. **62 C4** 24 58S 146 0 E
Warren, *Australia* .... **63 E4** 31 42S 147 51 E
Warren, *Ark., U.S.A.* **81 J8** 33 37N 92 4W
Warren, *Mich., U.S.A.* ... **76 D4** 42 30N 83 0W
Warren, *Minn., U.S.A.* ... **80 A6** 48 12N 96 46W
Warren, *Ohio, U.S.A.* **78 E4** 41 14N 80 49W
Warren, *Pa., U.S.A.* **78 E5** 41 51N 79 9W
Warrenpoint, *U.K.* **13 B5** 54 6N 6 15W
Warrensburg, *U.S.A.* **80 F8** 38 46N 93 44W
Warrenton, *S. Africa* .... **56 D3** 28 9S 24 47 E
Warrenton, *U.S.A.* **84 D3** 46 10N 123 56W
Warrenville, *Australia* ... **63 D4** 25 48S 147 22 E
Warri, *Nigeria* .... **50 G7** 5 30N 5 41 E
Warrina, *Australia* ...... **63 D2** 28 12S 135 50 E
Warrington, *U.K.* **10 D5** 53 24N 2 35W
Warrington, *U.S.A.* **77 K2** 30 23N 87 17W
Warrington □, *U.K.* **10 D5** 53 24N 2 35W
Warrnambool, *Australia* .. **63 F3** 38 25S 142 30 E
Warroad, *U.S.A.* **80 A7** 48 54N 95 19W
Warsa, *Indonesia* .... **37 E9** 0 47S 135 55 E
Warsaw = Warszawa, *Poland* .... **17 B11** 52 13N 21 0 E
Warsaw, *Ind., U.S.A.* **76 E3** 41 14N 85 51W
Warsaw, *N.Y., U.S.A.* **78 D6** 42 45N 78 8W
Warsaw, *Ohio, U.S.A.* ... **78 F3** 40 20N 82 0W
Warszawa, *Poland* ...... **17 B11** 52 13N 21 0 E
Warta →, *Poland* ...... **16 B8** 52 35N 14 39 E
Warthe = Warta →, *Poland* .... **16 B8** 52 35N 14 39 E
Waru, *Indonesia* .... **37 E8** 3 30S 130 36 E
Warwick, *Australia* ..... **63 D5** 28 10S 152 1 E
Warwick, *U.K.* **11 E6** 52 18N 1 35W
Warwick, *U.S.A.* **79 E13** 41 42N 71 28W
Warwickshire □, *U.K.* ... **11 E6** 52 14N 1 38W
Wasaga Beach, *Canada* .. **78 B4** 44 31N 80 1W
Wasatch Ra., *U.S.A.* **82 F8** 40 30N 111 15W
Wasbank, *S. Africa* ..... **57 D5** 28 15S 30 9 E
Wasco, *Calif., U.S.A.* **85 K7** 35 36N 119 20W
Wasco, *Oreg., U.S.A.* ... **82 D3** 45 36N 120 42W
Waseca, *U.S.A.* **80 C8** 44 5N 93 30W
Wasekamio L., *Canada* .. **73 B7** 56 45N 108 45W
Wash, The, *U.K.* .... **10 E8** 52 58N 0 20 E
Washago, *Canada* **78 B5** 44 45N 79 20W
Washburn, *N. Dak., U.S.A.* **80 B4** 47 17N 101 2W
Washburn, *Wis., U.S.A.* .. **80 B9** 46 40N 90 54W
Washim, *India* .... **40 J10** 20 3N 77 0 E
Washington, *U.K.* **10 C6** 54 55N 1 30W
Washington, *D.C., U.S.A.* **76 F7** 38 54N 77 2W
Washington, *Ga., U.S.A.* . **77 J4** 33 44N 82 44W
Washington, *Ind., U.S.A.* . **76 F2** 38 40N 87 10W
Washington, *Iowa, U.S.A.* **80 E9** 41 18N 91 42W
Washington, *Mo., U.S.A.* . **80 F9** 38 33N 91 1W
Washington, *N.C., U.S.A.* . **77 H7** 35 33N 77 3W
Washington, *N.J., U.S.A.* . **79 F10** 40 46N 74 59W
Washington, *Pa., U.S.A.* . **78 F4** 40 10N 80 15W
Washington, *Utah, U.S.A.* **83 H7** 37 8N 113 31W
Washington □, *U.S.A.* ... **82 C3** 47 30N 120 30W
Washington, Mt., *U.S.A.* . **79 B13** 44 16N 71 18W
Washington I., *U.S.A.* ... **76 C2** 45 23N 86 54W
Washougal, *U.S.A.* **84 E4** 45 35N 122 21W
Wasian, *Indonesia* ...... **37 E8** 1 47S 133 19 E
Wasior, *Indonesia* ...... **37 E8** 2 43S 134 30 E
Waskaganish, *Canada* ... **70 B4** 51 30N 78 40W
Waskaiowaka, L., *Canada* **73 B9** 56 33N 96 23W
Waskesiu Lake, *Canada* .. **73 C7** 53 55N 106 5W
Wasserkuppe, *Germany* . **16 C5** 50 29N 9 55 E
Waswanipi, *Canada* **70 C4** 49 40N 76 29W
Waswanipi, L., *Canada* .. **70 C4** 49 35N 76 40W
Watampone, *Indonesia* .. **37 E6** 4 29S 120 25 E
Water Park Pt., *Australia* . **62 C5** 22 56S 150 47 E
Water Valley, *U.S.A.* **81 H10** 34 10N 89 38W
Waterberge, *S. Africa* ... **57 C4** 24 10S 28 0 E
Waterbury, *Conn., U.S.A.* **79 E11** 41 33N 73 3W
Waterbury, *Vt., U.S.A.* ... **79 B12** 44 20N 72 46W
Waterbury L., *Canada* ... **73 B8** 58 10N 104 22W
Waterdown, *Canada* **78 C5** 43 20N 79 53W
Waterford, *Canada* **78 D4** 42 56N 80 17W
Waterford, *Ireland* **13 D4** 52 15N 7 8W
Waterford, *U.S.A.* **84 H6** 37 38N 120 46W
Waterford □, *Ireland* ... **13 D4** 52 10N 7 40W
Waterford Harbour, *Ireland* **13 D5** 52 8N 6 58W
Waterhen L., *Man., Canada* **73 C9** 52 10N 99 40W
Waterhen L., *Sask., Canada* **73 C7** 54 28N 108 25W
Waterloo, *Belgium* ...... **15 D4** 50 43N 4 25 E
Waterloo, *Ont., Canada* .. **70 D3** 43 30N 80 32W
Waterloo, *Qué., Canada* .. **79 A12** 45 22N 72 32W
Waterloo, *Ill., U.S.A.* **80 F9** 38 20N 90 9W
Waterloo, *Iowa, U.S.A.* ... **80 D8** 42 30N 92 21W
Waterloo, *N.Y., U.S.A.* ... **78 D8** 42 54N 76 52W
Watersmeet, *U.S.A.* **80 B10** 46 16N 89 11W
Waterton-Glacier International Peace Park, *U.S.A.* **82 B7** 48 45N 115 0W
Watertown, *Conn., U.S.A.* **79 E11** 41 36N 73 7W
Watertown, *N.Y., U.S.A.* . **79 C9** 43 59N 75 55W
Watertown, *S. Dak., U.S.A.* **80 C6** 44 54N 97 7W
Watertown, *Wis., U.S.A.* . **80 D10** 43 12N 88 43W
Waterval-Boven, *S. Africa* **57 D5** 25 40S 30 18 E
Waterville, *Canada* **79 A13** 45 16N 71 54W
Waterville, *Maine, U.S.A.* **71 D6** 44 33N 69 38W
Waterville, *N.Y., U.S.A.* .. **79 D9** 42 56N 75 23W
Waterville, *Pa., U.S.A.* ... **78 E7** 41 19N 77 21W
Waterville, *Wash., U.S.A.* **82 C3** 47 39N 120 4W
Watervliet, *U.S.A.* **79 D11** 42 44N 73 42W
Wates, *Indonesia* .... **37 G14** 7 51S 110 10 E
Watford, *Canada* **78 D3** 42 57N 81 53W
Watford, *U.K.* **11 F7** 51 40N 0 24W
Watford City, *U.S.A.* **80 B3** 47 48N 103 17W
Wathaman →, *Canada* .. **73 B8** 57 16N 102 59W
Watheroo, *Australia* .... **61 F2** 30 15S 116 0 E
Wating, *China* .... **34 G4** 35 40N 106 38 E
Watkins Glen, *U.S.A.* **78 D8** 42 23N 76 52W
Watling I. = San Salvador, *Bahamas* **89 B5** 24 0N 74 40W
Watonga, *U.S.A.* **81 H5** 35 51N 98 25W
Watrous, *Canada* **73 C7** 51 40N 105 25W
Watrous, *U.S.A.* **81 H2** 35 48N 104 59W
Watsa, *Dem. Rep. of the Congo* **54 B2** 3 4N 29 30 E
Watseka, *U.S.A.* **76 E2** 40 47N 87 44W
Watson, *Australia* ...... **61 F5** 30 29S 131 31 E
Watson, *Canada* **73 C8** 52 10N 104 30W
Watson Lake, *Canada* ... **72 A3** 60 6N 128 49W
Watsonville, *U.S.A.* **84 J5** 36 55N 121 45W
Wattiwarriganna Cr. →, *Australia* .... **63 D2** 28 57S 136 10 E
Watuata = Batuata, *Indonesia* .... **37 F6** 6 12S 122 42 E
Watubela, Kepulauan, *Indonesia* .... **37 E8** 4 28S 131 35 E
Watubela Is. = Watubela, Kepulauan, *Indonesia* . **37 E8** 4 28S 131 35 E
Wau, *Sudan* .... **49 F6** 7 45N 28 1 E
Waubamik, *Canada* **78 A4** 45 27N 80 1W
Waubay, *U.S.A.* **80 C6** 45 20N 97 18W
Waubra, *Australia* ...... **63 F3** 37 21S 143 39 E
Wauchope, *Australia* .... **63 E5** 31 28S 152 45 E
Wauchula, *U.S.A.* **77 M5** 27 33N 81 49W
Waugh, *Canada* **73 D9** 49 40N 95 11W
Waukarlycarly, L., *Australia* .... **60 D3** 21 18S 121 56 E
Waukegan, *U.S.A.* **76 D2** 42 22N 87 50W
Waukesha, *U.S.A.* **76 D1** 43 1N 88 14W
Waukon, *U.S.A.* **80 D9** 43 16N 91 29W
Wauneta, *U.S.A.* **80 E4** 40 25N 101 23W
Waupaca, *U.S.A.* **80 C10** 44 21N 89 5W
Waupun, *U.S.A.* **80 D10** 43 38N 88 44W
Waurika, *U.S.A.* **81 H6** 34 10N 98 0W
Wausau, *U.S.A.* **80 C10** 44 58N 89 38W
Wautoma, *U.S.A.* **80 C10** 44 4N 89 18W
Wauwatosa, *U.S.A.* **76 D2** 43 3N 88 0W
Wave Hill, *Australia* ..... **60 C5** 17 32S 131 0 E
Waveney →, *U.K.* ...... **11 E9** 52 35N 1 39 E
Waverley, *N.Z.* .... **59 H5** 39 46S 174 37 E
Waverly, *Iowa, U.S.A.* ... **80 D8** 42 44N 92 29W
Waverly, *N.Y., U.S.A.* ... **79 E8** 42 1N 76 32W
Wavre, *Belgium* .... **15 D4** 50 43N 4 38 E
Wâw, *Sudan* .... **51 G11** 7 45N 28 1 E
Wāw al Kabīr, *Libya* ..... **51 C9** 25 20N 16 43 E
Wawa, *Canada* **70 C3** 47 59N 84 47W
Wawanesa, *Canada* **73 D9** 49 36N 99 40W
Wawona, *U.S.A.* **84 H7** 37 32N 119 39W
Waxahachie, *U.S.A.* **81 J6** 32 24N 96 51W
Way, L., *Australia* .... **61 E3** 26 45S 120 16 E
Wayatinah, *Australia* .... **62 G4** 42 19S 146 27 E
Waycross, *U.S.A.* **77 K4** 31 13N 82 21W
Wayne, *Nebr., U.S.A.* ... **80 D6** 42 14N 97 1W
Wayne, *W. Va., U.S.A.* ... **76 F4** 38 13N 82 27W
Waynesboro, *Ga., U.S.A.* **77 J4** 33 6N 82 1W
Waynesboro, *Miss., U.S.A.* **77 K1** 31 40N 88 39W
Waynesboro, *Pa., U.S.A.* . **76 F7** 39 45N 77 35W
Waynesboro, *Va., U.S.A.* . **76 F6** 38 4N 78 53W
Waynesburg, *U.S.A.* **76 F5** 39 54N 80 11W
Waynesville, *U.S.A.* **77 H4** 35 28N 82 58W
Waynoka, *U.S.A.* **81 G5** 36 35N 98 53W
Wazirabad, *Pakistan* .... **42 C6** 32 30N 74 8 E
We, *Indonesia* .... **36 C1** 5 51N 95 18 E
Weald, The, *U.K.* .... **11 F8** 51 4N 0 20 E
Wear →, *U.K.* **10 C6** 54 55N 1 23W
Weatherford, *Okla., U.S.A.* **81 H5** 35 32N 98 43W
Weatherford, *Tex., U.S.A.* **81 J6** 32 46N 97 48W
Weaverville, *U.S.A.* **82 F2** 40 44N 122 56W
Webb City, *U.S.A.* **81 G7** 37 9N 94 28W
Webster, *Mass., U.S.A.* .. **79 D13** 42 3N 71 53W
Webster, *N.Y., U.S.A.* ... **78 C7** 43 13N 77 26W
Webster, *S. Dak., U.S.A.* . **80 C6** 45 20N 97 31W
Webster, *Wis., U.S.A.* ... **80 C8** 45 53N 92 22W
Webster City, *U.S.A.* **80 D8** 42 28N 93 49W
Webster Green, *U.S.A.* .. **80 F9** 38 38N 90 20W
Webster Springs, *U.S.A.* . **76 F5** 38 29N 80 25W
Weda, *Indonesia* .... **37 D7** 0 21N 127 50 E
Weda, Teluk, *Indonesia* .. **37 D7** 0 30N 127 50 E
Weddell I., *Falk. Is.* **96 G4** 51 50S 61 0W
Weddell Sea, *Antarctica* . **5 D1** 72 30S 40 0W
Wedderburn, *Australia* .. **63 F3** 36 26S 143 33 E
Wedgeport, *Canada* **71 D6** 43 44N 65 59W
Wedza, *Zimbabwe* ...... **55 F3** 18 40S 31 33 E
Wee Waa, *Australia* ..... **63 E4** 30 11S 149 26 E
Weed, *U.S.A.* **82 F2** 41 25N 122 23W
Weed Heights, *U.S.A.* ... **84 G7** 38 59N 119 13W
Weedsport, *U.S.A.* **79 C8** 43 3N 76 35W
Weedville, *U.S.A.* **78 E6** 41 17N 78 30W
Weemelah, *Australia* .... **63 D4** 29 2S 149 15 E
Weenen, *S. Africa* ...... **57 D5** 28 48S 30 7 E
Weert, *Neths.* .... **15 C5** 51 15N 5 43 E
Wei He →, *Hebei, China* **34 F8** 36 10N 115 45 E
Wei He →, *Shaanxi, China* .... **34 G6** 34 38N 110 15 E
Weichang, *China* .... **35 D9** 41 58N 117 49 E
Weichuan, *China* .... **34 G7** 34 20N 113 59 E
Weiden, *Germany* ...... **16 D7** 49 41N 12 10 E
Weifang, *China* .... **35 F10** 36 44N 119 7 E
Weihai, *China* .... **35 F12** 37 30N 122 6 E
Weimar, *Germany* ...... **16 C6** 50 58N 11 19 E
Weinan, *China* .... **34 G5** 34 31N 109 29 E
Weipa, *Australia* .... **62 A3** 12 40S 141 50 E
Weir →, *Australia* ..... **63 D4** 28 20S 149 50 E
Weir →, *Canada* **73 B10** 56 54N 93 21W
Weir River, *Canada* **73 B10** 56 49N 94 6W
Weirton, *U.S.A.* **78 F4** 40 24N 80 35W
Weiser, *U.S.A.* **82 D5** 44 10N 117 0W
Weishan, *China* .... **35 G9** 34 47N 117 5 E
Weiyuan, *China* .... **34 G3** 35 7N 104 10 E
Wejherowo, *Poland* ..... **17 A10** 54 35N 18 12 E
Wekusko L., *Canada* **73 C9** 54 40N 99 50W
Welbourn Hill, *Australia* . **63 D1** 27 21S 134 6 E
Welch, *U.S.A.* **76 G5** 37 26N 81 35W
Welkom, *S. Africa* ...... **56 D4** 28 0S 26 46 E
Welland, *Canada* **70 D4** 43 0N 79 15W
Welland →, *U.K.* **11 E7** 52 51N 0 5W
Wellesley Is., *Australia* .. **62 B2** 16 42S 139 30 E
Wellingborough, *U.K.* ... **11 E7** 52 19N 0 41W
Wellington, *Australia* ... **63 E4** 32 35S 148 59 E
Wellington, *Canada* **70 D4** 43 57N 77 20W
Wellington, *N.Z.* .... **59 J5** 41 19S 174 46 E
Wellington, *S. Africa* .... **56 E2** 33 38S 19 1 E
Wellington, *Somst., U.K.* . **11 G4** 50 58N 3 13W
Wellington, *Telford & Wrekin, U.K.* **11 E5** 52 42N 2 30W
Wellington, *Colo., U.S.A.* . **80 E2** 40 42N 105 0W
Wellington, *Kans., U.S.A.* **81 G6** 37 16N 97 24W
Wellington, *Nev., U.S.A.* . **84 G7** 38 45N 119 23W
Wellington, *Ohio, U.S.A.* . **78 E2** 41 10N 82 13W
Wellington, *Tex., U.S.A.* . **81 H4** 34 51N 100 13W
Wellington, I., *Chile* **96 F2** 49 30S 75 0W
Wellington, L., *Australia* . **63 F4** 38 6S 147 20 E
Wells, *U.K.* **11 F5** 51 13N 2 39W
Wells, *Maine, U.S.A.* **79 C14** 43 20N 70 35W
Wells, *Minn., U.S.A.* **80 D8** 43 45N 93 44W
Wells, *Nev., U.S.A.* **82 F6** 41 7N 114 58W
Wells, L., *Australia* ..... **61 E3** 26 44S 123 15 E
Wells Gray Prov. Park, *Canada* **72 C4** 52 30N 120 15W
Wells-next-the-Sea, *U.K.* . **10 E8** 52 57N 0 51 E
Wells River, *U.S.A.* **79 B12** 44 9N 72 4W
Wellsboro, *U.S.A.* **78 E7** 41 45N 77 18W
Wellsburg, *U.S.A.* **78 F4** 40 16N 80 37W
Wellsville, *Mo., U.S.A.* ... **80 F9** 39 4N 91 34W
Wellsville, *N.Y., U.S.A.* .. **78 D7** 42 7N 77 57W
Wellsville, *Ohio, U.S.A.* . **78 F4** 40 36N 80 39W
Wellsville, *Utah, U.S.A.* . **82 F8** 41 38N 111 56W
Wellton, *U.S.A.* **83 K6** 32 40N 114 8W
Wels, *Austria* .... **16 D8** 48 9N 14 1 E
Welshpool, *U.K.* **11 E4** 52 39N 3 8W
Welwyn Garden City, *U.K.* **11 F7** 51 48N 0 12W
Wem, *U.K.* **10 E5** 52 52N 2 44W
Wembere →, *Tanzania* . **54 C3** 4 10S 34 15 E
Wemindji, *Canada* **70 B4** 53 0N 78 49W
Wen Xian, *Gansu, China* . **34 H3** 32 43N 104 36 E
Wen Xian, *Henan, China* . **34 G7** 34 55N 113 5 E
Wenatchee, *U.S.A.* **82 C3** 47 25N 120 19W
Wenchang, *China* .... **38 C8** 19 38N 110 42 E
Wenchi, *Ghana* **50 G5** 7 46N 2 8W
Wenchow = Wenzhou, *China* .... **33 D7** 28 0N 120 38 E
Wendell, *U.S.A.* **82 E6** 42 47N 114 42W
Wenden, *U.S.A.* **85 M13** 33 49N 113 33W
Wendeng, *China* .... **35 F12** 37 15N 122 5 E
Wendesi, *Indonesia* ..... **37 E8** 2 30S 134 17 E
Wendover, *U.S.A.* **82 F6** 40 44N 114 2W
Wenlock →, *Australia* .. **62 A3** 12 2S 141 55 E
Wenshan, *China* .... **32 D5** 23 20N 104 18 E
Wenshang, *China* .... **34 G9** 35 45N 116 30 E
Wenshui, *China* .... **34 F7** 37 26N 112 1 E
Wensleydale, *U.K.* **10 C6** 54 17N 2 0W
Wensu, *China* .... **32 B3** 41 15N 80 10 E
Wensum →, *U.K.* ...... **10 E8** 52 40N 1 15 E
Wentworth, *Australia* ... **63 E3** 34 2S 141 54 E
Wenut, *Indonesia* .... **37 E8** 3 11S 133 19 E
Wenxi, *China* .... **34 G6** 35 20N 111 10 E
Wenzhou, *China* .... **33 D7** 28 0N 120 38 E
Weott, *U.S.A.* **82 F2** 40 20N 123 55W
Wepener, *S. Africa* ...... **56 D4** 29 42S 27 3 E
Werda, *Botswana* ...... **56 D3** 25 24S 23 15 E
Weri, *Indonesia* .... **37 E8** 3 10S 132 38 E
Werra →, *Germany* .... **16 C5** 51 24N 9 39 E
Werribee, *Australia* ..... **63 F3** 37 54S 144 40 E
Werrimull, *Australia* .... **63 E3** 34 25S 141 38 E
Werris Creek, *Australia* .. **63 E5** 31 18S 150 38 E
Weser →, *Germany* .... **16 B5** 53 36N 8 28 E
Wesiri, *Indonesia* .... **37 F7** 7 30S 126 30 E
Wesley Vale, *U.S.A.* **83 J10** 35 3N 106 2W
Wesleyville, *Canada* **71 C9** 49 8N 53 36W
Wesleyville, *U.S.A.* **78 D4** 42 9N 80 0W
Wessel, C., *Australia* .... **62 A2** 10 59S 136 46 E
Wessel Is., *Australia* .... **62 A2** 11 10S 136 45 E
Wessington, *U.S.A.* **80 C5** 44 27N 98 42W
Wessington Springs, *U.S.A.* **80 C5** 44 5N 98 34W
West, *U.S.A.* **81 K6** 31 48N 97 6W
West Allis, *U.S.A.* **76 D1** 43 1N 88 0W
West B., *U.S.A.* **81 L10** 29 3N 89 22W
West Baines →, *Australia* **60 C4** 15 38S 129 59 E
West Bank □, *Asia* ...... **47 C4** 32 6N 35 13 E
West Bend, *U.S.A.* **76 D1** 43 25N 88 11W
West Bengal □, *India* ... **43 H13** 23 0N 88 0 E
West Berkshire □, *U.K.* .. **11 F6** 51 25N 1 17W
West Beskids = Západné Beskydy, *Europe* ...... **17 D10** 49 30N 19 0 E
West Branch, *U.S.A.* **76 C3** 44 17N 84 14W
West Bromwich, *U.K.* ... **11 E6** 52 32N 1 59W
West Burra, *U.K.* **12 A7** 60 5N 1 21W
West Cape Howe, *Australia* .... **61 G2** 35 8S 117 36 E
West Chazy, *U.S.A.* **79 B11** 44 49N 73 28W
West Chester, *U.S.A.* ... **76 F8** 39 58N 75 36W
West Columbia, *U.S.A.* .. **81 L7** 29 9N 95 39W
West Covina, *U.S.A.* **85 L9** 34 4N 117 54W
West Des Moines, *U.S.A.* **80 E8** 41 35N 93 43W
West Dunbartonshire □, *U.K.* **12 F4** 55 59N 4 30W
West End, *Bahamas* **88 A4** 26 41N 78 58W
West Falkland, *Falk. Is.* .. **96 G5** 51 40S 60 0W
West Fjord = Vestfjorden, *Norway* .... **8 C15** 67 55N 14 0 E
West Frankfort, *U.S.A.* ... **80 G10** 37 54N 88 55W
West Hartford, *U.S.A.* ... **79 E12** 41 45N 72 44W
West Haven, *U.S.A.* **79 E12** 41 17N 72 57W
West Helena, *U.S.A.* **81 H9** 34 33N 90 38W
West Ice Shelf, *Antarctica* **5 C7** 67 0S 85 0 E
West Indies, *Cent. Amer.* **89 D7** 15 0N 65 0W
West Lorne, *Canada* **78 D3** 42 36N 81 36W
West Lothian □, *U.K.* ... **12 F5** 55 54N 3 36W
West Lunga →, *Zambia* **55 E1** 13 6S 24 39 E
West Memphis, *U.S.A.* .. **81 H9** 35 9N 90 11W
West Midlands □, *U.K.* .. **11 E6** 52 26N 2 0W
West Mifflin, *U.S.A.* **78 F5** 40 22N 79 52W
West Monroe, *U.S.A.* **81 J8** 32 31N 92 9W
West Newton, *U.S.A.* **78 F5** 40 14N 79 46W
West Nicholson, *Zimbabwe* .... **55 G2** 21 2S 29 20 E
West Palm Beach, *U.S.A.* **77 M5** 26 43N 80 3W
West Plains, *U.S.A.* **81 G9** 36 44N 91 51W
West Point, *Ga., U.S.A.* .. **77 J3** 32 53N 85 11W
West Point, *Miss., U.S.A.* **77 J1** 33 36N 88 39W
West Point, *Nebr., U.S.A.* **80 E6** 41 51N 96 43W
West Point, *Va., U.S.A.* .. **76 G7** 37 32N 76 48W
West Pokot □, *Kenya* ... **54 B4** 1 30N 35 15 E
West Pt. = Ouest, Pte., *Canada* **71 C7** 49 52N 64 40W
West Pt., *Australia* ...... **63 F2** 35 1S 135 56 E
West Road →, *Canada* . **72 C4** 53 18N 122 53W
West Rutland, *U.S.A.* ... **79 C11** 43 38N 73 5W
West Schelde = Westerschelde →, *Neths.* .... **15 C3** 51 25N 3 25 E
West Seneca, *U.S.A.* **78 D6** 42 51N 78 48W
West Siberian Plain, *Russia* .... **28 C11** 62 0N 75 0 E
West Sussex □, *U.K.* **11 G7** 50 55N 0 30W
West-Terschelling, *Neths.* **15 A5** 53 22N 5 13 E
West Valley City, *U.S.A.* . **82 F8** 40 42N 111 57W
West Virginia □, *U.S.A.* .. **76 F5** 38 45N 80 30W
West-Vlaanderen □, *Belgium* .... **15 D2** 51 0N 3 0 E
West Walker →, *U.S.A.* . **84 G7** 38 54N 119 9W
West Wyalong, *Australia* **63 E4** 33 56S 147 10 E
West Yellowstone, *U.S.A.* **82 D8** 44 40N 111 6W
West Yorkshire □, *U.K.* .. **10 D6** 53 45N 1 40W
Westall Pt., *Australia* ... **63 E1** 32 55S 134 4 E
Westbrook, *Maine, U.S.A.* **77 D10** 43 41N 70 22W
Westbrook, *Tex., U.S.A.* . **81 J4** 32 21N 101 1W
Westbury, *Australia* ..... **62 G4** 41 30S 146 51 E
Westby, *U.S.A.* **80 A2** 48 52N 104 3W
Westend, *U.S.A.* **85 K9** 35 42N 117 24W
Westerland, *Germany* ... **9 J13** 54 54N 8 17 E
Western □, *Kenya* ...... **54 B3** 0 30N 34 30 E
Western □, *Uganda* ..... **54 B3** 1 45N 31 30 E
Western □, *Zambia* ..... **55 F1** 15 15S 24 30 E
Western Australia □, *Australia* .... **61 E2** 25 0S 118 0 E
Western Cape □, *S. Africa* **56 E3** 34 0S 20 0 E
Western Dvina = Daugava →, *Latvia* .. **24 C3** 57 4N 24 3 E
Western Ghats, *India* .... **40 N9** 14 0N 75 0 E
Western Isles □, *U.K.* ... **12 D1** 57 30N 7 10W
Western Sahara ■, *Africa* **50 D3** 25 0N 13 0W
Western Samoa ■, *Pac. Oc.* **59 B13** 14 0S 172 0W
Westernport, *U.S.A.* **76 F6** 39 29N 79 3W
Westerschelde →, *Neths.* **15 C3** 51 25N 3 25 E
Westerwald, *Germany* ... **16 C4** 50 38N 7 56 E
Westfield, *Mass., U.S.A.* . **79 D12** 42 7N 72 45W
Westfield, *N.Y., U.S.A.* .. **78 D5** 42 20N 79 35W
Westfield, *Pa., U.S.A.* ... **78 E7** 41 55N 77 32W
Westhill, *U.K.* **12 D6** 57 9N 2 19W
Westhope, *U.S.A.* **80 A4** 48 55N 101 1W
Westland Bight, *N.Z.* .... **59 K3** 42 55S 170 5 E
Westlock, *Canada* **72 C6** 54 9N 113 55W
Westmeath □, *Ireland* ... **13 C4** 53 33N 7 34W

175

World: Regions in the News

Maps show the situation in June 1998

TAIWAN

0	50	100	150	200 km

☐ Territory of People's Republic of China

▨ Territory of Republic of China (Taiwan)

SOUTH CHINA SEA

0	250	500 km	

▲ Philippine terr.
▼ Vietnamese terr.
■ Chinese terr.
● Taiwanese terr.
—·— Philippine claim
——— Vietnamese claim
—+— Chinese claim
······· Malaysian claim

FORMER YUGOSLAVIA

0	50	100	150	200 km

—··— International boundaries
—·—· Republic boundaries
– – – Province boundaries
■ Capital cities
——— Dayton Peace Agreement Boundary
▨ Muslim-Croat Federation
▨ Bosnian Serb Republic

THE BREAK-UP OF YUGOSLAVIA
The former country of Yugoslavia comprised six republics. In 1991 Slovenia and Croatia declared independence. Bosnia-Herzegovina followed in 1992 and Macedonia in 1993. Yugoslavia now comprises the remaining two republics, Serbia and Montenegro.

YUGOSLAVIA
Population: 10,881,000 (Serb 62.6%, Albanian 16.5%, Montenegrin 5%, Hungarian 3.3%, Muslim 3.2%)

Serbia Population: 6,060,000 (Serb 87.7%, excluding the former autonomous provinces of Kosovo and Vojvodina)
  Kosovo Population: 1,989,050 (Albanian 81.6%, Serb 9.9%)
  Vojvodina Population: 2,131,900 (Serb 56.8%, Hungarian 16.9%)

Montenegro Population: 700,050 (Montenegrin 61.9%, Muslim 14.6%, Albanian 7%)

CROATIA
Population: 4,850,000 (Croat 78.1%, Serb 12.2%)

SLOVENIA
Population: 2,000,000 (Slovene 88%)

MACEDONIA (F. Y. R. O. M.)
Population: 2,150,000 (Macedonian 64%, Albanian 21.7%, Turkish 5%)

BOSNIA-HERZEGOVINA
Population: 3,600,000 (Muslim 49%, Serb 31.2%, Croat 17.2%)

THE CAUCASUS

0	100	200 km

—·— International boundaries
—·—· Republic boundaries

Georgia, Armenia and Azerbaijan achieved independence in 1991. Abkhazia, Ajaria and South Ossetia seek independence from Georgia. Chechenia has been trying to break away from Russia since 1991, but Russia has resisted with military force. Hostility also continues between Armenia and Azerbaijan over the enclave of Nagorno-Karabakh.

COUNTRIES AND REPUBLICS OF THE CAUCASUS REGION

RUSSIAN REPUBLICS IN THE NEWS

North Ossetia (Alania) Population: 695,000 (Ossetian 53%, Russian 29%, Chechen 5.2%, Armenian 1.9%)

Chechenia Population: 1,308,000 (Chechen and Ingush 70.7%, Russian 23.1%, Armenian 1.2%)

Ingushetia (Split from Chechenia in June 1993) Population: 250,000

GEORGIA
Population: 5,450,000 (Georgian 70.1%, Armenian 8.1%, Russian 6.3%, Azerbaijani 5.7%, Ossetian 3%, Greek 2%, Abkhazian 2%)

Abkhazia Population: 537,500 (Georgian 45.7%, Abkhazian 17.8%, Armenian 14.6%, Russian 14.3%)

Ajaria Population: 382,000 (Georgian 82.8%, Russian 7.7%, Armenian 4%)

ARMENIA
Population: 3,800,000 (Armenian 93%, Azerbaijani 3%)

Nagorno-Karabakh Population: 192,400 (Armenian 76.9%, Azerbaijani 21.5%)

AZERBAIJAN
Population: 7,650,000 (Azerbaijani 83%, Russian 6%, Armenian 6%, Lezgin 2%)

Naxçivan Population: 300,400

ISRAEL
Population: 5,900,000 (inc. East Jerusalem and Jewish settlers in the areas under Israeli administration. (Jewish 82%, Arab Muslim 13.8%, Arab Christian 2.5%, Druze 1.7%)

West Bank
Population: 1,122,900 (Palestinian Arabs 97% [of whom Arab Muslim 85%, Jewish 7%, Christian 8%])

Gaza Strip
Population: 748,400 (Arab Muslim 98%)

JORDAN
Population: 5,600,000 (Arab 99% [of whom about 50% are Palestinian Arab])

—··— 1949 Armistice Line

– – – 1974 Cease-fire Lines

● *Efrata* Main Jewish settlements in the West Bank and Gaza Strip

■ *Halhul* Main Palestinian Arab towns in the West Bank and Gaza Strip

■ *'Amman* Capital cities

THE NEAR EAST

0	25	50 km

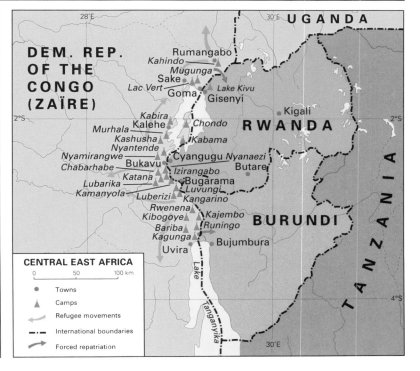

CENTRAL EAST AFRICA

0	50	100 km

● Towns
▲ Camps
⇦ Refugee movements
—·—· International boundaries
⇨ Forced repatriation

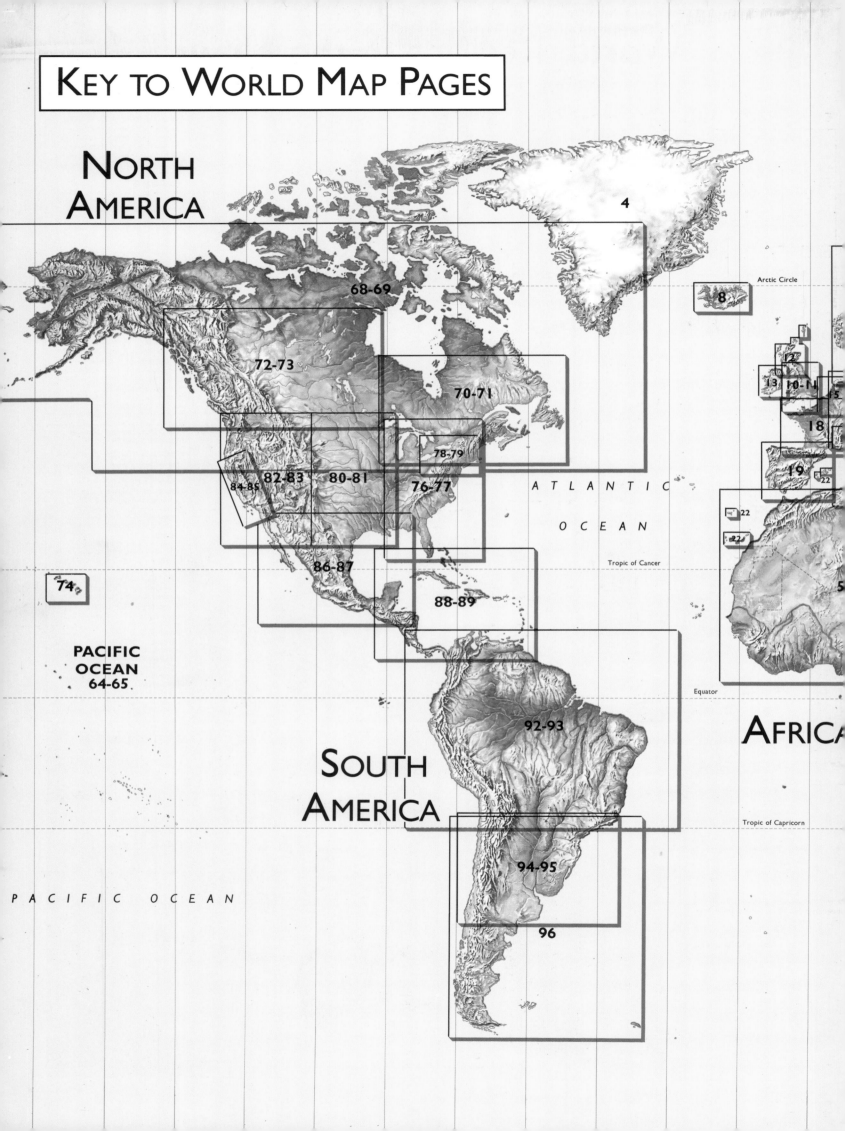

KEY TO WORLD MAP PAGES

NORTH AMERICA

SOUTH AMERICA

AFRICA

PACIFIC OCEAN 64-65

PACIFIC OCEAN

ATLANTIC OCEAN

Arctic Circle

Tropic of Cancer

Equator

Tropic of Capricorn

4

8

12

13

10-11

15

18

19

22

22

22

5

74

68-69

72-73

70-71

78-79

82-83

80-81

76-77

84-85

86-87

88-89

92-93

94-95

96